THE MARK TWAIN PAPERS

Mark Twain's Letters
Volume 1: 1853–1866

THE MARK TWAIN PAPERS AND WORKS OF MARK TWAIN
is a comprehensive edition for scholars of the private papers
and published works of Mark Twain (Samuel L. Clemens).

THE MARK TWAIN LIBRARY
is a selected edition reprinted from the Papers and Works for
students and the general reader. Both series of books are published
by the University of California Press and edited by members of the

MARK TWAIN PROJECT
with headquarters in The Bancroft Library,
University of California, Berkeley.

Editorial work for all volumes is jointly supported by grants from the

DIVISION OF RESEARCH PROGRAMS,
NATIONAL ENDOWMENT FOR THE HUMANITIES,
an independent federal agency,
and by public and private donations,
matched equally by the Endowment, to

THE FRIENDS OF THE BANCROFT LIBRARY

Letters, Volume 1: 1853–1866
Editors: Edgar Marquess Branch, Michael B. Frank,
and Kenneth M. Sanderson
Associate Editors: Harriet Elinor Smith,
Lin Salamo, and Richard Bucci
1988

THE WORKS OF MARK TWAIN
Roughing It
Edited by Franklin R. Rogers and Paul Baender
1972

What Is Man? and Other Philosophical Writings
Edited by Paul Baender
1973

A Connecticut Yankee in King Arthur's Court
Edited by Bernard L. Stein,
with an Introduction by Henry Nash Smith
1979

The Prince and the Pauper
Edited by Victor Fischer and Lin Salamo,
with the assistance of Mary Jane Jones
1979

Early Tales & Sketches, Volume 1 (1851–1864)
Edited by Edgar Marquess Branch and Robert H. Hirst,
with the assistance of Harriet Elinor Smith
1979

*The Adventures of Tom Sawyer · Tom Sawyer Abroad
Tom Sawyer, Detective*
Edited by John C. Gerber, Paul Baender, and Terry Firkins
1980

Early Tales & Sketches, Volume 2 (1864–1865)
Edited by Edgar Marquess Branch and Robert H. Hirst,
with the assistance of Harriet Elinor Smith
1981

THE MARK TWAIN LIBRARY
No. 44, The Mysterious Stranger
Edited by John S. Tuckey and William M. Gibson
1982

The Adventures of Tom Sawyer
Edited by John C. Gerber and Paul Baender
1982

Tom Sawyer Abroad · *Tom Sawyer, Detective*
Edited by John C. Gerber and Terry Firkins
1982

The Prince and the Pauper
Edited by Victor Fischer and Michael B. Frank
1983

A Connecticut Yankee in King Arthur's Court
Edited by Bernard L. Stein
1983

Adventures of Huckleberry Finn
Edited by Walter Blair and Victor Fischer
1985

OTHER MARK TWAIN PROJECT PUBLICATIONS

The Devil's Race-Track: Mark Twain's Great Dark Writings
The Best from Which Was the Dream? *and* Fables of Man
Edited by John S. Tuckey
1980

Union Catalog of Clemens Letters
Edited by Paul Machlis
1986

Samuel L. Clemens, 1853.
Courtesy of Vassar College Library (NPV).

THE MARK TWAIN PAPERS

General Editor

ROBERT H. HIRST

Contributing Editors for this Volume
DAHLIA ARMON
PRISCILLA BOTSFORD
JANICE E. BRAUN
ROBERT PACK BROWNING
VICTOR FISCHER
PAUL MACHLIS
DANIEL J. WIDAWSKY

A Publication of the Mark Twain Project
of The Bancroft Library

MARK TWAIN'S
LETTERS

VOLUME 1 ❦ 1853–1866

Editors

EDGAR MARQUESS BRANCH
MICHAEL B. FRANK
KENNETH M. SANDERSON

Associate Editors

HARRIET ELINOR SMITH
LIN SALAMO
RICHARD BUCCI

Mark Twain

UNIVERSITY OF CALIFORNIA PRESS

Berkeley · Los Angeles · London

1988

Publication of this volume was assisted by
a grant from the

PUBLICATION SUBVENTION PROGRAM,
DIVISION OF RESEARCH PROGRAMS,
NATIONAL ENDOWMENT FOR THE HUMANITIES,
an independent federal agency.

University of California Press
Berkeley and Los Angeles, California

University of California Press, Ltd.
London, England

Manufactured in the United States of America

Library of Congress Cataloging-in-Publication Data

Twain, Mark, 1835–1910
Mark Twain's letters.

Bibliography: v. 1, p.
Includes index.
Contents: v. 1. 1853–1866.
1. Twain, Mark, 1835–1910—Correspondence. 2. Authors,
American—19th century—Correspondence. 3. Humorists,
American—19th century—Correspondence. I. Branch,
Edgar Marquess, 1913–   . II. Frank, Michael B.
III. Sanderson, Kenneth M. IV. Title.
PS1331.A4   1987   818'.409 [B]   87-5963
ISBN 0-520-03668-9 (v. 1: alk. paper)

Editorial work for this volume has been supported by a grant to
The Friends of The Bancroft Library from the

MARK TWAIN FOUNDATION

and by matching funds from the
DIVISION OF RESEARCH PROGRAMS,
NATIONAL ENDOWMENT FOR THE HUMANITIES,
an independent federal agency.

Without such generous support, this volume could
not have been produced.

Contents

Acknowledgments

THE LONG SUSTAINED and necessarily intensive editorial labor represented by this volume, and by those soon to follow it, would have been impossible without the generous support of the American taxpayer, and the professional encouragement of scholars who, between 1976 and 1985, recommended funding for five successive grants to the Mark Twain Project from the Texts Program, Division of Research Programs, of the National Endowment for the Humanities, an independent federal agency. The University of California Press was likewise assisted by a grant from the Publication Subvention Program in the Division of Research Programs at the Endowment. We are grateful for this intellectual and material support, part of which the Endowment was able to grant by matching, dollar for dollar, a major contribution from the Mark Twain Foundation to The Friends of The Bancroft Library on behalf of the Project.

In addition, since 1976 more than sixty individual and institutional donors—only a handful of whom can be mentioned here—contributed funds that have been matched by the Endowment in its continuing support of the Mark Twain Project. We are grateful to the Heller Charitable and Educational Fund; the Koret Foundation; Mrs. Calvin K. Townsend; The House of Bernstein, Inc.; the Evelyn and Walter Haas, Jr., Fund; the Crescent Porter Hale Foundation; Constance Bowles Hart; Clarence E. Heller; Dr. Myra Karstadt; Theodore H. Koundakjian; the Estate of Helen F. Pierce; William M. Roth; Marion B. and Willis S. Slusser; the Henry Nash Smith Memorial Fund; and the Wells Fargo Foundation. Robert S. Livermore greatly facilitated completion of the editorial work with his gift of a Zendex 95/35 multi-user computer system.

The Mark Twain Committee of the Council of The Friends of The Bancroft Library is chiefly responsible for persuading these and other private donors to lend their support to the ongoing editorial work of the Project. Our thanks go to present and former members of this committee: John W. Rosston and Willis S. Slusser, co-chairmen; Henry K. Evers, Stephen G. Herrick, and David J. McDaniel, former chairmen; William P. Barlow, Jr., Henry M. Bowles, Launce E. Gamble, Constance Bowles Hart, James D. Hart, Roger W. Heyns, Kenneth E. Hill, James E. O'Brien, Joseph A. Rosenthal, Herbert E. Stansbury, Jr., and Norman H. Strouse, as well as Kimberley Massingale, secretary to the Council.

Several members of the Mark Twain Project's Board of Directors have been particularly helpful in sustaining the preparations required for this volume. James D. Hart, Director of The Bancroft Library, and Joseph A. Rosenthal, University Librarian, both at the University of California, Berkeley, have been steadfast and unfailingly resourceful in their support of the Project, intellectually and materially. William J. McClung, Editorial Director of the University of California Press, has been generous in his support, especially of the typographical experiments required to develop the system of transcription, which is used here for the first time. Henry Nash Smith, former Editor and Interim Editor of the Mark Twain Papers, has been for us what he doubtless was for others—a model and an inspiration for what it means to contribute usefully to scholarship on any subject.

Locating, collecting, and publishing Mark Twain's letters has occupied at least three generations of scholars. We are indebted to all of them, but particularly to Albert Bigelow Paine and his successors as Editor of the Mark Twain Papers: Bernard DeVoto, Dixon Wecter, Henry Nash Smith, and Frederick Anderson.

Editing Mark Twain's letters has required continuing and demanding research assistance. For such valuable aid over many years we are especially thankful to Donald E. Oehlerts, Director of the Miami University Libraries, and the staff of the Edgar Weld King Library, Miami University, Oxford, Ohio; the staff of The Bancroft Library, particularly Brenda J. Bailey, Anthony S. Bliss, Peter E. Hanff, Irene M. Moran, and William M. Roberts; Evelyn M. Kiresen, Leon D. Megrian, Jo Lynn Milardovich, and Donald G. Williams of the Interlibrary Borrowing Service, Philip Hoehn of the Map Room, and Daniel L. Johnston of the Photographic Service, all in the Library, University of California, Berkeley. We would also like to thank Nancy H. Harris in the Conservation Department of the Library, who has helped us preserve manuscript letters for posterity, even as we prepared their texts for publication.

Manuscripts as well as unique, nonoriginal forms of Mark Twain's letters are dispersed among libraries and private collections worldwide. Most of the letters in this volume, however, are transcribed from the original documents in two locations: the Mark Twain Papers in The Bancroft Library, and the Jean Webster McKinney Family Papers in the Vassar College Library, Poughkeepsie, New York. At Vassar, Frances Goudy, Barbara LaMont, Eleanor Rogers, and especially and most recently, Lisa Browar, permitted timely access to unique Clemens materials and graciously answered our repeated requests for supporting documents, photocopies, and information. Similar assistance, less frequent but no less crucial, was provided by John Chalmers and Cathy Henderson of the Harry Ransom Humanities Research Center, University of Texas, Austin; Gregory Johnson of the Alderman Library, University of Virginia, Charlottesville; Eric N. Moody of the Nevada Historical Society, Reno; Guy Louis Rocha of the Nevada State Library and Archives, Reno; Robert Nylen of the Nevada State Museum, Carson City; William D. Tammeus of the Kansas City *Star*, Kansas City, Missouri; Shirley Dick, Doris A. Foley, Karl Kiedaisch, Jr., and Betty Peters of the Keokuk Public Library, Keokuk, Iowa; Barbara Bublitz, Sheila Chaudoin, and Opal Tanner of the Musser Public Library, Muscatine, Iowa; David Crosson, Leda L. Greene, Soudi Janssens, Nancy Kraft, Karon Moll, and Vernon Tyler of the State Historical Society of Iowa at Des Moines; Debbie O'Brine of the Iowa Masonic Library, Grand Lodge of Iowa, Cedar Rapids; and Raymond H. Nartker of the University of Dayton Library. All of the institutions mentioned in this paragraph have generously given permission to publish letters from their holdings.

In addition, Todd M. Axelrod, Robert Daley, Robert A. Gates, and Victor Jacobs made it possible to include letters or to quote from Clemens documents in their several private collections. The remarkable collection acquired by The Bancroft Library from James and John M. Tufts in 1971, and the outstanding collection of Mark Twain materials donated to The Bancroft Library by Mr. and Mrs. Kurt E. Appert in 1973 and 1977, both provided letters not otherwise available. To all of these collectors we express our special gratitude for their enterprise and their cooperation.

In the course of annotating these letters we asked for, and received, help from the following, who have our thanks: Donald C. Gallup, David E. Schoonover, and the staff of the Beinecke Rare Book and Manuscript Library, Yale University; Henry Sweets of the Mark Twain Museum, Hannibal, Missouri; Herbert A. Wisbey, Jr., of the Center for Mark Twain Studies, Elmira College, Elmira, New York; Kenneth B. Holmes, Floyd C. Shoemaker, and Alma Vaughan of the State Historical Society of Missouri at Columbia; Deborah W. Bolas and Stephanie A. Klein of the Missouri Historical Society, St. Louis; Elizabeth Kirchner and the staff of the St. Louis Mercantile Library; Fred O. Hahn of Polar Star Masonic Lodge No. 79, St. Louis; Russell B. Thimmig, Sr., of the Scottish Rite Library, St. Louis; Susan Shaner of the Hawaii State Archives, Honolulu; Clive E. Driver of the Rosenbach Museum & Library, Philadelphia; Mrs. Elmer S. Forman and the staff of the Cincinnati Historical Society; Yeatman Anderson, III, and the staff of the Rare Book Room, Cincinnati Public Library; Helen Burkes of the Tulane University Library; Jane P. Kleiner of the Louisiana State University Library at Baton Rouge; Wayne Eberhardt and Collin B. Hamer of the New Orleans Public Library; Ardie Kelly of the Mariners' Museum, Newport News, Virginia; James Harkins of the Memphis Public Library; the staff of the John W. Brister Library, Memphis State University; the staff of the Illinois State Historical Society, Springfield; Paul Boswell of the Newspaper and Current Periodical Room of the Library of Congress; Kenneth Hall of the National Archives; Alice C. Dalligan and Mary Karshner of the Burton Historical Collection, Detroit Public Library; Robert E. Blesse of the Special Collections Department, University of Nevada Reno Library; Roberta Waddell, Curator of Prints, New York Public Library; Mabel Bartenhagen; Miriam Jacobs; and Coralee Paull. We extend a particular word of thanks to Michael H. Marleau, who provided us with copies of deeds and other documents gleaned from obscure Nevada mining records.

We greatly appreciate the collaboration of several individuals who shared information and documents that have notably enriched the annotation. Fred Clagett provided biographical details about his grandfather, Clemens's friend William H. Clagett, as well as a copy of a receipt in Clemens's handwriting, transcribed in a note. Mrs. Kate Gilmore, a distant relative of Clemens's mother, allowed us to publish a rare photograph of Pamela A. Moffett, his sister. Mr. and Mrs. Robert M. Gunn made available family records of Mr. Gunn's grandparents, Clemens's close

friends Robert M. and Louise Howland, including the photograph of
Robert reproduced here. Gladys Hill provided information about the
three Taylor sisters, who were friends of Clemens's in Keokuk, Iowa.
Mrs. Helen Jackson donated to The Bancroft Library an original photograph of her great-aunt, Laura Wright, one of Clemens's more memorable sweethearts, which we publish here for the first time. Jervis Langdon, Jr., responded generously to our requests for genealogical
information about the Clemens and Langdon families. And H. LeRoy
Oliver furnished facts about his great-grandfather, Augustus W. Oliver,
another of Clemens's early associates in the West.

Throughout the process of design and typesetting for this volume we
have had expert assistance from several individuals. At the University of
California Press, we want to thank Czeslaw Jan Grycz, Steve Renick, and
especially Fran Mitchell, for their expert and always timely advice and
guidance. Our typesetters, Wilsted & Taylor Publishing Services of Oakland, California, provided patient, expert help in designing the typographical aspect of the new system of transcription, as well as attentive,
informed, and exceptionally accurate typesetting of the volume itself.
Clemens himself might have felt a shock of recognition at this thoughtful
and ingenious application of modern technology to the best traditions of
typography. For their commitment to realizing Clemens's handwritten
letters in type, and to every other aspect of the editorial matter, we are
grateful and the reader is indebted to Burwell Davis, Nancy Evans, Andrew Joron, Matthew Lasar, Jane Ellen Long, Henry Mooney, Rosemary
Northcraft, Gary Pierce, Vivian Scholl, Fronia Simpson, Christine Taylor, Mary VanClay, Sherwood Williams, and LeRoy Wilsted. John R.
Parsons and Mark Williams of Eureka Cartography, in Berkeley, California, expertly redrew the maps of Nevada Territory (Appendix C) from
drafts prepared by the editors. Allen McKinney of Graphic Impressions,
Emeryville, California, prepared the half-tones for the MS facsimile re-
productions and other illustrations. Albert Burkhardt conceived the
original type and book design, which has been slightly modified and
adapted for this first volume of *Mark Twain's Letters.* Jane Moore checked
transcriptions against original letters at the Nevada Historical Society,
the Nevada State Library and Archives, and the University of Nevada
Reno. In 1977, on behalf of the Modern Language Association's Committee on Scholarly Editions, Thomas Wortham carried out a helpful advi-
sory inspection of preliminary editorial work for this volume. Robert

Sattelmeyer was the perceptive and constructive inspector of the completed volume, which received the Committee's seal of approval in 1987. For invaluable advice and support during the evolution of editorial policy, we would also like to thank Helen C. Agüera, Jo Ann Boydston, Don Cook, Kathy Fuller, Michael Millgate, Hershel Parker, and Elizabeth Witherell.

Finally, we wish to thank our associates in the Mark Twain Project for their selfless labors on our behalf. All members of the editorial staff gave enthusiastically of their special expertise, while also sharing the burden of mundane tasks like proofreading, collating, and checking. Dahlia Armon prepared the genealogy of the Clemens family, now the most complete available, reproduced in Appendix A. Priscilla Botsford helped draft the maps of Nevada Territory. Janice E. Braun contributed materially to the accuracy of the texts as well as the index. Robert Pack Browning painstakingly checked manuscript letters at several public and private collections against the transcriptions prepared for this volume. Victor Fischer brought his exceptional familiarity with Clemens's handwriting and his experience with typography and design to bear on vexing problems of transcription and on the evolution of editorial policy. Paul Machlis's *Union Catalog of Clemens Letters* (1986) was essential to the preparation of this volume—as it will be to all later volumes—of letters. His deft command of detail is evident in that catalog and in the index to the present volume, which he supervised. Daniel J. Widawsky assisted in the preparation and verification of the textual apparatuses and the index. The work of these editors was complemented by the efforts of a succession of student assistants—Elizabeth Bishop, Susan Gillman, David J. Goodwin, Penny Johnson, and Nancy Davis Spriggs—and by the steady support of Janet Leigh and Dorothy Gottberg, former and present administrative assistants to the Project. Their efficient and willing dispatch of a formidable host of duties, from budgeting to computer procurement, has expedited every aspect of the editorial process. All of these good colleagues and good friends have made the editing of Mark Twain's letters, always a stimulating enterprise, a congenial one as well.

                                    E.M.B.   M.B.F.   K.M.S.
                                      H.E.S.   L.S.   R.B.

Introduction

THIS VOLUME opens with an 1853 letter in which a brash, seventeen-year-old journeyman typesetter, writing from New York City, gives his mother an account of some of his activities since his recent unexpected departure from their home in Hannibal, Missouri. It closes with an 1866 letter in which an established thirty-one-year-old journalist, writing from San Francisco on the eve of returning home for the first time in six years, shares with his mother his gratification in the wide recognition and acquaintance he has achieved.

In the interval between these letters Samuel L. Clemens had lived a footloose existence, restlessly sampling a variety of companions, places, and occupations. Between 1853 and 1857, while an itinerant printer seeking employment and amusement in St. Louis, New York, Philadelphia, Washington, D.C., Muscatine and Keokuk, Iowa, and Cincinnati, he had tried his hand as a travel correspondent for his older brother Orion's struggling village newspapers, the Hannibal *Journal* and later the Muscatine *Journal*, and, under the pseudonym Thomas Jefferson Snodgrass, experimented with comic letters to the Keokuk *Post*. In 1857 he set off to make his fortune in Brazil, but got only as far as New Orleans before deciding instead to become an apprentice pilot on the Mississippi River. He was a Mississippi steersman and pilot, and an occasional contributor to newspapers in St. Louis and New Orleans, until the outbreak of the Civil War in 1861. In the summer of 1861, after a farcical two weeks as a Confederate irregular, he went west with Orion, then the newly appointed secretary of Nevada Territory, expecting to be gone for three months. He remained in Nevada for nearly three years, however, during which time he was a clerk for the territorial legislature, a gold and silver miner, a laborer in a quartz mill, an irrepressible speculator in mining stock, a notary public, and, as Mark Twain, a boisterously inventive, controversial, and highly visible local reporter and editor for the Virginia

City *Territorial Enterprise*. In 1864—after his published affront to the women of Carson City and his quarrel in print with one of the proprietors of the rival Virginia City *Union* almost resulted in duels—he moved to San Francisco. He spent most of the next two and a half years there, earning a precarious living and honing his rambunctious personal and journalistic style as a reporter and writer for several papers, principally the *Morning Call*, a popular daily, and the *Californian*, a literary weekly. At the end of 1864 he escaped hard times by retreating to rustic Tuolumne and Calaveras counties, where he did some pocket mining when not passing the time exchanging tall tales with garrulous miners and local residents. He used some of this material in sketches for the *Californian* upon his return to San Francisco in early 1865. Eastern reprintings of Clemens's *Californian* pieces paid him nothing, but won unanticipated praise in New York City, as did a story he published virtually by accident in the New York *Saturday Press* in November 1865, "Jim Smiley and His Jumping Frog." By late 1865 Clemens had come to rely for his income on his post as San Francisco correspondent of the *Territorial Enterprise*, a daily grind that, in early 1866, gave way to an idyllic four months as Hawaiian correspondent of the Sacramento *Union*. In the fall of that year, encouraged by San Francisco friends, he delivered a lecture based on his Hawaiian experiences. Making the most of its success, he took to the road, performing in the towns of northern California and western Nevada. This tour, a forerunner of the more extensive ones he was to make in the years to come, confirmed his status as a local celebrity. By December 1866 he could confidently exult in his sense of accomplishment and in a secure source of income as he prepared to sail for New York with a new commission as roving correspondent for the San Francisco *Alta California*.

The transformation of the cocksure but callow printer of 1853 into the worldly journalist and public figure of 1866 is vividly and reliably documented in the letters gathered here, the only ones known to survive for the period. They demonstrate the profound degree to which, in Clemens's case, the boy was father to the man. The earliest letters—even when padded, for the benefit of Orion Clemens's newspaper readers, with borrowings from other papers and from guidebooks—evidence the ready humor, the sure command of colloquial speech, and the keen eye for detail that characterize Mark Twain's best writing. In his mature work—especially *Roughing It* (1872), *Life on the Mississippi* (1883), and the Autobiographical Dictations that occupied him in his last years—Clemens returned to the material he first recorded in these letters to his family and friends. The letters, however, preserve this matter in its least self-conscious, unelaborated, and, often, most affecting form. Clemens's description in his 18 June 1858 letter to his sister-in-law, Mollie Clemens, of his younger brother Henry's sufferings and his own guilt-ridden remorse after the explosion of the steamer *Pennsylvania* is hardly less moving now than it must have been then. His Nevada letters, recording his determined acceptance of harsh living conditions and the backbreaking labor that might make him rich, manifest the entrepreneurial ambition that throughout his life co-existed, and sometimes interfered, with his literary impulse. Clemens's mercurial temperament is apparent here not only in his waxing and waning hopes as a miner, but also in his vacillation over commitment to the literary career that, in retrospect, seemed inevitable even to him. In October 1865, driven and despondent, he writes to Orion and Mollie Clemens, belittling his " 'call' to literature of a low order—*i.e.* humorous," but resigning himself to "excite the **laughter** of God's creatures" and thereby strive for an "unworthy & evanescent" fame. Nevertheless, just three months later, he is comfortable enough with this calling to send his mother and sister favorable notices of his work and reel off an ambitious array of literary projects, among them a book along the lines of *Life on the Mississippi*. In short, the youth Samuel Clemens was, and the man he became and remained, are captured in the letters published in this volume, more than forty of them for the first time. They present the most complete and intimate documentary account now available for this critical period in his life.

E. M. B.
M. B. F.
K. M. S.

Guide to Editorial Practice

THE AIM OF *Mark Twain's Letters* is to publish, in chronological order, the most reliable and the most legible text possible for every personal and business letter written by or for Samuel L. Clemens, and to publish the letters he received, selectively, as a part of the annotation. The editorial aim for that annotation is to explain whatever in the letters requires explanation, either in notes appended to the letter or, as necessary, in brief narrative passages between letters. The process of establishing the text for each letter is separately documented in the textual commentaries at the back of the volume.

The text for the letters themselves is an inclusive but critical transcription of the original documents sent or, lacking the originals, a critical text established from the most authoritative derived sources available. The goal in either case is a text that is optimally legible and, at the same time, maximally faithful to the text that Clemens himself transmitted. The original documents are therefore emended as little as possible and mainly in order to simplify or omit what would otherwise threaten to make the transcription unreadable or less than fully intelligible in its own right. But when the originals do not survive in an undamaged state, the nonoriginal sources are emended partly for the same reasons, but mainly, and as much as necessary, in order to restore the readings of the original letter, insofar as the evidence permits. In either case, each departure from the source of the text is recorded as an emendation and published in the textual commentary, barring only the most trivial kinds of change, which are *not* reported item by item, but described briefly at the end of this guide.

Exceptions to this form of the text will occur, but infrequently. For example, two letters that Clemens typed in 1874 (joking the while about his difficulties with the typewriter) clearly exceed the capacity of transcription to capture all their significant details, particularly the typing errors to which he alludes in them. Partly because they were typed, however, the original documents are relatively easy to read and therefore can be published in photographic facsimile, preserving most of their details without at the same time making them any harder to read than the originals. But in general, facsimile cannot provide an optimally reliable and readable text, even of Clemens's very legible holograph letters, which comprise at least eight thousand of the approximately ten thousand letters now known to survive. Facsimile does serve to represent *within* a transcription most elements of a manuscript which would not be rendered more clearly or more faithfully by being transcribed (newspaper clippings, for instance), or that cannot be faithfully transcribed, redrawn, or simulated (drawings, maps, rebuses, to name just a few of the possibilities). Indeed, for a representative handful of letters in each volume, we provide a complete facsimile as a supplement to and a potential test of the transcription, but in no sense as a replacement for it.

The letters have been transcribed using a system of notation and a rationale for emendation which have not before been used to edit letters. We call the result "plain text," in contrast both to "clear text" and its opposite, "genetic text."[1] We require two things of every transcription in plain text: (a) it must be sufficiently faithful to the text of the letter to serve as a *reliable substitute* for it; and (b) it must be *easier to read than the original letter*, so long as its reliability is preserved intact. To the extent that maximum fidelity and maximum legibility come into conflict, this way of linking them constrains the pursuit of either virtue at undue expense to the other. But most letters, most of the time, easily satisfy both requirements, yielding a transcription in type which, although clearly not a replacement for the original, can still be read and quoted from as if it *were* the original.

We have kept the number of newly introduced conventions to a minimum, and for those that are new, we have often adapted familiar conventions of both handwriting and typography in order to transcribe what has tended to be problematic, or else simply ignored, in more traditional kinds of transcription. For instance, to render printed letterhead intelligible at a glance, plain text uses EXTRA-SMALL SMALL CAPITALS for the printed words, and a dotted underscore below whatever Clemens put in the blanks, as for the date and place. And in order to represent all acts of deletion and insertion without making the transcription unreadable, plain text uses l̶i̶n̶e̶-̶t̶h̶r̶o̶u̶g̶h̶ cross-outs, ⸜slashes,⸝ and ˌinferiorˌ carets.

Most of these devices can now be set with the type itself, making them economical both to set and to print, and many of them can fairly be characterized as type-identical with their handwritten counterparts. A cross-out line through type, for instance, needs no interpretation: it simply *means* deleted, just as it would in manuscript. The effect may be compared with the effect of arbitrary symbols, such as "pointed brackets to the left or right, arrows, bars, and so on"—conventions that are ⟨of necessity⟩ ↑ both ↓ new and numerous, that may mean something different from one edition to the next, and that must, in any case, be consciously construed at each occurrence. At the same time, the risk of type-identical signs is that their editorial function as *signs* will be forgotten—that they will seem to picture rather than to transcribe the original manuscript. It is necessary to emphasize, therefore, that despite its greater visual resemblance to the handwritten originals, plain text is emphatically not a type facsimile of them.[2] Like all diplomatic transcription, and indeed any kind of transcription except type facsimile, plain text does not reproduce the original lineation, pagination, or any nonsemantic aspect of the manuscript unless the writer intended it to bear meaning, which is exactly why it does reproduce many nonsemantic features in the form of typographical conventions that have more or less exact equivalents in manuscript.

Clemens's letters lend themselves to such treatment in part because his training as a printer seems to have given rise to a lifelong fascination with all typographical matters, and in part because he lived at a time when the equivalents between handwriting and type were probably more fully developed and more widely accepted than they had ever been before—or are ever likely to be again. For while, on the one hand, it is clear that Clemens did not intend his private and business letters to be set in type, on the other hand, either by force of habit, or from a certain pride in his expertise, he used the handwritten forms of a great many typographical conventions as consistently and precisely in letters as he did in manuscripts that were intended for the printer. This habitual practice makes it possible to transcribe the letters very much *as if* they were intended to be set in type—to use the system of equivalents employed by nineteenth-century writers to communicate precisely with their typesetters—but in reverse, to communicate precisely instead with the modern reader. Clemens's typographical expertise, in short, makes his letters easier to transcribe fully and precisely, as well as to read in transcription, than they otherwise would be, assuming that we understand the meaning of his

signs and the code for their typographical equivalents exactly as he did—
an assumption, unfortunately, that cannot always be taken as granted.

1. The Author's Signs

A few of the signs to be encountered in these letters may seem unfamiliar,
if not wholly exotic. Others may be familiar, even though today they lack
the precise and accepted meaning they had when Clemens used them.
Especially because some of these signs have fallen into disuse and (partly
for that reason) have been adapted by modern editors for their own purposes, it is the more necessary to insist that in our transcriptions of Clemens's letters, they bear only the meaning given them by the writer and his
contemporaries. Purely editorial signs in the text are identified on pages
xxxviii–xl below, and because some of these purposely adapt typographical conventions, they must be discriminated from authorial signs. But
no editorial sign has been used that would entail displacing a normal,
easily recognized typographical equivalent for one of the author's signs.

A problem arises, however, precisely because the historical (authorial)
meaning of certain handwritten and typographical signs has changed, or
become lost altogether. The problem is twofold: how to explicate those
signs whose authorial meaning differed from the modern meaning, but
can still be recovered, at least in part; and how to represent authorial signs
whose earlier typographical equivalent, if any, remains unknown, at least
to the editors.

The following Glossary of Special Sorts and table of Emphasis Equivalents are intended to alert the reader to those changes in meaning that we
are now able to identify, and to describe the handwritten forms for which
the typographical forms are taken to be equivalent—or, in a few cases,
for which they have been made equivalent because we lack a better alternative. The glossary includes signs that do not appear in every volume of
Mark Twain's Letters, much less in every letter, and doubtless omits some
signs that will need to be added in future volumes. Like the glossary, the
table of emphasis equivalents provides some information that was, and
often still is, regarded as common knowledge. That no table of compara-
ble detail has so far been found in any nineteenth- or twentieth-century
grammar, printers' handbook, dictionary, or encyclopedia would appear
to indicate that the system of emphasis was almost completely taken for
granted, hence rarely made fully explicit even by those who relied upon

it. At any rate, the particular meaning for Clemens of all such equivalents, including underscores, has had to be deduced or inferred from the letters themselves, and from countless examples of his practice in preparing literary manuscripts for the typist or typesetter (sometimes with the additional evidence of how they responded to his instructions), as well as from the consistent but usually partial testimony found in a variety of printer's handbooks, encyclopedias, manuals of forms, and other documents bearing on what we take to be the system of equivalents between handwriting and type.[3]

Glossary of Special Sorts

asterisks * * * Always called "stars" by Clemens and by printers generally, asterisks appear in his manuscript as simple crosses (✕) or, often when used singly, in a somewhat more elaborate variant of the cross (✳). In letters, Clemens used the asterisk as a standard reference mark, either to signal his occasional footnotes, or to refer one part of a letter to another part. He also used asterisks for a kind of ellipsis that was then standard and is still recognizable, and for one now virtually obsolete—the "line of stars"—in which evenly spaced asterisks occupy a line by themselves to indicate a major omission or, for Clemens at any rate, the passage of time. In transcribing the standard ellipsis, we reproduce exactly the number of asterisks in the original, thus: * * * * . In transcribing the line of stars, however, the exact number of asterisks becomes irrelevant, since the device is intended to fill the line, whether in manuscript or in type. The line of stars in our transcriptions is, therefore, always represented by seven asterisks, evenly separated and indented from both margins:

* * * * * * *

(The conventional order of the standard reference marks was as follows: *, †, ‡, §, ||, ¶, and, by the end of the century, ☞.)

braces } ⏟ { { Clemens drew the brace as a wavy vertical line that did not much resemble the brace in type, except that it clearly grouped two or three lines of text together. He drew braces intended for more than three lines as straight (nonwavy) lines with squared corners, like a large bracket, usually in the margin. He occasionally used the two- and three-line braces in pairs, vertically and horizontally, to box or partly enclose just one line of text. The one-line brace ({ }) was not known to Clemens and would probably have seemed a contradiction in terms. It appears to be a modern invention, but has sometimes proved useful in the transcription when the original lineation cannot be reproduced or readily simulated (see page 219). Otherwise, the transcription prints a brace and preserves, or at least simulates, the original lineation wherever Clemens drew a brace or a nonoriginal copy-text printed one.

fist   ☞   Clemens used the "fist," as it was called by printers (also
        ☜   "hand," "index," "index-mark," "mutton-fist," and
doubtless other names), not so much as the seventh of the standard reference marks, but for its much commoner purpose of calling special attention to some point in a text. As late as 1871 the *American Encyclopedia of Printing* characterized the device as used "chiefly in handbills, posters, direction placards, and in newspaper work" (Ringwalt, 217), but Clemens used it often—and without apology—in his letters. We transcribe it by a standard typographical device, either right- or left-pointing, as appropriate, except in special circumstances. For instance, in the following case, Clemens clearly meant to play upon the term "fist" by drawing and using the device as a distinctly *open hand*:

              ☞ "Put it *there*, Charlie!"

(Envelope of SLC to Charles J. and Olivia L. Langdon, 12 Dec 68, CU-MARK.) In all such cases we necessarily reproduce the fist in facsimile, rather than by typographic device.

paragraph   ¶   The paragraph sign is both a mark of emphasis and the
           sixth of the reference marks. It is actually "P" reversed
(left for right, and white for black) to distinguish it from that character. Clemens, however, commonly miswrote it as a "P," drawing the hollow stem with large, flat feet, but not the left/right or white/black reversal in the loop. Whenever the sign is used in a letter, we transcribe it by the standard typographical device, with a record of emendation when it has been misdrawn. Clemens used the paragraph sign as a reference mark and as shorthand for the word "paragraph," but most commonly in letters to indicate a change of subject within a passage, one of its earliest meanings. When he inserted the paragraph sign in text intended for a typesetter, he was doubtless specifying paragraph indention. But when he used it in a letter, he was usually invoking the earlier meaning as a substitute

for indention. The transcription always prints the sign itself, even when it was inserted (¶) or was manifestly an instruction to a typesetter. In the textual commentary, however, the paragraph sign in brackets [¶] is *editorial* shorthand for "paragraph indention."

paraph —⁓— Clemens drew the paraph, or signature flourish, in a wide variety of forms, from the very simple to the elaborate. Although nineteenth-century typography certainly used decorative flourishes, a typesetter would not ordinarily transcribe a paraph at all. We do transcribe it, in part because Clemens used the same or similar flourishes apart from his signature, much as a typesetter might use fancy dash rules. In our transcriptions, all flourishes (including paraphs) are rendered by the same arbitrary sign, varied only as necessary to accommodate differing signature lengths.

rules Rules (or rule dashes) in manuscript are usually, but not
═══ (a) ═══ invariably, centered on a line by themselves, serving to
═══ (b) ═══ separate sections of the text. When used within a line of
─── (c) ─── text, they are positioned like an ordinary em dash and
may serve as a common form of ellipsis, or simply to fill blank space in a line. This last function may be compared with the original purpose of the eighteenth-century flourish, namely to prevent forged additions in otherwise blank space. But as with the flourish, this function had in Clemens's day long since dissolved into a mainly decorative one. Rules appear in Clemens's manuscript in three distinguishable species, each with two variant forms. The historical names for the typographical rules appear to be obsolete, even though the rules themselves are still relatively familiar. We construe wavy lines in manuscript as "thick" rules, and straight lines as "thin" rules, regularizing length as necessary. (a) *Double rules* appear in manuscript as two parallel lines, one wavy and the other straight, in either order. (b) *Parallel rules* appear in manuscript as two parallel lines, either both wavy or both straight (thick or thin). (c) *Plain rules* appear as single lines, either wavy or straight (thick or thin).

Emphasis Equivalents

Clemens used the standard nineteenth-century system of underscoring to indicate emphasis, both relative and absolute, and both within and between words. He indubitably understood the equivalents in type for the various kinds of underscore, but even if he had not, they could probably be relied on for the transcription of his underscored words, simply because the handwritten and the typographical systems were mutually translatable. Although we may not understand this system as well as Clemens apparently did, it is still clear that he used it habitually and consistently, and that anomalies are much more likely to result from our, rather than his, ignorance or error.

Occasionally Clemens used what appear to be two variations of a single underscore—a broken underscore (when *not* prompted by descenders from the underscored word) and a wavy underscore (when more distinctly wavy than normally occurs with any hand-drawn line). If these are in fact variations of a single underscore, they evidently indicate a more deliberate, or a slightly greater, emphasis than single underscore would imply. They have been transcribed in *l e t t e r s p a c e d   i t a l i c* and **boldface** type, respectively, even though we do not know what, if any, typographical equivalent existed for them (both are marked ★ in the table). Clemens occasionally used letterspacing (with or without hyphens) as an a-l-t-e-r-n-a-t-i-v-e to italic, but he seems not to have combined it with italic, so that this editorial combination always signifies broken underscore. Wavy underscore in manuscript prepared for a printer did mean

MANUSCRIPT	TYPE
lowercase	roman lowercase
Capitals and Lowercase	Roman Capitals and Lowercase
lowercase	*italic lowercase*
Capitals and Lowercase	*Italic Capitals and Lowercase*
★Capitals and Lowercase	★*Italic Letterspaced*
★Capitals and Lowercase	★**Boldface Capitals and Lowercase**
lowercase	ROMAN SMALL CAPITALS
Capitals and Lowercase	ROMAN CAPITALS AND SMALL CAPITALS
CAPITALS or lowercase	ROMAN CAPITALS
CAPITALS or lowercase	*ITALIC CAPITALS*
★CAPITALS	★*ITALIC CAPITALS*
★1, 2, 3, 4, 5	★*1, 2, 3, 4, 5*

boldface, or some other fullface type, at least by 1900, but it is not clear for how long this convention had been in place.[4] And in any case, **boldface** would ordinarily be used for a level of emphasis higher than ROMAN CAPITALS or *ITALIC CAPITALS*. The use of boldface type to represent wavy underscore is thus an editorial convention.

Clemens also sometimes emphasized capital letters and numerals in ways that appear to exceed the normal limits of the typographical system as we know it. In such cases (also marked * in the table), we extend the fundamental logic of the underscoring system and simulate one underscore for each manuscript underscore that exceeds the highest known typographical convention. Thus when the pronoun "I" has been underscored twice in manuscript, it is transcribed as an italic capital with one underscore: "*I*". Otherwise, underscores in the original letter are simulated only (a) when Clemens included in his letter something he intended to have set in type, in which case his instructions to the typesetter must be reproduced, not construed, if they are to be intelligibly transcribed; and (b) when he deleted his underscore, in which case the transcription simulates it by using the standard manuscript convention for deleting an underscore.

Since underscores in manuscript may be revisions (added as an afterthought, even if not demonstrably so), one virtue of the system of equivalents is that it allows the transcription to encode exactly how the manuscript was marked without resorting to simulation. There are, however, some ambiguities in this reversed use of the code: for example, a word inscribed initially as "Knight" or as "knight" and then underscored three times would in either case appear in type as "KNIGHT." Clemens also sometimes used block or noncursive capitals or small capitals, simulating rather than signing "KNIGHT" or "ᴋɴɪɢʜᴛ." Ambiguities of this kind do not affect the final form in the text, but whenever Clemens used block or noncursive letters, or when other uncertainties about the form in the manuscript arise, they are noted or clarified in the record of emendations.

2. The Author's Revisions and Corrections

The transcription always represents authorial *revisions* where they occur in the text, as it does all but the most ephemeral kinds of *self-correction*. Either kind of change is wholly given in the transcription, except when giving all cases of a phenomenon, or all details of an occurrence, would destroy its legibility. But whenever revision occurs, the transcription in-

cludes at least the initial and the final reading, with intermediate stages
(if any) described in the record of emendations. Self-corrections are
emended more frequently than revisions, either to omit or to simplify
them, because many could not, for instance, be easily distinguished from
revisions except by consulting the textual commentary, even though this
distinction is perfectly intelligible in the original letter. Causal evidence
in the original, such as a line ending (misspel-|ling) or physical defect
resulting in an error, cannot be represented in the text without adding a
heavy burden of arbitrary editorial signs. And corrected errors internal
to a word are so frequent in manuscript that more than one kind of emendation has had to be invoked to bring their presence in the transcription
within manageable, which is to say readable, limits.

The transcription does not distinguish between *simple deletions* and
deletions by superimposition, in which the writer deleted one word by writing another on top of it. Because we have no way to make this distinction
legible in the transcription, we represent all deletions as simple deletions,
but record as an emendation each instance of deletion by superimposition. For example,

> 252.11   ~~the str~~ Montgomery • ['Mont' *over* 'the str']

Since insertions and deletions are always signaled, however, the transcription is almost always as informative as the manuscript about the
timing of any change—that is, whether it was made immediately, or on
review, or not demonstrably either. Most deletions were immediate, but
occasionally the immediacy of a change may be undetectable from the
transcription, even though it is clear in the manuscript. For example,
"Do~~nt~~ you own" includes a deletion that appears to be either immediate
or on review. But the manuscript shows conclusively that Clemens superimposed "you" on "nt," thereby deleting it immediately: he never wrote
"Dont you own" but only "Dont" then "Do~~nt~~ you own." The exact timing of some few changes, therefore, can be gathered only from the record
of emendations, which in this case reads:

> 203.12   Do~~nt~~ you • ['y' *over* 'nt']

All deletions that have been transcribed are, perforce, legible to the
editors, and were therefore arguably so to the original recipient. But
Clemens did occasionally make some deletions easier—or more difficult—to read than usual. Those obviously intended to be read, or not,
are identified in the notes when their special character is not otherwise
apparent from the transcription. Deletions by unusual but meaningful

methods are simulated in the transcription or, if that is unfeasible, described in a note, or both: see page 210, for instance. But in general, the transcription does not discriminate the various degrees of thoroughness Clemens used in deleting any part of his text. It may be added that some deletions in manuscript, especially of punctuation, were indicated there only by methods that are not themselves transcribable. For instance, when a sentence period has been superseded because Clemens added one or more words to his initial sentence, the initial period has rarely been struck out. Instead, Clemens signaled his intention simply by leaving only the usual word-space between the original last word and his addition, rather than the larger space always left following a sentence period. All such *implied deletions* are transcribed as if they had been normally deleted, and the fact is recorded as an emendation.

DELETIONS

■ Single characters as words, word fragments, or within words, as well as underscores are deleted with slash marks:

$$, \; \flat \; \ell \; \ell \; \chi \; \kappa \; \nu \; \prime \; \prime \; l \; \jmath \; + \; + \; \acute{a} \; \flat \; \cancel{c} \; \cancel{d} \; \cancel{\jmath} \; \cancel{k} \; \cancel{l} \; \cancel{v} \; \cancel{w} \; \cancel{x} \; \cancel{y} \; \cancel{z} \; \cancel{l} \; \cancel{p} \; \cancel{3} \; \cancel{4} \; \cancel{6}$$
$$\cancel{A} \; \cancel{B} \; \cancel{C} \; \cancel{D} \; \cancel{E} \; \cancel{F} \; \cancel{G} \; \cancel{H} \; \cancel{I} \; \cancel{J} \; \cancel{K} \; \cancel{L} \; \cancel{M} \; \cancel{N} \; \cancel{O} \; \cancel{P} \; \cancel{Q} \; \cancel{R} \; \cancel{S} \; \cancel{T} \; \cancel{U} \; \cancel{V} \; \cancel{W} \; \cancel{X} \; \cancel{Y} \; \cancel{Z} \; \cancel{\$} \; \cancel{\&}$$

'Annie is *well*' (66.22)

'I was slow to ȼ take up' (97.24)

'Ƚ Trip before last' (103.18)

'an absence of ȼ 3 weeks' (77.17)

'sacrifice ȧ feet in that claim' (141.1)

'Iȴ reckon you girls' (100.28)

'cheerfulȴness' (109.22)

■ Two or more characters as words, word fragments, or within words are deleted by a horizontal rule:

'the clerks were out ~~in town~~ on business' (108.5)

'~~had this ca~~ it was well that this calamity' (109.29–30)

'with~~out~~ the greatest interest' (112.17)

■ Separate, successive deletions of two or more characters are shown by gaps or breaks in the rule:

'light ~~seeming~~ ~~some~~ ~~a little sun~~ spreading away' (89.10–11)

These gaps never coincide with line ends in the transcription; rules that continue from the end of one line to the beginning of the next thus always signify continuous deletion, never separate deletions.

■ Deletions within deletions are shown by combining the slash mark and the horizontal rule (for single characters) or by two horizontal rules (for two or more characters):

> 'then ~~the gallant vessels~~ she bore away to windward.' (352.25–26)
>
> 'It was ~~Emma Ro Rowe,~~ Emma Roe, wasn't it?' (248.17–18)
>
> '~~5 W a .50 & 110 Col~~' (80.10)

The earlier of the two deletions is always represented by the shorter line. To read the first stage, mentally *peel away* the longer line, which undeletes the second stage.

INSERTIONS

■ Single characters inserted between words or within a word:

> 'voice to a ghastly confidential tone' (303.14–15)
>
> '(when I . . . take Ma to Ky;)'(19.23–24)
>
> 'darned if I know which!' (21.20–21)
>
> 'and some is a beautiful snowy white' (21.11–12)
>
> 'to their room' (304.8)
>
> 'It *can't be*, though.' (100.17)
>
> 'said some very startling things' (112.18)

■ Two or more characters inserted between words or within a word:

> 'We (Van. B. & I,) descended the Ophir incline' (153.24)
>
> 'if I hadn't thoughtlessly got you into the notion' (157.11–12)

INSERTIONS WITH DELETIONS

■ Insertions with deletions of one or more words, combined in various sequences:

> 'worth knowing, ~~the King included, I believe.~~' (333.9)
>
> '~~Eighteen months~~ A short time, ago' (268.11)
>
> 'intended to say, Aunt Betsey, that, probably' (94.1)

■ Insertions with deletions combined within a word or numeral:

> 'mMay-tree' ['may-tree' *altered to* 'May-tree'] (89.36)
>
> 'wishesing' ['es' *over* 'ing' *to make* 'wishes'] (66.17)
>
> 'necessitary' ['it' *over* 'ar' *of* 'necessary' *to make* 'necessity'] (163.11)

Note that in the above cases the caret indicating insertion is used to identify characters that have usually been superimposed on earlier written characters, thereby deleting them. Superimposition is, in such cases, a kind of insertion designed to place new characters next to standing characters: Clemens might have achieved much the same thing, albeit with greater trouble, by literally interlining the characters. The timing of insertions internal to a word must be understood as pertaining only *within* the sequence of change to that word, *not* as later than any other part of the text: such changes are, in fact, almost invariably immediate.

Alterations within a word are transcribed in the text only if the original form was a complete word, even though not a possible word in context, or if it was a misspelling or start of a word possible in context. Thus the reader will find 'literaᴖture' (322.20) in the text because it contains the beginning of 'literary', but will not find 'excursiᴖon' (255.19–20) except in the report of emendations because it contains no other word or part of a word possible in context, nor is it a genuine misspelling. This rule of thumb has been invoked because the notation for internally altered words is unconventional, and because such words occur very frequently in manuscript, so that they would pose a serious threat to overall legibility if always transcribed. To further reduce the impediment within manageable limits, we simplify internally altered words, whether or not the original form was a word or start of a word possible in context, *whenever Clemens reused three or fewer characters*, counting quotation marks, parentheses, dollar signs, and the like. In all such cases we transcribe the initial and final forms as if they had been separately inscribed. Altered numerals are always simplified in this way, even if Clemens reused more than three digits.

'~~and~~ any' ['anyᴖ' *simplified*] (97.11)

'~~asking~~ getting' ['askₐgetting' *simplified*] (195.10–11)

'~~$20~~ $40' ['$ᴖ40' *simplified*] (186.9)

' "A "Snag' [' "Snagₐ' *simplified*] (100.30)

To quote the letters without including the author's alterations, simply omit carets and crossed-out matter, closing up the space left by their omission. For the correct forms of compound words divided at the end of a line in this edition, see the list of emendations for each letter.

3. The Editors' Signs

The editorial heading for each letter gives the name of the person or persons addressed, the date or dates of composition, the place or places of composition, as well as joint correspondents, persons writing on Clemens's behalf, and his amanuensis, if any. A final, separate line in smaller type briefly identifies the source documents used for the text, separated by a colon from their location, usually given as an abbreviation defined in References.

EDITORIAL HEADING

To . . . From . . .	Clemens himself is not named in the heading when he is the sole author of the letter. When someone else is writing on his behalf, or jointly with him, both Clemens and his agent or coauthor are named in the order of their first appearance in that letter.
per . . .	With documents inscribed or typed for Clemens, the amanuensis is identified following "*per.*"
3? October	The question mark indicates a conjecture: probably 3 October, but possibly a little later or earlier.
24–29 June	A span of dates joined by an en dash indicates a less specific conjecture: the date or dates of composition are thought to fall within this span.
2 and 3 May	Not a conjecture, but an assertion that the letter was written in part on each date given.
MS	Manuscript (MS) unmodified in the source line means the transcription has been checked against the original document sent. *Modifications* in this volume include:
author's copy	The source document is in Clemens's hand, but is his *copy* of the document actually sent.
damage emended	The source document is damaged and the transcription includes emendation to restore portions of text no longer visible. See the textual commentary, which usually includes a facsimile of the damaged source.
draft not sent	The source document is in Clemens's hand, but is a draft of the document actually sent.
draft telegram	The source document is in Clemens's hand, but is a draft of the telegram, not the copy received.
facsimile	The source document is a photographic facsimile, published or unpublished, of the original document sent.

paraphrase   The source document is a paraphrase judged to preserve at least some of the original words.

transcript   The source document is a printed, handwritten, or typed transcription (omitted when manifestly published).

LETTER TEXT

VIRGINIA CITY   Extra-small small capitals with no initial capitals identify printed text that was not originated by Clemens, such as letterhead or the postmark.

Feb. 19th   Dotted underscores signify a blank in the source document, whether or not the blank was so printed in the source, and whether or not Clemens filled it.

                    Ruled borders are an editorial device to represent the edge of printed or partly printed documents, such as telegram blanks, and are not transcribed from them.

.   .   .   .   Editorial ellipses, four periods centered in an otherwise blank line, signify an unknown amount of text missing. All other ellipses are transcribed as they appear in the source document.

a em deletion   Deletions are signaled by slash marks through single characters or underscores, and by rules through two or more characters.

making it up   Insertions are signaled by an inferior caret below single characters, and by a pair of carets enclosing two or more characters.

letter text   Shaded background identifies text *not originated* by Clemens, but by someone writing jointly with him. Not used for text *originated* by Clemens but written in another hand, or text of *any* origin transcribed below the envelope rule.

[ ]   Clemens's brackets are rendered in this form to avoid any confusion with editorial brackets.

[ ]   Editorial brackets enclose [*editorial description, which is always italicized*]; or text omitted inadvertently by the writer an[d] here interpolated by [the] editors; or text modified by description [*in margin:* All well].

d◇◇m◇nd   The diamond is an editorial sign representing any alpha-
                   betical character, numeral, or punctuation mark which
                   the editors cannot read or reliably conjecture. It *never*
                   signifies word-space. When the number of unread char-
                   acters cannot be estimated, the problematic text is de-
                   scribed, as in [*about three words illegible*].

letter[1] text.[2] Superscript numbers signal editorial notes, which follow
                   the letter itself.

Sam*l*   Superscript ell is always rendered italic to prevent confu-
                   sion between superscript one ([1]) and superscript ell ([l]).

✉———————   The envelope and full-measure rule indicate that all text
                   transcribed below them was written or printed on the
                   envelope at the time of transmission, or on the letter itself
                   as an address, receiver's endorsement, or docket.

| The vertical rule signifies the end of a line in the source
                   document. It is used only below the envelope rule, in
                   notes, and in the textual commentary.

4. Emendation of the Copy-Text

We emend original documents as little as possible, and nonoriginal documents as much as necessary, but basically for only two reasons: to prevent the transcription from including an error, ambiguity, or puzzle that
either (a) *is not in the original* or (b) is in the original but *cannot be intelligibly transcribed* without correcting, resolving, or simplifying it.

With the system of notation used in plain text, it is technically feasible
to transcribe much more detail than is consistent with maximum legibility. For example, the two words 'yourself about' (17.9) might have been
transcribed 'yourse/lf abo/ut', as indeed they are in the record of emendations, which reports the omission from the transcription of these two
self-corrections. But if the transcription were to include *all* such self-
corrections, instead of only those permitted by the several rules of thumb
already described, their sheer number, in combination with this still unconventional notation, would seriously impair the overall legibility of the
letters as a whole. This result is typical, and it means that the crucial
factor in deciding whether or not to emend is usually *not* whether includ-

ing this or that detail would make the text more reliable or complete (it would), but whether the detail *can* be intelligibly and consistently transcribed. By and large, if it can, it is, and if it cannot, it is emended.

This practical criterion for deciding "what to put in and what to leave out" does not, however, tell a reader exactly what to expect. Indeed, the more customary way to discriminate between transcribed and untranscribed details is to say, or imply, that the omitted details are not "significant." But there is, in fact, no necessary or obvious hypothetical limit on which details have "significance" in the text of personal letters, and we must assume that almost any semantic or nonsemantic detail of a letter *might* be "significant" to someone, in some circumstances.

But if there is no clear hypothetical limit on what to transcribe, there *is* a practical limit, which is jointly determined by the system of notation used and the purpose for which transcription is undertaken in the first place. Since our system of notation can represent more detail than can be made fully legible, nothing would be easier than to produce transcriptions that were *more difficult to read than the original letters*. But we assume that for most readers, most of the time—including readers interested in these ephemeral details of the original—the basic purpose of transcription is to make the letters easier to read than they are in the widely dispersed original documents. This is not to say that the criterion of legibility amounts to a magic wand, automatically producing reliable texts because they are made legible: with a less flexible system of notation, legibility most surely would not guarantee reliability. Legibility has become the decisive factor for plain text only because its system of notation is capable of including more, and doing so more legibly, than any other system known to us (not to say that it is beyond improvement). But whether or not plain text succeeds in omitting nothing of consequence from the transcription, and nothing that *may be* of consequence from the record of emendation, is a question that only experience with the result can answer satisfactorily. Meanwhile, it may be helpful at least to survey some recognizable categories of detail that are in fact frequently or invariably emended.

Authorial errors are not emended if they can be intelligibly transcribed. Some few errors are corrected within brackets—specifically those that can be fully and decisively repaired by *interpolating* what the writer has inadvertently omitted. Such interpolations may be necessary to construe the text at all, let alone to read it easily, and they can coexist with an otherwise uncorrected text because they correct errors without conceal-ing them. Strictly speaking, interpolations are not emendations, because like superscript numbers for notes they are always recognizably editorial from the text alone. Interpolations are therefore not routinely recorded as emendations.

Errors in a nonoriginal copy-text, such as a newspaper printing, are al-ways emended when the odds favor even a less than certain recovery of the reading in the lost original. Clemens's precise, even finicky habits make it more, rather than less, likely that errors in such a printing are the typesetter's, especially since the typesetter was in general not committed to an exact transcription but rather to a corrected form of the document being set in type. If an error in a newspaper text is deemed typical or characteristic of Clemens, however, it is *not* emended, although if it is a simple omission it may be corrected by interpolation. Likewise, when a nonoriginal copy-text seems to depart from the original (for example, in a signature printed as "CLEMENS"), no emendation would be made unless the editors *also* had substantial evidence of how the signature was in fact written. In short, whenever the text depends upon nonoriginal documents derived from the lost originals, the editors emend the copy-text when reliable evidence suggests not just that its reading is mistaken, but also what the likely reading of the original really *was*.

Damaged texts (usually, but not necessarily, the original manuscripts) are likewise emended whenever possible to restore the original, though now invisible, reading. Emendation in such cases is, despite some ap-pearance to the contrary, still based on documentary evidence: some-times a copy of the original made before it was damaged, or damaged to its present extent—but more commonly evidence still in the original doc-uments, such as fragments of the original characters, the size and shape of the missing pieces, the regularity of inscribed characters (or type) and of margin formation, the grammar and syntax of a partly missing sen-tence, and, more generally, Clemens's documented habits of spelling, punctuation, and diction. We undertake such emendations even though they are inevitably conjectural, in part because the alternative is to render the text even less complete than it is in the damaged original (since sen-tence fragments are unintelligible without *some* conjecture, however ten-tative, about the whole sentence), and in part because only a definite, albeit uncertain, conjecture is likely to elicit any effort to improve upon what the editors have been able to perform. For this same reason, a facsimile of any seriously damaged document is always provided, either in an appendix or in the textual commentary.

Alterations in the manuscript, meaning both revisions and self-corrections, are fully represented in the transcription, except when they are emended because they are too complicated to be readily intelligible in transcription; or because they are self-corrections (corrected false starts, miswritten characters, and the like) which cannot be transcribed intelligibly as corrections; or because one or another kind of detail, such as deletion by superimposition, is not yet susceptible of clear transcription.

End-line occurrences requiring some adjustment in transcription seem nearly infinite in their variety, and are probably the most common occasion for emendation. For example, all ambiguously hyphenated compounds ("water-|wheel") must be rendered unambiguously in the transcription ("waterwheel" *or* "water-wheel"), since their division at a line end cannot be duplicated. Even noncompound words divided at the end of a line may sometimes be ambiguous in ways that cannot be legibly preserved in the transcription: "*wit-|ness*" in the original must be either "*witness*" or "*witness*." Dittography of words or punctuation likewise occurs most frequently at line ends, physical evidence that makes it readily intelligible as an error in the source but that is lost in a transcription which abandons the original lineation. In other words, dittography becomes *more* difficult to construe readily when it is simply copied, and it is therefore emended. (This decision in turn requires that intralinear dittography also be emended in order not to give a distorted impression of this overall class of error in the original documents.)

One frequent (and frequently misunderstood) end-line occurrence that is always emended occurs in both original and nonoriginal copy-texts, although for slightly different reasons: the em dash following terminal punctuation *and* at a line end (not to be confused with the intralinear period-dash that for some of Clemens's contemporaries, but not for Clemens himself, was quite ordinary terminal punctuation). The period-dash combination in Clemens's manuscript virtually always occurs at a line end, at least until about the mid-1880s, when he seems to have trained himself not to use it at all, probably because typesetters so often misinterpreted it. The typographical use of "period.—|End line" probably originated as an inexpensive way to justify a line of type (especially in narrow measure, as for a newspaper) when a sentence ended so near the right margin that there was not room to set both the standard em quad (space) after the period and at least the first syllable of the first word in the next sentence. But Clemens used this same device in his manuscript whenever the last word in a sentence fell too near his right margin to permit the normal space and at least the beginning of the next word. The dash indicates that the slightly short line does *not* portend a new paragraph, but it may also have some familial relation to the eighteenth-century flourish used to prevent forged additions, since it sometimes occurs at the end of short lines that *are* followed by a new paragraph. Its function may be generally compared to that of a hyphen used at the end of a line to indicate that, even though a word has been divided, it is still to be understood as one word. In any case, whenever a dash in manuscript follows a period (or other clearly terminal punctuation) and also falls at the end of a line, the dash cannot be intelligibly transcribed because its meaning is a function of its position at the end of a short line. The dash is therefore emended and the change recorded, much the way "ob-|vious" would be transcribed, albeit silently, as "obvious." When "period.—|End line" occurs in a newspaper or other printing of a lost manuscript letter, it doubtless reflects the typesetter's own use of this method for right justification, and is necessarily emended. And when "period.—Dash" (that is, period-dash *within* a line) occurs in such a printing, it is almost certainly the result of the typesetter's misunderstanding the convention in Clemens's manuscript, and is likewise emended.

To save space, we transcribe only routine addresses on envelopes by using the vertical rule (|) to signify line end; nonroutine text on envelopes is transcribed by most of the same conventions used for the letters themselves. The text of preprinted letterhead is reproduced in EXTRA-SMALL SMALL CAPITALS, usually in its entirety, but when unusually verbose, only to the extent that Clemens may be said to adopt or refer to it ("I'm down here at the office"). Only substantive omissions from this preprinted, nonauthorial matter are reported as emendations. Whenever Clemens used any of the following typographical conventions in his manuscript, or whenever they occur in nonoriginal copy-texts and are deemed authorial, the transcription reproduces or simulates them: diagonal indention; hanging indention; half-diamond indention; squared indention; text centered on a line; the flush-left paragraph and the half-line of extra space (its collateral convention); text positioned flush-right; quotations set off by quotation marks, indention, reduced space between lines (reduced leading in type), extra space above, below (or both), smaller characters in manuscript (type size in nonoriginals), or any combination of these conventions. In *Volume 1*, normal paragraph indention is standardized at two ems, with variations of one em and three ems often occurring in the same letter.

We silently eliminate minor, presumably unintended variation in the size of all indentions, and we place datelines, salutations, complimentary closings, and signatures in a default position when this is not contradicted by the manuscript. Likewise, unmistakably large variation in the size of indention is treated as deliberate, or as an error, and reproduced or simulated, not corrected or made uniform. Notes which Clemens specifically did not insert within the letter text but wrote instead in its margin are nevertheless transcribed at the most appropriate place within the text, identified by editorial description: [*in margin:* All well], or [*in bottom margin:* over]. Regardless of where postscripts are written, they are transcribed in the order they were supposed to be read, as specified by various means in the original, such as "P.P.S." (clearly intended to be read after "P.S."). Postscripts inserted above the beginning of a letter, therefore, are transcribed at the beginning so long as they were inscribed in the same orientation as the letter itself. When written across or at an angle to the main text—a sign they are not to be read before or in conjunction with the text they precede or cross—they are transcribed at the end of the letter. Only *changes* in writing media are noted where they occur in the text, as in [*postscript in pencil:*], from which it may also be reliably inferred that all preceding text was in ink. Line endings, page endings, and page numbers are silently omitted from the transcription, but where they affect the text or its emendation, they are given in the record of emendation.

July 1987 R. H. H.

[1] According to Fredson Bowers, "General methods of transcription divide neatly in two," which is to say *clear text* (with supplementary apparatus containing all details of revision) or *genetic text* (without apparatus because the text itself contains all details of revision). A clear text transcribes the revised form of a manuscript "diplomatically," meaning that the "transcription exactly follows the forms of the manuscript in spelling, punctuation, word-division, italics (for underlining), and capitalization, but not in matters of spacing or in line-division, nor is a facsimile visual presentation of alterations attempted." A genetic text, on the other hand, includes authorial alterations in place "by means of a number of arbitrary symbols like pointed brackets to the left or right, arrows, bars, and so on," with the common result that it is "difficult to read the original text consecutively; [and] it is impossible to read the revised text at all in a coherent sequence" ("Transcription of Manuscripts: The Record of Variants," *Studies in Bibliography*

[1976], 29:213–14, 248). *Plain text*, however, descends from a kind of transcription not mentioned by Bowers, in which the myriad details of a manuscript (particularly details of the author's alterations) are systematically divided between the text and its apparatus, precisely in order to make the text as complete and informative as possible without destroying its legibility (see *N&J1*, 575–84). The practical result of this division is radically improved by adopting a less obtrusive and more readable system of notation than has been used in the past: plain text simultaneously increases both the amount of detail that can be included in the text and its overall legibility.

[2] It is also not a "literal" text, even though it is probably as inclusive as most texts for which that claim is made. Nor is it, strictly speaking, a "noncritical" text, as defined by G. Thomas Tanselle, since even though it "aims at reproducing a given earlier text [the original letter] as exactly as possible," the editor defines what is possible by what he is able to transcribe legibly. He is therefore "making decisions about how the new text will differ from the text in the document," and the result is necessarily a text that "then becomes a critical text" ("Textual Scholarship" in *Introduction to Scholarship in Modern Languages and Literatures*, edited by Joseph Gibaldi [New York: Modern Language Association, 1981], 32, 47).

[3] This is not the place for a full bibliography of relevant sources, but it may be helpful to name at least those found most frequently useful and pertinent: Thomas F. Adams, *Typographia; or, the Printer's Instructor* (Philadelphia: L. Johnson and Co., 1857; copyrighted 1845); Theodore Low De Vinne, *Correct Composition*, 3d ed. (New York: Century Company, 1910; copyrighted 1901); [George A. Gaskell], *Gaskell's American Manual and Compendium of Forms*, new and revised edition by Loomis T. Palmer (Chicago: M. A. Donohue and Co., 1903); Thomas MacKellar, *The American Printer: A Manual of Typography*, facsimile of the "fifteenth edition—revised and enlarged" (Philadelphia: MacKellar, Smiths and Jordan, 1885; facsimile by Harold A. Berliner, Nevada City, Calif., 1977); Lindley Murray, *An English Grammar: Comprehending the Principles and Rules of the Language . . . In Two Volumes* (New York: Collins and Perkins, 1810); [Wesley Washington Pasko], *American Dictionary of Printing and Bookmaking* (New York: Howard Lockwood and Co., 1894; facsimile edition, Detroit: Gale Research Company, 1967); J. Luther Ringwalt, ed., *American Encyclopaedia of Printing* (Philadelphia: Menamim and Ringwalt, J. B. Lippincott and Co., 1871); A. A. Stewart, *The Printer's Dictionary of Technical Terms* (Boston: School of Printing, North End Union, 1912); and C. Stower, *The Printer's Grammar; or, Introduction to the Art of Printing* (London: B. Crosby and Co., 1808).

[4] Citing "Mr. J. Stearns Cushing of the Norwood Press" for his information about "underscorings for display in school-books," including wavy underscore for boldface, De Vinne demonstrates that the convention was well established when he first copyrighted *Correct Composition* in 1901 (De Vinne, 340). But the date of its origin remains in doubt.

Letters: 1853–1866

Sometime in the first two weeks of June 1853, Samuel L. Clemens (aged seventeen) left his home and family in Hannibal, Missouri, for the first time, stopping initially in St. Louis and then going on to New York City, supporting himself as a journeyman printer in both places. Precisely when Clemens boarded the regular evening packet for St. Louis is not known: in his autobiography he said simply that he "disappeared one night and fled to St. Louis" (AD, 29 Mar 1906, CU-MARK, in *MTA*, 2:287). On 26 October 1853, however, he mentioned that he had first departed Hannibal "more than four months ago" (26–?28 Oct 53 to OC and HC). Since it would have been exactly four months on that day if he had left Hannibal on 26 June, Clemens himself seems to place his departure in the early weeks of that month.

Having sworn to his mother that he would not "throw a card or drink a drop of liquor" during his absence from home, Clemens was somewhat less than candid with her about his real plans, which, as Albert Bigelow Paine reported, were even then "to go farther than St. Louis" (*MTB*, 1:93). Three years later, in fact, when Clemens decided to conceal his true plans for traveling to Brazil from his older brother, Orion, she slyly acknowledged his earlier deceit: "Ma knows my determination," he wrote his younger brother, Henry, "but *even she* counsels me to keep it from Orion. She says I can treat him as I did her when I started to St. Louis and went to New York—I can start to New York and go to South America.!" (5 Aug 56 to HC).

Clemens's incentive for leaving home had been building for more than two years. In January 1851 he had cheerfully joined with Henry in going to work for Orion, who had just begun his efforts to publish the Hannibal *Western Union* and, a few months later, to revive the moribund Hannibal *Journal*. In part, Clemens's willingness simply derived from the relief he felt at ending his apprenticeship under Joseph P. Ament of the Hannibal

Missouri Courier. But as Orion later admitted, his brother's hopes for an easier and more independent berth were to be disappointed. "I was tyrannical and unjust to Sam," Orion recalled somewhat lugubriously in 1880.

He was as swift and as clean as a good journeyman. I gave him tasks, and if he got through well I begrudged him the time and made him work more. He set a clean proof, and Henry a very dirty one. The correcting was left to be done in the form the day before publication. Once we were kept late, and Sam complained with tears of bitterness that he was held till midnight on Henry's dirty proofs. (*MTB*, 1:85)

When Clemens ventured to enliven the Hannibal *Journal* by writing controversial satire for it (as he did in 1852 and 1853, while left briefly in charge), Orion's response was not unequivocally encouraging (*ET&S1*, 6–7, 102). Only when matters seemed near a crisis did Orion think to gratify his brother's literary impulse by instituting a feature he called, pointedly, "Our Assistant's Column." Clemens contributed this column only three times (on 23, 25, and 26 May 1853), and by the time of its second appearance, Orion was already looking for a replacement for his brother: "WANTED! AN APPRENTICE TO THE PRINTING BUSINESS! APPLY SOON" first ran on 25 May and continued daily through 10 June, evidently without success, for on the tenth Orion was obliged to suspend publication for a month—a clear sign that his brother had left him without adequate help (Wecter, 263).

In St. Louis Clemens was free to please himself. He probably stayed with his older sister, Pamela Ann, who in 1851 had married William A. Moffett (1816–65), later described by Clemens as "a merchant, a Virginian—a fine man in every way" (AD, 29 Mar 1906, in *MTA*, 2:289). Formerly in business in Hannibal, Moffett was now a partner in Moffett, Stillwell and Company, St. Louis commission merchants. The Moffetts' first child, Annie, had been born on 1 July 1852, but they were still not keeping house: they rented their home on Pine Street and boarded nearby, with an aunt (see 5 Dec 53 to PAM, n. 3).

Clemens's principal job was as a typesetter for the St. Louis *Evening News*, but he also worked on several other weekly journals published in the city. He may have tried to publish some sketches with the St. Louis *Missouri Republican* at this time, but his first months as a professional typesetter probably left him little time for literature (*ET&S1*, 8–9). A fellow printer recalled that "while the rest of us were drawing our $12 a week, it was all Sam Clemens could do to make $8 or $9. He always had so many errors marked in his proofs that it took most of his time correcting them. He could not have set up an advertisement in acceptable form to save his life" (Anthony Kennedy, 560). This description is somewhat suspect, but Clemens probably did have a bit yet to learn about his craft.

His two-month stay in St. Louis ended on 19 August, when he "ran away . . . & visited the World's Fair" in New York City (SLC 1899a, 3). He arrived in New York on 24 August, the date of his first surviving letter, which Orion promptly published in the *Journal*.

To Jane Lampton Clemens
24 August 1853 • New York, N.Y.
(Hannibal *Journal*, 5 Sept 53)

NEW YORK, ⎱
Wednesday, August 24th, 1853. ⎰

MY DEAR MOTHER: you will doubtless be a little surprised, and somewhat angry when you receive this, and find me so far from home; but you must bear a little with me, for you know I was always the best boy you had, and perhaps you remember the people used to say to their children—"Now don't do like Orion and Henry Clemens but take Sam for your guide!"[1]

Well, I was out of work in St. Louis, and didn't fancy loafing in such a dry place, where there is no pleasure to be seen without paying well for it, and so I thought I might as well go to New York. I packed up my "duds" and left for this village, where I arrived, all right, this morning.

It took a day, by steamboat and cars, to go from St. Louis to Bloomington, Ill; another day by railroad, from there to Chicago, where I laid over all day Sunday; from Chicago to Monroe, in Michigan, by railroad, another day; from Monroe, across Lake Erie, in the fine Lake palace, "Southern Michigan," to Buffalo, another day; from Buffalo to Albany, by railroad, another day; and from Albany to New York, by Hudson river steamboat, another day—an awful trip, taking five days, where it should have been only three.[2] I shall wait a day or so for my insides to get settled, after the jolting they received, when I shall look out for a sit;[3] for they say there is plenty of work to be had for *sober* compositors.[4]

The trip, however, was a very pleasant one. Rochester, famous on account of the "Spirit Rappings" was of course interesting;[5] and when I saw the Court House in Syracuse, it called to mind the time when it was surrounded with chains and companies of soldiers, to prevent the rescue of McReynolds' nigger, by the infernal abolitionists. I reckon I had better black my face, for in these Eastern States niggers are considerably better than white people.[6]

I saw a curiosity to-day, but I don't know what to call it. Two beings, about like common people, with the exception of their faces, which are more like the "phiz"[7] of an orang-outang, than human. They are white, though, like other people. Imagine a person about the size of Harvel Jordan's oldest boy,[8] with small lips and full breast, with a constant uneasy, fidgety motion, bright, intelligent eyes, that seems as if they would look through you, and you have these *things*. They were found in the island of Borneo (the only ones of the species ever discovered,) about twenty years ago. One of them is twenty three, and the other twenty five years of age. They possess amazing strength; the smallest one would shoulder three hundred pounds as easily as I would a plug of tobacco; they are supposed to be a cross between man and orang-outang; one is the best natured being in the world, while the other would tear a stranger to pieces, if he did but touch him; they wear their hair "Samson" fashion, down to their waists. They have no apple in their throats, whatever, and can therefore scarcely make a sound; no memory either; what transpires to-day, they have forgotten before to-morrow; they look like one mass of muscle, and can walk either on all fours or upright; when let alone, they will walk to and fro across the room, thirteen hours out of the twenty-four; not a day passes but they walk twenty-five or thirty miles, without resting thirty minutes; I watched them about an hour and they were "tramping" the whole time. The little one bent his arm with the elbow in front, and the hand pointing upward, and no two strapping six footers in the room could pull it out straight. Their faces and eyes are those of the beast, and when they fix their glittering orbs on you with a steady, unflinching gaze, you instinctively draw back a step, and a very unpleasant sensation steals through your veins. They are both males and brothers, and very small, though I do not know their exact hight.[9] I have given you a very lengthy description of the animals, but I have nothing else to write about, and nothing from here would be interesting anyhow. The Crystal

Palace is a beautiful building[10]—so is the Marble Palace.[11] If I can find nothing better to write about, I will say something about these in my next.

[*closing and signature missing*]

[1] To introduce this letter in the Hannibal *Journal*, Orion Clemens wrote: "The free and easy impudence of the writer of the following letter will be appreciated by those who recognize him. We should be pleased to have more of his letters." As Orion implied, newspaper decorum required him to remove or disguise personal references when publishing a private letter. He therefore omitted the signature and modified several proper names that would have been recognized in Hannibal. For instance, he printed "Now don't do like O. and H. C— but take S. for your guide!"—a cryptic form that Clemens would not have used in a letter to his own mother. In this sentence and one other (see note 8), the likely readings of the original have been adopted instead of Orion's departures from it; the emendations are recorded in the textual apparatus.

[2] Clemens's account, together with contemporary advertisements, suggests the following itinerary:

Day 1: Friday, 19 August. 8:00 A.M., from St. Louis to Alton, Illinois, by the steamer *Cornelia*; 11:00 A.M., from Alton to Springfield on the partly completed Chicago and Mississippi Railroad; by Frink's stage to Bloomington.

Day 2: Saturday, 20 August. From Bloomington to Chicago via La Salle on the Illinois Central and the Chicago and Rock Island railroads, arriving at 7:00 P.M.

Day 3: Sunday, 21 August. 9:00 P.M., after a twenty-six hour layover, from Chicago to Toledo, and from Toledo to Monroe, Michigan, on the Michigan Central and the Northern Indiana and Michigan Southern railroads.

Day 4: Monday, 22 August. 8:00 A.M., from Monroe across Lake Erie to Buffalo, New York, by the steamer *Southern Michigan*.

Day 5: Tuesday, 23 August. 7:00 A.M., from Buffalo to Albany via Rochester and Syracuse on the New York "Lightning Express"; 7:00 P.M., en route via the Hudson River to New York City on the steamer *Isaac Newton*.

Day 6: Wednesday, 24 August. 5:00 A.M., arrives in New York City aboard the steamer *Isaac Newton*.

[3] Short for "situation": printers' slang for "position" or "post of employment" (Jacobi, 125).

[4] Clemens alludes to his promise not to drink while away from Hannibal (*MTB*, 1:93). Anthony Kennedy, who had set type with him in St. Louis during "the spring of 1853," recalled more than fifty years later: "The most remarkable thing I remember about Clemens . . . is the fact that he was not 'one of the boys.' Then, more than now, it was the proud prerogative of printers to be able to drink more red whisky than men of any other trade. But Clemens, so far as I can remember, never took a drink" (Anthony Kennedy, 560).

[5] In 1848, Margaret and Kate Fox, sisters aged thirteen and twelve respectively, made Rochester famous by attributing to "spirits" the inexplicable knocking sounds, or "rappings," which they in fact created by cracking the joints of their

toes. Forty years later, Margaret confessed the ruse, long after it had precipitated the American spiritualist craze, which peaked in the 1850s and again in the 1870s (Kerr, 3–9, 119).

[6] On 1 October 1851, Jerry McHenry, a slave owned by John McReynolds (a prosperous landowner just outside Hannibal), had been arrested as a fugitive in Syracuse, New York, where he had been living for several years. An angry crowd twice stormed the courthouse, ultimately freeing the victim when the militia refused to cooperate further with the police. Like other controversial efforts to enforce the Fugitive Slave Act of 1850, this one received wide publicity in the newspapers (McDougall, 48–49; "Slave Catching in Syracuse—Intense Excitement," *Liberator* 21 [10 Oct 51]: 2). The attitude Clemens exhibits here—hardly unusual for a seventeen-year-old white Southerner on his first visit to the North—would change radically by 1861.

[7] Face or visage, used humorously or in contempt; an abbreviation of "physiognomy."

[8] Harvel Jordan (b. 1814 or 1815) had been a livery keeper in Hannibal since 1846. Born in Virginia, he moved with his parents to Missouri in 1831. In 1839 he married Lucy A. Dornes, with whom he had had five children by 1850, including two sons, Samuel and Milton, who in 1853 would have been twelve and seven, respectively (*Hannibal Census*, 313; Holcombe, 960). Jordan had recently joined the partnership of Shoot, Jordan and Davis, "the largest and most splendid Stable outside of St. Louis" (advertisement for Monroe House, Hannibal *Journal*, 11 May 53, 2). Orion's compositors appear to have misread Clemens's "H" as "F" and, in disguising Jordan's name, set "F.———J———'s" (emended; see the textual apparatus). No one listed in the 1850 Hannibal census had these initials (F. J.) and two sons of appropriate age.

[9] Some thirty years later, P. T. Barnum was to exhibit the "Wild Men of Borneo," supposedly captured in 1848. Known as Plutano and Waino, Hiram and Barney Davis were born in 1825 and 1827, respectively, and may be the *"things"* Clemens describes here. On 22 September 1853, Horace Greeley's New York *Tribune* inveighed against the custom whereby "Broadway is never without one or more damnable monsters on exhibition" ("Disgusting Exhibitions," 4).

[10] This was the main hall of the Exhibition of the Industry of All Nations, New York's first world's fair, which had opened on 14 July while Clemens was still in St. Louis. A large, domed building of glass and cast iron, it enclosed nearly six acres of exhibition space on two floors and stood at what was then the northern end of the city in Reservoir Square, facing Sixth Avenue between Fortieth and Forty-second streets (Greeley, 13–16; *Exhibition Catalogue*, 7–10). The Crystal Palace and its exhibits had been widely publicized in American newspapers, including those Clemens read in Hannibal and St. Louis. Probably he himself had remarked in the Hannibal *Journal* of 26 May: "From fifteen to twenty thousand persons are continually congregated around the new Crystal Palace in New York city, and drunkenness and debauchery are carried on to their fullest extent" (SLC 1853, 3).

[11] The grandiose dry-goods store built by multimillionaire Alexander T. Stewart (1803–76) in 1846, and enlarged in 1850, stood at Broadway and Chambers Street. Faced entirely with white marble, it was advertised as the most costly building ever occupied by an individual merchant. On 28 May 1867, having re-

New York's Crystal Palace with Latting Observatory at left, 1853. Original lithograph by N. Currier in the J. Clarence Davies Collection, Museum of the City of New York.

Interior of the Crystal Palace, 1853 (Joseph M. Wilson, xxix).

turned to New York as a reporter for the San Francisco *Alta California*, Clemens criticized Stewart's similarly ostentatious home on Fifth Avenue at Thirty-fourth Street, saying that it looked "like a mausoleum": "Verily it is one thing to have cash and another to know how to spend it" (SLC 1867c, 1).

To Jane Lampton Clemens
31 August 1853 • New York, N.Y.
(Hannibal *Journal*, 10 Sept 53)

NEW YORK, Aug. 31, 1853.

My dear Mother:

New York is at present overstocked with printers; and I suppose they are from the South, driven North by the yellow fever.[1] I got a permanent situation on Monday morning, in a book and job office, and went to work. The printers here are badly organized, and therefore have to work for various prices. These prices are 23, 25, 28, 30, 32, and 35 cents per 1,000 ems. The price I get is 23 cents; but I did very well to get a place at all, for there are thirty or forty—yes, fifty good printers in the city with no work at all; besides, my situation is permanent, and I shall keep it till I can get a better one.[2] The office I work in is John A. Gray's, 97 Cliff street, and, next to Harper's, is the most extensive in the city. In the room in which I work I have forty compositors for company. Taking compositors, pressmen, stereotypers, and all, there are about two hundred persons employed in the concern.[3] The "Knickerbocker," "New York Recorder," "Choral Advocate," "Jewish Chronicle," "Littell's Living Age," "Irish ——," and half a dozen other papers and periodicals are printed here, besides an immense number of books.[4] They are very particular about spacing, justification, proofs, etc., and even if I do not make much money, I will learn a great deal. I thought Ustick was particular enough, but acknowledge now that he was not old-maidish.[5] Why, you must put exactly the same space between every two words, and *every line must be spaced alike*. They think it dreadful to space one line with three em spaces, and the next one with five ems. However, I expected this, and worked accordingly from the beginning; and out of all the proofs I saw, without boasting, I can say mine was by far the cleanest. In St. Louis, Mr. Baird said my proofs were the cleanest that were ever set in his office. The foreman of the Anzeiger told me the same—foreman of the Watchman the same; and with all this evidence, I believe I *do* set a clean proof.[6]

My boarding house is more than a mile from the office;[7] and I can hear the signal calling the hands to work before I start down; they use a steam whistle for that purpose. I work in the fifth story; and from one window I have a pretty good view of the city, while another commands a view of the shipping beyond the Battery; and the "forest of masts," with all sorts of flags flying, is no mean sight. You have everything in the shape of water craft, from a fishing smack to the steamships and men-of-war; but packed so closely together for miles, that when close to them you can scarcely distinguish one from another.

Of all the commodities, manufactures—or whatever you please to call it—in New York, trundle-bed trash—children I mean—take the lead. Why, from Cliff street, up Frankfort to Nassau street, six or seven squares—my road to dinner—I think I could count two hundred brats. Niggers, mulattoes, quadroons, Chinese, and some the Lord no doubt originally intended to be white, but the dirt on whose faces leaves one uncertain as to that fact, block up the little, narrow street; and to wade through this mass of human vermin, would raise the ire of the most patient person that ever lived. In going to and from my meals, I go by the way of Broadway—and to *cross* Broadway is the rub—but once across, it is *the* rub for two or three squares. My plan—and how could I choose another, when there *is* no other—is to get into the crowd; and when I get in, I am borne, and rubbed, and crowded along, and need scarcely trouble myself about using my own legs; and when I get out, it seems like I had been pulled to pieces and very badly put together again.[8]

Last night I was in what is known as one of *the* finest fruit saloons in the world. The whole length of the huge, glittering hall is filled with beautiful ornamented marble slab tables, covered with the finest fruit I ever saw in my life. I suppose the fruit could not be mentioned with which they could not supply you. It is a perfect palace. The gas lamps hang in clusters of half a dozen together—representing grapes, I suppose—all over the hall.[9]

[closing and signature missing]

P. S. The printers have two libraries in town, entirely free to the craft; and in these I can spend my evenings most pleasantly. If books are not good company, where will I find it?[10]

---

[1] The disease had become epidemic in New Orleans, where it caused more than five thousand deaths in the next eighteen months. While Clemens was in New

York, the city's printers raised money to assist sick and destitute printers in New Orleans.

² "Monday morning" was 29 August. In January 1873, Clemens recalled that after his apprenticeship in Hannibal he worked as a printer "in St Louis, Cincinnati, Philadelphia & New York while yet a boy—& belonged to the Typographical Unions in those cities, by a courtesy which forebore to enforce the rule requiring 21 years of age for eligibility" (SLC 1873, 1–2). St. Louis Typographical Union No. 8, a charter member of the National Typographical Union founded in May 1852, represented a significant number of that city's printers, including some of Clemens's friends at this time. (Its membership records for 1853–55 have been lost.) By contrast, New York printers were split between two unions: New York Typographical Union No. 6 (also a charter member of the National) and the New York Printers' Co-operative Union, founded on 13 April 1853 to represent book and job printers. This division of loyalties had inhibited the printers' ability to establish uniform wage rates in keeping with rates paid elsewhere. In 1906 Clemens remembered the rate of pay he received in New York as "villainous" (AD, 29 Mar 1906, CU-MARK, in *MTA*, 2:287; see George A. Stevens, 2:206, 245–75; Morgan, 47–55).

³ John A. Gray's five-story book and job printing house was at 95–97 Cliff Street on the corner of Frankfort Street; Harper and Brothers was nearby, with five buildings fronting on Cliff Street and five more behind them on Pearl Street. Twenty-six of Gray's employees were members of the Printers' Co-operative Union (for book and job printers) in May 1853 (Rode 1853a, 267; "Destructive Fire," New York *Times*, 12 Dec 53, 1; George A. Stevens, 2:267).

⁴ Clemens mentions: the *Knickerbocker; or, New-York Monthly Magazine*, a well-known literary, humor, travel, and arts journal, published 1833–65; the *New York Recorder*, a Baptist weekly, published 1845–55; the *Musical Review and Choral Advocate; A Companion for the Choir, the Singing School, and the Fireside*, a New York monthly published 1850–73 under various titles; *The Jewish Chronicle*, a New York monthly published 1844–55 "under the direction of the American Society for Meliorating the Condition of the Jews" (i.e., converting them), one of whose directors was Clemens's employer, John A. Gray; *Littell's Living Age*, published 1844–1941, a Boston weekly that reprinted poetry, fiction, and political and social commentary from British journals, edited at this time by its founder, Eliakim Littell; and, probably, the *Irish-American*, a New York political and religious weekly, published 1849–1916. The ellipsis here is presumed to be in the original manuscript, but it may have been imposed by Orion Clemens when he printed the letter in the Hannibal *Journal*. Since both Clemens brothers had strong nativist views at this time, either of them might have regarded the conjunction of "American" with "Irish" as a sort of blasphemy (Mott 1939, 606–14, 747–49; Mott 1938, 76 n.134, 197; Titus, 3:2164, 2448, 2802, 4:3039, 3051; Winifred Gregory, 470).

⁵ Clemens refers to his recent experience as a journeyman in the book and job office of Thomas Watt Ustick (b. 1800 or 1801), a prominent St. Louis printer with offices on Main Street between Olive and Pine streets (Montague, 109). Ustick's office set type for the St. Louis *Evening News* and probably for other journals on which Clemens worked in June, July, and August 1853. Orion Clemens had also had first-hand experience of Ustick's exacting standards, for, as Clemens recalled in 1897, Orion had gone "to St. L to learn to be a printer, in

Ustick's job office" in about 1842 ("Villagers of 1840–3," *Inds*, 105). In introducing this letter in the *Journal*, Orion expressed some pride at the training he had helped give his brother in Hannibal: "The following letter is some encouragement to apprentices in country printing offices, as it shows that it is practicable to acquire enough knowledge of the business in a Western country office, to command the best situations, West or East. There are a great many who suppose that no mechanical business can be learned well in the West."

⁶ The Reverend E. Thompson Baird was editor of the St. Louis *Presbyterian*, a struggling religious weekly, from September 1852, when he arrived in St. Louis, until October 1854, when he departed to become agent of the Board of Domestic Missions of the Presbyterian Church. In June of 1853 Baird claimed that he was his "own editor, foreman, compositor, clerk, and man of all work," but Clemens evidently set type for him later that summer ("Circular," St. Louis *Presbyterian*, 23 June 53, 2–3). Clemens indicates here that he also set type for the *Anzeiger des Westens*, the city's leading German language daily, edited by Henry Boernstein, and for the *Western Watchman*, a weekly Baptist family journal, edited by William Crowell and the Reverend S. B. Johnson. The printing foremen of these journals have not been identified ("The St. Louis Presbyterian," St. Louis *Missouri Republican*, 7 Oct 54, 2; Montague, 121, 122).

⁷ "I found board in a sufficiently villainous mechanics' boarding-house in Duane Street," Clemens said in 1906 (AD, 29 Mar 1906, CU-MARK, in *MTA*, 2:287). There were, in fact, numerous boardinghouses on Duane Street (Rode 1853b, 9–11). Paine reported that Clemens "did not like the board. He had been accustomed to the Southern mode of cooking, and wrote home complaining that New-Yorkers did not have 'hot-bread' or biscuits, but ate 'light-bread,' which they allowed to get stale, seeming to prefer it in that way" (*MTB*, 1:96). If Clemens made his complaint in a letter, as Paine asserts, it is not known to survive.

⁸ From John A. Gray's establishment on the East River side of lower Manhattan, it was about a ten-block walk across town to Duane Street near Broadway on the West Side, where Clemens lived and boarded. Broadway was notably wider than the typical "little, narrow street" of lower Manhattan; it was also packed with carts, hacks, coaches, and omnibuses, not to mention pedestrians.

⁹ Possibly the Washington Market, on Washington Street between Vesey and Fulton streets on the Hudson River, which in 1852 grossed $28.4 million, including $2.8 million for the sale of fruit (Saunders, 125).

¹⁰ The Printers' Free Library and Reading Room was founded by the New York Typographical Society, whose "members commenced making donations of books to establish a library in 1823. . . . Many valuable donations of books have been received from publishers and others" (Jewett, 96–97). Sometime in 1853 the society moved its headquarters from 300 Broadway to 3 Chambers Street, just a few blocks from Clemens's boardinghouse. Its library was open from 6:00 P.M. to 10:00 P.M. "for the use of Printers, Stereotypers, Bookbinders, Engravers, and all others connected with the book and newspaper business. All the principal papers are on file, and the Library contains 3,000 vols. There is no charge made, except where persons take books from the Library, for which privilege $1 a year only is charged" (H. Wilson, appendix, 56; Rode 1852, appendix, 36; Rode 1853b, appendix, 74). The second library Clemens mentions has not been identified.

To Pamela A. Moffett
3? September 1853 • New York, N.Y.
(Transcripts and MS facsimile: *MTL*, 1: 21–22, 31;
MTB, 1: 94–95; Paine, 48–49)

. . . From the gallery (second floor) you have a glorious sight—the flags of the different countries represented, the lofty dome, glittering jewelry, gaudy tapestry, &c., with the busy crowd passing to and fro—tis a perfect fairy palace—beautiful beyond description.[1]

The Machinery department is on the main floor, but I cannot enumerate any of it on account of the lateness of the hour (past 1 o'clock.) It would take more than a week to examine everything on exhibition; and as I was only in a little over two hours to-night, I only glanced at about one-third of the articles; and having a poor memory, I have enumerated scarcely any of even the principal objects. The visitors to the Palace average 6,000 daily—double the population of Hannibal. The price of admission being 50 cents, they take in about $3,000.[2]

The Latting Observatory (height about 280 feet) is near the Palace— from it you can obtain a grand view of the city and the country round.[3] The Croton Aqueduct, to supply the city with water, is the greatest wonder yet. Immense sewers are laid across the bed of the Hudson River, and pass through the country to Westchester county, where a whole river is turned from its course, and brought to New York. From the reservoir in the city to the Westchester county reservoir, the distance is *thirty-eight miles!* and if necessary, they could easily supply every family in New York with *one hundred barrels of water per day!*[4]

I am very sorry to learn that Henry has been sick. [*in margin:* Write, and let me know how Henry is.] He ought to go to the country and take exercise; for he is not half so healthy as Ma thinks he is. If he had my walking to do, he would be another boy entirely. Four times every day I walk a little over one mile; and working hard all day, and walking four miles, *is* exercise—I am used to it now, though, and it is no trouble. Where is it Orion's going to?[5] Tell Ma my promises are faithfully kept; and if I have my health I will take her to Ky. in the spring—I shall save money for this.[6] Tell Jim and all the rest of them to write, and give me all the news.[7] I am sorry to hear such bad news from Will and Captain

Bowen. I shall write to Will soon.[8] The Chatham-square Post Office and the Broadway office too, are out of my way, and I always go to the General Post Office; so you must write the direction of my letters plain, "New York City, N. Y.," without giving the street or anything of the kind, or they may go to some of the other offices. (It has just struck 2 A.M. and I always get up at 6, and am at work at 7.) You ask where I spend my evenings. Where would you suppose, with a free printers' library containing more than 4,000 volumes within a quarter of a mile of me, and nobody at home to talk to? I shall write to Ella soon.[9] ˌWrite soon.ˌ

Truly your Brother

Sam

P. S I have written this by a light so dim that you nor Ma could not read by it.

[1] The first page (or pages) of the manuscript were evidently missing when Paine published it in 1912; except for the fragment he reproduced in facsimile, the remainder has since been lost. Clemens, however, is clearly describing the main floor of the Crystal Palace, which was divided into four sections housing exhibits from (1) the United States; (2) Great Britain and Ireland; (3) Belgium, France, and Germany; and (4) "various countries," including Canada, Italy, Austria, Holland, and several others. The second-floor gallery gave an excellent view of sculpture displayed in the naves separating these divisions as well as in the central open space beneath the translucent dome. At night, the interior was illuminated by hundreds of gas lamps. The Machine Arcade, which Clemens mentions next, was along the east wall of the main floor and was filled with machines of every description, including the latest in printing equipment (*Exhibition Catalogue*, 7–23).

[2] Clemens probably wrote this letter in the early hours of 3 September, having visited the Crystal Palace the previous evening. September 2 was, in any case, the first day on which closing hour was extended until 10:00 P.M. Attendance for that day was reported at 6,125, close to the average of 6,300 in the week prior. Between 3 and 10 September, however, the average dropped well below 6,000, and between 12 and 16 September it jumped above 8,000. Given the "average 6,000 daily" Clemens reports here, it seems likely that he was writing before seeing any report of the temporary decline that began on 3 September (various notices, New York *Tribune* and New York *Times*, 23 Aug–16 Sept 53).

[3] The observatory built by Waring Latting, and opened to the public in July 1853, was actually 350 feet high. It stood between Forty-second and Forty-third streets, adjacent to the Crystal Palace (see illustration, p. 7). Telescopes on the upper levels, which one reached by steam-powered elevator, afforded a panoramic view of the city. In 1856 the tower was destroyed by fire, and two years later, the "indestructible" Crystal Palace likewise succumbed in a matter of minutes (Kouwenhoven, 243; Stokes, 44; "Amusements," New York *Times*, 8 July 53, 5).

[4] A distributing reservoir for the Croton Aqueduct was adjacent to the Crystal Palace on Forty-second Street. Completed in 1842, the Croton aqueduct system

was an engineering feat that attracted tourists and that delivered abundant water to a growing city for the rest of the century (Stokes, 44).

[5] Pamela seems to have written to Clemens as soon as she learned his whereabouts, presumably from seeing his 24 August letter to their mother on about 28 August. In reporting Orion's plans to leave Hannibal, she evidently failed to mention his destination, possibly because Orion had not yet fully formed his plans. Not until 7 September did he notify subscribers to the Hannibal *Journal* that, because of "a large amount of business demanding undivided attention . . . for three or four weeks to come," he was placing "the editorial department" in the hands of the Reverend Daniel Emerson (OC 1853a, 2). It is likely that this "business" was Orion's plan to sell the Hannibal paper and move the family to Muscatine, Iowa, provided he could form a partnership with John Mahin to edit the Muscatine *Journal*. By 22 September he had reached an agreement with Mahin, for on that day he sold the Hannibal *Journal*, and on 30 September published his first issue in Muscatine.

[6] Jane Lampton Clemens hoped to visit her ancestral home in Kentucky where, thirty years before, she had met and married John Marshall Clemens, originally from Virginia. Plans for such a trip come up again in 26–?28 Oct 53 to OC and HC, and 28 Nov 53 to OC.

[7] Clemens probably refers to his uncle James Andrew Hays Lampton (1824–79), his mother's younger (by twenty-one years) half-brother, who had lived briefly next to the Clemenses in Hannibal in about 1845 or 1846. In 1897, Clemens remembered him as "a popular beau. . . . Good fellow, very handsome, full of life. Young doctor without practice, poor, but good family and considered a good catch. Captured by the arts of Ella Hunter, a loud vulgar beauty from a neighboring town—one of the earliest chipper and self-satisfied and idiotic correspondents of the back-country newspapers—an early Kate Field" ("Villagers of 1840–3," *Inds*, 98). Lampton took his medical training in St. Louis, married Ella Evelina Hunter (1834?–1904) in November 1849, and lived in New London, ten miles south of Hannibal, until returning to St. Louis, probably in 1853. According to one obituary, Lampton "early abandoned the practice of [medicine] . . . for other vocations more congenial to his inclinations and habits" (Garrett, 7). By 1854 he was an accountant in the St. Louis office of the surveyor general of Missouri and Illinois, a position he held until the mid-1860s (*Inds*, biographical directory; Selby, 107; Knox, 110, 188; Robert V. Kennedy: 1857, 130; 1859, 284; 1860, 303).

[8] In 1870 Clemens addressed William Bowen (1836–93) as "My First, & Oldest & Dearest Friend" (*MTLBowen*, 18). Originally from Hannibal, Bowen became a pilot before Clemens did, but the two men were briefly associated on the steamers *Alfred T. Lacey*, *A. B. Chambers*, and *Alonzo Child* between 1859 and 1861. Bowen piloted for the North during the Civil War and then left the river to enter the insurance business in 1868, first in St. Louis and later in Texas. If Clemens in fact wrote to him "soon," his letter is not known to survive, but the two men did correspond until within a few years of Bowen's death. Clemens based Joe Harper in *Tom Sawyer* and *Huckleberry Finn* on Bowen. Bowen's father, Samuel Adams Bowen, Sr. (1790–1853), had been a steamboatman early in life, and later a prosperous Hannibal merchant and insurance agent. The "bad news" from Will was doubtless of the Captain's "protracted and painful illness," which proved fatal on

2 November ("Died," Canton [Mo.] *Northeast Reporter*, 10 Nov 53, 2; Ferris, 19;
see *Inds*, biographical directory).
  [9] Although Paine identified "Ella" as Clemens's "cousin and one-time sweetheart, Ella Creel" (*MTL*, 1:23), Creel lived in Keokuk, Iowa, which Clemens first
visited in June 1855. It therefore seems more likely that the reference here is to
Ella Hunter Lampton.

To Pamela A. Moffett
8 October 1853 • New York, N.Y.
(MS, *damage emended:* CU-MARK)

New York, ~~ix~~ x, Oct., Saturday, 1853.[1]

My Dear Sister:

I have not written to any of the family for some time, from the fact,
firstly, that I didn't know where they were, and *secondly*, because I have
been fooling myself with the idea that I was going to leave New York,
every day for the last two weeks. I have taken a liking to the abominable
place, and every time I get ready to leave, I put it off a day or so, from
some unaccountable cause. It is just as hard on my conscience to leave
New York as it was *easy* to leave Hannibal. I think I shall get off Tuesday,
though.

Edwin Forrest has been playing, for the last sixteen days, at the
Broadway Theatre, but I never went to see him till last night. The play
was the "Gladiator." I did not like parts of it much, but other portions
were really splendid. In the latter part of the last act, where the "Gladiator" (Forrest) dies at his brother's feet, (in all the fierce pleasure of grati-
fied revenge,) after working the latter's revenge, the man's whole soul
seems absorbed in the part he is playing; and it is really startling to see
him. I am sorry I did not see him play "Damon and Pythias"—the former
character being his greatest. He appears in Philadelphia on Monday
night.[2]

I have not received a letter from home lately, but got a "*Journal*" the
other day, in which I see the office has been sold. I suppose Ma, Orion
and Henry are in St. Louis now. If Orion has no other project in ~~that~~ his
head, he ought to take the contract for getting out some weekly paper, if
he cannot get a foremanship. Now, for such a paper as the "*Presbyterian*"

he cou (containing about 60,000,) he could get $20 or $25 per week, and he and Henry could easily do the work:—nothing to do but set the type and make up the forms. I mean they could easily do the work if $5.00 for 25,000 (per week) could beat a little work in to into (no offence to him) Henry's lazy bones![3] Orion must get Jim. Wolfe a sit. in St. Louis. He can get 20 cents per 1.000.[4] The foreman of Gray's office[5] has taken a great fancy to go to St. Louis, and has got everything out of me that I know about the place, and I shouldn't be surprised if he should go, there.

If my letters do not come often, you need not bother yourself about me; for if you have a brother nearly eighteen years of age, who is not able to take care of himself a few miles from home, such a brother is not worth one's thoughts: and if I don't manage to take care of $N^{o.}$ *1.*, be assured you will never know it. I am not afraid, however: I shall ꝑ ask favors from no one, and endeavor to be, (and *shall* be,) as "independent as a wood-sawyer's clerk."[6]

I never saw such a place for military companies, as New York. Go on the street when you will, you are sure to meet a company in full uniform, with all the usual appendages of drums, fifes, &c. I saw a large company of the soldiers of the war of 1812, the other day, with a '76 veteran scattered here and there in the ranks. And when I passed through one of the parks lately, I came upon a company of *boys* on parade. Their uniforms were neat, and their muskets about half the common size. Some of them were not more than seven or eight years of age; but had evidently been well drilled.[7]

Passage to Albany (160 miles) in the finest steamers that ply the Hudson, is now 25 cents—cheap enough, but is generally cheaper than that in the summer.[8]

I want you to write as soon as I tell you where to direct your letter. I would let you know now, if I knew myself. I may perhaps be here a week longer; but I cannot tell. When you ʄ write tell me the whereabouts of the family. My love to Mr. Moffett and Ella.[9] Tell Ella I intend to write to her soon, whether she wants me to or not.

                                          Truly your Brother,
                                          Saml. L. Clemens.

[1] The manuscript of this letter (the earliest known to survive in holograph) has been damaged: several dozen words, letters, and marks of punctuation have been obliterated, including the last two digits of the year in Clemens's dateline. Fortunately, most of the affected text can be confidently (albeit conjecturally) restored:

see the textual apparatus for a detailed report of these emendations. Context establishes the year as 1853 and shows that Clemens twice mistook the day of the month while correctly naming the day of the week.

[2] Clemens attended a Friday evening performance of *The Gladiator* by Robert Montgomery Bird (1806–54), then a proprietor and literary editor of the Philadelphia *North American and United States Gazette*. From 19 September through the date of this letter, Edwin Forrest (1806–72), for whom Bird wrote this play, had been appearing at the Broadway Theatre in a variety of roles, including Spartacus in *The Gladiator* (30 September and 7 October) and Damon in John Banim's popular 1821 tragedy *Damon and Pythias* (19 and 24 September). On Monday, 10 October, Forrest began an engagement at Philadelphia's Walnut Street Theatre ("Amusements," New York *Tribune*, 19 Sept–9 Oct 53; "Mr. Forrest" and "Amusements," Philadelphia *Public Ledger*, 10 Oct 53, 2, 4).

[3] Clemens was unsure of his family's whereabouts because, probably sometime between 2 and 6 October, he had received the final, 22 September issue of the Hannibal *Journal*, which contained Orion's valediction:

Notice to the Public.

Notice is hereby given that I have this day sold the "Journal" office, with its patronage to Wm T. League, Esq., Proprietor of the "Whig Messenger." The "Hannibal Journal" will therefore after this date cease to be published. (OC 1853b, 3)

The "Notice" did not explain, however, that Orion had moved the family to Muscatine, Iowa, where he soon began publishing the Muscatine *Journal*.

[4] Jim Wolfe (or Wolf) had been "printer's devil" and then apprentice printer on Orion's Hannibal *Western Union* (later the Hannibal *Journal*) since 1851. Wolfe boarded with the Clemens family during much of this time. "A Gallant Fireman," the first sketch Clemens is known to have published, tells of Wolfe's dim-witted effort to be of assistance during a January 1851 fire at the shop next door to the *Western Union* (*ET&S1*, 62). He is likewise characterized as simple and rather gullible in an 1867 sketch, "Jim Wolf and the Tom-Cats," based on another humorous incident in Hannibal (*ET&S3*, no. 212). And in 1880, he would appear in chapter 23 of *A Tramp Abroad* as the "inconceivably green and confiding" Nicodemus Dodge, "a butt to play jokes on."

[5] Unidentified.

[6] The simile derives from the "advantageous and strategic position occupied by the wood-sawyer, which was naturally reflected in the attitude of his clerk," during "the pressing demand for wood in the days of early steamboat travel" (*Lex*, 261).

[7] On 17 October the New York *Tribune* called the prevalence of soldiers in the city "a new and frightful form of spotted fever": "The peculiar symptom . . . is a species of insanity which induces the patient, at all hours of the day and night, to suddenly rush from the bosom of his family and imagine himself a soldier!" To the "detestation of pedestrians, ladies and omnibus-drivers," the victims appeared dressed variously in "scarlet, blue, green and yellow. . . . These unhappy beings, ranged in platoons, sections, squadrons, hollow-squares, and other military positions, and preceded by a band furiously blowing upon a number of brass stovepipes, parade the town from morning to night, making it appear a beleaguered city" ("The Spotted Fever," 6).

[8] Although he soon went to Philadelphia, Clemens may have considered Albany, New York, as an alternative.

[9] Ella Hunter Lampton.

To Orion and Henry Clemens
26–?28 October 1853 • Philadelphia, Pa.
(MS and transcript: NPV and Muscatine *Journal*, 11 Nov 53)

Philadelphia, Pa. Oct. 26, 1853.

My Dear Brother:

I[t] was at least two weeks before I left New York, that I ~~left~~ received my last letter from home: and since then, devil take the word have I heard from any of you. And now, since I think of it, it wasn't a letter, either, but the last number of the "Daily Journal," saying that that paper was sold, and I very naturally supposed from that, that the family had disbanded, and taken up winter quarters in St Louis. Therefore, I have been writing to Pamela, till I'm tired of it, and have received no answer. I have been wanting for the last two or ~~the~~ three weeks, to send Ma some money, but ~~b~~ devil take me if I knew where she was, and so the money has slipped out of my pocket somehow or other, but I have a dollar left, and a good ~~del~~ deal owing to me, which will be paid next ~~m~~Monday.[1] I shall enclose the dollar in this letter, and you can hand it to her. I know it's a small amount, but then it will buy her a hankerchief, and at the same time serve as a specimen of the kind of stuff we are paid with in Philadelphia. You see it's against the law in Pennsylvania to keep or pass a bill of less denomination than $5. I have only seen two or three bank bills since I have been in the State. On Monday the hands are paid off in sparkling gold, fresh of the Mint; so your dreams are not troubled, with the fear of having doubtful money in your pocket.[2]

I am subbing at the Inquirer office.[3] One man has engaged me to work for him every Sunday till the first of next April, ~~will~~ (when I shall return home to take Ma to Ky;) and another has engaged my services for the 24th of next month; and if I want it, I can get subbing *every night* of the week. I go to work at 7 o'clock in the evening, and work till 3 o'clock the next morning. I can go to the theatre and stay till 12 o'clock, and then go to the office, and get work from that till 3 the next morning; when I go to bed, and sleep till 11 o'clock, then get up and loaf the rest of the day. The type is mostly agate and minion, with some bourgeois; and when one gets a good agate take, he is sure to make money.[4] I made $2.50 last Sunday, and was laughed at by all the hands, the poorest of whom sets 11,000 on Sunday; and if I don't set 10,000, at least, next Sunday, I'll give them leave to laugh as much as the[y] want to. Out of the 22 compositors in this office, 12 at least, set 15,000 on Sunday.

Unlike New York, I like this Phila amazingly, and the people in it. There is only one thing that gets my "dander" up—and that is the hands are always *encouraging* me: telling me ⅄ "it's no use to get discouraged—no use to be down-hearted, for there is more work here than you can do!" "Downhearted," the devil! I have not had a particle of such a feeling since I left Hannibal, more than four months ago. I fancy they'll have to wait some time till they see me downhearted or afraid of starving while I have strength to work and am in a city of 400,000 inhabitants. When I was in Hannibal; before I had scarcely stepped out of the town limits, nothing could have convinced me than I would starve as soon as I got a little way from home.

The grave of Franklin is in Christ Church-yard, cor. of Fifth and Arch streets. They keep the gates locked, and one can only see the flat slab that lies over his remains and that of his wife; but you cannot see the inscription distinctly enough to read th it. This inscription, I believe, reads thus:

$$\left.\begin{array}{c} \text{``Benjamin} \\ \text{and} \\ \text{Deborah} \end{array}\right\} \text{Franklin."}$$

I counted 27 cannons (6 pounders) planted in the edge of the side walk on in Water st. the other day. They are driven into the ground, about a foot, with the mouth end upwards. A ball is driven fast into the mouth of each, to exclude the water; they look like so many posts. They were put there during the war. I have also seen them planted in this manner, round the old churches, in N.Y.

The Exchange is we where the different omnibus lines have their starting or stopping place. That is it is the head-quarters; and from this they radiate to the different parts, of the city.[5] Well, as I was going to say, I went to the Exchange, yesterday, and deposited myself in a Fairmount stage, paid my sixpence, or "fip," as these heathen call it, and started.[6] We rolled along till we began to get towards the out-skirts of the city, where the prettiest part of a large city *always* is. We passed a ⅄ large house, which looked like a public p̸ building. It was built entirely of great blocks of red granite. The pillars in front were all finished but one. These pillars were beautiful ornamented fluted columns, considerably larger than a hogshead at the base, and about as high as Caplinger's second story front windows.[7] No marble pillar is as pretty as ~~this~~ these sombre red granite ones; and then to see some of them finished and standing, and then the huge blocks lying about of which the other was to be built, it looks so massy; and carries one in imagination, to the ruined piles of ancient Babylon. I despise the infernal bogus brick columns, plastered over with mortar. Marble is the cheapest building stone about Phila. This marble is the most beautiful I ever saw. I[t] takes a very high polish. Some of it is as black as Egypt,[8] with thin streaks of white running through it, and some is a beautiful snowy white; while the most of it is magnificent black, clouded with white.

But I must go on with my trip. We soon passed long rows of houses, (private dwellings) all the work about the doors, stoop, &c., of which, was composed of this pretty marble, glittering in the sun, ~~lie~~ like glass. We arrived at Fairmount,—got out of the stage, and ~~pe~~ prepared to look around. The hill, (Fairmount) is very high, and on top of it is the great reservoir. After leaving the stage, I passed up the road, till I came to the wire bridge which stretches across the Schuylkill (or Delaware, darned if I know which!—the former, I believe,—but you, know, for you are a better scholar than I am). This is the first bridge of the kind I ever saw.[9] Here I saw, a little above, the fine dam, which hold[s] back the water for the use of the Water Works. It forms ~~n~~ quite a nice water-fall. Seeing a park at the foot of the hill, I entered—and found it one of the nicest little places about. Fat marble Cupids, in big marble vases, squirted water ~~every~~ upward incessantly. Here stands in a kind of mausoleum, (is that proper?) ~~a~~ a well executed piece of sculpture, with the inscription— "Erected by the City Council of Philadelphia, to the memory of Peter Graff, the founder and inventor of the Fairmount Water Works." The bust looks toward the dam. It is all of the purest white marble. I passed along the pavement by the pump-house (I don't know what else to call it) and seeing a door left open by somebody, I went in. I saw immense water-wheels, &c., but if you will get a back-number of the Lady's ~~b~~Book, you will find a better description of the Works, than I can give you.[10] I passed on further, and saw small steamboats, with their signs up—"For Wissa-hickon and Manayunk—25 cts." Geo. Lippard, in his "Legends of Wash-

ington and his Generals," has rendered the ~~Wa~~ Wissahickon sacred in my
eyes, and I shall make that trip,—as well as one to Germantown, soon.[11]

But to proceed, again. Here was a long flight of stairs, leading to the
summit of the hill. I went up—of course. But I forgot to say, that at the
foot of this hill a pretty white marble Naiad stands on a projecting rock,
and this, I must say is the prettiest fountain I have seen lately. A nice half-
inch jet of water is thrown straight up ten or twelve feet, and descends in
a shower, all over the fair water spirit. Fountains also gush out of the
rock at ~~the~~ her feet, in every direction.[12] Well, arrived at the top of the
hill, I see nothing but a respectable-sized lake, which [looks] rather out
of place in its elevated situationed. I can't say I saw *nothing* else, either:—
for here I had a magnificent view of the city. Tired of this, I passed up
Coates streets, 5 or six squares from the hill, and came to the immense
(distributin) branch of the Works. It is built of a kind of dirty yellow
stone, and in the style of an ancient feudal Castle. Passing on, I took a
squint at the "House of Refuge," (of which we used to read at Sunday
School),—then I took a look at the marble Girard College, with its long
rows of marble pillars—then jumped into a 'bus, and posted back to the
Exchange.[13]

There is one fine custom observed in Phila. A gentleman is always
expected to hand up a lady's money for her. Yesterday, I sat in the front
end of the 'bus, directly under the driver's box—a lady sat opposite me.
She handed me her money, which was right. But, Lord! a St. Louis lady
would think herself ruined, if she should be so familiar with a stranger.
In St. Louis, a man will ~~stan~~ sit, in the front end of the stage, and see a
lady ~~star~~ stagger from the far end, to pay her fare. The Phila. 'bus drivers
cannot cheat. In the front end of the stage is a thing like and office clock,
with figures, from 0 to 40, marked on its face. When the stage starts, the
hands of the clock is turned toward the 0. When you get in and pay your
fare, the driver strikes a bell, and the hand moves to the fig. 1—that is,
"one fare, and paid for," and there is ~~re~~ your receipt, as good as if you had
it in your pocket. When a passenger pays his fare and the driver does not
strike the bell immediately, he is greeted "Strike that bell! will you?"

I must close now. I intend visiting the Navy Yard, Mint, &c. before
I write again. You must write often. You see I have nothing to write interesting to you, while you can write nothing that will not interest me. Don't
say my letters are not *long* enough. Tell Jim to write. Tell all the boys

where I am, and to write. Jim Robinson,[14] particularly. I wrote to him from N.Y. Tell me all that is going on in H—l.[15]

Truly your brother

Sam

. . . .

Philadelphia is rich in Revolutionary associations.[16] I stepped into the State House yesterday to see the sights. In one of the halls, on a pedestal, is the old cracked "Independence Bell," bearing the inscription "Proclaim liberty throughout the land," or something to that effect. It was cast 25 or 30 years before it made this proclamation. It was rung for the first time on "Independence Day," when it "proclaimed liberty" by calling the people together to hear the Declaration of Independence read.[17] It is an interesting relic. A small pine bench or pew in this Hall bears this inscription—"Washington, Franklin and Bishop White[18] sat on this Bench." Of course, I "sot down" on it. I would have whittled off a chip, if I had got half a chance. On the pedestal of the statue of Washington, in the same Hall, is a small block of granite, with the inscription—"A piece of the step on which the Secretary's foot rested when he read the Declaration of Independence." Full length portraits of William Penn and Lafayette hang in this Hall. There is another thing which should have a place in this Hall. It is a flag which I saw in New York. It was the personal property of Washington, and was planted on the Battery when the British evacuated New York. After that, it was not used until the laying of the corner stone of the Washington Monument. Then this faded and tattered, though time-honored relic of "the days that tried men's souls,"[19] was taken to Washington and unfurled to the breeze at that ceremony. It is said that when the procession reached the Monumental ground in Washington, the flag was unfurled and the announcement made—"This flag belonged to Washington; it proudly waved defiance to the British from the Battery when they evacuated New York; it is here now to display the stars and stripes under which its illustrious owner so nobly fought"— the multitude gazed on it for a moment, and then a shout went up that would have sent the blood from the cheek of a tyrant.

I came here from New York by way of the Camden and Amboy railroad—the same on which the collision occurred some time since. I never thought of this till our train stopped, "all of a sudden," and then began to go backwards like blazes. Then ran back half a mile, and switched off on another track, and stopped; and the next moment a large passenger train came round a bend in the road, and whistled past us like lightning! Ugh! ejaculated I, as I looked to see if Mr. Clemens's bones were all safe. If we had been three seconds later getting off that track, the two locomotives would have come together, and we should no doubt have been helped off. The conductors silenced all questions by not answering them.[20]

S. C.

[*crosswise over the first paragraph:*] Please send this to Henry if he is not in St. Louis

Sam

[1] Since Clemens reveals in his second paragraph that he was at work in Philadelphia by Sunday, 23 October, his further statement that he received the "last number" of Orion's Hannibal *Journal* "at least two weeks before I left New York," together with his earlier comment that he had received it "the other day" (8 Oct 53 to PAM), suggests that he made the trip by steamboat and rail on the afternoon of 19, 20, or 21 October. See also note 20.

[2] Clemens presumably enclosed a "Liberty Head" gold dollar, the only such coin then in circulation. Between 1849 and 1854 the United States Treasury minted more than 12.6 million of these dollars, which each weighed about one-twentieth of an ounce and measured one-half inch in diameter (Reed, 195).

[3] Jesper Harding's *Pennsylvania Inquirer and National Gazette* was the city's largest morning newspaper, located at 57 South Third Street in the heart of the newspaper district between Market and Chestnut streets (McElroy, 112). In contrast with Clemens's "permanent situation" in New York (see 31 Aug 53 to JLC), his employment in Philadelphia consisted of substituting temporarily for one or another of the *Inquirer*'s regular compositors ("subbing"). Under this system, which was used only on newspapers, he was paid on a piecework basis, although probably at somewhat higher rates than a compositor could earn in a book and job office.

[4] Of the three type sizes that Clemens names, agate was the smallest and bourgeois the largest. His comment about a "good agate take," or assignment of copy, implies that somewhat higher wages were paid for work done in the smallest type sizes: agate, pearl, and (the smallest) diamond.

[5] Twenty-nine omnibus routes (utilizing 275 four- and six-horse coaches) radiated from the Merchants' Exchange and Post Office Building at Walnut, Dock, and Third streets, near the Camden and Amboy ferry slip ("Omnibus Travel," Philadelphia *Public Ledger*, 17 July 54, 2).

[6] "Fip" was a local term meaning "fippenny," or fivepenny, bit (called a "sixpence" in New York). This silver coin, actually a Spanish half real, circulated in the United States until 1857; it was the equivalent of about six cents (one-sixteenth of a Spanish dollar).

[7] The building under construction has not been identified. Clemens compares the height of its pillars to George W. Caplinger's Hannibal grocery store, on Main Street, between Bird and Centre streets ("Mr. G. W. Caplinger . . . ," Hannibal

Journal, 16 Sept 52, 3; *Hannibal Census*, 311). When Orion published this letter in the Muscatine *Journal*, he substituted the phrase "25 or 30 feet high" for "about as high as Caplinger's second story front windows."

[8] Compare Exodus 10:21–22. "Egyptian darkness" or "Egyptian night," meaning unrelieved, impenetrable blackness, was one of Clemens's favorite metaphors.

[9] Fairmount Bridge, about three hundred and fifty feet long, spanned the Schuylkill, not the Delaware. It was the first cable suspension bridge in the United States. Designed and built by Col. Charles Ellet, Jr. (1810–62), it served the city from 1842 to 1875 (Jackson, 4:1200–1201). Orion omitted Clemens's parenthetical comment here, as well as one a few lines further on—"(is that proper?)." Both were presumably too personal to be published in the Muscatine *Journal*.

[10] Clemens probably refers not to a description proper, but to an engraving, captioned "Schuylkill Water Works," that appeared as a frontispiece in the September 1840 issue of *Godey's Lady's Book, and Ladies' American Magazine*, published in Philadelphia and edited by Sarah J. Hale, Lydia H. Sigourney, and Louis A. Godey. The engraving was intended to illustrate a poem published in the same issue, "Fairmount," by Catherine L. Brooke (142). Philadelphia's famous waterworks at Fairmount had been constructed in 1812–15. By 1822 the Schuylkill had been dammed to provide the necessary power (replacing the original use of steam) to raise the river water to the reservoirs atop Fairmount, about one hundred feet. Clemens mentions this dam and the building which housed the waterwheels and pumps. At the foot of the hill was Fairmount Gardens, where the city had placed an elaborate cenotaph containing the white marble bust of Frederick Graff (1774–1847), superintendent and chief designer and engineer of the water-supply system. The monument was engraved on one side, "To the Memory of Frederick Graff Who Designed and Executed the Fairmount Water Works"; and on the other side, "Erected by the City Councils of Philadelphia June 1 1848" (R. A. Smith, 45–51; Jackson, 3:733–35).

[11] Germantown was just north of the city proper, adjacent to Manayunk, a small manufacturing town on the east bank of the Schuylkill, a source of ample water power. Just below Manayunk, picturesque Wissahickon Creek flowed into the Schuylkill. Philadelphia journalist, author of romances, and visionary George Lippard (1822–54) was particularly enamored of the Wissahickon: he was married on its banks, he lived for a time near it, and he used it as a setting in several of his books. *Legends of the American Revolution; or, Washington and His Generals* (1847) was, according to its dedication, "an earnest attempt to embody the scenes of the Past, in a series of Historical pictures" (iii). Lippard died in Philadelphia on 9 February 1854, shortly before Clemens left the city ("George Lippard . . . ," Philadelphia *Public Ledger*, 10 Feb 54, 2).

[12] Probably "Spirit of the Schuylkill," one of several works by the American sculptor William Rush (1756–1833) which stood in Fairmount Gardens.

[13] Clemens appears to have mistaken Eastern Penitentiary, on Coates Street between Schuylkill Front and Schuylkill Third streets, for the distributing branch of the waterworks. No such building is described in his own guidebook to Philadelphia, but (as its map shows) the penitentiary was just four or five blocks along Coates. This was a very large structure. "The front is in the castellated style of architecture, having heavy square towers sixty-five feet high, and a splendid

Schuylkill Water Works, engraving by W. H. Bartlett
(frontispiece, *Godey's Lady's Book*, September 1840; see p. 25, n. 10).

arched gateway, with portcullis and central tower" (Scharf and Westcott, 3:1834–35), easily mistaken for "the style of an ancient feudal Castle." The House of Refuge was just another six blocks along Coates, between Schuylkill Seventh and Eighth streets, near the intersection with Ridge Road. It was a reform school for white juveniles, which received its first inmate in December 1828. The school had recently expanded, building anew at the corner of Parrish and William streets, to accommodate blacks, but Clemens appears to have seen only the older building (R. A. Smith, 141–43). If he then turned northwest on Ridge Road, he was within five blocks of Girard College. Founded by the American shipping magnate and financier Stephen Girard (1750–1831), who provided $3 million for construction and an endowment, the college had offered free education to white, male orphans since 1848. An engraving of the college's main building, designed after a Greek temple, with thirty-four Corinthian columns each fifty-five feet high, was the frontispiece for Clemens's guidebook, R. A. Smith's *Philadelphia as It Is, in 1852*, which also gave a very full description in the text (Scharf and Westcott, 3:1944–48; R. A. Smith, 119–31; Jackson, 3:726).

[14] Neither "Jim" nor Jim Robinson has been identified.

[15] Clemens's abbreviation for "Hannibal" ("H—l") was calculated to remind Orion of the time he had gone to St. Louis, leaving his brother in charge of the Hannibal *Journal* for the week of 6–13 May 1853. Clemens had seized this opportunity to generate a mock feud over the ambiguity of a dedication, "To Miss Katie of H—l," to the poem entitled "Love Concealed." Upon his return to Hannibal, Orion publicly dismissed the fuss as "a great bore to us, and doubtless to the public generally" (*ET&S1*, 7, 91–102).

[16] Beginning with this sentence (and barring the final postscript, which is in manuscript) the only surviving text is in the Muscatine *Journal*, where Orion published what he described as an "extract from a private letter to the senior editor." The extant manuscript shows that he omitted the first three paragraphs of the letter (indicating the omission with asterisks), as well as the two paragraphs immediately preceding the signature, the signature itself, and an unknown amount of text following it. The exact status of these two paragraphs following the signature remains problematic, but there is no decisive evidence to refute Orion's statement that he published an extract from a single letter. Since the paragraphs report further sightseeing performed "yesterday," they must have been written at least one or two days after the part of the letter written on 26 October. Although these passages do not mention either the mint or the navy yard, which Clemens had earlier promised to visit, they do mention the State House (within a few blocks of the mint), and they allude directly to Clemens's recent trip from New York to Philadelphia. Presumably Clemens added a postscript to the original letter (which ends with a blank verso) by starting on a fresh sheet with a new date: but Orion omitted this part of the text along with the concluding paragraphs of the first section, making the two parts read continuously as a letter written on 26 October. It is conceivable that Clemens actually sent two letters, but the sole documentary basis for this part of the letter (or letters) represents it as a single document.

[17] The inscription is from Leviticus 25:10: "Proclaim Liberty throughout all the Land unto all the Inhabitants Thereof." Originally cast in 1752, and then recast twice in 1753, the bell hung for many years in the tower of the State House.

It was rung on 8 July 1776 at the first reading of the Declaration of Independence in Independence Square. The bell cracked in 1835, and again in 1846.

[18] The Right Reverend William White (1748–1836), rector of Christ Church in Philadelphia for most of his life, became a chaplain of Congress during the Revolution and numbered many of its leaders among his congregation. In 1786 he was elected the first bishop of the new diocese of Pennsylvania, and in 1796 he became the Protestant Episcopal church's presiding bishop.

[19] Thomas Paine in *The American Crisis* (1776–83): "These are the times that try men's souls."

[20] Clemens presumably took the 2:00 P.M. Express Line (cost, three dollars) to Philadelphia. This trip lasted four and a half hours: by steamboat from New York to South Amboy, New Jersey, and from there by rail to Camden, and by ferry across the Delaware River to the wharf at Walnut Street (advertisement, New York *Tribune*, 6 Oct 53, 3; R. A. Smith, 411). The collision Clemens recalls was one between two passenger trains on the Camden and Amboy line which occurred on 9 August 1853. Four passengers were killed, and several others seriously injured, when the trains collided head on on a curve near Old Bridge, New Jersey ("Another Railroad Tragedy," New York *Times*, 10 Aug 53, 1; "The Camden and Amboy Railroad Accident—Verdict of the Jury," Philadelphia *Public Ledger*, 13 Aug 53, 1).

To Orion Clemens
28 November 1853 • Philadelphia, Pa.
(MS, *damage emended:* NPV)

Philadelphia, Nov. 28th 1853.

My Dear Brother:

I received your letter to-day. I think Ma ought to spend the winter in St Louis. I don't believe in that climate—it's too cold for her.[1]

The printer's annual ball and supper came off the other night. The proceeds amounted to about $1.000. The printers, as well as other people are endeavoring to raise money to erect a monument to Franklin, but there are so many abominable foreigners here (and among printers, too,) who hate everything American, that I am very certain as much money for such a purpose could be raised in St Louis, as in Philadelphia[.][2] I was in Franklin's old office this morning,—the "North American" (formerly "Philadelphia Gazette"), and there were at least one foreigner for every ~~ot~~ ¢ American at work there.[3]

How many subscribers has the Journal got? ~~How m~~ What does the job-work pay? and what ~~th~~ does the whole concern pay? I have not seen a copy of the paper yet.

I intend to take Ma to Ky., anyhow, and if I possibly have the money, I will attend to the deeds too.[4]

I will try to write for the paper occasionally, but I fear my letters will be very uninteresting, for this incessant night work dulls one['s] ideas amazingly.

From some cause, I cannot set type near so fast as when I was at home. Sunday is a long day, and while others set 12 and 15,000, yesterday, I only set 10,000. However, I will shake this laziness off, soon, I reckon.

I always thought the eastern people were patterns of uprightness,; but I never ~~below~~ before saw so many whisky-swilling, God-despising heathens as I find in this part of the country. I believe I am the only person in the Inquirer office that does not drink. One young fellow makes $18 for a few weeks, and gets on a grand "bender" and spends every cent of it.

How do you like "free-soil?[5] I would like amazingly to see a good, old-fashioned negro." My love to all

Truly your brother

$ Sam.

[1] The somewhat colder climate of Muscatine, Iowa.

[2] The third anniversary ball and banquet of Philadelphia Typographical Union No. 2 took place on 23 November at Sansom Street Hall. On 1 November, editors, authors, publishers, and printers had met at the County Court House to devise means to erect a suitable monument to Benjamin Franklin. Jesper Harding, proprietor of the *Pennsylvania Inquirer*, was chosen chairman of the Franklin Monument Association and early in December appointed an executive committee to take charge of the project (Philadelphia *Pennsylvanian*: untitled notice, 1 Nov 53, 2; "Respect to the Memory of Benjamin Franklin," 2 Nov 53, 3; "Franklin Monument Association," Philadelphia *Public Ledger*, 5 Dec 53, 2).

[3] Clemens had visited the offices of the Philadelphia *North American and United States Gazette* at 66 South Third Street, a few doors away from the *Inquirer* office. In 1845, two years before its merger with the *United States Gazette*, the *North American* had absorbed the Philadelphia *Gazette and Daily Advertiser*, the direct descendant of Franklin's *Pennsylvania Gazette*. Clemens's spelling ("foreighner") was probably intended to represent an Irish accent. The Irish in Philadelphia at this time were the victims of widespread hostility (McElroy, 712; Hudson, 77–79, 182–83; Mott 1962, 26–28, 188, 260; *NIM*, 406; Clark, 29, 34).

[4] Presumably the deeds to the Clemens family's Tennessee land (see 9 Mar 58 to OC and MEC, n. 11).

[5] Clemens refers to Orion's move from Missouri, a slave state, to Iowa, a free state. He mistakenly placed closing quotation marks at the end of the next sentence instead of this one.

To the Muscatine *Journal*
4 December 1853 • Philadelphia, Pa.
(Muscatine *Journal*, 16 Dec 53)

PHILADELPHIA, Dec. 4, 1853.

There is very little news of consequence stirring just now. The steamer, due several days ago, has not yet arrived, and fears are entertained that something has befallen her.[1] Mitchell, the Irish patriot, is the lion in New York at present. I suppose he will be here soon.[2]

Philadelphia is one of the healthiest places in the Union. The air is pure and fresh—almost like the country. The deaths for the week are 147.[3]

It was about 1682 that this city was laid out. The first settlers came over the year previously, in the "Sarah and John," Capt. Smith. The city now extends from Southwark to Richmond—about five miles—and from the Delaware to the Schuylkill—something over two miles. The streets are wide and straight, and cross each other at right angles, running north and south and east and west. Penn's original design was to leave Front street free, and allow no buildings to be erected upon it. This would have afforded a beautiful promenade, as well as a fine view of the Delaware. But this plan was not carried out. What is now the crooked Dock street was once a beautiful brook, running through the heart of the city. In old times vessels came up this creek as high as third street.

The old State House in Chesnut street, is an object of great interest to the stranger; and though it has often been repaired, the old model and appearance are still preserved. It is a substantial brick edifice, and its original cost was £5,600 ($28,000). In the east room of the first story the mighty Declaration of Independence was passed by Congress, July 4th, 1776.

When a stranger enters this room for the first time, an unaccountable feeling of awe and reverence comes over him, and every memento of the past his eye rests upon whispers that he is treading upon sacred ground. Yes, everything in that old hall reminds him that he stands where mighty men have stood; he gazes around him, almost expecting to see a Franklin or an Adams rise before him. In this room is to be seen the old "Independence Bell," which called the people together to hear the Declaration read, and also a rude bench, on which Washington, Franklin and Bishop White once sat.

It is hard to get tired of Philadelphia, for amusements are not scarce. We have what is called a "free-and-easy," at the saloons on Saturday nights. At a free-and-easy, a chairman is appointed, who calls on any of the assembled company for a song or a recitation, and as there are plenty of singers and spouters, one may laugh himself to fits at a very small expense.[4]

Ole Bull, Jullien, and Sontag have flourished and gone,[5] and left the two fat women, one weighing 764, and the other 769 pounds, to "astonish the natives." I stepped in to see one of these the other evening, and was disappointed. She is a pretty extensive piece of meat, but not much to brag about; however, I suppose she would bring a fair price in the Cannibal Islands. She is a married woman! If I were her husband, I think I could yield with becoming fortitude to the dispensations of Providence, if He, in his infinite goodness, should see fit to take her away! With this human being of the elephant species, there is also a "*Swiss* Warbler"— bah! I earnestly hope he may live to see his native land for the first time.[6]

W.[7]

[1] The SS *Europa* (British and North American Royal Mail Steam Ship line) had left Liverpool for New York on 19 November; since 2 December Philadelphia newspapers had repeatedly described the ship as overdue. It finally arrived safely on the morning of 6 December (advertisement, London *Times*, 9 Nov 53, 1; various notices, Philadelphia *Public Ledger*, 2–7 Dec 53; "Three Days Later from Europe," New York *Times*, 7 Dec 53, 3).

[2] John Mitchel (1815–75), an Irish nationalist and newspaper editor, had been convicted in 1848 of treason against the Crown and sentenced to fourteen years' transportation. In the summer of 1853 he escaped from Tasmania and fled via Australia, the Sandwich Islands, and Tahiti, to San Francisco. On 29 November he had arrived in New York, met by an enthusiastic public welcome. Clemens's remark echoes the Philadelphia *Public Ledger*'s observation that "John Mitchel is just now the lion in New York" ("Sketch of the Life of John Mitchel," 2 Dec 53, 1, reprinting the New York *Times*, 30 Nov 53, 3). Philadelphia held at least three meetings to plan a reception for Mitchel (on 26 November and 5 December 1853, and 3 January 1854), but no indication has been found that he ever visited the city. In January 1854, Mitchel alienated many of his admirers by publishing his adamant proslavery views in the New York *Citizen*, the weekly newspaper he founded (Dillon, 1:230–48, 2:1–34, 39–49; Philadelphia *Public Ledger*: "Reception of Mitchell," 28 Nov 53, 2; "John Mitchell, the Irish Patriot," 5 Dec 53, 2; "A Welcome to John Mitchell," 4 Jan 54, 2).

[3] On 6 January 1854, the Philadelphia *Public Ledger* reported that the city's death rate, "compared with the population . . . at the lowest computation,

400,000, is about the ratio of one to every forty-one of the inhabitants annually, more favorable than any other large city in the United States" ("The Mortality in Philadelphia," 2). Clemens's source for this observation, and for much of the factual material he included here and in his letter of 24 December to the Muscatine *Journal*, was R. A. Smith's *Philadelphia as It Is, in 1852* (Philadelphia: Lindsay and Blakiston, 1852), first identified in Lorch 1946, 348–52.

⁴These popular entertainments also offered food, stage shows, poultry raffles, and such performers as "Mr. Lovett, the Celebrated Bell Ringer" ("Amusements," Philadelphia *Public Ledger*, 3 Dec 53, 3).

⁵Norwegian violinist Ole Bull (1810–80), assisted by ten-year-old soprano Adelina Patti (1843–1919) and pianist Maurice Strakosch (1825–87), gave concerts on 2 and 4 November at Philadelphia's Musical Fund Hall. These were for the benefit of the suffering colonists of Oleana, the Norwegian agricultural settlement that, from September 1852 to September 1853, Bull had attempted to establish in Pennsylvania, unfortunately on land not suitable for farming. Between 9 and 21 November, the flamboyant French conductor and composer Louis Antoine Jullien (1812–60), who was touring the United States under the management of P. T. Barnum, gave eleven elaborate "Orchestral and Vocal Concerts" at Philadelphia's Concert Hall. Responding to popular and critical acclaim, he returned for three additional concerts from 1 to 3 December. German soprano Henriette Sontag (1806–54), assisted on the violin by boy prodigy Paul Julien (1841–66), appeared several times in Musical Fund Hall in October and November. Such performances attracted great crowds in American cities, where there was growing interest in classical music and European concert artists (*NGD*, 3:445–46, 9:748; *ICMM*, 1089; "Amusements," Philadelphia *Public Ledger*, 21 Oct–3 Dec 53).

⁶The eighteen-year-old, 769-pound "American Giant Girl," Miss Hannah Crouse, held "Levees" in "Bloomer Costume" in early December "in the beautiful and spacious room, in Ninth St., first door north of Chesnut st., between the hours of 10, A. M. and 10 o'clock P. M." On hand with her was the Swiss Warbler, whose mission was to "astonish and delight the audience with music on the Jewish Symbols, Accompanied by Warbling in Imitation of Birds." A rival attraction, which Clemens "stepped in to see," was Mrs. Scholley, the "Largest Lady in the World," weighing 764 pounds, and appearing "Day and Evening" with a different (or ubiquitous) Swiss Warbler at "Col. Wood's . . . At 142 Chesnut Street, Most Fashionable Resort in Town" ("Amusements," Philadelphia *Public Ledger*, 2 Dec 53, 4).

⁷"W." was probably short for "W. Epaminondas Adrastus Blab," a pseudonym Clemens had used (sometimes abbreviated as W. E. A. B.) in the Hannibal *Journal* in September 1852. The signature "W."—repeated in his letters of 24 Dec 53, 3 Feb 54, and 17 and 18 Feb 54, all to the Muscatine *Journal*—suggests that he had decided to have Blab fulfill an old promise to write travel correspondence (Branch 1942, 9–10; *ET&S1*, 83–84).

To Pamela A. Moffett
5 December 1853 • Philadelphia, Pa.
(MS, *damage emended:* NPV)

Philadelphia, Dec. 5

My Dear Sister:

I have already written two letters within the last two hours, and you will excuse me if this is not lengthy. If I had the money, I would come to St. Louis now, while the river is open;[1] but in the last two or three weeks I have spent about thirty dollars for clothing, so I suppose I shall remain where I am. I only want to return to avoid night work, which is injuring my eyes. I have received one or two letters from home, but they are not written as they should be; and know no more about what is going on there, than the man in the moon. One only has to leave home to learn how to write an interesting [letter][2] to an absent friend when he gets back. I suppose you board at Mrs. Hunter's yet—and that, I think, is somewhere in Olive street above Fifth.[3] Phila is one of the healthiest places in the Union. I wanted to spend this winter in a warm climate; but it is too late now. I don't like our present prospect for cold ~~wh~~ weather at all.

Truly your brother

Sam.

---

[1] That is, before the winter freeze closed the Mississippi.

[2] Clemens omitted the required noun, possibly because "interesting" fell at a line end in the manuscript. At some later date, Orion Clemens wrote "letter" in the margin, a likely correction which is adopted here.

[3] By 1854, and almost certainly in 1853, William and Pamela Moffett were renting a home in St. Louis on Pine Street between Fifth and Sixth streets (Knox, 133). Clemens recalls here that, while he was staying with them in the summer of 1853, the Moffetts had boarded with Ann E. Hunter, mother of his and Pamela's aunt Ella Hunter Lampton. St. Louis directories for the 1850s, less than comprehensive, do not give an Olive Street address for Ann Hunter and only in 1851 list her as the keeper of a boardinghouse, at 138 Market Street (Green, 177). It remains possible, however, that she did have such an establishment "in Olive street above Fifth" or that she simply lived there and provided meals for the Moffetts alone.

To the Muscatine *Journal*
24 December 1853 • Philadelphia, Pa.
(Muscatine *Journal*, 6 Jan 54)

PHILADELPHIA, Dec. 24, 1853.

The weather last night was intensely cold, and the wind blew almost a hurricane. During the week we have also had slight falls of snow.

On Thursday night last, there was an extensive fire in N. Third street, during the progress of which, the wall (only nine inches thick!) of a burning, four-story building came down with a terrible crash, burying several men who were engaged in extinguishing the fire. One of these unfortunates lay for some three hours, pressed down by the rubbish, and unable to extricate himself, in sight of his friends, who were alike unable to render him any assistance. He was at length, however, delivered from his perilous situation, and conveyed to his home, but at last accounts his injuries were such as to leave very little hope of his recovery. Another man, a policeman, was completely buried; and when found, he had long been dead. His feet were burned off, his face burnt to a crisp, and his head crushed in.[1]

The markets, as well as shops of all kinds, are crowded to-day, with people making their Christmas purchases. Turkeys and fowls of all kinds, are vanishing from the markets as if by magic. I asked a lady what the best turkeys were selling at. She replied that she had priced several fine ones, which were *seven dollars apiece!* This seems a high figure, but everything else is in proportion. Couldn't you forward us a few hundred of the birds?

During the week I have visited several places of note near Philadelphia. The first of these places was Germantown, where the Americans made the terrible charge upon the British, quartered in the celebrated "Chew's House." This building is still standing, and is at present occupied as a dwelling-house. It does not appear near as old as others in its immediate vicinity. It is built in the real old English style, and still bears the cannon and musket ball marks received in the conflict which made it famous. Germantown is rich in old buildings, some bearing the dates of 1743, 1760, &c.[2]

At the corner of Little Dock and Second streets, stands the queer looking old house occupied by the heroic Lydia Darrah. It was here, if I remember the story aright, that she left the British officer, and taking her flour bag, set off to inform Gen. Washington of the intended attack of the British upon his camp: and her heroic conduct defeated the plans of the red-coats, and saved the Americans. Well does she deserve a monument; but no such monument is hers. As one might almost guess, her old mansion is now occupied by a Jew, as a clothing store.[3]

The next place of note is the old "Slate-Roof House," which was the first house in the city covered with that material. It is situated in Second street, at the corner of Norris's alley. It was erected about one hundred and sixty years ago, in the old English style of architecture. It was occupied by Wm. Penn, in the year 1700, and John Penn, "the American," who was born under its roof. In this house Gen. Forbes, second in command, and afterwards successor to Gen. Braddock, died, and from it was borne to the grave, with imposing military honors. In after years, it was the temporary abode of John Adams, John Hancock, and many other distinguished members of the first Congress, and also of Baron De Kalb, who fell, fighting for American independence, at the battle of Camden. The brave General Lee also breathed his last in this house, and was buried in Christ Churchyard. This noble old relic is also desecrated in the same manner as the Darrah House. Unless measures are shortly taken for its preservation, it will soon go to decay and be remembered as one of the things that were.[4]

Carpenter's Hall, situated in Carpenter's Court, is a pile dear to every American, for within its walls, the first Congress of the United States assembled—a fact which should entitle it to a place in the heart of every true lover of his country. "The building is of brick, two stories high, and surmounted by a cupola. The facade is in the Roman style of architecture. The principal entrance leads to the Assembly Room, in which Congress first met. It is now occupied as an auction mart."[5] By an auction mart— the old story. Alas! that these old buildings, so intimately connected with the principal scenes in the history of our country, should thus be profaned. Why do not those who make such magnificent donations to our colleges and other institutions, give a mite toward their preservation of these monuments of the past? Surely their liberality would be well bestowed. It is painful to look upon these time-honored edifices, and feel that they will soon fall into decay and be forgotten.

This communication is already too long to be interesting, and I will stop.

W.

[1] Clemens may have drawn on an account of the fire published in the Philadelphia *Public Ledger* of 23 December. On the night of Wednesday, 21 December, the blaze was first noted at 198 and 200 Third Street, shortly before it spread through a partition "only nine inches thick" to 196 Third Street. All three buildings were destroyed, and police officer Hiram Hammer was found dead in the rubble the next day ("The Third Street Fire," 1). Jacob Albright, the "delivered" officer, died on 25 December ("Death of Officer Albright," Philadelphia *Public Ledger*, 28 Dec 53, 1).

[2] Cliveden, commonly known as "Chew House," was a handsome stone dwelling built in 1761 by Benjamin Chew (1722–1810), who had served colonial Pennsylvania as attorney general, and later chief justice of its supreme court. During the battle of Germantown on 4 October 1777, English troops barricaded themselves in Cliveden and successfully defended it against forces under George Washington (Eberlein and Hubbard, 324–38).

[3] In December 1777 Lydia Darragh (1729–89), a Quaker nurse and midwife, supposedly secured passage through British lines by claiming she had to buy flour, displaying an empty flour sack as proof. She then sent word to George Washington of an impending attack on his army camped near Philadelphia. Modern historians have long regarded the story of Darragh's heroism as largely a myth (Westcott, 192–95; *NAW*, 1:434–35). Loxley House, her residence at the time, was built in 1759 or 1760 by Benjamin Loxley, a Philadelphia carpenter and man of property. In "style and appearance" it "was exceptional and unlike any other building, public or private, to be found in the city," with a unique second-story railed gallery and a first story whose unusual storefront-type windows made it readily adaptable to commercial use (Westcott, 190–91). Clemens's source for this paragraph and for the rest of this letter noted that Loxley House was "at present occupied as a clothing depot" (R. A. Smith, 429).

[4] According to Clemens's source, "This house, once so honoured and renowned, now, alas! wears a sadly-neglected appearance,—the front rooms of the lower story being occupied as a huckster's shop, and those in the rear as a saw manufactory, while the upper stories are used by a cabinet-maker as a varnish-room" (R. A. Smith, 427–29). The same source incorrectly reported that the house contained the deathbed of "the brave but eccentric General Lee." In fact, Charles Lee (1731–82) was only buried from Slate Roof House after dying in a Market Street inn. No mere eccentric, Lee was contentious, egotistical, and mercenary. Appointed second major-general of the Continental Army in 1775, he was court-martialed in 1778 for disobeying orders, misconduct in the face of the enemy, and disrespect to George Washington. Lee was suspended from the army for a year, then was dismissed in 1780 after further offensive behavior. The discovery in 1858 of Lee's plan for defeating the American forces, written in 1777 while he was in British captivity, permanently tarnished his reputation (Jackson, 4:1094; *DAB*, 11:98–101).

[5] Quoted from *Philadelphia as It Is, in 1852* (R. A. Smith, 431–33).

To the Muscatine *Journal*
3 February 1854 • Philadelphia, Pa.

(Muscatine *Journal*, 17 Feb 54)

PHILADELPHIA, Feb. 3, 1854.

The Consolidation Bill, which has kept our citizens in such an excitement so long, has at length passed both houses of the Legislature, and when the Governor's signature is affixed to it, Southwark, the Northern Liberties, &c., will be among the things that were. This bill brings the various Districts, boroughs, &c., and also Philadelphia county under one municipal government.[1] Philadelphia as consolidated, is now the largest city in the United States. Although New York has much the larger population, Philadelphia has a far greater number of houses, and covers a much larger space than New York, or any other city in the Union. The police came out yesterday in their uniform. It is very neat, and gives them a kind of military appearance.[2]

I went, with a few friends, yesterday, to the Exchange, to see the reception of the two lions, Captains Low and Crighton. The Reading Room, at 12 o'clock, was densely crowded. About five minutes past twelve the two heroes made their appearance, and were received with three times three by the assembled populace. After a few remarks by the President of the Testimonial Committee, the shaking of hands commenced, and the two Captains were borne through the crowd, to the great danger of their lives and limbs, and were thus squeezed and cheered into the street, where a carriage was in waiting to convey them to the State House. The crowd followed them on a run, yelling and huzzaing till they were out of sight. The money subscribed for each, I believe, was about $2,500, in addition to which they will receive several medals. Capt. Crighton is about thirty-three years of age, and is a native of New England.[3]

The people here seem very fond of tacking a bit of poetry (?) to the notices of the death of friends, published in the Ledger. Here are a few lines of most villainous doggerel, and worse measure, which may be found in the "death" column of that paper three or four times every day. This will serve as a contrast with the pretty gems of your fair correspondents "Nannette" and "Virginia," &c.:

"Ah! dry your tears, and shed no more.
Because your child, husband, and brother has gone before;
In love he lived, in peace he died,
His life was asked, but was denied."

What do you think of that? Will not Byron lose some of his popularity now?[4]

The great California tree, or rather part of it, has just arrived here, and is now lying in Front street. It was sawed off about seven feet above the roots, and is about 23 feet in diameter. It is quite a curiosity. Some of the sailors of the ship in which it came, are Chinese.[5]

The Sabbath School children of the Methodist E. Churches, of Philadelphia, have contributed a block of marble for the Washington Monument. It bears an appropriate inscription.[6]

The journeymen rope makers of Philadelphia, have demanded an advance of 25 cents a day on their wages. This demand has generally been complied with.

They have lately placed a new chime of bells in the tower of St. Stephen's Church, here, the largest one of which weighs 2800 pounds. This is a large bell.

W.

[1] Climaxing ten years of effort by advocates of consolidation, on 2 February Governor William Bigler of Pennsylvania signed the bill bringing the original two-square-mile city of Philadelphia and the twenty-eight districts, townships, and boroughs of the county of Philadelphia under one government (Philadelphia *Public Ledger*: "Passage of the Consolidation Bill," 1 Feb 54, 2; "The Consolidation Bill," 4 Feb 54, 2; Jackson, 2:516–17).

[2] On 11 November 1853 the Philadelphia Board of Police had passed a resolution requiring all policemen to be in uniform by 1 February 1854. Improved police discipline, performance, and recognizability outweighed objections that uniforms were undemocratic and inappropriate to the American character. A number of the city's policemen, accustomed to wear only a star insignia, protested against the new uniform—a blue cloth cap, a navy-blue frock coat with standing collar and gilded buttons, and dark-gray trousers—particularly since they were obliged to pay the fourteen dollars it cost (Philadelphia *North American and United States Gazette*: "Police Uniform," 28 Nov 53, 1; "Police Reform," 16 Dec 53, 2; Philadelphia *Public Ledger*: "The Police Board," 12 Nov 53, 1; "Opposition to the Police Uniform," 17 Jan 54, 1; "The Police Uniform," 21 Jan 54, 1).

[3] This reception, in the rotunda of the Philadelphia Merchants' Exchange, was for two national heroes: Captain E. T. Low of the Boston bark *Kilby* and Captain Robert Creighton of the steamer *Three Bells* out of Glasgow, Scotland. The *Kilby* and the *Three Bells* had led in rescuing survivors of the steamer *San Francisco*, which lost some three hundred of its seven hundred passengers and crew to

drowning and cholera after a gale wrecked it and set it adrift in the mid-Atlantic on 25 December 1853. After their arrival at American ports in mid-January, Captains Low and Creighton went from city to city in triumph. Philadelphia awarded $1,000 to Low and $2,000 to Creighton (New York *Times*: "Total Loss of the San Francisco," 14 Jan 54, 1; "Wreck of the San Francisco," 16 Jan 54, 1; "Arrival of the Bark Kilby," 19 Jan 54, 6; Philadelphia *Public Ledger*: "The San Francisco Testimonial Fund," 2 Feb 54, 2; "Enthusiastic Reception of Captains Creighton and Low," 3 Feb 54, 1).

⁴In his 1870 essay "Post-Mortem Poetry," Clemens gave a tongue-in-cheek account of the *Ledger*'s custom of

appending to published death-notices a little verse or two of comforting poetry. Any one who is in the habit of reading the daily Philadelphia "Ledger," must frequently be touched by these plaintive tributes to extinguished worth. . . . There is an element about some poetry which is able to make even physical suffering and death cheerful things to contemplate and consummations to be desired. This element is present in the mortuary poetry of Philadelphia, and in a noticeable degree of development. (SLC 1870c, 864–65)

Paine reported that Clemens unsuccessfully submitted his own "contributions to the Philadelphia *Ledger*—mainly poetry of an obituary kind. Perhaps it was burlesque; he never confessed that, but it seems unlikely that any other obituary poetry would have failed of print" (*MTB*, 1:98). Clemens himself, speaking in Philadelphia in 1885, denied the "dreadful assertion" that he had written "obituary poetry in the Philadelphia *Ledger*," admitting, however, that "once, when a compositor in the *Ledger* establishment, I did set up some of that poetry, but for a worse offense than that no indictment can be found against me. I did not write that poetry—at least, not all of it" (SLC 1885a, 194). The verses Clemens quotes in this letter appeared in the *Public Ledger* three times between 30 January and 3 February. The Muscatine *Journal* had published sentimental poetry by "Virginia" on 11 November and 9 December 1853 ("The Lock of Hair" and "Lines on Visiting Home"). It published a sentimental poem and a tearful story by "Nannette" ("The Poets' Wreath for '54" and "Nathalie. A New-Years Tale") on 6 January 1854, and another poem by her ("To *————") on 20 January. Both women were regular "correspondents" of the *Journal*.

⁵On 27 January the clipper *Messenger* out of San Francisco brought to Philadelphia a ten-foot, hollowed-out section of a giant redwood from California, a tree some three thousand years old and three hundred and twenty-five feet in height. Approximately ninety feet in circumference, the section could easily enclose one hundred standing men. From Philadelphia it was taken for exhibit to Boston and New York (various notices, Philadelphia *Pennsylvanian* and Philadelphia *Public Ledger*, 28 Jan–15 Feb 54).

⁶The inscription read: "A preached Gospel—a free press. Washington—we revere his memory" ("Another Block for the Washington Monument," Philadelphia *Public Ledger*, 22 Feb 54, 1). The contribution of such blocks was encouraged by the Washington National Monument Society as a means of funding construction (Harvey, 48–49, 125–29).

To the Muscatine *Journal*
17 and 18 February 1854 • Washington, D.C.

(Muscatine *Journal*, 24 Mar 54)

WASHINGTON, Feb. 18, 1854.

When I came out on the street this morning to take a view of Washington, the ground was perfectly white, and it was snowing as though the heavens were to be emptied, and that, too, in as short a time as possible. The snow was falling so thickly that I could scarcely see across the street. I started toward the capitol, but there being no sidewalk, I sank ankle deep in mud and snow at every step. When at last I reached the capitol, I found that Congress did not sit till 11 o'clock; so I thought I would stroll around the city for an hour or two.[1]

The Treasury Building is a pretty edifice, with a long row of columns in front, and stands about a square from the President's house. Passing into the park in front of the White House, I amused myself with a gaze at Clark Mills' great equestrian statue of Jackson. It is a beautiful thing, and well worth a long walk on a stormy day to see.[2] The public buildings of Washington are all fine specimens of architecture, and would add greatly to the embellishment of such a city as New York—but here they are sadly out of place looking like so many palaces in a Hottentot village. The streets, indeed are fine—wide, straight, and level as a floor. But the buildings, almost invariably, are very poor—two and three story brick houses, and strewed about in clusters; you seldom see a compact square off Pennsylvania Avenue. They look as though they might have been emptied out of a sack by some Brobdignagian gentleman, and when falling, been scattered abroad by the winds. There are scarcely any pavements, and I might almost say *no* gas, off *the* thoroughfare, Pennsylvania Avenue. Then, if you should be seized with a desire to go to the Capitol, or somewhere else, you may stand in a puddle of water, with the snow driving in your face for fifteen minutes or more, before an omnibus rolls lazily by; and when one does come, ten to one there are nineteen passengers inside and fourteen outside, and while the driver casts on you a look of commiseration, you have the inexpressible satisfaction of knowing that you closely resemble a very moist dish-rag, (and *feel* so, too,) at the same time that you are unable to discover what benefit you have derived from your fifteen minutes' soak-

ing; and so, driving your fists into the inmost recesses of your breeches
pockets, you stride away in despair, with a step and a grimace that would
make the fortune of a tragedy actor, while your "onery" appearance is
greeted with "screems of laftur" from a pack of vagabond boys over the
way. Such is life, and such is Washington!

The Capitol is a very fine building, but it has been so often described, that I will not attempt another portrait. The statuary with which
it is adorned is most beautiful; but as I am no connoisseur in such matters,
I will let that pass also. The large hall between the two Congressional
Chambers is embellished with numerous large paintings, portraying
some of the principal events in American history. One, the "Embarkation
of the Pilgrims in the May Flower," struck me as very fine—so fresh and
natural. The "Baptism of Pocahontus" is also a noble picture, and worthy
the place it occupies.[3]

I passed into the Senate Chamber to see the men who give the people
the benefit of their wisdom and learning for a little glory and eight dollars
a day. The Senate is now composed of a different material from what it
once was. Its glory hath departed. Its halls no longer echo the words of a
Clay, or Webster, or Calhoun. They have played their parts and retired
from the stage; and though they are still occupied by others, the void is
felt. The Senators dress very plainly as they should, and all avoid display,
and do not speak unless they have something to say—and that cannot be
said of the Representatives. Mr. Cass is a fine looking old man; Mr. Douglass, or "Young America," looks like a lawyer's clerk, and Mr. Seward is a
slim, dark, bony individual, and looks like a respectable wind would blow
him out of the country.[4]

In the House nearly every man seemed to have something weighing
on his mind on which the salvation of the Republic depended, and which
he appeared very anxious to ease himself of; and so there were generally
half a dozen of them on the floor, and "Mr. Chairman! Mr. Chairman!"
was echoed from every part of the house. Mr. Benton sits silent and
gloomy in the midst of the din, like a lion imprisoned in a cage of mon-
keys, who, feeling his superiority, disdains to notice their chattering.[5]

February 19.

The Smithsonian Institute is a large, fine building, in the same style
of architecture as the Trinity Church of New York. It is composed of the
same kind of stone as that edifice, and looks like a half-church and half-

castle. It has a fine library, and also an extensive gallery of paintings. Lectures are delivered in it almost every evening.[6] Park Benjamin lectures there this evening.[7]

If there is anything in Washington, worth a visit, it is the Museum of the Patent Office. It is free to visitors at all times of the day, and is by far the largest collection of curiosities in the United States. The first story of this magnificent building is occupied by the models of patents. The second story is occupied by the museum. I spent a very pleasant four hours in this part of the building, looking at the thousands upon thousands of wonders it contains.[8] In one department were several Peruvian mummies of great antiquity. The hair was perfect, and remained plaited just as it was perhaps centuries ago; but the bodies were black, dry, and crisp, and what the appearance of the faces were during life, it was impossible to determine, for nothing remained but a shapeless mass of skin and flesh. The printing press used by Franklin, in London, nearly one hundred and twenty years ago, was an object worthy of notice. The bed is of wood and is not unlike a very shallow box. The platen is only half the size of the bed, thus requiring two pulls of the lever to each full-size sheet. What vast progress has been made in the art of printing! This press is capable of printing about 125 sheets per hour; and after seeing it, I have watched Hoe's great machine throwing off its 20,000 sheets in the same space of time, with an interest I never before felt.[9] In other cases are to be seen the suits of clothes worn by Washington when he resigned his commission as Commander-in-Chief of the American forces; the coat worn by Jackson at the battle of New Orleans; Washington's sword, war-tent, cooking utensils, knives and forks, &c., and camp equippage generally; the treaty of the United States with Turkey (a horrible specimen of Oriental chirography;)[10] the original Declaration of Independence; autographs of Bonaparte and several kings of Europe; pagan idols; part of the costumes of Atahualpa and Cortes, and thousands of other things of equal interest.

The Washington Monument is as yet but a plain white marble obelisk 150 feet high. It will no doubt be very beautiful when finished. When completed, an iron staircase will run up within 25 feet of the top. It is to be 550 feet high. If Congress would appropriate $200,000 to the Monument fund, this sum, with the contributions of the people, would build it in four years.[11]

Mr. Forrest played Othello at the National Theatre last night, to a good audience.[12] This is a very large theatre, and the only one of consequence in Washington.

W.

[1] Congress did not convene on Saturday, 18 February 1854. Clemens's "stroll" actually took place on 17 February.

[2] The statue by Mills (1810–83), cast from bronze cannons captured by Jackson in the War of 1812, was dedicated in January 1853. It represents the uniformed Jackson on a rearing horse, doffing his cap.

[3] Filling two of the eight panels in the Capitol rotunda, these paintings were by Robert W. Weir (1803–89) and John G. Chapman (1808–89), respectively.

[4] Clemens refers to: Lewis Cass (1782–1866), Democratic senator from Michigan; Stephen A. Douglas (1813–61), Democratic senator from Illinois, who in 1852 had been backed unsuccessfully for the Democratic presidential nomination by the party's "Young America" faction; and William H. Seward (1801–72), Whig senator from New York. At this time the Senate was heatedly debating Douglas's proposed Kansas-Nebraska Act, which, passed in May 1854, repealed the Missouri Compromise of 1820–21, ending its limitation on the extension of slavery. On 17 February, the day Clemens was in the gallery, Seward spoke for three hours in support of the Missouri Compromise (*DAH*, 3:197–98, 428; "Thirty-third Congress," Washington *National Intelligencer*, 18 Feb 54, 3; "Doings of Congress," Washington *Evening Star*, 18 Feb 54, 2).

[5] House proceedings on 17 February were notable for the unusual amount of bickering and procedural wrangling that preceded and followed debate on the Kansas-Nebraska Act (see *Congressional Globe*, 28 [I]:442–46). Almost fourteen years later Clemens vividly recreated the scene he describes in this paragraph, recalling that most of the legislators

seemed to be a mob of empty headed whipper-snappers that had only come to Congress to make incessant motions, propose eternal amendments, and rise to everlasting points of order. They glanced at the galleries oftener than they looked at the Speaker; they put their feet on their desks as if they were in a beer-mill; they made more racket than a rookery, and let on to know more than any body of men ever did know or ever could know by any possibility whatsoever. (SLC 1867d, no page)

Thomas Hart Benton (1782–1858), Democratic senator from Missouri from 1821 to 1851, served one term in the House (1853–55).

[6] The red sandstone "Castle on the Mall," designed in Norman style, had been occupied since 1849 but was not completed until 1855. At the time of Clemens's visit the building contained a library of about thirty-two thousand volumes, an art gallery, and a lecture hall accommodating two thousand people (Goode, 251–59).

[7] Park Benjamin (1809–64), an editor, critic, publisher, and poet, was also a popular lecturer, specializing in humorous and satirical "entertainments" in verse and prose. On 17 February he performed at the Smithsonian Institution, reciting "Fashion," his poem ridiculing styles in clothing and other fads. His next performance, a lecture on "Americanisms," was scheduled for 20 February, but was postponed a day because of a snowstorm (various notices, Washington *Evening Star*, 18–21 Feb 54).

[8] The United States Patent Office Building was modeled on the Parthenon. At this time, in addition to the Patent Office, it housed the Department of the Interior and the National Museum (Oehser, 161–64).

[9] The rotary-style press invented by Richard M. Hoe (1812–86) was first put into use, in 1846, by the Philadelphia *Public Ledger* and then widely adopted by other metropolitan newspapers (Hoe, 31–32). The fact that Clemens observed a Hoe press at work in a Washington newspaper office may suggest that he had been looking for work.

[10] The Turkish version of a treaty signed at Constantinople on 7 May 1830, establishing guidelines for commerce and navigation between the United States and the Ottoman Empire. The American negotiator had signed a French translation and exchanged it for the Turkish original signed by the representative of the Sublime Porte. This was the only treaty between the United States and the Ottoman Empire in force by 1854 (Hunter Miller, 3:541–98).

[11] In September 1833 the Washington National Monument Society was organized to raise funds by public subscription for a memorial to Washington, a project that Congress had been considering, inconclusively, since 1783. It was not until 4 July 1848, however, that the cornerstone of the monument was laid. Although by March 1854 the obelisk had been brought to a height of 153 feet at a cost of $230,000, work stopped a few months later when funds ran low. An appropriation of $200,000 was proposed in Congress, but for a variety of reasons—including dissension within the Society, doubts about the integrity of the construction already accomplished, and the Civil War—the money was not made available until 1876. Construction was finally completed on 6 December 1884, at a total cost of over $1 million. Dedicated on 21 February 1885, the monument was then the tallest structure in the world, rising to just over 555 feet (Harvey, 3–13, 45–46, 52–108; Appleton, 798–99).

[12] Edwin Forrest appeared for the "first and only time" as Othello at the National Theatre on 17 February ("National Theatre," Washington *National Intelligencer*, 17 Feb 54, 5).

BIOGRAPHICAL information is scant for Clemens's next twelve months, a period for which no letters have been discovered. His visit to Washington, D.C., probably lasted only a long weekend, from 16 through 20 February (or possibly through Washington's birthday) 1854. He himself called his stay a "flying trip," and Paine said that it "was comparatively brief, and he did not work there" (AD, 29 Mar 1906, CU-MARK, in *MTA*, 2:287; *MTB*, 1:101). No doubt relying upon information supplied by Clemens, Paine reported that he then returned to Philadelphia, where he "worked for a time on the *Ledger* and *North American*. Finally he went back to New York" (*MTB*, 1:101).

Clemens's removal to New York very likely occurred about two weeks after his return to Philadelphia. On 10 March and again on 17 March there were unclaimed letters for him in Philadelphia, an indication that by then he had left the city ("List of Letters Remaining in the Philadelphia Post Office," Philadelphia *Public Ledger*, 11 and 20 Mar 54, 4). Paine reported, "His second experience in New York appears not to have been recorded, and in later years was only vaguely remembered" (*MTB*, 1:101–2). Perhaps Clemens erased this period from his memory because it was a time of financial distress and bruised pride. His former confidence in his ability to "take care of himself a few miles from home" (8 Oct 53 to PAM) must have been shaken in the spring of 1854. Unemployment among New York printers was high, at least in part the result of the destruction by fire of two major publishing houses, Harper and Brothers and George F. Cooledge and Brothers, in December 1853 ("Destructive Fire," New York *Times*, 12 Dec 53, 1). Forty-five years later Clemens acknowledged that he had been "obliged by financial stress" to return home (SLC 1899a, 3).

In 1906 Clemens described this return trip: "I went back to the Mississippi Valley, sitting upright in the smoking-car two or three days and nights. When I reached St. Louis I was exhausted. I went to bed on board a steamboat that was bound for Muscatine. I fell asleep at once, with my clothes on, and didn't wake again for thirty-six hours" (AD, 29 Mar 1906, CU-MARK, in *MTA*, 2:287–88). Paine wrote that Clemens stopped off in St. Louis "only a few hours to see Pamela. It was his mother [in Muscatine, Iowa] he was anxious for." Paine also believed that Clemens had been away in the East for a year, from August 1853 to August 1854, and that "it was late in the summer of 1854 when he finally set out on his return to the West" (*MTB*, 1:102).

In fact, given the hard times in New York, it is reasonable to speculate that Clemens's return to the West came as early as April 1854. His appearance in Muscatine—a thriving town of about fifty-five hundred people located on the Mississippi River some three hundred and ten miles above St. Louis—occasioned a joyful reunion with his mother and brothers. Muscatine tradition contradicts Paine's contention that, unable to "afford the luxury of working for Orion" on the Muscatine *Journal*, Clemens quickly returned to St. Louis and his former job on the *Evening News* (*MTB*, 1:103). Local opinion holds that Clemens "remained in Muscatine several months before going to St. Louis, and that he worked for a time at the *Journal* office" (Lorch 1929a, 414; see also "Famous Humorist

Once Lived in Muscatine," Muscatine *Journal*, 26 Apr 1910, 3; "'Mark
Twain' in Muscatine," Muscatine *Weekly Journal*, 26 May 82, 6; Rich-
man, 1:391). Clemens's own detailed recollections of Muscatine in chapter 57 of *Life on the Mississippi* support this notion of a stay of some duration. He did not, however, remain until "the late fall of 1854 or the winter
of 1855" (Lorch 1929a, 417). "S. A. Clemens," almost certainly a mis-
print of his name, appears in a mail-to-be-claimed list in the St. Louis
Missouri Republican for 8 July ("List of Letters," 3), suggesting that
someone expected him to be there. He may well have been in St. Louis at
that point, working on the *Evening News* and perhaps other newspapers.
Certainly he was settled in St. Louis by 7 August, the first day of the
Know Nothing election riots in which he briefly participated as a citizen
policeman (*Life on the Mississippi*, chapter 51). Misremembering the time
as "1852 or 1853," Clemens recalled that he boarded "with the Paveys
[formerly of Hannibal], corner of 4th & Wash streets. It was a large,
cheap place, & had in it a good many young fellows who were students at
a Commercial college" (15 Dec 1900 to Frank E. Burrough, MoCgS).
Very little else is known about his activities in St. Louis until mid-Febru-
ary 1855, when he wrote the next letter for the Muscatine *Journal*—now
edited by Orion and Charles E. H. Wilson, successor to John Mahin, who
had withdrawn from partnership in the paper at the end of December
1854 ("Valedictory," Muscatine *Tri-Weekly Journal*, 29 Dec 54, 2).

To the Editors of the Muscatine *Tri-Weekly Journal*
(Orion Clemens and Charles E. H. Wilson)
16 February 1855 • St. Louis, Mo.
(Muscatine *Tri-Weekly Journal*, 28 Feb 55)

ST. LOUIS, Feb. 16, 1855.

Eds. Journal: Whether it is because of the wagon loads of valentines,
or the huge heaps of delayed mail matter that have just come to hand, I
cannot say; but there has been a heavy run on our Post Office for about a
week. It is almost impossible to get into the office at all, so great is the
rush—and to get to the deliveries, after ten in the morning, *is* an impos-
sibility.[1] For a week or so, nothing could be seen in the bookstores but

thousands upon thousands of valentines. One of our stationers has sold about $1,200 worth of this kind of nonsense.

A widow woman with five children, destitute of money, half starved and almost naked, reached this city yesterday, from some where in Arkansas, and were on their way to join some relations in Illinois. They had suffered dreadfully from cold and fatigue during their journey, and were truly objects of charity. The sight brought to mind the handsome sum our preacher collected in church last Sunday to obtain food and raiment for the poor, ignorant heathen in some far off part of the world; I thought, too, of the passage in the Bible instructing the disciples to carry their good works into all the world—*beginning first at Jerusalem.*[2]

An extension of the city limits seems to be exciting a good deal of attention just now, and meetings are held every day or two to consider the subject.[3]

The first train went through to Washington, on the Pacific railroad, on the 9th. The cars started from the new depot in Seventh street. The work on this road is progressing finely, and I hear no more complaint about a want of funds.[4]

A new evening paper is about to be started here, to be called the Evening Mirror. I do not know who are to be its editors. A new Catholic paper (bad luck to it) is also soon to be established, for the purpose of keeping the Know Nothing organ straight.[5]

The livery stable of T. Turner, Broadway, near Carr street, was burned on the night of the 14th. Seventeen or eighteen horses perished, among which were "Know Nothing," worth $800, and another fine horse, valued at $500. The whole loss is about $13,000, with an insurance of $8,000. The building burned very rapidly, and threw a light into my room (it was but a square and a half distant) sufficient to read by. Though half asleep, I could hear the shrieks of the poor horses as they madly struggled to escape from the cruel element.[6]

Policemen are queer animals and have remarkably nice notions as to the great law of self-preservation. I doubt if the man is now living that ever caught one at a riot. To find "a needle in a hay stack" is a much easier matter than to scare up one of these gentry when he's wanted. Late last night, hearing a fuss in the street, I got up to see what was the matter. I saw a man—somewhat inebriated—marching up the street, armed with a barrel stave, and driving a woman before him. He was talking very energetically, and applying the aforesaid stave most industriously to the poor woman's shoulders. The following remarks, which I overheard, will serve to enlighten you as to his reason for "lamming" the lady: "Curse you! (bang! went the stave;) by this kind of conduct (energetic application of the stave,) you have grieved me till you have broken my heart; (bang!) and I'll break your d—d neck for it!" (bang!—bang!—bang!) And thus the gentleman amused himself until out of sight and hearing, and failed to stumble upon a single policeman. I felt sorry for the poor heart-broken creature, and wished with all my heart it might please Providence to remove him from his troubles by putting it into the Sheriff's head to hang the scoundrel before morning. On this beast's account am I sorry that there is no purgatory for the brute creation.[7]

A Thespian Society, called the Young Mens' Dramatic Association, have played once or twice lately at the Varieties Theatre. I saw them play "The Merchant of Venice." I had always thought that this was a comedy, until they made a *farce* of it. The prompters found it a hard matter to get the actors on the stage, and when they did get them on, it was harder still to get them *off* again. "Jessica" was always "thar" when she wasn't wanted, and never would turn up when her services were required. They'll do better, next time.[8]

Rev. Dr. Cox will deliver the last of his course of historical lectures before the Young Mens' Christian Association, soon. He is an eloquent and interesting speaker, and never fails to attract large audiences.[9]

S. L. C.

[1] Clemens culled most of the news items in this letter from St. Louis papers, primarily the *Missouri Republican* and the *Missouri Democrat* of 15 and 16 February. On 14 February the St. Louis *Missouri Republican* reported the arrival of some five hundred sacks of letters and newspapers ("Mails," 2). This was mail from the East and North that had been delayed more than a week by heavy snowfalls in Illinois. On the day of the present letter the St. Louis *Evening News* noted that "our P.O. has been turned into a regular Sebastopol, which all manner of people unite in the morning to assault" ("Attack on the P.O.," 2).

[2] Clemens was reflecting on Luke 24:47, "And that repentance and remission of sins should be preached in his name among all nations, beginning at Jerusalem." The preacher was probably the Reverend Artemas Bullard, pastor of the First Presbyterian Church of St. Louis (see 30 July . . . 20 Aug 66 to JLC and PAM, n. 1). Clemens may have been acquainted at this time with Bullard's fifteen-year-old son Henry, who in 1867 became a fellow passenger on the *Quaker City* excursion to the Holy Land ("Illness Fatal to Dr. Bullard," St. Joseph [Mo.] *Gazette*, 17 May 1911, 1–2).

[3] St. Louis was debating the merits of a bill, proposed by the city council on 27 December 1854, to redistrict the city into ten wards and triple its area. Under the

proposal the city would extend roughly three miles east to west and seven miles along the Mississippi River. Voters ultimately approved the bill, which took effect on 5 December 1855 (St. Louis *Missouri Republican*: "City Extension," 29 Dec 54, 2; "The City Extension," 30 Dec 54, 2; "Extension Meeting," 16 Feb 55, 2; Scharf, 1:161; Primm, 197).

[4] The Pacific Railroad had been incorporated by Missouri on 12 March 1849. It was intended to run between St. Louis and Kansas City (about two hundred and eighty miles) and eventually to be part of the central route linking the two coasts. Liberally funded by the legislature, the railroad had just opened a fifty-four-mile section to Washington, Missouri, on 10 February. The *Missouri Democrat* predicted that "at no very distant day" the railroad would "bring to our city's lap not only the wealth of golden California, but the richer and more enduring treasures of the world's trade with the Indies and the East" ("Opening of the Pacific Railroad to Washington on the Missouri," 12 Feb 55, 2). Despite government assistance, however, a lack of funds impeded construction and the line was not completed to Kansas City until 1865. It eventually became part of the "Southwestern system," which extended to the Pacific coast (Scharf, 2:1142–67; Primm, 214–22; Belcher, 78–81).

[5] The St. Louis *Evening Mirror* made its debut on 19 February. The St. Louis *Leader*, a Catholic political and literary paper edited by novelist and poet Jedediah V. Huntington (1815–62), first appeared on 10 March. Clemens's "Know Nothing organ" was probably the St. Louis *Intelligencer*, a nativist daily established in 1850, or perhaps the blatantly xenophobic *True Shepherd of the Valley; or, St. Louis Know-Nothing*, established in September 1854 ("A New Paper—the Mirror," St. Louis *Missouri Republican*, 20 Feb 55, 2; "Prospectus of a New Catholic Paper, in the City of St. Louis," St. Louis *Missouri Democrat*, 11 Jan 55, 3; "The Leader," St. Louis *Intelligencer*, 13 Mar 55, 2; "A Know-Nothing Paper," St. Louis *Evening News*, 30 Sept 54, 2; Winifred Gregory, 371).

[6] On 15 February the St. Louis newspapers reported that a 5:00 A.M. fire "yesterday" at Tracy P. Turner's livery stables—at 321 Broadway—killed sixteen horses (Knox, 194).

[7] This and the next item were *not* derived from the St. Louis newspapers.

[8] Clemens describes the second 1855 performance, on 13 February, of the St. Louis Amateur Dramatic Association ("Amateur Dramatic Association—Benefit of the Poor," St. Louis *Missouri Republican*, 13 Feb 55, 2).

[9] Samuel Hanson Cox, D.D. (1793–1880), of Brooklyn, a "New School" Presbyterian minister and educator known as the "Great Conversationalist," gave a series of eight lectures on historical topics between 26 January and 16 February, closing with "Historic Poetry," which concentrated on the verse of Sir Walter Scott. Cox was a controversial figure: falsely accused of being an abolitionist, he had nevertheless helped organize a Presbyterian church for blacks in St. Louis, the first such church in Missouri ("Rev. Samuel H. Cox, D.D.," St. Louis *Missouri Democrat*, 26 Jan 55, 2; St. Louis *Missouri Republican*: "Dr. Cox—His Position," 26 Jan 55, 2; "Dr. Cox's Lecture," 28 Jan 55, 2; "Dr. Cox delivers . . . ," 16 Feb 55, 2; "Interesting Occasion," 20 Feb 55, 2).

To the Muscatine *Tri-Weekly Journal*
24–26 February 1855 • St. Louis, Mo.
(Muscatine *Tri-Weekly Journal*, 9 Mar 55)

ST. LOUIS, Feb. 24, 1855.
An arrangement has been made by which our California mails will
go direct from St. Louis to San Francisco without being overhauled at
New-York as has heretofore been the case. By the new plan, considerable
delay will be avoided. Hereafter, our California mails will be made up and
dispatched eastward on the 15th and last days of each month.[1]

Washington's Birth-day passed off rather tamely here, a military parade and a speech or so, making up the transactions of the day.

A heavy Banking House will be opened in St. Louis in a few days, to
be called the Missouri Savings Institution, by Messrs. Chouteau, Harrison, Valle, Pratte, Berthoud, Sam Gaty, Giles F. Filley and Chas. S. Ken-
net—all gentlemen of high standing and wealth. It is supposed that this
Bank will wield a great influence in the commercial affairs of St. Louis.[2]

Messrs. Smith, Kennedy & Co., who were fitting up an extensive
clothing and furnishing store on fourth street, were arrested and committed to jail on the 22d, charged by their Philadelphia creditors with obtaining goods under false pretences. The goods were sold at auction on the
day following for the benefit of the creditors.[3]

A man was found lying on the side walk in Main street yesterday
morning, badly frozen, and apparently in a dying condition. His nose,
feet, ears and hands were entirely frozen. He was taken to the Police
office, and from thence to the City Hospital. His name could not be ascer-
tained.[4]

It was reported yesterday that a riot was in progress among the laborers on the seventh section of the North Division Railroad, the result of a
"strike" for higher wages. A Deputy Sheriff with a posse of policemen
was dispatched to the spot to quell the disturbance; but finding that nothing serious had occurred, ten men were left to keep order, and the balance
returned to the city.[5]

A panorama of Australia, China, and the Japanese Expedition, is
now on exhibition at Wyman's Hall, which far exceeds any thing of the

kind in beauty, interest, excellence, and truthfulness to nature, which it has ever been my good fortune to witness. One portion of this painting in particular, (and it was all good)—a sun-set scene in China—was enchantingly beautiful: even more so than Muscatine sun-sets in summer.[6] This is a home work. It was commenced, carried through, and finished, in St. Louis, by a St. Louis artist, Mr. Boneau, a worthy follower in the footsteps of Pomarede and Banvard. If ever you have the opportunity, do not fail to visit the panorama.[7]

The negro girl Chlo Ann Harris, who was arrested and brought before the Criminal Court as a runaway slave, some three weeks since, and discharged by that Court, on the ground that the proper forms of law were not carried out in making the arrest, was yesterday taken before the Law Commissioner's Court on a writ of habeas corpus, tried, and again discharged. It was proved beyond a doubt that she was a free girl. She had entered the State without a license, and was passing as a slave to avoid the consequences of this breach of the law. She will doubtless be more careful in the future.[8]

Highly important news was received from New Mexico this morning. The Indians are becoming worse and worse, and seem to have things pretty much their own way on the frontier. Fourteen men were butchered, and a number severely wounded at the Pueblo of Arkansas, and the women and children carried off by the savages. The work was perfect, the whole settlement being broken up and the inhabitants murdered. The Utahs and Apaches, the tribe said to be the perpetrators of this massacre, seem determined upon the destruction of the whites, and unless a check is put upon them soon, terrible consequences will ensue. The people of Texas and New Mexico are greatly alarmed and excited, and a general breaking out of hostilities is anticipated.

Capt. Newell of the First Dragoons fought a band of Muscarilla Apaches at the Sacramento mountains, on the 20th ult. Four white men (Capt. H. W. Stanton and three privates,) and twelve Indians were killed in the skirmish.

General Garland has called into service against the Indians five companies of volunteers, for a term of six months, and has asked Congress to defray the expenses.

Maj. Cunningham, Paymaster at Santa Fe, was attacked in his quarters by robbers, who, after taking from him the key, unlocked the safe and took therefrom $40,000, Government money. A Mr. Chavis was also robbed of $2,000.[9]

Our eastern mails are again delayed, on account of snow on the Chicago route.

ST. LOUIS MARKET.

Very little produce in market. A little doing in wheat for future delivery. Not much flour in market—tending upward. It is said $9 were declined for a lot of city extra, to be delivered in thirty days. In bacon and buckwheat small sales are reported; 75 bales good undressed hemp sold at $100; 20 do prime $105 per ton. Galena lead, soft, $5 55, Missouri do, $5 50. Flour—sales at $9; $8 refused for city mills superfine; 25 bbls unbranded $7 50. Wheat $1 50a$1 65; corn—mixed 65; white 70c. Oats 50a60c. Whisky advancing—no sales. Bacon—shoulders 5c; ribbed sides 6c; hams 8c per pound. Hogs 4 1-2a5 3-4c. Freights to New Orleans—flour $7 1-2; pork $1 25; whisky $1 50; corn 60c per sack. Pound freight 45a55.—Stock $11.[10]

S. L. C.

[1] Mail for California would no longer be held in New York for processing. The St. Louis mail of the fifteenth would leave New York on a San Francisco–bound steamer on the twentieth of the month; the end-of-month mail would leave New York on the fifth of the new month ("California Mails," St. Louis *Missouri Republican*, 21 Feb 55, 2). Almost all of the items in this letter derived from St. Louis newspapers, primarily the *Missouri Republican* and the *Evening News* of 23 and 24 February.

[2] The Missouri Savings Institution was presumably founded as a response to the financial panic that had followed the 13 January failure of Page and Bacon, a prestigious St. Louis banking firm. The organizers of the new bank were prominent industrialists, merchants, bankers, and civic leaders, including Pierre Chouteau, Jr., James Harrison, Jules Vallé, Bernard Pratte, Augustus N. Berthoud, Samuel Gaty, Giles F. Filley, and, probably, Luther M. Kennett ("New Banking House in St. Louis," St. Louis *Evening News*, 23 Feb 55, 2; Conard, 1:590–91, 2:430–31, 3:9–10, 193, 528, 5:202; Knox, 13; Scharf, 2:1268–69, 1374–76).

[3] A tangled affair, given confused coverage in the St. Louis newspapers. Three former partners in a Philadelphia firm had attempted to set up shop in St. Louis. The three, including a J. Smith Kennedy, were arrested on 22 February but released after a few hours. A reward was offered for a fugitive fourth man, who had victimized partners and creditors alike (St. Louis *Missouri Republican*: "Arrest of Fourth Street Merchants," 23 Feb 55, 2; "The Fourth Street Case," 25 Feb 55, 2; St. Louis *Missouri Democrat*: "Important Arrests and Important Charges and Discharges," 24 Feb 55, 3).

[4] Clemens summarizes "Man Frozen" (St. Louis *Evening News*, 23 Feb 55, 3) and "Frozen" (St. Louis *Missouri Republican*, 24 Feb 55, 2).

[5] This riot occurred on the North Missouri Railroad and was dismissed by the St. Louis *Evening News* as an inconsequential "Irish shindy" ("The Railroad Riot," 24 Feb 55, 3; "Railroad Riot," 23 Feb 55, 3).

[6] Clemens later praised Muscatine sunsets at greater length in chapter 57 of *Life on the Mississippi* (1883).

[7] The artist Clemens admired was Edward Boneau (b. 1812), a native of Poland, listed in St. Louis directories as a "house and sign painter" and as a partner in a "painter shop" (Montague, 34; Knox, 17). The St. Louis *Missouri Republican* observed that Boneau's work exhibited "a nicety and care of touch which a finished artist would bestow upon a portrait" ("Boneau's Panorama," 24 Feb 55, 2). After the closing of the St. Louis show on 24 March, the panorama was scheduled for a European tour, and in the spring of 1858 was exhibited in Baltimore. Leon Pomarede (1807–92), a French-born panoramist, landscape painter, and religious muralist, was well known in St. Louis for his decoration of the Mercantile Library Hall and several churches. He first showed his "Panorama of the Mississippi River and Indian Life," reported to be as long as 1800 yards, in St. Louis in 1849. John Banvard (1815–91), a writer and painter, began exhibiting his famous "Panorama of the Mississippi," said to cover three miles of canvas, in 1846 (Morrison, 28; Arrington, 261–73; McDermott 1949, 8–18; McDermott 1958, 18–31, 145–60; Samuels and Samuels, 20–21, 376).

[8] The Missouri statutes of 1855 "in regard to free colored persons were very severe":

No colored person could live in this State without a license, and these licenses were to be issued only to certain classes of them; moreover, bond, not exceeding a thousand dollars, had to be given in security for good behavior. The negro was not allowed to retain in his possession the license or other free papers, though he could obtain them in the event of his moving from one county to another, as they had to be filed with the clerk of the county court where he resided. No free negro or mulatto could emigrate into the State or enter the State unless in the service of a white man, or for the purpose of passing through. In either case the time that he could remain in the borders was limited. If he stayed longer he was liable to arrest, a fine of $10, and expulsion. If the fine was not paid he was further liable to not more than twenty lashes, and the court could either order that he immediately leave the State or else hire him out until the fine, costs and expenses of imprisonment had been paid for by his labor. (Conard, 5:604–5)

Chloe Ann Harris's release came on 23 February when her papers arrived from Mount Pleasant, Ohio (St. Louis *Evening News*: "Slave Case," 1 Feb 55, 3; "Interesting Slave Case," 24 Feb 55, 3). Clemens probably had the 1855 laws in mind in 1876, while writing chapter 6 of *Huckleberry Finn*. There Pap Finn inveighs against the "govment" for refusing to sell "a free nigger" from Ohio "till he's been in the State six months" (see *HF*, notes to 33–34).

[9] This and the three preceding paragraphs derive from "Letter from Santa Fe" and "Late and Important from New Mexico" (St. Louis *Missouri Republican*, 24 Feb 55, 2).

[10] Clemens appears to have adapted this report from "Semi-Weekly Review St. Louis Market," dated 24 February (St. Louis *Missouri Republican*, 26 Feb 55, 2), indicating that he wrote at least this part of his letter as late as 26 February.

To the Muscatine *Tri-Weekly Journal*
1 March 1855 • St. Louis, Mo.
(Muscatine *Tri-Weekly Journal*, 12 Mar 55)

St. Louis, March 1, '55.

Yesterday afternoon, about 1 o'clock, an affray occurred in the saloon of the Planters' House, between the noted desperado, Bob O'Blennis, and Benjamin F. Brand, Deputy Marshal, which resulted in the death of the latter in a few hours.[1]

According to the published evidence, the two men commenced quarrelling, while standing at the bar. Harsh language passed on both sides. O'Blennis left the saloon, but soon returned, and said to Brand, "I suppose you have something against me, and now is the time to settle it." Brand said he was ready. Both drew their revolvers at the same time, but Brand did not shoot. O'Blennis fired four shots, one shattering B.'s hand, another entering his wrist, the third taking effect in the arm, near the shoulder, and the fourth and fatal ball entered the side, passed through the lungs, and lodged in the back bone. Brand lived about three hours. His wife, who visited him, was almost frantic. Mr. B. was about thirty years of age, and leaves three interesting children.

O'Blennis was taken before Justice Butler and examined.[2] He rambled about the streets, after the murder, accompanied by an officer part of the time, and part of the time entirely at liberty.

Bob O'Blennis has long been celebrated as the most abandoned and reckless outlaw in St. Louis—and but for his money, would have been roasting in the infernal regions long before this. Mr. Brand is not the first man he ever killed.[3] If all the curses I have heard heaped upon his head to-day were to go into effect, I almost doubt if a place could be invented hot enough for him.

S. L. C.

[1] Most of the details in this letter came from "The Murder Yesterday" (St. Louis *Missouri Republican*, 1 Mar 55, 2). Robert McO'Blenis (sometimes O'Blennis) was one of four partners in the company that operated the St. Louis omnibus lines. A wealthy gambler and livery-stable owner known for his arrogant and violent disposition, he supplied the drivers and horses for the street cars. Despite public outrage over his killing of Brand, McO'Blenis was convicted merely of second-degree murder. On 21 November 1855 he received a sentence of ten years'

imprisonment, but served only until 1857, when Governor Robert M. Stewart pardoned him ("The O'Blennis Trial," St. Louis *Missouri Republican*, 22 Nov 55, 2; Grissom, 94–95; Primm, 198–99; Hyde and Conard, 1:177).

[2] Edward Mann Butler (1784–1855) was a distinguished historian of Kentucky and the Ohio Valley. He held degrees in law and medicine, and for many years was a professor at Transylvania University in Lexington (forerunner of the University of Kentucky) and other Kentucky colleges. For the last years of his life he was a justice of the peace in St. Louis. Butler conducted the preliminary investigation of Brand's murder and denied bail to McO'Blenis (Collins, 1:641–42; Conard, 3:3; Green, 74; Morrison, 39; Montague, 38; Knox, 26; St. Louis *Missouri Democrat*: "A Painful Tragedy," 1 Mar 55, 2; "The McO'Blenis Tragedy," 2 Mar 55, 2).

[3] In December 1854 McO'Blenis had slightly injured a man with a knife in a bar fight. No charge was brought against him at that time (St. Louis *Missouri Republican*: "Affray," 28 Dec 54, 2; "No Prosecution," 29 Dec 54, 2).

To the Muscatine *Tri-Weekly Journal*
5 March 1855 • St. Louis, Mo.
(Muscatine *Tri-Weekly Journal*, 14 Mar 55)

ST. LOUIS, March 5th.

Business on the levee to-day was rather brisk, and several boats went out. Yesterday and to-day were as bright and pleasant as any one could wish, and fires were abolished, I hope for the season. March has "come in like a lamb," but many fear it will "go out like a lion." The river is on a stand at present, but not a particle of ice visible. The James Trabue was lost on the Red River on the 17th ult.[1]

James Reilly, lately book-keeper at the Democrat office, in this city, went with a friend to take a buggy ride in Illinois, day before yesterday, but had not proceeded far on their excursion when they met two Germans in a wagon, with whom they had a dispute, in the course of which Reilly shot one of the Germans, wounding him. The two St. Louisans then hastened back to the ferry landing, for the purpose of escaping to the city, but the officers of the boat having heard of the transaction, detained them until they were arrested by a constable. Reilly was drunk at the time of the occurrence.[2]

The examination of witnesses in the O'Blennis murder case will be concluded to-night. The excitement which this tragedy created has subsided, but the people are still anxious to know how the trial will terminate—though, to tell the truth, few expect *justice* to be done. I doubt if there are a hundred people in St. Louis that do not think O'Blennis ought to be hung, and the number is still less that *expect* him to be punished at all. Since Jackson and Ward escaped hanging, people seem to have very little confidence in courts of justice.[3]

The Hospital returns for the past week number 52; the cemetery report I have not seen, though I think sickness is on the increase. There is some small pox in the city, but the number of cases is unimportant. Persons afflicted with this disease are immediately conveyed to the pest hospital, and it is thus prevented from spreading.

Jamieson, the tragedian, is playing an engagement at the People's Theatre. He appears as Ingomar to-night.[4] Sol. Smith has purchased Bate's Theatre, and will open with a new company shortly.[5] The Varieties is idle.

The March term of the Criminal Court opened this morning, with one hundred and fifty-five cases on docket, but not a single murder in the list, which is something unusual.

Fourteen convicts were sent off by the Banner State for Jefferson City, to-day. Hyde, the poet, who recently attempted to commit suicide in jail, could not go, the state of his wound not yet permitting him to travel.[6]

ST. LOUIS MARKET.

Hemp $95 to $105. Lead $5 50. Flour ranges from $8 to $9 50. Wheat, fair white, from $1 65 to $1 80; red, from $1 70 to $1 85. Oats 50c. Barley $1 45. Mess Pork $12 50. Prime Lard 8c. Hay 85 to 90c per 100 lbs. Potatoes $2 to $2 25 per bushel. Navy Beans range from $1 50 to 2 per bushel. Eggs (retail) 30c per dozen—other articles in proportion.[7]

S. L. C.

[1] Clemens was interested in the *James Trabue* because, for six months before its trip to the Red River (where it sank near Campti, Louisiana, on 17 February), it had been in the St. Louis–New Orleans trade. For this letter he again drew on news items from the St. Louis press, primarily the *Missouri Republican* of 5 March.

[2] On 12 March, Reilly was acquitted of the charge of wounding Hugo Meir, on the grounds that he was acting in self-defense ("The Illinoistown Murder," St. Louis *Missouri Democrat*, 13 Mar 55, 3).

[3] In May 1854 William A. Jackson shot and killed James B. Laidlaw while on a buggy ride. Jackson, a dancer, and Laidlaw, a scenery painter, were both employed at the People's Theatre in St. Louis. After Jackson's capture that August he was indicted for first-degree murder, but on 7 December, after only twenty-

four hours' deliberation, the jury acquitted him, much to the public's dismay ("Jackson Acquitted," St. Louis *Missouri Democrat*, 8 Dec 54, 3; St. Louis *Missouri Republican*: "Murder," 6 May 54, 2; "To Be Tried for Murder," 20 Aug 54, 3; "Jackson's Trial," 10 Dec 54, 2). In November 1853 the wealthy and socially prominent Matthew F. Ward shot and killed William H. G. Butler, a respected high-school teacher and principal in Louisville, Kentucky, in the presence of his students. Butler had reprimanded Ward's younger brother, one of his students, for lying. Brought to trial in April 1854, Ward was found not guilty. Clemens was in Philadelphia at the time of the murder, which received detailed coverage in the local newspapers (for example, "The Louisville Tragedy," Philadelphia *Public Ledger*, 14 Nov 53, 1). Several current reports in St. Louis papers had mentioned Ward as a notorious unpunished murderer ("The Cry of Blood throughout the Land," St. Louis *Intelligencer*, 5 Mar 55, 2; "In the Hands of the Law," St. Louis *Evening News*, 5 Mar 55, 2).

[4] George W. Jamieson (1812–68) had been an important actor and playwright in Edwin Forrest's company before being named chief corespondent in the scandalous Forrest divorce case of 1851, which permanently blighted his career. The *Missouri Republican* called his 5 March performance in the title role of *Ingomar the Barbarian*—Maria A. Lovell's popular translation of *Der Sohn der Wildnis* by Friedrich Halm (Baron Eligius von Münch-Bellinghausen)—"finely conceived and admirably executed" ("People's Theatre," 6 Mar 55, 3; Mantle and Sherwood, 461).

[5] Clemens was apparently repeating a rumor here, source unknown. Solomon F. Smith (1801–69), the famed comedian and theatrical manager, had withdrawn from his extensive management concerns in 1853 and begun to practice law in St. Louis. Although on 1 May 1855 the theater formerly owned by John Bates reopened as the St. Louis Theatre (the name that Smith and his partner, Noah M. Ludlow [1795–1886], had previously used for their playhouse), there is no evidence that either Smith or Ludlow was connected with it ("The St. Louis Theatre," St. Louis *Missouri Republican*, 30 Apr 55, 2; Noah M. Ludlow, 708–9). Both men published exhaustive memoirs of their theater years in which they made no mention of an involvement with a second St. Louis Theatre (see the reference list).

[6] Jefferson City was the site of the Missouri state penitentiary. Thomas L. Hyde, a nineteen-year-old Louisianan, became known as the "felon poet" for the newspaper verse he wrote from his prison cell. Convicted in January 1855 for burglary and larceny, Hyde slashed his left arm at the elbow in late February. Following his pardon and a subsequent conviction and release, Hyde killed himself by swallowing arsenic in March 1858 (St. Louis *Missouri Republican*: "Criminal Court," 18 Jan 55, 3; "Suicide Attempted by a Jail Prisoner," 25 Feb 55, 3; "Suicide of Thomas L. Hyde," 22 Mar 58, 2; St. Louis *Missouri Democrat*: "Crazed," 23 Oct 57, 3).

[7] Clemens's source was "Semi-Weekly Review St. Louis Market" (St. Louis *Missouri Republican*, 5 Mar 55, 2).

No LETTERS are known to survive for the next fourteen and a half months. Probably Clemens remained in St. Louis, working as a typesetter, until mid-June 1855 before moving to Keokuk, Iowa. Keokuk was a bustling frontier town, population about sixty-five hundred, some two hundred miles above St. Louis on the Mississippi River. Orion Clemens had married Mary Eleanor (Mollie) Stotts, a Keokuk native, on 19 December 1854. On 9 June 1855, after Orion sold his share in the Muscatine *Journal* to James W. Logan earlier that week, the couple moved to Keokuk. There, on 11 June, Orion became the new owner of the Ben Franklin Book and Job Office (MEC, 3; Lorch 1929a, 418; "Sold Out," Keokuk *Morning Glory*, 6 June 55, 2; OC and Wilson, 2; OC 1855, 2). Naturally restless and wary of being trapped by what he considered a job without a future, Clemens may well have seen his older brother's new enterprise as an opportunity. By mid-June he seems to have left St. Louis for Keokuk, for his name appeared in a 16 June "List of Letters" unclaimed at the St. Louis post office (*Missouri Republican*, 16 June 55, 3). It evidently was Clemens whom the Keokuk *Dispatch* of 29 June described as follows:

> We know a man in this city who would make a *prime editor*, and we believe that if he has any "genus" at all, it runs in that direction, " 'cos" he says there is not a *single* paper published in town worth reading—and he says that not one of them has any news—and if he published a paper, he says he would *make news*, and lots of it, and spirited news, too.
>
> We propose to have all the papers in the city to club together and secure the services of this chap, and have *spirited news*; it will pay—we bet on it. What do you all say about hiring this editorial genius? He will save the expense of a telegraph. Everybody in the morning will be up at four to get the new *spirited news*, and everybody will take the paper. Our private opinion is that the thing must be "did," for he is the only population in the country. (Untitled notice, Keokuk *Weekly Dispatch*, 5 July 55, 1, reprinting the Keokuk *Dispatch* of 29 June 55)

If this local "genus" was indeed Clemens, then it is clear that he made his mid-July visits to Hannibal and the nearby villages of Paris and Florida on a downriver trip *after* he settled in Keokuk and not while en route from St. Louis, as previously thought (see *N&J1*, 14, 18–38; *MTBus*, 20–28; and Ralph Gregory: 1963, 9; 1971, 3). In the three small towns Clemens arranged for the care and disposition of family property before continuing downriver to St. Louis. There he attended to several errands, among them an effort to become a Mississippi River cub pilot. He had with him a letter from Orion introducing him to wealthy James Clemens, Jr. (1791–1878), a distant cousin, who he hoped would help him realize that ambition. James Clemens later told Orion that only illness prevented him from interceding with a friend "who is Pilot of one of the large boats," despite a conviction that "your brother should stick to his present trade or art" (letter of 6 Aug 55, CU-MARK; see *N&J1*, 36 n. 40).

Following his trip to St. Louis, Clemens returned to Keokuk and Orion's print shop. There is persuasive evidence that briefly toward the end of 1855, and perhaps into 1856, he left Orion's employ to set type on a newspaper published across the Mississippi in Warsaw, Illinois (Branch 1983–84, 201–5). But by 17 January 1856 at the latest, when he spoke at the Keokuk printers' celebration of Franklin's birth, Clemens was back in Orion's shop, working alongside their brother Henry and earning, according to Paine, "five dollars a week and board" (*MTB*, 1:104).

To Ann E. Taylor
21 and 25 May 1856 • Keokuk, Iowa
(*Kansas City Star Magazine*, 21 Mar 1926)

. . . .

of the hurricane deck is still visible above the water. Here is another "Royal George"—I think I shall have to be a second Cowper, and write her requiem.[1]

                                    Sunday, May 25.

Well, Annie, I was not permitted to finish my letter Wednesday evening.[2] I believe Henry, who commenced his a day later, has beaten me. However, if my friends will let me alone I will go through today. Bugs! Yes, B-U-G-S! What of the bugs? Why, perdition take the bugs! That is all. Night before last I stood at the little press until nearly 2 o'clock, and the flaring gas light over my head attracted all the varieties of bugs which are to be found in natural history, and they all had the same praiseworthy recklessness about flying into the fire. They at first came in little social crowds of a dozen or so, but soon increased in numbers, until a religious mass meeting of several millions was assembled on the board before me, presided over by a venerable beetle, who occupied the most prominent lock of my hair as his chair of state, while innumerable lesser dignitaries of the same tribe were clustered around him, keeping order, and at the same time endeavoring to attract the attention of the vast assemblage to their own importance by industriously grating their teeth. It must have been an interesting occasion—perhaps a great bug jubilee commemorating the triumph of the locusts over Pharaoh's crops in Egypt many centuries ago. At least, good seats, commanding an unobstructed view of the scene, were in great demand; and I have no doubt small fortunes were made by certain delegates from Yankee land by disposing of comfortable places on my shoulders at round premiums. In fact, the advantages which my altitude afforded were so well appreciated that I soon began to look like one of those big cards in the museum covered with insects impaled on pins.

The big "president" beetle (who, when he frowned, closely resembled Isbell when the pupils are out of time)[3] rose and ducked his head and, crossing his arms over his shoulders, stroked them down to the tip of his nose several times, and after thus disposing of the perspiration, stuck his hands under his wings, propped his back against a lock of hair, and then, bobbing his head at the congregation, remarked, "B-u-z-z!" To which the congregation devoutly responded, "B-u-z-z!" Satisfied with this promptness on the part of his flock, he took a more imposing perpendicular against another lock of hair and, lifting his hands to command silence, gave another melodious "b-u-z-z!" on a louder key (which I suppose to have been the key-note) and after a moment's silence the whole congregation burst into a grand anthem, three dignified daddy longlegs, perched near the gas burner, beating quadruple time during the performance. Soon two of the parts in the great chorus maintained silence, while a treble and alto duet, sung by forty-seven thousand mosquitoes and twenty-three thousand house flies, came in, and then, after another chorus, a tenor and bass duet by thirty-two thousand locusts and ninety-seven thousand pinch bugs was sung—then another grand chorus, "Let Every Bug Rejoice and Sing" (we used to sing "heart" instead of "bug"),[4] terminated the performance, during which eleven treble singers split their throats from head to heels, and the patriotic "daddies" who beat time hadn't a stump of a leg left.

It would take a ream of paper to give all the ceremonies of this great mass meeting. Suffice it to say that the little press "chawed up" half a bushel of the devotees, and I combed 976 beetles out of my hair the next morning, every one of whose throats was stretched wide open, for their gentle spirits had passed away while yet they sung—and who shall say they will not receive their reward? I buried their motionless forms with musical honors in John's hat.[5]

Now, Annie, don't say anything about how long *my* letter was in going, for I didn't receive *yours* until Wednesday—and don't forget that I *tried* to answer it the same day, though I was doomed to fail. I wonder if you will do as much?

Yes, the loss of that bridge[6] almost finished my earthly career. There is still a slight nausea about my stomach (for certain malicious persons say that my heart lies in that vicinity) whenever I think of it, and I believe I should have evaporated and vanished away like a blue cloud if John—indefatigable, unconquerable John—had not recovered from his illness to relieve me of a portion of my troubles. I think I can survive it now. John says "der chills kill a white boy, but sie (pronounced see) can't kill a *Detch-man*."

I have not now the slightest doubt, Annie, that your beautiful sketch is *perfect*. It looks more and more like what I suppose "Mt. Unpleasant" to be every time I look at it. It is really a pity that you could not get the shrubbery in, for your dog fennel is such a tasteful ornament to any yard. Still, I am entirely satisfied to get the principal beauties of the place, and will not grieve over the loss. I have delighted Henry's little heart by delivering your message. Give the respected councilman the Latin letter by all means.[7] If I understood the lingo well enough I would write you a Dutch one for him. Tell Mane[8] I don't know what Henry thinks of the verb "amo," but for some time past I have discovered various fragments of paper scattered about bearing the single word "amite," and since the receipt of her letter the fragments have greatly multiplied and the word has suddenly warmed into "amour"—all written in the same hand, and that, if I mistake not, Henry's, for the latter is the only French word he has any particular affection for. Ah, Annie, I have a slight horror of writing essays myself; and if I were inclined to write one I should be afraid to do it, knowing you could do it so much better if you would only get industrious once and try. Don't you be frightened—I guess Mane is afraid to write anything bad about you, or else her heart softens before she succeeds in doing it. Don't fail to remember me to her—for I perceive she is aware that my funeral has not yet been preached. Ete paid us a visit yesterday, and we are going to return the kindness this afternoon.[9] Good-by.

Your friend,

Sam.

[1] On Tuesday, 20 May, the steam ferry between Keokuk and Hamilton (Illinois) had struck a snag and sunk up to the guards near the Illinois shore, leaving only its top deck above water. Although it was heavily loaded with fifty men, women, and children, seven two-horse wagons, and fifteen cattle, no lives were lost ("Ferry Boat Sunk": Keokuk *Gate City*, Keokuk *Daily Post*, Keokuk *Des Moines Valley Whig*, all 21 May 56, 3). Most of the first part of Clemens's letter—evidently written on Wednesday, 21 May—is missing, but its concluding sentence, as well as the fifth paragraph of the part written on 25 May, strongly imply that he was one of the fifty passengers. William Cowper's "On the Loss of the Royal George" was written in 1782 to memorialize the eight hundred men who died when the English man-of-war *Royal George* capsized.

[2] Ann Elizabeth (Annie) Taylor (1840–1916), daughter of Hawkins Taylor (see note 7), was attending Iowa Wesleyan University at nearby Mount Pleasant ("Death of Mrs. Cunningham," Carrollton [Mo.] *Democrat*, 28 Jan 1916, 3; Lorch 1929a, 426–28).

[3] Oliver C. Isbell was the proprietor of the Keokuk "music rooms," where he offered voice, piano, and melodeon lessons and conducted the Mendelssohn Choral Society, which gave an annual series of concerts under his direction. His studio was on the second floor of the Ogden building, immediately below Orion's print shop. Clemens reportedly joined one of Isbell's singing classes and also took piano lessons from him (advertisements in the Keokuk *Gate City*, Nov 55–Mar 56; OC 1856, 78, 89; *MTB*, 1:104–5; Varble, 223).

[4] "Let Every Heart Rejoice and Sing" was a hymn written by Henry S. Washburn (1813–1903) in 1842 (Julian, 1235).

[5] John W. Kerr was a printer working for Orion. It seems highly likely that Kerr is the "German apprentice" called only "Fritz" whom Orion mentioned in his (now lost) autobiography (*MTB*, 1:107–8; Lorch 1929a, 425–26).

[6] Possibly a mistranscription of the manuscript reading "barge," meaning the sunken ferryboat presumably described in the now-missing part of the letter. No other information has been found to explain the reference to a lost "bridge."

[7] Hawkins Taylor (b. 1810 or 1811), Annie's father, was an alderman on the Keokuk city council and would become mayor in 1857. Formerly a steamboat captain and now a prominent businessman, he was a literate, articulate man interested in promoting education and known for his "sprightly writings along nearly the whole line of the Annals of Iowa" (Stiles, 118–19; OC 1856, 45; *Keokuk Census* [1850], 416; Lorch 1929a, 427–28). The author of "the Latin letter" remains unknown.

[8] Mary Jane Taylor, Annie's nineteen-year-old sister, also a student at Iowa Wesleyan University (Lorch 1929a, 426).

[9] "Ete" was Annie and Mary Jane's twenty-one-year-old sister, Esther (*Keokuk Census* [1850], 416; family information courtesy of Gladys Hill).

To Jane Lampton Clemens and Pamela A. Moffett
10 June 1856 • Keokuk, Iowa
(MS: NPV)

THE BEN FRANKLIN BOOK AND JOB OFFICE,
O. CLEMENS, PROPRIETOR, 52 MAIN STREET,
THIRD STORY, OVER THE "CITY BOOK STORE."
CARDS, CIRCULARS, BILL HEADS, BILLS LADING,
POSTERS, AND COLORED WORK, PRINTED.

KEOKUK, IOWA, June 10th 1856.

M y Dear Mother & Sister:[1]

I have nothing to write. Everything is going on well. The Directory is coming on finely.[2] I have to work on it occasionally, which I don't like a particle. I don't like to work at too many things at once. They take Henry and Dick[3] away from me too. Before we commenced the Directory, I could tell before breakfast just how much work could be done during the day, and manage accordingly—but now, they throw all my plans into disorder by taking my hands away from their work. I have nothing to do with the book[4]—if I ~~do~~ did I would the two book hands do more work than they do, or else I would drop. It is not a mere *supposition* that they do not work fast enough—I *know* it; for yesterday the two book hands were at work all day, Henry and Dick all the afternoon, on the advertisements, and they set up ~~tw~~ five pages and a half—and I set up two pages and a quarter of the same matter *after supper* night before last, and I don't work fast on such things. They are either excessively slow motioned or very lazy. I am not getting along well with the job work. I can't work blindly—without system. I gave Dick a job yesterday, which I calculated he could set in two hours and I could work off in three, and therefore just finish it by supper time, but he was transferred to the Directory, and the job, promised this morning, remains untouched. Through all the great pressure of job work lately, I never before failed in a promise of the kind.

John is gone—disappeared. I think he has ran away to get away from his brutal old father.[5]

Your son
Sam.

Excuse brevity—this is my 3[d] letter to-night.

Keokuk, Iowa, June 10th 1856.

My Dear Brother & Sister:

I have nothing to write. Every Thing is going on well. The Directory is coming on finely. I have to work on it occasionally which I don't like a particle. I don't like to work at too many things at once. They take Henry and Dick away from me too. Before we commenced the Directory, I could tell before breakfast just how much work could be done during the day, and manage accordingly up — but now, they throw all my plans into disorder by taking my hands away from their work. I have nothing to do with the book — if I did I would the two book hands do more work than they do, or else I would drop. It is not a mere supposition that they do not work fast enough — I know it, for yes—

[1] Jane Clemens was now living in St. Louis with her daughter and son-in-law, but it is not known when she moved there. She had been in Muscatine, Iowa, with Orion and Henry Clemens, at least as late as the spring of 1854. Possibly she did not go to St. Louis until June 1855, when Orion and his wife, Mollie, and Henry moved to Keokuk; conceivably she lived with them for a time in Keokuk before joining the Moffetts.

[2] Orion had begun assembling information for his *Keokuk City Directory* immediately after his arrival in Keokuk in June 1855. The first edition was available, for one dollar, by 12 July 1856 (Lorch 1929a, 431). Orion anticipated criticisms from the local press: "Errors in this Directory," he stated, "apologise for themselves, because the attempt is the first in Keokuk, and it would be a novelty among directories, if there were no mistakes; yet to prevent them neither pains nor labor has been spared. . . . we shall have an opportunity to improve in our next" (OC 1856, preface). Orion published a second edition of the directory in 1857, but profits from it failed to meet expectations because he printed several hundred copies too many (Rees, 401–2).

[3] Apprentice printer Richard Higham, a "good-natured, simple-minded, winning lad of seventeen" (AD, 26 Mar 1906, CU-MARK, in *MTA*, 2:251–52). After learning of Higham's death during the Civil War, Clemens reminisced fondly about him (see 2 Apr 62 to JLC).

[4] Clemens wrote at least one line of the *Keokuk City Directory*: his own listing, which identified him as "*Antiquarian.*" In 1888 an unidentified Keokuk "gentleman" remarked that Clemens "claimed the profession of antiquarian because of his researches among the ancient and venerable bugs of the hotel in which he boarded" (reported in Curtis, 1).

[5] Kerr's father remains unidentified.

To Henry Clemens
5 August 1856 • Keokuk, Iowa
(MS: NPV)

Keokuk, August 5th

My Dear Brother:

    Annie is well.[1] Got your letter, postmarked 5th about two hours ago—come d—d quick, (to be a little profane.)[2] Ward and I ~~have~~ held a long consultation, Sunday morning, and the result was that us two have determined to start to Brazil, if possible, in *six weeks* from now, in order to look carefully into matters there (by the way, I forgot to mention that *Annie* is well,) and report to D[r.] Martin in time for him to follow on the first of March.[3] We propose going *via.* New York. Now, between you and I and the fence you must say nothing about this to Orion, for he thinks that Ward is to go clear through alone, and that I am to stop at New York or New Orleans until he reports. But that don't suit me. My confidence in human nature does not extend quite that far. I won't depend upon Ward's judgment, or anybody's else,—I want to see with my own eyes, and form my own opinion. But you know what Orion is. When he gets a notion into his head, and more especially if it is an erroneous one, the Devil can't get it out again. So I nev knew better than to combat his arguments long, but apparently yielded, inwardly determined to go clear through. Ma knows my determination, but *even she* counsels me to keep it from Orion. She says I can treat him as I did her when I started to St. Louis and went to New York—I can start to New York and go to South America.! (This reminds me that—Annie *is* well.) Although Orion talks grandly about furnishing me with a h fifty or a hundred dollars in six weeks, I am not such an ass as to think he will retain the same opinion such an eternity of time—in all probability he will be *entirely* out of the notion by that time. Though I don't like to attribute selfish motives to him, you could see yourself that his object in favoring my wishesing was that I might take all the hell of pioneering in a foreign land, and then when everything was placed on a firm basis, and beyond all risk, he could follow himself. But you would soon discover, when the time arrived, that he couldn't leave Mollie and that lu "love of a baby."[4] With these facts before my eyes, (I must not forget to say that Annie is *well*,) I could not depend upon Orion for ten dollars, so I have "feelers" out in several directions, and have already asked for a hundred dollars from one source (keep it to yourself.)[5] I will lay on my oars for a while, and see how the wind sets, when I may probably try to get more. Mrs. Creel is a great friend of mine, and has some influence over with Ma and Orion, though I reckon they would not acknowledge it.[6] I am going up there to-morrow, to press her into my service. I shall take care that Ma and Orion are plentifully supplied with South American books. They have Herndon's Report, now.[7] Ward and the D[r.] and myself will hold a grand consultation to-night, at the office. We have agreed that no more shall be admitted into our company.

Emma Graham has got home, and Bettie Barrett has gone up the country.[8] I may as well remark that *Annie is well*. I spent Sunday afternoon up there,[9] and brought away a bo big bouquet of Ete's d—d stinking flowers, (I mean no disrespect for to her, or her taste,)[.] Any sink single one of the lot smells worse than a Sebastopol "stink-pot."[10] Between you and I, ~~be~~ I believe that the secret of Ma's willingness to ~~w~~ allow me to go to South America lies in the fact that she is afraid I am going to get married! Success to the hallucination. Annie has not heard from the girls yet. I believe the Guards went down to Quincy to-day to escort *our first locomotive* home.[11]

The report that Belle and Isbell are about to be married, is still going.[12] Dick was engaged in sticking up Whig office hand bills at last accounts.[13]

Write soon.

Your Brother,

Sam

P. S. I will just add that *Annie* IS WELL.

[1] Annie Taylor, apparently now in Keokuk for the summer, her college term having ended in the first week of July ("Commencement exercises . . . ," Keokuk *Gate City*, 7 July 56, 2). (Samuel C. Webster mistakenly identified "Annie" as Annie Moffett in *MTBus*, 28.)

[2] Henry was presumably in St. Louis, with his mother and sister.

[3] The proposed expedition reflected Clemens's recent reading (see note 7). Joseph S. Martin, a Keokuk physician, board-of-health member, and "Lecturer on Chemistry and Toxicology" at the Iowa Medical College in Keokuk, was evidently to be one of his companions. The 1856–57 Keokuk directory has partial listings for three persons named Ward, but it is impossible to say which was Clemens's prospective partner (OC 1856, 45, 103, and advertisements, 35; Harris, 214). Paine reported that Martin and Ward "gave up the plan, probably for lack of means" (*MTL*, 1:35); Clemens, however, apparently nursed his interest in Brazil until 1857, when he became a cub pilot.

[4] Orion and Mollie's daughter, Jennie, was born on 14 September 1855 (MEC, 6).

[5] The potential source mentioned here has not been identified. By the time Clemens left Keokuk in mid-October 1856, however, he had made an arrangement to write travel letters for the Keokuk *Post*. He was to be paid five dollars per letter, a rate he subsequently negotiated up to seven and a half dollars (Lorch 1929a, 434–38; Rees, 399–400). In fact he wrote only three letters, dated 18 October 1856 from St. Louis, and 14 November 1856 and 14 March 1857 from Cincinnati (SLC 1856a, 1856b, 1857). Written in the guise of a loutish bumpkin, Thomas Jefferson Snodgrass, the letters were among his first efforts to sustain the vernacular voice that he perfected in his mature writings. Not long after the last of them appeared, Clemens gave up the idea of a Brazilian excursion in favor of becoming a pilot.

[6] Mary Ann Creel (b. 1822 or 1823), Mollie Clemens's cousin, was the eldest daughter of Colonel William S. Patterson (1802–89), Iowa pioneer and legislator and Keokuk pork packer, postmaster, and later three-time mayor. She was married to Jane Clemens's cousin Robert P. Creel (b. 1815), a brickmason who owned a successful construction business. In 1856 he was a member of the Iowa legisla-

ture, and in 1862 became mayor of Keokuk (Ivins, 64, 96; *History of Lee County*, 664, 690; Reid, 165; *Keokuk Census* [1860], 152; OC 1856, 63; OC 1857, 21, 167; *Biographical Review*, 489–92; JLC to "Livy Children & Sam," 24 Jan 85, Davis 1981, 2; "Death of T. B. Patterson," Keokuk *Gate City*, 29 July 90, clipping in Scrapbook 20:107, CU-MARK).

[7] *Exploration of the Valley of the Amazon, Made under Direction of the Navy Department* (1853–54), in two volumes, by William Lewis Herndon and Lardner Gibbon. Clemens evidently read only the first volume, by Herndon. In 1910, in "The Turning Point of My Life," he recalled that it "told an astonishing tale about *coca*, a vegetable product of miraculous powers; asserting that it was so nourishing and so strength-giving that the native of the mountains of the Madeira region would tramp up-hill and down all day on a pinch of powdered coca and require no other sustenance." As a result, Clemens "was fired with a longing to ascend the Amazon. Also with a longing to open up a trade in coca with all the world. During months I dreamed that dream, and tried to contrive ways to get to Para and spring that splendid enterprise upon an unsuspecting planet" (*WIM*, 459; see also AD, 29 Mar 1906, CU-MARK, in *MTA*, 2:289). This ambition must also have been fed by newspaper reports of the Amazon Valley. Between 1853 and 1856 dozens of articles published in the cities where Clemens lived extolled the wonders and opportunities of the region and urged that it be opened to commerce.

[8] Emma Graham may be Emaline Graham, aged about sixteen, the daughter of James B. Graham, a carpenter (*Keokuk Census* [1860], 145). Bettie Barrett has not been identified.

[9] Hawkins Taylor owned a tract of land in a fashionable area on the Mississippi, a few miles above Keokuk. Clemens evidently had gone "up there" to visit Annie Taylor. His remark that he intended "going up there" to visit Mrs. Creel suggests that the spot was a summer retreat for prominent Keokuk families, including the Pattersons and the Creels.

[10] The allusion has not been precisely identified. A "stink-pot" was either a weapon designed to release acrid vapors when burned, or a device similarly used to combat cholera by fumigation. Both devices might have been used in the siege of Sevastopol (October 1854–September 1855) in the Crimean War, but no specific reference has been found to either in the voluminous contemporary reports of that battle. "Ete" was Esther Taylor.

[11] Escorted by the Keokuk Guards and welcomed by a booming cannon and exultant speeches by the city fathers, Keokuk's first steam locomotive, the *J. K. Hornish*, arrived at the levee at 9:00 A.M. on 8 August, via barge from Quincy, Illinois. The *Hornish* was intended for the Keokuk, Mount Pleasant, and Muscatine Railroad. It was named for the company's general agent, who had been instrumental in obtaining construction financing for the line. By reducing the cost of transporting freight around the Keokuk rapids from two dollars to fifty cents per ton, the railroad greatly benefited the town's economy ("Steam Engine J. K. Hornish," Keokuk *Post*, 9 Aug 56, 3; "Hurrah for the Iron Horse!" Keokuk *Saturday Post*, 9 Aug 56, 2; "The Locomotive . . . ," Keokuk *Gate City*, 9 Aug 56, 3; *History of Lee County*, 510–11).

[12] Mollie Clemens's nineteen-year-old sister, Susan Isabella (Belle) Stotts (b. 1837), was a soloist with Keokuk's Mendelssohn Choral Society, as was its director, Oliver Isbell ("Concert. The Mendelssohn Choral Society," Keokuk *Gate City*, 13 Mar 56, 2). The rumor of an attachment between the two apparently was

persistent, for in a letter of 28 May 1858, Orion Clemens asked his wife, "What made Mrs. Isbell jealous of Belle? What did Isbell do to make Pa [Mollie's father, William Stotts] so angry?" (CU-MARK). Belle married Thomas B. Bohon on 1 October 1861.
[13] Richard Higham's new employer was James B. Howell, one of Orion's competitors. Howell and Company edited and published two Whig newspapers in Keokuk, the daily *Gate City* and the weekly *Des Moines Valley Whig* (OC 1856, 76; OC 1857, 38, 121; Harris, 324).

NO LETTERS have been recovered for the next ten months. Dissatisfied with his position in Orion Clemens's mismanaged Ben Franklin Book and Job Office and hoping to venture profitably into Brazil, Clemens decided to abandon Keokuk. His own account of his departure, elliptical and influenced by time and imagination, occurs in his autobiography:

> One day in the midwinter of 1856 or 1857—I think it was 1856—I was coming along the main street of Keokuk in the middle of the forenoon. It was bitter weather—so bitter that that street was deserted, almost. A light dry snow was blowing here and there on the ground and on the pavement, swirling this way and that way and making all sorts of beautiful figures, but very chilly to look at. The wind blew a piece of paper past me and it lodged against a wall of a house. Something about the look of it attracted my attention and I gathered it in. It was a fifty-dollar bill, the only one I had ever seen, and the largest assemblage of money I had ever seen in one spot. I advertised it in the papers and suffered more than a thousand dollars' worth of solicitude and fear and distress during the next few days lest the owner should see the advertisement and come and take my fortune away. As many as four days went by without an applicant; then I could endure this kind of misery no longer. I felt sure that another four could not go by in this safe and secure way. I felt that I must take that money out of danger. So I bought a ticket for Cincinnati and went to that city. (AD, 29 Mar 1906, CU-MARK, in *MTA*, 2:288–89)

Actually, Clemens left Keokuk in October 1856, not in "midwinter." He made a brief visit to St. Louis, where he evidently attended the opening day, 13 October, of the St. Louis Agricultural and Mechanical Association Fair and wrote a sketch about it ("The Great Fair at St. Louis," *ET&S1*, 378–81). He also wrote his first Thomas Jefferson Snodgrass letter in St. Louis, on 18 October.

Having spent about a week with his mother and sister, Clemens left St. Louis. It is likely that he departed on 18 October and arrived in Keokuk the following day, intending to determine what George Rees, editor of the Keokuk *Post*, thought of "the first Snodgrass letter and to bargain for higher payment" (Baker, 301). He then went on by river packet to Quincy, Illinois, then by train through Chicago and Indianapolis to Cincinnati, probably arriving on 24 October. There he found employment at T. Wrightson and Company, one of the city's leading printers, where he continued to work into the spring of 1857 (Baker, 301–7). Little else is known of his activities during this period, which he skimmed over in his autobiography (*MTA*, 2:289), in "The Turning Point of My Life" (*WIM*, 459), and in *Life on the Mississippi* (chapter 5). Other than his two final Snodgrass letters, dated 14 November 1856 and 14 March 1857 from Cincinnati, only one piece during this period has even been attributed to him: an untitled sketch, dated 8 November 1856, about a Cincinnati boardinghouse (*ET&S1*, 382–86).

On 15 April 1857 Clemens took passage for New Orleans on the packet *Paul Jones* (Bates 1968, 33). Probably the "great idea" of the Amazon journey was still alive in his mind as he later claimed (*MTA*, 2:289), but within two weeks his old ambition to become a Mississippi pilot was rekindled. During daylight watches he began "doing a lot of steering" for Horace E. Bixby, pilot of the *Paul Jones*, whose sore foot made standing at the wheel painful (*MTA*, 2:289; *MTB*, 1:119). Bixby (1826–1912), later a noted captain as well as pilot, recalled after Clemens's death:

> I first met him at Cincinnati in the spring of 1857 as a passenger on the steamer Paul Jones. He was on his way to Central America for his health. I got acquainted with him on the trip and he thought he would like to be a pilot and asked me on what conditions he could become my assistant. I told him that I did not want any assistant, as they were generally more in the way than anything else, and that the only way I would accept him would be for a money consideration. I told him that I would instruct him till he became a competent pilot for $500. We made terms and he was with me two years, until he got his license. (Bixby 1910, 3)

Although Bixby consistently indicated that he and Clemens came to terms either at their first meeting or quite soon after, Mark Twain three times explicitly designated New Orleans as the place where he approached Bixby about becoming his steersman and where they reached an agreement (*MTB*, 1:117–20; Bixby 1882, 3; Bixby 1910, 3; *MTA*, 2:289; SLC 1875, 217; *WIM*, 461). Clemens's version seems the more probable. Not until the *Paul Jones* reached New Orleans on 26 April did Clemens learn that he "couldn't get to the Amazon": the obstacles were insuperable (*MTA*, 2:289). Moreover, it is reasonable to assume that, before agreeing to instruct him, Bixby would have used the entire trip to New Orleans to test his ability at handling the wheel.

At any rate, the *Paul Jones* left New Orleans on 30 April with Clemens installed as the new cub and arrived in St. Louis on 9 May (Bates 1968, 34; see *N&J1*, 41–43, for Clemens's river notes on this trip). While in St. Louis Clemens took steps to secure the $100 that Bixby required as a down payment on his instructional fee. (It is unclear how much of the total fee Clemens ultimately paid: see 25 Oct 61 to JLC and PAM, n. 5). Some forty years afterward, in notes for his autobiography, he reminded himself that he went to his cousin James Clemens, Jr., "to borrow the $100 to pay Bixby—before I got to the subject he was wailing about having to pay $25,000 taxes in N.Y. City—said it makes a man poor! So I didn't ask him" (SLC [1898?], 5). Clemens borrowed the money instead from his brother-in-law, William A. Moffett, and rejoined Bixby (*MTBus*, 32–33). The *Paul Jones* was laid up for repairs—not sunk, as previously conjectured (Bates 1968, 43)—so they transferred to the *Crescent City*. That boat left St. Louis on 22 May and arrived in New Orleans on 27 May, just a few days before Clemens wrote the next letter, to Ann E. Taylor. (For a record of the boats Clemens is known, or thought, to have served on during his piloting career, see the Steamboat Calendar.)

To Ann E. Taylor
1 June 1857 • New Orleans, La.
(Transcript and MS facsimile: *Kansas City Star Magazine*, 21 Mar 1926)

[*postscript in pencil:*]
‚P. S.—I have just returned from another cemetery—brought away an orange leaf as a memorial—I inclose it.‚

New Orleans, June 1ˢᵗ· 1857.

My Dear Friend Annie

I am not certain what day of the month this is, (the weather being so warm,) but I expect I have made a pretty close guess.

Well, you wouldn't answer the last letter I wrote from Cincinnati? I just ˌthought, I would write again, anyhow, taking for an excuse the fact that you might have written and the letter miscarried. I have been very unfortunate with my correspondence; for, during my stay of nearly four months in Cincinnati,[1] I did not get more than three or four letters beside those coming from members of our own family. You did write once, though, Annie, and that rather "set me up," for I imagined that as you had got started once more, you would continue to write with your ancient punctuality. From some cause or other, however, I was disappointed— though it could hardly have been any fault of mine, for I sat down and answered your letter as soon as I received it, I think, although I was sick at the time. Orion wrote to me at St. Louis, saying that Mane told him she would correspond with me if I would ask her. I lost no time in writing to her—got no reply—and thus ended another brief *correspondence*. I wish you would tell Mane that the Lord won't love her if she does so.

However, I reckon one page of this is sufficient.

I visited the French market yesterday (Sunday) morning. I think it would have done my very boots good to have met half a dozen Keokuk girls there, as I used to meet them at market in the Gate City. But it could not be. However, I did find several acquaintances—two pretty girls, with their two beaux—sipping coffee at one of the stalls. I thought I had seen all kinds of markets before—but that was a great mistake—this being a place such as I had never dreamed of before. Everything was arranged in such beautiful order, and had such an air of cleanliness and neatness that it was a pleasure to wander among the stalls. The pretty pyramids of fresh fruit looked so delicious. Oranges, lemons, pineapples, bananas, figs, plantains, watermelons, blackberries, raspberries, plums, and various other fruits were to be seen on one table, while the next one bore a load of radishes, onions, squashes, peas, beans, sweet potatoes—well, every-thing imaginable in the vegetable line—and still further on were lobsters, oysters, clams—then milk, cheese, cakes, coffee, tea, nuts, apples, hot rolls, butter, etc.—then the various kinds of meats and poultry. Of course, the place was crowded (as most places in New Orleans are) with men, women and children of every age, color and nation. Out on the pavement were groups of Italians, French, Dutch, Irish, Spaniards, In-dians, Chinese, Americans, English, and the Lord knows how many more different kinds of people, selling all kinds of articles—even clothing of every description, from a handkerchief down to a pair of boots, umbrellas, pins, combs, matches—in fact, anything you could possibly want—and keeping up a terrible din with their various cries.

Today I visited one of the cemeteries—a veritable little city, for they *bury* everybody *above* ground here. All round the sides of the inclosure, which is in the heart of the city, there extends a large vault, about twelve feet high, containing three or four tiers of holes or tombs (they put the coffins into these holes endways, and then close up the opening with brick), one above another, and looking like a long 3- or 4-story house. The graveyard is laid off in regular, straight streets, strewed with white shells, and the fine, tall marble tombs (numbers of them containing but one corpse) fronting them and looking like so many miniature dwelling houses. You can find wreaths of flowers and crosses, cups of water, mottoes, small statuettes, etc., hanging in front of nearly every tomb. I noticed one beautiful white marble tomb, with a white lace curtain in front of it, under which, on a little shelf, were vases of fresh flowers, several little statuettes, and cups of water, while on the ground under the shelf were little orange and magnolia trees. It looked so pretty. The inscription was in French—said the occupant was a girl of 17, and finished by a wish from the mother that the stranger would drop a tear there, and thus aid her whose sorrow was more than one could bear. They say that the flowers upon many of these tombs are replaced every day by fresh ones. These were fresh, and the poor girl had been dead *five years*. There's depth of affection! On another was the inscription, "To My Dear Mother," with fresh flowers. The lady was 62 years old when she died, and she had been dead *seven years*. I spent half an hour watching the chameleons—strange animals, to change their clothes so often! I found a dingy looking one, drove him on a black rag, and he turned black as ink—drove him under a fresh leaf, and he turned the brightest green color you ever saw.

I wish you would write to me at St. Louis (I'll be there next week) for I don't believe you have forgotten how, yet. ˎTell Mane and Ete[2] "howdy" for me.ˎ

Your old friend
Sam. L. Clemens.

[1] This stay was nearly six months, from around 24 October 1856 to 15 April 1857.
[2] Mary Jane and Esther Taylor.

NONE of the letters Clemens must have written during the next nine months is known to survive. He re-created his experiences of this period in "Old Times on the Mississippi" (SLC 1875) and again in 1883 in *Life on the Mississippi* (especially chapters 5–13). In brief, he continued as Horace Bixby's cub pilot aboard the *Crescent City* until 7 July 1857, when the boat laid up in St. Louis. Probably at that time Bixby transferred to a Missouri River packet and assigned Clemens, who (according to Bixby) did not wish to learn the Missouri River, to the pilot of another St. Louis–New Orleans steamer (*Life on the Mississippi*, chapter 13; *MTB*, 1:128). The pilot is unknown, but the boat evidently was the *R. J. Lackland*, a mammoth freighter rated at 710 tons and launched in March 1857 under the command of William B. Miller (Way 1983, 384). Apparently Clemens made one round trip on the *Lackland* between 11 July and 3 August; he recorded river data for part of that trip in his notebook (*N&J1*, 46; Branch 1982b, 500, 503–4). His next assignment, probably also arranged by Bixby, was to the *John J. Roe*. The *Roe* was captained by Mark Leavenworth and piloted by his brother Zebulon (1830–77) and by Sobieski (Beck) Jolly (1831–1905), both of whom became close friends of Clemens's. A large freighter, rated at 691 tons, the *Roe* frequently took "guests" of the captain, but was not licensed to carry passengers (Way 1983, 252). Clemens remembered that it was "a delightful old tug, and she had a very spacious boiler-deck—just the place for moonlight dancing and daylight frolics, and such things were always happening." He recalled Mark and Zeb Leavenworth as "hospitable and good-natured," and said that the "clerks, the mates, the chief steward, and all officials, big and little, of the *John J. Roe*, were simple-hearted folk and overflowing with good-fellowship and the milk of human kindness. . . . It was the same delight to me to meet and shake hands with the Leavenworths and the rest of that dear family of steamboating backwoodsmen and hay-seeds as if they had all been blood kin to me" (AD, 30 July 1906, CU-MARK, in *AMT*, 79–80).

Clemens's convivial tenure aboard the *Roe* was short, lasting for only two St. Louis–New Orleans round trips, between 5 August and 24 September, at which time the boat laid up. Bixby may have returned about then for "a trip or two" with his cub, but if so, the boat they piloted has not been identified (*MTB*, 1:129). There is some possibility that it was the *William M. Morrison*, captained by John N. Bofinger, and that Clemens and Bixby were aboard it between 9 and 26 October. At any rate, probably by 2 November, and certainly by 18 November, Bixby had assigned Clemens to William Brown, pilot of the *Pennsylvania*, the "ignorant, stingy, malicious, snarling, fault-finding, mote-magnifying tyrant" so vividly portrayed in chapters 13, 18, and 19 of *Life on the Mississippi*. A passenger and mail carrier built in 1854, the *Pennsylvania* was noted for its "beautiful proportions" and "magnificent style" ("River News," Pittsburgh *Gazette*, 15 Feb 54, 3). Its master, John S. Klinefelter (1810–85), captained many steamboats on the Ohio and Mississippi rivers between 1835 and his retirement in 1863.

On 26 November the *Pennsylvania* was severely damaged in a collision with the *Vicksburg* thirty miles above New Orleans. It was then laid up for nearly eleven weeks near New Orleans, for repairs and a general overhauling and refitting. How Clemens supported himself during this period is not known. He later recalled that during his apprenticeship he "always had a job" in New Orleans between the arrival and departure of his boats: "It was my privilege to watch the freight piles from seven in the evening until seven in the morning, and get three dollars for it" (AD, 13 Jan 1906, CU-MARK, in *MTA*, 1:309). Nevertheless, such employment could not have been congenial or remunerative enough to keep him in New Orleans for the entire period the *Pennsylvania* was out of commission. It is probable that Clemens returned to his family in St. Louis, and that he did so by accepting a berth as steersman aboard the *D. A. January*, captained by Patrick Yore and piloted by Joseph Edward Montgomery. (Clemens possibly had this trip in mind when, in chapter 49 of *Life on the Mississippi*, he recalled steering for Montgomery, who was usually a boat captain and only infrequently a pilot; see 27? June 60 to OC, n. 3.) The *January* left New Orleans on 13 December and arrived in St. Louis nine days later. Clemens presumably would have remained with his family for the Christmas and New Year's holidays before returning to New Orleans to resume his post on a repaired *Pennsylvania*. He may have made the downriver trip on the recently built *New Falls City*, commanded by Montgomery, possibly doing some steering in exchange for his passage. The *News Falls City* left St. Louis on 14 January 1858 and arrived in New Orleans on the twentieth of the month. Clemens was aboard the *Pennsylvania* when it

went back into service on 6 February 1858, departing New Orleans on
that date and reaching St. Louis eight days later. The harrowing return
trip is described at the beginning of the following letter.

To Orion and Mary E. (Mollie) Clemens
9 March 1858 • St. Louis, Mo.
(MS: NPV)

Saint Louis, March 9[th,] 1858.

Dear Brother and Sister:

I must take advantage of the opportunity now presented to write
you, but I shall necessarily be dull, as I feel uncommonly stupid. We have
had a hard trip this time.[1] Left Saint Louis three weeks ago on the Pennsylvania. The weather was very cold, and the ice running densely. We got
15 miles below town, landed the boat, and then one pilot, Second Mate
and four deck hands took the sounding boat and shoved out in the ice to
hunt the channel.[2] They failed to find it, and the ice drifted them ashore.
The pilot left the men with the boat and walked back to us, a mile and a
half. Then the other pilot and myself, with a larger crew of men started
out and met with the same fate. We drifted ashore just below the other
boat. Then the fun commenced. We made fast a line ~~50~~ 20 fathoms long,
to the bow of the yawl, and put the men, ˄(both crews)˄ to it like horses,
on the shore. Brown, the pilot, stood in the bow, with an oar, to keep her
head out, ~~with~~ and I took the tiller. We would start the men, and all would
go well till the yawl would bring up on a heavy cake of ice, and then the
men would drop like so many ten-pins, while ƀ Brown assumed the horizontal in the bottom of the boat. After an hour's hard work we got back,
with ice half an inch thick on the oars. Sent back and warped up the other
yawl, and then George (the first mentioned pilot,) and myself, took a
double crew of fresh men and tried it again. This time we found the
channel in less than an hour, and landed on ȧ island till the Pennsylvania
came along and took us off. The next day was colder still.[3] I was out in the
yawl twice, and then we got through, but the infernal steamboat came
near running over us. We went ten miles further, landed, and George and

I cleared out again—found the channel first trial, but got caught in the gorge and drifted helplessly down the river. The Ocean Spray came along and started into the ice after us, but although she didn't succeed in her kind intention of taking us aboard, her waves washed us out, and that was all we wanted. We landed on an island, built a big fire and waited for the boat. She started, and ran aground![4] It commenced raining and sleeting, and a very interesting time we had on that barren sandbar for the next four hours, when the boat got off and took us aboard. The next day was *terribly* cold. We sounded Hat Island,[5] warped up around a bar and sounded again—but in order to understand our situation you will have to read D[r.] Kane.[6] It would have been impossible to get back to the boat. But the Maria Denning was aground at the head of the island—they hailed us,—we ran alongside and they hoisted us in and thawed us out.[7] We had then been out in the yawl from 4 o'clock in the morning till half past 9 without being near a fire. There was a thick coating of ice over men, yawl, ropes, and everything else, and we looked like rock-candy statuary. ¶We got to Saint Louis this morning, after an absence of ~~2~~ 3 weeks—that boat generally makes the trip in 2.[8]

Henry was doing little or nothing here, and I sent him to our clerk to work his way for a trip, by measuring woodpiles, counting coal boxes, and other clerkly duties, which he performed satisfactorily. He may go down with us again, for I expect he likes our bill of fare better than that of his boarding house.[9]

I got your letter at Memphis as I went down. That is the best place to write me at. The post office here is always out of my route, somehow or other. Remember the direction: "S.L.C., Steamer Pennsylvania, Care Duval & Algeo, Wharfboat, Memphis."[10] I cannot correspond with a paper, because when one is learning the river, he is not allowed to do or think about anything else.

I am glad to see you in such high spirits about the land, and I hope will remain so, if you never get richer. I seldom venture to think about our landed wealth, for "hope deferred maketh the heart sick."[11]

I *did* intend to *answer* your letter, but I am too lazy and too sleepy, now. We had had a rough time during the last 24 hours working through the ice between Cairo and Saint Louis, and I have had but little rest.

I got here too late to see the funeral of the 10 victims by the burning of the Pacific hotel in 7th street. Ma says there were 10 hearses, with the fire companies (their engines in mourning—firemen in uniform,)—the various benevolent societies in uniform and mourning, and a multitude of citizens and strangers, forming, altogether, a procession of 30,000 persons! One steam fire-engine was drawn by four white horses, with crape festoons on their heads.[12]

Well, I am—just—about—asleep—

Your brother
Sam[13]

[1] The trip described here began about 10:00 A.M. on 17 February in a falling, ice-choked river made particularly treacherous by a rapidly changing channel. The captains of most New Orleans boats at the St. Louis levee elected to await better conditions before sailing. Captain Klinefelter's decision to get under way was based on his belief that the *Pennsylvania* had "power enough to plow through the ice even if the river should be full of it" ("Pennsylvania for New Orleans," St. Louis *Missouri Republican*, 16 Feb 58, 3).

[2] The pilot was George G. Ealer, a respected St. Louis–New Orleans riverman who served on the *Crescent City*, the *Pennsylvania*, and other major packets. Clemens wrote warmly of Ealer—a devotee of Shakespeare, Goldsmith, chess, and the flute—whose kindly disposition was in contrast to William Brown's maliciousness (see *Life on the Mississippi*, chapters 18, 19, 24, and "Is Shakespeare Dead?" SLC 1909b, 4–19). Unfortunately for Clemens it was Brown who was his direct superior on the *Pennsylvania*. The *Pennsylvania*'s second mate was James M. Thompson of Georgetown, Pennsylvania.

[3] By daybreak on 18 February, after twenty-one hours on the river, the *Pennsylvania* had managed to reach only Rush Tower, just forty miles below St. Louis ("Steamer Rodolph's Memoranda," St. Louis *Missouri Republican*, 19 Feb 58, 3).

[4] Captain Waldo P. Marsh's *Ocean Spray*, coming upriver from New Orleans with one wheel damaged by the ice, reported reaching "the foot of Ste. Genevieve Island [sixty miles below St. Louis], where we found Pennsylvania sounding. While we were trying to get over she grounded. We crossed below her on 5½ feet water, at 9 A. M." ("Memoranda," St. Louis *Missouri Republican*, 21 Feb 58, 3).

[5] A dangerous crossing near Wittenburg, Missouri, about a hundred miles below St. Louis and eighty above Cairo, Illinois. In chapter 7 of *Life on the Mississippi* it is the site of some spectacular piloting by Horace Bixby.

[6] Elisha Kent Kane (1820–57), a U.S. Navy surgeon, participated in two unsuccessful Arctic expeditions in the 1850s in search of Sir John Franklin, the explorer who died in 1847 while trying to find a northwest passage to the Orient. Kane published two popular accounts of the expeditions: *The U.S. Grinnell Expedition in Search of Sir John Franklin: A Personal Narrative* (1853), and *Arctic Explorations: The Second Grinnell Expedition in Search of Sir John Franklin, 1853, '54, '55* (1856).

[7] Soon after Clemens and the sounding crew were thawed out on board Captain Hercules Carrel's *Maria Denning*, the *Pennsylvania* got under way and arrived at Cairo on Friday afternoon, 19 February (Way 1983, 307; "Pennsylvania Arrived at Cairo—Special Dispatch," St. Louis *Missouri Republican*, 21 Feb 58, 3). The

Denning, bound for St. Louis, remained aground at Hat Island for at least five days.

[8] The *Pennsylvania* docked at St. Louis in the early morning of 9 March, having taken twenty days, six or seven more than usual, to complete the trip to New Orleans and back.

[9] Henry Clemens returned for five more trips as a "mud-clerk" on the *Pennsylvania*. The mud clerk was "so called because it was his duty to go on shore, often at a mere mud-bank, to receive or check off freight" (*Lex*, 150). "Mud clerks received no salary," Clemens recalled in 1906, "but they were in the line of promotion. They could become, presently, third clerk and second clerk, then chief clerk—that is to say, purser" (AD, 13 Jan 1906, CU-MARK, in *MTA*, 1:307). The regular clerks at the time of this letter were Lewis J. Black and William Drum.

[10] Duval, Algeo and Company of Memphis, Tennessee, were steamboat agents and receiving, forwarding, and commission merchants for the Ohio and Mississippi Railroad, specializing in cotton shipments to eastern terminals. They had purchased the unprofitable steamer *St. Louis* and in 1856 converted it to a wharfboat anchored at the lower Memphis levee, where it remained until it sank on 9 December 1860 (advertisement, Memphis *Appeal*, 13 Oct 58, 2; "River Intelligence," St. Louis *Missouri Democrat*, 14 Dec 60, 3; Way 1983, 412).

[11] Clemens's quotation is from Proverbs 13:12. He alludes to the tract of some seventy-five thousand acres near Jamestown, Fentress County, Tennessee, that John Marshall Clemens had purchased for $400 in about 1830, thereby saddling his family with the "heavy curse of prospective wealth" ("The Tennessee Land," CU-MARK, in *MTA*, 1:3–7). Although after the father's death in 1847 responsibility for realizing income from the land fell chiefly to Orion, every member of the Clemens family, at one time or another, cherished schemes for exploiting it. Orion, having sold his Keokuk print shop in June 1857, had been in Jamestown with his wife since October of that year. There he studied law, was admitted to the bar, and also surveyed the family land, no doubt in hopes of a sale. Mollie Clemens returned to Keokuk in late April 1858, and Orion followed her that July, without having disposed of any of the property (MEC, 6–9).

[12] On 20 February 1858, three days after the *Pennsylvania* left St. Louis, fire destroyed the new Pacific Hotel, killing twenty-one guests (Scharf, 2:1446; St. Louis *Missouri Republican*: "The Late Catastrophe," 24 Feb 58, 2; "Two More Victims," 25 Feb 58, 2). St. Louis civic leaders organized an impressive funeral procession to Bellefontaine Cemetery for ten of the victims on 24 February. The *Missouri Republican* of the following day expressed confidence that the citizens in the procession and the twenty-five thousand spectators were inspired by sorrow and respect, rather than a "love of funeral pomp" or "mere curiosity" ("Burial of the Pacific Hotel Victims," 25 Feb 58, 2). Annie Moffett Webster later recalled attending the procession with her grandmother, Jane Clemens, who *did* love such occasions (see *MTBus*, 41).

[13] Clemens artfully inscribed his closing and signature to suggest a gradual loss of control over his pencil.

To William A. Moffett
per Telegraph Operator
15 June 1858 • Memphis, Tenn.
(MS: CU-MARK)

ILLINOIS & MISSISSIPPI TELEGRAPH COMPANY
CATON LINES.

St Louis June 16 185 8

BY TELEGRAPH

FROM Memphis 15   185

TO W A Moffett 168 Locust st
Henrys recovery is very doubtful[1]
Saml Clements

[*canceled in pencil:*]
5 ₩ a .50 & 110 Col[2]

---

[1] Henry Clemens was severely injured in the explosion of three or four of the
Pennsylvania's boilers at about 6:00 A.M. on 13 June 1858. He was brought to
Memphis, about sixty miles upriver, with many of the other victims.
[2] That is, five words at $.50 each, plus $1.10, collect. The line was canceled,
presumably as a form of receipt, upon delivery and payment.

To Mary E. (Mollie) Clemens
18 June 1858 • Memphis, Tenn.
(MS: CU-MARK)

Memphis, Tenn., Friday, June 18th, 1858.
Dear Sister Mollie:
Long before this reaches you, my poor Henry,—my darling, my
pride, my glory, my *all*, will have finished his blameless career, and the
light of my life will have gone out in utter darkness. O, God! this is hard
to bear. Hardened, hopeless,—aye, lost—lost—lost and ruined sinner as
I am—I, even *I*, have humbled myself to the ground and prayed as never

man prayed before, that the great God might let this cup pass from me,—
that he would strike me to the earth, but spare my brother—that he would
pour out the fulness of his just wrath upon my wicked head, but have
mercy, mercy, mercy upon that unoffending boy. The horrors of three
days have swept over me—they have blasted my youth and left me an old
man before my time. Mollie, there are grey hairs in my head to-night. For
forty-eight hours I labored at the bedside of my poor burned and bruised,
but uncomplaining brother, and then the star of my hope went out and
left me in the gloom of despair. Then poor wretched me, that was once so
proud, was humbled to the very dust,—lower than the dust—for the
vilest beggar in the streets of Saint Louis could never conceive of a humiliation like mine. Men take me by the hand and *congratulate* me, and call
me "**lucky**" beg because I was not on the Pennsylvania when she blew up!
My God forgive them, for they know not what they say.[1]

Mollie you do not understand why I was not on that boat—I will tell
you. I left Saint Louis on her, but on they was way down, Mr. Brown, the
pilot that was killed by the explosion (poor fellow,) quarreled with Henry
without cause, while I was steering—Henry started out of the pilot-
house—Brown jumped up and collared him—turned him half way
around and *struck him in the face!*—Bro and him nearly six feet high—
struck my little brother. I was wild from that moment. I left the boat to
steer herself, and avenged the insult—and the Captain said I was right—
that he would discharge Brown in N. Orleans if he could get another pilot,
and would do it in St. Louis anyhow.[2] Of course both of us could not
return to St. Louis on the same boat—no pilot could be found, and the
Captain sent me to the A. T. Lacey, with orders to her Captain to bring
me to Saint Louis.[3] Had another pilot been found, poor Brown would
have been the "lucky" man.[4]

I was on the Pennsylvania five minutes before she left N. Orleans,
and I must tell you the truth, Mollie—**three hundred** human beings perished by that fearful disaster.[5] Henry was asleep—was blown up—then
fell back on the hot boilers, and I suppose that rubbish fell on him, for he
is injured internally. He got into the water and swam to shore, and got
into the flatboat with the other survivors.[6] He had nothing on but his wet
shirt, and he lay there burning up with a southern sun and freezing in the
wind till the Kate Frisbee came along. His wounds were not dressed till
M he got to Memphis, 15 hours after the explosion. He was senseless and
motionless for 12 hours after that.[7] But may God bless Memphis, the
noblest city on the face of the earth. She has done her duty by these poor

afflicted creatures—especially Henry, for he has had five—aye, ten, fifteen, *twenty* times the care and attention that any one else has had.[8] Dr. Peyton, the best physician in Memphis (he is exactly like the portraits of Webster,) st sat by him for 36 hours. There are 32 scalded men in that room, and you would know Dr. Peyton better than I can describe him, if you could follow him around and hear each ɸ man murmur as he passes— "May the God of Heaven bless you, Doctor!"[9] The ladies have done well, too. Our second Mate, a handsome, noble-hearted young fellow, will die. Yesterday a beautiful girl of 15 stooped timidly down by his side and handed him a pretty bouquet. The poor suffering boy's eyes kindled, his lips quivered out a gentle "God bless you, Miss," and he burst into tears. He made them write he[r] name on a card for him, that he might not forget it.[10]

Pray for me, Mollie, and pray for my poor sinless brother.

Your unfortunate Brother,
Sam[l]. L. Clemens.

P. S. I got here two days after Henry.

[1] One Memphis journalist later remembered that Clemens was "almost crazed with grief" at the sight of Henry, whose "fair young face . . . was almost the only one unmarred by steam and flame" (" 'Mark Twain.' A Sad Incident of His Early Life Recalled," Memphis *Avalanche*, 5 Nov 76, 4, clipping in Scrapbook 8:13, CU-MARK, facsimile in Branch 1985a, 37–39). Another observer provided the following account of Clemens's arrival at the Memphis Exchange, temporarily converted into a hospital for the *Pennsylvania* victims:

> We witnessed one of the most affecting scenes at the Exchange yesterday that has ever been seen. The brother of Mr. Henry Clemens, second clerk of the Pennsylvania, who now lies dangerously ill from the injuries received by the explosion of that boat, arrived in the city yesterday afternoon, on the steamer A. T. Lacy. He hurried to the Exchange to see his brother, and on approaching the bedside of the wounded man, his feelings so much overcame him, at the scalded and emaciated form before him, that he sunk to the floor overpowered. There was scarcely a dry eye in the house; the poor sufferers shed tears at the sight. This brother had been pilot on the Pennsylvania, but fortunately for him, had remained in New Orleans when the boat started up. ("A Sad Meeting," St. Louis *News and Intelligencer*, 19 June 58, reprinting the Memphis *Eagle and Enquirer*, 16 June 58, clipping in Scrapbook 1:7, CU-MARK)

[2] In 1882 Clemens placed his fight with William Brown in Eagle Bend at Island 103 (Pawpaw Island), approximately eighteen miles above Vicksburg (see *N&J2*, 454, 555). Known details of the *Pennsylvania*'s movements on this trip indicate that the incident occurred Thursday morning, 3 June 1858. Clemens described the fight and its aftermath in chapters 19 and 20 of *Life on the Mississippi*.

[3] Like the *Pennsylvania*, the *Alfred T. Lacey* (sometimes *Lacy*), captained by John P. Rodney, belonged to the St. Louis, Cairo, and New Orleans Railroad Line of steamboats. Rodney's pilot was Clemens's Hannibal friend Barton S. Bowen (see 7 May 66 to William Bowen, n. 4). The *Lacey* departed New Orleans

for St. Louis on 11 June 1858, two days after the *Pennsylvania*. Word of the explosion reached it at stops before Memphis, where it docked on 15 June. In 1897 Clemens recalled that Bowen gave him twenty dollars, presumably to help defray his expenses in Memphis, but the money was stolen ("Villagers of 1840–3," *Inds*, 97).

[4]Brown, who had probably gone off duty at 4:00 A.M., about two hours before the explosion, was blown into the river. Reed Young, a coalboat pilot taking passage on the *Pennsylvania*, was also blown into the river. He seized a floating life preserver and grasped the injured Brown, who soon slipped away. Brown's last words, as reported by Young, were "my poor wife and children" ("The Explosion of the Pennsylvania!" Louisville *Courier*, 17 June 58, 3).

[5]Contemporary newspaper reports, some based on the opinions of surviving crew members, estimated that of the more than three hundred aboard the *Pennsylvania*, passengers and crew, between one and three hundred lost their lives. Captain Klinefelter at first asserted that only twenty-five to thirty had died, a figure that he and pilot George Ealer later revised to thirty-eight. St. Louis steamboat inspectors, having investigated the explosion, first put the number at between one hundred fifty and one hundred sixty, then scaled it down to sixty. William M. Lytle's "Losses of United States Merchant Steam Vessels, 1807–1867" reported only twenty fatalities (Lytle, 247). Weighing all available evidence, eighty to one hundred deaths seems a reasonable estimate, but the loss of the ship's register and papers and the inconclusiveness of missing persons data, especially for an unknown number of immigrants traveling deck passage, leave any estimate in doubt ("Burning of the Steamer Pennsylvania," St. Louis *Missouri Democrat*, 16 June 58, 2; "The Pennsylvania Disaster," St. Louis *Missouri Republican*, 18 June 58, 2; "Further Particulars of the Pennsylvania Disaster," New Orleans *True Delta*, 16 June 58, 2; "Terrible Steamboat Disaster," Memphis *Morning Bulletin*, 15 June 58, 2; "The Steamer Pennsylvania," St. Louis *Missouri Republican*, 18 July 58, 2, clipping in Scrapbook 1:7, CU-MARK; "Report Relative to the Explosion of the Boilers of Steamer Pennsylvania," St. Louis *Missouri Republican*, 8 Aug 58, 3; U.S. Congress, Senate, 6 [pt. 2]: 271–72; Way 1983, 367).

[6]The explosion had occurred less than a mile below the foot of Bordeaux's (sometimes Burdeau's or Burdoo's) Chute and about sixty miles below Memphis, and approximately four miles above the head of Ship Island and twenty miles above Helena, Arkansas. According to eyewitness George C. Harrison, the boat was "not more than one or two hundred yards" off the Mississippi shore and "some three or four hundred yards" above the Harrisons' woodyard landing. Harrison, his father, and two friends manned a large flatboat and propelled it to meet the wrecked steamer, which was drifting downriver:

> The passengers were very slow in embarking at first, many being more anxious to save their property than to assist others to get on board. Fortunately the fire did not break out for some thirty or forty minutes (perhaps longer) after the explosion. So soon as the fire did break out, they then began to tumble in pell-mell, by which some were hurt. Some already on board were slightly hurt by trunks being thrown upon them. When the fire broke out, it spread with the greatest rapidity. We remained along side of the burning mass until it was with the greatest difficulty that we extricated the wood-boat from her perilous situation. Had we remained one minute longer it would have been impossible to have escaped. The heat was most intense as we passed around the stern of the burning and floating mass, and made a landing on a towhead just below. . . . On board the wood-boat, as near as we could ascertain, were from 180 to 200. (Harrison, 2)

The burned-out hulk of the *Pennsylvania* sank several miles below the point of explosion, near the Mississippi shore and above Austin, Mississippi, and Ship Island—a location that remained memorable to Clemens (see *N&J2*, 536). His fullest account of the disaster is in chapters 18–20 of *Life on the Mississippi*, although his narrative of the destruction of the *Amaranth* in chapter 4 of *The Gilded Age* also draws heavily on the *Pennsylvania* disaster. For a detailed reconstruction of the event, see Branch 1985a, 11–25.

[7] According to reports in Memphis newspapers, Henry arrived at Memphis on the *Kate Frisbee* (Captain Richard M. Mason) at 3:00 A.M. on 14 June, about twenty-one hours after the explosion. He and thirty-one other victims were then placed in the Memphis Exchange, where mattresses had been hastily assembled and arranged into five "wards," attended by the city's physicians, nurses, and many volunteers. Clemens provided further details of Henry's injuries and sufferings in a tribute he published, probably in late June or early July:

Henry's stateroom was directly over the boilers, and he was asleep when the explosion occurred. He was never able to give an account of the matter himself, but from what others have said, and also from the nature of his injuries, it is supposed that he was thrown up, then fell back on the heated boilers, and some heavy substance falling upon him, injured him internally. His terrible burns did not seem as if they had been caused by steam or boiling water. After extricating himself, he escaped on a mattrass to a raft or open wood boat, where he lay exposed (with a hundred others,) to the wind and the scorching rays of a Southern sun, for eight hours, when he was taken on board the Kate Frisbee and conveyed to Memphis. He arrived there in a senseless, and almost lifeless condition. He lingered in fearful agony seven days and a half, during which time he had full possession of his senses, only at long intervals, and then but for a few moments at a time. His brain was injured by the concussion, and from that moment his great intellect was a ruin. We were not sorry his wounds proved fatal, for if he had lived he would have been but the wreck of his former self. (SLC [1858], 1:15)

Clemens later presented a different scenario in chapter 20 of *Life on the Mississippi*. There he claimed that after Henry was flung in the river by the force of the explosion he returned to the burning boat to help others before finally succumbing to his injuries.

[8] Clemens's gratitude toward Memphis was not diminished by time. This is evident from his 25 October 1876 letter in reply to a Memphis woman (possibly the "Miss Wood" to whom Orion Clemens wrote in 1858; see *MTB*, 3:1591–92) who had watched over Henry. After apologizing for failing to remember her in particular, Clemens wrote:

What I do remember, without the least trouble in the world, is, that when those sixty scalded and mutilated people were thrown upon her hands, Memphis came forward with a perfectly lavish outpouring of money and sympathy, and that this did not fail and die out, but lasted through to the end. . . . Do you remember how the physicians worked?—and the students—the ladies—and everybody? I do. If the rest of my wretched memory was taken away, I should still remember that. ("'Mark Twain.' A Sad Incident of His Early Life Recalled," Memphis *Avalanche*, 5 Nov 76, 4, clipping in Scrapbook 8:13, CU-MARK)

Clemens's belief that Henry received special attention is borne out by the *Avalanche*, which observed: "Every one had been attracted by this young boy Henry, whose youth and slight physique were called upon to endure so much, and whose refined, graceful manner made it a gladness to do for him what could be done in the absence of a mother and sister for whom his heart grew sick."

[9] "What a magnificent man he was!" Clemens remarked of Thomas F. Peyton in his 25 October 1876 letter; "what healing it was just to look at him and hear his

voice!" Almost thirty years later he recalled Peyton as "a fine and large-hearted old physician of great reputation in the community" (AD, 13 Jan 1906, CU-MARK, in *MTA*, 1:311). Peyton, who attended patients in the third ward at the Memphis Exchange, provided this description of the treatment he gave to the *Pennsylvania* victims:

> The free use of white lead in linseed oil, such as is used in ordinary painting, and covering the part well with soft carded cotton, kept on until signs of sloughing, then remove, and re-apply to all parts not deeply injured, to the deep sloughs; apply fine olive oil and lime water, equal parts, on soft linen, and as the wound heals dress twice daily, with ointment of the sub-acetate of lead. ("The Treatment Generally Pursued with the Sufferers by the Steamer *Pennsylvania*," St. Louis *Missouri Republican*, 18 July 58, 2, clipping in Scrapbook 1:7, CU-MARK)

[10] The *Pennsylvania*'s badly scalded second mate, James M. Thompson, died at the Memphis Exchange on 27 June, six days after Henry Clemens ("The Pennsylvania Disaster. Additional Particulars," Memphis *Avalanche*, undated clipping in Scrapbook 1:11, CU-MARK; "The Sufferers," Memphis *Appeal*, 29 June 58, 2).

To William A. Moffett
per Telegraph Operator
21 June 1858 • Memphis, Tenn.
(MS: CU-MARK)

WESTERN UNION TELEGRAPH CO.
CONSOLIDATED LINES.

SEND THE FOLLOWING MESSAGE SUBJECT TO THE ABOVE CONDITIONS:[1]

Memphis June 21 185 8.

TO W^m A Moffitt
  Cor Com^l & Chesnut

Henry Died this morning leave tomorrow with the Corpse[2]

Saml. Clemens.

[*canceled in pencil:*]

~~9 a 50 & 110~~ Col

---

[1] In the original document about two hundred words, printed in very small type below the company's name, describe the "terms and conditions" for anyone relying on its services. This information, like other highly detailed verbiage printed

on such telegram blanks or on letter stationery, is not transcribed as part of the letter text. In this case, the "terms and conditions" are reproduced in full in the textual apparatus.

[2] Family records give the date of Henry Clemens's death as 20 June 1858, but this telegram and a report in the Memphis *Appeal* of 22 June ("The Victims," 2) indicate that he died on the twenty-first. Death came "about dawn," Clemens later recalled, attributing it, possibly inaccurately (see Bates 1968, 87–91), to an overdose of morphine administered at midnight by Dr. Peyton's assistants, "young fellows hardly out of the medical college," after Peyton had declared Henry "out of danger" (AD, 13 Jan 1906, CU-MARK, in *MTA*, 1:311). Dazed and exhausted, Clemens rested for a few hours in a Memphis household before making arrangements to convey Henry's body by steamer to the Moffett home in St. Louis. His niece Annie Moffett Webster remembered that the sympathetic people of Memphis "sent a young man up to St. Louis with Uncle Sam, who was so overcome with grief that they were afraid he would go insane" (*MTBus*, 36)— perhaps the unidentified individual whose kindness and financial assistance Orion Clemens acknowledged in 1858 (see *MTB*, 3:1592). On 18 June, the same day Clemens wrote the previous letter to Mollie Clemens (then in Keokuk), William Moffett telegraphed him in Memphis: "Will it be better for your mother to come down" (CU-MARK). Clemens must have discouraged such a course. Orion, who was in Jamestown, Tennessee, when the *Pennsylvania* exploded, hurried to Memphis, conceivably arriving in time to join Clemens in bringing Henry's remains to St. Louis, but more probably joining him there (*MTB*, 1:143; MEC, 7–8; OC to MEC, 9 Sept 61, CU-MARK). Henry's body arrived in Hannibal on 25 June aboard the steamer *Hannibal City*, accompanied by "some of his relatives" ("Funereal," Hannibal *Tri-Weekly Messenger*, 26 June 58, clipping in Scrapbook 1:8, CU-MARK). In addition to Sam and Orion, the cortege almost certainly included Jane Clemens and William and Pamela Moffett. Henry was buried that same day in Hannibal's Baptist cemetery beside John Marshall Clemens. In 1876 both bodies were moved to the newer Mount Olivet Cemetery.

No letters are known to survive for a period of almost nine months following the death of Henry Clemens. The exact date of Clemens's return to the river remains undetermined. Possibly he resumed his piloting apprenticeship in July 1858. He later recalled that he once steered a trip for Bart Bowen on the *Alfred T. Lacey* (26 Feb 99 to John B. Downing, *MTL*, 2:675). The *Lacey*'s 11–28 July St. Louis–New Orleans round trip, the only one it made that month, may well have been the assignment Clemens remembered. If so, the boat's second pilot was another old friend—for Clemens reportedly "returned to the river as steersman for George Ealer, whom he loved" (*MTB*, 1:145).

In August—perhaps as early as the fourth and no later than the twenty-fifth—Clemens began working as a steersman aboard the *John H. Dickey*, a packet in the St. Louis–Memphis trade piloted by the youngest of the Bowen brothers, Samuel (1838?–78). He remained with the *Dickey* through October, except for one round trip, from the twentieth to the twenty-sixth of the month, with the *White Cloud*, a packet that replaced the *Dickey* while it was laid up for repairs. (For a discussion of Clemens's activities while on the *Dickey*, including the texts of three articles he published in the St. Louis *Missouri Democrat* [1 Sept 58], the St. Louis *Missouri Republican* [22 Oct 58], and the Memphis *Appeal* [24 Oct 58], see Branch 1982a, 195–208.)

There is a strong possibility that Clemens's next berth, from 30 October to 8 December, was as steersman for Horace Bixby aboard the *New Falls City* during two St. Louis–New Orleans round trips. Following that assignment Clemens moved with Bixby to the *Aleck Scott*. Robert A. Reilly, the new master of the *Scott*, had thoroughly repaired the boat during November and early December 1858 ("Aleck Scott—Railroad Line Packet for New Orleans To-day," St. Louis *Missouri Republican*, 13 Dec 58, 3). Very likely Clemens joined the refitted and restaffed *Scott* on its 13 December run to New Orleans and remained for five St. Louis–New Orleans round trips, leaving it on 8 April 1859, the day before he acquired his pilot's license.

To Pamela A. Moffett
9 and 11 March 1859 • New Orleans, La.
(MS: CU-MARK)

. . . .

beginning of Lent, and all good Catholics eat and drink freely of what they please, and, in fact, *do* what they please, in order that they may be the better able to keep sober and quiet during the coming fast. It has been said that a Scotchman has not seen the world until he has seen Edinburgh; and I think that I may say that an American has not seen the United States until he has seen Mardi-Gras in New Orleans.

I posted off up town yesterday morning as soon as the boat landed,

in blissful ignorance of the great day.[1] At the corner of Good-Children
and Tchoupitoulas streets, I beheld an apparition!—and my first impulse
was to dodge behind a lamp-post. It was a woman—a hay-stack of curtain
calico, ten feet high—sweeping majestically down the middle of the street
(for what pavement in the world could accommodate hoops of such vast
proportions?) Next I saw a girl of eighteen, mounted on a fine horse, and
dressed as a Spanish Cavalier, with long rapier, flowing curls, blue satin
doublet and half-breeches, trimmed with broad white lace—(the balance of her dainty legs cased in flesh-colored silk stockings)—white kid
gloves—and a nodding crimson feather in the coquettishest little cap in
the world. She rep removed said cap and bowed low to me, and nothing
loth loath, I bowed in return—but I could n't help murmuring, "By the
beard of the Prophet, Miss, but you've mistaken your man this time—
for I never saw your silk mask before,—nor the balance of your costume,
either, for that matter." And then I saw a hundred men, women and children in fine, fancy, splendid, ugly, coarse, ridiculous, grotesque, laugh-
able costumes, and the truth flashed upon me—"This is Mardi-Gras!" It
was Mardi-gras—and that young lady had a perfect right to bow to, shake
hands with, or speak to, me, or any body else she pleased. The streets
were soon full of "Mardi-gras," representing giants, Indians, nigger min-
strels, monks, priests, clowns,— every birds, beasts,—everything, in
fact, that one could imagine. The "free-and-easy" women turned out *en
masse*—and their costumes and actions were very trying to modest eyes.
The finest sight I saw during the day was a band of twenty stalwart men,
f splendidly arrayed as Comanche Indians, flying and yelling down the
street on horses as finely decorated as themselves. It was worth going a
long distance to see the performances of the day—but bless me! how
insignificant they seemed in comparison with those of the night, when
the grand torchlight procession of the "Mystic Krewe of Comus" were
was added. *f* At half past seven in the evening I went up to St. Charles
street, and found both its pavements, for many squares, packed and
jammed with thousands of men and women, waiting to see the Mystic
Krewe. I managed to get an eligible place near the middle of the street
opposite the St. Charles Hotel, where I waited—yes, I waited—standing
on both feet as long as I could—then on one—then on tother—and was
just preparing to stand on my head awhile, when a shout of "*Here* they
come!" kept me still in the ‚proper‚ position of a box of glassware. But it
was a false alarm—and after a while we had another false alarm—and

then another—each repetition stirring up the impatience and anxiety of
the crowd & setting it to heaving and surging at a fearful rate. At last the
distant tinkling of lively music was heard—and then the tag-end of a great
huzza that had battered nearly all the life out of itself by butting against
many squares of hard brick houses before it reached us—and again the
tinkling music, and again the faint huzza—and five thousand people near
me were tip-toeing & bobbing & peeping down the long street, & wondering why the devil it ˏdidn't˲ come along *faster*—if it *ever* expected to
come get in sight. Impatience was growing, now,—for ever so far away
down the street we could see a flare of light seeming some a little sun
spreading away from a line of dancing colored spots. They approached
faster, then, & pretty soon, *we* took up the fainting huzza, & breathed
new life into it. And here was the procession at last. The torches were of
all colors, but their shapes represented the spots on a pack of cards—an
endless line of hearts, and clubs, &c., The procession was led by a
mounted Knight of the Crusader in blazing gilt armor from head to foot,
and I think one might never tire of looking at the splendid picture. Then
followed tall, grotesque maskers representing some ancient game—then
an odd figure covered with checks, with a huge chess board & chessmen
for a hat—then another quaint fellow gleaming in backgammon stripes,
with two great dice for a hat—then the kings of each suit of cards dressed
ˏinˏ royal regalia of ermine, satin & gold—then queern figures representing various other games,—then the Queen of the Fairies, with an winged
troop of beauties, in airy costumes at her heels—then the King & Queen
of the Genii, I suppose (eight or ten feet high,) with vast rolls of flaxen
curls, bowing majestically to the crowd—followed by a couple of infini-
tesimal dwarfs,—and again by other genii, in costumes grotesque, hideous & beautiful in turn—then figures whose bodies were vast drums,
trumpets, clarinets, fiddles, &c.,—followed by others whose bodies were
pitchers, punch-bowls, goblets, &c., terminated by two tremendous &
very unsteady black wine bottles—then gigantic chickens, turkeys,
bears, & other beasts & birds—then a big Christmas tree, followed by
Santa Claus, with fur cap, short pipe, &c., and surrounded by a great
basket filled with toys—and then—well, I don't remember half. There
were transparencies, marking the divisions, with a band of music to each.
Under "May-day" was a beautifully decorated rhMay-tree & a rhMay-
pole;—after "Twelfth-Night" followed Ҡ a troupe of the most outrageously hideous figures, half-beast,-half-human, that one could imag-

ine;—Santa Claus & his crew followed "Christmas"—the games, &c., followed "Comus at his old English tricks, & again," and if there were any other transparencies, I have forgotten them. The ~~whole~~ long procession blazed with bran-new silk and satin, and the whole thing seemed to have been gotten up without any regard to cost.

Certainly New Orleans seldom does things by halves.

New Orleans, Friday 11th.

I saw our little Princesses, Countesses, or whatever they are—the Piccolominis—in St. Charles street, ‚yesterday.‚ They came down from Memphis in the cars, I believe. Their first concert takes place to-night, and we shall leave this afternoon. So we shall not hear the young lady sing.[2] We had a souvenir of the warbler written on our ~~sla~~ old slate, but some sacrilegious scoundrel rubbed it out. It was "Je suis fachèr qu'il faut que nous allons de ce batteau à la Memphis." ~~To which~~ ("I am sorry that we must leave the boat at Memphis.") To which I replied *en mauvais française*, "Nous seront nous aussi très fachèr." (We shall be very sorry, also.) Ben[3] was going to "head" it "The Lament of the Irish Emigrant,"[4] & sell the old slate to Barnum for five hundred dollars. Ben said he had a very interesting conversation with the "old dowager," Madame Pic. He remarked—"I imagine, Madame, that if it would only drizzle a little more, the weather would soon be in splendid condition for young ducks!" And she replied—"Ah, mio, mio,—une petè—I not can *on*dersthand not!" "Yes'm, it's a great pity you can't ondersthand not, for it has cost you the loss of a very sage remark." And she followed with a tremendous gush of the musical language. Then Benjamin—"Yes, madame, you're very right—very right indeed. I acknowlege the justice of your remarks, but the devil of it is, I'm a little in the dark as to what you've been saying all the time!"

In eight days from this, I shall be in Saint Louis, but I am afraid if I am not careful I'll beat this letter there.

My love to all,

Your brother

Sam

---

[1] The *Aleck Scott* left St. Louis on 1 March and arrived in New Orleans on Mardi Gras, 8 March.

[2] Since her first appearance in Florence in 1852, at the age of seventeen, Maria Piccolomini had enjoyed great popularity in Italy, the British Isles, and elsewhere in Europe. Because her family was one of the oldest in Tuscany, she claimed "the

honorary title of Princess" on "the Italian principle of children and grand-children participating in the family honors" ("Piccolomini," New Orleans *True Delta*, 30 Oct 58, supplement, 1). The singer and her company had performed in St. Louis on 28 February and 1 March, then immediately left for Memphis at 11:00 P.M. on the *Aleck Scott*, en route to New Orleans. The travel party included Piccolomini's mother, sister, and other family members. Her Memphis audience had been typical of American audiences, which found her vivacious personality more captivating than her voice. The Memphis *Appeal* called her "not a musician of incredible skill, but a girl of inexpressible fascinations that fills the mind" and praised her "merry, gleeful, cheery way" ("The Concert Last Night," 5 Mar 59, 3). Piccolomini performed in New Orleans for ten days beginning on 11 March, the day the *Aleck Scott* left for St. Louis at 5:00 P.M.

  [3]Probably the engineer of the *Aleck Scott*. In chapter 13 of *Life on the Mississippi* Clemens recalled how, in a moment of panic at the wheel, he called to the engineer, "Oh, Ben, if you love me, *back* her! Quick, Ben! Oh, back the immortal *soul* out of her!"

  [4]A popular sentimental song expressing a lover's bereavement, by Lady Dufferin (Helen Selina Sheridan).

To John T. Moore
6 July 1859 • Memphis, Tenn.
(Arkansaw Traveler, 14 July 83)

MEMPHIS, July 6, 1859.

MY DEAR JOHN:—

  I have made many attempts to answer your letter which received a warmth of welcome perspiringly in keeping with the present system of hot weather; but somehow I have failed. Now, however, I screw myself down to the pleasant task. It is a task, let me tell you, and it is only by the courtesy of friendship that I can call it pleasant.[1]

  I have been wondering lately what in the name of Mexican cultivation and flatboat morality is to become of people, anyhow. Years, now, I have been waiting for the summers to become cooler, but up to the present moment of agony I see no change. I wish there was some arrangement by which we could have the kind of weather we want; but then I suppose I would call for an arrangement by which we could make a living without work. What a fool old Adam was. Had everything his own way; had succeeded in gaining the love of the best looking girl in the neighborhood, but yet unsatisfied with his conquest he had to eat a miserable little apple.

Ah, John, if you had been in his place you would not have eaten a mouthful of the apple, that is if it had required any exertion. I have often noticed that you shun exertion. There comes in the difference between us. I court exertion. I love to work. Why, sir, when I have a piece of work to perform, I go away to myself, sit down in the shade and muse over the coming enjoyment. Sometimes I am so industrious that I muse too long.

No, I am not in love at present. I saw a young lady in Vicksburg the other day whom I thought I'd like to love, but John, the weather is too devilish hot to talk about love; but oh, that I had a cool, shady place, where I could sit among gurgling fountains of perfumed ice-water, an' be loved into a premature death of rapture. I would give the world for this— I'd love to die such a glorious and luxurient death.

Yours,

SAM CLEMENS.[2]

[1] Known as "Tom" (presumably his middle name), Moore had clerked on the *John J. Roe* for two years, beginning in 1856 or 1857. His whereabouts at the time of this letter are not known. By 1866 he had risen to the rank of captain, for he was in command of the *Ida Handy* when it burned at St. Louis on 2 June of that year. In 1867 he retired from the river, eventually becoming the owner of several large sugar plantations near New Orleans, as well as the father of seven children (index of steamboat officers, MoShi; Way 1983, 220). He and Clemens had been acquainted since at least August and September 1857, when Clemens was cub pilot on the *Roe*. Twenty-five years later, on his final visit to New Orleans, Clemens went out of his way to find and visit his old friend: "I hunted up Tom Moore, who used to be mud clerk on the John J Roe when I was cub. He is short, & unwieldy with flesh, is a rich & respected burgher, & looks it. Good fellow is Tom; am going to his house to see his wife & six children, tomorrow" (4 May 82 to Olivia Clemens, CU-MARK, in *N&J2*, 465 n. 116). Moore died near New Orleans in May 1909.

[2] The authenticity of this letter remains in doubt: the manuscript has not been found, and the text therefore derives from what Opie P. Read, editor of the *Arkansaw Traveler* (Little Rock), published on 14 July 1883, with this introduction: "The following letter, written by Samuel Clemens—'Mark Twain'—has never heretofore been published. It was addressed to an old river man, once of New Orleans but now of Little Rock." Three weeks later, however, Read said his Mark Twain letter was a hoax, a "very rough imitation . . . purporting to have been written in Memphis in 1859" (Read 1883b, 4; Burns, 90–92). Yet the hoax may be Read's retraction, not the letter itself. Clemens was furious when, also in July 1883, another of his letters, to Joseph Twichell, was published in Hartford (see *N&J3*, 28 n. 47). Since Read's publication "was immediately reproduced by many of the leading papers in the country," it is likely that Clemens knew of it, and may even have asked for the retraction. "Our motive in publishing this exposure of the fraud," wrote Read, "is to exculpate the author of 'Innocents Abroad' from any odium that might fall upon him in consequence of the letter." But whether or not Clemens called for a retraction, the available circumstantial evi-

dence supports the letter's authenticity: Moore clearly fits Read's description of "an old river man, once of New Orleans," even though he was not "now of Little Rock"; Paine, who apparently received a copy of the letter from Stephen E. Gillis in 1907, identified Clemens's correspondent as "John T. Moore, a young clerk on the *John J. Roe*," information he could scarcely have learned from anyone but Clemens himself (*MTB*, 1:156; Davis 1956b, 2). Existing evidence suggests that Clemens was in Memphis on the date Read gave for the letter. It is now thought that between 25 June and 28 July 1859 he made two St. Louis–New Orleans round trips as pilot of the *J. C. Swon*, captained by Isaac H. Jones. On the first of these trips the *Swon* left St. Louis on 25 June, arrived at New Orleans on 1 July, and started back upriver two days later. Noted for its fast upriver passages, the *Swon* definitely reached Memphis by 7 July and in fact may well have arrived there by midnight of the sixth. In any case, the likelihood is small that any hoaxer writing in 1883 would be able to approximate the facts of Clemens's whereabouts in 1859 so closely. The letter writer's elaborate pretense of laziness, his interest in "what a fool old Adam was," and the joking about his love life (including a young lady he saw "the other day" in Vicksburg, before reaching Memphis) all strongly suggest Clemens's manner, while the tone greatly resembles the tone of a letter he is known to have written as "Soleather" and deliberately published just two weeks later, in the 21 July New Orleans *Crescent* (SLC 1859, 4).

To Elizabeth W. Smith
13? October 1859 • St. Louis, Mo.
(MS facsimile: Daley)

Saint Louis, Thursday,—*M*.[1]

Dear Aunt Betsey:[2]

Ma has not written you, because she did not ˌknowˌ when I would get started down the river again—and sh I could not write, because, between you and I, Aunt Betsey, for once in my life I *didn't know any more than my own mother*—she could not tell when she and the coal-tinted white tom-cat might hope to get rid of me, and I was in the same lamentable state of ignorance myself.

You see, Aunt Betsey, I made but one trip on the packet after you left, and then concluded to remain at home awhile.[3] I have just discovered, this morning, that I am to go to New Orleans on the Col. Chambers—"fine, light-draught, swift running passenger steamer—all modern accommodations—and improvements—through with dispatch—for freight or passage apply on board or to"—but—I have forgotten the agent's name—however, it makes no difference[4]—and as I was saying, or had intended to say, Aunt Betsey, ~~that~~ probably, if you are ready to come up, you had better take the "Ben Lewis," the best boat in the packet line. She will be at Cape Girardeau at noon on Saturday (day after to-morrow,) and will reach here at breakfast time Sunday.[5] If Mr. Hamilton is Chief Clerk,—very well. I am slightly acquainted with him.[6] And if Messrs. Carter, Gray and Dean Somebody (I have forgotten his other name,) ~~very well~~ are in the pilot-house—very well again—I am ac-quainted with them.[7] Just tell Mr. Gray, Aunt Betsey—that I wish him to place himself at your command.

All the family are well except myself—*I* am in a bad way again—disease, *Love*, in its most malignant form. Hopes are entertained of my recovery, however. At the dinner-table, *I*—excellent symptom—I am still as "terrible as an army with banners."[8]

Aunt Betsey—the wickedness of this world—but I haven't time to moralize this morning.

Good-bye.

Sam. Clemens

P. S.—All send their love.

[1]Paine, when printing this letter in *MTL* (1:44–45), indicated that the source of his text gave the date as "Oct. 31"; he conjectured that the year was "probably 1859." It seems reasonable to suppose that Paine's copy of the letter was not the manuscript but a transcript, whose maker supplied the month and day of writing, but not the year. Unfortunately, 31 October 1859 was not a Thursday. A date of Thursday, 13 October 1859, is assigned here on the assumption that a simple transposition of numbers accounts for the transcriber's error. This date is consis-tent with the schedule of the *A. B. Chambers*, which Clemens was about to join as pilot (see note 4). The boat's first advertisement for the Mississippi trade ap-peared in the *Missouri Republican* on 20 October, before which time the owners would certainly have completed the hiring of the pilots.

[2]Mrs. Elizabeth W. Smith (b. 1794 or 1795), an old friend of the Clemens family's in Hannibal, was now living in Jackson, Missouri, just a few miles north-west of Cape Girardeau (*Hannibal Census*, 318; *MTL*, 1:44). She was remembered by Annie Moffett Webster as a frequent and welcome visitor in St. Louis (*MTBus*, 49). Clemens characterized her, both in his autobiographical dictations and in several fictions, as his mother's companion and "chum":

She wasn't anybody's aunt in particular, she was aunt to the whole town of Hannibal; this was because of her sweet and generous and benevolent nature and the winning simplicity of her character. . . . She and my mother were very much alive; their age counted for nothing; they were fond of excitement, fond of novelties, fond of anything going that was of a sort proper for members of the church to indulge in. . . . they were always ready for Fourth of July processions, Sunday-school processions, lectures, conventions, camp-meetings, reviv-als in the church—in fact, for any and every kind of dissipation that could not be proven to have anything irreligious about it—and they never missed a funeral. (AD, 30 Nov 1906, CU-MARK, in *AMT*, 62)

In 1894 Clemens used Elizabeth Smith and his mother as the models for Aunt Patsy Cooper and Aunt Betsy Hale in "Those Extraordinary Twins." In 1897 he used Mrs. Smith as the model for "old aunt Betsy Davis" in "Hellfire Hotchkiss" (*Inds*, 109–33), and a year later for the "widow Dawson" in the "Schoolhouse Hill" version of *The Mysterious Stranger* (*MSM*, 175–220).

³On 2 August 1859 Clemens began piloting the *Edward J. Gay*, captained by Bart Bowen, in the St. Louis–New Orleans trade. The *Gay*, an "elegantly furnished and fully appointed" packet on its maiden voyage, was the newest addition to the St. Louis and New Orleans Railroad Line ("River News," St. Louis *Missouri Republican*, 25 July 59, 3). Presumably the third round trip of the *Gay*, which began on 13 September and ended on 1 October, was Clemens's last, the "one trip" he made after Aunt Betsey's visit. He then remained "at home awhile" in St. Louis with his mother and Pamela and William Moffett, until learning that he was to pilot the *A. B. Chambers*.

⁴The *A. B. Chambers* was a Missouri River steamboat that sometimes switched to the Mississippi when winter conditions made the shallower Missouri impassable. In the winter of 1859–60, the *Chambers*, captained by George W. Bowman, began its first trip south in the St. Louis–New Orleans trade on 26 October. It is not known for certain when Clemens joined the crew, but it is probable that he was hired for the first trip and remained until 24 February 1860, when the *Chambers* prepared to return to the Missouri River. His later remarks indicate only that he had Will Bowen as his partner for one trip, and that he was aboard when the *Chambers* grounded near Goose Island (26 Feb 99 to John B. Downing, *MTL*, 2:674–75; *N&J2*, 529; see also Bixby 1910, 3). Riverman Grant Marsh reportedly recalled that only one of the pilots hired for the first trip of the *Chambers* that season remained with the boat. This "smooth-faced young fellow, whose quiet and retiring manner did not prevent his being very popular with all his associates, proved a most excellent navigator, knowing his river thoroughly and possessing the judgment to make the best use of his knowledge. This young man was familiarly known as Sam Clemens" (Hanson, 26–27). In an earlier account of his friendship with Clemens, Marsh specified that they were on the *Chambers* together during "the winter I was married, in '59 and '60" (Grant Marsh 1878, 7). On 22 or 23 December 1859, during its third run from St. Louis, the *Chambers* grounded on a bar five miles south of Commerce, Missouri, and thirty miles above Cairo, where the channel passed between Power's Island and Goose Island—a notorious trouble spot. It was soon "hard aground in the middle of the river, in the course of the former channel, with the ice piled up all around" ("Cairo Correspondence," St. Louis *Missouri Republican*, 28 Dec 59, 4). Marsh, who was first mate at the time, recalled an exploit of Clemens's:

I believe he once saved my life, his own and six others. Our steamer was lying above Cairo on a sand-bar. We were out of wood, and the captain ordered Sam, me and the six roustabouts to get in a yawl and row up the river and bring down a flat-boat loaded with wood. The river was full of floating ice. We rowed up on the opposite bank from the flat-boat. The ice was running almost solid, with an occasional opening by the ice blocking up. We took advantage of these openings to shoot across the river. When we got into the channel a short distance I saw the danger we were encountering. The ice was liable to close in on us and drown the whole outfit. I appealed to Sam to row back. There was an opening in the rear. Sam resolutely said "No." In another minute the ice broke in the path behind the boat and crushed by with terrific force. Had we turned back when I suggested it, we would have been "goners," every mother's son of us. Sam's judgment was not questioned again on that trip. (Grant Marsh 1881, no page)

Clemens later confirmed this account (marginal comment on Joseph M. Hanson to SLC, 9 July 1906, CU-MARK) and in turn praised Marsh's skill in piloting the flatboat down to the stranded steamer:

When we were taking that wood flat down to the Chambers, which was aground, I soon saw that I was a perfect lubber at piloting such a thing. I saw that I could never hit the Chambers with it, so I resigned in Marsh's favor, and he accomplished the task to my admiration. We should all have gone to mischief if I had remained in authority. (Ca. late Aug 81 to John B. Downing, *MTL*, 2:496–97, misdated 1888)

The *Chambers* finally reached Cairo safely on 29 December, and continued downriver to New Orleans on 31 December ("River News," St. Louis *Missouri Republican*, 30 Dec 59, 5). The boat subsequently grounded at about the site of the December grounding on 3 February 1860, while on its fourth and final trip before returning to the Missouri trade, but the weather conditions on that occasion do not correspond to those in Marsh's account.

⁵The *Ben W. Lewis* was built in 1857–58 for the Missouri River trade. In August 1859, it was leased by the St. Louis and Memphis United States Packet Line (whose president was Clemens's friend Captain Dan Able), which ran it regularly out of St. Louis on Mondays and out of Memphis on Thursdays ("River Intelligence," St. Louis *Missouri Democrat*, 6 Aug 59, 3; "Port of Memphis," Memphis *Appeal*, 7 Sept 59, 3). With this schedule in mind, Clemens advised his correspondent to board the *Ben Lewis* in Cape Girardeau (about three hundred miles above Memphis) on Saturday, to arrive in St. Louis (another one hundred and thirty-five miles upriver) on Sunday morning.

⁶There was a John P. Hamilton working as clerk on the *Ben Lewis* at this time, but it was probably not the same John Hamilton who was a pilot friend of Clemens's ("River News," St. Louis *Missouri Republican*, 17 Oct 59, 3; Robert V. Kennedy 1859, 207; *N&J1*, 37; *N&J2*, 456).

⁷Possibly one of the brothers Edmund or Lemuel Gray (pilots of the *Gold Dust* during Clemens's 1882 river trip) and their brother-in-law, pilot Andrew Jackson Carter, all working on the river at this time. "Dean Somebody" remains unidentified.

⁸Song of Solomon 6:10.

To Orion Clemens
27? June 1860 • *City of Memphis* en route
from Memphis, Tenn., to St. Louis, Mo.
(Transcript and MS: *MTB*, 1:146, and NPV)

· · · ·

What is a government without energy? And what is *a man* without energy? Nothing—nothing at all. What is the grandest thing in "Paradise Lost"—the Arch-Fiend's terrible energy! What was the greatest feature in Napoleon's character? His unconquerable energy! Sum all the gifts that man is endowed with, and we give our greatest share of admiration to his energy. And to-day, if I were a heathen, I would rear a statue to Energy, and fall down and worship it!

I want a man to—I want *you* to—take up a line of action, and *follow* it out, in spite of the very devil.[1]

.   .   .   .

yourself from the reputation of a visionary. I am not talking nonsense, now—I am in earnest. I want you to keep your troubles and your plans out of the reach of meddlers,,—until the latter are consummated—so that, in case you fail, no one will know it but yourself. Above all things (between you and I,) never tell Ma ~~and~~ any of your troubles. She never slept a wink the night your last letter came,, and she looks distressed yet.[2] Write only cheerful news to her. You know that she will not be satisfied so long as she thinks anything is going that she is ignorant of,—and she makes a bitter fuss about it when her suspicions are ~~con~~ awakened:—but that makes no difference—*I* ~~that~~ know that it is better that she be kept in the dark concerning all things of an unpleasant nature. She upbraids me occasionally for giving her only the bright side of my affairs—(but unfortunately for her she has to put up with it, for I know that troubles which I curse awhile and forget, would disturb her slumbers for some time.) (Par. N⁰· 2.—Possibly because she is deprived of the soothing consolation of swearing.) Tell ~~me~~ her the good news and me the bad.

Putting all things together, I begin to think I am rather lucky than otherwise—a notion which I was slow to ¢ take up. The other night I was about to round to for a storm—but concluded ~~to~~ that I could find a smoother bank somewhere. I landed 5 miles below. The storm came—passed away and did not injure us. ɪ Coming up, day before yesterday, I looked at the spot I first chose, and half the trees on the bank were torn to shreds. We couldn't have lived 5 minutes in such a tornado.[3] And I am also lucky in having a berth, while all the other young pilots are idle. This *is* the luckiest circumstance that ever befell me. Not on account of the wages—for that is a secondary consideration—but from the fact that the City of Memphis is the largest boat in the trade and the hardest to pilot, *and* consequently I can get a *r e p u t a t i o n* on her, which is a thing I never could accomplish on a transient boat. I can "bank" in the neighborhood of $100 a month on her, and that will satisfy me for the present (principally because the other youngsters *are sucking their fingers*.) Bless me! what a pleasure there is in revenge!—and what ẃ vast respect ᵱProsperity

commands! Why, six months ago, I could enter the "Rooms,"[4] and receive only the customary fraternal greeting—but now they say, "Why
how *are* you, old fellow—when did you get in?" And the young pilots,
who used to tell me, patronizingly, that I could never learn the river,
cannot keep from showing a little of their chagrin at seeing me so far ahead
of them. Permit me to "blow my horn," for I derive a *living* pleasure from
these things. And I must confess that when I go to pay my dues, I rather
like to let the d—d rascals get a glimpse of a hundred dollar bill peeping
out from amongst notes of smaller dimensions, whose faces I do *not* exhibit! You will despise this egotism, but I tell you there is a "stern joy" in
it.[5]

.   .   .   .

[1] The two fragments printed here (connected by the editorial ellipsis) are probably, but not demonstrably, parts of a single letter, which remains incomplete.
The first part survives only in Paine's transcription; the second survives in manuscript, found among Pamela Moffett's papers now at Vassar (NPV). As early as
1880, Orion Clemens noted on this manuscript that "the balance is lost." Yet this
may mean only that the beginning pages of the letter were misplaced with some
other member of the family, and that Paine managed to see both fragments (separately), noticed their common theme, but did not recognize them as belonging
to the same letter. Paine said of the first that it was "from a letter written toward
the end of the year" (1858), ostensibly reflecting Clemens's new-found confidence
and wealth following upon his being licensed as a pilot. He gave a similar charac-
terization of the second fragment, assigning it to 1859. But Paine was mistaken
about when Clemens received his license, placing that event on 9 September 1858
instead of the correct date, 9 April 1859 (*MTB*, 1:145–48; *MTL*, 1:42–44).
Moreover, the second fragment, in which Clemens specifies that his prosperity is
a development of the past six months, can be firmly connected with events of June
1860 (see note 3). With these facts in mind, therefore, Paine's own reasoning
about the first fragment places it in 1860, not 1858. So while it remains possible
that the two fragments are from separate letters which just happened to share the
same theme and to have been written in 1860, it seems somewhat more likely that
their common date and common theme, as well as their being fragments in the
first place, mean that they belong to the same letter.
[2] According to his wife's journal, Orion again left Keokuk in May 1860, moving
to Memphis, Missouri, in an effort to establish a law practice there. His distress-
ing letter presumably described his tribulations in this latest effort to "take up a
line of action, and *follow* it out." Orion brought Mollie and Jennie to Memphis in
August of this year (MEC, 6–9).
[3] Probably since 25 March, Clemens had been one of the pilots on the *City of
Memphis*, under Captain Joseph Edward Montgomery (usually known as J. Ed.
Montgomery), a well-known pilot and commander who later became commodore
of the Confederate River Fleet. Clemens's berth on the *City of Memphis*, together
with a contemporary report of the storm he mentions, supplies the circumstantial
evidence for assigning this letter the date of 27 June 1860. According to their
published memoranda, the pilots of the *J. C. Swon*, traveling upstream, encoun-

tered a storm at about 11:00 A.M. on 19 June, while negotiating Terrapin Bend, some twenty-eight miles above Vicksburg. "A severe storm of wind accompanied with rain and hail" was said to have "done a great deal of damage to the crops, and destroyed a great amount of timber" ("Memoranda," St. Louis *Missouri Democrat*, 25 June 60, 3). A few hours later, the *Swon* met the *City of Memphis*, heading downstream, at Stack Island (Island No. 94), near Lake Providence, Louisiana, some thirty-five miles above Terrapin Bend. The *City of Memphis* is known to have reached New Orleans on 22 June, and to have departed upriver again on the twenty-fourth at 10:00 A.M. It arrived at Cairo late on 28 June, and at St. Louis on 1 or 2 July. Since Clemens says that he revisited the storm area the "day before yesterday," he probably wrote this letter aboard ship about 27 June, soon after picking up his mail at Memphis, Tennessee, just about two days' travel above Terrapin Bend, the site of the storm. At any rate, he clearly wrote the letter before reaching St. Louis, when his service on the *City of Memphis* came to an end.

⁴The office and meeting room of the Western Boatman's Benevolent Association, the organization of pilots in the St. Louis–New Orleans trade.

⁵The allusion is to Scott's *Lady of the Lake* (1810): "And the stern joy which warriors feel" (canto 5, stanza 10). Clemens's pride in his post was soon ended. The day he reached St. Louis, the *Evening News* reported that "the steamer *City of Memphis* has laid up for a while, and will now make some few necessary repairs. Capt. [William J.] Kountz [half-owner and regular master of the boat] has again taken charge of her" ("River News," 2 July 60, 3; Way 1983, 94). Clemens's 1882 notebook reveals the likely reason for the repairs: "One time I mistook Capt. Ed. Montgomery's coat hanging on the big bell for the Capt. himself and waiting for him to tell me to back I ran into a steamboat at New Orleans" (*N&J2*, 536; see also chapter 49 of *Life on the Mississippi*, where Clemens mistakenly identified the steamboat as the *Crescent City*). Since the captain's authority over a boat's movements while entering or leaving a port was absolute, Montgomery acted correctly when he absolved his young pilot of blame and, as Clemens recalled in 1874, "shouldered the responsibility like a man" (28 Mar 74 to Meriwether Jeff Thompson, in St. Louis *Missouri Republican*, 28 Apr 74, 3). The *City of Memphis* was back at the landing by 25 July, with Captain Kountz in command and neither Montgomery nor Clemens among its officers. There is no evidence, however, that either man was dismissed punitively.

To Susan I. (Belle) Stotts
11 August 1860 • Cairo, Ill.
(MS: NPV)

Cairo, Saturday, Aug. 11.

Dear Belle:

    *Con*found me if I wouldn't *eat up* half a dozen of you small girls if I just had the merest shadow of a chance this morning. Here I am, now, about 3 weeks out from Keokuk, and 2 from St. Louis, and yet I have not heard a word from you—and may not, possibly, for 2 or 3 more weeks, as we shall go no further up the river at present, but turn back from here and go to New Orleans.[1]

Just *go on*, though—*go on*. I have had a pleasant trip, and there is consolation in that. I quarreled with the mate,[2] and "made it up" with him; and I quarreled with him again, and made it up again; and quarreled and "made up" the third time—and I have got the shell of half a watermelon by me now, ready to drop on his head as soon as he comes out of the "Texas,"—which will produce quarrel N$^{o\cdot}$ 4, if I have made my calculations properly.

Yes, and I have disobeyed the Captain's orders over and over again, which produced a "state of feeling" in his breast, much to my satisfaction—(bless your soul, I always keep the *law* on my side, you see, when the Chief Officer is concerned,) and I am ready now to quarrel with anybody in the world that can't whip me.[3] Ah me, I feel as strong as a yoke of oxen, this morning, and nothing could afford me greater pleasure than a pitched battle with you three girls.[4] It *can't be*, though. However, I̶f̶ *I'll* "fix" the mate when *he* comes out.

Belle, you ought to see the letter I wrote last night for a friend of mine. He is fearfully love-sick, and he feared he should die, if he didn't "pour out his soul" (*he* said—"*stomach*," I should say,) in an epistolary form to the "*being*," (Ella Creel knows what *that* word means,) who has entrapped his virgin affections. Poor devil—he said "Make i̶t̶ the letter sweet—fill it *full* of love," *and* I did, as sure as you live. But if the dose don't turn the young lady inside out, she must certainly h̶a̶ be endowed with the stomach of an ostrich.

But did you girls see the Aurora Borealis last night (Friday?) It was very beautiful, but it did not last long. I̶f̶ reckon you girls had been home from choir-meeting about an hour when I saw it—or perhaps you were out on the bluff. ⸜Somebody remarked ⸜A "Snag ahead!" and I lost the finest part of the sight.

Now, Belle, can't you write to me, *right away*, to "Care of *Eclipse* Wharf Boat, Memphis, Tenn?"[5] *Of course* you can, if you will. I sent you 2 pieces of instrumental music and a song to Ella Creel from Vicksburgh—did they arrive safely?

Oh, confound Cairo.

Good-bye my dear

Sam

[1] Having left his berth on the *City of Memphis*, Clemens visited Keokuk during the first three weeks of July before returning to St. Louis for a new assignment: he was aboard the *Arago* for its 28 July departure for Vicksburg. A small, recently built steamer under Captain George P. Sloan, the *Arago* was not, as previously conjectured (Bates 1967, 102–3), operating as a "transient" or "tramp steamboat," but as a scheduled boat for a major company, the St. Louis and Vicksburg Mail Packet Line. On Clemens's first trip, the *Arago* did not reach St. Louis in time for its regularly scheduled departure (Saturday, 11 August), having spent about two days lightening off the *City of Memphis*, which had grounded on a sandbar near Greenville, Mississippi. The *Arago*'s owners earned $1,300 for this service, but were obliged to substitute another boat in the schedule. Captain Sloan transferred his St. Louis–bound freight at Cairo and began loading there for the return trip south, departing on 12 August. Clemens remained as one of the *Arago*'s pilots (the other was J. W. Hood) until 31 August. He apparently was no longer aboard when, on 9 September, the boat struck a snag and sank near Goose Island; contemporary reports of the accident do not mention him. The *Arago* was soon refloated and, by mid-October, ready for business, but Clemens was by then established as a pilot of the *Alonzo Child*, a berth he assumed on 19 September (Bates 1968, 148).

[2] Unidentified.

[3] Captain Sloan, who owned a two-thirds interest in the *Arago*, was characterized in the river columns as a well-known, popular steamboat commander. Clemens's disobedience of his orders presumably involved navigational decisions made while the boat was under way in the river. At such a time the pilot's authority was absolute, as Clemens reported in chapter 14 of *Life on the Mississippi*:

> The captain could stand upon the hurricane deck, in the pomp of a very brief authority, and give him [the pilot] five or six orders while the vessel backed into the stream, and then that skipper's reign was over. The moment that the boat was under way in the river, she was under the sole and unquestioned control of the pilot. He could do with her exactly as he pleased, run her when and whither he chose, and tie her up to the bank whenever his judgment said that that course was best. His movements were entirely free; he consulted no one, he received commands from nobody, he promptly resented even the merest suggestions. Indeed, the law of the United States forbade him to listen to commands or suggestions, rightly considering that the pilot necessarily knew better how to handle the boat than anybody could tell him.

[4] Probably (in addition to Belle Stotts herself) Eleanor J. (Ella) Patterson, born in 1840, and Mary E. (Ella) Creel, born in 1840 or 1841. Paine reported that Clemens's "favorite companions" during the Keokuk years were "Ella Creel, a cousin on the Lampton side, a great belle; also Ella Patterson (related through Orion's wife and generally known as 'Ick'), and Belle Stotts" (*MTB*, 1:106). Belle Stotts and Ella Patterson were cousins. Ella Patterson, though virtually the same age as Ella Creel, was nevertheless her aunt. And Ella Creel was Clemens's second cousin, the daughter of his mother's cousin Robert P. Creel and Ella Patterson's oldest sister, Mary Ann (see 5 Aug 56 to HC, n. 6). Ella Patterson was never known as "Ick," who in fact was one of her sisters, Margaret Patterson Starkweather. By all accounts the two Ellas were good friends and frequent companions. In her diary for 11 April 1862, for instance, Mollie Clemens noted, "Went to Ick Starkweathers, E. C, E P. there had a nice time" (MEC, 40). Paine's report that Ella Creel was Clemens's "one-time sweetheart" (*MTL*, 1:23) has not been confirmed (*Biographical Review*, 492; *Keokuk Census* [1850], 423, 433; *Keokuk*

Census [1860], 151–52; JLC to "Livy Children & Sam," 24 Jan 85, Davis 1981, 2).

[5] The *Eclipse* was "the longest, largest, most elegant, and just about the fastest" steamboat on the Mississippi from the time of its construction in 1852 until February 1860 when, severely damaged in a storm, it was dismantled (Way 1975, 40, 46). J. D. Morton and Company had purchased the hull and, on 28 July, anchored it as a wharfboat on the upper levee at Memphis. Clemens later commemorated the *Eclipse* in *Life on the Mississippi* (chapter 30).

To Orion Clemens
29 September 1860 • New Orleans, La.
(MS: NPV)

"Alonzo Child," N. Orleans, Sept. 28th.

Dear Brother:

I just received yours and Mollies letters yesterday—they had been here ~~3~~ 2 weeks—forwarded from St Louis. We got here yesterday—will leave at Noon, to-day.[1] Of course I have had no time, in 24 hours, to do anything—therefore I'll answer after we are under way again. Yesterday I had many things to do, but Bixby[2] and I got with the pilots of two other boats and went off ~~disa~~ dissipating on a ten dollars dinner at a French restaurant—breathe it not unto Ma!—where we ate Sheep-head-fish with mushrooms, shrimps and oysters—birds—coffee with brandy burnt in it, &c &c,—ate, drank & smoked, from 1 P. M. until 5 o'clock, and then—then—the day was too far gone to do anything.

To-day I ordered the alligator boots—$12⁰⁰. Will send 'em up next trip. Please find enclosed—and acknowledge receipt of $20⁰⁰

In haste

Sam. L. Clemens

[1] Clemens misdated this letter, for New Orleans newspapers show that the *Alonzo Child* arrived there on 28 September and departed the next day. The regular captain of the *Child*, which ran in the St. Louis and New Orleans Railroad Line, was David DeHaven (1826–76), who was on duty in September. On many subsequent trips, however, DeHaven was too ill to serve and was replaced by Captain James O'Neal (see 6 Feb 61 to OC and MEC, n. 2). The *Child* was the last boat that Clemens piloted. One of his two surviving river notebooks contains details of some of the trips he made between November 1860 and March 1861 (see *N&J1*, 53–56).

[2] Horace E. Bixby, Clemens's former mentor, was again his fellow pilot.

To Orion Clemens and Family
21 November 1860 • St. Louis, Mo.
(MS: CU-MARK)

Saint Louis, Wednesday, Nov. 20.[1]

My Dear Brother:

At last, I have succeeded in scraping together moments enough to write you. And it's all owing to my own enterprise, too—for, running in the fog, on the coast, in order to beat another boat, I grounded the "Child" on the bank, at nearly flood-tide, where we had to stay until the "great" tide ebbed and flowed again (24 hours,) before she floated off. And that dry-bank spell so warped and twisted the packet, and caused her to leak at such a rate, that she had to enter protest and go on the dock, here, which delays us until Friday morning.[2] We had intended to leave to-day. As soon as we arrived here last Sunday morning, I jumped aboard the "McDowell" and went down to look at the river—grounded 100 miles below here—25 miles this side of the "crossing" which I started down to look at—stayed aground 24 hours—and by that time I grew tired and returned here to be ready for to-day. I am sorry now that I did not hail a down-stream boat and go on—I would have had plenty of time.[3]

The New Orleans market fluctuates. If any man doubts this proposition, let him try it once. ⅃ Trip before last, chickens sold rapidly on the levee at $7⁰⁰ per doz—last trip they were not worth $3⁰⁰. Trip before last, eggs were worth $35 @ 40ᶜ per doz—last trip they were selling at 12½— which was rather discouraging, considering that *we* were in the market with 3,600 dozen, which we paid *15* cents for—together with 18 barrels of apples, which were not worth a d—m— We *expected* to get $6 or 7 per bbl. for them. We *stored* the infernal produce, and shall wait for the market to *fluctuate* again. But in the meantime, *Nil desperandum*—I am deep in another egg purchase, *now.*

I am ashamed of myself for not having sent you any money for such a long time. But the fact is, I'll be darned if I *had* it. I went to the clerk awhile ago and asked him "how we stood?" "Twenty-two days' wages— $183.33⅓." "Deduct my egg speculation and give me the balance." And he handed me *$35⁰⁰!* So much for eggs. I gave the money to Ma. However, we shall have been here 4 days to-morrow. I'll go and collect *that* and divide with you.

When I go to Memphis, Mo, I will see what can be done about produce in your part of the country.

Now, as I understand the "house," business, you can get a big, respectable house to live in for $110°° a year—per. centage—which is cheap enough rent it seems to me—and 10 years to pay the principal—in law. *Take it*—and take the whole town on the same terms if you can get it. Furnish the house nicely, and move into it—and then, if you'll invite me, I'll be happy to pay you a visit. Let me know how much money you want to furnish the house with. About the other house I can tell nothing. If it be best to purchase—why—*pitch in*. I'll raise the money in some way. You owe Uncle Billy Patterson and old Jimmy Clemens Jr. money—and if they were to die, ~~ther~~ their administrators would "gobble up" everything you've got.[4] Therefore, put no property in your own name—either put your share in Ma's name and my half in my own, or else put it *all* in Ma's or mine—*Ma's* will do me—and you, too, I reckon. If you can buy both houses with "law and 10 per cent," *take them*—but see that the contract is carefully written out. Because, for *one* reason, the law business of an influential man like Downing[5] is worth a great deal more money in the influence *it* carries with it, than ~~the~~ simply the money which is paid for it. Yes—you might advertize for cheap lots in your local paper. But perhaps you had better wait until I see whether this last egg speculation of mine is going to "smash" me or not.

Blast it—you didn't ask Belle where she got that stone—and if I don't get another pretty soon I'll lose the setting—and it's fine gold, and I want to save it.

"In conclusion"—Pamela has got a *baby*—which you may have heard before this. She is now reposing on her honors—seemingly well satisfied with the personal appearance of the very unexpected but not unwelcome young stranger—and deeming the matter "glory enough for one day."[6] (*Sub rosa*—a very small amount of this kind of glory would go a good way with the subscriber—*if* I were married—"which" I am *not* married, owing to the will of Providence and the "flickering" of my last.) And her nurse is *almost* the counterpart of Mrs. Gamp in "Martin Chuzzlewit"—who used to say—"No,—M no—which them is the very words I have said more nor once to Mrs. Harris—No, m'a'm—I am oppoged to drinking, I says—not that I mean to say that I do nor I don't, or I will or I won't, myself. But what *I* say, is, 'leave the bottle on the mankle-shelf, and let me put my lips to it when I'm so dispoged.[']" I don't mean to say that *this* Mrs. Gamp drinks—but I *do* say she *looks* just like the other Mrs. Gamp.[7]

Like all the letters of the family, *this* is to you and Mollie and Jennie[8]—*all*. And as I am "strapped"—and pushed for time, we'll sing the doxology, as follows—hoping to hear from all of you soon:

> "In the world's great field of battle,
> In the bivuac of life,
> Be not like dumb, driven cattle—
> Be a *hero* in the strife."[9]
>
> *Amen.*

> Vôtre frère,
> Sam. L. Clemens[10]

[1] It was actually Wednesday, 21 November. Clemens could not have returned from his trip on the *Augustus McDowell* by 20 November (see note 3).

[2] In the early hours of 11 November Clemens grounded the upward-bound *Alonzo Child* on the right-hand bank of the Mississippi, at the Houmas plantation, about seventy-three miles above New Orleans. No details of his effort "to beat another boat" have been discovered. Although the *General Quitman* attempted to pull the *Child* free, it remained stuck for twenty-eight hours, until a rising tide floated it off, and it did not arrive in St. Louis until early Sunday morning, 18 November. The following day, after Captain O'Neal had entered protest (that is, made formal explanation of the grounding), the *Child* went on the docks for repairs to its hull. It returned to the levee on 21 November, "looking as gay as a lark" ("Boats Leaving This Day," St. Louis *Missouri Republican*, 22 Nov 60, 4), but its departure for New Orleans was delayed by a heavy snowfall until 10:00 A.M. on Friday, 23 November ("River News," St. Louis *Evening News*, 15 Nov 60, 3; "River Intelligence," St. Louis *Missouri Democrat*, 16 Nov 60, 3; "Memoranda," St. Louis *Missouri Republican*, 19 Nov 60, 3).

[3] The *Augustus McDowell* was a New Orleans packet piloted by Jesse Jamison, a friend of Clemens's. Judging by the mileage figures reported here, the *McDowell* went aground on Monday, 19 November, in the Hat Island area, about twenty-five miles above Devil's Island Bend, which was probably the crossing Clemens wished to inspect before his next turn at the wheel of the *Child*. He returned to St. Louis by Wednesday, 21 November, presumably by hailing a passing upstream boat.

[4] William S. Patterson was aged fifty-eight; cousin James Clemens, Jr., was sixty-nine.

[5] Unidentified.

[6] Pamela Moffett's second child, Samuel Erasmus Moffett, was born in St. Louis on 5 November. Clemens implies the birth was premature.

[7] Dickens's *Life and Adventures of Martin Chuzzlewit* was originally published in 1843–44.

[8] Orion and Mollie's five-year-old daughter. In August she and Mollie had joined Orion in Memphis, Missouri (MEC, 9).

[9] Longfellow's "Psalm of Life" (stanza 5), collected in his first volume of verse, *Voices of the Night* (Cambridge, Mass.: John Owen, 1839).

[10] Before forwarding this letter, probably to her sister Belle Stotts in Keokuk, Mollie wrote the following in the margins and blank spaces of the original:

> Orion Cliant that was to bring us wood for a fee has disappinted us and Orion has just enguaged 5 cord hicory 2 dollars per cord all write often tell us all the news it is dull.
> Orion seams lowe spirited again
> I "hooked" ,crotched, Orion a pair of mittens last week, cost 15ᶜ
> Tell Miss Christfield to be care ful how she uses pain kill her I will write her soon.
> Hura for the weddings and woe to them this time next year
> Annie Martin wishes to get a guitar instructor like Rets upon my recomendation; she will send the money by Tom and you can tell him whare to get it or let him enquire of Ret when he goes. I think the price is $2,50ᶜ. She had a copy of your likeness taken from the one I have I asked Jennie what I should write for her she said you need not write for me I will write to them next Sunday. I am very sorry indeed to hear of Mary Anns family being sick I advise you to go thare (when you are in town) and help wait on them and there by heap coals of fire on her head I reproach myself for not going to see Ann, she has erred but she is yet a sister in name if not in action I think I will write her a letter soon Jennie requests me to say she got a new book 2 weeks today & she has learned it nearly all through but I will not tell her what is in it but I will read it to her when I go over thare.

Mollie also glossed Clemens's phrase *"Sub rosa"* with an asterisk and note: "Under my breath or in a whisper."

To the Worshipful Master, Wardens, and Brethren of Polar Star Lodge No. 79 of the Ancient, Free, and Accepted Order of Masons, *per* John M. Leavenworth

26 December 1860 • St. Louis, Mo.

(MS facsimile: *Masonic Light*, Feb 1926)

Saint Louis December 26 1860

To the W. M. Wardens and Bretheren of Polar Star Lodge No 79 A. F. and A. M.[1]

The subscriber residing in St Louis of lawful age and by occupation a Pilot begs leave to state that unbiased by friends and uninfluenced by mercenary motives he freely and voluntary offers himself as a candidate for the mysteries of Masonry and that he is prompted to solicit this privilege by a favorable opinion conceived of the Institution a desire of knowledge and a sincere wish of being serviceable to his fellow creatures. Should his petition be granted he will cheerfully conform to all the Ancient established usages and customs of the Fraternity

Recommended by   Signed
John M. Leavenworth
Tom Moore[2]   Sam. L. Clemens[3]
Comm.–
    H. T. Taylor
    Defriez
    Wannall[4]

[1] Polar Star Lodge No. 79, of St. Louis, had more members than any other Missouri lodge, among them many rivermen (Jones, 363–64).

[2] Moore and Clemens had been friends at least since they served together on the *John J. Roe* (see 6 July 59 to Moore). John M. Leavenworth was a clerk with the St. Louis wholesale grocery firm of William L. Ewing and Company (Robert V. Kennedy 1860, 161). He was also the brother of Mark and Zebulon Leavenworth, captain and pilot, respectively, of the *John J. Roe*, which Clemens had steered in August and September 1857.

[3] The signature is in Clemens's hand. Leavenworth and Moore also signed their own names.

[4] The members of the committee appointed to consider Clemens's petition have not been further identified. (One of them, evidently, inscribed these final four lines.) They reported favorably, and Clemens was elected on 13 February 1861. He received his first degree (Entered Apprentice) on 22 May, his second degree (Fellow Craft) on 12 June, and his third degree (Master Mason) on 10 July 1861. Although Clemens let his membership in Polar Star Lodge lapse while he was in the Far West, he did attend meetings of the Carson City and Angels Camp lodges on 24 March 1862 and 8 February 1865, respectively (Mace, 162). After reinstatement in Polar Star Lodge on 24 April 1867, he remained a Mason only until 8 October 1869, when the lodge granted his request for a demit, thereby accepting his resignation. (For a discussion of the Masonic influence on Clemens's thought and work, see Jones, 363–73.)

To Orion and Mary E. (Mollie) Clemens
6 February 1861 • Cairo, Ill.
(MS: NPV)

Ą Steamer "Alonzo Child,"
Cairo, Feb. 6th, 1861.

My Dear Brother:

After promising Mrs. Holliday a dozen times—(without anything further than a *very* remote intention of fulfilling the same,) to visit *the* fortune teller—Mad. Caprell—I have at last done so.[1] We lay in New Orleans a week; and towards the last, novelties begun to grow alarmingly scarce; *I* did not know what ∅ to do next—Will Bowen had given the matter up, and gone to bed for the balance of the trip; the Captain was on the Sugar Levee, and the clerks were out ~~in town~~ on business.[2] I was revolving in my mind another foray among the shipping, in search of beautiful figure-heads or paragons of nautical architecture, when I ~~remembered~~ happened to think of Mrs. Holliday; and as the Devil never comes unattended, I naturally thought of Mad. Caprell immediately after, and then I started toward the St. Charles Hotel for the express purpose of picking up one of the enchantress's bills, with a view to ascertaining her whereabouts—or, in ~~ot~~ simpler language, where she was supposed to "hang out." The bill said 37 Conti, above Tchoupitoulas—terms, \$2 for gentlemen in my situation, i.e. unaccompanied by a lady.

Arrived at the place, the bell was answered by a middle-aged lady (who certainly pitied me—I saw it in her eye,) who kindly informed me that I was at the wrong door—turn to the left. Which I did. And stood in the Awful Presence. She is a very pleasant little lady—rather pretty—about 28—say 5 feet 2¼—would weigh 116—has black eyes and hair—is polite and intelligent—uses good language, and talks much faster than *I* do.

She invited me into the little back parlor, closed the door; and we were—alone. We sat down facing each other. Then she asked my age. And then she put her hand before her eyes a moment, and commenced talking as if she had a good deal to say, and not much time to say it in. Something after this style:

"Yours is a watery planet; you gain your livelihood on the water; but you should have been a lawyer—there is where your talents lie; you might ∅ have distinguished yourself as an orator; or as an editor; you have written a great deal; you write well—but you are rather out of practice; no matter—you will be *in* practice some day;[3] you have a superb constitution; and as excellent health as any man in the world; you have great powers of endurance; in your profession, your are strength holds out against the longest sieges without flagging; still, the upper part of your lungs—the top of them, is slightly affected—and you must take more care of yourself; you do not drink, but you use *entirely* too much tobacco; and you must stop it; mind, not moderate, but *stop* the use of it, totally;[4] then, I can almost promise you 86, when you will surely die; otherwise, look out for 28, 31, 34, 47 and 65; be careful—for you are not of a long-

lived race, that is, on your *father's* side; you are the only healthy member
of your family, and the only one in it ~~with~~ who has any thing like the
certainty of attaining to a great age—so, stop using tobacco, and be careful of yourself; in nearly all respects, you are the best sheep in your flock;
your brother has an excellent mind, but it is not as well balanced as yours;
I should call yours the best mind, altogether; there is more unswerving
strength of will, & set purpose, and determination and energy in you than
in all the balance of your family put together; in some respects you take
after your father, but you are much *more* like your mother, who belongs
to the long-lived, energetic side of the house. (But Madam, you are too
fast—you have given me too much of these qualities.) No, I have not.
Don't interrupt me. I am telling the truth. And I'll prove it. Thus: ~~in reck~~
you never brought all your energies to bear upon an object, but what you
accomplished it—for instance, you are self-made, self-educated. (Which
proves nothing.) Don't interrupt. When you sought your present occupation, you found a thousand ~~gh~~ obstacles in your way—obstacles which
would have deterred nineteen out of any twenty men—obstacles unknown,—not even suspected by any save you and I, since you keep such
matters to yourself,—but you fought your way through them, during a
weary, weary length of time, and never flinched, or quailed, or ~~wis~~ never
once wished to give over the battle—and hid the long struggle under a
mask of cheerfulⁱness, which saved your friends anxiety on your account.
To do all this requires the qualities which I have named. (You flatter well,
Madam.) *Don't* interrupt. ¥ Up to within a short time, you had always
lived from hand to mouth—now, you are in easy circumstances—for
which you need give credit to no one but yourself. The turning-point in
your life occurred in 1847–8 (Which was?)—a death, perhaps; and this
threw you upon the world and made you what you are; it was always
intended that you should make yourself; therefore, ~~had this ca~~ it was well
that this calamity occurred as early as it did;[5] you will never die *of* water,
although your career upon it in the future seems well sprinkled with misfortune; but I *intreat* you to remember this: no matter *what* your circumstances are, in *September*, of the year ¥ in which you are 28, *don't* go *near*
the water—I will *not* tell you why, but by all that is true and good, I charge
you, while that month lasts, keep away from the water (which she repeated several times, with much show of earnestness—"make a note
on't,"[6] & let's see how much the woman knows.) Your life will be menaced
in the years I have before-mentioned— ~~im~~ will be in *imminent* peril when
you are 31—if you escape, then when you are 34—neither 47 or 65 look

so badly; you will continue upon the water for some time yet; you will not retire finally until ten years from now; *two* years from now, ~~on~~ or a little more, ~~you will be~~ *a child will be born to you!* (Permit me to hope, Madam, in view of this prospective good luck, that I may also have the jolly good-fortune to be *married* before that time.) Well, you are a free-spoken young man. *Of course* you will. (Make another note, Orion—I think I've caught her up a played-out chute in a falling river *this* time—but who knows?) And *mind*—your whole future welfare depends upon your getting married as soon as you can; don't smile—don't *laugh*—for it is just as true as truth itself; if you fail to marry within two years from now, you will regret that you paid so little attention to what I am saying now; don't be foolish, but go and marry—your future depends upon it; you can get the girl you have in your eye, if you are a better man than her mother—she (the girl) is; the old gentleman is not in the way, but the mother is decidedly *cranky*, and much in the way; *she* caused the trouble and produced the coolness which has existed between yourself and the young lady for so many months past—and you ought to break through this ice; you won't commence, and the girld won't—you are both entirely too proud—a well-matched pair, truly; the young lady is—(but I didn't ask after the young lady, Madam, and I don't want to hear about her.) *There*, just as I said—*she* would have spoken to me just as you have done. For shame! I must goń on. She is 17—not remarkably pretty, but very intelligent—is educated, and accomplished—and has property—5 feet 3 inches—is slender—dark-brown hair and eyes—you don't want to see her? Oh, no—but you will, nevertheless, before this year is out—here in New Orleans (mark that,) too—and then—look out! The fact of her being so far away now—which is the case, is it not?—doesn't affect the matter.[7] You will marry *twice*—your first wife will live (I have forgotten the number of years,)—your second choice will be a widow—you[r] family, finally, all told, will number *ten* children (slow—Madam—slow—and stand by to ship up[8]—for I know you are out of the channel,) some of them will live, and some will not at- (there's consolation in the latter, at least.) Yes, ten is the number. (You must think I am *fond* of children.) And you *are*, although you pretend the contrary—which is an ugly habit; quit it; I grant you that you do not like to *handle* them, though. What is your brother's age? 33?—and a lawyer?—and in pursuit of an office?[9] Well, he stands a better chance than the other two, and, he *may* get it—he must do his best—and not trust too much to others, either—which is the very reason why he is so far behind, now; he never *does* do anything, if he can get anybody else to do it for him; which is bad; he never goes steadily on till he attains an object, but nearly always drops it when the battle is half won; he is too visionary—is always flying off on a new hobby; this will never do—tell him I said so. He is a good lawyer—a *very* good lawyer—and a fine speaker—is very popular, and much respected, and makes many friends; but although he retains their friendship, he loses their confidence, by displaying his instability of character; he wants to speculate in lands, and *will*, some day, with very good success; the land he has now will be very valuable after a while (say 250 years hence, or thereabouts, Madam,)—no—less time—but never mind the land, that is a secondary consideration—let him drop that for the present, and devote himself to his business and politics, with all his might, for he must hold offices under government, and 6 or 8 years from this time, he will run for Congress. You will marry, and will finally live in the South—do not live in the northwest; you will not succeed well; you will live in the South, and after a while you will possess a good deal of property—retire at the end of ten years—after which your pursuits will be literary—try the law—you will certainly succeed. I am done, now. If you have any questions to ask—ask them freely—and if it be in my power, I will answer without reserve[*]—without reserve."

I asked a few questions of minor importance—paid her $2 and left—under the decided impression that going to the fortune-teller's was just as good as going to the Opera, and cost scarcely a trifle more—*ergo*, I would disguise myself and go again, one of these days, when other amusements failed.

Now isn't she the devil? That is to say, isn't she a right smart little woman? I have given you almost her very language to me, and nothing extenuated, nor set down aught in malice.[10] Whenever she said anything pointed about you, she would ask me to tell you of it, so that you might profit by it—and confound me if I don't think she read you a good deal better than she did me. That Congress business amused me a little, for she wasn't far wide of the mark you set yourself, as to time. And Pa's death in '47–8, and the turning-point in my life, was very good. I wonder if there is a Past and future chronological table of events in a man's life written in his forehead for the special convenience of these clairvoyants? She said Pa's side of the house was not long-lived, but that *he* doctored himself to death. I do not know about that, though.[11] She said that up to 7 years, I had no health, and then mentioned several dates after that when my health had been very bad.[12] But that about that girl's [mother] being "cranky," and playing the devil with me, *was* about the neatest thing she performed—for although I have never spoken of the matter, I happen to know that she spoke truth. The young lady has been beaten by the old one, ˌthough,ˌ through the romantic agency of intercepted letters, and the girl still thinks *I* was in fault—and always will, I reckon, for I don't see how she'll ever find out the contrary. And the woman had the impudence to say that although I was eternally falling in love, still, when I went to bed at night, I somehow always happened to think of Miss Laura before I thought of my last new flame—and it always would be the case (which will be devilish comfortable, won't it, when both she and I (like one of Dickens' characters,) are Another's?[)]¹³ But drat the woman, she *did* tell the truth, and I won't deny it. But she said *I* would speak to Miss Laura first—and I'll stake my last shirt on it, she missed it there.¹⁴

So much for Madame Caprell. Although of course, I p̸ have no faith in her pretended powers, I listened to her in silence for half an hour, with~~out~~ the greatest interest, and I am willing to acknowledge that she said some very startˌling things, and made some wonderful guesses. Upon leaving, she said I must take care of myself; that it had cost me ˌseveral, years to build up my constitution to its present state of perfection, and now I must watch it. And she would give me this motto: "L'ouvrage de l'année est détruit dans un jour,"—which means, if you don't know it, "The work of a year is destroyed in a day."

We shall not go to St. Louis. Turn back from here, to-morrow or next day. When you want money, let Ma know, and she will send it. She and Pamela are always fussing about small change, so I sent them a hundred and twenty *quarters* yesterday—fiddler's change enough to last till I get back, I reckon.

                                   Ɏ Votre frère,
                                          Sam.

Dear Mollie:
      You owe me one.   (over

                     (To be continued.)

                                   Ɏ Ton ♭ Ƒ frère,
                                          Sam Clemens

<hr>

¹ Mrs. Richard Holliday (b. Melicent S. McDonald, ca. 1800) was a well-to-do, twice-widowed resident of Hannibal, the acknowledged prototype for Widow Douglas in *Tom Sawyer* and *Huckleberry Finn*. Annie Moffett Webster recalled

her as a frequent visitor at the Moffett home in St. Louis. In "Villagers of 1840–3," Clemens described her as "Well off. Hospitable. Fond of having parties of young people. Widow. Old, but anxious to marry. Always consulting fortune-tellers; always managed to make them understand that she had been promised 3 [husbands] by the first fraud. They always confirmed the prophecy. She finally died before the prophecies had a full chance" (*Inds*, 96 and biographical directory; *MTBus*, 49). Madame Caprell practiced her trade between 1857 and 1861 not only in New Orleans, but in Memphis and St. Louis as well. In various newspaper advertisements she boasted that, being endowed with "Spirit Vision" at birth, she could calculate horoscopes, reveal "all that was in the past, all that is in the present, and . . . all that will be in the future," "minutely point out and properly prescribe for all diseases of the human frame," and "answer any question relating to . . . Marriage or Absent Friends, and . . . future partners." All this she accomplished merely by inquiring "the age of the person, and then, by consulting the planets" (New Orleans *Picayune*: "Madame Caprell," 15 Mar 60, 4; "M'me Caprell," 5 Mar 61, 6; "Madame Caprell . . . Has Arrived in Town," Memphis *Appeal*, 9 Nov 58, 2). In her encounter with Clemens, Madame Caprell indubitably profited from her acquaintance with Mrs. Holliday, whom Samuel C. Webster characterized as "a fluent talker, even without encouragement," who "knew the whole background of the Clemens family" (*MTBus*, 58).

[2] The *Alonzo Child* was in New Orleans from 24 through 29 January. William Bowen, with whom Clemens had served briefly on the *A. B. Chambers*, was his co-pilot. The *Child*'s clerks were William B. McBride, Ed Lee Bready, and a Mr. Matsenbaugh (or Metzenbaugh). The captain was James O'Neal (d. 1899), who in his more than fifty years on the Ohio, Missouri, and Mississippi rivers held virtually every position of responsibility in steamboating, serving as clerk, pilot, master, boat designer and builder, superintendent of the Anchor Line, and United States supervising inspector of steam vessels. Clemens recalled him affectionately in 1866 (see 25 Aug 66 to Bowen).

[3] Clemens is thought to have written only one sketch since August 1859—"Pilot's Memoranda," published in the St. Louis *Missouri Republican* on 30 August 1860 (*ET&S1*, 142–45).

[4] In 1880, Orion Clemens commented on several points in this letter, which he planned to publish as part of his autobiography. One of these notes survives on the letter itself; the others only in a copy that Mark Twain read into his own autobiographical dictation many years later. About tobacco Orion simply observed that "Sam smoked too much for many years, and still smokes" (AD, 29 Jan 1907, CU-MARK). On 26 August 1907, Clemens recalled his early attitudes toward smoking. According to a note made that day by his secretary, Isabel Lyon:

He was speaking of the power of breaking away from a habit & said that when he was a cub pilot he made up his mind not to chew tobacco any longer. He had the plug in his pocket, & he didn't throw it away & so burn his bridges behind him—no,—he kept the plug in his pocket until it was in a powder, & he never chewed again. He said probably some outside influence was the cause of his reform. Then he decided twice to stop smoking, once when he was a young man in Keokuk I should say & he was firm in his resolve until he decided to resume again. Then just before he married he stopped again. (Lyon, 238)

[5] In 1880 Orion noted, "My father died March 24, 1847, Sam being then 11 years of age. My mother took him from school, and set him to learning the printing business" (AD, 29 Jan 1907, CU-MARK). Clemens was apprenticed to printer Henry La Cossitt in 1847 and subsequently to Joseph P. Ament, probably

in May 1848, but he clearly continued in school for part of the time until at least 1849 (Wecter, 200–202; *Inds*, biographical directory).

[6] One of the recurrent locutions of Captain Ned Cuttle in Dickens's *Dombey and Son* (1846–48).

[7] When Clemens first met Laura M. Wright (1844–1932) in May 1858, she was visiting New Orleans aboard the *John J. Roe* as the guest of her uncle, William C. Youngblood, a pilot friend of Clemens's. Clemens recalled in 1906 that "she wasn't yet fifteen when I knew her. It was in the summertime, and she had gone down the Mississippi from St. Louis to New Orleans" on the *Roe*, "a steamboat whose officers I knew very well" (AD, 30 July 1906, CU-MARK, in *AMT*, 79). Laura Wright was from Warsaw, Missouri, on the Osage River some one hundred and fifty miles west of St. Louis. Her father, Foster Pellatier Wright (b. 1809), had married her mother, Nancy Jacqueline McClanahan (b. ca. 1820), in 1837, the same year he had been appointed judge of the seventh circuit in Missouri and moved to Warsaw (Laura Wright Dake biographical documents, PH in CU-MARK, courtesy of Howard G. Baetzhold). By September 1864, Laura had presumably married Mr. Dake: "What has become of that girl of mine that got married?" Clemens wrote his mother on 25 September 1864. "I mean Laura Wright." Despite Clemens's repeated claim that he met and parted from Laura only once, it is clear that the two corresponded over an unknown period of time, and that Clemens made at least one trip to Warsaw itself. Thomas Murray wrote him in 1880, for instance, "I remember a young man, (and often have I thought of him,) bearing your honored name. I met him at Warsaw, Mo., before the war, 'fighting for his *Wright's.*' I was then chief clerk of the Missouri Legislature—he, a sailor on the Father of Waters. We met at Judge Wright's: he, courting Laura; I, eating Brandy peaches with the Mother" (Murray to SLC, 8 May 80, CU-MARK). Even before receiving this letter, however, Clemens acknowledged his memory of Laura in a letter to one of her pupils: "She was a very little girl, with a very large spirit, a long memory, a wise head, a great appetite for books, a good mental digestion, with grave ways, & inclined to introspection—an unusual girl" (20 May 80 to D. W. Bowser, TxU, in Covici, 108). See also note 14.

[8] The full phrase is "to ship up to back," meaning "to stop both sidewheels and get ready to reverse them, in order to back the steamboat" (*Lex*, 204).

[9] Born on 17 July 1825, Orion Clemens was in fact thirty-five. On 7 January 1861 he had written from Memphis, Missouri, to Clemens, enclosing

a letter introducing you to Mr. Glover. I think if not very busy he will immediately write you a letter of introduction to Mr. Bates, and also a letter recommending me for a clerkship. He would do this with you sitting by him, when probably he would not take the trouble or time to do so if I merely wrote directly to him. . . . It will be a great advantage to me to get some such office, as I can then support myself and family, which will be a huge gratification, and probably be able to pay some debts, which will also be gratifying. (CU-MARK)

The upshot of this process was that Edward Bates (1793–1869), Lincoln's attorney general, secured Orion's appointment as secretary of the newly formed Nevada Territory. Orion "received notice of his appointment on the 27 of March" (MEC, 10).

[10] *Othello*, act 5, scene 2.

[11] In 1880, Orion wrote on the last page of the original letter:

Reading the foregoing letter after 20 years, I thought she might have read Sam's mind, till I came to the paragraph in which he states that he did not know that our father doctored

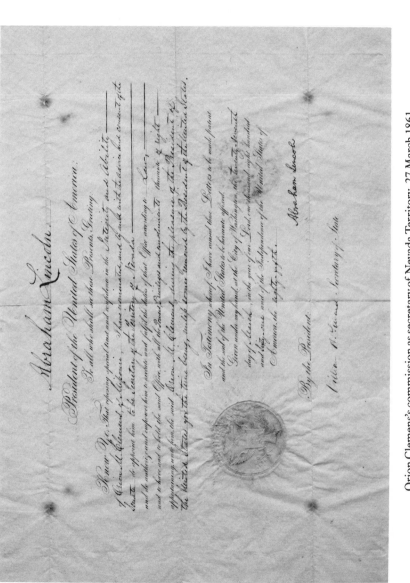

Orion Clemens's commission as secretary of Nevada Territory, 27 March 1861. Mark Twain Papers, The Bancroft Library (CU-MARK).

himself to death. He doctored himself from my earliest remembrance. During the latter part of his life he bought Cook's pills by the box, and took some daily. He was very dexterous at throwing a pill to the root of his tongue, washing it down with a sip of water.

And in the notes preserved in Clemens's autobiographical dictation, he somewhat expanded this comment:

> My mother's mother died when my mother was 13 years of age. Her father died at the age of 63. Her grandfather on her father's side lived beyond 60, and his widow beyond 80. On my father's side his father was killed accidentally when my father was 7 years old. My father's mother lived beyond 60. My father died at 48. My mother is now (1880) 78. My father may have hastened the ending of his life by the use of too much medicine. He doctored himself from my earliest remembrance. During the latter part of his life he bought Cook's pills by the box and took one or more daily. In taking a pill he held it between his right thumb and forefinger, turned his head back, cast the pill to the root of his tongue, and from a glass of water in his left hand, took a sup and washed down the bitter dose. (AD, 29 Jan 1907, CU-MARK)

Family records indicate that pneumonia was the immediate cause of John Marshall Clemens's death.

[12] In 1880 Orion noted, "Sam was delicate when a child" (AD, 29 Jan 1907, CU-MARK).

[13] Clemens alludes to the lovelorn Augustus Moddle in *Martin Chuzzlewit*.

[14] In 1907 Clemens was still impressed by the accuracy of Madame Caprell's words: "Her references to my sweetheart, and her description of the sweetheart, and of how our estrangement was brought about, is so exactly in accordance with the facts, that I feel sure she pumped these things out of me without my being aware of it" (AD, 27 Jan 1907, CU-MARK). In 1917 Laura Wright Dake told Paine, "*I* understand why Mr. C. *thought* his letters were intercepted" (Dake to Albert Bigelow Paine, 26 Jan 1917, PH in CU-MARK, courtesy of Robert Daley), but she did not explain the true cause of their disaffection. Whatever the cause, Clemens's memory of Laura proved remarkably persistent: it is she who appears and reappears as his "dream-sweetheart" in "My Platonic Sweetheart," written in 1898 and published posthumously by Paine (SLC 1912, 14–20; see Baetzhold, 414–29).

To Orion Clemens
18 March 1861 • St. Louis, Mo.
(Transcript and MS, *damage emended:*
MTL, 1:45–47, and NPV)

St. Louis, Mch 18.[1]

My Dear Bro.,

Your last has just come to hand. It reminds me strongly of Tom Hood's letters to his family, (which I have been reading lately).[2] But yours only *remind* me of his, for although there is a striking likeness, your humour is much finer than his, and far better expressed. Tom Hood's *wit*, (in his letters) has a savor of *labor* about it which is very disagreeable. Your letter is good. That portion of it wherein the old sow figures is the very best thing I have seen lately. Its quiet style resembles Goldsmith's "Citizen of the World," and "Don Quixote,"—which are my *beau ideals* of fine writing.

You have paid the preacher! Well, that is good, also. What a man wants with religion in these breadless times, surpasses my comprehension.

Pamela and I have just returned from a visit to the most wonderfully beautiful painting which this city has ever seen—Church's "Heart of the Andes"—which represents a lovely valley with its rich vegetation in all the bloom and glory of a tropical summer—dotted with birds and flowers of all colors and shades of color, and sunny slopes, and shady corners, and twilight groves, and cool cascades—all grandly set off with a majestic mountain in the background with its gleaming summit clothed in everlasting ice and snow! I have seen it several times, but it is always a new picture—*totally* new—you seem to see nothing the second time which you saw the first. We took the opera glass, and examined its beauties minutely, for the naked eye cannot discern the little wayside flowers, and soft shadows and patches of sunshine, and half-hidden bunches of grass and jets of water which form some of its most enchanting features. There is no slurring of perspective effect about it—the most distant—the minutest object in it has a marked and distinct *personality*—so that you may count the very leaves on the trees. When you first see the tame, ordinary-looking picture, your first impulse is to turn your back upon it, and say "Humbug"—but your third visit will find your brain *gasping* and straining with futile efforts to take all the wonder in—and appreciate it in its fulness—and understand how such a miracle could have been conceived and executed by human brain and human hands. You will never get tired of looking at the picture, but your reflections—your efforts to grasp an intelligible Something—you hardly know what—will grow so painful that you will have to go away from the thing, in order to obtain relief. You may find relief, but you cannot banish the picture—it remains with you still. It is in my mind now—and the smallest feature could not be removed without my detecting it. So much for the "Heart of the Andes."[3]

Ma was delighted with her trip, but she was disgusted with the girls for allowing me to embrace and kiss them—and she was horrified at the

Schottische as performed by Miss Castle and me. She was perfectly willing for me to dance until 12 o'clock at the imminent peril of my going to
sleep on the after watch—but then she would top off with a very inconsis-
tent sermon on dancing in general; ending with a terrific broadside aimed
at that heresy of heresies, the Schottische.[4]

I took Ma and the girls in a carriage, round that portion of New
Orleans where the finest gardens and residences are to be seen, and although it was a blazing hot dusty day, they seemed hugely delighted. To
use an expression which is commonly ignored in polite society, they were
"hell-bent" on stealing some of the luscious-looking oranges from
branches which overhung the fences, but I restrained them. They were
not aware before that shrubbery could be made to take any queer shape
which a skilful gardener might choose to twist it into, so they found not
only beauty but novelty in their visit. We went out to Lake Pontchartrain
in the cars.

Your Brother

Sam. Clemens

P. S. Ma has got a ,($25), check for the money and asked me to enclose it.

P. P. S.—I owe Mollie one!

[1] In the absence of all but a few fragments of the original manuscript, the principal source for this letter is Paine's text in *MTL*, where he printed the year as
1860—probably a guess necessitated by the manuscript's giving place and day
but no year. The correct year is established by Clemens's subsequent reference to
Church's *Heart of the Andes*, first exhibited in St. Louis between 27 February and
21 March 1861 ("Amusements," St. Louis *Missouri Republican*, 27 Feb and 18
Mar 61, 4).

[2] Clemens was probably referring to Thomas Hood's *Up the Rhine* (1839), an
epistolary novel recounting a family's holiday in Germany (see Brashear, 218–22).

[3] Frederic Edwin Church (1826–1900) first exhibited this painting in the spring
of 1859 at his New York studio, drawing crowds of thousands willing to pay
twenty-five cents to view it. After showings in London and Edinburgh, *Heart of
the Andes* was returned to New York and subsequently exhibited in Boston, Philadelphia, Cincinnati, Chicago, and St. Louis (Huntington, 5–6). Clemens's "several" visits to see it at the Western Academy of Art must have occurred between
15 and 18 March (see note 4). Almost thirty years later Clemens became friends
with Church, visiting him at Olana, his mansion on the Hudson River (Church to
SLC, 16 Dec 87, CU-MARK).

[4] Clemens had taken his mother, a Miss Castle from St. Louis, and an otherwise
unidentified young woman to New Orleans aboard the *Alonzo Child*. On 27 February, the *Child* left St. Louis carrying twenty to thirty couples of young people
from Boonville, Missouri—for many years Captain David DeHaven's home—for
a pleasure trip south. "They were a gay party, and came in a body as a special

Heart of the Andes by Frederic E. Church, oil on canvas, 1859.
The Metropolitan Museum of Art, Bequest of Mrs. David Dows, 1909 (09.95).

compliment to Captain D. DeHaven, who has just resumed command of his fine boat, after a protracted illness" ("River News," St. Louis *Evening News*, 28 Feb 61, 3). The *Child* reached New Orleans on 6 March, departed two days later, and arrived back in St. Louis on 15 March. A "fine band of music," which presumably played for the schottische (a dance similar to the polka), reportedly accompanied the party ("River News," St. Louis *Missouri Republican*, 16 Mar 61, 4). Paine identified the third guest, with varying degrees of certainty, as Clemens's cousin Ella Creel (see *MTB*, 1:156, and *MTL*, 1:47).

To Orion Clemens
26 April 1861 • *Hannibal City* en route
from St. Louis to Hannibal, Mo.
(MS: NPV)

Steamer "Hannibal City"
Under Way, Apl. 26.

My dear Brother:

I am on the wing for ~~Louisiana,~~[1] ˏHannibal, to collect money due me. I shall return to St Louis to-morrow.[2]

Orion bring down "Armageddon" with you if you have it. If not, *buy* it.[3]

Yr. Brother
Sam. Clemens

---

[1] Louisiana, Missouri, some twenty-five miles below Hannibal.

[2] Clemens arrived at St. Louis aboard the *Alonzo Child* on 25 April. Paine has hinted, and Samuel C. Webster has suggested, that Clemens's purpose in making this trip was to size up the small group of his rebel friends which may even then have been forming in Hannibal (*MTB*, 1:163; *MTBus*, 61). But Clemens's brief military experience came almost seven weeks later. It is more likely that, as he states, his purpose was to collect on outstanding debts. William Bowen, for one, had borrowed $200 from him, promising—but failing—to repay the loan on 26 February 1861. Clemens may have hoped to settle this debt now, although later he claimed that he had never intended to collect it (see 25 Aug 66 to Bowen). Bowen, who had left the *Child*, had just completed supervising the construction of a Hannibal boardinghouse to be run by his mother—"a commodious and taste-fully finished building, three stories high and containing 20 rooms. These have been furnished in magnificent style at considerable trouble and expense" ("A New Private Boarding House," Hannibal *Weekly Messenger*, 18 Apr 61, 2). Clemens probably returned to St. Louis on 28 April as a passenger on the *Die Vernon*.

[3]*Armageddon*, by Samuel D. Baldwin, was first published in about 1845. In 1880 Orion described it in a note on Clemens's letter:

"Armageddon" was a book written by a Baptist preacher of Nashville, to prove that the end of the world would come about 1860 to 1875. The author located Armageddon in the Mississippi Valley. In the battle of Armageddon the United States would defeat Russia and other European powers, after which Republicanism and the milennium would reign universally.

Orion was expected in St. Louis to confer about his plans to move to the West. On 27 March notice of his appointment as secretary of Nevada Territory reached him in Memphis, Missouri, and his commission itself arrived on 20 April. Six days later he left Memphis with his wife and daughter, arriving with them in Keokuk, Iowa, Mollie Clemens's home, on 27 April. That night he started alone for St. Louis to see his mother, brother, and sister (MEC, 10). The North and South had now been at war for two weeks, and Orion, before returning to Keokuk to prepare to assume his Nevada post, may have suggested that Clemens accompany him to the new territory.

NO LETTERS are known to survive for the next five months. After spending a few days with his family in St. Louis at the end of April 1861, Clemens rejoined the *Alonzo Child* for its 2 May departure, arriving in New Orleans six days later. The *Child*'s flamboyantly secessionist captain, David DeHaven, decided not to return north, but to run the boat instead in the Memphis–New Orleans trade. The best evidence indicates that Clemens left the *Child* and went north as a passenger on the *Nebraska*, departing New Orleans on 14 May and arriving at St. Louis on 21 May. The *Nebraska* was the last boat to gain free passage to the upper Mississippi through the Union blockade at Memphis, which put a virtual end to commercial traffic on the river (see Mattson, 398–409). After a little more than two years as a licensed pilot, Clemens was forced to abandon his profession.

Annie Moffett Webster later recalled that in the weeks following his arrival in St. Louis, Clemens spent most of his time in the Moffett home, hiding for fear "that he might be arrested by government agents and forced to act as pilot on a government gunboat" (*MTBus*, 60). In mid-June Clemens went to Hannibal and there joined the Marion Rangers, a desultory band of would-be Confederate volunteers. This connection with the Southern cause—depicted with humor and pathos in "The Private History of a Campaign That Failed" (SLC 1885b, 193–204)—ended after about two weeks. By early July Clemens was back in St. Louis. On the fourth of that month Orion Clemens, who was now ready to take up

Receipt for Orion and Samuel Clemens's stagecoach passage from
St. Joseph, Missouri, to Carson City, Nevada Territory. Orion paid $300 the
day before their 26 July departure, and promised to pay the balance within
thirty days. Mark Twain Papers, The Bancroft Library (CU-MARK).

his post as secretary of Nevada Territory, came down from Keokuk,
where he was leaving his family. Orion

prevailed on his Brother Sam to go to his new home with him. They left St Louis
on the 18 of July on the Soux City, for St Joe. There they took passage in the Over
land Coach—a mail conveyance which began to run daily between St Joe. Missouri and Sacramento California

They left St Joe. on the 26 of July Arrived in Carson City Nevada Territory on
the 14 of Aug 1700 miles from St Joe. and 580 miles West of Great Salt Lake City.
(MEC, 11)

Clemens gave his own account of the western journey in the first twenty
chapters of *Roughing It.* (Some important corrections, particularly in regard to his financial arrangements with and employment by Orion, can
be found in William C. Miller, 1–9; for Orion's recollections of the trip
see *RI*, supplement D, 546–50.) Early in September he made his first
visit to Aurora, in the Esmeralda mining district, evidently remaining at
least until the tenth of the month (see 25 Oct 61 to JLC and PAM, n. 4).
Allowing time for travel he probably arrived back in Carson City on 12
September. There he wrote the next letter.

To Mary E. (Mollie) Clemens
12? September 1861 • Carson City, Nev. Terr.
(MS, *damage emended:* NPV)

. . . .

well, although I believe I never had the pleasure of her acquaintance,) and left for California the same day; and I told him plainly that I did not believe it, and wouldn't, if he ⱴ swore it—for I didn't, Mollie, and did[n't] think Billy could be as stupid as that. On the contrary, I thought he was the most talented boy that Keokuk had ever produced. But when I got back, Orion confirmed Billy's statement—so, you see, I am *forced* to believe that—(that they are both liars.) If *I* ever ‸were to‸ marry, I should would certainly stay at home a week, even if the Devil were in town with a writ for my arrest.[1]

Why don't Ma and Pamela write? Please kiss Jennie for me[2]——

(P. S.—And tell her when she is fifteen years old, I will kiss her my-self——)

(P. S.—If she is good-looking.)

P. S.—Don't get "huffy."

P. S.—Write.

Thine,

Sam. L. Clemens

---

[1] Clemens knew William Horace Clagett (1838–1901) while Clagett was studying law in Keokuk in 1856 and 1857. Admitted to the bar in September 1858, Clagett "practiced law in Keokuk and made his first political speeches for [Stephen] Douglas in the campaign of 1860. In the spring of 1861 he was married to Miss Mary E. Hart. . . . On the day of his marriage he, with his brother George, started across the plains for California. . . . He had a hard trip across the plains, and finding nothing better to do, went to work cutting and hauling wood near Dayton, Nevada" (Dixon, 249–50; see also Andrew J. Marsh, 698). Clagett briefly practiced law in Carson City before accompanying Clemens to the Humboldt district in December 1861, eventually settling in Unionville. Mary Clagett (b. 1840 or 1841) was the daughter of a Keokuk merchant. In the fall of 1862 she accompanied Mollie Clemens to Nevada when both women came to rejoin their husbands (*Keokuk Census* [1860], 48; MEC to OC, 1 Sept 62, CU-MARK). Clemens's remarks on marriage may have been evoked in part by a 2 August letter in which Mollie informed Orion of her sister's imminent wedding (see the next let-

ter, n. 6). Mollie's letter reached Carson City on 9 September, and Clemens could have seen it on the twelfth, the estimated date of his return from Aurora.

[2] Jennie Clemens's sixth birthday, on 14 September 1861, presumably was the occasion for Clemens's "kiss" and the joking that follows.

To Jane Lampton Clemens
18–21 September 1861 • Carson City, Nev. Terr.
(*MTL*, 1:56–59)

. . . The level ranks of flame were relieved at intervals by the standard-bearers, as we called the tall dead trees, wrapped in fire, and waving their blazing banners a hundred feet in the air. Then we could turn from this scene to the Lake, and see every branch, and leaf, and cataract of flame upon its bank perfectly reflected as in a gleaming, fiery mirror. The mighty roaring of the conflagration, together with our solitary and somewhat unsafe position (for there was no one within six miles of us,) rendered the scene very impressive. Occasionally, one of us would remove his pipe from his mouth and say,—"*Superb! magnificent! Beautiful!*—but—by the Lord God Almighty, if we attempt to sleep in this little patch to-night, we'll never live till morning!—for if we don't burn up, we'll certainly suffocate." But he was persuaded to sit up until we felt pretty safe as far as the *fire* was concerned, and then we turned in, with many misgivings. When we got up in the morning, we found that the fire had burned small pieces of drift wood within six feet of our boat, and had made its way to within 4 or 5 steps of us on the South side. We looked like *lava* men, covered as we were with ashes, and begrimed with smoke. We were very black in the face, but we soon washed ourselves white again.[1]

John D. Kinney, a Cincinnati boy, and a first-rate fellow, too, who came out with Judge Turner, was my comrade.[2] We staid at the Lake four days[3]—I had plenty of fun, for John constantly reminded me of Sam Bowen when we were on our campaign in Missouri. But first and foremost, for *Annie's*, Mollie's, and Pamela's comfort, be it known that I have never been guilty of profane language since I have been in this Territory, and Kinney hardly ever swears.[4] But *sometimes* human nature gets the better of him. On the second day we started to go by land to the lower camp, a distance of three miles, over the mountains, each carrying an axe.[5] I don't think we got *lost* exactly, but we wandered four hours over the steepest, rockiest and most dangerous piece of country in the world. I couldn't keep from laughing at Kinney's distress, so I kept behind, so that he could not see me. After he would get over a dangerous place, with infinite labor and constant apprehension, he would stop, lean on his axe, and look around, then behind, then ahead, and then drop his head and ruminate awhile. Then he would draw a long sigh, and say: "Well—could any Billygoat have scaled that place without breaking his —— neck?" And I would reply, "No,—I don't think he could." "No—you don't think he could—" (mimicking me,) "Why don't you *curse* the infernal place? You know you *want* to. *I* do, and *will* curse the ———— thieving country as long as I live." Then we would toil on in silence for awhile. Finally I told him—"Well, John, what if we *don't* find our way out of this today— we'll know all about the country when we *do* get out." "Oh stuff—I know enough—and *too much* about the d—d villainous locality already." Finally, we reached the camp. But as we brought no provisions with us, the first subject that presented itself to us was, how to get back. John swore he wouldn't *walk* back, so we rolled a drift log apiece into the Lake, and set about making paddles, intending to straddle the logs and paddle ourselves back home sometime or other. But the Lake objected—got stormy, and we had to give it up. So we set out for the only house on this side of the Lake—three miles from there, down the shore. We found the way without any trouble, reached there before sundown, played three games of cribbage, borrowed a dug-out and pulled back six miles to the upper camp. As we had eaten nothing since sunrise, we did not waste time in cooking our supper or in eating it, either. After supper we got out our pipes—built a rousing camp fire in the open air—established a faro bank (an institution of this country,) on our huge flat granite dining table, and bet white beans till one o'clock, when John went to bed. We were up before the sun the next morning, went out on the Lake and caught a fine trout for breakfast. But unfortunately, I spoilt part of the breakfast. We had coffee and tea boiling on the fire, in coffee-pots and fearing they might not be strong enough, I added more ground coffee, and more tea, but—you know mistakes will happen. I put the tea in the coffee-pot, and the coffee in the tea-pot—and if you imagine that they were not villainous mixtures, just try the effect once.

And so Belle is to be married on the 1st of Oct.[6] Well, I send her and her husband my very best wishes, and—I may not be here—but wherever I am on that night, we'll have a rousing camp-fire and a jollification in honor of the event.

In a day or two we shall probably go to the Lake and build another cabin and fence, and get everything into satisfactory trim before our trip to Esmeralda about the first of November.[7]

What has become of Sam Bowen? I would give my last shirt to have him out here. I will make no promises, but I believe if John would give him a thousand dollars and send him out here he would not regret it. He might possibly do very well here, but he could do little without capital.[8]

Remember me to all my St. Louis and Keokuk friends, and tell Challie and Hallie Benson that I heard a military band play "What are the Wild Waves Saying?" the other night, and it reminded me very forcibly of them.[9] It brought Ella Creel and Belle across the Desert too in an instant, for they sang the song in Orion's yard the first time I ever heard it. It was like meeting an old friend. I tell you I could have swallowed that whole band, trombone and all, if such a compliment would have been any gratification to them.

Love to the young folks,[10]

Sam.

[1] In chapter 23 of *Roughing It*, Clemens confessed to having caused this conflagration at Lake Bigler (Tahoe) while preparing to cook dinner over a camp fire. Some of the details included in the book probably also appeared in the missing portion of this letter.

[2] Kinney (1840–78), described in *Roughing It* as the "young son of an Ohio nabob" (chapter 22), had been a teller in his father's Cincinnati bank. He had come overland from St. Louis with George Turner and Horatio M. Jones, the recently appointed chief justice and associate justice of Nevada Territory, arriving in Carson City the second week of September 1861—probably on the tenth or eleventh. (Hence the trip to Lake Bigler described here could not have taken place around "the end of August," as Mark Twain mistakenly recalled in *Roughing It.*) In Carson City, Kinney was a real-estate dealer and mining speculator until early in March 1862, when he returned to his father's bank (see 8 and 9 Mar 62 to Clagett). He twice volunteered for service in the Civil War: before coming to Nevada he enlisted in the Sixth Ohio Infantry, and after returning to Ohio he became a captain in the Seventh Ohio Cavalry (C. S. Williams: 1861, 211; 1863, 220; "Letter from St. Louis," San Francisco *Evening Bulletin*, 10 Sept 61, 1; Liberal, 3; Kelly 1862, 83; deeds and PH of Kinney's military-service records in CU-MARK, courtesy of Michael H. Marleau).

[3] It seems probable that Clemens and Kinney met in Carson City on 12 or 13 September and then went together to Lake Bigler between the fourteenth and seventeenth of the month. Since they spent four days at the lake, a reasonable range of dates for the composition of this letter is 18–21 September.

[4] Kinney must have been a formidable swearer if he reminded Clemens of Samuel A. Bowen. During the Marion Rangers' June 1861 "campaign in Missouri," which Clemens surely had described to his family before going West, Bowen swore continually, cursing Clemens, cursing picket duty, and even cursing in his sleep. Joe Bowers, the character based on Bowen in "The Private History of a Campaign That Failed," exhibits a similar propensity (SLC 1885b, 197; working notes for SLC 1885b, CU-MARK). Clemens enjoyed teasing his mother and sister about the pledge not to swear which they had extracted from him (see 8 and 9 Feb 62 to JLC and PAM).

[5] The camps mentioned in this letter had been set up and stocked with provisions in August by eleven Carson City friends and retainers of territorial governor James W. Nye (members of the "Irish Brigade" in chapter 21 of *Roughing It*). These men formed John Nye and Company, named for the governor's brother, which on 24 August had entered timber claims located on the northeastern shore of Lake Bigler (memorandum of agreement and copartnership, 24 Aug 61, PH in CU-MARK, courtesy of Michael H. Marleau; Mack 1936, 222).

[6] On 9 September Orion replied to a 2 August letter from Mollie, "I think Tom Bohon will do very well for Belle" (CU-MARK). His wife's younger sister did marry Thomas B. Bohon on 1 October 1861.

[7] In order to locate a claim on timber land it was necessary to build a fence around the property and a house on it—requirements that Clemens and Kinney met by felling "three trees apiece" (the fence) and building a house of brush barely distinguishable from "the surrounding vegetation" (*Roughing It*, chapter 22). Of course their handiwork was obliterated by the forest fire. Paine asserted that the two men made later trips to Lake Bigler and "located other claims—claims in which the 'folks at home' . . . were included" (*MTB*, 1:180; see also 25 Oct 61 to JLC and PAM). Very possibly one such trip was made between 22 and 28 September. A stay of several days then, coming after the initial four-day visit in the middle of the month, would help account for Clemens's later impression that he and Kinney spent "two or three weeks" at the lake (*Roughing It*, chapter 23). Clemens delayed his second trip to Esmeralda until early April 1862.

[8] Sam Bowen was evidently a Union prisoner at this time because of his Southern sympathies (see 11 and 12 May 62 to OC, n. 22). John Henley Bowen (1822–91), Sam's older brother, had settled in St. Louis and in the 1850s was a commission agent, then a steamboat agent and a representative of the Hannibal and St. Joseph Railroad. He became a successful contractor with the Union army. In "Villagers of 1840–3," Clemens recalled him as "steamboat agent in St. Louis; army contractor, later—rich" (*Inds*, 97 and biographical directory).

[9] "What Are the Wild Waves Saying?" was a song for two voices composed in 1850 by Stephen Glover and Joseph E. Carpenter. It derives from Paul Dombey's wistful query to his sister Florence in Dickens's *Dombey and Son* (BBC, 4:1174). The Benson girls were the young daughters of James L. Benson of St. Louis, a flour inspector for the Merchants' Exchange there. In 1866 Haille Benson (b. 1847)—whose name was sometimes spelled "Hallie"—married William Hyde, then assistant editor of the St. Louis *Missouri Republican* (Conard, 3:341, 343, 5:59; Scharf, 1:919). No information has been discovered about her sister Chaille (or Challie).

[10] Annie Moffett, Samuel Erasmus Moffett, and Jennie Clemens, aged nine, ten months, and six, respectively.

From George Turner (*per* William M. Gillespie)
and Samuel L. Clemens to Orion Clemens
18–30 September 1861 • Carson City, Nev. Terr.
(MS: CU-MARK)

Form for message, transmitting to the Council, House Bills for concurrence.

━━━━━━━━━

                                        Territory of Nevada.
                                        House of Representatives
                                        Carson _____ 1861.
To the Hon: the Council.
    The House ~~sends~~ transmits ~~for the concurr~~ herewith for the
concurrence of the Hon: the Council, the following Bills:
    An act &c
    An act &c
    An act &c

                                        Respl'y

                                        ━ ━ ━ ━ ━ ━

                                                Clerk.[1]

[*in pencil:*]
    From Hon. Chief Justice Turner[2]—I send your book by Dorsey,
Orion—why the devil didn't Turner send it to you himself while he was
in the States?[3]

                                        Yrs
                                        Sam.

[1]This "Form for message" is in the hand of William Martin Gillespie (1838–
85), originally from New York, who was chief clerk of the House of Representatives of the first Territorial Legislature, in session from 1 October through 29
November 1861. He served in the same capacity for the second Territorial Legislature (11 November–20 December 1862) and subsequently held a succession of
other offices. The fact that Gillespie left blanks for the name of the clerk suggests
that he prepared the form before he was formally elected to the post on 1 October
(Andrew J. Marsh, 12, 668–69 n. 29).
    [2]George Turner (d. 1885), an Ohio lawyer, had been appointed chief justice of
Nevada Territory by Abraham Lincoln in March 1861. After arriving in Carson
City in the second week of September of that year, Turner served until 1864 when

he and the rest of the judiciary resigned following accusations of corruption made by the Nevada press (Andrew J. Marsh, 670 n. 41). He apparently devised the "Form for message" which Gillespie transcribed.

[3]Clemens was Orion's eight-dollar-a-day clerk throughout the legislative session (William C. Miller, 2–5). He presumably sent Orion this note after his return to Carson City from Lake Bigler and before the legislature convened on 1 October. During that two-week period, Orion frequently must have been occupied preparing the legislative headquarters, two rooms in "the Capitol that is to be. It is located in the upper story of a lonely stone building, nearly two miles east of Carson City and on the opposite side of the narrow alkali plain on which the city is built" (Andrew J. Marsh, 2). On 1 October both Orion and Turner were in the House of Representatives—the former to preside until the election of officers, the latter to administer the oath of office to the members. They then could have attended to the matter of the book, probably a volume containing handwritten model forms drafted by Turner and Gillespie, without Clemens's intervention. The present "Form for message" was at one time pasted in a scrapbook (which Orion afterward used for clippings) facing a model form for recording House passage of a bill, also in Gillespie's hand (Scrapbook 2, CU-MARK). It is likely that this scrapbook, which contains a number of House transmittal documents and receipts later penned by Gillespie, *was* the book Clemens sent "by Dorsey," who remains unidentified. In any event, Turner could not have had such a book "while he was in the States," since he could only have collaborated on it with Gillespie after arriving in Nevada Territory.

To Pamela A. Moffett and Jane Lampton Clemens
25 October 1861 • Carson City, Nev. Terr.
(MS: NPV)

Carson City, Oct. 25, 1861.

My Dear Sister:

I have just finished reading your letter and Ma's, of Sept. 8th. How in the world could they have been so long coming? You ask if I have forgotten my promise to lay a claim for Mr. Moffett? By no means. I have already laid a timber claim on the borders of a Lake (Bigler) which throws Como in the shade—and if we succeed in getting one Mr. Jones to move his saw-mill up there, Mr. Moffett can just consider that claim better than bank stock. Jones says he will move his mill up next Spring.[1] In that claim I took up about two miles in length by one in width—and the names in it are as follows: "Sam. L. Clemens, W^m· A. Moffett, Thos. Nye" and ~~two o~~ three others. It is situated on "Sam Clemens' Bay"—so named by Capt.

Nye[2]—and it goes by that name among the inhabitants of that region. I had better stop about "the Lake," though—for whenever I think of it I want to go there and *die*, the place is so beautiful. I'll build a country seat there one of these days that will make the Devil's mouth water if he ⅄ ever visits the earth. Jim Lampton will never know whether I laid a claim there for him or not until he comes here *himself*.[3] We have now got about 1,650 feet of mining ground—and if it proves *good*, Mr. Moffett's name will go in—if not, I can get "feet" for him in the Spring which *will* be good. You see, Pamela, the trouble does not consist in getting mining ground—for that is plenty enough—but the money to work it with after you get it is the mischief. When I was in Esmeralda, a young fellow gave me fifty feet in the "Black Warrior"—an unprospected claim.[4] The other day he wrote me that he had gone down eight ⅞ feet on the ledge, and found it eight feet thick—and pretty good rock, too. He said he could take out rock *now* if there were a mill to crush it—but the mills are all engaged (there are only four of them,,) so, if I were willing, he would suspend work until Spring. I wrote him to let it alone at present—because, you see, in the Spring I can go down myself and help him look after it. There will then be twenty mills there. Orion and I have confidence enough in this country to think that if the war will let us alone we can make Mr. Moffett rich without its ever costing him a cent of money or a particle of trouble. We shall lay plenty of claims for him, but if they never *pay* him anything, they will never *cost* him anything. Neither Orion or I are financiers. Therefore, you *must* persuade Uncle Jim to come out here and help us in that line. I have written to him twice to come. I wrote him to-day. In both letters I told him not to let you or Ma know that we dealt in such romantic nonsense as "brilliant prospects," because I always *did* hate for any one to know what my plans or hopes or prospects were—for, if I kept people in ignorance in these matters, no one could be disappointed but myself, if they were never realized. You know I never told you that I went on the river under a promise to pay Bixby $500 until I had paid the money and cleared my skirts of the possibility of having my judgment criticised.[5] I would not say anything about our prospects now, if ~~I~~ we were nearer home. But I suppose at this distance you are more anxious than ‚you‚ would be if you saw us every ~~money~~ month—and therefore it is hardly fair to keep you in the dark. However, keep these matters to yourselves, and then if we fail, we'll keep the laugh in the family.

What we want now, ~~if~~ ‚is‚ something that will commence paying im-

mediately. We have got a chance to get into a claim where they say a tunnel
has been run 150 feet, and the ledge struck. I got a horse yesterday, and
went out with the Attorney General and the claim-owner—and we tried
to go to the claim by a new route, and got lost in the mountains—sunset
overtook us before we found the claim,—my horse got too lame to carry
me, and I got down and drove him ahead of me till within four miles of
town—then we sent Rice on ahead.[6] Bunker, (whose horse was in good
condition,) undertook to lead mine, and I followed after him. Darkness
shut him out from my view in less than a minute, and within the next
minute I lost the road and got to wandering in the sage brush. I would
find the road occasionally, and then loose lose it again in a minute or so. I
got to Carson about nine o'clock, at night, but not by the road I traveled
when I left it. The General says my horse did very well for awhile, but
soon refused to lead. Then he dismounted, and had a jolly time driving
both horses ahead of him and chasing them here and there through the
sage brush (it does my *soul* good when I think of it,) until he got to town,
when both animals deserted him, and he cursed them handsomely and
came home alone. Of course the horses went to their stables.

Tell Sammy I will lay a claim for him, and he must come out and
attend to it. He must get rid of that propensity for tumbling down,
though, for when we get fairly started here, I don't think we shall have
time to pick up those who fall.

I got Perry Smith's letter, for which I was very grateful. I wrote to
him the other day. If I thought Hallie and Margaret were in earnest about
writing to me, I would write to them first,—but I am afraid their time is
too much occupied by concerns of greater interest.[7] Still, tell them I wish
they *would* write—and then I'll tell them all about the World's Fair when
I get to London (for you know without my telling you, that I'll attend that
Fair if the thing is within the range of possibility.) And they *do* say that
where there's a will there's a way.[8]

Well, I must say, that either Annie spells with a fearful latitude, or I
read very crazily. Still, I was trying to put the most reasonable construction on her letter. I don't suppose, with her notorious Sunday school
proclivities, that she would willingly foster crime? ¢ Certainly not. Very
well, then. Every body knows it is a crime to be poor—and every body
knows that it is *not* a crime to be a fool. So, it would have been well enough
to help the fools along—but who cares what becomes of those hardened
sinners, the poor? When she has grown old in worldly wisdom, like her

venerable uncle, she will understand these things. Tell her that although I used to try to persuade her to trade her testament for lager beer, I'll never sell mine.[9]

That is Slaughter's house, I expect, that Cousin Jim has moved into. This is just the country for Cousin Jim to live in. I don't believe it would take him six months to make $100,000 here, if he had $3,000 dollars to commence with. I suppose he can't leave his family though.[10]

Tell Mrs. Benson[11] I never intend to be a lawyer. I have been a slave several times in my ~~lo~~ life, but I'll never be one again. I always intend to be so situated (*unless* I marry,) that I can "pull up stakes" and clear out whenever I feel like it.

We are very thankful to you, Pamela, for the papers you send. We have received half a dozen or more, and, next to letters, they are the most welcome visitors we have.

I am going out again, in a day or two, to look for that claim again—I hope with better success than my former attempt.

Write *oftener*, Pamela. Remember me to Mrs. S. to M., Mrs. B., H. and Chaillè.

Yr. Brother
Sam.

My Dear Mother: I hope you WILL all come out here some day. But *I* shan't consent to invite you, until we can receive you in *style*. But I guess we shall be able to do that, one of these days. I ~~mean~~ intend that Pamela shall live on *I* Lake Bigler until she can knock a bull down with her fist— say, about three months.

"Tell everything as it is—no better, and no worse." Well, "Gold Hill" sells at $5,000 per foot, cash down; "Wildcat" isn't worth ten cents.[12] The country is fabulously rich in gold, silver, copper, lead, coal, iron, quicksilver, marble, granite, chalk, plaster of Paris, (gypsum,) thieves, murderers, desperadoes, ladies, children, lawyers, Christians, Indians, Chinamen, Spaniards, gamblers, sharpers, cuyotès (pronounced ~~ky~~ ki-yo-ties,) ~~chin~~ poets, preachers, and jackass rabbits. I overheard a gentleman say, the other day, that it was "the d—dest country under the ~~so~~ sun."—and that comprehensive conception I fully subscribe, to. It never rains here, and the dew never falls. No flowers grow here, and no green thing gladdens the eye. The birds that fly over the land carry their provisions with them. Only the crow and the raven tarry with us. Our city lies in the midst of a desert of the purest—most unadulterated, and uncompromising *sand*—in which infernal soil nothing but that fag-end of vegetable creation, "sage-brush," ventures to grow. ~~Just~~ ₍If you will₎ take a lilliputian cedar tree for a model, and build a dozen imitations of it with the stiffest article of telegraph wire—set them one foot apart and then try to walk through them, ~~and~~ you'll understand (provided the floor is covered 12 inches deep with sand,) what it is to wander through a sage-brush desert. When crushed, sage brush emits an ~~order~~ odor which isn't exactly magnolia and equally isn't exactly polecat—but, ~~is,~~ a sort of compromise between the two. It looks a good deal like grease-wood, and is the ugliest ~~thing~~ ₍plant₎ that was ever conceived of. It is gray in color. On the plains, sage brush and grease wood grow₍ about twice as large as the common geranium—and in my opinion they are a very good substitute for that useless vegetable. Grease-wood is a *perfect*—*most* perfect imitation ~~of~~ in miniature of a live oak tree—"barring" the color of it. As to the *other* fruits and flowers of the country, there ain't any, except "Pulu" or "Tulu," or whatever they call it,—a species of unpoetical willow that grows on the banks of the Carson[13]—a *river*, 20 yards wide, knee-deep, and so ~~infernally~~ ₍villainously₎ rapid and crooked, that it looks like it had wandered into the country without intending it, and had run about ~~an~~ in a bewildered way and got lost, in its hurry to get out ~~of~~ again before some thirsty man came along and drank it up. I said we are situated in a flat, sandy desert—true. And ~~surrounded by~~ surrounded on all sides by such prodigious mountains, that when you gaze at them awhile,— ~~until you~~ ₍and₎ begin to conceive of their grandeur—and ₍next to₎ *feel* their vastness ~~exten~~ expanding your soul like a bladder—and ₍ultimately₎ find yourself growing and swelling and spreading into a giant—I say when this point is reached, you look disdainfully down upon the insignificant village of ~~ca~~ Carson, and in that instant you are seized with a burning desire to stretch forth your hand, put the city in your pocket, and walk off with it.

As to churches, I believe they *have* got a Catholic one here, but like ~~than~~ that one the New York fireman spoke of, I believe "they don't ₍h₎ run her now."[14] Now, although we are *surrounded* by sand, the ₍p₎ greatest part of the town is built upon what was once a very pretty grassy spot; and the streams of pure water that ~~once~~ ₍used to₎ poke₍ about it in ~~wil~~ rural ₍sloth and₎ solitude, now ~~prome~~ pass through our ~~streets~~ dusty streets and gladden the hearts of men by reminding them that there is at least something here that hath its prototype among the homes they left behind them. And

up "King's Cañon," (please pronounce *can-yon,*⟩ after the manner of the
natives,) there are "ranches," or farms, where they say hay grows, and
grass, and beets, and onions, and turnips, and other "truck" which is
suitable food for cows—yea, and even Irish potatoes,—a ~~vegi~~ vegetable
eminently proper for *human* consumption; also, cabbages, peas &
beans.[15]

The houses are mostly frame, unplastered, but "papered" inside
with ~~cot~~ flour-sacks ~~sow~~ sewed together—and the handsomer the
"brand" upon the sacks is, the neater the house looks. Occasionallyᴌy,
you stumble on a stone house. On account of the dryness of the country,
the shingles on the houses warp till they look like ⟩ short joints of stove
pipe split lengthwise.[16]

                                     .   .   .   .

[1] Charles Jones was co-owner of the Clear Creek Mill, a steam-powered sawmill
in Clear Creek Cañon west of Carson City in the Sierra Nevada foothills. The mill
did not relocate: in 1863, operating as "Chas. Jones & Co.," it was still situated
on Clear Creek (Kelly 1862, 60; Kelly 1863, 86; Angel, 531, 534).

[2] Captain John Nye was the governor's brother. He was an enthusiastic entre-
preneur in mining and timber projects and an incorporator of the Aurora and
Walker River Railroad, franchised by the Nevada Territorial Legislature in 1861
(Angel, 274). Clemens lauded his "conversational powers," "singular 'handi-
ness,'" and "spirit of accommodation" in chapter 35 of *Roughing It*. Nye's son
Thomas, about eighteen, was a clerk—boarding at Mrs. Margret Murphy's in
Carson City (Bridget O'Flannigan's "ranch" in chapter 21 of *Roughing It*)—and
afterward private secretary to Governor Nye (Kelly 1863, 9; Nye-Starr, 94–95).

[3] Clemens's uncle James A. H. Lampton longed to join his nephew in Nevada.
On 17 November, Jane Clemens reported that Lampton and his wife, Ella, had
visited that evening: "I told them they should not see my letters, but Will [Mof-
fett] is so well pleased he delights in reading the letters and they were all read out
and Ellas remarks going on all the time. James said if he was a single man or had
means to leave to Ella he would have gone before this time" (JLC to OC and SLC,
17 Nov 61, CU-MARK).

[4] On 8 September Horatio G. Phillips had sold Clemens fifty feet (i.e., shares)
worth $10 each in the discovery claims of the Black Warrior Gold and Silver
Mining Company on Martinez Hill, Aurora, Esmeralda district (deed recorded
10 Sept 61, in CU-MARK). A report from Aurora, dated 21 October, in the
Carson City *Silver Age*—possibly written by Phillips, who is mentioned prominently—identified the Black Warrior as one of Aurora's "undoubtedly rich" lodes
("From the Esmeralda Mines," San Francisco *Evening Bulletin*, 1 Nov 61, 3,
reprinting the *Silver Age* of unknown date). It is not known how much of the
nominal price of $500 Clemens actually paid Phillips. Mining feet were not costly,
being obtainable for a small advance payment, in exchange for labor on a ledge,
or through share bartering.

[5] Before accepting Clemens as his apprentice pilot in 1857, Horace Bixby had
demanded $500—one-fifth payable in advance, which Clemens borrowed from

William A. Moffett. In 1899 Bixby implied that he reduced the fee somewhat when he turned Clemens's training over to William Brown (see Bassford, 515). Nine years later he gave this account of Clemens's payments: "We made a bargain that he was to pay me $500 to teach him the river, $100 down and the rest in installments. I never did get the whole amount, but I got $300. He paid the $100 when I took him with me, and I didn't get any more until we were running a boat together, some years later. At this time he paid me $200, and, as the Irishman says, 'I fergive him the debt' " (Baskerville, 1). But Jane Clemens reported that in 1862 Bixby claimed to have "knocked off" only $100 of Clemens's fee "because he was sorry for him, he was a young man just setting out in the world." And she added, "I have been told by a pilot since you left that no man ever paid such a price as you did" (JLC to "all in the Territory," 12 and 14 Oct 62, NPV, in *MTBus*, 73). Exorbitant apprenticeship fees were common. Just six months after Clemens came to the river, two prominent St. Louis–New Orleans pilots, Charles M. Scott and William Gallaher, publicly condemned "the cupidity of several who were in the habit of taking steersmen, receiving . . . $500 for learning them" (Scott and Gallaher, 2).

⁶ The attorney general of Nevada Territory was Benjamin B. Bunker (b. 1815), from New Hampshire, appointed in 1861 by Abraham Lincoln and removed by him in June 1863 for inattention to duty (Anderson and Branch, 9–13; see 7 Aug 62 to OC, n. 4). In August 1863 Clemens characterized Bunker as "the densest intellect the President ever conferred upon the Territory" (*ET&S1*, 281). The claim owner was Clement T. Rice, reporter for the Carson City *Silver Age*, who was to become Clemens's close friend and journalistic collaborator (Andrew J. Marsh, 693).

⁷ Clemens alludes here to Haille Benson, of St. Louis, and to Margaret Sexton, who, along with her mother, Louise, had boarded with the Clemenses in Hannibal (*Inds*, biographical directory). The Sextons evidently were now living in St. Louis. Perry Smith probably was the "friend of Uncle Sam's" named Smith who, according to Annie Moffett Webster, was the originator of the "wild project" of forming the Marion Rangers (see *MTBus*, 60). In "The Private History of a Campaign That Failed," Clemens recalled that one of that ragtag company was "Smith, the blacksmith's apprentice. This vast donkey had some pluck, of a slow and sluggish nature, but a soft heart; at one time he would knock a horse down for some impropriety, and at another he would get homesick and cry. However, he had one ultimate credit to his account which some of us hadn't: he stuck to the war, and was killed in battle at last" (SLC 1885b, 194).

⁸ The International Exhibition of 1862, in London, ran from May through October of that year. Clemens did not attend (London *Times*: "International Exhibition Opening," 1 May 62, 10; "The International Exhibition," 1 Nov 62, 5).

⁹ Clemens enjoyed hearing from his nine-year-old niece, Annie Moffett. He later incorporated what he claimed was one of her "model" letters into "An Open Letter to the American People," published in the New York *Weekly Review* on 17 February 1866 (*ET&S3*, no. 181).

¹⁰ "Cousin Jim" was Jane Clemens's flamboyant first cousin, James J. Lampton (not to be confused with "Uncle Jim," James A. H. Lampton). He was the prototype for Colonel Sellers, the impecunious but irrepressible speculator in *The Gilded Age*. Slaughter has not been identified.

¹¹ Mrs. James L. Benson, mother of Clemens's friends Haille and Chaille.

¹²The Gold Hill Gold and Silver Mining Company claim was located at the north end of the main lode running through Gold Hill, a richly laden, easily exploited "mound-like mass of quartz rock" just south of Virginia City (Kelly 1862, 169; "Gold Hill Claims," Virginia City *Territorial Enterprise*, 5 Mar 63, clipping in Scrapbook 2:17, CU-MARK). A few days after Clemens wrote this letter, the company's stock was reported to have sold for as much as $3,000 a foot, the highest price paid in the Gold Hill district (Paul 1861, 1). "Wildcat" mines, according to chapter 44 of *Roughing It*, were "not mines, but holes in the ground over imaginary mines" and "in general terms, *any* claim not located on the mother vein, *i.e.*, the 'Comstock.' " Such properties inevitably attracted the gullible. See 11 and 12 Apr 63 to JLC and PAM, n. 3.

¹³ "Together with the cattails, the tules grew in dense, gray-green clumps that covered acre after acre of the marshes. Tules are tall, round reeds that bear a plume of seeds near the tip." Indians of the wetlands of western Nevada used tules (pronounced "*too*-lees") for making boats and rafts (Wheat, 6, 40).

¹⁴Possibly an allusion to an incident in *The New York Fireman*, a melodrama that told the "inspiring story of a brave fireman, who married an heiress, and demonstrated emphatically that honest hearts are more than dollars" (Odell, 5:552). Originally produced in 1850, it remained popular, and was regularly reprised, for many years.

¹⁵King's Cañon, running west from Carson City toward Lake Bigler, was the site of an early road intended as part of the overland route to California but soon abandoned (Angel, 34).

¹⁶The remainder of the letter has been lost, but the version published in the Keokuk *Gate City* (the next letter) provides a sense of at least some of the missing material.

To Jane Lampton Clemens
26 October 1861 • Carson City, Nev. Terr.
(Keokuk *Gate City*, 20 Nov 61)

CARSON CITY, Nevada Ter., ⎱
October 26, '61.¹ ⎰

DEAR MOTHER: You ask me in your last to tell you about the country—tell everything just as it is—no better and no worse—and *do* let nonsense alone. Very well, then, ma, since you wasted a considerable portion of your life in an unprofitable effort to teach me to tell the truth on all occasions, I will repay you by dealing strictly in facts just this once, and by avoiding that "nonsense" for which you seem to entertain a mild sort of horror.

Thus: "Gold Hill" (which is the name of the finest gold bearing quartz ledge in this vicinity,) sells at $5,000 a foot, cash down; 'Wildcat' isn't worth 10 cents. And thus: Nevada Territory is fabulously rich in gold, silver, copper, lead, coal, iron, quicksilver, marble, granite, chalk, slate, plaster of Paris (gypsum,) thieves, murderers, desperadoes, ladies, children, lawyers, Christians, gamblers, Indians, Chinamen, Spaniards, sharpers, cuyotes, (pronounced ki-yo-ties,) preachers, poets and jackass-rabbits.

Furthermore: it never rains here, and the dew never falls. No flowers grow here, and no green thing gladdens the eye. The birds that fly over the land carry their provisions with them. Only the crow and the raven tarry with us. Our city lies in the midst of a desert of the purest, most unadulterated and uncompromising sand—in which infernal soil nothing but that fag-end of vegetable creation, "sage-brush," is mean enough to grow. If you will take a liliputian cedar tree for a model, and build a dozen imitations of it with the stiffest article of telegraph wire—set them one foot apart and then try to walk through them—you will understand, (provided the floor is covered twelve inches deep with sand) what it is to travel through a sage-brush desert. When crushed, sage-brush emits an odor which isn't exactly magnolia, and equally isn't exactly polecat, but a sort of compromise between the two. It looks a good deal like grease-wood, and is probably the ugliest plant that was ever conceived of. It is gray in color. On the plains sage-brush and grease-wood grow to about twice the size of common geranium, and, to my thinking, are very good substitutes for that very useless vegetable. Greasewood is a perfect imitation, in miniature, of the live-oak tree, 'barring' the color of it. As to the other fruits and flowers of the country, there ain't any except 'Tula,' a species of unpoetical rush, that grows on the banks of the Carson, —a RIVER, *ma mere*, twenty yards wide, knee-deep, and so villainously rapid and crooked, that it looks like it had wandered into the country without intending it, and had run about in a bewildered way and got lost in its hurry to get out again before some thirsty man came along and drank it up.

I said we are situated in a flat, sandy desert. True. And surrounded on all sides by such prodigious mountains that when you stand at a distance from Carson and gaze at them awhile,—until, by mentally measuring them, and comparing them with things of smaller size, you begin to conceive of their grandeur, and next to feel their vastness expanding your soul like a balloon, and ultimately find yourself growing, and swelling, and spreading into a colossus,—I say when this point is reached, you look disdainfully down upon the insignificant village of Carson, reposing like a cheap print away yonder at the foot of the big hills, and in that instant you are seized with a burning desire to stretch forth your hand, put the city in your pocket, and walk off with it.

Now, although we are *surrounded* by sand, the greater part of the town is built upon what was once a very pretty grassy spot; and the streams of pure water that used to poke about it in rural sloth and solitude, now pass through our dusty streets and gladden the hearts of men by reminding them that there is at least something here that hath its prototype among the homes they left behind them.

And up "King's Canon," (please pronounce *can-yon*, after the manner of the natives,) there are ranches, or farms, where they say hay grows; and grass, and beets, and onions, and turnips and other "truck," which cows are fond of—yea, and even potatoes grow there—a vegetable eminently proper for human consumption; also cabbages, peas and beans.

The houses are mostly frame, and unplastered; but "papered" inside with flour-sacks sewed together—with the addition, in favor of the parlor, of a second papering composed of engravings cut from "Harper's Weekly;" so you will easily perceive that the handsomer the "brand" upon the flour-sacks is, and the more spirited the pictures are, the finer the house looks. There are several stone buildings here, and in the course of time, Ma, there will be several more. On account of the dryness of the atmosphere, the shingles on the houses warp until they look very much like they would be glad to turn over, and lie awhile on the other side.

Notwithstanding the extraordinary mixture of folks which I mentioned in the beginning of my letter, one can find as good society, here, of both sexes, as any Christian need desire. Please do not forget that.

Behold, I have spoken the truth concerning this land. And now, for your other questions, which shall be answered tersely, promptly, and to the point: First—"Do I go to church every Sunday?" Answer—"Scasely." Second—"Have you a Church in Carson?" We have—a Catholic one—but, to use a fireman's expression, I believe "they don't run her now." We have also Protestant service nearly every Sabbath in the school house. Third—"Are there many ladies in Carson?" Multitudes—probably the handsomest in the world. Fourth—"Are the citizens generally moral and religious?" Prodigiously so. Fifth—"When my old friends ask me how you like Nevada, what reply shall I make?" Tell them I am *de-*

lighted with it. It is the dustiest country on the face of the earth—but I rather like dust. And the days are very hot—but you know I am fond of hot days. And the nights are cold—but one always sleeps well under blankets. And it never rains here—but I despise a country where rain and mud are fashionable. And there are no mosquitoes here—but then I can get along without them. And there are scorpions here—and tarantulas or spiders, as big as a mouse—but I am passionately fond of spiders. Tell them I never liked any country so well before—and my word for it, you will tell them the truth.

Tell aunt Mary[2] that I am sorry she thought I intended to study law, because to my mind, that is proof positive that her excellent judgment has erred this time. I do not love the law. And besides, there are many young lawyers here, and I am too generous to allow the glare from my lamp of genius to dim the feeble lustre of their two-penny dips. In a word, you know—I don't want to be the means of showing them how little the Lord has done for them. And while on the subject, let me hint to the craft that fees in this Territory are large—and also, that although there is a shining array of legal talent here, there is still room in the firmament for another star or so.

While at breakfast this morning I received a telegraphic dispatch worded as follows, and I have delayed my letter in order to insert it:

China Town,[3] Oct. 26,—8 a. m.

"DEAR SAM.:—My brother George died this morning at half past two o'clock—come down.

WM. H. CLAGETT."[4]

I shall go down in the stage at noon and render Billy all the assistance in my power, in this, his hour of distress. For the present, good-bye.

S. L. C.

---

[1] The editor of the Keokuk *Gate City* prefaced his text with these words: "The following letter in answer to certain questions, will be found peculiar and interesting, and probably quite satisfactory." Clemens evidently prepared the manuscript published in the *Gate City* by copying and revising the letter he sent his family. Although the newspaper printing contains some errors (which are here emended by reference to the holograph of the preceding letter) and may have been otherwise edited, most of the differences between the two letters are plainly authorial.

[2] A fictitious person, Clemens's substitute for Mrs. Benson in the preceding letter.

[3] A small settlement on the Carson River at the mouth of Gold Cañon, about ten

miles northeast of Carson City, so named because of the large number of Chinese laborers living there. At a citizen mass meeting on 28 October 1861 the town was renamed Dayton ("Dayton, Not Chinatown," San Francisco *Alta California*, 2 Nov 61, 1, reprinting the Carson City *Silver Age* of 29 Oct 61).

[4] The news about George Clagett—a former resident of Keokuk like his brother William—brought this reaction from Mollie Clemens: "It made me very sad indeed to hear of the death of George Clagett, I think it will be a severe trial to his relatives, I know Will C, must feel very very sad.—how strange, to think he had to go through all the toil of the journey and privation attending it—to die alone in a strange land—I pray he was prepared for the great change—and hope Will will take it to heart and be a better man" (MEC to OC, 17 and 18 Nov 61, CU-MARK).

To Horatio G. Phillips
29 October 1861 • Carson City, Nev. Terr.
(MS: TxU)

$$\left.\begin{array}{c}\text{Carson City,—}\\\text{Tuesday, Oct. 29/61.}\end{array}\right\}$$

Dear 'Ratio:[1]

Bob[2] showed me your letter yesterday, in which you say that the "Averill Mill" is crushing our "Black Warrior" rock for its contents.[3] All success to the "Black Warrior" and Horatio G. Phillips! Amen. This looks like business—and hath an encouraging sound to it. I wish they would "strike it rich" shortly, for I want to ∧send∧ a fine "Black Warrior" specimen to the London World's Fair ~~when~~ by the Nevada commissioner, when he is appointed.[4] From a despatch received by Tom Nye to-day from his father, the Captain, we are led to hope that that noisy old youth will arrive here about next Saturday. I have no doubt the "Cap." would be very much pleased to received a slice of the "Black Warrior."

My brother is very particularly delighted with the "Black Warrior["]—and I have told him that some day I'll *give him a foot!* He is looking for money every day, now, from Washington.[5] And when it comes, I shall expect to take you by the hand again in Aurora.

Bob has got such a jolly long tongue, and keeps it wagging so comfortably, that I have not been able to ask him yet, whether he succeeded in selling your "Fresno" or not. Did he?—and have you saved your mother's place?—because I would like to know these things, as I have a mother at home myself, and naturally feel interested. I was sorry, though, that you were obliged to ~~sell~~ sacrifice ⫽ feet in that claim, for I am told that it is very fine. Since it *had* to go, though, I was sorry I was not able to buy it myself.[6]

I told Bob that you ought to come up here ⫽ and see about getting the county clerkship down there, and I explained to him *why* you ought to come up. I was talking to my brother, though, a while ago, and he says the Governor will make no appointments down there until the California Legislature adjourns, so that he may have the sense of that body upon the boundary question.[7] *One* thing I have *thought* of often, but have not spoken of—and that is, that the Governor may be absent when those appointments are made, and then my brother will have to make them himself. (Burn this letter, Ratio.)

Verily, it is *raining*—the first specimen of that kind that has fallen under my notice since I have been in Carson. It is pleasant to the sight, and refreshing to the senses—yea, "even as the shadow of a great rock in a weary land."[8]

The wings of Death overshadow us to-day—for this clouded sun is the last that one of our boys will ever look upon in life. Wagner, the civil engineer. I believe you do not know him. He surveyed with Lander's party for two years.[9] He is one of the few at whom the shafts of ⫽Slander were never aimed, and ~~in whose presence~~ against whom the hand of Mali*f*ce was never lifted. The fact of his dying here among comparative strangers, with no relative within thousands of miles of him and no *woman* to lay the *blessing* of her hand upon his aching head; and soothe ˏhisˏ weary heart to its last sleep with the music of her woman's voice, will shed a gloom over us all, when the sad event is consummated. May you die *at home*, Ratio, is the aspiration of

Your Friend,
Sam. L. Clemens

Write me often—and I will reply promptly.

[1] Horatio G. Phillips, a former resident of Nevada City, California, had probably arrived in Aurora, in the Esmeralda mining district, early in 1861. There he located numerous claims and worked several mines. He and Clemens probably first met in Carson City during the last week of August 1861, while Phillips was serving as a delegate from Esmeralda to the Union Convention called to nominate a candidate for territorial delegate to the United States Congress. Early the next month Clemens may have accompanied Phillips to Aurora where, on 8 September, Phillips sold him fifty feet in the Black Warrior claim for $500. Clemens later purchased feet in at least five other Aurora ledges from Phillips. The two men also owned jointly in several claims, including the Horatio and Derby ledge and an extension of the Wide West (Angel, 402; deeds in CU-MARK).

[2]Clemens first met Robert Muir Howland (1838–90), a native of New York State who had settled in Aurora in the summer of 1861, late that August when Howland, like Horatio Phillips, was in Carson City as a delegate to the Union Convention. At the time, Howland and Phillips were sharing a cabin. In Aurora, during the next few years, Howland was superintendent of the Federal Union, Union Star, and Magdalena mines, and co-owner of the Pride of Esmeralda Gold and Silver Mining Company and the Miners' Foundry. He served as marshal of Aurora and in 1864 was appointed warden of the territorial prison at Carson City. In 1883 he was appointed United States deputy marshal for California (Howland, 1–5; San Francisco *Alta California*: "Letter from Esmeralda—No. 6," 10 Nov 62, 1; "The Pride of Esmeralda," 18 Feb 63, 1; Dale, 3; Howland deputy-marshal appointment, 18 June 83, PH in CU-MARK; Colcord, 117; "Deaths," San Francisco *Evening Bulletin*, 18 Jan 90, 3). Clemens remained friendly with Howland until the latter's death, recalling him in 1906 as "a slender, good-natured, amiable, gentle, kindly little skeleton of a man, with a sweet blue eye that would win your heart when it smiled upon you, or turn cold and freeze it, according to the nature of the occasion" (AD, 19 Jan 1906, in *MTA*, 1:352–53). Presumably the "sweet blue eye" turned cold on the occasion when, while serving as prison warden, Howland heated a steel bar "on one end to a red heat" and used it to subdue a defiant prisoner (Angel, 546).

[3]Anson Averill was a resident of Aurora. The Averill Mill was in Esmeralda ravine, about two miles below the town (Kelly 1862, 245; San Francisco *Evening Bulletin*: "The Esmeralda Mines," mistakenly listing the mill as the "Avery," 28 Oct 61, 2; "From the Esmeralda Mines," 1 Nov 61, 3, reprinting the Carson City *Silver Age* of unknown date; "The Mining Roll Continued," 16 Mar 63, 3).

[4]On 21 October Governor Nye informed the first Territorial Legislature that California had already appointed commissioners to represent the western states and territories in London at the International Exhibition of 1862. He urged the legislature to name an independent Nevada commissioner and to appropriate funds for a specimen collection of Nevada minerals. The legislature completed passage of the necessary bill on 29 November, the last day of the legislative session, and Nye signed it immediately, but no evidence has been found to indicate that a commissioner was actually sent. Nevada was impressively represented, nevertheless: Joseph Mosheimer, a San Francisco chemist and assayer, won a medal in the category of "mining, quarrying, metallurgy and mineral products" for a "collection illustrating the newly-explored mineral wealth of the Territory of Nevada" ("The Great Exhibition: Award of the Jurors," New York *Times*, 26 July 62, 5; *Journal of the Council*, 83–84, 106, 251; *Journal of the House*, 92, 124, 329, 332; Lord, 59).

[5]Orion Clemens finally received $925, his salary for the period 27 March–30 September 1861, in late November (OC to Elisha Whittlesey, 20 Nov 61, NvU-NSP).

[6]The Fresno was a claim on Martinez Hill, Aurora. On 22 December Phillips wrote to Orion Clemens: "We are expecting to strike the Ledge in our Fresno soon & when we do if it is as rich as we all have every reason to believe I will let you know if we strike it as rich in the Tunnel as the top indicates it will be worth a few Hundred Dollars a foot. J. D. Kinney has been buying all he can get He got fifty feet at six dollars" (NPV). Samuel Clemens paid Kinney $1,000 on 1 March 1862 for Kinney's holdings of over 1,400 feet in sixteen claims, including 100 feet in the Fresno and 200 feet in the first north extension of the Fresno (deed in CU-

MARK). Clemens's letter of 23 July 1862 to Orion suggests that his faith in the Fresno's potential richness remained undiminished until the end of his Aurora residence.

[7] Although Nevada's limits had been roughly laid out by Congress in March 1861, the new territory was expected to establish its western border by arbitration with California. At the time of the present letter, that boundary, both north and south of Lake Bigler, was in dispute, and mineral-rich Aurora was claimed by both Mono County, California, and Esmeralda County, Nevada. Four days before Clemens wrote this letter, Governor Nye requested the Territorial Legislature to appoint a commission to ask the California legislature to "grant unto this Territory all that portion of her State lying east of the summit of the Sierra Nevada mountains" (Andrew J. Marsh, 158). Meanwhile, Nye preferred to leave the administration of Esmeralda County business in the hands of the already elected Mono County officers, with the exception of a county surveyor and a district attorney whom he appointed. The commission he requested was never created, and the boundary dispute continued, sometimes violently, for almost two years (Chalfant, 77–78; Angel, 100). Clemens's letters for the period comment repeatedly on the conflict.

[8] Isaiah 32:2.

[9] Will H. Wagner was a member of John Nye and Company (Wagner to John Nye, 7 Sept 61, PH in CU-MARK, courtesy of Michael H. Marleau; see 18–21 Sept 61 to JLC and PAM, n. 5). Frederick West Lander (1821–62), engineer, explorer, and soldier, led or participated in five transcontinental survey expeditions in the 1850s, most notably those for the Northern Pacific Railroad route and for the overland wagon road north of Carson City (Angel, 164).

From Orion and Samuel L. Clemens
to Mary E. (Mollie) Clemens
29, 30, and 31 January 1862 • Carson City, Nev. Terr.
(MS: CU-MARK)

A member of the Academy of Sciences, of Paris, has discovered a simple and unexpensive process for rendering muslins, laces and all sorts of light stuffs incombustible. It simply consists of adding to the starch used in stiffening them, one-half its weight of the carbonate of lime, usually known as "Spanish White."[1]

Carson City, N. T.,
January 29th 1862.

My Dear Wife:—

The Silver Age of this morning, contains an announcement that Governor Nye has received the appointment of Brigadier General, and that he will leave us. The Governor tells me I shall soon be Governor. We will see.[2]

The Indians prophecy more storms—they say "heap snow," "heap rain."

Jan. 30 Poor Mrs. Upton who had a baby last week is very low, and fears are entertained that she will not recover.

January 31—Poor Upton has met with the severest loss ʎ that can befall a man. His wife died this evening about two hours ago. Since I commenced this paragraph he came into my office, took my hand, sat down and cried. He says she is happy, for she was a pure, good woman; and he will meet her some day if he behaves himself; that she was too good for him, was the reason she was taken. He has been thoughtless, but not bad.[3]

It is cold and dry to-night.

I am told that female society here is not much better than the male society. There is a fashion of loose language among them that disgusts men of refinement. Loose manners are frequent. In California great numbers of the women are loose characters. Mrs. Upton was among the exceptions, and was an excellent woman.

Dear Mollie:

"Paint-Brush" in the hands of the enemy![4] God forgive me! this is the first time I have felt melancholy since I left the United States. And he is doing service for the enemy. But *against his will*. Ah, me, Mollie—there would be consolation—priceless consolation in the fact which I have italicised, were it not that *that* is a natural failing with the poor devil—everything ɇ he ever *did* do, he did against his will. His most insignificant services, even for *me*, were done under protest. Of course I mean that whenever he *did* condescend to ₓdoₓ anything in accordance with my wishes, ₓand that was not an everyday occurrence, at all,ₓ he showed his unwillingness in a marked manner—but h̶i̶s̶ he was a willing soul to do things after his own fashion. And of course he generally consulted his own judgment—because: You remember, (as I perceive by your language,) that between me and the pillow on the saddle, there was a very Mine of trouble—and between the saddle and the ground w̶a̶s̶ there was another Mine of trouble, viz; the Mule. And the saddle was always loose,—therefore, I was afraid it might turn; and I could not cinch it tighter, as i̶t̶ ̶w̶a̶s̶ the cinch was old, and I feared it might break. So, you see, when in the saddle, I lived as u̶p̶ one astraddle of a magazine—for, had I combatted the mule's wishes to any ʎ great extent, he would have retaliated by jumping gullies, or rolling on the ground, or running away—and the consequences, to me, of such conduct, would have been a matter of small concern to *him*.

But if I had the "Paint Brush" here, Mollie, I would "feed fat the ancient grudge I bear him."[5] I would f board him on sage-brush, and cinch him till he couldn't breathe, and ride him sixty miles a day. He would be a wonderfully useful animal to me. However, if he has gone over to the enemy, let him go. ~~Han~~ He can't be depended on anyhow—he'll desert at the first opportunity; if he don't fall in a camp-kettle and get drowned.

Well, Mollie, I think July will be soon enough, because I think that by that time some of our claims will be paying handsomely, and you can come in "high-tone" style, as Tom Nye, says. And we could have a house fit to live in—and servants to do your work. You know it is all very well for a man's wife to talk about w how much work she *can* do—but actually *doing* it is a thing that don't suit my notions. That part of the business belongs to the servants. I am not married yet, and I never *will* marry until I can afford to have servants enough to leave my wife in the position for which I designed her, viz:—as a *companion*. I don't want to sleep with a three-fold ƀBeing who is cook, chambermaid and washerwoman all in one. I don't mind sleeping with female servants as long as I am a bachelor—by *no* means—but *after* I marry, that sort of thing will be "played out," you know. (But Lord bless you, Mollie, don't *hint* this depravity to the girls.) No, Madam, I am anxious for you to stay just where you are until you can live here in a handsome house and boss your own servants—even if it should be until the first July after the Millenium! If you come here before you ought to come, Mollie, and I hear people say "the Secretary's wife does her own cooking"—I'll tell every such person that the Secretary's wife is ~~such~~ subject to fits of derangement! Mind, now, I'm not going to have any one-horse business here after *you* arrive. D-o-n-'t get in a hurry, Madam. The world wasn't made in a day.[6]

· · · · ·

[1]Orion pasted this clipping, possibly from the Carson City *Silver Age* of 29 January, in the upper left-hand corner of the first page of the letter.

[2]James W. Nye (1815–76) had formerly been a district attorney (1839) and judge (1844–51) in New York State and the first president of the Metropolitan Board of Police in New York City (1857–60). He reputedly felt that "the job of being governor of the Territory of Nevada was only an interlude between his political activities in New York City and some position he would get out of creat-

ing a state of the Territory of Nevada. And when he found that living in frontier Carson City was a drab existence . . . he didn't intend to spend any more time there than he could help" (Mack 1961a, 84). Orion served as acting governor during Nye's frequent trips to California, Washington, D.C., and New York, the longest such substitution coming between December 1862 and July 1863. Nye later became a Republican senator from the state of Nevada, serving from 1864 to 1873 (McMullin and Walker, 231–33).

[3] M. Upton was a partner, with G. F. Crowell, in Upton and Company, a Carson City grocery and dry-goods establishment (Kelly 1862, 70, 90; Kelly 1863, 98, 111, 115).

[4] Paint-Brush was the mule that Clemens rode during his stint as a Confederate volunteer in June 1861—"a disagreeable animal, in every way" (SLC 1885b, 196). According to the recollections of a fellow campaigner, Absalom Grimes, Paint-Brush was a "little yellow mule, as frisky as a jack-rabbit. He had long, erect ears, was about four feet high, and carried his tail sticking straight out on a dead level with his back. . . . His tail was shaved as with a razor to within six inches of the end—which resembled a painter's only tool. He was promptly christened 'Paint Brush' by his master" (Grimes, 6).

[5] *The Merchant of Venice*, act 1, scene 3.

[6] Mollie Clemens was increasingly eager to join her husband in Carson City, but was deterred by both Orion and Samuel Clemens for the reasons set forth in this letter and because of the difficulty of finding a suitable traveling companion for the long trip to Nevada. Mollie and Jennie Clemens finally made the journey, by way of New York and thence by steamer, accompanied by William Clagett's wife, Mary, in September 1862. They arrived in Carson City on 12 October 1862 (MEC to OC, 1 Sept 62, CU-MARK; MEC, 13–14).

To Jane Lampton Clemens
30 January 1862 • Carson City, Nev. Terr.
(Keokuk *Gate City*, 6 Mar 62)

CARSON CITY, Jan. 30, '62.[1]

MY DEAR MOTHER:—

> "How sleep the brave who sink to rest,
>   Far, far from the battle-field's dreadful array,
>   With cheerful ease and succulent repast,
>   Nor ask the sun to lend his streaming ray."

Bully, isn't it? I mean the poetry, madam, of course. Doesn't it make you feel just a little "stuck up" to think that your son is a—Bard? And I have attained to this proud eminence without an effort, almost. You see, madam, my method is very simple and easy—thus: When I wish to write a great poem, I just take a few lines from Tom, Dick and Harry, Shakspeare, and other poets, and by patching them together so as to make them rhyme occasionally, I have accomplished my object. Never mind the *sense*—sense, madam, has but little to do with poetry. By this wonderful method, any body can be a poet—or a bard—which sounds better, you know.[2]

But I have other things to talk about, now—so, if you please, we will drop the subject of poetry. You wish to know where I am, and where I have been? And, verily, you shall be satisfied. Behold, I am in the middle of the universe—at the centre of gravitation—even Carson City. And I have been to the land that floweth with gold and silver—Humboldt.[3] (Now, do not make any ridiculous attempt, ma, to pronounce the "d," because you can't do it, you know.) I went to the Humboldt with Billy C., and Gus., and old Mr. Tillou.[4] With a two-horse wagon, loaded with eighteen hundred pounds of provisions and blankets—necessaries of life—to which the following luxuries were added, viz: Ten pounds of Killikinick,[5] two dogs, Watt's Hymns, fourteen decks of cards, "Dombey and Son," a cribbage board, one small keg of lager beer and the "*carminia sacrae.*"[6]

At first, Billy drove, and we pushed behind the wagon. Not because we were fond of it, ma—Oh, no—but on Bunker's account. Bunker was the "near" horse, on the larboard side. Named after the Attorney General of this Territory. My horse—you are acquainted with him, by reputation, already—and I am sorry you do not know him personally, ma, for I feel towards him, sometimes, as if he were a blood relation of our family—he is so infernally lazy, you know—my horse, I was going to say—was the "off" horse on the starboard side. But it was on Bunker's account, principally, that we pushed behind the wagon. For whenever we came to a hard piece of road, that poor, lean, infatuated cuss would fall into a deep reverie about something or other, and stop perfectly still, and it would generally take a vast amount of black-snaking and shoving and profanity to get him started again; and as soon as he was fairly under way, he would take up the thread of his reflections where he left off, and go on thinking, and pondering, and getting himself more and more mixed up and tangled in his subject, until he would get regularly stuck again, and stop to review the question.

And always in the meanest piece of road he could find.

In fact, Ma, that horse had something on his mind, all the way from here to Humboldt; and he had not got rid of it when I left there—for when I departed, I saw him standing, solitary and alone, away up on the highest peak of a mountain, where no horse ever ventured before, with his pensive figure darkly defined against the sky—still thinking about it.

Our dog, Tom, which we borrowed at Chinatown without asking the owner's permission, was a beautiful hound pup, eight months old.[7] He was a love of a dog, and much addicted to fleas. He always slept with Billy and me. Whenever we selected our camp, and began to cook supper, Tom, aided and abetted by us three boys, immediately commenced laying his plans to steal a portion of the latter; and with our assistance, he generally succeeded in inserting his long, handsome nose into every dish before anybody else. This was wrong, Ma, and we know it—so, to atone for it, we made Mr. Tillou's dog stand around whenever he attempted any such liberties. And when our jolly supper was swallowed, and the night was on the wane, and we had finished smoking our pipes, and singing songs, and spinning yarns, and telling lies, and quoting scripture, and all that sort of thing, and had begun to look for a soft place on the ground to spread our blankets on, Tom, with immense sagacity, always assisted in the search, and then with becoming modesty, rewarded himself by taking first choice between the blankets. No wonder we loved the dog.

But, Mr. Tillou's dog, "Curney," we utterly despised. He was not a long, slender, graceful dog like Tom, but a little mean, white, curly, grinning whelp, no bigger than a cat—with a wretched, envious, snappish, selfish disposition, and a tail like an all-wool capital O, curled immodestly over his back, and apparently wrenched and twisted to its place so tightly that it seemed to lift his hind legs off the ground sometimes. And we made Tom pester him; and bite his tail; and his ears; and stumble over him; and we heaped trouble and humiliation upon the brute to that degree that his life became a burden to him. And Billy, hating the dog, and thirsting for his blood, prophesied that Curney would come to grief. And Gus and I said Amen. And it came to pass according to the words of the prophet. Thus.

On the fifth day out, we left the village of Ragtown, and entered upon the Forty-five mile Desert, where the sand is of unknown depth, and locomotion of every kind is very difficult; where the road is strewn thickly with the skeletons and carcasses of dead beasts of burden, and charred remains of wagons; and chains, and bolts and screws, and gun-barrels, and such things of a like heavy nature as weary, thirsty emigrants, grown desperate, have thrown away, in the grand hope of being able, when less encumbered, to reach water.[8] We left Ragtown, Ma, at nine o'clock in the morning, and the moment we began to plow through that horrible sand, Bunker, true to his instincts, fell into a reverie so dense, so profound, that it required all the black-snaking and shoving and profanity at our disposal to keep him on the move five minutes at a time. But we did shove, and whip and blaspheme all day and all night, without stopping to rest or eat, scarcely, (and alas! we had nothing to drink, then.) And long before daylight we struck the Big Alkali Flat—and Curney came to grief; for the poor devil got *alkalied*—in the seat of honor. You see he got tired, traveling all day and all night, nearly—immensely tired—and sat himself down by the way-side to rest. And lo! the iron entered his soul (poetical figure, Ma.) And when he rose from that fiery seat, he began to turn somersets, and roll over and over and kick up his heels in the most frantic manner, and shriek, and yelp and bark, and make desperate grabs at his tail, which he could not reach on account of his excitement and a tendency to roll over; and he would drag himself over the ground in a sitting posture, (which afforded him small relief, you know,) and then jump up and yelp, and scour away like the wind, and make a circuit of three hundred yards, for all the world as if he were on the Pony Express. And we three weary and worn and thirsty wretches forgot our troubles, and fell upon the ground and laughed until all life and sense passed out of us, and the colic came to our relief and brought us to again, while old Mr. Tillou wiped his spectacles, and put them on, and looked over them, and under them, and around them, in a bewildered way, and "wondered," every now and then, "what in the h—ll was the matter with Curney."

We thought,—yea, we fondly hoped, ma,—that Curney's time had come. But it was otherwise ordained. Mr. Tillou was much exercised on account of his dog's misery, and, sharing his misery, we recommended a bullet as a speedy remedy, but the old gentleman put his trust in tallow, and Curney became himself again, except that he walked behind the wagon for many hours with humble mien, and tail transformed from a brave all-wool capital O to a limp and all-wool capital J, and gave no sign when Tom bit his ears or stumbled over him.

We took up our abode at Unionville, in Buena Vista Mining District, Humboldt county, after pushing that wagon nearly 200 miles, and taking eleven days to do it in.[9] And we found that the "National" lead there was selling at $50 per foot, and assayed $2,496 per ton at the Mint in San Francisco. And the "Alba Nueva," "Peru," "Delirio," "Congress," "Independence," and others, were immensely rich leads.[10] And moreover, having winning ways with us, we could get "feet" enough to make us all rich one of these days. And again that mills would be in operation there by the 1st of June.[11] And in the Star District, O. B. O'Bannon, of Keokuk, was flourishing, and had plenty of "feet," and in the Santa Clara District, Harroun and Jo. Byers of Memphis, Mo., likewise and ditto.[12] And Billy put up his shingle as Notary Public, and Gus put up his as Probate Judge, and I mounted my horse (in company with the Captain and the Colonel) and journeyed back to Carson, leaving them making preparations for a prospecting tour;[13] and before I can go to Esmeralda and get back to Humboldt, they will have laid, with the certainty of fate, the foundation of their fortunes. It's a great country, ma.

Now, ma, I could tell you how, on our way back here, the Colonel and the Captain and I got fearfully and desperately lousy; and how I got used to it and didn't mind it, and slept with the Attorney General, who wasn't used to it, and *did* mind it;[14] but I fear my letter is already too long. Therefore—*sic transit gloria mundi, e pluribus unum forever!* Amen. (Latin, madam—which you don't understand, you know).

S. L. C.

----

[1] The editor of the *Gate City* provided this heading for Clemens's letter: "It is hardly necessary to say how this letter fell into our hands. Let it suffice that we know it was intended for publication."

[2] Clemens's pastiche begins with the opening line of William Collins's ode "How Sleep the Brave," written in 1746. Sources for the other lines have not been identified.

[3] An irreverent allusion to Exodus 3:8—". . . unto a land flowing with milk and honey." The Humboldt mining area, located approximately one hundred and seventy-five miles northeast of Carson City in the Humboldt Mountain Range, had become the new El Dorado of Nevada Territory by December 1861. Clemens left Carson City for Humboldt sometime in the second week of that month. The excursion that followed lasted approximately seven weeks. It included, on the return trip, eight water-bound days at Honey Lake Smith's, a trading post on the road to Carson City, and, beginning on 19 January, at least another week floodbound in Virginia City. Given the constant rain and snow that washed out the roads, travel to Carson City would have been hazardous if not impossible before the end of January ("Humboldt," Marysville *Appeal*, 2 Feb 62, 3; "From the Humboldt Mines," Stockton *Weekly Independent*, 8 Feb 62, 2). Clemens later described his Humboldt trip in detail in chapters 27–33 of *Roughing It*. He also recalled it in a letter dated 12 February 1866 to the Virginia City *Territorial Enterprise* (*ET&S3*, no. 179) and in chapter 27 of *The Innocents Abroad*.

[4] Clemens's companions were: his Keokuk friend William H. Clagett, recently appointed notary public of Unionville, the Humboldt County seat; Cornbury S. Tillou, a Carson City blacksmith and jack-of-all-trades (Kelly 1862, 89); and Augustus W. (Gus) Oliver, appointed probate judge of Humboldt County by Governor Nye on 10 December 1861. Born in Maine in 1835 and trained as a lawyer,

Oliver had migrated to California in 1860 and, before going to Unionville, had worked as a Carson City journalist reporting the first Territorial Legislature. His later career took him back to California, where he was a schoolteacher and principal in San Diego and Gilroy, and a judge in Perris (Angel, 448; Andrew J. Marsh, 693 n. 287; San Diego *Union*: "San Diego Academy," 16 Jan 72, 3; "Personal," 5 Aug 73, 3; "Township Officers," 22 Nov 92, 3; Oliver biographical information courtesy of H. LeRoy Oliver). Oliver and Tillou figure under their real names in Clemens's 12 February 1866 letter to the *Territorial Enterprise*, and in *Roughing It* as Oliphant and Ballou. In *The Innocents Abroad*, Clemens described Oliver as the "mildest-mannered man that ever was" (chapter 27). For Oliver's 1910 recollections of the Humboldt journey, see DeLaney, 1–3.

[5] Or kinnikinnick, a smoking mixture. Clemens described the "miraculous conglomerate they call 'Killickinick' " in his "Answers to Correspondents," originally published in the *Californian* on 17 June 1865:

It is composed of equal parts of tobacco stems, chopped straw, "old soldiers," fine shavings, oak leaves, dog-fennel, corn-shucks, sun-flower petals, outside leaves of the cabbage plant, and any refuse of any description whatever that costs nothing and will burn. After the ingredients are thoroughly mixed together, they are run through a chopping-machine. The mass is then sprinkled with fragrant Scotch snuff, packed into various seductive shapes, labelled "Genuine Killickinick, from the old original manufactory at Richmond," and sold to consumers at a dollar a pound. (*ET&S2*, 192)

[6] Lowell Mason's *Carmina Sacra; or, Boston Collection of Church Music*, originally published in 1841 or 1842. Like Isaac Watts's *Hymns*, first published in 1707, Mason's collection of church music was a work of enduring popularity, frequently reprinted.

[7] Clemens later claimed the party was accompanied by three dogs: Tillou's "small pup 'the Colonel,' and our hound pup named 'Tom Nye,' and a beautiful pointer stolen from John H. Kinkead" (letter of 12 Feb 66 to the *Territorial Enterprise*). Kinkead was a Carson City merchant and the territorial treasurer (Kelly 1862, 10, 83).

[8] Ragtown was on the Carson River at the junction of the old pioneer Reese River and Humboldt roads—a place "where horses can be shod 'when the blacksmith is not in jail' " ("The Humboldt Mining District of Nevada Territory," San Francisco *Alta California*, 23 June 62, 1). From Ragtown the route to Unionville passed through miles of heavy sand, alkali flats, and the Humboldt slough area, all of it difficult for a heavily laden wagon to traverse and, according to one traveler, "the only place I ever saw that seemed fit to commit murder or suicide in" ("Letter from Nevada Territory," San Francisco *Alta California*, 18 June 63, 1).

[9] Unionville had been laid out in July 1861 along the stream that descended Buena Vista Cañon, a broad and beautiful east-west cut through the Humboldt Mountains. At the time of this letter the town had recently been designated the county seat of newly organized Humboldt County (Angel, 446, 458–59). In chapter 28 of *Roughing It* Clemens claimed that when he arrived in December 1861 Unionville "consisted of eleven cabins and a liberty-pole." Actually, the population of the three settlements in Humboldt County (Unionville, Humboldt City, and Star City) was reported to be as high as eight hundred by the beginning of 1862 (Kelly 1862, 237). A Unionville resident of the period described it as a lively place: "The numerous adobe, stone, brush and canvas habitations that line the broad and level streets impart to it a varied architectural beauty and picturesque appearance; and the county officials, speculators in 'feet,' limbs of the law, and

Pah-Utahs that have congregated here, reflect a business-like and heterogeneous air around the town" (Wyoming 1862a, 4).

[10] These six leads were near Unionville and had been located by September 1861. The National and the Alba Nueva were two of the more famous mines of the Buena Vista district of Humboldt County, the latter the first ledge opened there. Each of them was partly owned by Captain Hugo Pfersdorff (see note 13). They were on the same hill, had well-developed shafts by September 1861, and were praised in the press for their gold-bearing quartz. On 28 January 1862 Clemens purchased ten feet in the Alba Nueva ("The Humboldt Region," San Francisco *Alta California*, 17 Sept 61, 1; Wyoming 1862a, 4; Kelly 1862, 237; deeds in CU-MARK).

[11] John C. Fall's Pioneer Mill, near Unionville, did not begin operating until November 1862. It was the first mill in the Buena Vista district ("Letter from Nevada Territory," San Francisco *Alta California*, 15 Nov 62, 1; Nomad, 1).

[12] The Star mining district was about eleven miles north of Unionville on the eastern slope of the Humboldt Mountains. Clemens visited Star City, the main settlement of the district, in December 1861 while he was in the Humboldt area. (For an incident of that visit see *Roughing It*, chapter 57.) Orville B. O'Bannon, originally from Kentucky, had been a lawyer in Keokuk, Iowa, before relocating in Humboldt County; in his 12 February 1866 letter to the *Territorial Enterprise* Clemens described O'Bannon as "miner, lawyer, and late local editor of the Humboldt *Register*." By December 1861 O'Bannon had removed to the Santa Clara district, directly north of the Star district, where he helped systematize the mining laws and records (OC 1856, 89, and advertisements, 37; "Copy of the Proceedings of a Miners' Meeting," Red Bluff [Calif.] *Beacon*, 19 Dec 61, 2). De Witt Harroun and J. A. Byers evidently were Missouri acquaintances of Orion's. Documents among the Clemens brothers' mining deeds (CU-MARK) reveal that Harroun and Byers were partners in opening up six ledges in the Santa Clara district. By August 1864 Byers was established as secretary in the New York City office of the Mount Blanc Gold and Silver Consolidated Mining Company, in which Orion had invested and for which he served as both president and trustee (OC to Byers, 26 Aug 64, CU-MARK).

[13] Clemens made the arduous return trip from Unionville to Carson City with Captain Hugo Pfersdorff and Colonel John B. Onstine. In May 1861 Pfersdorff had been co-discoverer of the mineral deposits near the future site of Unionville. Subsequently he helped to lay out the town and to organize the Buena Vista mining district, and he was elected the district's first recorder, twice serving two-year terms (Angel, 458–59; Pioneer, 84). Onstine, from Ohio, had practiced law for ten years in the Midwest before setting up his law firm in Carson City in August 1861 and, a few months later, in Unionville ("Law Firm," Carson City *Silver Age*, 10 Aug 61, 2). Clemens gave a brief account of the return trip to Carson City in his 12 February 1866 *Territorial Enterprise* letter. In a longer version of the story (chapter 30 of *Roughing It*) he identified his companions as "Mr. Ballou and a gentleman named Ollendorff." There is no other known evidence, however, that Ballou's prototype, Cornbury S. Tillou, actually was along.

[14] The "Attorney General" here may be the horse Bunker, rather than Benjamin B. Bunker. Although the latter could have been in Virginia City in late January in time to join Clemens, Pfersdorff, and Onstine for the last leg of their Humboldt–Carson City trip, no evidence has been found to confirm this.

To William A. Moffett
30 January–1 February 1862 • Carson City, Nev. Terr.
(MS: NPV)

. . . .

In the little square package of "National" rock, (wrapped in writing paper,) there are particles of free gold which have become detached from the rock, while lying here in the office, and more will crumble away on the road—open carefully.[1] I have, in the same package, placed in a piece of the quartz in which no gold can be *seen*. If you doubt their being any in it, let Jim Lampton pulverize it in a mortar and wash it out.[2] The ledge is 8 inches wide on top, and 22 inches wide at a depth of 34 feet. It will probably grow wide enough before they reach China.

Open the Selenite crystals carefully. They are very delicate, and have already got battered. The strip which is tied to the prism, I split off with my knife. They are from the "Latrobe Tunnel," (at Virginia, City) which is being run by two brothers Van Bokkelen, San Francisco capitalists. They begun the tunnel 12 months ago, and will finish it 2 years from now. It is 6½ feet square, and is already 1,600 feet long. It has a wooden railway its throughout its whole length, and two air shafts; from who which air, in pipes, is conveyed to the workmen in the end of the tunnel.[3] I went into the tunnel ‚yesterday morning before I left Virginia,‚ in a small car, (which Mr. Van B. pushed from behind,) and carried the lights. I picked up some beautiful crystals (they are either mica or selenite,) in the extreme end of the tunnel, 1600 feet from its mouth and 200 feet below the surface of the ground—but I k have kept them, and I send you others which will stand the trip better, although they are not very pretty.

We ‚(Van. B. & I,)‚ descended the Ophir incline ‚190 feet‚ (I call it the Ophir perpendicular,) last Sunday Saturday night at 9 o'clock.[4] We went down lying [on] our backs in a little car—not room enough in the shaft to allow you to sit up—and we reached the bottom nearly as quickly as we would if we had jumped down the hole. The foreman told took us all through the mine (he is not allowed to admit visiters at night, but I was introduced as the Secretary of the Territory, and he said he would take the responsibility of disobeying his orders for once.)[5] We were around through the bowels of the earth generally, and the specimens I send you,

I picked up from a choice pile marked ~~(~~ "First class—N$^{o.}$ 2," ₍(worth 4 or $5,000 to the ton,)₎ at the extremest depth, where the ledge is 52 feet wide. The Ophir, you know, is Silver rock—with some gold in it, though. The yellow spots in the specimen are iron pyrites, (or possibly, they may be copper.) The Ophir has $2,000,000 worth of ore lying on the ground at the mouth of their ~~tunnel~~ incline, which they do not intend to crush until it can be crushed at $20 ~~at~~ ₍per₎ ton—they pay about $45 now, and crush only 1st 2^{d} and 3^{d} class rock, I believe.

There is one Selenite crystal which is neither tied up nor marked. All the other unlabeled specimens are water formations from Steamboat Springs, 15 miles from Virginia. These Springs effect some great cures in the rhumatic line. ~~The~~ Some of the springs are hot enough to boil a hog in.

In the box are specimens from the following ledges: ⸌National; Gov. Downey; Alba Nueva; Moonlight—and casing rock of the Sheba.[6]

Sam. L. Clemens

Love to the folks.

✉—————————————————————————————

[*on outside of letter as folded:*]

Read this before open-

ing the packages

[1]The initial page or pages of this letter are missing. Presumably written to Moffett, whose capital Clemens desired to sustain his mining ventures, the letter was evidently mailed inside the "box" of separately labeled "specimens" it goes on to describe. The ore from the National ledge, near Unionville in Humboldt County, seemingly has had at least a brief time, "lying there" in Orion's Carson City office, in which to begin to decompose. Clemens had arrived in Carson City from Humboldt, via Virginia City, by 30 January, and he probably wrote no later than 1 February (see note 4).

[2]Clemens's uncle James A. H. Lampton was hoping to come to Nevada. Being a physician, Lampton would have had the mortar and pestle to pulverize the quartz sample.

[3]The Latrobe Tunnel and Mining Company of San Francisco was incorporated on 29 January 1861. Its president was Jacob L. Van Bokkelen (d. 1873), of Virginia City, who was president of the Council of the first Territorial Legislature (1861) and served on the Council of the second Territorial Legislature (1862). He was probably the legislator mentioned in chapter 25 of *Roughing It* who proposed dispensing with the legislative chaplain and who "generally sat with his feet on his desk, eating raw turnips during the morning prayer": on 14 November 1862 he did offer a council resolution that, if passed, would have eliminated the post of chaplain. Van Bokkelen's brother William, a Virginia City notary public, is not

listed in Nevada territorial directories in connection with the Latrobe Tunnel and Mining Company. The company's tunnel, which was begun on 4 February 1861 on the flat below Virginia City, ultimately penetrated about three thousand feet, reportedly passing "entirely through the Comstock lode" without striking any ore (Foster, 117; Andrew J. Marsh, 3, 449, 666 n. 11; Kelly 1863, 289, 304–5; "A Trip to Washoe," Nevada City [Calif.] *Transcript*, 10 July 61, 2).

[4] Since Clemens arrived in Virginia City on 19 January and was back in Carson City by 30 January, his descent into the Ophir (in the Virginia mining district) had to have taken place on Saturday, 25 January. This circumstance helps limit the range of probable dates for the present letter. Clemens could not have written it after Saturday, 1 February, without implying that "last Saturday night" *was* 1 February, a date on which he could not have visited the Ophir.

[5] Although Clemens had himself listed in the first territorial directory as "Assistant Secretary Nevada Territory" (Kelly 1862, 69), the only office he actually held was that of Orion's clerk during the first legislative session, 1 October–29 November 1861 (William C. Miller, 2–3).

[6] All of these ledges were on the eastern slopes of the Humboldt Mountains, the first three on a single hill near Unionville in the Buena Vista district. The Moonlight became known as one of the richest mines in the Indian district, about seven miles to the south. The Sheba was the most productive mine in the Star district, to the north of Buena Vista Cañon. A casing was a zone of "material altered by vein-action" between the vein and "unaltered" rock (Raymond, 18, 25).

To Jane Lampton Clemens and Pamela A. Moffett
8 and 9 February 1862 • Carson City, Nev. Terr.
(MS: NPV)

Carson City, Feb. 8, 1862.

My Dear Mother/ and Sister:

By George, Pamela, I begin to fear that I have invoked a Spirit of ₐsomeₐ kind or other which I will find some difficulty in laying. I wasn't much terrified by your growing *inclinations*, but when you begin to call *presentiments* to your aid, I confess that I "weaken." Mr. Moffett is right, as I said before—and I am not much afraid of his going wrong. Men are easily dealt with—but when you get the women started, you are in for it, you know. But I have decided on two things, viz: Any of you, or all of you, may live in California, for that is the Garden of Eden reproduced—but you shall never live in Nevada; and secondly, none of you, save Mr. Moffett, shall ever cross the Plains. If you were only going to ~~Denver,~~ Pike's Peak, a little matter of 700 miles from St. Joe, you might take the coach, and I wouldn't say a word. But I consider it over 2,000 miles from St. Joe to Carson, and the first 6 or 800 miles is mere Fourth of July, compared to the balance of the route. But Lord bless you, a *man* enjoys every foot of it. If you ever come here or to California, it must be by sea, you know.[1] Mr. Moffett must come by overland *coach*, though, by all means. He would consider it the jolliest little trip he ever took in his life. Either June, July or August are the proper months to make the journey in. He could not suffer from heat, and three or four heavy army blankets would make the cold nights comfortable. If the coach were full of passengers, *two* good blankets would probably be sufficient. If he comes, and b[r]ings plenty of money, and fails to invest it to his entire satisfaction, I will prophecy no more.

But I will tell you a few things which you wouldn't have found out if I hadn't got myself into this scrape. I expect to return to St. Louis in July—per steamer. I don't say that I *will* return then, or that I shall *be able* to do it—but I *expect to*—you bet. I came down here from Humboldt, in order to look after our Esmeralda interests, & my sore-backed horse and the bad roads have prevented me from making the journey. Yesterday, one of my old Esmeralda friends, Bob Howland, arrived here, and I have had a talk with him. He owns with me in the "Horatio and Derby" ledge. He says our tunnel is in 52 feet, and a small stream of water has been struck, which bids fair to become a "big thing" by the time the ledge is reached—sufficient to supply a mill. Now, if you knew anything of the value of water, here, you would perceive at a glance that if the water should al amount to 50 or 100 inches, *we* wouldn't care whether school kept or not. If the ledge should prove to be worthless, we'd *sell the water* for money enough to give us quite a lift. But you see, the ledge *will not* prove to be worthless. We have located, near by, a fine site for a mill; and when we strike the ledge, you know, we'll have a mill-site, water power and pay-rock, all handy. *Then* we shan't care whether we have capital or not. Mill-folks will build us a mill, and wait for their pay. If nothing goes wrong, we'll strike the ledge in June—and if we do, I'll be home in July, you know.[2]

So, just keep your shirt on, Pamela, until I come. Don't you know that undemonstrated human calculations won't do to bet on? Don't you know that I have only *talked*, as yet, but proved nothing? Don't you know that I have expended money in this country but have made none myself? Don't you know that I ne have never held in my hands a gold or silver bar that belonged to me? Don't you know that its all talk and no cider so far? Don't you know that people who always feel jolly, no matter where they are or what happens to them—who ẇ have the organ of Hope preposterously developed—who are endowed with an uncongealable sanguine temperament[3]—who never feel concerned about the price of corn—and who cannot, by any possibility, discover any but the *bright* side of a picture—are *very* apt to go to extremes, and exaggerate, with 40-horse microscopic power? Of course I never tried to raise these suspicions in your mind, but ẏ then your knowledge of ‸the fact that‸ some people's poor frail human nature is a sort of crazy institution anyhow, ought to have suggested them to you. Now, if I hadn't ‸thoughtlessly‸ got you into the notion of coming out here, and thereby got myself into a scrape, I wouldn't have given you that highly-colored paragraph about the mill, &c., because, you know, if that pretty little picture should fail, and wash out, and go to the Devil generally, it wouldn't cost me the loss of an hour's sleep, but you fellows would be as much distressed on my account as I could possibly be if "circumstances beyond my control" ~~should~~ ‸were to‸ prevent my being present at my own funeral. But—but—

"In the bright lexicon of youth,
There's *no such word* as Fail"—

and I'll prove it![4]

And look here. I came near forgetting it. Don't you say a word to me about "trains" across the plains.[5] Because I am down on that arrangement. That sort of thing is "played out," you know. The Overland Coach or the Mail Steamer is the thing.

You want to know something about the route between California and Nevada Territory? Suppose you take my word for it, that it is exceedingly jolly. Or take, for a winter view, J. Ross Brown's picture, in Harper's Monthly, of pack mules, tumbling fifteen hundred feet down the side of a mountain.[6] Why bless you, there's *scenery* on that route. You can stand on some of those noble peaks and see Jerusalem and the Holy Land. And you can start a boulder, and ~~watch~~ send it tearing up the earth and crashing th over trees—down—down—down—to the very devil, Madam. And you would probably stand up there and look, and stare and wonder at the magnificence spread out before you till you starved to death, if let alone. But you should take some one along to keep you moving, you know. And the way to make that journey is not by coach, because, in that case, be you ~~man~~ ‸male‸ or ~~woman,~~ ‸female,‸ ~~male or fe~~ ‸man or woman,‸

you would be eternally scared to death, at the prospect of rolling down a mountain, and it would take up so much of your time to enjoy that sort of thing, you know, that you couldn't pay much attention to the scenery. But just take the steamer to Sacramento City, then the railroad to ʄ Folsom, then buy a good horse and shin it for the mountains. You wouldn't lose anything, then, because the horse would be worth as much or more here than he cost you in California.

Since you want to know, I will inform you that an eight-stamp water-mill, put up and ready for business would cost about $10,000 to $12,000. Then, the water to run it with would cost from $1,000 to $~~25,000~~, ₌$30,000—and even more,ₓ according to the location. What I mean by that, is, that water powers in *this* vicinity, are immensely valuable. So, also, in Esmeralda. But Humboldt is a *new* country, and things don't cost so much there yet. I saw a good water power sold there for $750⁰⁰. But here is the way the thing is managed. A man with a good water power on Carson river will lean his axe up against a tree (provided you find him chopping cord-wood at $~~2~~ $4 a day,) and talking his chalk pipe out of his mouth to afford him an opportunity to spit, and answer your questions, will look you coolly in the face and tell you his little property is worth forty or fifty-thousand dollars! But you can easily fix *him*, you know. You tell him that you'll build a quartz mill on his property, and make him a fourth or a third, or a half owner in said mill in consideration of the privilege of using said property—and that will bring him to his milk in a jiffy.[7] So he spits on his hands, and goes in again with his axe, until the mill is finished, when lo! out pops the quondam wood-chopper, arrayed in purple and fine linen, and prepared to deal in bank-stock, or bet on the races, or take governmentʃ loans, with an air, as to the *amount*, of the most don't-care-a-d—n-dest ₌unconcernₓ that you can conceive of, Madam. The reason why I tell Mr. Moffett to bring money *with* him is, because my experience here has been to this effect: that 999 men out of every 1000 who come into this Territory, make this remark after they have been here long enough to look around a little: "By George, if I *just* had a thousand dollars—*I'd* be all right!" Now there's the "Horatio," for instance. There are five or six shareholders in it, and I *know* I could buy half of ~~there~~ their interests at, say $20 per foot, now that flour is worth $50 per barrel and they are pressed for money. But I am hard up myself, and *can't* buy—and in June they'll strike the ledge, and then "good-bye canary," I can't get it for love or money. Twenty dollars a foot! Think of it. For ground that is *proven* to be rich. $ Twenty dollars, Madam—and we wouldn't part with a foot of our 75 for five times the sum.[8] So it will be in Humboldt next summer. The boys will get pushed and sell ground ~~wort~~ for a song that is worth a fortune. But I am at the helm, now. I have convinced Orion that he hasn't business talent enough to carry on a peanut stand, and he has solemnly promised me that he will meddle no more with mining, or other matters not connected with the Secretary's office. So, you see, if mines are to be bought or sold, or tunnels run or shafts sunk, parties have to come to me—and me only. I'm the "firm," you know.

"How long does it take one of those infernal trains to go through?" Well, anywhere between three and five months.

Tell Margaret[9] that if you ever come to live in California, that you can promise her a home for a hundred years, and a bully one—but she wouldn't like this country. Some people are malicious enough to think that if the devil were set at liberty and told to confine himself to Nevada Territory, that he would come here and loaf sadly around, awhile, and then get ∮ homesick and go back to hell again. But I hardly believe it, you know. I am saying, mind you, that *Margaret* wouldn't like the country, perhaps—nor the devil either, for that matter,—or any other man—but *I* like it. When it rains here, it ~~does~~ never lets up till it has done all the raining it has got ‚to‚ do—and after that, there's a dry spell, you bet. Why, I have had my whiskers and moustaches so full of alkali dust that you'd have thought I worked in a starch factory and boarded in a flour barrel. And it is very healthy here. The funeral bell, with its sad accompaniments of tearful eyes, and drooping heads, and [*ink blot*] (*blast* such a pen, anyhow—I *do* think they get up pens in this country that would make the oldest man in the world cuss—if he hadn't, like me, promised that he wouldn't‚). But its healthy here, you know, if you wear a heavy beard. That is what I was trying to come at.

Since we ~~haven't~~ been here there has not been a fire—although the houses are built of wood. They "holler" fire sometimes, though, but I am always too late to see the smoke before the ‚fire‚ ᴡ is out, if they ever have any. Now they raised a yell here in front of the office a moment ago. I put away my papers, and locked up everything of value, and changed my ~~coat,~~ boots, and pulled off my coat, and went and got a bucket of water, and came back to see what the matter was, remarking to myself, "I guess I'll be on hand *this* time, any way." But I met a friend on our pavement, and he said, "Where you been? Fire's out half an hour ago. Next door, you know." (Some people appear to think other people are Telegraphs. But I made a bucket of water by the operation). Orion was up at the Governor's.

Why, Sammy is a regular prodigy. *"Tries* to say *almost* every word you tell him." But he was further advanced than that, Madam, before I left home—for he used to try to play on the piano. Now let me give you some advice. As soon as he is old enough to understand you, just tell him, "Now, my boy, every time that you allow another boy to lam you, I'll lam you myself; and whenever a boy lams you, and you fail to pitch into that boy the very next time you see him, and lam *him*, I'll lam you *twice*." And you'll never be sorry for it. Pa wouldn't allow us to fight, and next month Orion will be Governor, in the Governor's absence,[10] and then he'll be sorry that his education was so much neglected. Now, you should never despise good advice, you know, and that is what I am giving you when I warn you to teach Sammy to fight, with the same care that you teach him to pray. If he don't learn it when he is a boy, he'll never learn it afterwards, and it will gain him more respect than ~~Go~~ any other accomplishment he can acquire.

Ma says Axtell was above "suspition"—but I have searched through Webster's Unabridged, and can't find the word. However, it's of no consequence—I hope he got down safely. I knew Axtell and his wife as well as I know Dan Haines.[11] Mrs. A. once tried to embarrass me in the presence of company by asking me to name her baby, when she was well aware that I didn't know the ~~na~~ sex of that Phenomenon. But I told her to call it Frances, and spell it to suit herself. That was about 9 years ago, and Axtell had no property, and could hardly support his family by his earnings. He was a pious cuss, though. Member of Margaret Sexton's church.

And Ma says "it looks like a man~~'t~~ can't hold public office and be honest." Why, certainly not, Madam. A man *can't* hold public office and be honest. It is like a white man attempting to play Washoe Injun—that is, trying to swallow cockroaches and grasshoppers alive and kicking— ~~the~~ it can't be *did*, you know. Lord bless you, Madam it is a common practice with Orion to go about town stealing little things that happen to be lying around loose. And I don't remember having heard him speak the truth since ~~I have~~ we have been in Nevada. He even tries to prevail upon *me* to do these things, Ma, but I wasn't brought up in that way, you know. You showed the public what *you* could do in that line when you raised me, ~~you know.~~ Madam. But then you ought to have raised me first, *ma mère,* and so that Orion could have had the benefit of my example. Do you know that he stole all the stamps out [of] an 8-stamp quartz mill one night, and brought them home under his over-coat and hid them in the back room? That "let *me* out," you know.

Much obliged for the picture of Camp Benton. But it don't look like the old Fair Grounds to me.[12] Pamela, if you are still anxious [to] come here, I will answer all your questions next time.

I wrote and mailed a letter to Zeb to-day, (the 9th of February[)].[13]

Yrs &c.

Sam.

[*in margin:*] Beck Jolly will read Ma's Chinese letter for her.[14]

---

[1]In a letter of 16 and 17 January 1862 Orion Clemens warned his wife of the sort of peril a lone woman could expect while traveling overland:

> Your coming by the stage will meet my approbation, if Billy's wife [Mary Clagett] or some other well known family, or your brother John [Stotts] comes with you, but no other way. . . . Traveling across the plains sometimes develops the d—l in people. But of all ways of traveling for a woman, the very last I have even tried is a stage. Half the time for three weeks it will be so dark in the stage you can't see your hand before you. The stage is rolling and tumbling, you may be asleep, your man company awake, but pretending to be asleep. His hand wanders over you. If you catch him he snores or yawns sleepily, and you don't know whether he was asleep or awake. They say the worst enemy a woman has is *opportunity*, and if I didn't know you to be incorruptible, I would be almost doubtful whether to sleep with you or not, if you came three weeks of dark nights, through a wilderness, with only a man acquaintance. (CU-MARK)

[2]The Horatio and the Derby were adjacent ledges on Martinez Hill, Aurora. Horatio G. Phillips, Robert M. Howland, and J. L. Snyder had claimed land, water, and tunneling rights on the hill in order to dig a tunnel into the Horatio, the Derby, and five other nearby lodes (plat dated 29 Dec 61, PH in CU-MARK, courtesy of Michael H. Marleau). Clemens's participation in the tunnel enterprise predated the filing of that claim, for in a letter of 8 December 1861 Phillips had notified him that "50 ft in the Horatio was located in your name," informed him that ten feet of tunnel had been completed, and assessed him $23 as his share of associated costs (NPV). The project seemed so promising that on 16 January 1862 Orion Clemens bought twenty-five feet in the Horatio from Phillips for $125 (deed in CU-MARK). Sometime between 1880 and 1882, while writing his autobiography, Orion commented that "all the ledges and tunnels and water rights . . . proved to be worthless, and our money was thrown away!" (note attached to Phillips to SLC, 8 Dec 61, NPV).

[3]Clemens here employs the jargon of phrenology, a pseudoscience that linked psychological dispositions to physical characteristics, particularly the shape of the skull, and divided mankind into groups according to "temperaments." He had made a study of phrenology in the summer of 1855, recording his observations in his notebook (see *N&J1*, 21–24, 27–29, 32–33).

[4]The verses are quoted freely from Edward Bulwer-Lytton's 1838 blank verse play, *Richelieu*, act 3, scene 1.

From the final installment of "A Peep at Washoe"
(J[ohn] Ross Browne, 301).

[5] That is, wagon trains. Construction on the transcontinental railroad did not begin until 1863.

[6] J. Ross Browne's three-part series "A Peep at Washoe"—a tongue-in-cheek account of his sojourn in Nevada—appeared in *Harper's New Monthly Magazine* from December 1860 to February 1861. The drawing of tumbling mules was in the final installment (see above).

[7] That is, to quickly bring him "to a proper realization of his duty, condition, etc." (Mathews, 2:1055).

[8] On 1 March 1862 Clemens acquired an additional twenty-five feet in the Horatio, bringing his and Orion's holdings to a total of one hundred feet. This acquisition was part of a package of shares in sixteen mining claims that he purchased for $1,000 from John D. Kinney (deed in CU-MARK).

[9] Clemens's friend Margaret Sexton, of St. Louis.

[10] For the explanation of James Nye's absence see 8 and 9 Mar 62 to Clagett, n. 6.

[11] On 3 January 1862 the St. Louis *Missouri Republican* reported that Stephen D. Axtell, chief clerk in the county collector's office and "heretofore considered a highly respectable citizen," had confessed to embezzling $30,000 of county funds and had agreed to convey "sufficient of his property to the county to cover his fraudulent transactions" ("Surprising Developments—Heavy Defalcation—An

Old Citizen Implicated," 3). Dan Haines was another of Clemens's St. Louis acquaintances (see 2 Apr 62 to JLC, n. 7).

[12] Camp Benton was established in August 1861 as a training center for federal troops. It housed up to twenty-three thousand men in barracks just west of the St. Louis fairgrounds (Scharf, 1:400–401). In a letter of 17 and 18 November 1861 to Orion, Mollie Clemens had described her visit to the camp (CU-MARK).

[13] Zebulon Leavenworth—one of the pilots of the *John J. Roe* in 1857, while Clemens was its steersman—lived near the Moffetts in St. Louis (Webster 1949, 1).

[14] According to Samuel C. Webster, Clemens had sent his mother a letter "marked in each corner 'Private,' 'Strictly Confidential,' and so on. The family were all on edge to hear what it was about, but Grandma Clemens refused even to open it in their presence. She marched upstairs to read it—but in a minute was down again, blazing with wrath. It was written in Chinese" (*MTBus*, 66). Sobieski (Beck) Jolly (1831–1905) was another of the pilots Clemens had known on the *John J. Roe*. In addition to his ostensible proficiency in Chinese (see also 25 Aug 66 to Bowen), Jolly was "very handsome, very graceful, very intelligent, companionable," with "a fine character" and "the manners of a duke" (AD, 30 July 1906, CU-MARK, in *AMT*, 79). His riverboat career, which began in 1846 and ended with his retirement in 1885, included service throughout the Civil War piloting Union steamboats on the Mississippi and its tributaries (Ferris, 14–16). In chapter 24 of *Life on the Mississippi*, Clemens comically acknowledged Jolly's superior piloting skills by including him among the reputed "A 1 alligator pilots."

To William H. Clagett
28 February 1862 • Carson City, Nev. Terr.
(MS, *damage emended:* ViU)

‚P.S. Frank Ayres says he will take out the opera glass for me. Tell Oliver that Col. O. will send his trunk out by Weaver, if Weave concludes to go.‚[1]

Carson City, Feb. 28, 1862.

Dear Billy:

The expressman has just arrived, bringing your letter and Capt. Pfersdorff's, and my deed and John Kinney's.[2] (Kinney leaves for the States to-morrow, overland.) Bully for you! You seem to be ~~my~~ getting along swimmingly. And a thousand thanks for your liberality to me. "We may be happy yet,"[3] you know. Damn the day I left Unionville before there was any necessitary for it. For I have been sitting here swearing like a trooper ever since I arrived—and so far from being able to get out of town, one can hardly even get into the street. I am glad you have secured that lot for me, for I think, myself, it is much the best of the two. Speaking of that "National" ground, P. W. Van Winkle told me to-day that he had been trying to buy a portion of it, but Mr. Fall had concluded not to sell, —is going to keep his ground, and go out to Unionville himself.[4] However, I will try and find Fall to-morrow myself; and if I can get the ground for Sam, it shall be done—you bet.[5] Bully for the "Annie Moffett["]! (have you spelled it right?) I wouldn't have had you forget Annie for anything. I shall think a good deal of that 300 feet.[6]

Well, Billy, I can't tell just when I shall get back to Humboldt, but I am going to Esmeralda with Bunker in a week or ten days from now.[7] It would suit me the best in the world to help shove the wagon out again,, and if you and Dad[8] think you will be in shortly, I will time myself accordingly. [*in margin:* Humboldt *is* the country for us—*you bet* it is.]

Keep your eye on the old man, Billy, and don't let him get too enthusiastic, because if he does, he will begin to feel young again, like he did when he fell in the river at Honey-Lake's;[9] and being a lecherous old cuss anyhow, he might ~~vi~~ ravish one of those Pi-Utes and bring on an Indian war, you know. So, just keep an eye on him.

Oh, d—n that dog. He was always an ungrateful brute. Still, we stole him, and it was but natural that we should overlook his faults and love the ~~so~~ long-legged son-of-a-bitch anyhow. ~~But~~ Alas, poor Tom! He had a good, kind countenance, and a tender heart, and a long nose—and he was always cold. But he hath gone the way of the beautiful—even as the flowers, that bloom, and wither and die, and are seen no more forever. Peace to his ashes, and damnation to his destroyer. Amen. But I know all about this business. "Kurney" is at the bottom of it. He always had designs against Tom's life ever since Tom lammed him at Willow Grove.[10] Now between you and I, Billy, I set that dog "Kurney" down for a bloodthirsty desperado, the first time I ever looked into his vindictive countenance. And I said to myself, "Now there is a dog which is capable of doing the darkest deeds—and mind, you, my boy, he'll die with his boots on." I am astonished that Dad should keep such a reckless beast about him—and still more astonished that he should permit him to run at large. "*Prodigious!*"

Good for Billy Dixon and Judge Clagett.[11] Which reminds me that ~~we~~ Orion received a letter yesterday from his wife, in which she said your wife was very low-spirited and uneasy, and that, save through our letters, she has not heard from you since Christmas. I answered the letter right away—and if she tells your wife half I intended her to be told, I don't think she will be uneasy any longer. May be I didn't confine myself strictly to the truth, you know, but *n'importe*, my friend, "the end justifies the means," always. She has received the letters *I* brought from Humboldt by this time, though. I must be on hand to help you build your house, Billy. I feel like an old hand at that business. Indeed, it ⚡ is a great source of gratification to me to review ₐmyₐ efforts up there in the gulch.[12] I hope I am not vain-glorious—*but*, if I do ₐpossess₎ one shining talent, ₐI think₎ it is that of building willow houses out of rocks and dirt and things.

"Played out?" Is it true, though? Hath it actually come to pass? *Amen*, then—and ⚡ Amen. Sic transit gloria mundi!, glory be to God. Amen. I have swung my hat and shouted, "A "So mote it be." Alas, how have the mighty fallen! Yet we will be merciful, and temper the wind to the shorn lamb.[13]

Orion went to the postoffice as soon as we had finished reading your letter, but the expressman had already been there and got everything that belonged to you. Orion told the P. M. to put your letters in our box hereafter, so that we can mail them in a large envelop. I prepaid the express on my letter to you, Billy. I hope you did not have to pay again. We intend to ₐsend₎ you the envelops by the expressman to-morrow, if he will take them.

Well, Billy, tell Tom Smith[14] that they've been and gone and done it. Old Curtis, you know. He has thrashed our Missourians like everything. But by the Lord, they didn't do it on the Sacred Soil, my boy. They had to chase 'em clear down into Arkansas before they could whip them. There's consolation in *that*. If they had remained on the Soil, Curtis couldn't have done it. It's all in the Soil, you know. Take a Missourian on his own soil, and he is invincible.[15] Now, when I was on the soil, I used to be as terrible as an army with banners;[16] but out here on this quartz foundation, you see, I don't amount to a Damn. That's what's the matter with *me*. And they have taken Fort Henry, and Fort Donelson, and the half of Tennessee—and the stars and stripes wave over the Capitol at Nashville.[17]

And tell old Sam Montgomery that I have written to several different persons concerning his brother Jim, and I guess I'll hear from some of them before long. Give my very best regards to the boys, and tell Tom to "stand by!" and be prepared to bet on the black horse[18]—for with the assistance of that animal and a euchre deck, we'll make paupers of you and Sam when I get back. But I'll be d—d if you shall starve, either of you, my lads, even ~~if~~ though you *are* Southerners. [*in margin:* Keep your eye skinned, Billy, and steal another dog—you and Dad.]

Convey unto Dad my most high-toned love and veneration, and tell him to learn to get up early. I get up as early as 7 8 o'clock, sometimes, on purpose to enjoy the gorgeous spectacle of *t* Sunrise. After signifying my approbation, I go back to bed, ˏagain.ˏ I have been practising this sort of thing for some, time, and I mean to keep it up, for I am already improving in health, and am convinced that early rising is the cause of it. By the way, has "the old man" built that chimney to Fort Briggs, yet?[19] I intended to show him how to do it before I left, but I forgot it. *T* However, tell him to copy ~~of~~ after the plan of the fire-place we built in the gulch, and it will do. I superintended that little piece ˏofˏ architecture, you know, and I confess that I am rather proud of it than otherwise.

And look here, you fellows. You can't depend on the Colonel and I, d—n you, but you must send your petitions for mail routes to the Governor. And you have had your trouble for your pains, and I am *not* sorry. You can just learn better, now, and get up your petitions again; for they have not been heard of since the expressman delivered them at the Governor's office. They are *lost*, my boy.

Billy, if you have altered your name in your seal,[20] perhaps you had better send Orion a new copy to be filed here. Orion sends his love.

Orion has written to Capt. Pfersdorff, and enclosed the last dispatches. If there is anything important in the morning paper, I will send it with this.

A lot of my old St. Louis chums will be out in the Spring—and when we get Billy Dixon & the other Keokuk boys here, Oh, no, we won't stuff ballot-boxes and go to Congress nor nothing. By no means. "I hope I'm not a oyster though I may not wish to live in crowds." Now I don't mean to say that Nipper's remark is ~~by~~ at all pertinent, you know, but I just happened to think of "them old Skettleses," and the quotation followed as a matter of course. And equally of course, the whole Dombey family come trooping after: Cap'en Ed'ard Cuttle, mariner, as Uncle Sol's successor, polishing the chronometers, and making calculations concerning the ebb and flow of the human tide in the street; and watching the stars with a growing interest, as if ˏheˏ felt that he had fallen ~~air~~ heir to a certain amount of stock in them; and that old fool of a nurse at Brighton, who thought the house was so "gashly;" and "that Innocent," Toots; and the fated Biler; and Florence, my darling; and "rough old Joey B., Sir;" and "Wal'r, my lad," and the Cap'en's eccentric timepiece, and his sugar tongs, and other little property which he "made over" jintly;" and looming grandly in the rear, comes ponderous Jack Bunsby! Oh, d—n it, I wish I had the book.[21] Good-bye to you all, Billy, & neglect no opportunity to write.

Your old friend
Sam.

[in pencil on a small scrap of paper, both sides:]

P. S.—Run for Recorder. We have bought a fine pair of hay-scales, and if we go to Humboldt after a while, we'll probably have them shipped there from Folsom to weigh your quartz with. How would that pay? Then we could weigh, work the "process" and do your Recorder business and leave you entirely free when legal business was pressing.[22] When you write me (to Carson, always,) mention all these things in such a way that Orion cannot understand them. I don't care a d—n for failures and disappointments, but they nearly kill him, you know.

P.P.S. Get the right from Supervisors to put our Scales where all the rock will have to pass over them on its way to the mills.

▣——————————————————————————————

[in ink:] W^m. H. Clagett, Esq. | Unionville, | Humboldt Co. | Nevada Ty
[no postage stamp]

[1]Mentioned here are Clemens's friends Augustus (Gus) Oliver and John B. Onstine. Ayres may have been "F. Aires," who, along with Clemens, reportedly was among the earliest prospectors to arrive in Unionville, "soon after the arrival of the first party of explorers" in May 1861 (Angel, 459). Weaver has not been identified.

[2]On 28 January 1862 Clemens had paid Hugo Pfersdorff $100 for ten feet in the Alba Nueva ledge in the Buena Vista district of Humboldt County. On the same date John D. Kinney paid Pfersdorff $500 for ten feet in the National ledge in the same district (deeds in CU-MARK).

[3]An aria from English composer Michael William Balfe's 1844 opera, *The Daughter of St. Mark*. The libretto was written by the English theatrical manager Alfred Bunn (Sears, 603; BBC, 1:57, 4:1161).

[4]P. W. Van Winkle was a Carson City notary public (advertisement, Carson City *Silver Age*, 15 Sept 61, 1; Kelly 1863, 111). John C. Fall, formerly of Marysville, California, was a Carson City banker and merchant. He was one of the initial investors in Humboldt County mining properties, and he owned the Pioneer Mill near Unionville, the first quartz mill in the Buena Vista district. As a major owner and superintendent of the rich Arizona mine, discovered near Unionville in 1863, he continued to be identified with the town's affairs into the 1870s (Angel, 450,

459, 555; Wyoming 1862b, 1). He may have regretted his decision not to sell his National holdings, for, like most other mines in the Buena Vista area, the coveted National failed to live up to early expectations.

[5] Sam Montgomery, of Unionville, was a southerner who had begun prospecting in the Buena Vista district soon after its exploration by Hugo Pfersdorff in May 1861 (Angel, 459).

[6] The "Anne Moffatt" ledge was located in the Buena Vista district, about one mile southwest of Unionville (Milleson map). No further information about this claim has been discovered.

[7] In fact, Clemens did not go to the Esmeralda mining district until early April 1862.

[8] Cornbury S. Tillou, Clemens's companion on his December 1861 trip to Humboldt County, also referred to as "the old man."

[9] Honey Lake Smith's, a trading post and stage station, earlier called Williams' Station, was on the north bank of the Carson River on the road from Carson City to Unionville. The site, near the present town of Silver Springs, is now covered by the waters of the Lahontan Reservoir (Gianella, 4–7). It was there that Clemens was marooned in January 1862 while returning from Unionville to Carson City. Since his companions at the time evidently did not include Tillou, it may be that the blacksmith fell in the Carson River on his way *to* Unionville with Clemens in December 1861 (see 30 Jan 62 to JLC, nn. 3, 4, 13).

[10] "Willow" was "the name of most frequent occurrence in Nevada, used principally for creeks and springs for willow trees growing there" (Carlson, 247). Clemens's Willow Grove has not been identified.

[11] William W. Dixon of Keokuk, Iowa, and William Clagett's father, Thomas W. Clagett, who served in the Iowa legislature and as a judge of the district court. Dixon, aged twenty-five, was a Keokuk notary public and lawyer, the son of Thomas Clagett's law partner, George C. Dixon. William Clagett's good news probably was that his father and Dixon would be coming to Nevada. Judge Clagett did not make the trip (see 8 and 9 Mar 62 to Clagett), but Dixon arrived in 1862 and served as prosecuting attorney for Humboldt County from 22 December 1862 until 9 January 1863 (Stiles, 348; OC 1856, 61, 65; OC 1857, 24; Dixon, 4:249; Angel, 448).

[12] Clemens alludes to the "small, rude cabin" that he, Clagett, Oliver, and Tillou had built in Unionville in December 1861 (see *Roughing It,* chapter 28).

[13] "So mote it be" was a prayer response in some Masonic initiation rites, including those for two of the degrees Clemens had attained in St. Louis in 1861: Entered Apprentice and Master Mason (Macoy, 24–25, 68). The concluding allusions are to 2 Samuel 1:25 ("How are the mighty fallen in the midst of the battle!") and Laurence Sterne's version of a French proverb: "God tempers the wind . . . to the shorn lamb" ("Maria," in *A Sentimental Journey through France and Italy,* 1768).

[14] A Unionville acquaintance (see also 17 May 62 to OC, n. 2).

[15] On 13 February 1862 General Samuel R. Curtis's Union forces moved southward through divided Missouri into Springfield, driving the rebel troops under General Sterling Price—"largely made up of Missouri militia"—across the state line into Arkansas. "This movement for the time, freed the State of the presence of armed opponents of the General government; and the St. Louis papers of February 22, announced with no little satisfaction, that 'the last vestige of military

insurrection had been swept away'" (Davis and Durrie, 172, 174). Clemens's remarks here, while they do not evidence any profound conviction or concern, show his sympathies to be with Price's defeated troops.

[16] Song of Solomon 6:10.

[17] Ulysses S. Grant had captured Fort Henry and Fort Donelson, both in Tennessee, on 6 February and 16 February 1862, respectively. These victories were the first major Union triumphs of the war; they opened the way for the advance on Nashville, the Confederate capital of Tennessee, which was occupied by Union troops on 25 February.

[18] The following bill of sale for this animal is entirely in Clemens's hand (Clagett, PH in CU-MARK):

Carson City, Dec. 1st, 1861

W[m.] H. Clagett,
    Bought of Sam. L. Clemens,
One Black Horse—white face—— $45.00
               Rec'd Payment,
               Sam. L. Clemens.

It is likely that this was the original of the "Genuine Mexican Plug," which, according to chapter 24 of *Roughing It*, Clemens was unable to sell or trade and finally gave "to a passing Arkansas emigrant whom fortune delivered into my hand."

[19] Possibly a reference to a house in Unionville being constructed by Tillou. He and Clagett owned adjoining lots there (Fred Clagett to Edgar M. Branch, 15 May 1984).

[20] Used by Clagett in his capacity as a Unionville notary public.

[21] *Dombey and Son*, which Clemens had taken with him to Humboldt in December 1861 (see 30 Jan 62 to JLC).

[22] Clagett never became the Humboldt County recorder. William Brayton, the incumbent at this time, had been elected in January 1862 and would be re-elected the following September (Angel, 448).

To William H. Clagett
8 and 9 March 1862 • Carson City, Nev. Terr.
(MS: ViU)

Carson City, March 8th 1862.

Dear Billy:

    As a good opportunity offers, I have embraced it to send you some legal and letter paper, and a copy of the laws.[1] I send the pencils, pens, &c., because I don't know whether you have run out of such things or not. If you have got plenty of stationery, maybe Sam and Tom[2] have not. I also send you some more envelops. The Colonel[3] proposes to start to-morrow or next day.

I hunted up Fall, but he would not sell me his ground for Sam. Then I told him he had better go to Unionville and "nurse" a good thing while he had it. He said he would.

John Kinney has gone to the States, *via* San Francisco.

Your Father has purchased the Keokuk "Journal,"—so he will hardly come out here this year—hey?[4]

I have heard from several reliable sources that Sewall will be here shortly, and has sworn to whip me on sight. Now what would you advise a fellow to do?—take a thrashing fo from the son-of-a-bitch, or bind him over to keep the peace? I don't see why he should dislike *me*. He is a yankee,—and I naturaly love a yankee.[5]

I stole a bully dog the other day—but he escaped again. Look out for one. That *other* dog, over whose fate a dark mystery hangs, has not revisited the glimpses of the moon yet, in this vicinity, although he has been seen in a certain locality—whereof it would be Treason to speak. D—n the beast—does he intend to haunt us like a nightmare for the balance of his days?

The Governor's Cavalcade left for California the other day. Some of the retainers I will name: the Governor and Gov. Roop, Boundary-line Commissioners; accompanied by Mr. Gillson, Mr. Kinkead and others— and followed by Bob Howland, Chief Valet de Chambre to His Excellency, and Bob Haslan, Principal Second Assistant ditto ditto.[6] What do you [make of] that, for instance? There were quite a number in the Cavalcade, and Haslan brought up the rear on a mule. Bob Howland expects to sell some ground in San Francisco.

You say the "Annie Moffett *Company*"—isn't that the name of the *ledge*, too? I hope so.

I would like to write you some news, Billy, but unfortunately, I haven't got any to write. I couldn't write it, though, if I had, for I am in a bad humor, and am only writing anyhow, because I hate to lose the opportunity. You see I have been playing cards with Bunker, and the d—d old Puritan wouldn't play fairly—and I made injurious remarks and jumped the game.

I send a St. Louis Republican for Tom. There is something in it from "Ethan Spike."[7]

Enclosed please find Mr. Cox's Speech.[8]

If you and Dad intend coming down, Billy, with the wagon, don't fail to write and say about what time you will be here. I leave for Esmeralda next week some time, with Major General BBBunker, L.L.D.,

Esq—provided "nothing happens." But this *do* happen in this country, constantly. In fact, it is about the d—est country in the world for things to happen in. *My* calculations never come out right. However, as I said before, We May be Happy Yet.

Remember me kindly to the boys—not forgetting "the old man," of course. I have labored hard to get a copy of "Fannie Hill"[9] for him to read, but I have failed sadly.

Sunday.—I intended to finish this letter to-day, but I went to church —and busted! For a man who can listen for an hour to Mr. White, the whining, nasal, Whangdoodle preacher, and then sit down and write, without shedding melancholy from his pen as a ducks water slides from a duck's back, is more than mortal. Or less. I fear I shall not feel cheerful again until the beans I had for dinner begin to operate.[10]

Which reminds me of that afternoon in Sacramento cañon,[11] when I gained such a brilliant victory of over Oliver and Mr. Tillouw, and drove them in confusion and dismay from behind my batteries.

We have not heard from home for some time, and I have only written two letters to St Louis since I arrived here.

John D. Winters has sold out his interest in the Ophir for a hundred thousand dollars.[12]

J. L. G. and his father[13] are still flourishing in Chinatown. Mr. Bunker saw them there the other day.

Tom Nye is down at Fort Churchill. Write, at your earlies[t] convenience.

Your sincere friend
Sam L. Clemens

W[m.] H. Clagett, Esq. | Unionville, | Humboldt Co. | N.T. [*no postage stamp*]

[1] *Laws of the Territory of Nevada, Passed at the First Regular Session of the Legislative Assembly* (San Francisco: Valentine and Company, 1862).

[2] Sam Montgomery and Tom Smith (or Messersmith).

[3] John B. Onstine.

[4] The Keokuk *Journal* ceased publication in November 1861 and reappeared the following month as the Keokuk *Constitution* (Winifred Gregory, 176). The *Constitution*, edited for many years by Judge Thomas W. Clagett, had a fiery history during the Civil War. Clagett, "aristocrat, capitalist, lawyer, politician, . . . published scurrilous articles that reflected on the bravery of the northern soldiers and the Union cause." Finally, on 19 February 1863, a group of soldiers enraged at Clagett's editorials marched on the newspaper office, dismantled the presses

and type cases, and threw them into the Mississippi River. "Eventually the presses were fished out, and the *Constitution* resumed publication, its sentiments cooled for the duration of the war" (Writers' Program, 61).

[5] Clemens and G. T. Sewall presumably became acquainted while Clemens was prospecting in Humboldt County in December 1861 and January 1862, but the precise cause of their antagonism is unknown. Sewall had lived in the area for approximately eight years, was active in mining, and had been appointed county judge by Governor Nye in December 1861. In 1861 Sewall was briefly associated with two of Nevada's three newspapers. According to Orion Clemens, writing in August of that year, the Silver City *Washoe Times* was "recently purchased by G. T. Sewall, who is now in partnership with Mr. [John C.] Lewis of the [Carson City] 'Silver Age,' in both papers, of which they will be editors" (OC to Elisha Whittlesey, 21 Aug 61, NvU-NSP). Lewis and Sewall were commissioned, with Orion Clemens's endorsement, to print the journals and laws of the first Territorial Legislature. Then in November 1861, in the middle of the legislative session, they acrimoniously dissolved their partnership, aborting their printing contract and causing considerable embarrassment and aggravation to Orion (see 25 June 62 to OC, n. 2). It is possible that his brother then took up the cudgels in his behalf. A remark in Clemens's 9 July 1862 letter to Orion suggests that he was irritated at Lewis as well as Sewall. Whatever the cause of the dispute, within a few months Clemens revenged himself by ridiculing Sewall in "Petrified Man" in the Virginia City *Territorial Enterprise* (see 21 Oct 62 to OC and MEC).

[6] Governor Nye was on his way to Sacramento to confer with the California legislature in an effort to settle the dispute over Nevada's western boundary. His cavalcade included: Isaac N. Roop (1822–69), head of the provisional government of Nevada Territory during 1859 and 1860 and currently a member of the territorial Council; George Gillson, Nye's special assistant for Indian affairs; John H. Kinkead (1826–1904), a Carson City merchant with numerous mining, milling, and real-estate interests, who was appointed territorial treasurer by Nye in February 1862, later served in the state constitutional conventions, and became Nevada's third governor (1879–82); Clemens's Aurora cohort Robert M. Howland, who enjoyed Nye's patronage as a result of their mutual friendship with Secretary of State William H. Seward; and Robert T. Haslan, page of the territorial House. Nye's mission was a failure. California refused to make concessions, and the boundary conflict continued (Andrew J. Marsh, 27, 666 n. 13, 690 n. 253; Mack 1936, 394–97; Mack 1961a, 30; Kelly 1862, 11).

[7] The Ethan Spike letters, a series of humorous dialect sketches that repeatedly condemned slavery and its supporters, were published in the Portland (Maine) *Transcript* between 1846 and 1863 and were widely reprinted in newspapers across the country. They were written by Matthew F. Whittier (1812–83), younger brother of John Greenleaf Whittier. His creation, Ethan Spike, was a New England backwoodsman whose letters, like the writings of Artemus Ward and Petroleum V. Nasby, were marked by cacography and malapropisms (Griffin, 646–63). On 3 February 1862 the St. Louis *Missouri Republican* (4) printed the following excerpt:

A DOWN EAST JURYMAN.

["Ethan Spike" contributes to the Portland Transcript a sketch of his experience as a juryman. The first cases he was called to try were capital ones—the criminals being a German and a "nigger" respectively.]

"Hev you formed any opinion for or agin the prisoners?" said the judge.

"Not perticular agin the Jermin," says I, "but I hate niggers as a general principle, and shall go for hanging this here old white wooled cuss, whether he killed Mr. Cooper or not," says I.

"Do you know the nature of an oath?" the clark axed me.

"I orter," says I. "I've used enough of 'em. I begun to swear when I was only about—"

"That'll do," says the clark. "You kin go bum," says he, "you won't be wanted in this ere case," says the clark, says he.

"What?" says I, "aint I to try this nigger at all?"

"No," says the clark.

"But I'm a jewryman," says I, "and you can't hang the nigger onless I've sot on him," says I.

"Pass on," says the clark, speaking rather cross.

"But," says I, "you mister, you don't mean as you say; I'm a regular jewryman, you know. Drawed aout of the box by the seelick man," says I. "I've ollers had a hankering to hang a nigger, and now, when a merciful dispensatory seems to have provided one for me, you say I shan't sit on him! Ar this your free institutions? Is this the nineteenth centry? And is this our boasted"— Here somebody hollored "Silence in Court."

"The Court be—!" I didn't finish the remark fore a couple of constables had holt of me, and in the twinkling of a bed post I was hustled down stairs into the street.

"Naow, Mr. Editor, let me ask, what are we comin' to, when jewrymen—legal, lawful jewrymen, kin be tossed about in this way? Talk about Cancers, Mormons, Spiritualism, free love and panics—whar are they in comparison? Here's a principle upsot. As an individual, perhaps, I'm of no great account; t'an't fur me to say; but when as an enlightened jewryman, I was tuk and carried down stairs by profane hands, just for assertin my right to sit on a nigger—why it seems to me the pillows of society were shook; that in my sacred person the hull State itself was, figgeratively speakin, kicked down stairs! If thar's law in the land I'll have this case brought under a writ of habeus Corpus or icksey Dicksit.

The 3 February *Republican*, presumably sent by Jane Clemens and Pamela Moffett, probably was Clemens's enclosure. It is conceivable that he enclosed a weekly *Republican* containing both the Ethan Spike excerpt and the speech discussed in note 8, but no copy of such a paper has been located. In chapter 6 of *Adventures of Huckleberry Finn* (1885), Clemens was to have the disreputable Pap Finn deliver an antigovernment, antiblack harangue similar to Ethan Spike's.

[8] On 31 January 1862, Ohio Democrat Samuel S. Cox (1824–89) delivered an address in the House of Representatives in defense of General George B. McClellan's handling of the war effort, and in favor of a Northern accommodation with slavery. Cox's speech was a rebuttal to remarks made the day before by Congressman John A. Gurley (1813–63), also of Ohio, who was a radical Republican and abolitionist. In an attempt to discredit Gurley's pro-Union sympathies, Cox in part berated him for "rehearsing again his contempt for the Union, which he expressed in his printed speech made at Cleveland on the day of John Brown's obsequies, when he said that no purer spirit than John Brown's had ever entered Paradise for the past thousand years; and that he would rend the Union to destroy slavery." Clemens probably enclosed the text of Cox's speech that filled more than four columns in the St. Louis *Missouri Republican* of 5 February 1862 ("Ohio vs. Ohio," 2). The speech soon issued in pamphlet form (Cox).

[9] The erotic novel by John Cleland. It appeared originally as *Memoirs of a Woman of Pleasure* (1749) and then, abridged by the author, as *Memoirs of Fanny Hill* (1750).

[10] The Reverend A. F. White arrived in Carson City from Gilroy, California, in September 1861 to act as pastor of the newly formed First Presbyterian Church, of which Orion Clemens was a member. White secured a series of political posts:

chaplain of the territorial House of Representatives during the October–November 1861 session; superintendent of Ormsby County schools, 1862–63; superintendent of public instruction for the territory and then the state of Nevada, 1863–66; and later, state mineralogist (Andrew J. Marsh, 670–71 n. 46). His nomination to the post of chaplain of the legislative Council in October 1861 sparked a comical controversy over the necessity for his services (see *Roughing It*, chapter 25, and Mack 1947, 89–90). White was widely known for his series of sermons on the pecuniary advantages of observing the gospel (for Clemens's jibes at White's worldliness, see SLC 1864b, 4:3, and SLC 1864d, 3). No doubt Clemens associated White's pulpit style with that of the "Hard-shell Baptist" preacher whose sermon, "Where the Lion Roareth and the Wang-Doodle Mourneth," was a staple of frontier humor (see *N&J2*, 362 n. 22). The "Whangdoodle," a "mysterious animal, like the 'gyascutis' of circus fame, has never been beheld of man and its attributes and habits are entirely unknown" (Maitland, 300).

[11] Located in the West Humboldt mountain range not far from the Buena Vista district, which Clemens had explored in December 1861 and January 1862.

[12] John D. Winters (1830–1900), a Carson City resident and a member of the 1861 territorial House of Representatives, had gone from Illinois to California in 1848 and then migrated to Nevada in 1857. He was the only one of the original discoverers of the Comstock lode to retain an interest after 1860. Winters owned quartz mills at Dayton and Aurora and held a one-eighteenth interest in the Ophir Silver Mining Company, which he had helped to organize (Andrew J. Marsh, 667 n. 19; Kelly 1862, 218; Ratay, 293). The day before Clemens wrote this letter, the Carson City *Silver Age* reported Winters's sale of his Ophir stock for "the snug sum of one hundred thousand dollars" ("Large Sale," San Francisco *Alta California*, 13 Mar 62, 1, reprinting the *Silver Age* of 7 Mar 62).

[13] Unidentified.

To Jane Lampton Clemens
20 March 1862 • Carson City, Nev. Terr.
(Keokuk *Gate City*, 25 June 62)

CARSON CITY, March 20, 1862.

MY DEAR MOTHER:—

Lo! the poor Indian, whose untutored mind,
Impels him, in order to raise the wind,
To double the pot and go it blind,
Until he's busted, you know.

I wrote the three last lines of that poem, Ma, and Daniel Webster wrote the other one[1]—which was really very good for Daniel, considering that he wasn't a natural poet. He used to say himself, that unabridged dictionaries was *his* strong suit. Now if you should happen to get aground on those two mysterious expressions in the third line, let me caution you, Madam, before you reach after that inevitable "Whole Duty of Man,"[2] that you'll not be likely to find any explanation of them in that useful and highly entertaining volume, because I've got that learned author cornered at last—got the dead-wood on him, Ma—and you'll get no consolation out of him, you know; for those are Poker expressions—technical terms made use of in the noble game of Poker. And Poker not being a duty of man at all, is probably not even mentioned in that book; therefore, I have got him, Madam, where he can neither trump nor follow suit.

Bully for me.

But you said in your last, "Do tell me all about the lordly sons of the forest, and the graceful and beautiful sq-squaws, (what an unpleasant word,) sweeping over the prairies on their fiery steeds, or chasing the timid deer, or reposing in the shade of some grand old tree, lulled by the soft music of murmuring brooks and warbling birds—*do*."

Gently, now,—gent-ly, Madam. You *can't* mean the Pi-Utes, or the Washoes, or the Shoshones, do you? Because if you do, you are barking up the wrong tree, you know; or in other words, you've got the wrong sow by the ear, Madam. For among those tribes there are no lordly sons of the forest, for the ferocious reason that there are no forests of any consequence here. At any rate, I am confident that those fellows are never designated by that name in this Territory. Generally speaking, we call them sons of the devil, when we can't think of anything worse. And they don't sweep over the prairies on their fiery steeds,—these Washoes, and Pi-Utes and Shoshones, don't,—because they haven't got any, you know. And there are no prairies, Ma, because sage-brush deserts don't come under that head, in this portion of Paradise Lost. Nor they don't chase the timid deer; nor they don't repose in the shade of some grand old tree; nor they don't get lulled by the soft music of murmuring brooks and warbling birds. None of them. Because, when the timid deer come prospecting around here, and find that hay is worth one hundred and fifty dollars a ton, and sage-brush isn't good to eat, they just turn their bob-tails toward the rising sun and skedaddle, my dear. And all that about these Pi-Utes sunning themselves in the shade of the grand old trees, is a grand old humbug, you know—on account of the scarcity of the raw material. Also the item about the warbling birds. Because there are no warbling birds here, except magpies and turkey-buzzards. And they don't warble any to signify, because, if they fooled their time away with that sort of nonsense they would starve to death, suddenly. I tell you, Madam, that when a buzzard moves his family into Nevada Territory, he soon discovers that he has got to shin around and earn his living by the sweat of his brow, and that singing is played out with *him*. Moreover, Ma, you know as well as any one what a great puffed-up, stupid buzzard looks like, so you can picture the bird to yourself as I invariably see him here— standing solemnly on a decomposed ox, (and looking for the world as if he had his hands under his coat-tails,) with his head canted to one side, his left leg advanced to steady himself, and chewing a fragrant thing of entrails with their ends dangling about his portly bosom. I ask you in all candor, Madam, if the best disposed buzzard in the world could warble under such circumstances? Scasely. But wouldn't it make a bully coat-of-arms for the Territory?—neat and appropriate, and all that? And wouldn't it look gay on the great seal, and the military commissions, and so forth, and so on, and cetera? I proposed it, but the Secretary of the Territory said it was "disgusting." So he got one put through the Legislature with star-spangled banners and quartz mills and things in it. And nary buzzard. It is all right, perhaps—but *I* know there are more buzzards than quartz-mills in Nevada Territory. I understand it though—*he* wanted the glory of discovering and inventing and designing the coat-of-arms of this great Territory—savvy?—with a lot of barbarous latin about *"Volens and Potens"*—(able and willing, you know,[)] which would have done just as well for my buzzard as it does for his quartz-mills.[3]

But if you want a full and correct account of these lovely Indians— not gleaned from Cooper's novels, Madam, but the result of personal observation—a strictly reliable account, which you could bet on with as much confidence as you could on four aces, you will find that on that subject I am a Fund of useful information to which the whole duty of man isn't a circumstance. For instance: imagine this warrior Hoop-de-doodle-do, head chief of the Washoes. He is five feet seven inches high; has a very broad face, whose coat of red paint is getting spotty and dim in consequence of accumulating dirt and grease; his hair is black and straight, and dangles about his shoulders; his battered stove-pipe hat is trimmed all over with bits of gaudy ribbon and tarnished artificial flowers, and he wears it sometimes over his eyes, with an exceedingly gallus air, and sometimes on the back of his head; on his feet he wears one boot and one shoe—very ancient; his imperial robe, which almost drags the ground, is composed of a vast number of light-gray rabbit-skins sewed together; but the crowning glory of his costume, (which he sports on great occasions in corduroy pants, and dispensing with the robe,) is a set of ladies' patent extension steel-spring hoops, presented to him by Gov. Nye—and when he gets that arrangement on, he looks like a very long and very bob-tailed bird in a cage that isn't big enough for him.[4] Now, Ma, you know what the warrior Hoop-de-doodle-doo looks like—and if you desire to know what he smells like, let him stand by the stove a moment, but have your hartshorn handy, for I tell you he could give the stink-pots of Sebastopol[5] four in the game and skunk them. Follow him, too, when he goes out, and burn gun powder in his footsteps; because wherever he walks he sheds vermin of such prodigious size that the smallest specimen could swallow a grain of wheat without straining at it, and still feel hungry. You must not suppose that the warrior drops these vermin from choice, though. By no means, Madam—for he knows something about them which you don't; viz, that they are good to eat. There now. Can you find anything like that in Cooper? Perhaps not. Yet I could go before a magistrate and testify that the portrait is correct in every particular. Old Hoop himself would say it was "heap good."

This morning I had a visit from three of the head-chief Hoop-de-doodle-doo's wives—graceful, beautiful creatures, called respectively, Timid-Rat, Soaring Lark and Gentle Wild-Cat. (You see, like all Indians, they glory in high-sounding names.) They had broad, flat faces, which were dirty to the extreme of fashion, they wore the royal rabbit skin robe, their stringy matted hair hung nearly to their waists, they had forgotten their shoes, and left their bonnets at home, only one of them wore jewelry, the Timid Rat around whose leathery throat was suspended a regal necklace composed of scraps of tin. Their shapelessness caused them to resemble three great muffs. The young chief Bottled Thunder was with the party, bottled up in a sort of long basket and strapped to the back of the Soaring Lark.

Also a juvenile muff, in the person of the Princess Invisible Rainbow, with a cigar box strapped to her back, containing a bogus infant made of rags—which leads me to suspect that a weakness for doll-babies is not a result of education, but an instinct, which comes as natural to any species of girl as keeping clothing store does to a jew.

You see, ma, I was taking breakfast with a friend, this morning, and the Princesses came and rested their elbows on the window sill and thrust their heads in, like three very ancient and smoky portraits trying to get out of their frame. They examined the breakfast leisurely, and criticised it in their own tongue; they pointed at each article of food, with their long, skinny fingers, and asked each other's opinion about it; and they kept an accurate record of each mouthful we took, and figured up the total, occasionally. After awhile the Gentle Wild Cat remarked: "May be whity man no heap eat um grass-hopper?" (their principal article of diet, ma,) and John replied, "May be whity man no heap like um grass-hop-per—*savvy!*" And thus the Lark: "May be bimeby Injun heap ketch um sage-hen." "Sage-hen heap good—bully!" said John. You see, these sav-ages speak broken English, madam, and you've got to answer accord-ingly, because they can't understand the unfractured article, you know. We held further conversation with them, of the same interesting charac-ter, after which we closed the "talk" by giving them a bar of soap and a cup of coffee for breakfast, and requesting them to leave, which they did, after they had begged a few old shirts, boots, hats, etc., and a deck of cards. They adjourned to the wood pile, and resolved to poker a little— for these Indians are inveterate gamblers, ma. First they "dealt" and "antied," threw up their "hands," and "doubled the pot," and dealt again. This time the Gentle Wild Cat "went blind," to the extent of a pair of boots; the Timid Rat "saw the blind," although it took a check shirt and a Peruvian hat to "come in;" the Soaring Lark "straddled the blind," which created a sensation, you know, and seemed to cause the other ladies great anxiety of mind, as to whether the Lark held an "ace full," or was only "bluffing." However, when an Indian gets to gambling he doesn't care a cent for expenses, so they rallied and "came in" handsomely. And the way old clothes were piled up there, when the betting had fairly com-menced, was interesting. As soon as one Princess would bet a hat, another would "see that hat" and "go a pair of socks better;" until the Timid Rat had staked her darling necklace, and the Gentle Wild Cat's last shirt was on the pile. At this stage of the game, great excitement prevailed, and the Soaring Lark was in despair, for she couldn't "come in." Presently, aware that she was the centre of an absorbing interest, and appreciating the grandeur of her position, she grew desperate and gallantly "called" her opponents, for she unstrapped the Bottled Thunder, and bet that mighty Prince against the game, and all hands said bully for the Lark. The de-nouement was thrilling. The Gentle Wild Cat showed four aces, and thereby "busted" the party, madam, because four aces can't be beaten, you know. Make a note of that on the fly-leaf of your Whole Duty of Man, for future reference. You will find it useful, if you ever turn Injun, for then your dusky compatriots will not think much of you if you don't gamble.

Now, if you are acquainted with any romantic young ladies or gentlemen who dote on these loves of Indians, send them out here before the disease strikes in.

S. L. C.

[1] The first line is from Alexander Pope's "Essay on Man" (1733–34).

[2] A standard religious work written in 1658. Its authors may have included Richard Allestree and Bishop John Fell.

[3] Orion Clemens suggested a design for the territorial seal to the legislature on 7 October 1861: "Mountains, with a stream of water coursing down their sides and falling on the overshot wheel of a quartz mill at their base. A miner leaning on his pick and upholding a United States flag. A motto expressing the two ideas of loyalty to the Union and the wealth to sustain it—'*volens et potens*' " (*Journal of the Council*, 42; also in Andrew J. Marsh, 44–45). The Territorial Legislature passed an act establishing the seal, as conceived by Orion, on 28 November 1861 (Andrew J. Marsh, 48, 370, 374).

Seal of the Territory of Nevada, designed by Orion Clemens.
Mark Twain Papers, The Bancroft Library (CU-MARK).

[4] Governor Nye and Indian Agent Warren H. Wasson had visited the Indian tribes at Walker River and Pyramid Lake in late July and early August 1861 (Mack 1936, 314–15). On 8 August the Marysville (Calif.) *Appeal* (2) carried this item: "HOOP-DE-DOODEN-DOO.—Among the presents brought out by Governor Nye, of Nevada Territory, for the Pah-Utes, is a full assortment of hoops, which the *Enterprise* thinks will not assist the wild squaws in the navigation of the sagebrush and chaparal. Probably they are of the peaceful sort, and are intended to

displace the obsolete war-*whoops*." The Virginia City *Territorial Enterprise*'s comment on the gift of hoops, published on 3 August, was: "The idea of an Indian maiden treading the forests in the full panoply of hoops, is a refinement on romance itself" (reprinted in "Gov. Nye's Doings," Marysville [Calif.] *Appeal*, 8 Aug 61, 3).
[5] See 5 Aug 56 to HC, n. 10.

To Jane Lampton Clemens
2 April 1862 • Carson City, Nev. Terr.
(MS: NPV)

Carson City, April 2, 1862.

My Dear Mother:

Yours of March 2[d], has just been received. I see I am in for it again—with Annie.[1] But she ought to know that I was always stupid. She used to try to teach me lessons from the Bible, but I never could understand them. Don't she remember telling me the story of Moses, one Sunday, last Spring, and how hard she tried to ~~make~~ explain it and simplify it so that I could understand it—but I *couldn't?* And how she said it was strange that while her ma and her grandma and her uncle Orion could understand anything in the world, I ~~couldn't~~ was so dull that I couldn't understand the "*ea-siest* thing?" And don't she remember that finally a light broke in upon me and I said it was all right—that I knew old Moses himself—and that he kept a clothing store in Market street? And then she went to her ma and ~~sh~~ said she didn't know what would become of her uncle Sam—he was too dull to learn anything—ever! And I'm just as dull yet. Now I have no doubt her letter was spelled right, and was correct in all particulars—but then I had to read it according to my lights; and they being inferior, she ought to overlook the mistakes I make—especially, as it is not *my* fault that I wasn't born with good sense. I am sure she will detect an encouraging ray of intelligence in that ₍last₎ argument.

Lord bless me, who can write where Orion is. I wish he had been endowed with some conception of music—for, with his diabolical notions of time and tune he is worse than the itch when he begins to whistle. And for some wise ~~not a~~ but not apparent reason, ~~p~~Providence has ordained that he shall *whistle* when he feels pleasant— ~~which~~ notwithstanding the fact that the barbarous sounds he produces are bound to drive comfort

away from every one else ˌwithin, in hear-shot of them. I have got to sit
still and be tortured with his infernal discords, and fag-ends of tunes
which were worn out and discarded before "B "Roll on—Sil-ver Moo-
oon" became popular, strung together without regard to taste, time, tune
melody, or the eternal fitness of things,[2] because, if I should boil over and
say I wish his music would bust him, there'd be a row, you know. For I
discovered, by accident, that he looks upon his Variations as a so as something of an accomplishment, and when he does warble, he warbles very
complacently. I told him once, on the plains, that I couldn't stand his
cursed din—that he was worse than a rusty wheel-barrow—and if he did
not stop it I would get out of the coach. Now he didn't *say* "get out and be
d—d," but I know he thought it, Ma, and if I were you I would just touch
him up a little, and give him á some advice about profane swearing—not
so as to hurt his feelings, you know, but just to give him to understand, in
a general way, that you don't lend your countenance to that sort of thing.
You're his mother, you know, and consequently, it is your right, and your
ḍ business and comes within the line of your duties, as laid down in the
Articles of War. Now *I* could do it—*I* could stir him up in such a way—*I*
could read him a lecture that would make him "grit his teeth" and d—n
all creation for a week, bless you. But then I am not his mother, you know,
consequently it is not in my line—it must come from you—don't you
see?

Now to my thinking, Miss Louisa Conradń and Miss Chipman are
young ladies of remarkably fine taste—and an honor to St. Louis. Did
Miss Conrad live "opposite" when I was at home? If she did, and you had
described her, I would know who you mean. When I was in St. Louis, no
young ladies lived "opposite" except those handsome Texas girls who
dressed in black,[3]—and *they* lived opposite Mr. Schroter's.[4]

I am waiting here, trying to rent a better office for Orion. I have got
the refusal for a ˌafter next, week of a room 16 × 50 on first floor of a fire-
proof brick—rent, eighteen hundred dollars a year. Don't know yet
whether we can get it or not. If it is not rented before the week is up,
we can.[5]

I was sorry to hear that Dick was killed.[6] I gave him his first lesson in
the musket drill. We had half a dozen muskets in our office ⌀ when it was
over Isbell's Music Rooms. I asked Isbell to invite me and the other boys
to come every Friday evening and hear his Choral Society, composed of
ladies and gentlemen, rehearse—but he refused, and I told him I would

spoil their fun. And I did, Madam. I enrolled Dick and Henry and the two Dutch boys into a military Company, took command of it, and ordered them to meet at the office every Friday evening for drill. I made them "order arms" oftener than necessary, perhaps, and they always did it with a will. And when those muskets would come down on the floor, it was of no use, you know—*somebody* had to have a headache,—and nobody could sing. Isbell said he would "give in," (Civil authorities, you know, are bound to knuckle to the military.) But he begged so hard that I relented, and compromised with, ,him., And "for and in consideration" of certain things expressed between us, I agreed not to drill on a certain special occasion, when he was to have ~~many~~ ,a number of, invited guests. ,ḁAnd we didn't drill., But I was too many for him, ,anyhow,, Madam. We got some round stones and some bottles, and we opened a ten-pin alley over his head, simultaneously with the opening of his concert. He said the ten-pin alley was worse than the drill—so we compromised again. But I wrote a burlesque on his principal anthem, and taught it to the boys. And the next Friday, when ~~we~~ our Choral Society opened its lungs, the other one had to "dry up." So we compromised again. And went back to the drill—and drilled, and drilled, until Isbell went into a decline— which culminated in his death at Pike's Peak. And served him right. Dick enjoyed the sport amazingly, and never missed a drill, no matter how the weather was, although he lived more than a mile from the office. He was a lubberly cuss, like me, and couldn't march gracefully, but he could "order arms" with any body. I couldn't very easily forget Dick, for besides these things, he assisted in many a villainous conspiracy against Isbell's peace of mind, wherein his Choral Class were not concerned.

Tell Carrie Schroter I will give her a lump of gold out of any mine or claim I have got—but she must send Dan Haines after it.[7] I want to see Dan, anyhow.

Of course we can excuse Pamela from writing, while her eyes are sore. It is a pity her eyes distress her so much. She will have to try what Lake Bigler can do for them one of these days. I feel certain that it would cure *any-body's* sore eyes, just to *look* at that Lake.

Ma, ~~if~~ I perceive that you have a passion for funerals and processions yet—and I suppose Annie has, ~~al~~ too. The paper Pamela sent has not arrived yet, containing an account of the celebration on the 22[d], and I am afraid it will not come before I leave here. I would like much to see it.[8]

Orion has heard of Mr. Mayor, but I have not, and I don't know where the devil to go to look for him. Why don't he come and see us? He knows we are here. Yes, I remember Miss Adda King.[9] She was very good-looking, too, God forever bless her everlasting soul, but I don't know her from John the Baptist—or any other man. However, I like to have them mentioned, you know. I must keep the run of every body.

I hope I am wearing the last white shirt that will embellish my person for many a day—for I do hope than that I shall be out of Carson long before this reaches you. Love to all.

> Very Respectfully
> Sam.

[1] Annie Moffett, Clemens's niece.

[2] This phrase is from *Tom Jones* (1749), book 4, chapter 4. "Roll on, Silver Moon" was an anonymous song of English origin. It reportedly was at the height of its popularity in the United States in 1847 (Lax and Smith, 325).

[3] In 1949 Annie Moffett Webster recalled some St. Louis neighbors of 1857–61:

Montgomery Brooks was a young man who lived opposite. He was very intimate with Uncle Sam. . . . He had a couple of sisters. I remember once in later years writing to Uncle Sam about the Brooks girls next door and he corrected me and said, "The Brooks girls live opposite." . . . The Conrad family was all mixed up. It was not a very large house and the Conrads had a large family of their own and then someone died and the children all came to the Conrads and somebody else died and more children came. . . . There were two older cousins, Lou and another cousin who seemed to be alone. Uncle Sam admired Lou Conrad. (Webster 1949, 1)

The Brooks sisters possibly were the "handsome Texas girls." Miss Chipman has not been identified.

[4] George Schroter (b. 1813 or 1814) had been William A. Moffett's partner in Moffett and Schroter, St. Louis commission merchants, since 1855 or 1856. St. Louis directories indicate that from 1857 through 1860 (no directory was published in 1861) Schroter and the Moffetts lived within a few blocks of each other, but never on the same street. Hence, so far as can be determined, the Brooks sisters could not have lived "opposite" both Schroter, as Clemens here states, and the Moffetts, as he "corrected" Annie Webster. No listing for Montgomery Brooks appears in the St. Louis directory until 1864, at which time his address is given as 183 Locust. In 1860, however, his widowed mother, Maria, lived at 183 Locust with Richard M. Brooks (possibly Richard *Montgomery* Brooks), while the Moffetts lived "opposite" at 168 Locust, and Schroter lived nearby at 222 Chesnut (*Hannibal Census*, 306; Robert V. Kennedy: 1857, 156, 197, 261; 1859, 337, 421; 1860, 75, 362, 456; Campbell and Richardson, 251; Edwards 1864, 159; Edwards 1865, 248).

[5] Clemens was anxious that his brother's accommodations reflect his position as secretary of Nevada Territory. For the first few months after his arrival in Nevada, Orion Clemens's office and living quarters were confined to one room in Mrs. Margret Murphy's boardinghouse in Carson City's main plaza (Bridget O'Flannigan's boardinghouse in chapter 21 of *Roughing It*), which he paid for himself. At the end of November 1861 he rented an office for fifty dollars a month and

furnished it, after the close of the first session of the Territorial Legislature, with "tables, chairs, desks and spitoons" from the legislative hall. The office had "one room with a little bed room back. The wind had blown in a large quantity of dust which had settled on the cloth ceiling, and was always sifting down. . . . The snow sometimes blew in and settled on the ceiling, and melted and dripped." A second office, also costing fifty dollars a month, had "similar annoyances . . . with the addition of a smoking stove, so that sometimes after making a fire in the morning I could not for awhile see from one end of the office to the other" (OC to William Hemphill Jones, 29 Apr 63, NvU-NSP). Attempts to improve Orion's lodgings continued for several months (see 13 Apr 62 and 11 and 12 May 62, both to OC).

⁶Richard Higham was a printer employed by Orion Clemens in Keokuk, Iowa, in 1856. He was killed at Fort Donelson in the advance of 15 February 1862, which was led by his regiment, the Second Iowa Infantry. Clemens included an account of Higham's death in his Autobiographical Dictation of 26 March 1906 (CU-MARK, in *MTA*, 2:251–52).

⁷Caroline (Carrie) Schroter (b. 1833 or 1834) was the wife of William A. Moffett's partner. Daniel Haines (b. 1836 or 1837) was her brother (*Hannibal Census*, 323). According to Jane Clemens, Haines wanted "to go out to Nevada for his health" (JLC to OC and SLC, 17 Nov 61, CU-MARK).

⁸A Washington's Birthday "Union Jubilee" on 22 February had been highlighted by a grand procession of thousands of "loyal" citizens through the flag-decorated streets of St. Louis. The *Missouri Republican* was moved to nationalistic fervor in its reaction to the scene: "When a great people, united, move forward in awakened power to the accomplishment of a sacred purpose—and that purpose is the preservation of a time-honored heritage, and that heritage the integrity of the freest and the mightiest government on earth—what shall go before the spectacle in grandeur and sublimity?" ("Washington's Birthday," 23 Feb 62, 2). Apparently there was no evidence of the city's bitterly divided loyalties during the celebration.

⁹Mayor and King have not been identified.

To Orion Clemens
10? April 1862 • Aurora, Calif./Nev. Terr.
(*MTB*, 1:198)

.   .   .   .

Send me \$50 or \$100, all you can spare; put away \$150 subject to my call—we shall need it soon for the tunnel.¹

.   .   .   .

¹Paine indicated that this sentence was from one of Mark Twain's Aurora letters to Orion, which were "full of such admonition" (*MTB*, 1:198). The sentence is

probably from a letter, now lost, that preceded the next two letters, which contain very similar "calls" upon Orion and mention tunnels on two Aurora claims: the Horatio and Derby, and the Red Bird. Since it is not known exactly when between 2 and 13 April Clemens arrived in Aurora, the assigned date remains conjectural.

To Orion Clemens
13 April 1862 • Aurora, Calif./Nev. Terr.
(MS: NPV)

ᴀP.S. Remember me   ᴀSend me some stamps—3 and 10 cent.ᴀ
  to Tom & Lockhart.ᴀ[1]

Esmeralda, 13th April, 1862.[2]

My Dear Brother:
        Wasson got here night before last, "from the wars." Tell Lockhart he is not wounded and not killed—is altogether unhurt. He says the whites left their stone fort before he and Lieut. Noble got there.ᴀ, and started to & A large amount of provisions and ammunition which they left behind them fell into the hands of the Indians. They had a pitched battle with the savages, some fifty miles from the fort, in which Scott, (sheriff,) and another man were killed. This was the day before the soldiers came up with them. I mean Noble's men and those under Cols. Evans and Mayfield, from Los Angeles. Evans assumed the chief command—and next morning the forces were divided into three parties, and marched against the enemyies. Col. Mayfield was killed, and Sargeant Gillespie also. One Noble's Corporal was wounded. The California troops went back home, and Noble remained, to help drive the stock over here.[3] And, as Cousin Sally Dillard says, tha this is all that I know about the fight.[4]
        Work not yet begun on the H. & Derby—haven't seen it yet. It is still in the snow. Shall begin on it within 3 or 4 weeks—strike the ledge in July. Guess it is good—worth from $30 to $50 a foot in California.
        Why didn't you send the "Live Yankee" deed—the very one I wanted? Have made no inquiries about it, much. Don't intend to until I get the deed.[5] Send it along—by *mail*—d—n the Express—have to pay 3 times for all express matter; once in Carson and twice here.[6] I don't expect to take the saddle-bags out of the Express office. I paid 25 cts for the Express deeds.

Man named Gebhart shot here yesterday while trying to defend a claim on Last Chance Hill. Expect he will die.[7]

Tell Mr. Upton that Green hasn't paid me yet—~~he's~~ he'll have no money for several days. Tell him the two men would not acknowledge the deed. All I can do is to get the *witness*, (Miller,) to acknowledge it. He will be in town in a day or two. I gave the deed to Mr. DeKay.[8]

These mills here are not worth a d—n—except Clayton's—and it is not in full working trim yet.[9]

Send me ~~$20~~ $40 or $50—by mail—immediately.

Write to Billy[10] not to be in a hurry, for I can't get things fixed to suit me here for some time—can't say how long.

The "Red Bird["] is probably good—can't work on the tunnel on account of snow. The "Pugh" I have thrown away—shan't re-locate it. It is nothing but bed-rock croppings—too much work to find the ledge, if there is one. Shan't record the "Farnum" until I know more about it— perhaps not ₐatₐ all.

"Governor" under the snow.

"Douglas["] & Red Bird are both recorded.[11]

I have had opportunities to get into several ledges, but refused all but three—expect to back out of two of them.

Stint yourself as much as possible, and lay up $100 or $150, subject to my call. I go to work to-morrow, with pick and shovel. Something's got to come, by G—, before I let go, here.

Col. Young's says you must rent Kinkead's room by all means— Government would rather pay $150 a month for your office than $75 for Gen. North's.[12] Says you are playing your hand very badly, for either the Government's good opinion or anybodyₐ'sₐ else, in keeping your office in a shanty. Says put Gov. Nye in your place and he would have a stylish office, and no objections would ever be made, either. When old Col. Youngs talks this way, I think it time to get a fine office. ~~And~~ I wish you would take that office, and fit it up handsomely, so that I can quit telling people that by this time you are handsomely located, when I know it is no such thing.

I am living with 'Ratio Phillips. Send him one of those black portfolios—*by the stage*, and put a couple of penholders and a dozen steel pens in it.

If you should have occasion to dispose of the long desk before I return, don't foget to break open the middle drawer and take out my things. Envelop my black cloth coat in a newspaper and hang it in the back room.

Don't buy *anything* while I am here—but save up some money for me. Don't send any money home. I shall have your next quarter's salary spent before you get it, I think. I mean to make or break here within the next 2 or 3 months.

Yrs,

Sam.

[1] Thomas C. Nye, the governor's nephew, and Jacob T. Lockhart, the United States Indian agent, both living in Carson City (Kelly 1862, 10, 85).

[2] Clemens was in Aurora, approximately one hundred miles southeast of Carson City, in the rich Esmeralda mining district, an area claimed by both Esmeralda County, Nevada Territory, and Mono County, California. With the exception of the next letter, the datelines of his extant Aurora letters reflect the fact that the United States Post Office Department designation for the Aurora post office—his mailing address—was Esmeralda, California. That post office was established on 9 September 1861, during Clemens's first visit to the town, which had been developing steadily since the discovery of mineral deposits in 1860. By July 1862 Aurora proudly claimed a population of nearly two thousand, with six hotels and restaurants, eleven billiard saloons, and ten quartz mills. This boom reached its peak in 1863–64, and by 1870 virtually all mining and milling had ceased. The Clemens brothers began investing in mining claims in the Esmeralda district in September 1861, and eventually owned feet, nominally worth $5,000, in at least thirty different ledges there. They never realized anything like the face value of their holdings, however, much less the great riches they anticipated ("Aurora," Nevada City [Calif.] *Transcript*, 26 July 62, 2, reprinting the Esmeralda *Star* of unknown date; Angel, 418; Kelly 1862, 241; Salley, 12, 70; deeds in CU-MARK).

[3] A condensed but essentially accurate account of the most recent battle in hostilities that began in the winter of 1861 between cattlemen in the Owens River area (south of Aurora) and Digger Indians defending their land. The cattlemen had gathered in a fortified spot above Owens Lake and had sent to Nevada and California for help. Eighteen men from Aurora, including Sheriff Scott, came to their aid in March 1862, and under the command of Colonel Mayfield, a private citizen, they sallied forth to engage the Indians, but were soon compelled to retreat. Meanwhile, Lieutenant H. Noble set forth from Fort Churchill, Nevada, with fifty soldiers of the Second Cavalry, California Volunteers, and in early April was joined near Aurora by acting Indian Agent and United States Marshal Warren H. Wasson, whose assignment was to attempt peace negotiations. At the scene of the hostilities, they combined forces with Lieutenant-Colonel George Evans, commanding forty soldiers also from the Second Cavalry, California Volunteers (who had set out from their post near Los Angeles). These forces, together with the cattlemen and their Aurora allies, were unable to defeat the Indians. The situation remained unresolved until October 1862, when a treaty was negotiated (Angel, 166–68).

[4] An allusion to "Cousin Sally Dilliard," Hamilton C. Jones's burlesque sketch

about a pompous young lawyer's embarrassment at the hands of a digressive witness. Sally Dilliard is talked about, but is not actually a character, in the sketch. The words Clemens attributes to her are in fact spoken by the witness. The piece first appeared in the New York weekly *Spirit of the Times: A Chronicle of the Turf, Agriculture, Field Sports, Literature and the Stage* on 18 May 1844 (134).

[5] The Live Yankee Gold and Silver Mining Company was incorporated on 13 September 1861 with a capital stock of $120,000 at $100 per share ("Mining and Other Corporations Formed in 1861," Sacramento *Union*, 1 Jan 62, 3). The mine was located in Middle Hill, Aurora. On 17 December 1861 Orion Clemens purchased twenty-five feet in the ledge for $500 from William E. Teall, a representative in the House of the first Territorial Legislature (deed in CU-MARK; Andrew J. Marsh, 2). That same day the Carson City *Silver Age* characterized the Live Yankee as a "small but very rich lead" ("Items from Esmeralda," San Francisco *Evening Bulletin*, 18 Dec 61, 3, reprinting the *Silver Age* of 12 Dec 61).

[6] Express service between Carson City and Aurora was provided by Wells, Fargo and Company and by William H. Brown and Company's Express Stage Line, which made one weekly round trip (Kelly 1862, 74). Clemens's irritation at express fees was not unique. Six months before he wrote this letter, an Aurora correspondent of the San Francisco *Evening Bulletin* complained about "Wells, Fargo & Co. charging 25 cents for transmitting letters, when they send to other parts of California for 10 cents . . . places at a greater distance from the central office" ("The Esmeralda Mines," 28 Oct 61, 2).

[7] Gebhart, head of his own mining company, and John Copeland, representing S. H. Chase and Company, both claimed ownership of the same lead on Last Chance Hill in Aurora. On 11 April Copeland, Chase, and two other partners confronted Gebhart and his laborers at the mine shaft, and a gun battle ensued in which Copeland shot Gebhart in the stomach and slightly wounded one of the men with him (Vox Populi 1862b, 4). Gebhart died some days later.

[8] Clemens's debt to Mr. Upton (presumably M. Upton, a Carson City dry-goods dealer) was still unpaid three months later (see 23 July 62 to OC). Green was probably Edmund Green, one of three supervisors of Esmeralda County, the superintendent of the Wide West mine, and a co-owner of the eight-stamp Pioneer Mill near Last Chance Hill—Aurora's first mill, erected in June 1861 (Wasson, 45; Angel, 401, 416). William De Kay was the deputy county clerk of the Esmeralda district (Kelly 1862, 247). He held an interest in the Flyaway and probably in other Aurora claims. Miller remains unidentified.

[9] Joshua Elliot Clayton, a well-known San Francisco civil and mining engineer, was a pioneer settler and prospector in Aurora who helped lay out the town and, with two others, located the important Real del Monte claim on Last Chance Hill in August 1860. His twelve-stamp mill on Martinez Hill, east of Aurora, was the only Esmeralda mill with machinery specifically designed for the efficient reduction of silver ore. It reportedly was in operation by February 1862 and by April was operating around the clock, seven days a week (Langley: 1861, 99; 1863, 100; 1865, 121; Silversmith 1861a, 4; Wasson, 44; Angel, 120, 416; Kelly 1862, 244; "Aurora," Marysville [Calif.] *Appeal*, 22 Feb 62, 2, reprinting the Carson City *Silver Age* of 16 Feb 62; "News from Esmeralda," Stockton *Weekly Independent*, 26 Apr 62, 2, reprinting the Carson City *Silver Age* of 18 Apr 62).

[10] William Dixon of Keokuk.

[11] Apparently the Red Bird, the Douglas, and the Governor (possibly the Gov-

ernor Nye) were claims that had interested Clemens for some time. In response to a letter from him (now lost), Horatio Phillips wrote on 8 December 1861: "I will find out where the 'Governor' is & the 'Douglass' & attend to them." He added that "the Red bird Co were at work starting a tunnel but I will attend to them all" (NPV). Clemens's correspondence contains no further mention of these claims nor of the Pugh. On 16 November 1861 he and Orion had paid Noah T. Carpenter $200 for twenty feet in the Farnum (or Farnham) lead, located in the Van Horn mining district east of Aurora (deed in CU-MARK; Kelly 1862, 253).

[12] Colonel Samuel Youngs (1803–90), formerly of New York, had been a prominent citizen of Aurora since November 1860 and from 1865 to 1870 operated a four-stamp mill there. A fervent Unionist, he was a member of the 1861 Territorial Legislature and a delegate to the 1863 state Constitutional Convention (Andrew J. Marsh, 667 n. 15; Zimmer, 46, 63; Angel, 414). "Old Col. Youngs is very friendly, and I like him much," Clemens wrote Orion on 4 July 1862, but late in 1863 he ridiculed Youngs in his *Territorial Enterprise* correspondence as an "estimable old fossil" and a "snuffling old granny" (SLC 1863j, 3:28; SLC 1863k, 3:55). John W. North (1815–90), a native of New York, was appointed surveyor general of Nevada Territory in June 1861 by President Lincoln, and from 1862 to 1864 was an associate justice of the territorial supreme court (Andrew J. Marsh, 692–93 n. 280). Reminiscing years later to a western correspondent, Clemens named North among the "unforgotten & unforgetable antiques" of his Nevada past (24 May 1905 to Robert L. Fulton, PH in CTcHi, in *MTL*, 2:773). For Kinkead, see 8 and 9 Mar 62 to Clagett, n. 6.

To Orion Clemens
17 and 19 April 1862 • Aurora, Calif./Nev. Terr.
(MS: CU-MARK)

‸P. S. I wrote for $40 or $50 & some 3 & 10ᶜᵗ stamps—get the letter?‸

‸"Stand by" to let me have $150 when I call for it.‸

Aurora, 17ᵗʰ/62.

My Dear Bro:

As to the "Live Yankee," I will see the President in the morning, and get the Secy's address.[1]

No, don't buy any ground, anywhere. The pick and shovel are the only claims I have any confidence in now. My back is sore and my hands blistered with handling them to-day. But something must come, you know.

We shall let a contract on the H. & Derby in a day or two. Most folks like these ledges. I don't. It will not cost much now, though, to test it with the tunnell.

I, too, have seen very rich specimens from East Walker.[2] Not quite so rich, and gold hardly as fine as that taken from the National, though.

The "Live Yankees," as you call them, are a pack of d—d fools. They have run a tunnel 100 ft long to strike the *croppings*.[3] They could have blasted, above ground, easier. It is the craziest piece of work I know of, except that wherein the owners of the "Esmeralda" discovery sold one-half their interests to get money to run a ~~tun~~ seventeen-thousand-dollar tunnel in, to strike the ledge just *under* the croppings, when said croppings are 100 feet high, and pay $300 a ton in Clayton's Mill[4]—which, by-the-bye, is an excellent mill, and cannot be beaten *any where*. It is the *only* mill here.

Oh, Dewy be d—d. Keep a chance at the "six" if you can, but pay Harroun no money.[5] If I can dig pay rock out of a ledge here *myself*, I will buy—not otherwise.

Yes—if we find good rock in the H. & Derby, ~~wil~~ we'll incorporate it. Raish and I would then have full control of it—we represent 750 feet in it.

Got Billy's letter. Tell him to be Recorder.[6]

Crooker[7] wants you to certify his claim, as enclosed, or, if it isn't figured up right, why, ~~ma~~ figure it up right yourself, get the scrip for it, and, if you can sell the scrip for 75 cents, do so, and forward the money—if not, forward the scrip. I told him it was a d—d sight easier to sell tracts than scrip in Carson. (It may be well enough, though, to sell enough to pay your fee for the seal, you know.)[8] Also, do ditto and likewise for R. M. Howland, who was Messenger, only, but traveled 30 miles more, (to Mono,) making 150 miles. You can sell his for 50 cents, ~~and~~ if any body offers that, and send ~~y~~ the money to me or Raish—don't collect your fee in *this* case, though. Crooker sent his bill by Kinney to Turner, once.

Well, things are so gloomy that I begin to feel really jolly and comfortable again.[9] I enjoy myself hugely now.

Saturday—I have fixed the "Live Yankee"—it is all right now. Portfolio & the Gen.'s letter came to hand all right.

.   .   .   .

✉————————————————————————————

O. Clemens, Esq. | ¢ Karson City | N. T. [*postmaster's hand:*] Esmeralda Cal, | April 21ˢᵗ 1862 [*brace*] [*postage stamp cut away*]

[1] A. D. Allen, president of the Live Yankee Mining Company, was an early locator on the Comstock lode and in the summer of 1860 was one of the organizers of the Bodie mining district (southwest of Esmeralda) and one of the locators of the Real del Monte mine in Aurora (Angel, 58; Wasson, 6, 44). Later, while working as foreman of the Wide West mine, he joined with Clemens and Calvin Higbie in the blind-lead project that supposedly made them millionaires for ten days (see 23 July 62 to OC, n. 1). Allen was reportedly among the successful Aurora miners who were "sure to sell stock in claims which have long since been given up by poor miners, while many rich ledges lie neglected because confidence is only reposed in the wealthy, and because of their [the poor miners'] inability to bring rock to the market" (Sahab, 1). The secretary of the Live Yankee Company has not been identified. Clemens possibly intended to contact him to get a copy of the deed Orion had failed to send (see 13 Apr 62 to OC).

[2] Clemens here refers to mining activity along the east fork of the Walker River and its tributaries in an area about thirty-five miles north of Aurora. In July a resident of the region would report that seventy-two well-defined leads had been discovered, and many of them prospected, in the East Walker River district (Veni, Vidi 1862c, 1).

[3] "That part of a vein which appears above the surface is called the *cropping* or *outcrop*" (Raymond, 26).

[4] The Esmeralda claim, on Silver Hill (also called Esmeralda Hill), Aurora, was located on 25 August 1860 by James M. Braly, J. M. Cory, and E. R. Hicks, the original discoverers of the rich mineral deposits in that area (Kelly 1862, 239–41; Kelly 1863, 408). "Any amount of mills," it was reported, "can be supplied from this mammoth lead," which yielded "big *boulders* of amalgam and bullion" ("Letter from Esmeralda," Stockton *Weekly Independent*, 21 June 62, 3).

[5] Between October 1861 and July 1862, Orion paid $600 for feet in six ledges that De Witt Harroun owned in the Santa Clara district of Humboldt County, and an unknown sum for feet in seven ledges that Harroun owned in the Star district of the same county (deeds in CU-MARK).

[6] The Clemens brothers' correspondent was William H. Clagett. As the next letter indicates, he had written on 2 April. See also 28 Feb 62 to Clagett, n. 22.

[7] D. C. Crooker, clerk at the district recorder's office in Aurora (Kelly 1862, 247). The claims by Crooker and Robert M. Howland discussed in this paragraph evidently concerned reimbursement of travel expenses.

[8] On 29 November 1861 "An Act to authorize the Secretary of the Territory to receive Compensation for certain Duties pertaining to his Office" had been passed. It permitted Orion to collect several fees, including one dollar "for attaching a certificate and the seal of his office to any instrument not pertaining to the government of said territory" (*Laws* 1862, 310; see also William C. Miller, 4–5). This act provided a significant supplement to Orion's salary (see Mack 1961, 81).

[9] Clemens echoes the determinedly cheerful words of Mark Tapley in Dickens's *Martin Chuzzlewit*. Tapley is mentioned explicitly in the next letter.

To William H. Clagett
18 April 1862 • Aurora, Calif./Nev. Terr.
(MS, *damage emended:* ViU)

ˌP.S.ˌ   ˌDo as I am doing now, Billy—
ˌDon't let my opinion of this   keep out of leads unless you
place get abroad.ˌ   *know* them to be good.ˌ

Esmeralda, April 18, 1862.

Dear Billy:

Yours of the 2ᵈ just received. As far as I can see, there are not more than half a dozen leads here that will do to bet on—only two, in fact, that a man would like to risk his whole pile on. Still, money will be made here as soon as $25-rock ~~will~~ can be crushed for $10 ~~or $15.~~ a ton. I discover that top-rock which *assays* $40 is considered "bully." ~~N~~ But the large majority of the ledges wouldn't assay $5 on top—the *large* majority, *I* think. I know, also, that I own in several such. Now I wouldn't give a d—n for any such claims. When I went and looked at my best purchase, I didn't *say* anything, but I just thought, "Now, about how many empty ginger-pop bottles would that fellow sell for in Buena Vista?"[1] Billy, if I hadn't started in here, I would clear out for Humboldt immediately. But since I *have* got interests here, I will hold on a little, and see if I can make anything out of them. 'Ratio Phillips says that if we fail with a lead we are going down on now, he will go to Buena Vista with me—so I am not very particular whether that lead succeeds or not—for I tell you, he would be no bad acquisition to our crowd. He thinks the "Horatio & Derby" is bully—but I told him what I thought was the truth, that so far from such a claim being considered rich up *our* way, I didn't even ~~though~~ think our boys would have taken the trouble to record it. Billy, I told you I would get you some claims here, and I could do it, without any trouble; but it strikes me that the fewer feet you own here, the richer you will be. You see, if you fail to do 2 days' work on each claim every month in the year, your property is jumpable at the first instance of neglect. Claims have been pointed out to me as re-locatable, and supposed to be good—but *I* didn't want them, and I thought you didn't,—so, they are re-locatable yet. I have been offered numerous feet for nothing, but I haven't accepted. Last summer, Orion paid $50 for 15 feet in a claim here. Yesterday one of the owners came and offered me 25 feet more for $50, with 30 days' time on half the amount. He said he hated to part with it, but then he wanted me to have a good "stake." I told him I appreciated his kindness to me, but that I was "on the sell" ˌmyselfˌ—that I would like to sell him my 15 feet at $1⁰⁰ a foot—$2⁰⁰ down, and the balance in thirteen annual instalments. Now, do you imagine that he took me up? Not by a *d—d* sight, my love. Oh, Shighte! (see Webster,) Tom and I can take a deck of cards, and my old black horse, and *win* feet enough from Sam in an hour to buy all Esmeralda.[2] There *are* 5 or 6 good leads here, but I am lucky enough not to own in them.

ˌ(*Private*).ˌ But Phillips and I have a project on foot that may amount to something. Mr. Clayton, who uses a "process" of his own, unknown to *any* one else, saves $300 a ton out of rock from the "Esmeralda" lode—about four times as much as any other mill in the camp can get out of it. He saves silver within 4 per cent., and gold within 20 per cent. of the fire assay.[3] This he *guarantees*. He has promised to teach his secret to Phillips (allowing him to teach it to me,) free of charge—and if we use it we are to pay him one-fourth of our profits. And, since you will share with me in this thing, I advise you before-hand *not* to sell out. Now, Billy, you understand why I want to stay here until I get some money out of one of these d—d leads, if the thing be possible. Because, you see, we want to attach this process to one of your Humboldt mills, and it̶ machinery, &c., will cost us $1,000 to do it with. Keep this entirely to yourself, you know. Clayton will assist us by experimenting with our infernal rock at half-price until we get some that will pay.[4] We haven't taken out any yet that will even do to experiment with. My love to Dad[5] and the boys—and tell Dad not to be discouraged, but "come out strong," like Mark Tapley.[6]

Yr. old friend

Sam L. C.

Wm. H. Clagett, Esq. | Unionville | Humboldt Co. | N. T. [*partly boxed, lower left:*] *Via* Carson [*postmaster's hand:*] Esmeralda Cal, | April 21st 1862 [*brace*] [*three-cent U.S. postage stamp, canceled with a pen*]

---

[1] The Buena Vista mining district in Humboldt County.
[2] Presumably Clemens's Humboldt friends Tom Smith (or Messersmith) and

Sam Montgomery. For discussion of the black horse see 28 Feb 62 to Clagett, n. 18.

[3] Joshua E. Clayton's mill employed the "Clayton & Veatch process for saving both silver and gold" (Kelly 1862, 244). John A. Veatch, who devised several processes for extracting gold and silver ores (see Silversmith 1861b, 4, and Kelly 1862, 260), was a San Francisco physician, mineralogist, and chemist (Langley: 1859, 273; 1860, 310; 1861, 337; 1862, 388). Clayton had evidently modified one of Veatch's techniques; no explanation of the resultant method has been discovered.

[4] So far as is known, Clemens did not own in any of the mines whose rock, according to newspaper reports, was crushed by Clayton's Mill.

[5] Cornbury Tillou.

[6] Young Martin Chuzzlewit's faithful companion in Dickens's novel.

To Orion Clemens
24 and 25 April 1862 • Aurora, Calif./Nev. Terr.
(MS: NPV)

Esmeralda, Thursday.

My Dear Bro:

Yours of 17th, per express, just received. Part of it pleased me exceedingly, and part of it didn't. Concerning the latter, for instance: You have *promised* me that you would leave all mining matters, and everything involving an outlay of money, in my hands. Now it may be a matter of no consequence at all to *you*, to keep your word with me, but I assure you *I* look upon it in a very different light. Indeed I fully expect you to deal as conscientiously with me as you would with any other man. Moreover, you know as well as ~~I,~~ I do, that the very best course that you and I can pursue will be, to keep on good terms with each other—notwithstanding which fact, we shall certainly split inside of six months if you go on in this way. You see I talk plainly. Because I know what is due me, and I would not put up with such treatment from any body but you. We discussed that Harroun business once before, and it was *decided*, then, that he was not to receive a cent of money.[1] But you have paid him $50. And you agreed to pay a portion of Perry's expenses, &c., although, as I gather from the tone of your letter, you ~~know that y~~ knew, at that very moment, that you were breaking your word with me, and also, that all the money you might expend in that project would go to the devil without every benefitting you a penny. As soon as Perry left your presence, you cursed yourself for being so easily persuaded, and resolved that he might pay his own prospecting expenses, without hope of assistance from you. Now wouldn't it have been better to have saved yourself all ~~that~~ this by simply pronouncing the talismanic "No," which always sticks in your throat? And would it not be ~~be~~ as well, even at this late day, to say to him that by a solemn promise made to me, you are debarred from expending money on ~~such~~ prospecting tours, ~~in~~ &c., in search of Mill Sites, (which is probably the *d—dest* strangest phantom that ever did flit before the dazed eyes of a prospector since that *genus* came into existence,) without first ~~asking~~ getting me to agree to it. That you have tried me, but it wouldn't work. That I have already backed down from paying Pfersdorff's expenses, and will never consent again, while the world stands, to help pay another man's expenses. I don't know where the ~~m~~Mountain House is, but I *do* know that if there is a mill site near the Mountain House worth having, Mr. Perry will arrive ~~that~~ there a long time after it was taken up. But as for all the ledges he can find between now and next Christmas, I would not supply his trip with lucifer matches for a half interest in them. Sending a man fooling around the country after *ledges*, for God's sake!—when there are hundreds of feet of them under my nose here, begging for owners, free of charge. G—d d—n it, I *don't want* any more feet, and I won't *touch* another foot—so you see, Orion, as far as any ledges of Perry's are concerned, (or *any other*, except what I examine first with my own eyes), I freely yield my right to share ownership with you.[2]

Now, Orion, I have given you a piece of my mind—you have it in full, and you deserved it—for you would be ashamed to acknowledge that you ever broke faith with another man as you have with me. I shall never look upon Ma's face again, or Pamela's, or get married, or revisit the "Banner State," until I am a rich man—so you can easily see that when you stand between me and my fortune (the one which I shall make, as surely as Fate itself,) you stand between me and *home*, friends, and all that I care for—and by the Lord God! you must clear the track, you know!

The balance of your letter, I say, pleases me exceedingly. Especially that about the H. & D. being worth from $30 to $50 in Cal. It pleases me because, if the ledges prove to be worthless, it will be a pleasant reflection to know that others were beaten worse than ourselves. 'Raish sold a man 30 feet, yesterday, at $20 a foot, although I was present at the sale, and

told the man the ground wasn't worth a d—n. He said he had been hankering after a few feet in the H. & D. for a long time, and he had got them
at last, and he couldn't help thingking he had secured a good thing. We
went and looked at the ledges, and both of them acknowledged that there
was nothing in them but good "indications." Yet the owners in the H. &
D. will part with anything else sooner than with feet in those ledges. Well,
the work goes slowly—*very* slowly on, in the tunnel, and we'll strike it
some day.[3] *But*—if we "strike it rich,"—I've lost my guess, that's all. I
expect that the way it got so high in Cal. was, that Raish's brother, over
there was offered $750°° for 20 feet of it, and he refused.

Yes, the saddlebags were all right. I had nothing to pay on them.
With letters, though, the case is different. Have to pay for them at both
ends of the route. Raish says money can't be sent by mail. It's a d—d
curious mail, isn't it.?

The next excellent news is the $50, although I did suppose I could
have worried along with something less for a week or two.

But the best news of all is, your resolution to take Kinkead's office,;
and when you come to furnish it, look at what the County paid in that
way for Turner's office, and see it if you can't "go" a few dollars "better."
But the carpet—let *that* eclipse everything in town. I feel very much relieved, to think you will be out of that d—d coop shortly.

Lieut. Noble and his men are here. Three deserted yesterday. One
was caught to-day and put in irons.[4]

Couldn't go on the hill to-day. It snowed. It *always* snows here, I
expect.

Don't you suppose they have pretty much quit writing, at home?

(over)

When you receive your next $\frac{1}{4}$'rs salary, don't send any of it here until
after you have told me you have got it. Remember this. I am afraid of that
H. & D.[5]

They have struck the ledge in the Live Yankee tunnel, and I told the
President, Mr. Allen, that it wasn't as good as the croppings. He said that
was true enough, but they would hang to until it *did* prove rich. He is
much of a gentleman, that man Allen.

Remember me to Tom Nye and Lockhart.

And tell ask Gasherie why the devil he don't send along my commission as Deputy Sheriff. The fact of my being in California, and out of his

county, would amount to a d—n with *me*, in the performance of my official duties.[6]

I have nothing to report, at present, except that I shall find out all I
want to know about this locality before I leave it.

Did you tell Upton what I told you in my last?

How do the Records pay?[7]

Yr. Bro.
Sam

P.S.—Put off Harroun, now, until his pay comes out of the ledges. Phillips and I will see him this summer.

[in pencil on a small scrap of paper, both sides:]

P. S.—Friday Morning.—I am in a better humor this morning, but as
you deserved a blowing-up, why, I will not deprive you of it. I am on my
way now, with picks, &c., to work on my pet claim. If it proves good, you
will know all about it some day—if it don't, you will never even learn its
name. So, wait, and banish hope—for I have *Resolved*, that it is like most
Esmeralda ledges, viz: worthless. ¶. = I went down with Lieut. Noble,
awhile ago, to get Wasson's order conveying the guns of the "Esmeralda
Rifles" to his (N.'s) ~~charge~~ custody. The people here regret being deprived of these arms, as the Secessionists have declared that in case Cal.
accedes to the new boundaries, Gov. Nye shall not assume jurisdiction
here. Noble will perhaps remain here a fortnight, and hopes are entertained that Gen. Wright may be prevailed upon to allow the arms to remain here. All this has been told the Governor in a letter sent from here
by mail. If that letter is still in *t* Carson (or the P.O.,) express it to Frisco.
It's in a white mail envelop thus directed: "His Excellency Gov. Nye,
Carson City, Nevada Territory." (true copy: teste.)[8]

[in ink, crosswise over the previous paragraph:]

Ratio, wishes you to ask Gen. Bunker, if he is still in Carson, to see
Cradlebaugh, when he gets to Washington, and get him to use his best
endeavors toward securing his brother's appointment to the *n* Naval
School.[9] Ratio will make the Gen. a handsome present of a good mining
claim for his trouble.

[1] As recently as 17 April Clemens had instructed Orion to "pay Harroun no
money."

[2] Orion's interest in recent mining "excitements" near Carson City found
expression in a letter of 10 May to the Keokuk *Gate City*. Among the discoveries

he described was one that presumably was the Mountain House ledge: "A ledge in the mountains, three or four miles west of Carson lately struck—must be good—one of the owners says it is" (OC 1862, 2). Nothing is known about Perry, whom Orion evidently had grubstaked.

[3] The tunnel into Martinez Hill, Aurora, that Clemens, Horatio G. Phillips, and others had been developing since late 1861 (see 8 and 9 Feb 62 to JLC and PAM, n. 2).

[4] Following their skirmishes with the Indians near the Owens River (see 13 Apr 62 to OC, n. 3), Lieutenant Noble and his men returned to Aurora, escorting settlers forced to flee the area of the hostilities. California military records identify two of the men who deserted at Aurora, on 21 April: Frederick Gramer and August Kertz. The third man is not listed, possibly because he was quickly apprehended (Vox Populi 1862c, 5; "By Telegraph to the Union," Sacramento *Union*, 2 May 62, 2; Orton, 205).

[5] Orion's salary of $450 for the first quarter of 1862 had been sent from Washington on 12 April but did not reach him in Carson City until 3 July, long after the Horatio and Derby ledge had ceased to interest Clemens (OC to Elisha Whittlesey, 3 May 62, 30 June 62, and 7 July 62, NvU-NSP).

[6] D. J. Gasherie served two terms (1862–64) as Ormsby County sheriff (Angel, 530). He is a minor character in two of Clemens's 1863 sketches for the Virginia City *Territorial Enterprise*: "A Sunday in Carson" and "A Bloody Massacre near Carson" (see *ET&S1*, 220–22, 320–26). Although Clemens here seems to accept California's claim to Aurora, he aligns himself later in this letter with the partisans of Nevada (see note 8). According to his friend Robert M. Howland, Aurora was considered by "most of the settlers here to be in Nevada Territory" (Howland to "Cousin Martha," 12 Jan 62, Gunn). That observation was confirmed by the Aurora correspondent of the Sacramento *Union*, who estimated the pro-Nevada majority as "seven-eighths of the people" (Vox Populi 1862a, 8).

[7] Clemens was probably referring to the fee law enacted on 29 November 1861 (see 17 and 19 Apr 62 to OC, n. 8). It allowed Orion Clemens to collect "thirty cents per folio, of one hundred words" on copies of "any law, joint resolution, transcript of record, or other document or paper, on file in his office" which he furnished to private individuals (*Laws* 1862, 310–11).

[8] In November 1861 the Territorial Legislature had appropriated funds for a survey to establish the California-Nevada boundary. The work of surveyors John Kidder and Butler Ives, completed by 14 August 1862, put Aurora, which California claimed as the seat of Mono County, within Nevada Territory. Reluctant to lose the mineral wealth of Aurora, California refused to accept the Kidder-Ives boundary (Nye, 14; Angel, 100, 401–2; Mack 1936, 394–98; Veni, Vidi 1862d, 1). This potentially explosive disagreement was exacerbated by national Civil War allegiances, the pro-California group in Aurora being vocal in its Southern sympathies. In March 1862, at the same time that Lieutenant Noble and his California cavalry troop were first sent to Aurora, Governor Nye requisitioned fifty government muskets for the use of Aurora citizens. Upon the arrival of the guns in early April, Aurora Unionists immediately organized the Esmeralda Rifles as home guards (Vox Populi 1862a, 8; "From Nevada Territory," San Francisco *Alta California*, 16 Apr 62, 1, reprinting the Carson City *Silver Age* of 11 Apr 62). Clemens notes here that the Esmeralda Rifles' weapons had been confiscated by the California military, leaving Aurora open to the depredations of the secessionist pro-

California faction. His concern for delivery of the letter to Nye clearly places him in the camp of the pro-Nevada, pro-Union Aurora residents. United States military authorities in California—Brigadier General George Wright was commandant of the Department of the Pacific, headquartered in San Francisco—were persuaded to re-arm the Esmeralda Rifles in August after violent secessionist demonstrations in Aurora. Lieutenant Noble, a strong Union supporter, led the action that quelled the disturbances (Angel, 266–67; Langley 1862, 545). For a discussion of Orion's part in the boundary dispute and the details of its settlement, see 11 and 12 Apr 63 to JLC and PAM, n. 5.

[9] John Cradlebaugh, a former associate justice for Utah Territory, had been elected on 31 August 1861 as Nevada's territorial delegate to the Thirty-seventh United States Congress. He served in Washington, D.C., from 2 December 1861 through 3 March 1863 (Andrew J. Marsh, 682 n. 160; Angel, 78). Attorney General Benjamin B. Bunker already had "left for the East" (OC to William M. Gillespie, 22 Apr 62, NvU-NSP).

To Orion Clemens
28 April 1862 • Aurora, Calif./Nev. Terr.
(MS: NPV)

Esmeralda, Apl. 28.

My Dear Bro:

Well, if Perry *has* found something, I take it all back. But I am dubious yet—*very* dubious—for I confess that I can't see anything but a little sulphate of copper and a few sulphurets, iron pyrites, &c., in the specimen which Bagley brought.[1] However, I mean to pan it out to-morrow, and then we shall see what we shall see—and I will hope for the best, until I see the ledges myself.

You have described exactly the spot on Dr. Ives'[2] hill where Bunker and I found very good specimens of silver quartz. We traced the ledge some distance, but didn't think it worth while to locate it. D—n Carson, I wouldn't have a claim that close to it. How is the "Lady Washington["] doing?[3] Why don't they go down *on the ledge* in your new claims? I am afraid of "shenanigan" and "wildcat" when a miner shirks his ledge.

I have been at work all day, blasting, and picking, and gadding[4] and d—ning one of our new claims—the "Dashaway,"—which I don't think a great deal of, but which I am willing to try. We are down, now, 10 or 12 feet. We are following down, *under* the ledge, but not taking it out. If we get up a windlass to-morrow, we shall take out the ledge, and see whether ~~is~~ it is worth anything or not.[5]

I mean that the "Live Yankee" is recorded, and that makes it all right, Allen says, because no transcript of the Records has yet been made by the Co.

Raish has been hunting for the ledge which produced the fine specimen shown you by Mr. Larue[6]—but this hunting needles in a haystack is "played out," you know.

Ma and Pamela seem to be down on my last to the Gate City. Well, what'r they going to *do* about it—be Jes–s?—(though I would hate to ask *them* the question, you bet.[)][7]

I have attended to Barstow.[8]

Yes, I got the money.

Touch the new claims carefully, you know, as far as cash is concerned. Don't *buy* anything, by *any* means.

Well, I shall know in the morning, but I *can't* see anything in the M. House specimen.

Y^{r.} Bro.

Sam.

Remember me to Tom[9]

[1] H. W. Bagley was the driver of William H. Brown and Company's weekly stage between Carson City and Aurora ("Aurora and Owens River," Stockton *Weekly Independent*, 12 Apr 62, 1, reprinting the Carson City *Silver Age* of 28 Mar 62). The specimen, given to Orion by the unidentified Perry, was from the Mountain House ledge near Carson City.

[2] Dr. John Ives had accompanied Governor James W. Nye from New York to Nevada. He practiced medicine in Carson City and was a member of John Nye and Company (see 18–21 Sept 61 to JLC and PAM, n. 5; Mack 1936, 222; Kelly 1862, 82).

[3] The Lady Washington, in the Gold Hill district of Storey County, was an "outside mine"—that is, a mine parallel to the Comstock lode. Such mines numbered "hundreds, perhaps thousands" and were located "in every conceivable place, and according to the most absurd theories." Nevertheless, the Lady Washington belonged to a cluster called "perhaps as promising a field as any of the outsides" (Angel, 616). Its proprietors incorporated it sometime before 1 June 1863, with a claimed capital value of $660,000 and shares worth $200 each (Kelly 1863, 11, 15).

[4] A "gad" was a "small iron punch with a wooden handle used to break up ore" (Raymond, 38).

[5] By 12 May Clemens owned one-fifth of the Dashaway claim, located on Silver Hill, Aurora (11 and 12 May 62 to OC). On 22 July he purchased from Horatio Phillips, as part of a package of stocks costing $300, seventy-five additional feet

in the claim (deed in CU-MARK). In March 1863, however, he was not listed among the "first trustees" who incorporated the Dashaway Gold and Silver Mining Company with a capital stock of $180,000 and shares valued at $300 each ("The Mining Roll Continued," San Francisco *Evening Bulletin*, 16 Mar 63, 3).

[6] J. D. LaRue, the local deputy recorder, was soon to be one of Clemens's partners in the Clemens Gold and Silver Mining Company (Kelly 1862, 249; Clemens Gold and Silver Mining Company trust deed, 9 May 62, PH in CU-MARK, courtesy of Michael H. Marleau).

[7] Clemens refers to his 30 January 1862 letter to his mother, which appeared in the Keokuk *Gate City*. Although by now his family must have received his 20 March letter about Nevada's Indians, which also appeared in the *Gate City*, their reactions to it probably had not reached him yet.

[8] About this time Clemens began contributing letters, under the pen name "Josh," to the Virginia City *Territorial Enterprise*. These letters, none of which survive, caught the eye of William H. Barstow, formerly assistant secretary of the Council of the first Territorial Legislature, who was now employed in the business office of the *Enterprise*. Barstow soon helped Clemens win a place on the newspaper's regular staff (see 30 July 62 to OC, n. 1). For a description of one of Clemens's "Josh" letters, see Daggett, 15.

[9] Thomas C. Nye.

To Orion Clemens
4 and 5 May 1862 • Aurora, Calif./Nev. Terr.
(MS: NPV)

ʌ("Prospect" from "M. H." ledge sticking to piece of yellow paper in middle of this page.)ʌ[1]

Esmeralda, Sunday, May — 1862.

My Dear Brother:

D—d— Well—if you haven't "struck it rich"—that is, if the piece of rock you sent me came from a *bona fide* LEDGE—and it looks as if it did. If that *is* a ledge, and you own 200 feet in it, why, it is a big thing—and I have nothing more to say. If you have actually made something by helping to pay somebody's prospecting expenses, it is a wonder of the first magnitude, and deserves to rank as such. If that rock came from a well-defined ledge, that particular vein must be at least an inch wide, judging

[*gold sample*]

from this specimen, which is fully that thick. When I came in the other evening, hungry and tired and ill-natured, and threw down my pick and shovel, Raish gave me your specimen—said Bagley brought it, and asked me if it were **cinnabar**. I examined it, by the waning daylight, and took the specks of fine gold for sulphurets—wrote you that I did not think much of it—and posted the letter immediately. But as soon as I looked at it in the broad light of day, I saw my mistake. During the week, we have made three horns, got a blow-pipe, &c., and yesterday, all prepared, we prospected the "Mountain House." I bo broke the specimen in two, and found it full of fine gold inside. Then we washed out one-fourth of it, and got a noble prospect. This we reduced with the blow-pipe, and got about two cents (herewith enclosed) in *pure* gold. As the fragment prospected weighed rather less than an ounce, this would give about $500 to the ton. We were eminently well satisfied. Therefore, hold on to the "Mountain House," for it is a "big thing." Touch it lightly, as far as money is concerned, though, for it is well to reverse the code of justice, in the matter of quartz ledges—that is, consider them all (& their owners) guilty (of "shenanigan") until they are proved innocent. If, without buying, you can get another interest in the "M. H.," do so—put it in my name—and I will give it to Raish, and we will go and freeze to it and put it through astonishingly—that is, work a shaft on every claim in it,—and a dozen more beside, if the mills could keep up with us. Get another claim of 100 or 200 feet if you can, but don't *buy* it. If the owners know knew R.'s talent for managing these things as well as I do, that they would willingly give him 10 or 15 feet apiece to get him to take charge of the mine. Try them.

La Rue probably showed you a remarkably fine specimen from here. Raish and I, and Mr. Fowler,[2] hunted for the ledge it came from, for 2 days, but we couldn't find it. It probably came from a mere boulder, or piece of float rock;[3] but that made no difference. If we could have found out what hill it was on, we could have found the ledge it came from. Which reminds me that if *your* specimen came from a boulder, the ledge is not far off, and can easily be found.

We have got interests in the first W. extension of the "Flyaway," and in second E. extension of the same.[4] Will get into the original if possible. Yesterday we took a spirit level and got the ∤ angle of the celebrated "Antelope" ledge, and to-morrow we shall commence a hunt after the second E. extension of it.[5] We may find it and we may not. The thing has often been tried before, but with no success. If we find it, our fortunes are made—if we don't,—they ain't. Of course. Unless the "M. H." proves "all my fancy painted her."[6] If I had a few thousands (to spare) I would make this search with a tunnel—the only probable way of finding it.

Still progressing slowly with the "H & D." tunnel. I had some notion of selling out this institution, but everybody seems to have so high an opinion of it that I concluded to "chance" it, and hold on, as it will cost but little to finish it now. It's d—d slowness is what I dislike.[7]

I have 75 feet in a *spur* of the "Antelope," which promises nothing save that it is an offshoot from a *good family*—and I am aristocrat enough to attach some importance to that sort of thing.[8]

Send me some money. If the article is scarce, $20 will do. Send by Bagley. I want to try his system of charges first once. However, if the Exp. won't charge more than the ratio of $2^{00} on $100^{00}—that is reasonable enough—and send it that way.

Dont you own in those water powers? If so—well, I recollect, you *do*—it is bully. Isn't confiscating *ten miles* of one of God Almighty's rivers coming ₐitₐ rather strong, perhaps? The more the better, though, if the thing can be stood. Tell us something more about ⱨ those ledges— whether they are well defined—how wide they are—width of the *pay* streak, &c. Raish is a great manager, and wi must be "corraled" into this arrangement. Finally—don't *sell* or *give away* a foot of the "M. H." until you at all. I will step over there one of these days, and look at the ledges— and *then*, if they prove worthless, we can sell out.

Please read this letter *twice*.

> Yr. Bro,
> Sam. L. Clemens.

P.S.—Monday—Ratio & I have bought one-half of a segregated claim[9] in the *original* "Flyaway," for $100^{00}—$50 down. We haven't a cent in the house. *We two* will work the ledge, and have full control, & pay all expenses. If you can spare $100 conveniently, let me have it—or $50, any how. Considering that I own *one-fourth* of this, it is of course more valuable than our ⅟₇ of the "Mountain House," although not so rich.

[*in a different ink on a torn half-sheet:*]

P.S. Continued.—I saw "F." rock taken to the mill the other day which I know ought to have paid $100 a ton—but it only yielded $38—from ten feet below the surface. If we strike the same kind of rock in our segregated claim, it will amply satisfy me. *We'll* get more than $38 out of it—by taking it to Clayton's. We may *not* find as good rock, but as we shall sink within a hundred feet of the "F" shaft, the probability is that we shall.

Hunted for "Antelope" to-day, and found a ledge—but hardly think it is the right one.

Crooker says, please sell his scrip for as much as it will bring, and send him the money. Send Dodd's[10] SCRIP to Crooker. (Deduct fees, of course.)

Four of us boys have dug two trenches, each 20 feet long and 6 feet deep, to-day, in the gravelly hill side. Finally, if we *do* find the "Antelope," we shan't care a d—n—any more. And if we don't do that but *do* strike it rich in the "Flyaway," we'll not care a da d—n anyhow whether school keeps or not.

I don't intend to pay Mrs. Derby that $75 until her share of feet in the tunnel are run.[11] Let me know when your money comes.[12]

Say nothing about what the "F." yielded in the mill.

[1] The gold sample from the Mountain House claim, near Carson City, remains attached to Clemens's holograph.

[2] Possibly B. C. or T. B. Fowler, residents of Aurora (Kelly 1863, 422).

[3] "Float-ore," that is, "water-worn particles of ore; fragments of vein-material found on the surface, away from the vein-outcrop" (Raymond, 36).

[4] During the week following the writing of this letter, Clemens was especially sure that the Flyaway was a rich lode, more valuable than even the Lady Washington or Orion's Mountain House. Before his hopes for it collapsed completely he owned substantially in the original claim and four of its extensions (deeds in CU-MARK). The Flyaway, on Middle Hill, was owned largely by William De Kay, from whose shaft (according to newspaper reports in May and June) rock was being taken that paid $150 a ton—and sometimes as much as $1 a pound. The Flyaway Gold and Silver Mining Company was incorporated on 22 September 1862, with capital stock of 600 shares valued at $60,000 ("Description of Esmeralda," San Francisco *Herald and Mirror*, 14 June 62, 3; "Mining and Other Corporations Formed in 1862," Sacramento *Union*, 1 Jan 63, 1).

[5] The Antelope claim, on Silver Hill, was one of the earliest made in Aurora, located on 1 September 1860. Its owners incorporated on 31 January 1861 as the Antelope Silver Mining Company, with capital stock of 1,200 shares valued at $600,000. The Antelope was considered one of the richest mines in Aurora, and from 1861 to 1863 newspapers quoted the market price of its stock at $200 to $600 a share. When Clemens wrote his letter, the Antelope shaft was down over seventy-five feet, with hundreds of tons of extracted rock piled up; a second shaft was being started, and a mill would soon be purchased. Despite its promise, however, the bulk of the Antelope's ore turned out to be low grade, averaging $50 a ton ("Mining Operations in Esmeralda District," Sacramento *Union*, 25 June 62, 3, reprinting the Esmeralda *Star* of 21 June 62; "Mining and Other Corporations Formed in 1861," Sacramento *Union*, 1 Jan 62, 2; Kelly 1863, 406, 408; Bunker, 6).

[6] From "Alice Gray," by English poet and journalist William Mee (Stevenson, 139, 2351).

[7] The Horatio and Derby tunnel had been in progress since late 1861 (see 8 and 9 Feb 62 to JLC and PAM, n. 2).

[8] A "spur" was "a branch leaving a vein, but not returning to it" (Raymond, 81). The "*good family*" spur may have been the one described in the Esmeralda

Star as "a vein shooting out of the main ledge; it is being worked and looks well. The First North Extension on the Antelope have got this ledge, and the rock resembles in character the Discovery; the owners feel highly elated, and value their interests in it high, none caring to sell for fear they might sell their fortunes" ("Mining Operations in Esmeralda District," Sacramento *Union*, 25 June 62, 3, reprinting the Esmeralda *Star* of 21 June 62).

[9]An individually owned section of a larger, jointly owned claim (Raymond, 75).

[10]Possibly C. H. Dodd, a tinsmith, listed in Kelly's first and second Aurora directories (Kelly 1862, 247; Kelly 1863, 421).

[11]Only one Derby, William, has been identified as an Aurora resident at this time (Kelly 1862, 247; Kelly 1863, 421). Presumably he was Horatio Phillips's claim partner in the Horatio and Derby mine and it was his wife who was Clemens's creditor. It is not known how, or if, Clemens's debt was related to the Horatio and Derby tunnel project.

[12]Orion's overdue salary (see 24 and 25 Apr 62 to OC, n. 5).

To Orion Clemens
11 and 12 May 1862 • Aurora, Calif./Nev. Terr.
(MS: NPV and CU-MARK)

Esmeralda, May 11, 1862.

My Dear Bro:

To use a French expression, I have "got my d—d satisfy" at last. Two years' time will make us capitalists, in spite of anything. Therefore, we need fret and fume, and worry and doubt no more, but just lie still and put up with priv/ations for six months. Perhaps 3 months will "let us out." Then, if Government refuses to pay the rent on your new office, we can do it ourselves. We have *got* to wait *six weeks*, anyhow, for a dividend, maybe longer—but that it *will* come, there is no *shadow* of a doubt. I have got the thing sifted down to a dead moral certainty. I own *one-eighth* of the new "Monitor Ledge, Clemens Company," and money can't buy a foot of it; because I *know* it to contain our fortune.[1] The ledge is 8 6 feet wide, and one needs no glass to see gold & silver in it. Phillips and I own one-half of a segregated claim in the "Flyaway" discovery, and good interests in two extensions on it. We put men to work on our part of the discovery yesterday, and last night they brought us some fine specimens. Rock taken from 10 feet below the surface on the other part of the discovery, *has* yielded $150°° to the ton, ₍in the mill₎ and we are at work 300 feet from their shaft. Now for the reason why we can't get a return for about 2 months. Clayton's is the *only* mill in camp which can save more than 25 per cent. of *any* rock. Any other mill here would be sure to run us in debt. Now Clayton is bound by contract to crush no rock for six months except "Esmeralda" and "Antelope," unless occasionally to work ab a batch of not less than 100 tons of outside rock. It would cost us $1000 to *get out* that much, maybe. But to-morrow, Raish commences, at Clayton's Mill, to learn his process. He will learn it inside of six weeks. By that time Dow's mill will be fitted up with Clayton machinery, and R. will take charge of the amalgamating department of it.[2] *Then*, when we get rock worked, it will be done properly. And shortly after that, if we can money holds out, I shall have the work on the led leads so far advanced that somebody with mining experience will have to relieve me—so, if Mr. Clayton will consent, R. will teach me the process, and when learned, leave me in the mill, and he will take charge of the mines. Looks like a d—d romance, don't it?

Say nothing about this mill arrangement. It is a big thing. Other mills here charge $16 $18 per ton for working rock, but Clayton charges $50. Save your money. If I had all the money we have spent foolishly lately since we have been in the Territory, I could use it now in sinking shafts. I am paying but little attention to our other claims. I have decided upon holding onto 3 claims, and letting the balance go for what they will bring. Having secured a *sure thing* now, we have will spend nothing on the other claims. Have you ever been paid by Gillespie?[3] How doƒ the Records pay? ˏHow's the "M. H?"ˏ[4]

Yr. Bro.
Sam.

I called for $150? Can you "see it?"

[*remainder in ink:*]

May 12—Yours by the mail received last night. "Eighteen hundred feet in the C. T. Rice's Company!"[5] Well. I am glad you did not accept of the 200 feet. Tell Rice to give it to some *poor* man. I have fully determined that the "Monitor," which is probably worth twenty-five Allen claims,[6] shall be divided in twain some day, because *800* feet is too much to have in one company. ˏ800 feet *can* be divided—but who wants to take risks on an untried portion [of] 1800, when in nine cases out of ten the ledge can't be traced half the distance?ˏ In all the claims I have here which I consider of any value, I own one-fourth, except this, ˏandˏ the 1st N S. ex. Flyaway (one-ninth.) The latter I will sell when I can. I own one-fifth of the Dash-away, and about the same, I believe, in the Antelope Spur. We want *no more* ground. If I could have *seen* the "M. H.," and satisfied myself that that specimen came from it, it would have been a dead-sure fortune. But as it is, it ~~wall~~ was well enough to deed it back to Perry. I am sorry I could not go and see the "M. H." But hereafter, when anybody holds up a glittering prospect before you, just argue in this wise, viz: That, if all spare change be devoted to working the "Monitor" and "Flyaway," 12 months, or 24 at furthest, will find all our earthly wishes satisfied, so far as money is concerned—and the more "feet" we have, the more anxiety we must bear—therefore, why not say "No—d—n your 'prospects,' I wait on a *sure* thing—and a man is less than a man, if he can't wait 2 years for a fortune?" When you and I came out here, we did not expect '63 or '64 to find us rich men—and if that proposition had been made, we would have accepted it gladly. Now, it *is* made.

Well, I am willing, now, that "Neary's tunnel," or ¢ anybody else's tunnel shall succeed.[7] Some of them may beat us a few months, but we shall be on hand in the fulness of time, as sure as fate. I would hate to swap chances with any member of the "tribe"—in fact, I am so lost to all sense and reason as to be capable of refusing to trade "Flyaway," (with but 200 feet in the Company of four,) ˏfoot for footˏ for that splendid "Lady Washington," with its list of capitalist proprietors, and its 35,000 feet of Priceless ground.

If Henry Hardy[8] will take you up a claim and pay all assessments on it himself, forevermore, it would be well enough. But I don't want it, even on those excellent terms.

Montgomery never gave me any deed at all. He sent me a *blank* deed, to be filled out in case I sold any ground for him. But I didn't.

I wouldn't mind being in some of those ¢ Clear Creek claims, if I lived in Carson & we could spare the money.[9] But I have struck my tent in Esmeralda, and I care for no mines but those which I can superintend myself. I am aˏ citizen here now, and I am satisfied—although ˏ R. and I are "strapped" and we haven't three days' rations in the house.

Raish is looking anxiously for money, and so am I. Send me whatever you can spare conveniently—and if you owe nothing on the Dayton lots, sell *one* of them for $100, or both for $150, if you can do no better, and ~~co~~ can't otherwise raise that amount conveniently.[10] I want it to work the Flyaway with. My fourth of that claim only cost me $50, ˏ(which isn't paid yet, though,)ₐ and I suppose I could sell it here in town for ten times that amount, to-day, but I shall probably hold on to it till the cows come home. I shall work the "Monitor" and the other claims with my own hands. I prospected ¾ of a pound of "M." yesterday, and ₐRaishₐ reduced it with the blow-pipe, and got about 10 or 12 cents in gold & silver, besides the other half of it which we spilt on the floor and *didn't* get. There was about 4 or 5 times as much in the button as there was in that one which I sent you ₐbut from ~~und~~ 10 or ~~11~~ 12 times as much rockₐ. Lieut. Noble has got it. We put him in for 100 ft. The specimen came from the croppings, but was a choice one, and showed much free gold to the naked eye. The rock is exactly like the Antelope, and the ledge is the same width. I hope it may prove as rich.

Raish wrote the "Carsonite" letter to the "Age," I only assisted him.[11]

It will not be necessary to apprise me before sending down that portion of your salary. My only reason for ~~$~~ it was, that I was afraid that if these Derbys got the money, they would not do their work in the tunnel, and that would be another "dead dog" you know. I am confident they did not intend to do the work. But they kept inquiring about the money until I told them that the matter was in my hands now, entirely, and I hardly ₐthoughtₐ that last payment would ever be made until the work was done on the feet they still hold. They said your promise was out. I told them it would probably stay out for awhile—that if it were still in your hands, you would keep your promise; but it wasn't, and I didn't mind such things much when I found they were likely to render worthless a good claim. They said they had no means to work it with. So they told Raish. And I sent them word that if it suited them, I would have it worked myself, and take my pay out of the $75. They said "all right"—(what else *could* they say, you know?)—and I have had the work done.

Well, I like the corner up-stairs office amazingly—provided, it has one fine, large front room superbly carpeted, for the safe and a $150-desk, or such a matter—one handsome room amidships, less handsomely gotten up, perhaps, for Records and consultations, and one goodsized bedroom and adjoining it a kitchen, neither of which latter can be entered by *anybody* but yourself[12]—and finally, when one of these ledges begins to pay, the whole to be kept in parlor order by two likely ~~cl~~ contrabands at big wages, the same to be free of expense to the Government.[13] You want the entire second story—no less room than you would have had in Harris

& Co.'s.[14] Make them fix for you *before* the 1st July—for maybe you might want to "come out strong" on the 4th, you know.

No, the Post Office is all right, and kept by a gentleman[15]—but W. F. Express isn't. They charge 25c to Express a letter *from* here, but I believe they have quit charging twice for letters that arrive prepaid.

Well, if Harroun calls for assessments, I would pay them when the call does not exceed $20 at a time and don't come too often. You see 50 feet in those Humboldt ledges of infernal proportions don't amount to much, and when they levy on you for $20, you may feel pretty sure that you are paying more than your share, because, in that case anybody who owned a full claim would be assessed $120°°—and who ever heard of such an assessment as that in an unincorporated company—more money than there is in Santa Clara. I think you can safely pay assessments, because $5 at a time would be a big one, to my thinking.

No, 50 feet in Boyd's ledge[16] would not be desirable, unless there were only 200 feet in the company, and you could *see* gold in the rock—and in when one owns a fourth, it necessarily costs like the devil to work a claim. For instance, you and I will have to pay about $90 towards sinking a shaft 22 feet on the Flyaway, alth as we own a fourth, and Raish and I are to foot all bills on the first 22 feet for working it. The "Flyaway" specimen I send you, (taken by myself from DeKay's shaft, 300 feet from where we are going to sink) cannot be called "choice," exactly—say something above medium, to be on the safe side. But I *have* seen *exceedingly* choice chunks from that shaft. My intention at first in sending the Antelope specimen was, that you might see that it resembles the Monitor—but, come to think, a man can tell absolutely nothing about that without seeing both ledges themselves. I tried to break a handsome chunk for from a huge piece of my darling Monitor a wh which we brought from the croppings yesterday, but it all splintered up, and I send you the scraps. I call that "choice"—any d—d fool would. Don't ask if it has been assayed, for it hasn't. It don't need it. It is amply able to speak for itself. It is 6 feet wide on top, and traversed through and through with veins whose color proclaims their worth. What the devil does a man want with any more feet when he owns in the Flyaway and the invincible bomb-proof Monitor?[17]

Have just heard some bully news. Raish has returned from the mill, where he went to take his first lesson, and says Clayton will crush 20 tons for us from either the F. or M. at $20 a ton. I think we can get rock from the top of either ledge that will ~~more than pay~~ at least pay expenses. You bet we will try.

Snow is the matter now, though. ₓday beforeₓ Yesterday we worked comfortably on the M,—now there's a foot of snow there, perhaps, and 3 or 4 inches down here—and still at it.

No, it is not best to segregate claims until they are paying in the mills. It costs too much to work a segregated claim. I wouldn't have one now. Can't work it by yourself, either if you wanted to—you *must* have assistance in a shaft—and I like to pick my company when at work. When every tub is able to stand on its own bottom, then it [is] early enough to begin.

I collected that $25.70—~~but can't Upton wait on me awhile?—especially when I have been running to Tom, Dick and Harry, trying to get this that house business of his properly arranged—and if I haven't succeeded yet, it wasn't my fault. If he *must* have it, though, pay him. I don't want~~ to keep it longer, ~~unless~~ he is able to stand ~~it~~.[18] But then again, suppose you *don't* pay, it. No, on second thoughts; don't pay him. Tell him I have spent $150 since I have been here, and you'll be d—d if you'll put up with it. (*I owe him one*, you know.) Tell him I spoke of the debt to you, and said ~~to~~ I would like to ~~take~~ have an extension on it. ₓ(**Entre nous,** I have already taken up the 1ˢᵗ N. Exten. on it.)ₓ And say you will pay no debts ₓat presentₓ except those of your own contracting—but that if I never pay it, he shall not lose it. You see it is not your debt, Orion, and I ~~pr~~ peremptorily forbid its payment at present. I must have money to open those ledges with.

How about the Governor's 40-stamp mill which he ~~w~~ is to bring here? It wouldn't set the camp back any.[19]

If I had anything more to say, I have forgotten what it was, unless, perhaps, that I want a sum of money—anywhere from $20 to $150, as soon as possible.

Raish sends regards. He or I one will drop a line to the "Age" occasionally. I suppose you saw my letters in the "Enterprize.["][20]

Yr. Bro,

Sam

P.S. I suppose Pamela never will regain her health, but she could *improve* it by coming to California,—provided the trip didn't kill her.

You see Bixby is on the flag-ship. He always was the best pilot ~~th~~ on the Mississippi, and deserves his "posish."[21] They have done a reckless thing, though, in putting Sam. Bowen on the "Swon,"—for if a bombshell happens to come his way, he will infallibly jump overboard. It would be refreshing if they would catch Will Bowen and hang him.[22]

If the snow will permit us, we shall probably commence taking out rock to-morrow—Clayton would prefer 30 tons—and if it even pays expenses, why, I shall put on some of the most disgusting airs you know—but if it *don't* pay,—why—I shan't care a d—n anyhow. There's plenty more rock in those ledges.

Send me another package of those envelops, per Bagley's coat pocket.

>•<————————————————————————————————

Orion Clemens Esq. | Carson City | N. T. [*upper left:*] ~~With specimens.~~ | [*rule canceled*] [*partly boxed, lower left:*] ~~Politeness of Mr La Rue.~~ [*postmaster's hand:*] Esmeralda Cal | May 13th 1862 [*brace*] [*postage stamp cut away*]

---

[1] Except for Clemens's references in this and succeeding letters, little is known of the Monitor ledge, located on Middle Hill, Aurora. The Clemens Gold and Silver Mining Company, consisting of Clemens, Calvin H. Higbie, Daniel H. Twing, and J. D. LaRue, was formed on 9 May 1862 in order to work 800 feet of the Monitor. When the company incorporated on 27 February 1863, with a capital stock of 700 shares valued at $140,000, it consisted of three partners: Twing, R. E. Brewster, and C. W. Buckingham. It retained its original name, however, and continued in existence for at least a few months (Clemens Gold and Silver Mining Company trust deed and certificate of incorporation, PH in CU-MARK, courtesy of Michael H. Marleau; "More Mining Corporations," San Francisco *Alta California*, 3 Mar 63, 1).

[2] The Aurora Mill was owned by Dow, Childs, and Batturs (Kelly 1862, 244). It was in the process of expanding from ten stamps to twenty and introducing a Veatch reduction process, evidently the one used at Clayton's Mill (see 18 Apr 62 to Clagett, n. 3).

[3] William M. Gillespie, clerk of the territorial House of Representatives. His indebtedness to Orion has not been explained. For an explanation of the "Records" Clemens asks about next, see 24 and 25 Apr 62 to OC, n. 7.

[4] The Mountain House ledge.

[5] Clemens's friend Clement T. Rice was an active mining investor.

[6] A. D. Allen, the highly successful Aurora miner.

[7] James Neary, a "speculator" boarding at Margret Murphy's in Carson City, was one of the "Irish Brigade" who accompanied Governor Nye to Nevada (Kelly 1862, 85; *Roughing It*, chapter 21). He was a member of John Nye and Company (see 18–21 Sept 61 to JLC and PAM, n. 5). Nothing is known about his tunnel project.

[8] Unidentified.

[9] The Clear Creek district, west of Carson City, experienced its major mining boom in 1859–60. Despite current hopes for it, the area proved relatively unproductive as mining property (Angel, 537).

[10] Orion Clemens had bought two lots in the town of Dayton, Lyon County, for $100 on 11 December 1861, but the deed was not filed for record until 16 June 1862 (deed in CU-MARK). About six weeks before Orion made his purchase Dayton (then still called Chinatown) was reported to be "fast growing in importance. It already has eight stores and seven saloons and hotels. . . . It is fast becoming the centre of a lively trade with the surrounding districts. . . . Town lots are on the rise" ("Items from Washoe," San Francisco *Evening Bulletin*, 30 Oct 61, 1, reprinting the Virginia City *Territorial Enterprise* of unknown date).

[11] The Carson City *Silver Age*, founded by former California newspaperman John C. Lewis, began as a weekly paper in November 1860 and then became a daily in September 1861. It was acquired around March 1862 by the "Age Association, consisting of John Church, S. A. Glessner and J. L. Laird, who, in November, 1862, moved the establishment to Virginia City, and started the Virginia *Daily Union*" (Angel, 312). Since the files of the *Silver Age* are no longer extant, the joint contribution that Clemens alludes to has not been recovered. In July, pressed for funds, he planned to make regular contributions to this paper (see 23 July 62 to OC).

[12] Late in 1862 Orion managed to secure an office much like the one described here, consisting of two rooms and a bedroom, "plastered overhead." He furnished it, at government expense, with: a bedstead and mattress, a table and ten chairs, a washstand, and "silk damask window curtains" with cornices, for a total of $339.25; a desk and chair costing $200.00; "Brussel's carpet" throughout for $142.70; and two stoves, cost unknown. Unfortunately, early in 1863 the Treasury Department questioned Orion's expenditures. He pleaded his inexperience in public office, explaining, "It was not my design to furnish my office . . . in an extravagant or unusual manner; but I never held an office before, except that I once had the honor to be clerk of an election, was never in Washington, never saw a Legislature in session, and never saw any office at the Capitol of any State or Territory." Nevertheless, he agreed to reimburse the government for the items costing $339.25 (OC to William Hemphill Jones, 29 Apr 63, NvU-NSP).

[13] A slave who fled behind Union lines or lived in an area captured by Union forces was generally regarded by the Lincoln administration as "contraband of war" and therefore liberated, although in some cases slaveowners loyal to the Union were allowed to reclaim runaways (Litwack, 52). "Contraband" became synonymous with "Negro" or "slave."

[14] H. Harris and Company, owners of the Pioneer Assay Office in Carson City (Kelly 1862, 80, 81).

[15] Daniel H. Pine was postmaster in Aurora (Salley, 70; Kelly 1862, 250).

[16] The owner of this ledge possibly was John Boyd, a Carson City cabinetmaker (Kelly 1862, 68).

[17] The Monitor ledge presumably was named for the ironclad Union warship, launched in early 1862. On 9 March the *Monitor* had fought a four-hour draw with the *Virginia* (formerly the *Merrimack*), the Confederate ironclad, at Hampton Roads, Virginia. This was the first battle ever between two such warships (*DAH*, 4:10).

[18] Clemens struck out the marked passage in a deliberate but uncharacteristic manner. He evidently intended his few long strokes to cancel the passage without impairing its legibility.

[19] James W. Nye reportedly was planning to establish a mill in Aurora, in part-

nership with the actor James Stark, but there is no indication that this plan was carried out (see 2 June 62 to OC, n. 4).

[20] Clemens's "Josh" letters in the Virginia City *Territorial Enterprise*.

[21] Horace E. Bixby served from September 1861 to August 1862 as pilot of the USS *Benton*, flagship of the Western Flotilla. In 1882, during his return to the Mississippi River, Clemens had his secretary record Bixby's account of his Civil War service (*N&J2*, 563–67; Way 1983, 49).

[22] Sam Bowen was evidently now piloting the Northern boat *J. C. Swon*, a circumstance that seems not to have signified a true change in his Southern sympathies. Although official records offer no information about Bowen's war service, pilot Absalom Grimes, in 1861 a member of the Marion Rangers with Clemens and Bowen, later recalled that immediately after that misadventure Bowen was

arrested by Federals and confined in the stockade at Hannibal, where he learned the trade of wood-sawing. . . . After he graduated as a wood-sawyer he went back to St. Louis, took the oath of allegiance to the United States, and went back to piloting again. After I became the Confederate mail-carrier, Sam Bowen and his sister, Miss Amanda Bowen, were untiring in their efforts to aid the Southern cause. He was pilot on the steamer *G. W. Graham*, a regular packet in the St. Louis and Memphis trade. His brother, Bart Bowen, was captain of the *Graham*. He was of untold assistance to the South in carrying the mail for the Rebel army between St. Louis and Memphis. (Grimes, 18)

It is unclear whether Clemens's present low opinion of Sam Bowen stemmed from political or personal differences. His animosity toward Will Bowen was in part political. Jane Clemens remembered that "when Sam and W B were on the Alonzo Chi they quarreled and Sam let go the wheel to whip Will for talking secesh and made Will hush" (JLC to "all in the Teritory," 12 and 14 Oct 62, NPV, in *MTBus*, 73). The antagonism also resulted from a financial "misunderstanding" (see 25 Aug 66 to Bowen).

To Orion Clemens
17 May 1862 • Aurora, Calif./Nev. Terr.
(MS: NPV)

Esmeralda, May 17.

My Dear Bro:

If you can't get the *whole* of the second story at Kinkead's, why, Gov. Johnson's seems pretty good,—except in the matter of binding yourself to take it for a year. I would not like to do that, for when the Capital buildings are erected, you will probably have rooms in them. The suggestion is worthy of attention. Wherever you go, fit up the office superbly. I don't like *J* Gov. J.'s as well as Harrington's, because the former is not on the principal business street.[1]

I thought it was a *blank* deed which Sam Montgomery ¢ sent me.

Send those Spanish spurs that hang in the office, out to "Thomas Messersmith,[2] care of Billy Clagett," by some safe person. I wore them in from Humboldt.

Yes, I have received the $100—much obliged. Stand by, now, for we shall let a contract on the Flyaway to-morrow, which will cost about $200—sink a shaft 25 feet deep.

No, let the Humboldt ground alone, but keep yourself posted about the rise of property in Dayton, so that you may know what you are about when you start in to sell those lots. And post yourself about Carson property, too—so that you can sell your town lot for all it is worth. The cards are the Flyaway and the Monitor—and we will stake the whole pile on them. If they win, we are all right—if they lose, I am busted.

That is well. Let Mollie stay where she is, for the present.

Perhaps you *had* better send me your note to Teall.[3]

Never send anything by that d—d stage again, that can come by MAIL, as I have said before. The pkg envelops cost me 50 cents.

You don't understand. A letter from here, by Express, must be enclosed in a W.F. envelop, and be additionally *prepaid* in *cash* and *cash* ONLY.

I hope Barstow will leave the "S.L.C." off my Gate City letters, in case he publishes them. Put my Enterprise letters in the scrap book—but send no extracts from them *East*.[4]

You perceive that I am not in a high good humor. For several reasons. One—Raish came home from the mill this morning, after working the whole night, and ~~rea~~ found a letter from Bob, in which he learned that no sale had been effected.[5] This reduced his spirits to the lowest possible notch, for he is out of money, ~~and~~ or nearly so, and he was making large calculations on Bob's replenishing his purse. Another thing is, two or three of the old "Salina" company entered our hole on the Monitor yesterday morning, before our men got there, and took possession, armed with revolvers. And according to the d—d laws of this forever d—d country, nothing but the District Court (and there ain't any) can touch the matter, unless it assumes the shape of an infernal humbug which they call "forcible entry and detainer," and in order to bring that about, you must compel the jumpers to use personal violence toward you! We went up and demanded possession, and they refused. Said they were in the hole, armed, and meant to die in it, if necessary. I got in it with them, and again demanded possession. They said I might stay in it as long as I pleased, and work—but they would do the same. I asked one of our company to take my place in the hole, while I went to ~~cut~~ consult a lawyer. He did so. The lawyer said it was no go. They must offer some "force." Our boys will try to be there first in the morning—in which case they may get possession and keep it. Now you understand the shooting scrape in which Gephart was killed the other day.[6] The Clemens Company—all of us— hate to resort ~~too~~ to arms in this matter, and ~~I~~ it will not be done until it becomes a forced hand—but I think that will be the end of it, nevertheless.

Remember me cordially to Capt. Nye, and ask the old cuss how "Bill" is. If I wasn't so glad to hear that the "old man" is back again, and if I hadn't been swearing so much to-day that I am about run out, I would give him a dose of slang just because I am at a safe distance and can do so with impunity. He be d—d *anyhow*—just for a starter.[7]

Ask Tom to give my dear love to Miss P.—she with the long curls, out there under the hill.[8]

Yr. Bro.
Sam.

[1] Territorial treasurer John H. Kinkead and William P. Harrington, Jr. (1826–1903), a representative in the House of the first Territorial Legislature, were partners in Kinkead, Harrington and Company, Carson City "importers and jobbers" of groceries, dry goods, and mining tools. Their establishment was centrally located on Carson Street, at the corner of the plaza. John Neely Johnson (1825–72), born in Indiana, practiced law in Keokuk, Iowa, before moving to California in 1849, subsequently serving as that state's fourth governor (1856–58). He was now a lawyer in Carson City and evidently had his office in his residence on Curry Street (Andrew J. Marsh, 667 n. 18, 690 n. 253; Marsh, Clemens, and Bowman, 465 n. 18; Kelly 1862, 76, 82; Kelly 1863, 105).

[2] Possibly the Humboldt acquaintance Clemens previously referred to as Tom Smith (see 28 Feb 62 to Clagett).

[3] The note was for Orion's purchase of shares in the Live Yankee lode (see 13 Apr 62 to OC, n. 5).

[4] William H. Barstow of the Virginia City *Territorial Enterprise*, impressed with Clemens's "Josh" letters, was interested in reprinting his letters about Nevada which had appeared in the Keokuk *Gate City* (26 Oct 61, 30 Jan 62, 20 Mar 62, all to JLC). Clemens was nettled by his mother's and sister's negative reactions to the second of these (see 28 Apr 62 to OC) and apparently anticipated that his *Enterprise* pieces would provoke a similar response. Neither Orion's scrapbook, containing clippings of the "Josh" letters, nor the *Enterprise* for this period is extant. It is not known whether Barstow actually reprinted Clemens's *Gate City* letters.

[5] Horatio Phillips was learning the quartz-milling process in use at Clayton's Mill. Phillips's Aurora cabinmate Robert Howland had gone to California with

Governor Nye's party in March in order to "sell some ground in San Francisco" (8 and 9 Mar 62 to Clagett).

[6]This shooting took place on 11 April (see 13 Apr 62 to OC, n. 7).

[7]Captain John Nye, the governor's brother, achieved an enduring notoriety as "one of the fiercest and most vehement talkers that is to be found anywhere. His anathemas would annihilate any man by their force, if sound and fury are good for anything" ("Jorkins at Washington," San Francisco *Evening Bulletin*, 14 Mar 68, 5). "Bill" has not been identified.

[8]The message was to be delivered by John Nye's son Thomas. "Miss P." was Carrie Pixley, the daughter of Carson City carpenter Seymour Pixley (Kelly 1862, 86). On 8 May 1907, then Mrs. Edward Headrick, she wrote to Clemens, requesting permission to make her reminiscences of their friendship available to Albert Bigelow Paine. She cautioned Clemens to "remember, in those days you were not a Chesterfield in deportment . . . being at that time—just Sam—the name that all ways makes one think of a big hearted, restless, lazy, good natured chap, that every one loved" (CU-MARK). For the information she sent to Paine, see Davis 1956c, 1–2, and *MTB*, 1:246.

To Orion Clemens
2 June 1862 • Aurora, Calif./Nev. Terr.
(MS: NPV)

Esmeralda, June 2[d], 1862.

My Dear Bro:

The "Monitor" suit was decided to-day. We, (plffs.) retain 700 feet, and restore the other 100 to defts. It was agreed to set the value of the lode at $200, so as to bring the title within jurisdiction of a justice's court. Therefore, this decision gives us title. They may appeal it to the Co. Court. If so, we will "stay with them."

Mr. Clayton seems inclined to help us all he can. I saw him yesterday, and he said that in the course of 5 or 6 weeks he expected to commence teaching me the process, and when I have learned it, he wants Raish and me to go out to Humboldt, get it used by Humboldt Mills, and stay there and work it. As soon as I commence learning it, I shall write to Billy C.[1] to begin puffing it up out there.

We haven't money enough to work the "Flyaway;" so, we shall hold on and see if we can financier it out without cash.

It costs me $8 or $10 per week to "batch" in this d—d place.

Send me all the money you can spare every week or so, without further orders. I have only $25 left.

I own 50 feet in the *"Monitor Co."* (same ledge), and we are taking pretty good rock out of it. Assessments have cost me $12—the ground nothing.

Yr. Bro.

Sam.

[*remainder in pencil:*]

If I do not forget it, I will send you, per next mail, a *pinch* of decom, which I pinched with thumb and finger, from Wide West ledge a while ago.[2] Raish and I have secured 200 out of a company with 400 ft. in it ͭ—aͭ which is a̶b̶ perhaps (the ledge, I mean,) a spur from the W. W.— our shaft is about 100 ft from the W. W shaft.[3] In order to get in, we agreed to sink 30 ft. We have sublet to another man for 50 ft, & we pay for powder & sharping tools. It is all right, if the latter can get somebody to go in with HIM for 25 ft. We are only taking desperate chances, this time, but it will not cost much.

Col. Vibbard wishes Gov. Nye to come down with Stark.[4] Tell him so.

Yrs,

Sam.

[1] William H. Clagett.

[2] The Wide West claim on Last Chance Hill, Aurora, was located in 1860 by Alec Gamble and his brother, who in 1863 received well in excess of $200,000 for their stock. The Wide West Mining Company was incorporated on 17 January 1861 with a capital stock of 2,400 shares valued at $600,000. Throughout 1861 it was known as a source of relatively rich ore, its rock bringing as much as $140 per ton (McGrath, 3; Colcord, 116–17; "Mining and Other Corporations Formed in 1861," Sacramento *Union*, 1 Jan 62, 2; Nevada City [Calif.] *Transcript*: "Letter from Esmeralda," 14 May 61, 2; "From Esmeralda," 4 Dec 61, 3). Around the time of the present letter a "remarkably rich" strike in the Wide West was reported: "The ledge is more than four feet wide, and the specimens are about as thickly spangled with gold, to say nothing of silver, as a turkey's egg is with specks" ("The Esmeralda Mines," San Francisco *Herald and Mirror*, 12 June 62, 1). Clemens later described ore from this ledge as "not hard rock, but black, decomposed stuff which could be crumbled in the hand like a baked potato, and when spread out on paper exhibited a thick sprinkling of gold and particles of 'native' silver" (*Roughing It*, chapter 40). Ultimately it was discovered that this "decom," a sample of which Clemens "pinched," did not come from the Wide West ledge. Its source actually was the Dimes blind lead (a blind lead was an ore vein that did not show at the earth's surface and hence was discoverable only by accident), which cut diagonally through the Wide West ledge (see 22 June 62 and 23 July 62, both to OC).

[3] The spur from the Wide West was the Annapolitan lead mentioned in the next few letters. No evidence has been found to confirm Clemens's later statement that he "purchased largely in the 'Wide West'" itself (SLC 1869b, 2).

[4] James Stark (b. 1818) was an actor well known on the East Coast since the late 1840s and in California since 1850. Following the completion of his company's tour of Nevada Territory, Stark had gone to Aurora in late December 1861, when Governor Nye was also there. The two men reportedly had plans to establish a mill. Before the end of the year, Nye purchased $25,000 in mining property in the region from Phillip G. Vibbard, an early settler of Aurora, one of its wealthiest landowners, and, along with Nye's brother John, an incorporator of the Aurora and Walker River Railroad. Stark also acquired mining interests in Esmeralda and in January 1863 became owner of the Aurora Mill—in partnership with wealthy San Francisco jeweler and mine investor John W. Tucker, not Governor Nye. Probably in response to the Vibbard request that Clemens here transmits, Nye came to Aurora on 22 June 1862. He, Vibbard, and Stark were soon partners in the Vibbard Gold and Silver Mining Company, incorporated on 12 September and operating on Last Chance Hill, eighty feet below and parallel to the Wide West ledge (Andrew J. Marsh, 693 n. 283; Marsh, Clemens, and Bowman, 470 n. 42; Angel, 274; Kelly 1862, 244, 252; Kelly 1863, 415; "Mining Enterprises in Esmeralda," Marysville [Calif.] *Appeal*, 28 Dec 61, 3; "The San Francisco Spirit of the Times . . . ," Nevada City [Calif.] *Transcript*, 18 Jan 62, 2; Veni, Vidi 1862a, 1; "Mining and Other Corporations Formed in 1862," Sacramento *Union*, 1 Jan 63, 1; Pioneer, 2; Keseph, 1; Langley 1862, 383; Briton, 1).

To Orion Clemens
9 June 1862 • Aurora, Calif./Nev. Terr.
(MS: NPV)

Esmeralda, June 9.

My Dear Bro.

I have received all the money you mentioned. $25 per week will be sufficient, but where is it to come from? Don't take any from the Gov't. funds, at all. I mean, don't draw ˏonˏ your salary until you receive it, if possible. But sell all your town lots when a good cash prrice is offered.

~~Das~~ "Flyaway" is down 16 feet,—$45 due from me on it. We shall have to sink 25 feet and then drift, before we find pay rock, I think—we could not have struck a more barren place on the whole ledge, I reckon.

The "Annipolitan" (which we hope will be the "Wide West's" rich ledge,) has cost us $36 so far.[1] We gave two men 100 feet to sink the 30-foot shaft which we contracted to sink. But we had to pay them $36 worth of powder & tools to do it with. However, we owed them that, for work done on other ledges for us.

But for God's sake get out of that d—d office. I am ashamed to send anybody to it. Consequently, I have told ~~Decay~~ DeKay to inquire for Gov. Johnson's—that he'll find you there. ₍Private₎ DeK is Deputy County Clerk, and "Secesh" they say.

Clayton's last improvement is a big thing. He can work as fast as a mill can crush. I know all the chemicals, and the manner of using them, shall begin practice in a week or so.

When do you move?

You must do all the writing home. I haven't written a ~~wort~~ word home since I left Carson.[2] I am afraid the folks will not hear from me again while I remain in this part of Calfornia.

Send me some 3ᶜᵗ stamps.

Did Bob Howland give you Crooker's receipts? If so, seend me the money for Crooker—just whatever you get for his scrip.

Yr. Bro.

[*in ink:*] O. Clemens, Esq. | Carson City | N. T. [*upper left:*] Introducing Mr. DeKay, | [*rule*] [*no postage stamp*]

[1] The Annapolitan ledge lay parallel to the Wide West lode on Last Chance Hill. Clemens hoped that it was an extension of the ledge from which the rich "decom" he had "pinched" was mistakenly thought to come. His faith in the Annapolitan is indicated by his two known purchases: on 22 July 1862 he bought 33 feet in its discovery lode from Horatio Phillips as part of a package of stocks costing $300; and on 1 August he bought 50 feet in its first north extension from Calvin Higbie for $200. Within a few months the Annapolitan was reported to be one of several claims that, because of proximity to the Wide West, were "increasing rapidly in value," allowing their owners to feel "well satisfied that they have large fortunes close at hand" ("Letter from Esmeralda," San Francisco *Alta California*, 27 Oct 62, 1). When the Annapolitan Consolidated Gold and Silver Mining Company filed its certificate of incorporation on 2 March 1863, it announced a capital stock of 800 shares valued at $800,000. Exactly a year later Clemens was the owner of 50 shares that the company offered at auction because he owed $25 in unpaid assessments. It is hardly credible, however, that these shares had the same value as those announced upon the company's incorporation (deeds in CU-MARK; San Francisco *Alta California*: "More Mining Incorporations," 3 Mar 63, 1; "Annapolitan Consolidated Gold and Silver Mining Company," 2 Mar 64, 3).

[2] Clemens had left Carson City for Esmeralda in the second week of April 1862.

To Orion Clemens
22 June 1862 • Aurora, Calif./Nev. Terr.
(MS: ViU)

Esmeralda, June 22, 1862.

My Dear Bro:

Things are going on pretty much as usual. Our men are still at work on the "Annipolitan" and "Flyaway," but we are doing nothing on the "Monitor," as the other parties have until the end of this month to appeal in. They have struck it fully as rich in the "Pride of Utah" as in the "Wide West." Here is the position of the ledges:[1]

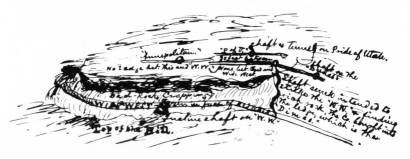

You see the grand rock comes from the "Dimes," in reality, and not from the W. W., although the latter said nothing about it until they had bought into the former.[2] The "Annipolitan" shaft is about 200 feet from the P. of Utah and Dimes-W. W. shafts. ~~These~~ These two ledges are so close together that I don't see how ours could be crowded between them —and we are most damnably "mixed" as to whether the "Annipolitan" will prove to be the "Dimes" or the "Pride of Utah." We want it to be the former—for in that case we can hold all our ground—but if it be the "Pride of Utah," we shall lose all of it except fifty feet, as the "P. of U." was located first. There is an extension on the "P. of U.," and in order to be on the safe side, we have given them notice not to work on it. We are in a good neighborhood, for, since the rich strikes on the "Dimes" and "Pride of Utah," they have resumed work on the "W. W." incline, and are getting out very handsome rock. McNear,[3] who owns one-half the "Annipolitan," says he would not sell an inch for even $2,000 a foot. He is the best pleased man I know. Well, it *does* seem like a dead sure thing,—but then it's the d—dest country for disappointments the world ever saw. However, sure or *not* sure, by the new law I can get a perpetual title to our ground very easily,[4] and I mean to do it and leave the country for a year, if we don't strike something soon. I am mighty impatient to see the shaft down on the "A.;"—but if 30 feet don't find it rich, we shall sink 30 more immediately—so I expect to be here 3 months longer, anyhow. I have now been here over two months, and have accomplished a great deal—but I know, and you know, that I cannot double that time in any one place without a miracle. I have been here as long, now, as it is in my nature to stay in one place—and from this out I shall feel as much like a prisoner as if I were in the county jail. I believe I have not spent six months in one place (unless I was in Keokuk, that long,) since 1853—ten years ago— and God knows I want to be moving to-day. Well, this is the first time I have uttered a complaint since I have been here, but it is not the first time I have *felt* one. Christ! how sick I am of these same ~~on~~ old humdrum scenes.

Those Enterprise fellows make perfect nonsense of my letters—like all d—d fool printers, they can't follow the punctuation as it is in the manuscript. They have, by this means made a mass of senseless, d—d stupidity out of my last letter.[5]

I received $25 from you nearly a week ago, I believe. I am sorry it has to come from the school fund,—for I am afraid it might be called for, you know. Did you get my letter about the ⌀ business of Barstow—and his letter? Do not hint to Gillesp anything about it.[6]

Put all of Josh's letters in my scrap book. I may have use for them some day.

If you should ever remove the long desk from your office, don't forget to take out my letters and traps from the middle drawer.

You have heard nothing from your last quarter's salary, I suppose.[7]

It is time now to begin your arrangements for a supply of stationery for the Legislature, I should think.[8]

I have quit writing for the "Gate."[9] I haven't got time to write. I half intended writing east to-night, but I hardly think I will. Tell Mollie I will not offend again. I see by ~~th~~ a Boston paper that Colorado Territory expects to export $40,000,000 (bullion, I believe,) this year. Nevada had better look to her laurels.[10]

⌀ Your Bro.

Sam

◄►

Orion Clemens, Esq. | Carson City | N. T. | [*rule*] [*postmaster's hand:*]
Esmeralda Cal | June 24th 1862 [*postage stamp cut away*]

[1] In the drawing Clemens has noted:
[*upper left:*] "Annipolitan." | No ledge bet. this and "W. W." [*upper center:*] "P of U." | 30
feet between | None bet. this and | Wide West. [*upper right:*] shaft & tunnel on Pride of
Utah. | shaft on the | "Dimes" | Shaft sunk intended to | strike the "W. W.", & finding | rich
rock, the Co. bought into | the ledge, which is the | "Dimes." [*lower left:*] Bed-Rock Crop-
pings | WIDE WEST—a vein in face of Bed Rock | Incline shaft on "W. W." | Top of the
Hill.
As Clemens's map shows, the Pride of Utah, like the Annapolitan, lay parallel to
the Wide West on Last Chance Hill and its claim line butted almost end to end
with that of the Annapolitan. The day after Clemens wrote this letter, the Aurora
correspondent of the Sacramento *Bee* noted the new strike made in the Pride of
Utah and ranked the mine equal to the Wide West in richness. "The 'Pride of
Utah,'" he continued, "is now yielding about a thousand dollars per day. The
rock is rotten quartz and easily worked. Clayton's mill cleaned up yesterday, after
a week's run on the 'Pride of Utah' rock, and the yield of gold was *one wooden pail
full*—more than a man could conveniently carry" (Veni, Vidi 1862a, 1). Since
Clemens was being trained in Clayton's Mill about this time, he probably had
first-hand knowledge of Pride of Utah rock. Eventually it became known that the
rich quartz coming out of the mine's shaft actually came from a vein (or blind
lead) intersecting the Pride of Utah ledge—the same vein, in fact, that intersected
the Wide West ledge at another point on the hill (see 23 July 62 to OC, n. 1).
    [2] By 16 January 1863 the Wide West owned fifty-two percent of the Dimes stock
(Tucker, 2).
    [3] George McNear of Aurora. He may have been the George McNeir who served
briefly in 1861 as clerk and auditor of Carson County, Utah Territory, before it
became part of Nevada Territory (Kelly 1862, 249; Angel, 75, 76; Mack 1936,
154–56).
    [4] Article 2 of the mining laws of Esmeralda district, passed at a miners' meeting
on 1 June 1862, reads: "All claims of (200) two hundred feet, or proportion
thereof, that shall have ($75) seventy-five dollars' worth of useful work done on or
for them, or in their proportion, shall give the owner or owners a perpetual title"
(*Mining Laws*, 6).
    [5] One of the nonextant "Josh" letters.
    [6] As the next letter indicates, William M. Gillespie was planning to start a news-
paper. Clemens seems to have feared that William H. Barstow's interest in publishing his Keokuk *Gate City* letters in the Virginia City *Territorial Enterprise*
would cost him the opportunity of writing for Gillespie's paper.
    [7] The overdue $450 did not arrive until 3 July.
    [8] On 16 July Orion Clemens wrote to Elisha Whittlesey, first comptroller of the
United States Treasury, requesting $5,000 "to purchase stationery for the next
session of the Legislature, before freights rise, and to pay the balance on the
printer's bills" (NvU-NSP).
    [9] The Keokuk *Gate City*.
    [10] In 1862 the mines of Colorado Territory produced bullion worth $3.4 mil-
lion. Nevada's mines produced nearly $6.3 million in bullion that year (Fossett,
426; Lord, 416).

To Orion Clemens
25 June 1862 • Aurora, Calif./Nev. Terr.
(MS: NPV and CU-MARK)

[dateline in pencil]   Esmeralda, 25th June
My Dear Bro:
The mail will close in a few moments. D—n Johnson and the
whole tribe. I am sick of that old crib you are in. I received $25 per
Express day before yesterday. If Gillespie gets up a large paper, it will suit
me exactly to correspond for it.[1] I shall not refuse pay, either, although
$4 or $5 a week ₩ could hardly be called extensive when you write by
the "*column*," you know. I am his man, though. Let me know further
about his paper—and let it not fail as utterly as the Laws did.[2]

No—haven't struck anything in the "Annipolitan." No—down 12
feet—am not afraid of it. It will come out well I think. It don't cost Flyaway $50 per ton for crushing—only $20. Clayton wanted to help the
boys. We shan't touch the Monitor until the 1st July, at least. Haven't got
an Enterprise of the 8th. Raish sent it to the Bay. I gave Crooker the bill.
He looked at the law and found 30 cents a mile allowed—which makes his
claim worth 30 or $35 *anyhow*. Thank you for writing home for me.
They've struck good pay rock in another shaft within 50 yards of Annipolitan hole. Assays $75.[3]

                                          Yr. Bro,
                                              Sam

✉️————————————————————————————————————

Orion Clemens Esq | Carson City | N. T. [*postmaster's hand:*] Esmeralda,
Cal | June 26th 1862 [*brace*] [*postage stamp cut away*]

---

[1] There is no evidence that William M. Gillespie ever started a newspaper in
Nevada. When the Virginia City *Old Piute* began publication in April 1864, he
was its associate editor. That paper suspended publication in January 1865 (Lingenfelter and Gash, 258).
    [2] The arrangements for the printing of the territorial laws and legislative jour-
nals were the responsibility of Orion Clemens, who encountered numerous difficulties in completing this task. In accord with a government directive that the
printing be done within the territory, Orion offered the contract to the proprietors of the Virginia City *Territorial Enterprise*. After the *Enterprise* declined the
work because the "terms of payment" were "unsatisfactory" (*Journal of the Council*, 98, 109), the contract was let to the firm of John C. Lewis and G. T. Sewall,

the only other printers in the territory, who published the Carson City *Silver Age*. About one hundred and fifty pages of the legislative journals had been printed when, in November 1861, Lewis and Sewall dissolved their print-shop partnership. Orion was unable to comply with their successors' demand for advance payment, and the remaining work was left undone. The territorial Council grew impatient with the delay, and in late November 1861 passed an act that "authorized and required" the secretary to contract with a printing firm in California (*Laws* 1862, 294). Orion finally let the work to Valentine and Company of San Francisco and dispatched William M. Gillespie to that city to oversee the printing. Gillespie apparently failed in this assignment, for Valentine and Company printed many volumes of the *Laws* with signatures missing and portions of the index omitted (William C. Miller, 4). In addition, the United States Treasury Department questioned Orion's decision to employ a California firm and balked at paying the full printing bill. The matter remained unsettled until the fall of 1863, when Orion received authorization to pay the outstanding balance of Valentine and Company's fee (Elisha Whittlesey to OC, 19 May 62; OC to Whittlesey, 3 Feb 62, 17 Sept 62, 23 Jan 63; OC to R. W. Taylor, 21 Sept 63: all in NvU-NSP).
    [3]Possibly the Star of Hope ledge on Last Chance Hill: on 16 June 1862 its rock was reported to have assayed from seventy to ninety dollars a ton ("From the Esmeralda Mining District," San Francisco *Alta California*, 23 June 62, 1, reprinting the Esmeralda *Star* of 16 June 62).

To Orion Clemens
9 July 1862 • Aurora, Calif./Nev. Terr.
(MS: CU-MARK)

Esmeralda, July 9, 1862

My Dear Bro:

    I am here again. Capt. Nye, as his disease grew worse, grew so peevish and abusive, that I quarreled with him and left. He required almost constant attention, day and night, but he made no effort to hire anyone to assist me. He said he nursed the Governor three weeks, day and night—which is a d—d lie, I suspect. He told Mrs. Gardiner he would take up the quarrel with me again when he gets well. He shall not find me unwilling. Mr. and Mrs. G. dislike ʎ him, and are very anxious to get rid of him.[1]

    Don't send me that $75, and do not let anyone find out that you have got your salary—above all, Phillips—but *no* one if not necessary. Pay off your indebtedness to the school fund when you can do so without having to pay a heavy discount on your draft, and put the balance away by itself, and keep a strict account of your disbursement of it.

₍**Private.**₎ I do not think these new placer diggings are a "steamboat." A friend of mine, C. H. Higbie, happened to pass through the locality two years ago, and intended paying it a quiet visit this summer—so last week when the news came, he said nothing, but got a horse, and left here at that night at midnight. I had a whispered message from him last night, in which he said he had arrived safely on the ground, and was in with the discoverers, turning the river out of its bed. They will allow no others to participate.[2] Higbie left here while I was with Capt. Nye. **Now keep all this entirely to yourself.** Nine-tenths of the people who leave here for⧸ the diggings, don't know where to go to. Higbie is a large, strong man, and has the perseverance of the devil. If there is anything there, he will find it. And when he gets discouraged and leaves, rest assured he will leave no one behind him. You can no more discourage him than you can frighten him. Visiting the Yo-Semite Falls, (100⧸ miles from here,) he carried for two-thirds of a day, a 60-pound pack on his back, and a rifle and shot-gun in his hands, and then, with this load, and all his company trying to dissuade him, he left the valley and climbed to the summit of the ridge, (which is 7,000 feet above the valley,) by a trail which the mountain goats are almost afraid of. I am telling you these things so that if you learn that Higbie calls the new diggings a steamboat, you can feel convinced that there is no gold in that part of the country.[3] I am freezing for him to send word for me to come out there—for God knows a respite from this same old, old place would be a blessing.

From what I can learn, the Pride of Utah and the Dimes have run together, at a depth of less than 100 feet, and now form one immense ledge, of fabulous richness. I suppose the Annipolitan will share the same fate. They are down 15 or 20 feet on the ledge, and have passed through a 2-inch vein of rich decomposed quartz—but they done nothing with it of course, as it was too narrow to be worth working. I[t] was a *cross* vein,[4] like all the rich rock in those claims.

I caught a violent cold at Clayton's, which lasted two weeks, and I came near getting salivated, working in the quicksilver and chemicals. I hardly think I shall try the experiment again. It is a confining business, and [I] will not be confined, for love nor money.

Gillespie talks reasonably now, and I shall try and be ready for him as soon as he starts his paper. Tell him not to secure a San Francisco correspondent for the winter, because they do nothing here ~~do~~ during the winter months, and I want the job myself. I want to spend the winter in California. When will his first number be published, and where?

Tell Church I would as soon write a correspondence for the "Age" as not, since Lewis is out of the concern, but want of time will not permit it.[5] Besides, I have no private room, and it is a torture to write when there is a crowd around, as is the case here, always.

The 100 feet cut off from the Monitor segregates itself, without further action.

Don't you know that when you let Gillespie read my letters you take all *privacy* away from them?

I do hope you will be able to get into your new office soon.

I shall go on a walking tour of 40 or 50 miles shortly, to ~~pass~~ get rid of this infernal place for a while. If I go, I will let you know. We projected the tour some time ago, but could not leave at that time.

Old Col. Youngs[6] is very friendly, and I like him much.

Rip goes the d—d mail again, once a week. So when you are in a hurry, you will have to send by Express, as before.

Yr. Bro.

Sam.

I got the States letters you sent.

[1] Three days after Clemens wrote this letter, the editor of the Esmeralda *Star* reported that John Nye, bedridden at Gardiner's Nine Mile Ranch, a few miles northwest of Aurora, was "an invalid, lying upon his back, all stiffened and swollen up by that excruciating disease—inflammatory rheumatism" ("Captain John Nye," Placer [Calif.] *Weekly Courier*, 26 July 62, 3, reprinting the Esmeralda *Star* of 12 July 62). In chapter 41 of *Roughing It* Clemens reported that he nursed Nye for nine days through a bout of "spasmodic rheumatism." Recalling Nye's violent bad temper, he excused it as the result of terrible discomfort and claimed he had been angered only "a little, at the moment" when Nye ordered him to leave. John Nye might have nursed his brother the governor on either of two occasions when the latter was ill, also with severe rheumatism: in late November 1861 and early June 1862 (Andrew J. Marsh, 354, 381; Marysville [Calif.] *Appeal*: "Gov. Nye . . . ," 1 Dec 61, 2; "Illness of Gov. Nye," 7 June 62, 2).

[2] These "new placer diggings" were an attempt to find the fabulously rich Whiteman "cement" mine, originally discovered in 1857 and then lost when its discoverer died in 1860, without ever exploiting it. Mark Twain later described this mine as a "curious vein of cement running along the ground, shot full of dull yellow metal. . . . The vein was about as wide as a curbstone, and fully two-thirds of it was pure gold" (*Roughing It*, chapter 37). The cement mine took its name from Gideon F. Whiteman, who played a prominent part in the intense searches

for it that began in 1861. On 3 July 1862, the Aurora correspondent of the Sacramento *Bee* commented on recent activity in the area suspected to contain it:

'Twas but a few days ago that the news was whispered round in a few private circles, that mines of gold had been discovered down across the Adobe meadows. Directly parties of horsemen were noticed to leave town during the still hours of night, stealthily moving away to the west. And the late watchers who saw them were mystified and told what they saw to others. . . . Well, the next day . . . another and another party quietly took themselves out of town. . . . The second night more departed, and thus has this town excited itself for three several days and nights, till anxious listening and watching has produced a violent fever. . . . To-day everybody has been making up their minds or their packs to travel by midnight hour or early dawn towards the goal of all their visions—"a heap of oro." (Veni, Vidi 1862b, 3)

Ten days later the same correspondent reported "The Cement Diggings, on Owen's river, about which there was such a wild excitement a week ago, will prove, I'm afraid, what the miners here call a 'steamboat sell.' There are about twenty men at work turning the river, and in a few days will prospect its bed and solve the problem whether or not there is gold in paying quantities in that region" (Veni, Vidi 1862c, 1). In fact the cement mine was never found again, although the search continued into the twentieth century (see James W. A. Wright, iv–vi, 11–16, and Chalfant, 43–50).

[3]Calvin H. Higbie (d. 1914), Clemens's cabinmate for a short time in Aurora and his partner in the blind-lead scheme, was the "Honest Man, . . . Genial Comrade, and . . . Steadfast Friend" to whom *Roughing It* is dedicated. After Clemens left Nevada in 1864, he and Higbie, who traveled for a number of years and then mined unprofitably for the rest of his life, communicated infrequently. In 1906, following a long silence, Higbie requested Clemens's "candid opinion" of "the recolections of our associations in Nevada," which he wished to submit to the New York *Herald* in order to earn "a little money" (Higbie to SLC, 15 Mar 1906, CU-MARK). Clemens read Higbie's manuscript, intending to help place it in the *Herald*. Unfortunately, he found it full of "such extravagant distortions of the actual facts that hardly an unimpeachable grain of truth is discoverable in them" and successfully urged its suppression (AD, 10 Aug 1906, CU-MARK). Portions of the manuscript published in 1920 do contain inaccuracies, among them Higbie's claim to have met Clemens through Orion, an assertion that the present letter, which in effect introduces Higbie *to* Orion, plainly refutes (see Phillips, 23, 69).

[4]An "intersecting vein" (Raymond, 27).

[5]John C. Lewis had founded the Carson City *Silver Age* in 1860. The paper had recently been taken over by the "Age Association," one of whose members was John Church (see 11 and 12 May 62 to OC, n. 11). Clemens's evident antipathy toward Lewis has not been explained, but seems likely to have been related to his "falling out" with Lewis's former partner, G. T. Sewall (see 8 and 9 Mar 62 to Clagett, n. 5).

[6]Colonel Samuel Youngs.

To Orion Clemens
23 July 1862 • Aurora, Calif./Nev. Terr.
(MS: NPV)

Esmeralda, July 23ᵈ.

My Dear Bro:

No, I don't own a foot in the "Johnson" ledge[1]—I will tell the story some day in a more intelligible manner than Tom has told it.[2] You needn't take the trouble to deny Tom's version, though. I own 25 feet ($^1/_{16}$) of the 1ˢᵗ east ex. on it—and Johnson himself has contracted to find the ledge for 100 feet.[3] Contract signed yesterday. But as the ledge will be difficult to find, he is allowed 6 months to find it in. An eighteenth of the Ophir was a fortune to John D. Winters—and the Ophir can't beat the Johnson any. I have promised a man ten dollars if he will get one of the owners to give me 25 feet more. I am very much afraid he can't manage it, though. Johnson has contracted to find the 1ˢᵗ W. ex. on the ᵈᵒ ᵈᵒ for 100 feet, and day before yesterday, when he thought he had struck it, one of the owners sold 25 feet of it for $600 cash. Johnson owns 400 ft in the discovery, and owns largely in the Pride of Utah, and also owns the Union Mill.

Well, I am willing Mollie should come, provided she brings John with her. John would do well here.[4] Are you in the new office yet?

I have written Judge Turner—but I didn't tell him Johnny[5] had written me—don't you. I have offered to sell all ~~the~~ my half the ground to him except the Fresno for $700—or $400, if he will give me his Fresno. I don't want the d—d ground. ~~I w~~ If Judge Turner is not there, and will not be there soon, take his letter out of the office and send it to him.

I have not your letter by me now, and I do not remember all that was in it. At any rate, with regard to Phillips, don't depart from my instructions in my last. He is a d—d rascal, and I can get the signatures of 25 men to this sentiment whenever I want them. He shall not be paid out of the Record fund. Tell him if he can't wait for the money, he can have his ground back, and welcome—that is, 12½ feet of it—or 25, for that matter, for it isn't worth a d—n, except that the work on it will hold it until the next great convulsion of nature injects gold and silver into it.[6]

My debts are greater than I thought for. I bought $25 worth of clothing, and sent ~~$20~~ $25 to Higbie, in the cement diggings. I owe about 45 or $50, and have got about $45 in my pocket. But how in the h—l I am going

to live on something over $100 until October or November, is singular.[7]
The fact is, I must have something to do, and that *shortly*, too. I want that
money to pay assessments with. And if Turner don't accept my offer right
away, I'll make a sale of that ground d—d soon. I don't want to sell any of
it, though until the Fresno tunnel is in. Then I'll sell the extension.

Now write to the Sacramento Union folks, or to Marsh,[8] and tell
them I'll write as many letters a week as they want, for $10 a week—my
board must be paid. Tell them I have corresponded with the N. Orleans
Crescent,[9] and other papers—and the Enterprise. California is full of
people who have interests here, and it's d—d seldom they hear from this
country. I can't write a specimen letter—now, at any rate—I'd rather
undertake to write a Greek poem. Tell 'em the mail & express leave here
three times a week, and it costs from 25 to 50 cents to send letters by that
blasted express. If they want letters from here, who'll run from morning
till night collecting materials cheaper. I'll write a short letter twice a
week for the present for the "Age," for $5 per week. Now it has been a
long time since I couldn't make my own living, and it shall be a long time
before I loaf another year.

No, you needn't pay Upton. I took all sorts of pains, and run after
men every day for two weeks trying to fix up that business of his here,
about his house, and d—n him, he has never even answered my letters on
the subject. If I sell any of Johnny's ground, he shall be paid.

I want to have a shaft sunk 100 feet on the Monitor, but I am afraid
to try it, for want of money. Don't send any money home.

If I can think of it I will enclose that scrap about the old scissors, and
you can paste it in my scrap book. Who the devil *was* that James Clemens,
I wonder? Pamela enters into no explanations.[10]

We can't decide what is to be done with the Fresno until DeKay gets
back from Mono.

If I get the other 25 feet in the Johnson ex., I shan't care a d—n. I'll
be willing to curse awhile and wait. And if I can't move the bowels of these
hills this fall, I will come up and clerk for you until I get money enough to
go over the mountains for the winter.

Yr. Bro,

Sam

[1] Peter Johnson was a principal owner of the Pride of Utah mine and a proprietor of the Union Mill on the edge of Aurora. On 1 July 1862 he located and
recorded the Johnson ledge, which was at the extremity of a drift that connected
with the Pride of Utah tunnel (Kelly 1862, 243; deeds, Mono County Archives,

Bridgeport, California, Book E:44, PH in CU-MARK, courtesy of Michael H. Marleau; "The Esmeralda Mines," San Francisco *Alta California*, 27 Dec 62, 1, reprinting the Esmeralda *Star* of 20 Dec 62). The Esmeralda correspondent of the Virginia City *Territorial Enterprise* (almost certainly Clemens), writing on 13 July, correctly reported that the Johnson ledge was "a cross ledge running through the Pride of Utah and the Wide West, and is the one from which these two companies have been taking their wonderful rock" (SLC 1862, 2). The segment of the cross ledge belonging to the Wide West was known as the Dimes ledge (Veni, Vidi 1862b, 3). In 1872, in *Roughing It*, Mark Twain identified the Johnson ledge as the rich blind lead that he, Calvin H. Higbie, and A. D. Allen planned to claim, but he inaccurately made it part of the Wide West mine instead of the Pride of Utah. He explained that he and his partners forfeited this great find (to Johnson) because, through miscommunication, they failed "to do a fair and reasonable amount of work on their new property within ten days after the date of the location" (chapters 40–41). Higbie, in his 1906 "recolections," did not remember any miscommunication; rather he contended that Clemens vowed to him to be solely responsible for the required work, but forgot about it while nursing John Nye (see Phillips, 70). For a detailed analysis of the blind-lead episode in *Roughing It*, see Branch 1985b, 234–48.

[2] Thomas Nye was evidently spreading an account of how his father John's illness had kept Clemens from securing title to the blind lead. For Clemens's version of the story see chapters 40 and 41 of *Roughing It*.

[3] A deed preserved by his family shows that on 21 July 1862 Clemens paid D. C. Crooker $500 for "an undivided interest of Twenty-five (25) feet in the First East Extension of the 'Johnson' Lode, situated on Last Chance Hill" (NPV). This deed was filed for record by Calvin H. Higbie on 3 October 1862. On 13 December the Esmeralda *Star* reported:

The owners of the First East Extension of the Johnson lode, on Last Chance Hill, have let a contract to Peter Johnson, the discoverer of the original claim, to sink a shaft one hundred feet on that lode. He has commenced the shaft, and has already reached the depth of twenty-five feet. The work is still progressing, and the company expect in the course of another month, to take out equally as rich rock as has been struck in the Johnson and Wide West claims. ("Mines in Aurora," Sacramento *Union*, 20 Dec 62, 3, reprinting the *Star*)

[4] John E. K. Stotts (b. 1828), Mollie Clemens's older brother, was a wholesale dry-goods salesman and a merchant in Keokuk, Iowa. He had lived in Orion and Mollie's home there in 1860 (MEC, 20; OC 1856, 99, 105; OC 1857, 67, 76; *Keokuk Census* [1860], 11).

[5] John D. Kinney of Cincinnati.

[6] On 16 January 1862, Orion had purchased 25 feet in the Horatio lode and the Horatio Company from Horatio G. Phillips. Apparently he still owed Phillips half the total price of $125. The day before writing this letter Clemens had purchased from Phillips, for $300, 274 feet distributed among five Aurora claims: the Dashaway, La Plata, Annapolitan, Flyaway, and Monitor (deeds in CU-MARK). The Monitor acquisition, 50 feet, was in addition to the *"one-eighth"* of this supposedly rich ledge that Clemens already owned (see 11 and 12 May 62 to OC). Given Clemens's current shortage of funds, as well as his distrust of Phillips, he presumably did not make full payment for his 22 July purchases.

[7] Clemens was counting on employment as Orion's clerk while the second Territorial Legislature was in session (11 November–20 December 1862). By then, however, he was local reporter for the Virginia City *Territorial Enterprise*.

⁸Andrew J. Marsh was the Nevada legislative correspondent of the Sacramento *Union*. He and Clemens later reported the proceedings of the first Nevada Constitutional Convention (2 November–11 December 1863) for the *Territorial Enterprise* (see Marsh, Clemens, and Bowman, passim).

⁹Two pieces by Clemens are known to have appeared in the New Orleans *Crescent*: the burlesque "River Intelligence" of 17 May 1859, satirizing Captain Isaiah Sellers (*ET&S1*, 126–33), and "Soleather Cultivates His Taste for Music," a comic sketch published on 21 July 1859 (see Branch 1982b, 497–510).

¹⁰Pamela A. Moffett's letter and enclosure do not survive; nor does the scrapbook that Orion was keeping for Clemens at this time. The James Clemens mentioned by Pamela has not been identified.

To Orion Clemens
30 July 1862 • Aurora, Calif./Nev. Terr.
(MS: NPV)

Esmeralda, July 30, 1862.

My Dear Bro:

Your letter to the Union was entirely satisfactory. I hope you will receive an answer right away, because Barstow has offered me the ~~local~~ post of local reporter for the Enterprise at $25 a week, and I have written him that I will let him know next mail if possible, whether I can take it or not. If G. is not *sure* of starting his paper within a month, I think I had better close with Barstow's offer.[1]

Old Snyder, who owns in the H & D says it's a big thing on account of the water and mill-site, even if it does have to lie still a while. Possibly he may be right.[2]

Yes, the 50 feet in the Monitor, is worth what we paid for the H & D. I acknowledge that much.

Of course I don't want to correspond with the Age until I know whether I shall remain here or not. So it makes no difference.

Yes—I wish John[3] *would* come. These claims of ours would soon sing a different song.

Oh, no, Johnny wasn't expert at drawing deeds, by a d—d sight. I think Turner will discover that he managed to worry along, though, at it. He's a d—d liar, too. He knows right well that his deed don't convey him all the ground. Certainly—certainly—I have no doubt we shall understand each other. He shall understand *me*, at least. He can't scare me with his legal threats either, such as he insinuated in his letter to me. He wants to know what I gave? Tell him that ranks as a "leading question." As to the balance, I *told* him my deed conveys *all* of the ground to me—and that Johnny told me to deed half of it to him if he had not returned by the 1ˢᵗ July. I should think my words were explicit enough. I wrote the Judge as soon as I heard he was in Carson. I don't care a d—n whose money bought the ground. Now I shan't answer the Judge's letter until I am in a good humor. I think my deed bears date March 1ˢᵗ, but I can't go up to the Co. C̶l̶e̶r̶k̶'̶s̶ Rec.'s to see to-night, and I have not thought of it sooner. I have had a sort of general offer of $25 for my 25 feet of Mountain Flower, & have accepted. I̶f̶ ̶h̶e̶ ̶s̶a̶y̶ ̶t̶h̶e̶ ̶w̶◊◊◊◊ ̶h̶e̶ I told my agent (I don't sell ground myself,) to sell the Judge's at the same price, according to the Judge's instructions to me, and he did so. The bargain will probably be closed within 3 or 4 days, and if the Judge don't like the price he must speak before it is too late. The price suits me, since I can do no better. The balance of the ground won't sell now, but the Fresno will be either valuable or worthless in a few weeks. I have started a man out to sell fifty feet in that t̶o̶ for Judge Turner.[4]

Oh, I don't blame the Captain[5] for being ill-natured when he was sick. The confinement made me so. I was what the yankees call "ugly," you know.

I suppose Billy will know what to do with the National ground. If he thinks it best to sell, I will send him J.'s letter ʃ as authority.[6]

What's the matter with the mill out there? What's the matter with Tillou? Why work the case-rock,[7] if the ledge is 4 feet wide. I would not think it impossible to work a 4-foot shaft.

Yr. Bro.

Sam.

---

[1] This offer from the Virginia City *Territorial Enterprise* was a tribute to the talent for humor that Clemens had displayed in his "Josh" letters to the paper. It was also the result of practical considerations: the *Enterprise* needed a substitute for Dan De Quille (William Wright), its local editor, who was planning a trip East; and the management was well aware of Clemens's potential political influence. "Orion and Sam. may have believed Sam. had been employed by the *Enterprise* because of the 'Josh' letters; Barstow and Goodman may have thought that it might be helpful to have Sam. on the staff when Orion gave out the contracts for the public printing" (Andrew J. Marsh, 674 n. 71). In fact, Joseph T. Goodman and Company, owners and publishers of the *Enterprise*, did secure the contract to print the laws passed by the second Territorial Legislature (*Laws* 1863). See also *ET&S1*, 14–18.

[2] J. L. Snyder was a partner, with Horatio G. Phillips, Robert M. Howland, and Clemens in the Horatio and Derby tunnel project on Martinez Hill in Aurora

(see 8 and 9 Feb 62 to JLC and PAM, n. 2). Their land claim on the hill included rights to "the water that may be obtained from the drifts & tunnels together with the right of a dump & Tunnelling & mill *Sight* & *priveledges* & all of the land for mining purposes with the necessary tail way from the mill" (plat dated 29 Dec 61, PH in CU-MARK, courtesy of Michael H. Marleau).

[3] John E. K. Stotts.

[4] Clemens did not let his agent sell George Turner's share of the mining stock discussed here. On 7 August (as he indicates in the next letter) he deeded to Turner, for $1,000, almost half of the 1,412½ feet in sixteen ledges he had acquired from John D. Kinney, for $1,000, on 1 March 1862, just before Kinney's return to Cincinnati (PH of deeds in CU-MARK, courtesy of Todd M. Axelrod). Among the shares Turner received were 50 feet in the Fresno, 100 feet in the first northeast extension of the Fresno, and 25 feet in the Mountain Flower. The latter had been described by the Carson City *Silver Age* as "a new lode of gold-bearing quartz" that was "richer than anything heretofore found in the district" ("Aurora," Marysville [Calif.] *Appeal*, 22 Feb 62, 2, reprinting the *Silver Age* of 16 Feb 62).

[5] John Nye.

[6] Orion Clemens was holding a deed of 28 January 1862 for John D. Kinney's purchase of ten feet in the National ledge in Humboldt County (deed in CU-MARK). Evidently Kinney had sent instructions from Cincinnati to sell out his mining interests. Clemens suggests here that Orion should consult William Clagett, who was living in Humboldt County, about the sale.

[7] Rock "altered by vein-action," between the vein and "unaltered" rock (Raymond, 18, 25).

To Orion Clemens
7 August 1862 • Aurora, Calif./Nev. Terr.
(MS: NPV)

Esmeralda, Aug. 7, 1862.

My Dear Bro:

Barstow wrote that if I wanted the place I could have it. I wrote him to let that I guessed I would take it, and asked him lo how long before I must come up there. I have not heard from him since.

Now I shall leave at midnight to-night, alone and on foot for a walk of 60 or 70 miles through a totally uninhabited country, and it is barely possible that mail facilities may prove infernally "slow" during the few weeks I expect to spend out there. But do you write Barstow that I have left here for a week or so, and in case he should want me he must write me here, or let me know through you. You see I want to know something about that country out yonnder.[1]

The Contractors say they will strike the Fresno next week. After fooling with those assayers a week, they concluded not to buy ͵"M. Flower"͵ at $50, ͮ although they would have given five times the sum for it four months ago. So I have made out a deed for one-half of all Johnny's ground and acknowledged and left it in Judge F. K. Bechtel's hands, and if Judge Turner wants it he must write to Bechtel and pay him his Notary fee of $1.50.[2] I would have paid that fee myself, but I want money now as I leave town to-night. However, if you think it isn't right, you can pay the fee to Judge Turner yourself.

Hang to your money now. I may want some when I get back.

Col. Youngs sends his regards, & says he will have our census completed & send up to you to-morrow, & we ought to have a larger representation—although the law said census must be taken in May—but he couldn't help it, d—n 'em they wouldn't run the line.[3]

Yes, I will scrape up some specimens—*have* got a lot—but they're a d—d nuisance about a cabin. I picked up some splendid agates & such things, but I expect they are all lost by this time.

No—I shan't pay Upton—just yet.

See that you keep out of debt—to *any*body[.] B̶u̶n̶k̶e̶r̶ Bully for Bunker. Write him that I would write him myself, but I am to take a walk to-night & haven't time. Tell him to bring his family out with him.[4] He can rely upon what I say—and I say the land has lost its ancient desolate appearance; the rose and the oleander have taken the place of the departed sage-brush; a rich black loam, garnished with moss, and flowers, and the greenest of grass, smiles to Heaven from the vanished sand-plains; the "endless snows" have all disappeared, and in their stead—or to repay us for their loss, the mountains rear their billowy heads aloft, crowned with a fadeless and eternal verdure; birds, and fountains, and trees—tropical trees—everywhere!—and the poet dreampt of Nevada when he wrote:

> "—and Sharon waves, in solemn praise,
> Her silent groves of palm."[5]

and to-day the royal Raven stands on ʄ a fragrant carcass and listens in a dreamy stupor to the songs of the thrush and the nightingale and the canary—and shudders when the gaudy-plumaged birds of the distant South sweep by him to the orange groves of Carson. Tell him he wouldn't recognise the d—d country. He ʄ should bring his family by all means.

I intended to write home, but I haven't done it.

                                                    Yr. Bro. Sam.

P. S. Put the enclosed slips in my scrap book.[6]

[1] Evidently Clemens planned at this time to visit the White Mountain district in eastern Mono County, California, and the area around Mono Lake—a trip that was postponed until the latter part of August (see 9 Sept 62 to Clagett).

[2] Clemens's conveyance to Turner totaled 581¼ feet, 125 feet short of half of "Johnny's ground"—whether by intention or inadvertence is not known. Frederick K. Bechtel (b. 1823) of Pennsylvania was a justice of the peace and a notary public, conveyancer, and commissioner of deeds for Nevada Territory in Aurora. He owned many mining properties. Clemens may have first met him in August 1861 in Carson City, where Bechtel represented Esmeralda County at the Union convention to nominate a candidate for delegate to Congress (Marsh, Clemens, and Bowman, 463 n. 7; Angel, 81, 402; Vox Populi 1862b, 4).

[3] In 1861 William E. Teall and Samuel Youngs had represented Esmeralda in the House of Representatives of the first Territorial Legislature. Esmeralda was to have four representatives in the 1862 second Territorial Legislature, but only three of them took their seats (Andrew J. Marsh, 2, 666 n. 14, 697 n. 347). The Esmeralda census was evidently delayed by the California-Nevada contention for jurisdiction over Aurora, part of the ongoing struggle over their mutual boundary.

[4] Benjamin B. Bunker, attorney general of Nevada Territory, returned to the States in May 1862 on a leave of absence so that he might move his family from the East Coast to Carson City. After receiving several extensions of his leave and having failed to resume his duties, he was removed from office by President Lincoln in June 1863 "on the ground that he does not attend to the office, nor, in fact, pass much time in the territory" (Lincoln to John P. Hale, 9 June 63, Lincoln, 6:255).

[5] From "Calm on the listening ear of night," a Christmas hymn written in 1834 by Edmund Hamilton Sears.

[6] The scrapbook is not extant.

To Pamela A. Moffett
15 August 1862 • Aurora, Calif./Nev. Terr.
(*MTL*, 1:85–86)

Esmeralda, Cal., Aug. 15, 1862.

My Dear Sister:

I mailed a letter to you and Ma this morning, but since then I have received yours to Orion and me. Therefore, I must answer right away, else I may leave town without doing it at all. What in thunder are pilot's wages to me? which question, I beg humbly to observe, is of a *general* nature, and not discharged particularly at you. But it is singular, isn't it, that such a matter should interest Orion, when it is of no earthly consequence to me? I never have *once* thought of returning home to go on the river again, and I never expect to do any more piloting at any price. My livelihood must be made in this country—and if I have to wait longer than I expected, let it be so—I have no fear of failure. You know I have extravagant hopes, for Orion tells you everything which he ought to keep to himself—but it's his nature to do that sort of thing, and I let him alone. I did think for awhile of going home this fall—but when I found that that was and had been the cherished intention and the darling aspiration every year, of these old care-worn Californians for twelve weary years—I felt a little uncomfortable, but I stole a march on Disappointment and said I would *not* go home this fall. I will spend the winter in San Francisco, if possible. Do not tell any one that I had any idea of piloting again at present—for it is all a mistake. This country suits me, and—it *shall* suit me, whether or no. . . .[1]

Dan Twing[2] and I and Dan's dog, "cabin" together—and will continue to do so for awhile—until I leave for—

The mansion is 10 × 12, with a "domestic" roof. Yesterday it rained —the first shower for five months. "Domestic," it appears to me, is not water-proof.[3] We went outside to keep from getting wet. Dan makes the bed when it is his turn to do it—and when it is my turn, I don't, you know. The dog is not a good hunter, and he isn't worth shucks to watch— but he scratches up the dirt floor of the cabin, and catches flies, and makes himself generally useful in the way of washing dishes. Dan gets up first in the morning and makes a fire—and I get up last and sit by it, while he cooks breakfast. We have a cold lunch at noon, and I cook supper—very much against my will. However, one must have *one* good meal a day, and if I were to live on Dan's abominable cookery, I should lose my appetite, you know. Dan attended Dr. Chorpenning's funeral yesterday,[4] and he felt as though he ought to wear a white shirt—and we had a jolly good time finding such an article. We turned over all our traps, and he found one at last—but I shall always think it was suffering from yellow fever. He also found an old black coat, greasy, and wrinkled to that degree that it appeared to have been quilted at some time or other. In this gorgeous costume he attended the funeral. And when he returned, his own dog drove him away from the cabin, not recognizing him. This is true.

You would not like to live in a country where flour was $40 a barrel? Very well, then, I suppose you would not like to live here, where flour was $100 a barrel when I first came here. And shortly afterwards, it couldn't be had at any price—and for one month the people lived on barley, beans and beef—and nothing beside. Oh, no—we didn't luxuriate then! Perhaps not. But we said wise and severe things about the vanity and wickedness of high living. We preached our doctrine and practised it. Which course I respectfully recommend to the clergymen of St. Louis.

Where is Beck Jolly? and Bixby?

Your Brother
Sam.

[1] Clemens may have had these remarks in mind when he wrote in chapter 42 of *Roughing It,*

I was a good average St. Louis and New Orleans pilot and by no means ashamed of my abilities in that line; wages were two hundred and fifty dollars a month and no board to pay, and I did long to stand behind a wheel again and never roam any more—but I had been making such an ass of myself lately in grandiloquent letters home about my blind lead and my European excursion that I did what many and many a poor disappointed miner had done before; said "It is all over with me now, and I will never go back home to be pitied—and snubbed."

The ellipsis at the end of this paragraph of the letter probably indicates an editorial omission in *MTL*, the only source for the present text.

[2] Before coming to Nevada Territory, Daniel H. Twing had emigrated from the East to California in 1859. He had interests in several Esmeralda ledges and was one of the partners in the Clemens Gold and Silver Mining Company. On 18 February 1863 Clemens assigned Twing a "special power of attorney" over his mining interests (PH in CU-MARK, courtesy of Michael H. Marleau). Twing was later known as "a pioneer real estate dealer of San Francisco and Sonoma county" ("Complete Fifty Years Together," San Francisco *Chronicle*, 19 Apr 1904, 13).

[3] Domestic was undyed domestically manufactured cotton fabric—in this case, probably canvas.

[4] Dr. F. Chorpenning of Aurora—formerly public administrator of Mono County, California, and superintendent of the Overland Mail Company—was an acting assistant surgeon with the Second Cavalry, California Volunteers. On 28 July 1862 William Pooler shot him "for being too attentive" to Pooler's estranged wife (Veni, Vidi 1862d, 1). Dr. Chorpenning died on 13 August, and his funeral the next day was attended by a large number of Aurora citizens ("Progress of Mining, etc., in Esmeralda," San Francisco *Evening Bulletin*, 23 Sept 61, 2, reprinting the Carson City *Silver Age* of 17 Sept 61; "Dr. Chorpenning Dead," San Francisco *Alta California*, 20 Aug 62, 2; Angel, 166, 344).

To William H. Clagett
9 September 1862 • Aurora, Calif./Nev. Terr.
(MS: ViU)

Esmeralda, Sept. 9, 1862.

Dear Billy:

Orion enclosed your letter to me, and informed me also that you were elected to represented Humboldt County in the Legislature. Bully for Humboldt, and bully for *you*, my boy! This is well, so far—but it is only the beginning. If you do not represent the *State* of Nevada in the U.S. Senate in the year of its birth you ought to be damned for a worthless cuss—the malediction might be modified, though, if you went to the Lower House.[1]

But, it appears to me that the very *existence* of the United States is threatened, just now. I am afraid we have been playing the game of brag about as recklessly as I have ever seen it played, even on an Arkansas steamboat—"going blind" and "doubling the pot" and "straddling" and "calling" on hands without a "pair," or even an "ace at the head." D—n it! only to think of this sickening boasting—these miserable self-complacent remarks about "twenty-four hours more will seal the fate of the bastard ¢ Confederacy—twenty-four hours more will behold the United States dictating terms to submissive and groveling rebeldom!" Great God! and at that very moment the national army were inaugurating a series of retreats more disastrous than bloody defeats on the battle-field! Think of it, my boy—last week the nation were blowing like school-boys of what they were going to do—this week they are trembling in their boots and whining and sniveling like threatened puppies—absolutely frantic with fear. God! what we were going to do!—and last night's dispatches come to hand—we all rush to see what the mountain in labor hath brought forth, and lo! the armies have fled back to Washington; its very suburbs are menaced by the foe; Baton Rouge is evacuated; the rebel hosts march through Kentucky and occupy city after city without firing a gun; Nashville is threatened; Memphis is threatened; Louisville quakes like an aspen; Cincinnati is stricken as with a palsy; Baltimore holds her breath and listens for the tread of the forty thousand; Pennsylvania shivers with a panic! Oh Christ! touching the clay of the sleeping Lazarus—

invoking a blush upon the crystal waters: behold the miracle ~~than~~ that man hath wrought!

Let us change the disgusting subject. Let us close our eyes and ~~ev~~ endeavor ˏtoˏ discover in these things profound, mysterious wonders of "strategy!" Ah me—I have often thought of it—what a crown of glory it would be to us to slip quietly out of Washington some night and when the rebels entered it in the morning, overwhelm them with the bitter humiliation that the whole transaction was a masterpiece of "strategy!" Strategy be d—d—all these astonishing feats of strategy which we have been treated to lately, and which we stared at with a stunned look, and dimly felt that it was a big thing—a wonderful thing—and said so in deadened tones bereft of inflection, although, to save our souls from being eternally damned we couldn't distinctly "see it"—all these "strategic" feats are beautiful—beautiful as early dawn—yet, like unto the ~~mill~~ mild and lovely juvenile show, "six pins admittance," they don't amount to a damn when the "shore-nuff" circus comes to town.

Strategy will bust this nation yet, if they just keep it up long enough, my boy.

Well, ~~les~~ let's make another effort to change the disgusting subject. For more than two weeks I have been slashing around in the White Mountain District, partly for pleasure and partly for other reasons. And old Van Horn was in the party. He knows your daddy and the whole family, and every ˏoldˏ citizen of Keokuk. He left there in '53.[2] He built parson Hummer's Pavilion[3]—and parson Williams' house,[4] and a dozen others. He says he used to go with your father when he stumped the district, and sing campaign songs. He is a comical old cuss, and can keep a camp alive with fun when he chooses. We had rare good times out there fishing for trout and hunting. I mean to go out there again before long.

I saw a man last June who swore that he knew of rich placer diggings within 100 miles of Humboldt City. What became of *our* placers, that we intended to visit last May?

Have you still a good opinion of those claims in Santa Clara?

Billy, I can't stand another winter in this climate, unless I am obliged to. I have a sneaking notion of going down to the Colorado mines 2 months from now.[5]

Remember me to Dad[6] and the boys.

Enclosed please find that power of Attorney.[7]

Times have never grown brisk here until this week. I don't think

much of the camp—not as much as I did. Old fashioned winter & snow
lasted until the middle of June.

Your old friend

Sam L C.

◥──

[*in ink:*] Hon. Wᵐ· H. Clagett, | Unionville | Humbol{dt Co. | Nevada
Ter'y. [*top part of the envelope torn away: postmaster's usual entry is presumably lost*] [*three-cent U.S. postage stamp, canceled with a pen*]

¹Clagett, who quickly earned a reputation as an orator in Unionville, represented Humboldt County in the House of the second and third territorial legisla-
tures (11 November–20 December 1862, 12 January–20 February 1864). Following strenuous campaigning for President Lincoln and the Republican ticket, he
served as state senator (elected from Storey County) from November 1864 until
he resigned in April 1865. In October 1865 Clagett was defeated in his bid to
become the Republican candidate for a seat in the United States House of Representatives. His subsequent history was varied: in 1866 he left Virginia City, where
he had been practicing law, and over the next thirty-five years was alternately a
lawyer and a miner in Montana, Dakota, Idaho, and Washington. He only once
held a national political office, serving as a Republican congressman from Montana from 1871 to 1873 (Dixon, 250, 252, 253, 254, 263; Andrew J. Marsh, 698 n.
350; Angel, 88–89, 447, 606).

²The White Mountains straddled Esmeralda County, Nevada Territory, and
Mono County, California. Clemens described his trip in chapters 37–39 of *Rough-
ing It*, placing it (out of chronological order) before the blind-lead episode.
Roughing It makes clear that one of his "other reasons" for "slashing around" in
the region was a desire to discover the Whiteman cement mine (see 9 July 62 to
OC, n. 2). William Van Horn (Mr. Van Dorn in *Roughing It*), aged about forty-
two, was originally from Tennessee and had worked as a joiner while living in
Keokuk (*Keokuk Census* [1850], 420). He was a prospecting companion of Gideon
F. Whiteman's and played a key role in the search for the lost mine. Van Horn and
a friend reportedly located the mine in 1862, but circumstances kept him from
exploiting his find (see James W. A. Wright, 25–27, and Chalfant, 45–46).

³Michael Hummer (b. 1800) was pastor of the First Presbyterian Church of
Iowa City from 1841 until 1848, when, having converted to Swedenborgianism
and spiritualism, he was tried by his congregation and expelled from the ministry.
He retreated to Keokuk, Iowa, where he joined with other spiritualists. Together
they chose a lot on Concert Street and began construction of a spiritualist church,
guided by the spirit communications of medium Mary Margrave. This "Pavillion" was of brick and wood and "completed with a steamboat roof and attic like
a Texas, with windows to open and shut that the spirits and angels might at their
pleasure fly in and out" ("Launching Spiritualism in Keokuk," Keokuk *Gate
City*, 28 Aug 1914, no page). The spiritualist excitement culminated in the adul-
tery trial of Hummer and Margrave, in which Hummer's lawyer entered the unprecedented plea of insanity. The spiritualists abandoned their Pavillion, and it
served as a private residence until it was razed in 1934 (Van Der Zee, 535–40;
Gallaher, 156; Garrison, 14–15).

⁴William H. Williams (b. 1803 or 1804) was a Keokuk Presbyterian clergyman. The house that Van Horn built for Williams presumably was a large one, since by 1850 his family consisted of a wife and seven children. By 1860, when he was preacher at Keokuk's New School Presbyterian Church and owned $79,000 in real estate and other property, Williams had added a seamstress, a gardener, and a servant to his household (*Keokuk Census* [1850], 412; *Keokuk Census* [1860], 6).

⁵There was considerable excitement at the moment about mining prospects in Colorado Territory. Dan De Quille of the Virginia City *Territorial Enterprise* visited the area early in 1863 and reported:

From what I saw of the Pike's Peak country, I am impressed with the belief that the Territory of Colorado is just now ready to burst forth into a season of blooming prosperity. . . . In the Colorado mines capital will find a fine and profitable field, while in the valleys of the country the poor man may build him up a happy home, and eventually as fine a fortune as a man of moderate desires could wish to possess. Those who imagine the Pike's Peak mines to be played out, are very much mistaken; their development is just now about to be commenced. (William Wright 1863, 2:33)

Although Clemens still hoped to make his fortune as a miner, by late September he was in Virginia City, working as local reporter for the *Territorial Enterprise*. His earliest extant articles for that paper appeared on 1 October 1862 (see *ET&S1*, 389–91).

⁶Cornbury S. Tillou.

⁷Clemens's enclosure is not known to survive.

To Orion and Mary E. (Mollie) Clemens
21 October 1862 • Virginia City, Nev. Terr.
(MS: NPV)

OFFICE OF THE DAILY TERRITORIAL ENTERPRISE.
GOODMAN & MᶜCARTHY, PROPRIETORS.

VIRGINIA CITY, N. T., Oct. 21 1862.

To the Hon. the Sec'y
and Deputy Sec. N. T.:¹

I wrote by Joe,² but he would not give me time to say all I wished to say, —but I hadn't a great deal to talk about anyhow. Nor have I now, being rather busy than otherwise.

But—the great wrong is consummated. In the Dist. Court last night, in "Chollar S. M. Co. vs. Potosi G. & S. M. Co.," the jury rendered verdict for Plff.³ This lets Virginia, & Judge Mott, and the Devil, & many others—"*out*"—and clinches my ancient opinion that hell is peopled with honester men than California.⁴ Joe can tell you what a preposterous thin wrong that decision last night, was. The case will be appealed⧸ I suppose, but if it isn't, why, look out for a miraculous feat—which is simply this: if that decision stands, the Ophir will open its mighty jaws and swallow Mount Davidson![5]

(*Between us*, now)—did you see that squib of mine headed "Petrified Man?" It is an unmitigated lie, made from whole cloth. I got it up to worry Sewall. Every day, I send him some California paper containing it; moreover, I am getting things so arranged that he will soon begin to receive letters from all parts of the country, purporting to come from scientific men, asking for further information concerning the wonderful stone man. If I had plenty of time, I would worry the life out of the poor cuss.[6]

.   .   .   .

[1] There was no such position in Nevada Territory; this was a playful reference to Mollie Clemens. She and seven-year-old Jennie Clemens had arrived in San Francisco on the steamer *Constitution* on 5 October. Orion met them there and the three left for Carson City on 10 October, arriving on the twelfth (MEC, 14).

[2] Joseph T. Goodman (1838–1917) emigrated from New York to California in 1854. He worked as a compositor and writer on San Francisco newspapers before he and Denis E. McCarthy (1841–85), a fellow typesetter on the San Francisco *Mirror* and the San Francisco *Golden Era*, bought into Jonathan Williams's Virginia City *Territorial Enterprise* on 2 March 1861. Later that year Dennis Driscoll (1823–76), the *Enterprise* bookkeeper, replaced Williams in the partnership. He withdrew in October 1863, leaving Goodman and McCarthy in control, the former having editorial charge of the *Enterprise* and the latter running its print shop. McCarthy left the paper in September 1865 and Goodman was sole proprietor until he sold out in February 1874 and moved to San Francisco. Quick to recognize Clemens's gift for humorous journalism, Goodman gave him encouragement and support and became a lifelong friend (Emrich, 263–64; Angel, 317, 322, 326; Goodman to Alfred B. Nye, 6 Nov 1905 and 17 Nov 1905, Alfred B. Nye Papers, CU-BANC; Weisenburger, 53, 60, 61, 62–63; Lingenfelter and Gash, 253–54).

[3] The first decision in the "remarkable case of the Chollar [Silver] Mining Company *vs.* the Potosi [Gold and Silver] Mining Company." This suit was "the immediate cause of the resignation of the whole territorial bench and a contention without a parallel in the history of the litigation of mining claims in its duration, fierceness, and cost" (Lord, 151). The proceedings had begun in January 1862 when the Chollar Company brought an action for ejectment against the Potosi Company, which had been extracting ore from a well-defined underground ledge, on the Comstock lode, which it had located and followed underneath the Chollar Company's surface claim, also on the Comstock. The Chollar Company asserted that its surface claim included rights to "all the dips, angles, spurs, and variations thereof, together with all the quartz, leads, and ledges and earths containing the precious metals," however deep such ore bodies might lie. The Potosi Company "denied the infringement of any rights . . . as they were not working in surface ground, but in a well-defined ledge located by them in accordance with the district laws" (Lord, 151, 152). In fact the existing laws were ambiguous in regard to such disputes. On 20 October 1862 a jury, with Judge Gordon N. Mott concurring, decided in favor of the Chollar Company. The Potosi Company was forced to relinquish its ledge, "and their rival possessed the fruit of their labors" (Lord,

Virginia City *Territorial Enterprise* building, 1864. Detail of original
lithograph at the Mackay School of Mines, University of Nevada, Reno.

154). The decision of Mott's court was upheld by the territorial supreme court in
March 1863. Nevertheless, the litigation, fed by political and judicial corruption,
continued into 1865, and the mining laws remained in dispute. The principals in
the suit resolved their conflict without a final judicial decision by merging as the
Chollar-Potosi Mining Company in April 1865 (see Lord, 151–73).

[4] Gordon N. Mott (1812–87)—a native of Ohio who had practiced law in California before moving to Nevada in 1861—was judge of the first district of Nevada
Territory, associate justice of the territorial supreme court, and, by election on 2
September 1862, territorial representative to the United States Congress. In September 1863, the managers of the Potosi Company, believing that Mott was biased
in favor of the Chollar Company, paid him $25,000 to relinquish his judicial posts
in favor of a lawyer more sympathetic to their claims (Andrew J. Marsh, 669 n.
35; Kelly 1862, 10; Angel, 80; *BDAC*, 1367; Lord, 154–55). Another erstwhile
Californian involved in the Chollar-Potosi suit was the attorney for the former
company, William M. Stewart (1827–1909). Originally from New York, Stewart
migrated to Nevada in 1860 after ten years in California, where he was acting
attorney general in 1854. He later (1864–75, 1887–1905) served as Republican
senator from the state of Nevada (Mack 1964, passim; Andrew J. Marsh, 665 n.
8, 675 n. 84).

[5] Virginia City "roosted royally midway up the steep side of Mount Davidson"
(*Roughing It*, chapter 43). By October 1862 the Ophir Company, owner of the first

claim located on the Comstock lode, on Mount Davidson, had already acquired
title to adjoining properties and was preparing an ejectment suit against the Burning Moscow Company, which was extracting ore directly to the west of Ophir
ground. William Stewart, counsel for the Ophir, was the region's leading advocate
of the "one-ledge theory," which held that all bodies of ore-bearing quartz on
Mount Davidson, even though separated by large strata of barren rock and earth,
were really only parts of one ledge. "If, then, there was only one ledge, and the
croppings on each side of it were adjudged to be spurs and angles instead of
distinct bodies, the locators along the line of that one ledge were the lawful pos-
sessors of the ore deposits throughout the whole basin and eastern hill slope"
(Lord, 99). Judge Mott's reasoning in his decision favoring the Chollar Company
gave legal support to one-ledge arguments; and as Clemens seems to have
guessed, the Ophir's coming suit against the Burning Moscow also was to be based
on such arguments. Joseph T. Goodman of the *Territorial Enterprise* was not alone
in opposing the one-ledge theory. The rival Virginia City *Union* strenuously opposed that concept and considered the Ophir to be a "great Grab All Company"
that sought to "steal the silver of other people" ("The Virginia (N.T.,) *Daily
Union* . . . ," San Francisco *Alta California*, 1 Nov 63, 1, reprinting the *Union* of
unknown date; see also A Subscriber, 1).

⁶Clemens's report of the discovery of an ancient "Petrified Man," a hoax aimed
primarily at Judge G. T. Sewall of Humboldt County (see 8 and 9 Mar 62 to
Clagett, n. 5), appeared in the *Territorial Enterprise* of 4 October 1862. Since the
bogus report was widely reprinted in California papers, Clemens might well have
sent Sewall daily clippings. It is less likely, however, that he was able to produce
the fraudulent letters from "scientific men" (see *ET&S1*, 155–59).

To Jane Lampton Clemens and Pamela A. Moffett
16 February 1863 • Virginia City, Nev. Terr.
(MS: NPV)

OFFICE DAILY TERRITORIAL ENTERPRISE,

VIRGINIA, Feb. 16, 186 3.

My Dʳ Mother & Sister:

I suppose I ought to write, but I hardly know what to write about.
I am not in a very good humor, to-night. I wanted to rush down and take
some comfort for a few days, in San Francisco, but there is no one here
now, to take my place. They let me go, about the first of the month,
to stay twenty-four hours in Carson, and I staid a week.[1] Perhaps they
haven't much confidence in me now. If they have, I am proud to say it is
misplaced. I am very well satisfied here. They pay me six dollars a day, and
I make 50 per cent. profit by only ~~dol~~ doing three dollars' worth of work.

Well, I have no news to report, unless it will interest you to know that they "struck it rich["] in the "Burnside" ledge last night. The stock was worth ten dollars a foot this morning. It sells at a hundred to-night.[2] I don't own it, ~~th~~Madam,, though I might have owned several hundred feet of it yesterday, you know, & I assure [you] I would, if I had known they were going to "strike it." None of us are prophets, though. However, I take an absorbing delight in the stock market. I love to watch the prices go up. My time will come after a while, & then I'll rob somebody. I pick up a foot or two occasionally for lying about somebody's mine. I shall sell out ~~w~~ one of these days, when I catch a susceptible emigrant. If Orion writes you a crazy letter about the "Emma Gold & Silver Mining Company," pay no attention to it. It is rich, but he owns very little stock in it.[3] If he gets an eighth share in the adjoining company, though let him blow. It will be all right. He may never get it, however.

What do you show my letters for? Can't you let me tell a lie occasionally to keep my hand in for the public, without exposing me?

I advertised for Mrs. Hubbard's brother[4] & David Anderson's son. Mr. Dreschler called on me two days afterward. He was in robust health; lives in Steamboat Valley, near here; I promised to visit him. He owns ranch & city property, & is well off. Mr. Ellison called on me the same day. He said John Anderson was on his ranch at the Sink of the Carson, 60 miles from here. Anderson will return to St. Louis in the Spring to go to the wars. I sent him some late St. Louis, Louisville and New Orleans papers, & promised to visit him some day. Remember me kindly to Mrs. Hubbard & Fannie.

Pamela, you do not say whether you are getting well or not? I think you will have to spend next Summer at the Fountain of Youth—the fabled spring which the weary Spaniards sought with such a hopeful yearning, and never found. But I have found it, and it is Lake Bigler. No foul disease may hope to live in the presence of such beauty as that. I send the paper to Moffett & Scroter every day; you will find in it all that you do not find in my letters.

I inclose a picture for Margaret Sexton. Had your letter arrived a little sooner, I could have sent it to her myself, as a Valentine.

Yrs affctnly
Sam. L. Clemens

Remember me to all.

---

[1] During his week in Carson City, Clemens sent off at least three letters to the *Territorial Enterprise*, including the first article he is known to have signed "Mark

Twain," which was probably written on 31 January and printed on 3 February 1863 (see *MTEnt*, 47–61, and *ET&S1*, 192–209).

[2]The Burnside Silver Mining Company, capitalized at $280,000 with 2,800 shares, was incorporated in San Francisco in late August 1862. Its claim was located on the western slope of Mount Davidson. In the first week of February 1863, the "Resident Correspondent" of the San Francisco *Alta California* credited the Burnside company with "doing wonders in developing their lead" and reported "quite an excitement . . . created by parties trying to buy up shares" (Quartz 1863a, 1; Quartz 1863b, 1). The price of the stock on the San Francisco market fluctuated during the next few months, reaching $69.50 a share in early May, but plunging to $19.00 a month later ("Mining and Other Corporations Formed in 1862," Sacramento *Union*, 1 Jan 63, 1; San Francisco *Evening Bulletin*: "San Francisco Mining Companies," 6 Jan 63, 3; "San Francisco Stock and Exchange Board," Feb–June 63). The following December the Virginia City *Evening Bulletin* charged that the local editors of the Virginia City *Union* and *Territorial Enterprise* "were 'sold' by the owners of a 'salted' claim—the Burnside—less than a year ago" ("The Lady Bryan Claim," 26 Dec 63, 2).

[3]The subject of Orion's "crazy letter" possibly was the Emma Frances mine, in the Silver Mountain district of Douglas County, about sixty-five miles south of Virginia City. Ore from the Emma Frances was sometimes, with scant reason, said to be "as rich as that of the 'Ophir'" ("The Mines of the Silver Mountain District," San Francisco *Alta California*, 3 Dec 62, 1). Clemens visited the Silver Mountain region in the final week of April 1864 (see *ET&S1*, 358). By then it had become part of California, a consequence of the California-Nevada boundary settlement (Kelly 1863, 74; Carlson, 150, 216).

[4]William H. C. Nash of Hannibal (b. 1829) was a childhood friend of Clemens's and brother of Mary Nash Hubbard. Nash emigrated to the West in 1849 and remained twenty years, after which he returned to Hannibal and became a merchant; in later years he was city assessor and president of the board of education (Greene, 281; Hannibal *Courier-Post*, 6 Mar 1935, 7B). None of the other people mentioned in this paragraph has been identified.

To Jane Lampton Clemens and Pamela A. Moffett
11 and 12 April 1863 • Virginia City, Nev. Terr.
(MS: NPV and CU-MARK)

ˏP. S. I have just heard five pistol shots down street—as such things are in my line, I will go and see about it.ˏ

ˏP. S. Nᵒ 2—5 A. M.—The pistol did its work well—one man—a M̶i̶ Jackson County m̶Missourian, shot two of my friends, (police officers,) through the heart—both died within three minutes. Murderer's name is John Campbell.ˏ[1]

Virginia, April 11.

My Dear Mother & Sister

It is very late at night, & I am writing in my room, which is not quite as large or as nice as the one I had at home. My board, washing & lodging cost me seventy-five dollars a month.

I have just received your letter, Ma, from Carson—the one in which you doubt my veracity about the tape worm, and also about statements I made in a letter to you. That's right. I don't recollect what the statements were, but I suppose they were mining statistics. [*in margin:* Ma, write on *whole* letter sheets—is paper scarce in St Louis?] I have just finished writing up my report for the morning paper, and giving the Unreliable a column of advice about how to conduct himself in church,[2] and now I will tell you a few more lies, while my hand is in. For instance, some of the boys made me a present of fifty feet in the East India G & S. M. Company, ten days ago.[3] I was offered ninety-five dollars a foot for it, yesterday, in gold. *I refused it*—not because I think the claim is worth a cent, ₓfor I *don't*,ₓ but because I had a curiosity to see how high it *would* go, before people find out how worthless it is. Besides, what if one mining claim *does* fool me?—I have got plenty more. I am not in a particular hurry to get rich. I suppose I couldn't well help getting rich here some time or other, i̶f̶ I̶ whether I wanted to or not. You folks do not believe in Nevada, and I am glad you don't. Just keep on thinking so.

I was at the Gould & Curry mine, the other day, and they had two or three tons of choice rock piled up, which was valued at $20,000 a ton. I gathered up a hat-full, ₓof chunks,ₓ on account of their beauty as specimens—they don't let everybody supply themselves so liberally. I send Mr. Moffett a little specimen ₓof it,ₓ for his cabinet. If you don't know what the white stuff on it is, I must inform you that i̶s̶ it is purer silver than ɏ minted coin. There is about as much gold in it as there is silver, but it is not visible. I will explain to you some day how to detect it.[4]

I suppose we are on the verge of war now. If Orion assumes jurisdiction over Esmeralda county, California[5]

[*two MS pages (about 800 words) missing*]

of great, dark, timbered chambers, with a lot of shapeless devils flitting about in the distance, with dim candles flickering in the gloom; and then s̶h̶o̶u̶l̶d̶ she could look far above her head, to the top of the shaft, and see a faint little square of daylight, apparently no bigger than one of the spots on a chess-board; or if she found nothing cheerful in these things, she could go to the express offices and see them ship two or three thousand pounds of silver bullion away on the coaches every day. I would show her a hundred proofs that in the course of ten years we shall make that blowing California sing almighty small.[6] How I *hate* everything that looks, or tastes, or smells like California!—and how I hate everybody that loves the cursed State! Californians hate Missourians,—consequently I take great pains to let them public know that "Mark Twain" hails from there. I never let an opportunity slip to blow my horn for Missouri—*you bet*—as these rotten, lop-eared, whopper-jawed, jack-legged California abscesses say—*blast* them! But I have struck it now—I *can* show Pamela something cheerful, in reality, if-s when she comes out: we *hang* one of these scabby, putrefied Californians every now and then—she shall see one of them get his neck stretched. I hate those fellows worse than I hate a Chinaman.[7]

O, say, Ma, *who was* that girl—that sweetheart of mine wh you say got married, and her father gave her husband $100 (so you said, but I suppose you meant $100,000,)? It was ~~Emma Ro Rowe,~~ Emma Roe, wasn't it? What in thunder did I want with *her?* ~~Espec~~ I mean, since she wouldn't have had as me if I had asked her to? Let her slide—I don't suppose her life has ever been, is now, or ever will be, any happier than mine.[8]

Remember me to Zeb, and Uncle Jim, and Aunt Ella, and Cousin Bettie, and tell the whole party to stay in St. Louis—it is such a slow, old fogy, easy-going humbug of a town. And don't forget to remember [me] to Mrs. Sexton and Margaret—has Margaret recovered from her illness? And be sure to remember me ~~kid~~ kindly to *our* Margaret at home.[9]

> Yrs aff
> Sam.

---

[1] In the early morning hours of 12 April 1863, John Campbell murdered two policemen, Dennis McMahon and Thomas Reed. Clemens mentioned the double murder in "Horrible Affair," published in the *Territorial Enterprise* sometime between 16 and 18 April (see *ET&S1*, 244–47).

[2] "Advice to the Unreliable on Church-Going" probably appeared in the *Enterprise* on 12 April (see *ET&S1*, 241–43). It was the latest installment in a continuing mock feud between Mark Twain and the Unreliable, Clement T. Rice, who was the local reporter for the Virginia City *Union* and a good friend. For Mark Twain's other contributions to this feud, see *ET&S1*, passim.

[3] The East India Gold and Silver Mining Company was incorporated on 31 March 1863, claiming a capital stock of $550,000 divided into 1,100 shares. Among the incorporators were Clemens's friends William M. Gillespie and Clem-

ent T. Rice, each of whom originally owned 100 shares. Company records indicate that Gillespie contributed 40 shares and Rice 10 shares to make up the gift to Clemens (East India Gold and Silver Mining Company documents, PH in CU-MARK, courtesy of Michael H. Marleau: certificate of incorporation, 31 Mar 63; trust deed, 31 Mar 63; power of attorney to Leonard M. Ferris, 4 Apr 63). The East India mine, located in the middle of C Street in Virginia City, turned out to be a "wildcat" claim—that is, a claim of dubious value (SLC 1868, 2). In chapter 44 of *Roughing It* Clemens acknowledged that the owners of such claims often gave reporters stock in exchange for publicity. East India stock, he recalled, "sold briskly although there was an ancient tunnel running directly under the claim and any man could go into it and see that it did not cut a quartz ledge or anything that remotely resembled one." No *Enterprise* notice of the East India claim is extant, although Clemens may well have published one in return for his gift. Clement T. Rice probably wrote the following puff, which appeared in the Virginia City *Union*, the paper he worked for, on 2 April: "The East India Company (Waterloo ledge) yesterday produced some very rich gold-bearing rock. The gold stuck out in big flakes in many places" (Rice 1863a, 4).

[4] Clemens apparently wrote the similar description of rich Gould and Curry ore which appeared in the *Enterprise* on 3 April (see *ET&S1*, 312).

[5] The Nevada-California boundary-line dispute (see 24 and 25 Apr 62 to OC, n. 8) had erupted into violence in February 1863, when officials of Roop (formerly Lake) County, Nevada, and Plumas County, California, took up arms over the issue of their respective jurisdictions along the disputed line. The war in Roop County brought the whole boundary matter to a crisis, with the primary issue being not the Roop County line, but whether Aurora was in Mono County, California, or Esmeralda County, Nevada. (There was no "Esmeralda county, California.") In March 1863 Orion Clemens, acting governor while James W. Nye was in the East, announced that he would begin to organize Esmeralda County (including Aurora), appointing Nevada officials to replace the incumbent Mono County officers, immediately after the California legislature adjourned on 8 April. He hoped that the legislature would act to resolve the dispute in Nevada's favor before that date. Governor Leland Stanford of California warned that if Nevada attempted "to include within its limits the thriving and important town of Aurora . . . together with some of the richest and most valuable mining localities," the action would "pave the way for serious difficulties" (Stanford, 2:35). To this challenge the *Enterprise* responded on 3 April with a long editorial, which said in part:

California has shown an ungraciousness throughout, regarding this boundary question, which is not calculated to beget a very conciliatory spirit on our part. . . . If the California Legislature, through neglect or obstinacy, fail to make a satisfactory settlement, and invite a collision of jurisdiction, let us accept the issue. We have used quite enough supplication and conciliatory means. If we have any rights—which we begin to doubt—let us claim for them a decent respect. California would engorge our whole Territory if she could. We have submitted to enough insolence. Our people are tired of this aggression, and before yielding another foot of ground will raise the standard of The Summit Boundary or Blood. ("The Boundary Question Again," Virginia City *Territorial Enterprise*, 3 Apr 63, clipping in Scrapbook 2:36, CU-MARK)

By 9 April Orion Clemens had decided to defer organizing Esmeralda County until sometime after 20 April, the rescheduled adjournment date of the California legislature. Although feelings remained high, in May a joint commission of California and Nevada surveyors was appointed to run a final boundary line. Partisans for both sides in Aurora remained in doubt until September, when the surveyors reached that area and determined, still amid some controversy, that it was in fact part of Nevada Territory. The boundary findings were formally accepted by the California legislature in April 1864 and by the Nevada state legislature in February 1865 (Angel 100–102, 401–3; Mack: 1936, 398–406; 1961a, 33; 1961b, 85; Virginia City *Territorial Enterprise*: "Further of the Boundary Question," 9 Apr 63, clipping in Scrapbook 2:37, CU-MARK; "The Boundary Line between California and Washoe," 17 Sept 63, clipping in Scrapbook 2:78, CU-MARK).

[6] That is, Californians would be humbled, made to qualify or retract their boasts, or even be forced "to be silent or dumb" (*OED*, 9:529 [second page sequence]).

[7] Clemens's distaste for California was not long-lived: in less than a month he and Clement T. Rice were to leave Virginia City to spend two months in San Francisco. His momentary antipathy is probably explained by the border dispute with California. Since this passage occurs in one manuscript fragment, while the allusion to being "on the verge of war" with California occurs in the other, it seems plausible, if not certain, that the two fragments belong to the same letter (see the textual apparatus for details). Clemens's efforts to identify Mark Twain as a Missourian cannot now be documented, probably because so little of what he wrote for the *Enterprise* between February (when he first signed the name) and April 1863 survives.

[8] Emma Comfort Roe (1844–1904) was the daughter of John J. Roe (1809–70), long identified with St. Louis commerce as commission merchant, steamboat owner, meat packer, railroad magnate, banker, insurance executive, and one of the city's wealthiest citizens. Clemens served on several boats—including the *John J. Roe*—in which Roe held an interest. On 26 August 1862 Emma Roe married John G. Copelin, who became her father's business partner. For decades she took an active role in the social life of the city's wealthiest class ("Death of a Prominent Citizen," St. Louis *Missouri Republican*, 15 Feb 70, 2; Walter B. Stevens, 2:453–54; "Deaths," St. Louis *Post-Dispatch*, 27 Mar 1904, sec. 5:2; Roe-Copelin marriage record, PH in CU-MARK).

[9] Among those to whom Clemens sends regards are Zeb Leavenworth, James and Ella Lampton, and the Moffett servant, Margaret. "Cousin Bettie" may be Elizabeth Ann Lampton (1823–1906), Jane Clemens's first cousin (Selby, 106). Clemens's ironic suggestion that "the whole party . . . stay in St. Louis—it is such a slow, old fogy, easy-going humbug of a town" echoes a note he had struck in the second paragraph ("You folks do not believe in Nevada, and I am glad you don't. Just keep on thinking so"). The compatibility of these statements, which occur in separate manuscript fragments, strongly suggests that the fragments are from a single letter. The statements reinforce Clemens's ironic argument, most of which is missing, that Pamela would find nothing of interest if she were to visit Nevada, except the inside of a mine shaft and the daily transporting of "two or three thousand pounds of silver bullion."

To Jane Lampton Clemens
16 April 1863 • Virginia City, Nev. Terr.
(MS: NPV)

. . . .

ladies ~~othe~~ at the other end, ~~whe~~ who, when they had finished their meal, came by & asked me to come into the parlor after dinner. I accepted, gladly, thinking I had my new friend "in the door" then—as the faro players say—but I was mistaken, you know. He proceeded with me to the parlor door—but for the sake of his friends & his innocence, I said nothing uncivil to him, but turned away & went up town, he still following. He staid with me bravely, until I had gone all my usual rounds & a few unusual ones, too, although a fearful snowstorm was raging at the time— and came back to the office with me, where he staid until 8 or 9 o'clock & then went out to feed his oxen—since which time I am happy to inform you, Madam, I have neither seen or heard of him. Remember me kindly to his folks, & especially to Mrs. Dr Douglas.[1]

Bully for Mrs Holliday—she owes me five or ten dollars. Tell Uncle Jim[2] I don't write, simply because I am too lazy. Nothing but that deep & abiding sense of duty which is a second nature with me, prompts me to write even to my gay & sprightly mother. It is misery to me to write letters. But I say, Ma, don't let your ~~y~~ kind heart be exercised about Poor John Anderson, because in that case I shall get the benefit of it in your next, you know. This country will take the "soft solder" out of *him*—just let him alone.

Why, certainly, if ~~m~~ Mr. Moffett will ~~I~~ advance you money on my account Ma, draw liberally—I'll foot the bill some day.

But I can't write any more. They have "struck it rich" in the "front ledge" in Gold Hill the other day, & I must go out and find out something more about it. The "front ledge"[3]

. . . .

---

[1] Neither Clemens's "new friend" nor Mrs. Douglas has been identified.

[2] James A. H. Lampton.

[3] By the evening of 16 April, probably just a few hours after writing this letter, Clemens had found out "something more." He included the following item in a

column he wrote that evening and published in the *Territorial Enterprise* on 17
April:

> The recent discovery at Gold Hill has materially advanced the rates of the claims on the
> main range, and is really of great importance. The discovery consists of a newly developed
> ledge, of surprising richness, immediately in front of what has been supposed to be the
> front vein in that locality. Should the new ledge prove to be permanent and continuous, it
> will doubtless be claimed as a portion of the main Gold Hill possessions. (SLC 1863b, 1)

On 24 April the *Enterprise*, recalling the "fearful excitements" caused by the
"front ledge" and other discoveries of the "past week," reported:

> The grand climax of the epidemic fell yesterday, and in the shape of another mineral discov-
> ery. Mr. Mark Twain and the Unreliable made it, somewhere in B street, and established
> their lines of location so ingeniously as to take in the Ophir, the Spanish and other of the
> richest claims on the Comstock lode. The croppings of the ledge especially taken up by
> these gentlemen look very imposing . . . look as natural as if they had been dumped on the
> spot from a cart. . . . The location "Notice" reads as follows: "Mr. Twain and the Unrelia-
> ble claim several thousand feet on this, the Mark Twain ledge, with the Comstock and all
> other spurs, dips, angles, variations and sinuosities, together with all the Crown property
> therein, thereupon, thereabouts, or remotely adjacent thereto. The company shall be
> known as the Unreliable Auriferous, Argentiferous, Metaliferous Mining Company."
> ("The Climax," clipping in Scrapbook 1:41, CU-MARK)

The *Enterprise* article concluded with a lengthy burlesque assay of "specimens"
from the Mark Twain ledge.

To Jane Lampton Clemens and Pamela A. Moffett
18? May 1863 • San Francisco, Calif.
(MS: CU-MARK)

[two MS pages (about 400 words) missing]

When I first came down here,[1] I was with Neil Moss[2] every day for
about two weeks, but he has gone down to Coso[3] now. He says he is about
to realize something from those mines there, after roughing it & working
hard for three years. He says he has had a very hard time ever since he has
been in California—has done pretty much all kinds of work to make a
living—keeping school in the country among other things. He looks just
like his father ~~be~~ did eight or ten years ago—though a little rougher &
more weather-beaten perhaps. The man whom I have heard people call
the "handsomest & finest-looking man in California," is Bill Briggs.[4] I
meet him on ~~the str~~ Montgomery street every day. He keeps a somewhat
extensive gambling hell opposite the Russ House.[5] I went up with him
once to see it.

I shall remain here ten days or two weeks longer, & then return to Virginia*,*, & go to work again.[6] They want me to correspond with one of thes[e] dailies here, & if they will pay me enough, [*about nine words torn away*] I'll do it.[7] [The pay is only a "blind"—I'll correspond anyhow. If I don't know how to make such a thing pay me—if I don't know how to levy black-mail on the mining companies,—who *does*, I should like to know?][8]
~~If I had Mr. Moffett here, the position would be worth $20,000 a year. For instance: I black-mailed a company to the extent of 40 feet, two months ago. Since I have been here, the stock went to $100°° a foot, & the Mr. Moffett or any other sensible man would have cleared it out at that figure; but I, and the rest of the fools went on pleasure-seeking, & let the opportunity go by. That stock will never breathe again for three months—maybe six.~~

Ma, I have got five twenty-dollar greenbacks—the first of that kind of money I ever had. I'll send them to you—one at a time, so that if one or two get lost, it will not amount to anything. I ~~m~~ have been mighty ~~careless~~ neglectful about remittances heretofore, Ma, but when I return to Virginia, I'll do better. I'll sell some wildcat every now & then, & send you some money. Enclosed you will find one of the rags I spoke of—it's a ratty-looking animal, anyway. Love to all.

Yrs affctiny

Sam

✉————————————————————————————

[*penciled notation by Jane Clemens on the first extant page:*] Nᵒ 1—$20—[9]

[1]Clemens was on his first visit to San Francisco. On 3 May 1863, in a column of verse and prose toasting his departure from Virginia City, the *Territorial Enterprise* playfully recognized that he had become a local celebrity:

Mark Twain has abdicated the local column of the ENTERPRISE, where, by the grace of Cheek, he so long reigned Monarch of Mining Items, Detailer of Events, Prince of Platitudes, Chief of Biographers, Expounder of Unwritten Law, Puffer of Wildcat, Profaner of Divinity, Detractor of Merit, Flatterer of Power, Recorder of Stage Arrivals, Pack Trains, Hay Wagons, and Things in General. . . . He has gone to display his ugly person and disgusting manners and wildcat on Montgomery street. In all of which he will be assisted by his protegee, the Unreliable. ("Mark Twain," clipping in Scrapbook 2:43, CU-MARK)

[2]The son of Russell Moss, the proprietor of a large pork-packing firm in Hannibal in the 1850s and one of the wealthiest men in the town. Clemens recalled Neil Moss (b. 1835 or 1836) in "Villagers of 1840–3" as an "envied rich boy. . . . Spoiled and of small account," who was sent to Yale and "came back in swell eastern clothes, and the young men dressed up the warped negro bell ringer in a travesty of him. . . . At 30 he was a graceless tramp in Nevada, living by mendi-

cancy and borrowed money. Disappeared" (*Inds*, 94; *Hannibal Census*, 312). It was Moss whom Clemens nicknamed "the Prodigal" in chapter 55 of *Roughing It*:

The son of wealthy parents, here he was, in a strange land, hungry, bootless, mantled in an ancient horse-blanket, roofed with a brimless hat, and so generally and so extravagantly dilapidated that he could have "taken the shine out of the Prodigal Son himself," as he pleasantly remarked. He wanted to borrow forty-six dollars—twenty-six to take him to San Francisco, and twenty for something else; to buy some soap with, maybe, for he needed it.

Clemens loaned the money to Moss—after borrowing it himself from a Virginia City banker (see 17 Sept 64 to Wright, n. 2).

[3] Around this time "the vast territory between Owens Lake [in California] and the Nevada line" was known as the Coso Diggings (Gudde, 72).

[4] The eldest son (b. 1830 or 1831) of William Briggs of Hannibal, Missouri, and brother of Clemens's childhood friend John Briggs (*Hannibal Census*, 316). In 1897 Clemens recalled Briggs in "Villagers of 1840–3": "Drifted to California in '50, and in '65 was a handsome bachelor and had a woman. Kept a faro-table" (*Inds*, 95). Amelia Ransome Neville, a wealthy San Francisco socialite, sketched Briggs as he was in the 1880s:

We knew Bill Briggs, successful professional gambler of that later time who came to Shasta Springs for summer visits. Conservative guests avoided him, but others found him an engaging person, devoted to his small son and talking of everything but cards. His profession he left at home, and nothing could persuade him into a game while he sojourned among us. But he wore his mustache and wide-awake hat and the largest solitaire diamond I have ever seen in a ring. When he died, he left a fortune to the little son, then at a military school, and a reputation for square dealing. (Neville, 41)

[5] One of San Francisco's leading hotels, built in 1861-62 on a site occupying the entire block between Pine and Bush on Montgomery Street (Bancroft 1891–92, 6:540; Langley 1862, xxxvii, 26).

[6] On 1 June Clemens wrote his mother and sister that he was "still" in San Francisco, suggesting that on that date, at the latest, they would have expected him to be in Virginia City. Hence, 18 May, exactly two weeks earlier, seems a likely date for the present letter. In fact Clemens remained in San Francisco through June and did not arrive back in Virginia City until 2 July (*ET&S1*, 26).

[7] Clemens reached an agreement with the San Francisco *Morning Call* and subsequently sent off a total of ten letters that appeared in the paper between 9 July and 19 November 1863.

[8] The opportunity for such "black-mail" was virtually unlimited, since mine owners were willing to give stock to reporters in exchange for favorable newspaper notices of their mines. See 11 and 12 Apr 63 to JLC and PAM, n. 3.

[9] Possibly a reproduction of a notation by Clemens on the missing first page of the letter. He sent at least twelve enclosures of greenbacks between May and August 1863. Only five additional letters bearing similar notations, in his hand, have been discovered (1 June 63, 4 June 63, 18 July 63, 5 Aug 63, and 19 Aug 63, all to JLC and PAM).

To Jane Lampton Clemens and Pamela A. Moffett
1 June 1863 • San Francisco, Calif.
(MS: NPV)

N°· 2—[$20⁰⁰ Enclosed]

Lick House, S. F. June 1.[1]

My Dear Mother & Sister

The Unreliable & myself are still here, & still enjoying ourselves. I suppose I know at least a thousand people here—some of them a great many of them citizens of San Francisco, but the majority belonging in Washoe—& when I go down Montgomery street, shaking hands with Tom, Dick & Harry, it is just like being in Main street in Hannibal & meeting the old familiar faces. I *do hate* to go back to Washoe. We ǵ fag ourselves completely out every day, and go to sleep without rocking, every night. We dine out, & we lunch out, and we eat, drink and are happy—as it were. After breakfast, I don't often see the hotel again until midnight—or after. I am going to the Dickens mighty fast. I know a regular village of families here in the house, but I never have time to call on them. Thunder! we'll know a little more about this town, before we leave, than some of the people who live in it. We take trips across the Bay to Oakland, and down to San Leandro, and Alameda, and those places, and we go out to the Willows, and Hayes Park, and Fort Point, and up to Benicia;[2] and yesterday we were invited out on a yachting excursion, & had a sail in the fastest yacht on the Pacific Coast. Rice says: "Oh, no—*we* are not having any fun, Mark—Oh, no, I reckon not—it's somebody else—it's probably the "gentleman in the wagon!" (popular slang phrase.) When I invite Rice to the Lick House to dinner, the proprietors send us champaign and claret, and then we *do* put on the most disgusting airs. Rice says our calibre is too light—we can't stand it to be noticed!

I rode down with a gentleman to the Ocean House, the other day, to see the sea-horses, and also to listen to the roar of the surf, and watch the ships drifting here about, here, & there, and far away at sea.[3] When I stood on the beach & let the surf wet my feet, I recollected doing the same thing on the shores of the Atlantic—& then I had a proper appreciation of the vastness of this country—for I had traveled from ocean to ocean across it, *on land*, with the exception of crossing Lake Erie—(and I wish I had gone around it.)[4]

Sam

[1] According to Clemens's letter of 16 May to the *Territorial Enterprise*, he and Clement T. Rice first stayed at San Francisco's Occidental Hotel at Bush and Montgomery streets (see *ET&S1*, 248–53). Evidently they had by this time moved to the more opulent Lick House at Montgomery and Sutter, opened just eleven months earlier. The Lick House, owned by the eccentric land speculator James Lick, was known for its active social life and boasted a dining room modeled on the banquet hall at the Palace of Versailles (Langley 1863, 7, 227, 278; James, 261–72).

[2] The Willows, at Mission and Eighteenth streets, and Hayes Park, at Laguna and Grove streets, were favorite pleasure resorts offering a variety of entertainments and recreational facilities. Fort Point, a massive brick fortification, is on the northernmost promontory of the San Francisco peninsula. Benicia, founded in 1847, is a town on the north shore of the Carquinez Strait. An important stop on the route to the California mines, and the state capital in 1853–54, it was the site of an army ordnance base and a coaling and repair base for Sacramento River boats (Estavan, 16:23–34; Motheral, 6–9; Hart, 36).

[3] The Ocean House hotel and restaurant, south of the Cliff House. The numerous sea lions visible on the rocky shoreline were a popular attraction (Lockwood, 121). Clemens's "sea-horse" (i.e., walrus) was a misnomer.

[4] Clemens crossed Lake Erie during his August 1853 trip from St. Louis to New York City (see 24 Aug 53 to JLC, n. 2).

To Jane Lampton Clemens and Pamela A. Moffett
4 June 1863 • San Francisco, Calif.
(MS: CU-MARK)

N° 3.—$20 enclosed.

Lick House, San Francisco
June 4, 1863.

My Dear Mother & Sister

My visit to San F is gradually drawing to a close, and it seems like going back to prison to go back to the snows & the deserts of Washoe, after living in this Paradise. But then I shall soon get used to it—all places are alike to me. I have put in the time here, "you bet." And I have lived like a lord—to make up for two years of privation, you know. I havent

written to the paper but twice, I believe.[1] I have always got something
more agreeable on hand.

At the opera to-night, I saw some one whom I took to be Bill Nash. I
know he was to have been here this week, & I am very sure it was him—I
never forget faces. I get fooled with them, sometimes, though, & I want
to give you an instance of it—a case which I consider very remarkable.
The first Sunday after I arrived here, I went, by previous engagement, to
take Mrs. J. B. Winters to church (I have a special friendship for her,
because she is the very image of Pamela.)[2] She introduced me to a pretty
girl—Miss Jennie Woodruff—some relative of Gov Stanford's, & of
course, I showed a particular friendship for the girl, also, for that day.
The next day, at noon, I met the young lady on the street, & bowed to
her—sweetly. She simply stared at me & looked a little indignant. I didn't
care a cent, & thought no more about it. Two days afterward, I met her
again, & kept my eye on her, but never thought of such a thing as bowing
to her—and lo! she smiled lovingly, & bowed to *me*. Shortly afterward—
two or three days—when I took my usual seat at the dinner table, I bel
beheld my fickle darling opposite me. I smiled—bowed—and blast my
skin if she didn't scowl at me as sour as thunder, & went on destroying her
hash without ever noticing me again. Well, I just thought to myself, this
acquaintance is too spotted—it don't pan out to suit me, & I'll move my
stakes & drop it. I met her the same afternoon, and she astounded me by
bowing to me in the most marked and peremptory manner![3] I couldn't do
anything

. . . . .

[1] Only one letter written to the Virginia City *Territorial Enterprise* from San
Francisco as of this date (4 June) survives; it is dated 16 May 1863 (see *ET&S1*,
248–53).

[2] The wife of Clemens's Carson City friend John B. Winters. On 19 June Mark
Twain wrote "All about the Latest Fashions" for the *Enterprise*, a mock fashion
report that included a playful description of "Mrs. J. B. W." In September 1863,
he included a similar fashion report in "The Lick House Ball," again mentioning
Mrs. Winters (*ET&S1*, 310, 317).

[3] Clemens may have been thinking of Jennie Woodruff in September 1863 when
he alluded to the "lady acquaintance, who, for reasons best known to herself,
don't see you when she looks at you" in "How to Cure a Cold" (*ET&S1*, 302).

To Orion and Mary E. (Mollie) Clemens
20 June 1863 • San Francisco, Calif.
(MS: CU-MARK)

Lick House, June 20.

My Dear Bro.

The Echo progresses! The terms of compromise were agreed on yesterday—I don't know what they are, yet—only that they are rather severe on us. But every inch saved is bully, you bet. You can make money at trading Emma for Echo at 5 feet for one. But I don't ‸want‸ to trade at that rate—nor any other, for that matter. Gould & Curry, it is conjectured, will advance to the neighborhood of a thousand dollars an inch within the next twelve months—and take my word for it, the Echo will make 'em hunt their holes within the next twenty-four. It is on the main Gold Hill lead, and the nastiest old ledge in Nevada Territory. I have ~~h~~ stores of information on hand, but ~~is~~ it is not for publication just yet. I have played my cards with a stiff upper lip since ~~I~~ my arrival here—sometimes flush, sometimes dead broke & in debt—have spent eight hundred dollars, & sent Ma~~s~~ two hundred—was strapped day before yesterday, but I'm on the upper side of the wheel again to-day, with twelve hundred dollars in the bank & out of debt—nine-tenths of it will be invested to-morrow, ~~—~~ & then I'll hold up & start home in a day or two. But through it all, I have kept strict watch over the Echo, & when money was to be spent in order to get into anybody's good graces or gain a point in the way of information, I have spent it like a Lord, & trusted to luck to get even again. Oh, I tell you I'm *on it*. And mind, if you can't sell your Echo at $3,000 a foot fifteen months from now, do you pack up your traps & go home—because then it will be proved that all promises fail in this country. As I told you before, let people imagine that you own about a thousand feet in it if they will. I've got Echo on my brain—that's what's the matter with *me*.[1]

Mollie, my Dear, I enclose some more pictures for those girls, if they want them. All hearty—how are you?[2]

Yr Bro

Sam

[1]The Echo Gold and Silver Mining Company had incorporated in San Francisco on 22 April 1863 ("Rush for Mining Claims Continued," San Francisco *Alta*

California, 23 Apr 63, 1). The mine was located a quarter mile north of Devil's Gate near the road to Gold Hill, Nevada. Evidence that Clemens had at least a small share in the Echo is provided by the surviving fragment of a 16 April 1870 letter (CU-MARK) in which an unidentified correspondent in Grand Rapids, Michigan, reminded him: "Sometime in the latter part of April 1863. You and I were at the Boston Mine afterwards known as the Echo Mine situated and being in Gold Hill near the devil's Gate. . . . it was on the occasion of my getting Fritz [J. S. Fretz, one of the Echo incorporators] to give you an order for ten (10) shares of the stock of that company. (The Echo)." Clemens's 1863 letters to the San Francisco *Morning Call* suggest that he desired to puff the value of Echo stock, possibly because he was a shareholder. On 12 July he wrote that the dollar value of Echo's "first-class ore goes clear out of sight into the thousands. The Echo is probably the richest mine in Gold Hill District" (SLC 1863d, 1). One week later he again informed his readers of progress in the mine's development and of its "very valuable stock" (SLC 1863f, 1). Finally, on 8 August he reported of the Echo that "from five to seven tons of ore, ranging in value from $1,500 to $3,000 a ton, have been taken from it daily and shipped to the Bay, with occasionally a few hundred pounds of $10,000 rock. The yield now is in the neighborhood of ten tons a day" (SLC 1863g, 1). This publicity may have helped inflate the market value of Echo stock, which in mid-July reached an asking price of $140 a share in San Francisco, with $100 bid. Within six months the stock was selling for $27 ("Stock Sales at the Bay Last Week," Virginia City *Evening Bulletin,* 20 July 63, 2; "San Francisco Stock and Exchange Board, Jan. 11, 1864," San Francisco *Alta California,* 12 Jan 64, 6). Clemens is not known to have made further mention of the Echo mine at this time. In May 1864, just prior to his departure from Virginia City for California, Echo miners uncovered a new "exceedingly rich streak" of gold-bearing rock, expected to assay "from $1,500 to $2,000 per ton" ("The Echo," Virginia City *Union,* 31 May 64, 3). These potential riches were apparently never realized. Four years later, when writing to the Chicago *Republican* about Nevada claims that had proved to be "essentially and outrageously wildcat," Clemens lamented: "Oh where is the wonderful Echo?" (SLC 1868, 2).

² Neither Clemens's enclosures nor "those girls" have been identified.

To Jane Lampton Clemens and Pamela A. Moffett
18 July 1863 • Virginia City, Nev. Terr.
(MS, *damage emended:* CU-MARK)

Nº· 10—$20 enclosed

Virginia, July 18.

My Dear Mother & Sister

Ma, you are slinging insinuations at me again. Such as "where did I get the money*!*?" and "the company I kept" in San Francisco." Why I sold "wildcat" mining ground that was given me, & my credit was always good at the bank for two or three thousand$ dollars, & is yet. I *never* gamble, in any shape or manner, and never drink anything stronger than claret or lager beer, which conduct is regarded as miraculously temperate in this country. As for my company, Ma, I went into the very best society to be found in San Francisco, & to do that, you must know, of course, that I had to keep myself ~~my~~ mighty straight. I also ~~keep~~ move in the best Society of Virginia, & actually have a *r e p u t a t i o n* to preserve.

As for money, I manage to make a living, but if I had any business tact, the office of reporter here would be worth $30,000 a year—whereas, if I get 4 or $5,000 out of it, it will be as much as I expect. I have stock in my possession, which, if I had sold when it was first given me, from time to time, ~~wou~~ in the last ◊ months, would have brought me $10,000—but I have carelessly let it go down to nothing again. I don't think I am any account, anyhow. Now, I raised the price of "North Ophir" from $13 a foot to $45 a foot, to-day, & they gave me five feet.[1] That will go the way of all the rest. I shall probably mislay it or throw it in my trunk & never get a dollar out of it. But I am telling you too many secrets, & I'll stop. One more. ⦀ A gentleman in San Francisco told me to call at his office, & he would give me five feet of "Overman." Well, do you know I never went after it? The stock is worth $400⁰⁰ a foot, now—$2,000 thrown away.[2] I don't care a straw, for myself, but I ought to have had more thought for you. Never mind, though, Ma—I will be more careful in future. I will take care that your expenses are paid,—SURE.

You and Pamela only pay $8 a week apiece for board (& lodging too?) Well, you are not in a very expensive part of the world, certainly. ⦀ My room-mate & I pay, together, $70 a month for our bedchamber, & $50 a month, each, for board, besides.[3] Put in my washing, & it costs me $100 a month to live.

Affectionately,

Mark[4]

---

[1] The North Ophir mine was located in the Argentine district in Washoe County, near Virginia City. The price for North Ophir stock in fact rose from $20 asked/$12 bid on 15 July to $45 asked/$23 bid on 18 July ("Stock Market," Virginia City *Evening Bulletin*, 15 and 18 July 63, 2). It is not known whether Clemens wrote an item on 18 July for the *Enterprise* puffing the North Ophir, for the paper of that date is not extant. But the next day, 19 July, he wrote to the San Francisco *Morning Call*:

The "North Ophir" is coming into favor again. As nuggets of pure silver as large as pieces of chalk were found in liberal quantities in the ledge, the mine was pronounced "salted," and the stock fell from $60 to $13 a foot. However, during the last day or two a hundred experienced miners have examined the claim, and laughed at the idea of its having been salted. . . . Their testimony has removed the stain from the North Ophir's character, and the stock has already begun to recover. (SLC 1863f, 1)

A charge that the North Ophir was salted with melted half-dollars had been made by the Virginia City *Evening Bulletin* on 6 July ("Fluctuations of North Ophir," 2). Clemens later admitted this to be the fact in a letter of 11 October 1869 to the New York Society of California Pioneers (New York *Tribune*, 14 Oct 69, 5, in *MTL*, 1:163–65) and in chapter 44 of *Roughing It*.

²Clemens gives a different account of this missed opportunity in chapter 44 of *Roughing It*:

I met three friends one afternoon, who said they had been buying "Overman" stock at auction at eight dollars a foot. One said if I would come up to his office he would give me fifteen feet; another said he would add fifteen; the third said he would do the same. But I was going after an inquest and could not stop. A few weeks afterward they sold all their "Overman" at six hundred dollars a foot and generously came around to tell me about it—and also to urge me to accept of the next forty-five feet of it that people tried to force on me.

The Overman was a productive mine on the Comstock lode in the Gold Hill district of Storey County. Clemens's claim about the value of its stock was accurate: the bid price had risen from $150 to $400 between 6 and 16 July ("Stock Market," Virginia City *Evening Bulletin*, 6 July 63, 2, and 16 July 63, 3).

³Clemens was living at the White House, a recently completed, "most elegantly furnished" boardinghouse on B Street, "perhaps one of the best finished buildings in the city" ("Large Conflagration—Loss About $30,000," Virginia City *Evening Bulletin*, 27 July 63, 3; Kelly 1863, 293). It was managed by Mrs. C. A. Williamson, whom Clemens had earlier known and liked as the proprietor of the Carson City White House (*ET&S1*, 397; Kelly 1862, 91). Two of Clemens's acquaintances, Clement T. Rice (the Unreliable) and William M. Gillespie, also lived at the White House. It is not known which of the two was his roommate.

⁴The earliest extant private use of this signature, which also appears on the next two letters, to Jane Clemens and Pamela Moffett. Clemens's family may have objected to the pseudonym, for "Mark" does not reoccur until 20 January 1866.

To Jane Lampton Clemens and Pamela A. Moffett
5 August 1863 • Virginia City, Nev. Terr.
(MS, *damage emended:* CU-MARK)

N⁰· 11—$20 enclosed

Va., Aug 5.

My Dear Mother & Sister

I got burned out about ten days ago—saved nothing but the clothes I had on—lost a couple of handsome suits that I had made in San Francisco.¹ The fire resulted in no benefit to me except that M̶r̶ Judge Ferris' wife offered me the use of t̶h̶e̶ ̶s̶p̶a̶r̶e̶ one of the spare chambers in her house until the Superintendent of the Ophir, who occupies it, returns from San Francisco.[2] Therefore, I shall live in some style for a while, at any rate, free of charge, in rooms worth $200 or $250 a month, I guess. I board at the Collins House.[3] They only charge me $10 a week there—so much for being a reporter. Mrs. Ferris (and everybody else,) has gone to Lake Bigler, & I shall go myself if I can get any one to report for me. However, I didn't lose so very much by the fire. A man whom I never saw before, gave me some "feet" as I went down town, & I sold the batch for $200 & fitted me myself out again half as good as new. The unknown scoundrel couldn't have done me a favor of the kind n when I needed it more.

Orion is in town. I saw him at the Theatre to-night. He says he has a letter from home at Carson.

He sent me your last the other day, with a fearful lecture to me on the subject of dissipation,, from himself. As I don't dissipate, & never expect to, & am man enough to have a good character & keep it, I didn't take the trouble to answer it. He will learn after a while, perhaps, that I am not an infant, that I know the value of a good name as well as he does, & stop writing such childish nonsense to me.

Now, I don't wo really work more than two hours a day, but then I am busy all the time, gadding about, you know, & consequently I don't expect to write you very often. You can hear from me by the paper, though. When I was in San Francisco I believe they thought I wasn't coming back & any more, & stopped your paper—but I started it again pretty suddenly when I returned. I am glad to hear you are all improving in health. I wish you would stay a with Dr Gross.[4]

Yrs affcty

Mark

---

[1] The fire at the White House occurred at about 11:00 A.M. on 26 July and was thought to be "the work of an incendiary" ("Large Conflagration—Loss About $30,000," Virginia City *Evening Bulletin*, 27 July 63, 3). The Virginia City *Union* of 28 July carried an account of the fire probably written by Clemens's fellow resident Clement T. Rice. It included the following information, which, the paper noted, was "supposed to be a 'goak'": "Sam. Clemens and W. M. Gillespie lost all their clothing, valued at about $15, besides an immense amount of 'wild cat,' variously estimated to be worth from ten cents to two hundred thousand dollars" (Rice 1863b, 2). Clemens's own account of his narrow escape appeared in the San Francisco *Morning Call* on 30 July:

I discovered that the room under mine was on fire, gave the alarm, and went down to see how extensive it was likely to be. . . . I came near not escaping from the house at all. I started to the door with my trunk, but I couldn't stand the smoke, wherefore I abandoned

that valuable piece of furniture in the hall, and returned and jumped out at the window. . . .
Now do you know that trunk was utterly consumed, together with its contents, consisting
of a pair of socks, a package of love-letters, and $300,000 worth of "wildcat" stocks? Yes,
Sir, it was; and I am a bankrupt community. Plug hat, numerous sets of complete harness—
all broadcloth—lost—eternally lost. However, the articles were borrowed, as a general
thing. I don't mind losing them. (*ET&S1*, 261)

[2] Leonard W. Ferris and his wife lived on B Street not far from the White
House. Ferris had been appointed probate judge of Storey County in December
1861 and was elected to the same position in September 1863. Edward B. Wilder
was superintendent of the Ophir mine. Clemens had talked with him in July while
visiting the Ophir during a series of cave-ins, afterward describing them in the
San Francisco *Morning Call* (SLC 1863e, 1, and SLC 1863f, 1). He may be referring, however, to the company's general superintendent, who supervised the
Ophir mine and also the mill and reduction works, Walter W. Palmer. Clemens
mentioned Palmer in the *Morning Call* (SLC 1864l, 3, and SLC 1864m, 1), and
later alluded to him in chapter 45 of *Roughing It* (Kelly 1863, 130–31, 210, 269,
293; Angel, 607).

[3] The Collins House, owned by John A. Collins, was Virginia City's newest
hotel. On opening night, 8 July 1863, Collins gave a banquet attended by prominent citizens. The *Evening Bulletin* reported that after the dinner "came the
champagne, the wisdom and the wit. . . . Perhaps *the* speech of the evening was
made by Sam. Clemens. Those not familiar with this young man, do not know the
depths of grave tenderness in his nature. He almost brought the house to tears by
his touching simple pathos" ("Opening of the Collins House," Virginia City *Evening Bulletin*, 9 July 63, 3).

[4] Unidentified.

To Jane Lampton Clemens and Pamela A. Moffett
19 August 1863 • Steamboat Springs, Nev. Terr.
(MS: NPV)

N[o.] 12—$20

Steamboat Springs,[1]
August 19.

My Dear Mother & Sister

Ma, you have given my vanity a deadly thrust. Behold, I am prone
to boast of having the widest reputation as a local editor, of any man on
the Pacific coast, & you gravely come forward & tell me "if I work hard &
attend closely to my business, I ¢ may *aspire* to a place on a big San Francisco daily, some day." There's a comment on human vanity for you!
Why, blast it, I was under the impression that I could get such a situation
as that any time I asked for it. But I don't want it. No paper in the United

States can afford to pay me what my place on the "Enterprise" is worth. If I were not naturally a lazy, idle, good for nothing vagabond, I could make it pay me $20,000 a year. But I don't suppose I shall ever be any account. I lead an easy life, though, & I don't care a cent whether school keeps or not. Everybody knows me, & I fare like a prince wherever I go, be it on this side of the mountains or the other. And I am proud to say I am the most conceited ass in the Territory.

You think that picture looks old? Well, I can't help it—in reality I am not as old as I was when I was eighteen.

I took a desperate cold more than a week ago, & I seduced Wilson (a Missouri boy, reporter of the Daily Union,) from his labors, & we went over to Lake Bigler.[2] But I failed to cure my cold. I found the "Lake House"[3] crowded with the wealth & fashion of Virginia, & I ~~had to~~ could not resist the temptation to take a hand in all the fun going. Those Virginians—men & women both—are a stirring set, & I found if I went with them on all their eternal excursions, I should bring the consumption home with me—so I left, day before yesterday, & came back into the Territory again. A lot of them had purchased a site for a town on the Lake shore, & they gave me a lot. When you come out, I'll build you a house on it. The Lake seems more supernaturally beautiful now than ever. It is the masterpiece of the Creator.

The hotel here at the Springs[4] is not as much crowded as usual, & I am having a very comfortable time of it. The hot, white steam puffs up out of fissures in the earth like the jets that come from a steamboat's 'scape pipes, & it makes a boiling, surging noise like a steamboat, too—hence the name. We put eggs in a hankerchief & dip them in the Springs—they "soft boil" in 2 minutes, & boil as hard as a rock in 4 minutes. These fissures extend more than a quarter of a mile, & the long line of steam columns looks very pretty. A large bath house is built over one of the Springs, & we go in it & steam ourselves as long as we can stand it, & then come out & take a cold shower bath. You get baths, board & lodging, all for $25 a week—cheaper than living in Virginia without baths.

We shall bud out into a State before many months, which will relieve Orion of his office. If I have influence enough, I mean to get him nominated a candidate for some fat office under the State Government, so that you can come out and live with him.[5] I am a pretty good hand at such things. I was a mighty heavy wire-puller at the last Legislature. I passed every bill I worked for, & on a bet, I killed a bill by a three-fourths vote in the House after it had passed the Council unanimously. Oh, I tell you a reporter in the Legislature can swing more votes than any member of the body. We'll have rare times the coming session, & in the State convention.

Yrs aff

Mark

[1] These mineral springs, discovered in 1860, were located in Steamboat Valley in Washoe County, about nine miles northwest of Virginia City (Angel, 644–45). Clemens described his visit to Steamboat Springs in letters to the *Territorial Enterprise*, published on 25 August, and the San Francisco *Morning Call*, published on 30 August (see *ET&S1*, 270–83).

[2] Adair Wilson (b. 1841) was the junior local editor of the Virginia City *Union*. Before coming to Nevada, Wilson had practiced law for two years in San Francisco. He left the *Union* in October 1863 to edit the *Reese River Reveille* in Austin, Nevada, left that post in 1864 to resume his San Francisco law practice, and in 1865–66 was a reporter for the San Francisco *American Flag*. After moving to Colorado in 1872 he became a state senator and a judge (*Portrait*, 321–25; Hall, 4:610; Angel, 303–4; Langley 1865, 458). Wilson figured in Clemens's *Territorial Enterprise* columns as "Young Wilson" and "the Unimportant." Clemens described their experiences at Lake Bigler in "How to Cure a Cold," published on 20 September 1863 in the San Francisco *Golden Era* (*ET&S1*, 296–303).

[3] Captain Augustus W. Pray's luxurious Lake Shore House at Glenbrook on Bigler's eastern shore had first opened earlier in the year (Scott, 265).

[4] Steamboat Springs Hotel, kept by A. W. Stowe and John Holmes (*ET&S1*, 281).

[5] Although voters approved statehood by better than four to one in a plebiscite held on 2 September 1863, it was late 1864 before Nevada entered the Union (Angel, 81, 87). Clemens's plans for Orion were never fully realized (see 2? Jan 64 to JLC, n. 4).

No LETTERS are known to survive for the next four and a half months. This was a period of frequent movement and varied activity for Clemens. He returned to Virginia City from Steamboat Springs on 23 August 1863, his cold still uncured, but remained there less than two weeks. Dan De Quille's arrival, on 5 September, after a nine-month visit to his Iowa home, freed Clemens from his *Territorial Enterprise* duties as local editor, enabling him to seek restored health in San Francisco. He left Virginia City that same day, evidently stopping over in Carson City and arriving in San Francisco on 8 September. During the next four weeks he enjoyed a pleasurable recuperation, attending balls and the theater and playing billiards with other residents of the luxurious Lick House. He described some of his experiences in contributions to the *Enterprise* and the San Francisco *Golden Era* (see *ET&S1*, 291–319, and SLC 1863h, 2:78).

Clemens departed San Francisco, probably around 9 October, to attend the First Annual Fair of the Washoe Agricultural, Mining and Mechanical Society, held in Carson City from the twelfth through the seventeenth of the month. He had been made recording secretary of that society by the 19 December 1862 legislative act that created it, with a salary not to exceed "the sum of three hundred dollars per annum" (*Laws* 1863, 97). He served until the conclusion of the fair, when the society elected its new officers and his friend William M. Gillespie was chosen to succeed him ("First Annual Fair of the Washoe Agricultural, Mining and Mechanical Society," Virginia City *Union*, 14 Oct 63, clipping in Scrapbook 2:90–91, CU-MARK; "The Territorial Fair," Virginia City *Evening Bulletin*, 19 Oct 63, 1). Clemens reported the events of the fair in at least two letters to the *Enterprise*, one of which, written on 19 October, has survived (see SLC 1863i, 2:99). Soon after that date he resumed his *Enterprise* post in Virginia City. At the end of October he and Dan De Quille rented rooms there together (see 17 Sept 64 to Wright, n. 3). A few days later, however, Clemens was again in Carson City, this time to collaborate in the *Enterprise* coverage of Nevada Territory's first Constitutional Convention, which ran from 2 November through 11 December 1863 (see Marsh, Clemens, and Bowman, passim, and SLC 1863j–m). He was still in Carson City on 13 December, when he sent a dispatch to the *Enterprise* reporting the burlesque proceedings of the Third House of the Constitutional Convention (see SLC 1863n, 3:55).

Clemens returned to Virginia City in time to enjoy an uproarious visit by Artemus Ward, which began on 18 December and apparently lasted until the twenty-ninth. On the evening of 29 December Clemens reported a Virginia City political meeting for the *Enterprise* (see SLC 1863o, 3:60–61). In his capacity as political reporter he probably went to Carson City the following day—to be on hand for the opening, on 31 December, of the Union party convention to select candidates for Nevada's first state election, scheduled for 19 January 1864. The convention was of personal, as well as professional, interest to Clemens: his brother Orion emerged as the party's candidate for secretary of state, while *Enterprise* editor Joseph T. Goodman failed to win its nomination for state printer (Angel, 84, 85). Following the convention, Clemens wrote the next letter.

To Jane Lampton Clemens
2? January 1864 • Carson City, Nev. Terr.
(MS: NPV and CU-MARK)

[*first two MS pages (about 300 words) missing*]

ment.[1] It was reported back from the Committee with a whole lot of blanks ‚in it,‚ (for dates—apportionment & number of members, amount of money appropriated to pay expenses of the Convention, &c.) The Council passed it without filling those blanks—the House did the same thing—it was duly enrolled, brought back & signed by the President of the Council & the Speaker of the House[2]—& then transmitted, a worthless, meaningless, ṗ & intentionally powerless instrument, to the Governor, for his signature—at night. And behold, a miracle! When the bill reached the Governor, there was not a solitary blank in it! Who filled them, ṭh nobody can tell,—but the ¢Enrolling Clerk[3] didn't, anyhow, as the enrolled bill in this office will show. Therefore, the bill was a fraud—the Constitutional Convention was a fraud—the Constitution is born of fraud—a State erected under it would be a fraudulent & impotent institution, & we should ultimately be kicked back into a Territorial status ‚again,‚ on account of it. Wherefore, when men say "let the Constitution slide," I say Amen.[4]

The reason why I haven't sent you any money lately, Ma, is because I have been in debt on mining account. But I shall be out again before long.

When Artemus Ward gets to St Louis, invite him up to the house & treat him well, for behold, he is a good fellow. But don't ask him too many questions about me & Christmas Eve, because he might tell tales out of school.[5] At his suggestion, I mean to write semi-occasionally for the New York Sunday Mercury. Of his own accord he wrote a flattering letter about "Mark Twain" to the editors of that paper;[6] & besides, I have promised to go with him to Europe in May or June (provided something don't turn up in the meantime to change my notion, you know.[)][7]

I can't write regularly for the Mercury, of course. I shan't have time. But I sometimes throw a pearl before these swine here (there's no self-conceit about that, I beg you to observe,) which ought, for the eternal welfare of my race, to have a more extended circulation than is afforded by a local daily paper.

And if Fitzhugh Ludlow, (author of the "Hasheesh Eater,") comes your way, treat him well also. He published a high encomium upon Mark Twain, (the same being eminently just & truthful, I beseech you to believe,) in a San Francisco paper.[8] Artemus Ward said that when my gorgeous talents were publicly acknowledged by such high authority, I ought to appreciate them myself—leave sage-brush obscurity, & journey to New York with him, as he wanted me to do. But I preferred not to burst upon the New York publicly too suddenly & brilliantly, & so I concluded to remain here.

Well, Ma, I will tell you something now which will suit your taste for the marvellous. ~~Eighteen months~~ ˌA short time, ago, a woman, about 18 years old & very pretty, arrived here, alone. Or rather, she had a young child with ⱳ her. She took up her residence in the outskirts of the town, & although the gossips went to work to ~~work~~ worm her private history out of her, they failed entirely. She would answer no questions. She would not even tell her own name, or that of her child—she said it had none & never would have. She was weary & ⱳ care worn, sad & melancholy, & spent half her time in crying bitterly in solitude. A sinister looking man was occasionally seen prowling about her premises at dusk, & always with a gun. He was suspected of some villainous design, & the neighbors made up their minds that he was no better than he ought to be. One evening, just ~~at sun~~ at twilight, they were paralized to see him thrust his gun through the lonely woman's back window, take deliberate aim, and [*illegible deletion, torn*][9]—I guess it's about time for me to go to bed, now.

Sam.

[1] "An Act to frame a Constitution and State Government for the State of Washoe," which authorized a constitutional convention, had been approved by the Territorial Legislature on 20 December 1862 (*Laws* 1863, 128–30). The surviving part of this letter begins with Clemens's remarks on the fraud involved in the passage of the act and the consequent invalidity of the convention, the constitution it produced, and any state government founded upon that constitution. Clemens concluded a 4 January letter from Carson City—published as "Doings in Nevada" by the New York *Sunday Mercury* (SLC 1864d, 3)—with a similar, sometimes verbatim account that suggests some of what is missing here:

> In the Legislature, last year, I was wielding the weapon which, under just such circumstances, is mightier than the sword, at the time that the Act authorizing the calling together of a Convention to form a State Constitution was passed; and I know the secret history of that document. It was reported back from the Committee with a lot of blanks in it (for dates, apportionment, and number of members, amount of money appropriated to defray expenses of the Convention, etc.). Both Houses passed the Bill without filling those blanks; it was duly enrolled, brought back, and signed by the presiding officers of the Legislature, and then transmitted, a worthless, meaningless, and intentionally powerless instrument—

to Gov. Nye for his signature—at night. And lo! a miracle. When the bill reached the Governor, there was not a solitary blank in it! Who filled them, is—is a great moral question for instance; but the enrolling clerk did not do it at any rate, since the amendations are in an unknown and atrocious handwriting. Therefore, the bill was a fraud; the convention created by it was a fraud; the fruit of the convention was an illegitimate infant constitution and a dead one at that; a State reared upon such a responsibility would be a fraudulent and impotent institution, and the result would be that we should ultimately be kicked back into a territorial condition again on account of it. Wherefore, when men say; "Let our constitution slide for the present", we say Amen.

[2] Dr. John W. Pugh, of Aurora, was president of the Council of the second Territorial Legislature; John H. Mills, a Gold Hill miner, was Speaker of the House of Representatives (*Laws* 1863, xiii; Andrew J. Marsh, 412, 417–18, 667 n. 22).

[3] Unidentified.

[4] The constitutional convention authorized by the fraudulent act met in Carson City from 2 November to 11 December 1863. From 31 December 1863 to 2 January 1864 the Union party held its convention there to nominate candidates for the 19 January election, at which the new constitution was to be ratified by the voters. It is likely that Clemens wrote the present letter to his mother on 2 January, the day the Union party convention concluded, to inform her immediately of Orion's nomination for the position of secretary of state. In addition to that news, the missing portion of the letter may have contained other information in the following passage of "Doings in Nevada":

> We do not fool away much time in this country. As soon as the Constitution was duly framed and ready for ratification or rejection by the people, a convention to nominate candidates for State offices met at Carson. It finished its labors day before yesterday. The following nominations were made: For Governor, M. N. Mitchell; Lieutenant-Governor, M. S. Thompson; Secretary of State, Orion Clemens; Treasurer, Wm. B. Hickok; Member of Congress, John B. Winters; Superintendant Public Instruction, Rev. A. F. White. Now, that ticket will be elected, but the Constitution won't.

As Clemens expected, the proposed state constitution was rejected on 19 January. Unfortunately, that meant that the election the same day of Orion and the other Union party candidates was nullified. A new constitution was approved on 7 September 1864, and on 31 October Nevada became the thirty-sixth state (Angel, 84–87; Mack 1936, 250–53). In 1866 Orion briefly served under the state government (see 18 Oct 64 to OC, n. 2).

[5] Humorist Charles Farrar Browne (1834–67), better known as Artemus Ward, arrived in Virginia City on 18 December 1863 and four days later lectured at recently built Maguire's Opera House ("Artemus Ward," Virginia City *Evening Bulletin*, 19 Dec 63, 3; Angel, 572). According to Dan De Quille, Ward "remained on the Comstock several days, making the *Enterprise* his headquarters. Mark Twain and I had the pleasure of showing him the town, and a real pleasure it was—a sort of circus, in fact" (William Wright 1893b, 14). Christmas Eve 1863, as Joseph T. Goodman recalled years later, was a typically raucous occasion:

> About midnight, as usual, he [Ward] turned up in the *Enterprise* office and commanded the editorial slaves to have done with their work, as his royal highness proposed to treat them to an oyster supper. . . . Artemus Ward, Mark Twain, Dan de Quille, Denis McCarthy, [Edward P.] Hingston [Ward's manager] and myself sat about the table. . . . Then begun a flow and reflow of humor it would be presumptuous in me to attempt to even outline. It was on that occasion that Mark Twain fully demonstrated his right to rank above the world's acknowledged foremost humorist. . . . Course succeeded course and wine followed wine,

until day began to break. . . . The first streaks of dawn were brightening the east when we went into the streets.

"I cant walk on the earth," said Artemus. "I feel like walking on the skies, but as I can't I'll walk on the roofs."

And he clambered up a shed to the tops of the one-story houses, with Mark Twain after him, and commenced a wild scramble from roof to roof. Following them along the street we saw a policeman crouched low, with his pistol drawn and cocked.

"What are you doing?"

"S-s-s-h! Do you see those burglars up there?"

"Burglars! Why, they are Artemus Ward and Mark Twain."

"Well, I'll be d——d!" said the vigilant watchman. "But you can just tell them for me that they had the closest call they are ever likely to get in their lives."

As the sun rose above the desert range and gilded the Sugar Loaf, Mount Davidson and Cedar Hill it shone likewise upon the porch of Fred Getzler's saloon, where, astride a barrel, sat Mark Twain, whom Artemus Ward, with a spoon, was diligently doping with mustard, while he inquired of bystanders if they had ever seen a more perfect presentment of a subjugated idiot. (Goodman, 1)

Ward left Virginia City by stagecoach, probably on 29 December, bound for Salt Lake City. Reaching Austin, Nevada, some two hundred miles from Virginia City, on 31 December, he stopped to lecture. On 1 January 1864 he wrote to Clemens from Austin, "I shall always remember Virginia as a bright spot in my existence, as all others must or rather cannot be, as it were" (CU-MARK, in *MTL*, 1:94). After lecturing in Utah, Ward performed in Colorado and then in several midwestern cities, including St. Louis. Illness prevented him from visiting the Moffett home, where Jane Clemens was living (Seitz, 128–62; *MTBus*, 81).

[6] Before leaving Virginia City, Ward had presumably promised to intercede with the *Mercury*, a pledge he reiterated in his 1 January letter: "I shall write, soon, a powerfully convincing note to my friends of 'The Mercury.'" Clemens did not receive Ward's letter until 10 January because it had been "sloshing around between Virginia and Carson for awhile" (SLC 1864a, 4:4). Evidently assuming that Ward had already contacted the New York paper, on 4 January 1864 Clemens wrote his "Doings in Nevada" letter to "*Editor T. T.*"—the editor of the *Mercury*'s "Sunday Table-Talk" column.

[7] Ward went to England, but not until June 1866 (Seitz, 184). At that time Clemens was in the Sandwich Islands.

[8] Fitz Hugh Ludlow (1836–70) was one of New York's Bohemians. He achieved notoriety with *The Hasheesh Eater: Being Passages from the Life of a Pythagorean* (1857), an account of his experience with drugs. He was an editor of *Vanity Fair* for two years (1858–60), and he contributed to several eastern journals. In the fall of 1863 he visited the West—including three days in Virginia City and a longer stay in San Francisco—and described his travels for the *Atlantic Monthly* in a series of articles published in 1864. Ludlow had been particularly welcomed by the Bohemian writers for the San Francisco *Golden Era* and became a contributor to that journal (Wilson and Fiske, 4:50–51; Walker 1969, 163–66). His "high encomium upon Mark Twain" appeared there on 22 November 1863: "In funny literature, that Irresistible Washoe Giant, Mark Twain, takes quite a unique position. He makes me laugh more than any Californian since poor Derby died. He imitates nobody. He is a school by himself" (Fitz Hugh Ludlow, 4).

[9] The illegible deletion appears to be at most three characters long, and it is possible that Clemens also tore the paper at this point in order to further tantalize his mother with a deletion clearly *not* intended to be read.

To Jane Lampton Clemens and Pamela A. Moffett
9 and 10 January 1864 • Carson City, Nev. Terr.
(MS: CU-MARK)

TERRITORY OF NEVADA,
SECRETARY'S OFFICE,
CARSON CITY, Jan. 9, 186 4.[1]

My ₫ Dear Mother & Sister

2 P. M. Sunday—I thought of writing you a letter, but I expect I shall not; I just got up a little while ago; went to bed at 7 o'clock this morning; I was out visiting the girls until 10 o'clock (they were in bed when we got there—but we were not in a hurry—we waited until the[y] got up & dressed again—they had been out to a ball all the previous night.) I wrote the balance of the night—an article for the New York Sunday Mercury. If I send it at all, it will be in a few days, & consequently it may appear the first Sunday or so after you get this. You tell Beck Jolly to get a ~~copy~~ lot of those papers & stick them around everywhere there is any one acquainted with Zeb Leavenworth, & drive the old fool into the river. The article contains ⱥ ˌan absurdˌ certificate for a patent medicine, purporting to come from "Mr. Zeb. Leavenworth, of St. Louis, Mo." I wrote it especially for Beck Jolly's useˌ—so he could pester Zeb.[2]

Well, I won't write any more now. Ma, we are going to send for you in the Spring. Make Aunt Betsy Smith[3] come out with you—~~sh~~ you two would enjoy yourselves in Carson & Virginia, you *bet* you! Then I could burlesque you occasionally, you know.

All are well. Good bye. ~~Lege~~ Legislature meets day after to-morrow.[4]

Yrs
Sam L. Clemens

---

[1] Clemens wrote his dateline, and probably his salutation, on Saturday, 9 January. He wrote the rest of the letter the following day.

[2] "Those Blasted Children," Mark Twain's second contribution to the New York *Sunday Mercury*, was published on 21 February 1864 (*ET&S1*, 347–56). It included a bogus letter addressed to "Mr. Mark Twain" by "Zeb. Leavenworth"

of St. Louis, testifying to Mark Twain's "sovereign remedy" for stammering children—sawing off the child's underjaw. Leavenworth and Jolly were pilot friends
of Clemens's from his days as a cub aboard the *John J. Roe.*
³ Elizabeth W. Smith.
⁴ The third Territorial Legislature met in Carson City from 12 January to 20
February 1864. Clemens reported the proceedings for the *Territorial Enterprise*
(see *MTEnt*, 130–78).

To Seymour Pixley and G. A. Sears
23 January 1864 • Carson City, Nev. Terr.
(Carson City *Independent*, 24 Jan 64)

CARSON, Jan. 23, 1864.

Gentlemen:—Certainly. If the public can find anything in a grave
state paper worth paying a dollar for, I am willing they should pay that
amount or any other. And although I am not a very dusty christian myself,
I take an absorbing interest in religious affairs, and would willingly inflict
my annual message upon the church itself if it might derive benefit thereby. You can charge what you please; I promise the public no amusement,
but I do promise a reasonable amount of instruction. I am responsible to
the Third House only, and I hope to be permitted to make it exceedingly
warm for that body, without caring whether the sympathies of the public
and the Church be enlisted in their favor and against myself or not.¹

Respectfully,

MARK TWAIN.

¹ Clemens was responding to the following request:

CARSON, Jan. 23, 1864.
    Gov. Mark Twain:—Understanding from certain members of the Third House of the
Territorial Legislature, that that body will have effected a permanent organization within a
day or two, and be ready for the reception of your Third Annual Message, we desire to ask
your permission, and that of the Third House, to turn the affair to the benefit of the Church
by charging toll-road, franchises, and other persons, a dollar apiece for the privilege of
listening to your communication.

S. PIXLEY,
G. A. SEARS.
Trustees
("Local Matters," Carson City *Independent*, undated clipping in Scrapbook 4:3, CU-
MARK)
    G. A. Sears and Seymour Pixley were trustees of the First Presbyterian Church in
Carson City, whose building, begun in the summer of 1862, was not completed
until May 1864 (Angel, 214–15). The Third House was a mock legislative body
in existence at least as late as 1901. At its informal meetings—in saloons, public

buildings, and the legislative chambers—legislators and other officials were frequently among those participating in burlesque deliberations and law making (*MTEnt*, 100–101; Doten 1973, 2:1572, 3:1658, 1839, 2098). Clemens had been elected president of the Third House at its meeting on 11 December 1863, after the adjournment of the first Nevada Constitutional Convention, and his remarks to that body were published in the *Enterprise* on 13 December (SLC 1863n, 3:55). But the text of his Third Annual Message to the Third House, delivered on 27 January 1864 at the Ormsby County Courthouse in Carson City while the third Territorial Legislature was in session, is not extant; probably he never acted on the promise he made in his 28 January legislative report to the *Enterprise* to "correct, amend and publish the message" (SLC 1864c, 3:140; see 18 Mar 64 to PAM). His friend Clement T. Rice, reporter for the Virginia City *Union*, commented on 29 January: "Mark Two's message only helped to keep up the effervescing spirit of the good work in behalf of that same, ever-present, gaping skeleton of a church. The benefit on this occasion was large—perhaps $200—which will take the institution in out of the weather and hasten its completion very materially" (Rice 1864, 1).

To J. T. Goodman and Company
29 February 1864 • Virginia City, Nev. Terr.
(MS: CU-MARK)

$150⁰⁰

Virginia, Feb 2̶8̶ 29, 1864.

J. T. Goodman & Co.

Please pay Orion Clemens One Hundred & Fifty Dollars ($150) upon delivery of this Order.

Sam L. Clemens

To Pamela A. Moffett
18 March 1864 • Virginia City, Nev. Terr.
(MS: CU-MARK and NPV)

Va, March 18/64.

My Dear M̶o̶t̶ Sister

(I will not write to Ma, b̶e̶c̶ this time, because in a day or two I shall write to her through the columns of the N. Y. Sunday Mercury.)[1] I would have m̶a̶i̶l̶e̶d̶ finished it to-day, but I took it over to show it to Miss

Menken, the actress—Orpheus C. Kerr's wife—she is a literary cuss herself.[2] Although I was acquainted with Orpheus, I didn't ˏknowˏ her from
the devil,[3] & the other day (I am acting in place of *both* the chief editors,
now, & Dan has the local all to himself,)[4] she sent a ~~note~~ brief note,
couched in stately terms & full of frozen dignity, addressed to "Mr Mark
Twain," asking if we would publish a sketch from her pen. Now you ought
to have seen my answer—ˏ(3 pages of "legal capˏ,")ˏ because I took a good
deal of pride in it. It was extravagantly sociable & familiar, but I swear it
had humor in it, because I laughed at it myself. It was bad enough as it
was when first finished—but I took it out of the envelop & added an extra
atrocity. She has a beautiful white hand—but her handwriting is infamous; she writes very fast, ~~but~~ ˏandˏ her ~~letters~~ chirography is of the door-
plate order—her letters are immense. I gave her a conundrum—thus:
"My Dear Madam—Why ought your hand to retain its present grace &
beauty always? Because you fool away devilish little of it on your manuscript."

I think I can safely say that woman was furious for a few days. But
that wasn't a matter of much consequence to me, & finally she got over it
of her own accord, & wrote another note. She is friendly, now.[5]

Pamela, you wouldn't do for a local reporter—because ~~do~~ you don't
appreciate the interest that attaches to *names*. An item is of no use unless
it speaks of some *person*, & ~~then~~ not then, unless that person's *name* is
distinctly mentioned. The most interesting letter one can write, to an
absent friend, is one that treats of *persons* he has been acquainted with,
rather than the public events of the day. Now you speak of a young lady
who wrote to Hallie Benson that she had seen me, & you didn't mention
her *name*. It was just a mere chance that I ever guessed who she was—but
I did, finally, though I don't remember her name, now. I was introduced
to her in San Francisco by Hon A. B. Paul,[6] & saw her afterwards in Gold
Hill. They were a very pleasant lot of girls—she & her sisters.

You say "we hear that Sam has grown very fleshy & remarkably
broad-shouldered—you must send us a full-length likeness, & let us see
the improvement." I'll do it—here it is:

[*four-line space (about two inches): portrait missing*]

I have no confidence in photographic artists, & I drew the picture myself,
so that I would *know* it was correct. I had to borrow the head from a
photograph, though—those fellows take heads very well. If this is too
broad for Annie's album, tell her she must paste it on the back of it. I

don't want it lost, because it cost me infinite pains & labor to make it. I would,n't, have undertaken such a job for anybody but her.[7]

I also send her full-length pictures of ~~Go~~ his Excellency Gov. Mark Twain, of the Third House, Hon Wm H. Clagett of the House of Representatives, and Hon. A. J. Simmons, Speaker of the same.[8] Ma will know Clagett by his frowsy hair & slovenly dress. He is the ~~greatest~~ ,ablest, public speaker in the Territory.

I can't send you my Message. It was written to be *spoken*—~~it~~ to write it so that it would *read* well, would be∮ too much trouble, & I shall probably never publish it. It was terribly severe on Gov. Nye, too, & since he has conferred on me one of the coveted Notarial appointments (without the formality of a *petition* from the people,) it would be a mean return to print it now.[9] If he had refused the appointment, though, I'd have delivered it in Virginia (I could have got the whole community at a dollar a head,) & published it afterward. You bet you. I got my satisfaction out of it, though—a larger audience than Artemus had[10]—the ~~satis~~ comfort of knowing that the ~~thieving, lousy~~ slow,,-going,, ~~ratty popul~~ careless population of Carson *could* be induced to fill a house *once,*—the gratification of ~~her~~ hearing good judges say it was the best thing of the kind they had ever listened to—& finally, a present of handsome $225^{00} gold watch, from Theodore Winters & Hon. A.W. Baldwin, inscribed "To Gov. Mark Twain," &c. &c.[11] I am ahead on the Message, anyhow.

Pepper saw Judge Mott, did he? I promised to write to Mott occasionally, & so did Orion, but I guess neither of us have ever done it.[12]

Remember me kindly to Mr P̸ & Mrs Pepper, & Zeb & Beck Jolly.

We had a little snow to-day, & once, 3 months ago, a few ~~flas~~ flakes fell—but at no time this winter has it been necessary to wear an overcoat. I have no recollection of having seen rain—either here or in California—for I don't know how long—nearly a year & a half, I suppose. [I went & raised the devil & had the paper started to Moffett & Schr again.[13] Tell me if it arrives regularly.

Sam.

(over

Joe Goodman is gone to the Sandwich Islands. I stipulated, when I took his place, that I should never be expected to write editorials about politics or ~~the~~ eastern news. I take no sort of interest in those matters. I wanted to go with Joe, but the news-editor[14] was expecting every day to get sick (he has since accomplished it,) & we could not all leave at once.[15]

Molly & Orion are all right, I guess.[16] They would write me if I would answer there letters—but I won't. It is torture to me to write a letter. And it is still *greater* torture to receive one—except yours & Ma's. My correspondents, being industriously neglected, are gradually dropping off, though, & I begin to ɟ feel really comfortable over the prospect of their drying up entirely. I think Ma inflicts a new correspondent on me every now & then (bel (beware how you leave this letter where Aunt Ella[17] can see it—I haven't answered her letter of 3 months ago) but she mustn't scare up any more, male or female, though I am really thankful to her for her intended & well-meant kindness.

Sam

---

[1] No such communication has been found in the *Mercury*. The sketch Clemens promises "may never have been written, or it may have been an early version of 'An Open Letter to the American People'. . . which teases his mother about her style of letter writing; it was not published in the *Mercury* but in the New York *Weekly Review*, almost two years later, on 17 February 1866" (*ET&S1*, 350; see *ET&S3*, no. 181).

[2] Adah Isaacs Menken (1835?–68) had arrived in Virginia City on 27 February 1864 after dazzling California audiences for some six months with a repertoire of her favorite plays. While in Virginia City throughout March, she titillated theater-goers in the title role of *Mazeppa*, Henry M. Milner's dramatic adaptation of Byron's poem, in which she wore flesh-colored tights to simulate nudity, earning the sobriquet "the great unadorned" ("Miss Menken," Unionville *Humboldt Register*, 19 Mar 64, 2). Nevada newspaper gossip suggests that offstage "the Menken" was almost as visible. She was rumored to have abandoned her third husband, satirist Orpheus C. Kerr (Robert Henry Newell, 1836–1901), who was traveling with her, in favor of a local horse trainer. She engaged in a jealous quarrel with an actress in her troupe. And in public ceremonies she received a silver brick and honorary membership in Fire Engine Company No. 2. Menken characterized her Virginia City stay as "one of the pleasantest months of my life" (" 'The Dying Menken' Thinks of Virginia City," Virginia City *Territorial Enterprise*, 16 Sept 68, 2). A would-be poet as well as an actress, Menken had published some of her unrestrained free verse in the San Francisco *Golden Era* and elsewhere; *Infelicia* (London, 1868), a collection of her poems, appeared posthumously ("Menken," Virginia City *Union*, 27 Feb 64, 3; *NAW*, 2:526–27).

[3] Clemens had, however, seen Menken in September 1863 in San Francisco performances of *Mazeppa* and John Thomas Haines's *The French Spy*, both of which he reviewed for the *Territorial Enterprise* of 17 September. Her acting in the former play, he felt, resembled the contortions of a violent "lunatic": "She bends herself back like a bow; she pitches headforemost at the atmosphere like a battering-ram; she works her arms, and her legs, and her whole body like a dancing-jack. . . . she 'whallops' herself down on the stage, and rolls over as does the sportive pack-mule after his burden is removed." But in *The French Spy*, in the role of "a frisky Frenchman . . . as dumb as an oyster," her "extravagant gesticulations do not seem so overdone. . . . She don't talk well, and as she goes on her

Adah Isaacs Menken as Mazeppa,
from a contemporary showbill (Lyman, facing 269).

shape and her acting, the character of a fidgety 'dummy' is peculiarly suited to her line of business" (SLC 1863h, 2:78).

[4] By "chief editors," Clemens meant Joseph T. Goodman, co-owner of the *Enterprise*, and, possibly, Rollin M. Daggett (see 17 Sept 64 to Wright, n. 3). Denis E. McCarthy, Goodman's partner, managed the *Enterprise* print shop. Dan De Quille (William Wright, 1829–98) was local editor of the paper from 1862 to 1898. He was born in Ohio and lived there and then in Iowa until 1857, when he migrated to California. A miner in both California and Nevada before joining the staff of the *Enterprise*, Wright became widely recognized as an authority on mining, as well as a humorist. His *History of the Big Bonanza* (Hartford: American Publishing Company, 1876), written with Clemens's encouragement and published with his assistance, remains a definitive account of the mines of the Comstock lode (see William Wright 1876, vii–xxv).

[5] Menken soon became friendly enough to invite Clemens to an unusual literary dinner in her hotel room, the only other guests being Dan De Quille and the Bohemian poet Ada Clare (Jane McElhinney, 1836?–74). Menken's husband was

barred from the room. According to Dan De Quille, the evening terminated ignominiously when Clemens, aiming a kick at one of the actress's numerous dogs, accidentally "hit the Menken's pet corn, causing her to bound from her seat, throw herself on a lounge and roll and roar in agony. . . . Mark disliked the Menken and would have avoided the arrangement that seated him by her side had it been possible. After this mishap nothing could propitiate Mark. He very soon imagined a pressing engagement and begged to be excused" (William Wright 1893b, 14).

[6] Almarin B. Paul (1823–1909) was a prominent quartz miner and mill operator from Nevada City, California. According to most authorities, in August 1860 he began operating the first mill in Nevada Territory, the Pioneer Mill of the Washoe Gold and Silver Mining Company at Devil's Gate in Gold Cañon. He was also a discoverer of the Washoe wet process of crushing ore and the inventor of an improved type of separator. By the time of Clemens's letter, Paul—a Gold Hill banker and the owner of several mills and extensive mining and timber lands—was reputed to be one of Nevada's wealthiest men (Irvine, 2:671–73; Paul 1927, 54; Angel, 68, 503; Lord, 84–88; Lyman, 136–37; Elliott, 95–96; Kelly 1863, 329, 345; Paul 1861, 1).

[7] The beneficiary of Clemens's efforts was his niece, Annie Moffett.

[8] Clemens and A. J. Simmons may have met while both were prospecting in the Humboldt region. Simmons migrated to the Santa Clara district, Humboldt County, in the summer of 1861 from Red Bluff, California, and sent back letters to the Sacramento *Union* and the Red Bluff *Beacon*. He located numerous claims, helped draft resolutions governing the district organization of mining companies, and became an officer in several of those companies. On 27 December 1862 he sold Clemens, for $1,000, ten feet in the Butte ledge, Tehama Mining Company, and ten feet in the Kentucky ledge, Union Tunnel Company, both in the Santa Clara district of Humboldt County (deed in CU-MARK). Simmons was elected a Humboldt representative to the 1862 second Territorial Legislature, and was chosen Speaker of the House in the 1864 third Territorial Legislature (Simmons 1861a, 1; Simmons 1861b, 1; "A. J. Simmons," Red Bluff [Calif.] *Beacon*, 27 Dec 62, 3). The photograph Clemens sent has not been found, but it was probably another print of the one reproduced here—presumably without the inscription, which has not been explained.

[9] "An Act to provide for the Appointment of Notaries Public, and Defining their Duties," passed on 9 February and effective on 1 March, revoked the more than two hundred existing notary licenses. It limited the number of new notaries to a total of seventy-two for Nevada Territory's ten existing counties, allotted six to any new county created, and specified that all notaries be appointed by the governor (*Laws* 1864, 46–48). In a letter to the *Territorial Enterprise* written on 6 February, Clemens described the fierce competition for these lucrative positions which developed in anticipation of this law: "There are seventeen hundred and forty-two applications for notaryships already on file in the Governor's office" (SLC 1864e, 3:103). In fact at least one thousand applications, many accompanied by lengthy petitions signed by influential backers, were filed. Clemens himself was "seized with the fatal distemper" and "wrote a petition with frantic haste, appended a copy of the Directory of Nevada Territory to it, and . . . fled down the deserted streets to the Governor's office" (SLC 1864e, 3:103). The petition accompanying Clemens's application was signed by Orion Clemens, Thomas C.

William H. Clagett, Mark Twain, and A. J. Simmons, January 1864,
the third Territorial Legislature, Carson City (Lyman, facing 253).

Nye (the governor's nephew), Territorial Auditor William W. Ross, and Ross's
clerk and legislative attaché, F. A. Hollister. On 1 March Governor Nye appointed Clemens to a two-year term as notary for Storey County, and two days
later an advertisement for Henry L. Blodgett and Sam. L. Clemens, notaries
public, with quarters in the post office, began running in the Virginia City *Evening Bulletin*. For reasons Clemens never made clear, on 14 April he wrote the
next letter, relinquishing his appointment (see Rocha and Smith, 83–90, and
Nevada, 5).

[10] Artemus Ward had lectured in Virginia City on 22 December 1863.

[11] Theodore Winters (1823–1906), brother of John D. Winters, was an Illi-
noisan who settled in Washoe Valley in 1857 and soon became wealthy through
his holdings in the Ophir and Spanish mines. For many years he was a successful
rancher and stockman, specializing in the breeding and racing of horses. In Feb-

ruary 1864 Clemens had attended a lavish party at his mansion near Washoe City (see *ET&S1*, 339–42). Alexander W. (Sandy) Baldwin (1840–69) was a Georgian who emigrated to California and then to Nevada. He was considered an outstanding attorney, and became William M. Stewart's law partner. Baldwin was a councilman from Storey County in the third Territorial Legislature (1864) and in 1865 was appointed United States district judge for Nevada (Andrew J. Marsh, 681 n. 147). On 27 November 1869, after Baldwin's death in a railway accident, Clemens eulogized him in the Buffalo *Express* (SLC 1869b, 2). In his 28 January 1864 dispatch to the *Territorial Enterprise*, Clemens called Baldwin's and Winters's gift to him "a pretty good result for an incipient oratorical slouch like me" (SLC 1864c, 3:140).

[12] Judge Gordon N. Mott had resigned from the Nevada bench in September 1863 as a consequence of the Chollar-Potosi suit (see 21 Oct 62 to OC and MEC, nn. 3, 4). In November 1863 he had returned to Washington, D.C., to resume his duties as territorial representative to Congress. Samuel Pepper (1820–93), a clerk aboard the *John J. Roe* during Clemens's piloting days and in 1862 captain of the steamboat *Champion*, lived near the Moffetts in St. Louis. He was the brother-in-law of Zebulon Leavenworth, pilot of the *Roe*, mentioned in the next paragraph ("Samuel Pepper Dead," unidentified clipping in MoSHi; *N&J2*, 465 nn. 114, 118).

[13] That is, the firm of William A. Moffett and George Schroter, St. Louis commission merchants.

[14] Possibly Charles A. V. Putnam, "telegraph, paragraph and scissoring editor" of the *Enterprise*, one of several men who at various times had news-editing responsibilities (Doten 1973, 3:2227–28; William Wright 1893a, 15). He later was Nevada state printer.

[15] In chapter 55 of *Roughing It*, Clemens gave this account of his stint as Goodman's replacement:

Mr. Goodman went away for a week and left me the post of chief editor. It destroyed me. The first day, I wrote my "leader" in the forenoon. The second day, I had no subject and put it off till the afternoon. The third day I put it off till evening, and then copied an elaborate editorial out of the "American Cyclopedia," that steadfast friend of the editor, all over the land. The fourth day I "fooled around" till midnight, and then fell back on the Cyclopedia again. The fifth day I cudgeled my brain till midnight, and then kept the press waiting while I penned some bitter personalities on six different people. The sixth day I labored in anguish till far into the night and brought forth—nothing. The paper went to press without an editorial. The seventh day I resigned. On the eighth, Mr. Goodman returned and found six duels on his hands—my personalities had borne fruit.

In fact, Goodman was away until 8 April ("Arrivals Yesterday," Virginia City *Union*, 9 Apr 64, 3). There is no indication that he faced any challenges as a result of Clemens's temporary editorship.

[16] Orion and Mollie Clemens's only child, eight-year-old Jennie, had died of "spotted fever" (cerebrospinal meningitis) on 1 February 1864 in Carson City (MEC, 15).

[17] Ella Hunter Lampton.

To Orion Clemens
14 April 1864 • Virginia City, Nev. Terr.
(*Proclamations*, 251: Nv-Ar)

Virginia N.T. April 14ᵗʰ 1864

Hon O Clemens
    Acting Governor &c
    I hereby resign my Commission as a Notary Public in and for the County of Storey N.T. The same having been granted me on or about the 1ˢᵗ of March of the present year.

Sam' L. Clemens

[*Orion Clemens's notation on the letter:*]
Received and accepted ⎱
April 15th 1864   ⎰
    Orion Clemens
    Acting Governor N.T.

To Jane Lampton Clemens and Pamela A. Moffett
17 May 1864 • Virginia City, Nev. Terr.
(Unidentified newspaper clipping: CU-MARK)

VIRGINIA CITY, Nevada Territory, midnight.—I don't know the day of the month or of the week; consult the postmark.[1]

My Dear Mother and Sister: I had rather die in Washoe than *live* in some countries. The old California motto is applicable here: "We have lived like paupers that we might give like princes."[2] Virginia is only a small town, about three times as large as Hannibal, and Gold Hill is about the same size as Hannibal. Silver City and Dayton are mere villages—but you ought to see them roll out the twenty dollar pieces when their blood is up. It makes no difference what the object is, if you just get them stirred up once they are bound to respond.

I think they like that Sanitary Fund because it affords them such a bully opportunity of giving away their money.[3] They are slow until you move them, though. When Pamela wrote us to try and do something for the St. Louis Fair,[4] I went after the President of the Storey County Sanitary Commission, who is an old St. Louisian[5]—I had never taken much interest in sanitary matters before.[6] He went to work sending calls to the several counties to contribute, and I, being chief of our editorial corps, then, went to scribbling editorials. But we couldn't make the riffle.[7]

Paul got the ladies of Gold Hill to give a ball, and a silver brick worth $3,000 was the result, but that wouldn't go far, you know.[8] Then we got up a meeting in Virginia, and only got $1,500 or $1,800, and that made us sick. We tried it again, and almost concluded to disband the audience without trying to do anything—but we went on, kept it up all the afternoon and raised $3,500, and had about concluded it was no use to try to get up a sanitary excitement.[9] We began to think we were going to make a mighty poor show at the St. Louis Fair, when along came RUEL GRIDLEY, (you remember him) whom I hadn't seen for 15 years, and he brought help. He is a Copperhead, or as he calls himself, "Union to the backbone, but a Copperhead in sympathies."[10] He lives in Austin, Reese river—a town half as big as Hannibal. He made an eccentric wager with a Republican named Hereford[11] that if a Republican Mayor were elected there, he would give Hereford a 50-pound sack of flour, and carry it to him on his shoulder, a mile and a quarter, with a brass band at his heels playing "John Brown," and if a Democrat were elected, Hereford was to carry the flour to the tune of "Dixie." Ruel lost the bet,[12] and carried the flour, with the band and the whole town at his heels. Hereford gave the flour back to Ruel, and about that time one of Paul's letters arrived, and Ruel put the flour up at auction and sold it for the benefit of the St. Louis Fair for five thousand three hundred dollars. The news came here, but it didn't work on the people much. However, when Ruel got here yesterday, with his sack, on his way to the States,[13] Paul thought we might make some use of it. We put it up at auction and it only brought five or six hundred dollars.[14] He lives in Gold Hill, and he said he was so disgusted with Virginia that he would try his own town, and if she failed he would leave the country. This morning at eleven o'clock he had two open carriages—one for reporters and the other for the speakers—got a brass band and we started for Gold Hill. When we got there Ruel gave the history of the flour sack, and said that from what he could see people outside of Austin didn't care much for flour. But they soon made him sing small. Gold Hill raised Austin out of her boots, and paid nearly seven thousand dollars in gold for the sack of flour. Ruel threw up the sponge![15]

Then we went down to little Silver City and sold it for $1,500 or $1,700. From there we went to the village of Dayton and sold it for somewhere in the neighborhood of $2,000. Carson is considerably larger than either of these three towns, but it has a lousy, lazy, worthless, poverty-stricken population, and the universal opinion was that we couldn't raise $500 dollars there. So we started home again about $10,000 better off than when we left in the morning.

We got to Gold Hill at 4 in the afternoon, and found the streets crowded, and they hailed us from all sides with "Virginia's boomin'!" "Virginia's mad!" "Virginia's got her back up!" "You better go 'long to Virginia; they say they'll be d—d if the whole Territory combined shall beat them!" and a hundred other such exclamations. Wherefore we journeyed into Virginia with a long procession at our heels, coming up to see the fun.[16] We got to the meeting place after dark, and found the neighboring buildings illuminated and the adjacent streets completely blocked up with people. Then the fun commenced, and I wished Pamela could have been there to see her own private project bringing forth its fruit and culminating in such a sweeping excitement away out here among barren mountains, while she herself, unconscious of what her hands had done, and unaware of the row she was kicking up, was probably sitting quietly at home and thinking it a dreary sort of a world, full of disappointments, and labors unrequited, and hopes unblessed with fruition. I speak of the row as hers, for if she had not written us, the St. Louis Fair would probably have never heard from Washoe. She has certainly secured $30,000 or $40,000 worth of greenbacks from us by her own efforts.[17]

Well, the fun commenced, and the very first dash made Austin take a back seat, and strode half way up the Gold Hill. It was a bid for the sack of flour by the men employed in the Gould & Curry mine and mill, of three thousand five hundred dollars! They went ahead of Austin two hundred dollars. Then followed half a dozen bids of five hundred dollars each, and the thing was fairly under way. In two hours and a half Virginia cleaned out the Territory and paid nearly $13,000 for the sack of flour! How's that? Nearly a dollar a head for every man, woman and child in the camp, in two hours and a half; and on four hours' notice. New York couldn't come up to that ratio in the same length of time. And then the offices of all our big mines are located in San Francisco, and when that city makes a big dash for the Sanitary fund, the heaviest end of it comes always from those very offices.

The other day the *Daily Union* gave $200, and I gave $300, under instructions from the proprietors always to "go them a hundred better." To-night the *Union* bid $100, and I bid $150 for the *Enterprise*. I had to go to the office to make up my report, and the *Union* fellows came back and bid another $100. It was provoking, because I had orders to run our bid up to $1,000, if necessary, and I only struck the *Union* lightly to draw them on. But I guess we'll make them hunt their holes yet, before we are done with them.[18]

If I have time to-morrow, I will send a dispatch, by request, to the St. Louis *Republican*.[19]

I stated in the paper once that Virginia could raise half a ton of pure silver in six hours for the St. Louis Fair, if they could get her mad—she went over that weight to-night in two hours and a half. If all our bars for the St. Louis Fair had no gold in them, their weight would not fall far short of a ton.

Yours affectionately,

SAM.

[1] Clemens's account in this letter of events of 15 and 16 May 1864 establishes that the date was Tuesday, 17 May. The St. Louis newspaper that published the letter gave it the following introduction: "A lady of this city put the ball in motion which rolled on and raised for our Sanitary Fair the gold bricks and silver bars from Nevada. The following interesting letter gives the *modus operandi* of 'raising the wind' in Washoe. It is very readable both for its style and its facts." The "lady of this city" was Pamela A. Moffett, who clearly was also responsible for publication of her brother's letter.

[2] Unidentified.

[3] Two major "sanitary" organizations were established in 1861 to raise funds for the relief of sick and wounded Union soldiers: the United States Sanitary Commission, headed by the Reverend Henry Whitney Bellows; and the Western Sanitary Commission, headed by James E. Yeatman and based in St. Louis, whose relief operations extended only to the armies of the Western Department. By January 1866, the combined organizations had raised about $5.7 million in cash and an estimated $18.5 million worth of supplies. California's and Nevada's cash contributions were $1,234,000 and $108,000, respectively (Scharf, 1:542, 549; Stillé, 69, 546, 548–49).

[4] In February 1864 a group of St. Louis citizens, with the backing of Generals Ulysses S. Grant and William S. Rosecrans, laid plans for a Mississippi Valley Sanitary Fair to raise funds for the Western Sanitary Commission. With the strong support of leading merchants, bankers, and local chapters of the Ladies' Union Aid Society and the Ladies' Loyal League, the fair opened in St. Louis on

17 May 1864, ran for about a month, and realized approximately $600,000 (Scharf, 1:553–55).

⁵Almarin B. Paul, who had lived in St. Louis from 1833 to 1845 and was a graduate of St. Louis University (Irvine, 2:671). On 23 March 1864, Paul had distributed a circular issued by the officers of the Mississippi Valley Sanitary Fair, which Pamela Moffett doubtless had forwarded to Clemens. In it the fair's officers appealed for contributions of money and goods of all kinds. Paul accompanied the circular with his own appeal to all of Nevada, which included this promise: "The citizens of Storey county, whose liberal outpourings have netted about $45,000 to the New York Commission, intend sending a contribution of silver bars to this St. Louis Fair" (Paul 1864a, 2). Paul's efforts were officially recognized on 27 April with his appointment by the fair's honorary president, General William S. Rosecrans, as "a Special Agent . . . to solicit donations from auxiliary societies, and co-operate generally for the benefit of said Fair" (Rosecrans, 3). Throughout April the Virginia City *Evening Bulletin* and the *Union* publicized the fair and appealed for donations. The *Enterprise* very likely did the same, although this cannot be verified since no complete files survive for this period.

⁶Clemens had evidently given little notice in print to sanitary-fund activities. His surviving remarks, all supportive, appeared in the *Territorial Enterprise* on 10 January and 10 November 1863 and 28 April 1864, and in the San Francisco *Morning Call* on 3 September 1863 (see: *ET&S1*, 183–87, 284–87, 400; SLC 1863i, 2:110; and SLC 1864f, 3:144). He was about to become embroiled in controversy as a result of sanitary-fund commentaries he published in the *Enterprise* on the day of this letter and the day following it.

⁷"To make the riffle" was "to cross a riffle or rapid, to succeed in an undertaking." The expression also had mining associations since a riffle could be "a bar, slat, or other obstruction placed across the bottom of a sluice box or other gold-washing apparatus to arrest particles of gold" (Mathews, 2:1395).

⁸The Gold Hill ball was held on Wednesday night, 20 April, and took in $3,080 after expenses (Virginia City *Union*: "Concert and Ball To-night," 20 Apr 64, 3; "Sanitary Society at Gold Hill," 27 Apr 64, 3).

⁹At the first of these meetings, held in Maguire's Opera House on 1 May, a small audience subscribed about $1,800. The speakers then were Almarin B. Paul and Thomas Fitch, the well-known lawyer, editor, and orator (see 11 Nov 64 to OC, n. 4). The second, larger gathering took place on 15 May, also in the opera house. The speakers were Fitch, William H. Clagett, and Emma Hardinge, an "Inspirational Speaker," who was in Virginia City to lecture on "Spiritualism and Kindred Sciences" ("New To-day," Virginia City *Union*, 15 May 64, 2). More than $3,700 in cash, mining stock, and a silver brick was raised (Virginia City *Union*: "Sanitary Meeting," 3 May 64, 3; "The Sanitary Meeting Sunday Afternoon," 17 May 64, 3).

¹⁰Reuel Colt Gridley (1829–70), although older than Clemens, had been a schoolmate of his in Hannibal. (Clemens—or the compositor—misspelled "Reuel" throughout this letter.) In 1846 or 1847, Gridley had joined an infantry company and gone off to fight in the Mexican War. He was now a partner in the grocery firm of Gridley, Hobart and Jacobs in Austin, Lander County, Nevada (Angel, 268).

¹¹Actually Dr. H. S. Herrick, "Republican, a native of New York, then holding a Federal position in connection with the Internal Revenue Department, and

Reuel Colt Gridley and the sack of
flour (Mack 1947, facing 289).

subsequently Superintendent of Schools" for Lander County. Herrick had also
been elected county assessor on 2 September 1863. Clemens may have confused
him with A. P. Hereford, elected senator from Lander County on 19 January 1864
under the defeated state constitution (Angel, 268, 462–64).

[12] On 19 April 1864, Charles Holbrook, the Republican candidate, defeated
David E. Buel, a Democrat, in the Austin mayoral election (Angel, 268).

[13] After auctioning the sack of flour repeatedly in Nevada and California, Gridley took it around the eastern states, spending more than a year on the road at his
own expense. He supposedly raised $175,000 (also reported as $275,000), in the
process "becoming from a positive secessionist an ardent Unionist. . . . Returning to Austin in poor health, he found his business much depressed and himself
overwhelmed in debt" (Angel, 270). He died a poor man in Paradise, California
(Elizabeth H. Smith, 11–18). Clemens included an account of Gridley's wager
and his efforts on behalf of the sanitary fund in chapter 45 of *Roughing It* and in
an Autobiographical Dictation of 16 March 1906 (CU-MARK, in *MTA*, 2:216–
18).

[14] During the 15 May meeting in Virginia City (see note 9) Gridley arrived from
Austin with the flour sack and put it up briefly for auction, bringing in $570 of the
total amount raised.

[15] In Austin, following the loss of his wager, Gridley had "performed the ceremony of delivering the sack, throwing up the sponge in token of surrender" (Angel, 269). He carried the same sponge with him to Gold Hill (SLC 1864g, 5).

[16] On 21 May, writing to the San Francisco *Evening Bulletin* under his pen name, "Cosmos," Almarin B. Paul gave an extended account of the daylong procession of carriages, bands, horsemen, foot soldiers, and pedestrians which—like other news reports—corroborates Clemens's present version. Paul credited Mark Twain, "a well known local reporter here," with dubbing the money-raising caravan the "Army of the Lord" (Paul 1864b, 1). For Clemens's published contemporary accounts of the event, see SLC 1864g, 5, and SLC 1864i, 1.

[17] By 6 June Storey County had sent almost $22,000 in gold and silver bars to the fair. The equivalent of approximately $39,000 in greenbacks, this was nearly two-thirds of Nevada Territory's entire contribution to that date. The treasurer of the fair, Samuel Copp, responded gratefully: "Well done, Storey county! She stands ahead—next to St. Louis in her liberal gifts to the M.S.V. Fair" (Copp, 3; "Progress of the Great Fair," St. Louis *Missouri Democrat*, 1 June 64, 4; Paul 1864c, 3; Virginia City *Union*: "Shipment of Sanitary Bars," 1 June 64, 3; "The Sanitary Bars," 8 June 64, 3).

[18] In response to the *Union*'s second bid of $100, Clemens published the following item in the *Enterprise* of 18 May:

How Is It?—While we had no representative at the mass meeting on Monday evening, the UNION overbid us for the flour—or at least ex-Alderman Bolan bid for that paper, and said that he would be responsible for the extra hundred dollars. He may have an opportunity, as we are told that the UNION (or its employés, whichever it is,) has repudiated the bid. We would like to know about this matter, if we may make so free. (SLC 1864h, 2)

[19] Clemens evidently did not fulfill this request: no dispatch likely to have been sent by him has been identified in the St. Louis *Missouri Republican*.

To Mary E. (Mollie) Clemens
20 May 1864 • Virginia City, Nev. Terr.
(MS: CU-MARK)

Virginia, May 20.

My Dear Mollie:

I have had nothing but trouble & vexation since the Sanitary trip, & now this letter comes to aggravate me a thousand times worse. If it were from a man, I would answer it with a challenge, as the easiest way of getting out of a bad scrape, although I know I am in the wrong & would not be justified in doing such a thing. I wrote the squib the ladies letter refers to, & although I could give the names of the parties who made the offensive remarks I shall not do it, because they were said in drunken jest and no harm was meant by them. But for a misfortune of my own, they never would have seen the light. That misfortune was, that that item about the sack of flour slipped into the paper without either my consent or Dan's.[1] We kept that Sanitary spree up for several days, & I wrote &

laid that ~I~ item before Dan when I was not sober (I shall not get drunk again, Mollie,)—and said he, "Is this a joke?" I told him "Yes." He said he would not like such a joke as that to be perpetrated upon him, & that it would wound the feelings of the ladies of Carson. He asked me if I wanted to do that, & I said "No, of course not." ~He threw it on the table~ While we were talking, the manuscript lay on the table, & we forgot it & left it there when we went to the theatre, & ~we~ I never thought of it again until I received this letter tonight, for I have not read a copy of the Enterprise for a week. I suppose the foreman, prospecting for copy, found it, & seeing that it was in my handwriting, thought it was to be published, & carried it off.[2]

Now Mollie, whatever blame there is, rests with me alone, for if I had not ~been just~ had just sense enough to submit the article to Dan's better judgment, it would have been published all the same, & not by any mistake, either. Since it has made the ladies angry, I am sorry the thing occurred, & that is all I can do, for you will see yourself that their communication is altogether unanswerable. I cannot publish that, & explain it by saying the affair was a silly joke, & that I & all concerned were drunk. No—I'll die first.

Therefore, do one of two things: Either satisfy those ladies that I dealt honorably by them when I consented to let Dan suppress that article upon his assertion that its ~would~ publication would wound their feelings—or else make them appoint a man to avenge the wrong done them, with weapons in fair & open field.

They will understand at a glance that I cannot submit to the humiliation of publishing myself as a liar (according to the terms of their letter,) ~& they will also understand~ so long as I have the other alternative of either challenging or being challenged.

Mollie, the Sanitary expedition has been very disastrous to me. Aside from this trouble, (which I feel ~worst,~ deepest,) I have two other quarrels on my hands, engendered on that day~,~, & as yet I cannot tell how either of them is to end.[3]

Mollie, I shall say nothing about this business until I hear from you. If they insist upon ~pu~ the publication of that letter, I shall still refuse, but Dr Ross shall hear from me, for I suspect that he is at the bottom of the whole business.[4]

> Your affectionate
> Brother,
> Sam

¹ Dan De Quille.

² Clemens's "joke"—ostensibly reporting an offensive rumor about the proceeds of a ball held in Carson City on 5 May for the benefit of the United States Sanitary Commission—appeared in the *Enterprise* on 17 May. The following day the members of the event's organizing committee sent a letter of protest to the *Enterprise*, which never printed it. The exchange survives only as published in the Virginia City *Union* (2), in the form of a public notice, on 25, 26, and 27 May:

THE "ENTERPRISE" LIBEL OF THE LADIES OF CARSON.
CARSON CITY, May 21st, 1864.

VIRGINIA DAILY UNION: The following communication, in reply to a libelous article which appeared in the Enterprise of the 18th inst. [actually 17 May], was sent to that journal for publication, but thus far no notice has been taken of it. By inserting it in your columns, you will confer a favor upon the ladies whose names are appended, and, *perhaps*, draw a reply from "Mark Twain," the author of the scurrilous item.

CITIZEN.

CARSON CITY, May 18th, 1864.

EDITORS OF ENTERPRISE: In your issue of yesterday, you state "that the reason the Flour Sack was not taken from Dayton to Carson, was because it was stated that the money raised at the Sanitary Fancy Dress Ball, recently held in Carson for the St. Louis Fair, had been diverted from its legitimate course, and was to be sent to aid a Miscegenation Society somewhere in the East; and it was feared the proceeds of the sack might be similarly disposed of." You apparently mollify the statement by saying "that it was a hoax, but not all a hoax, for an effort is being made to divert those funds from their proper course."

In behalf of the ladies who originated and assisted in carrying out the programme, let us say that the whole statement is a *tissue of falsehoods*, made for *malicious* purposes, and we demand the name of the author. The ball was gotten up in aid of the Sanitary Commission, and *not* for the St. Louis Fair. At a meeting of the ladies, held in this city last week, no decision was arrived at as to whether the proceeds of the ball should be sent to St. Louis or New York, but one thing *was decided*, that they should go to the aid of the sick and wounded soldiers, who are fighting the battles of our country, *and for no other purpose*. The only discussion had upon the subject was, whether the funds should be forwarded to St. Louis or New York, and this grew out of a circular received from St. Louis, by one of the members, stating "that a portion of the proceeds of the St. Louis Fair, were to be applied to the aid of the Freedmen's Society." In order to have no mistake in the matter, and that the funds should all be applied to the Sanitary Commission, it was proposed by some of the ladies that the money be sent to New York, but no final decision was arrived at. In conclusion, let us say that the ladies having the matter in charge, consider themselves capable of deciding as to what shall be done with the money, without the aid of outsiders, who are probably desirous of acquiring some *glory* by appropriating the efforts of the ladies to themselves.

MRS. W. K. CUTLER, President.
MRS. H. F. RICE, Vice President.
MRS. S. D. KING, Treasurer.
MRS. H. H. ROSS, Sec'y San. Ball.

The ladies signing the above card, sent it to the editors of the "Enterprise," and not to any individual. The assumption in "Enterprise" of May 24th, that they were expecting an answer from "Mark Twain," except through the "Enterprise," is his, not theirs.

CITIZEN.

³ Only one of these quarrels has been identified. It was the result of Clemens's "How Is It?" (see the preceding letter, n. 18). On 19 May the Virginia City *Union* had responded with a long and bitter editorial that reprinted "How Is It?" and included a 17 May receipt for the *Union*'s sanitary-fund contributions, pointing out that the *Enterprise* had not yet fulfilled its own pledges, a "characteristic" omission:

When a question is first sounded it [the *Enterprise*] inhales much of the wind of the occasion, bubbles up high, shows out empty, braggart-like, and then goes down sniveling or sneering. In the instance of patriotism and philanthropy its sensibility is excited while the drums beat, then it is irrepressibly prominent and liberal. Returning to the even course of its instincts, it regrets its gifts and sublimates its manners into the most contemptible self praise, introduced through falsifying insinuations against its neighbors.

Calling the *Enterprise*'s insinuations "despicable" and without "parallel in unmanly public journalism," the *Union* charged: "Such an item could only emanate from a person whose employer can find in his services a machine very suitable to his own manliness" (" 'How Is It?'—How It Is," Virginia City *Union*, 19 May 64, 2). Clemens immediately replied with an *Enterprise* editorial, which provoked the responses he protests in the next letter.

⁴Dr. H. H. Ross was husband of the secretary of the Sanitary Ball committee. Clemens may have believed that Ross was "CITIZEN."

To James L. Laird
21 May 1864 • Virginia City, Nev. Terr.
(Virginia City *Territorial Enterprise*, 24 May 64)

ENTERPRISE OFFICE,⎱
SATURDAY, May 21, 1864 ⎰

JAMES LAIRD, ESQ.¹—*Sir:* In your paper of the present date appeared two anonymous articles, in which a series of insults were leveled at the writer of an editorial in Thursday's ENTERPRISE, headed "How is it?—How it is." I wrote that editorial.²

Some time since it was stated in the Virginia *Union* that its proprietors were alone responsible for all articles published in its columns. You being the proper person, by seniority, to apply to in cases of this kind, I demand of you a public retraction of the insulting articles I have mentioned, or satisfaction. I require an immediate answer to this note. The bearer of this—Mr. Stephen Gillis—will receive any communication you may see fit to make.³

SAM. L. CLEMENS.

¹A partner in John Church and Co., publishers of the Virginia City *Union*. Church and S. A. Glessner were the other members of the firm.
²The full text of Clemens's editorial of Thursday, 19 May, is not known to survive. A fragment of it appears toward the end of the following, one of the "anonymous articles" published in the *Union* on 21 May (2):
"HOW IT IS."
VIRGINIA DAILY UNION:—The editor of the Daily Enterprise has, during the last two days, in his anxiety to injure a cotemporary, seen fit to place before the public in a false light,

and slander in a cowardly manner the printers of this city. We refer to his misrepresentation of the circumstance attending our donation to the Sanitary Fund. We wish it distinctly understood that we have no sympathy whatever in any issue between the proprietors of the UNION and Enterprise. Nor do we entertain any feeling of rivalry toward our fellow-craftsmen employed on that paper. We consider that what redounds to our credit is equally due to them. The editor of the Enterprise has asserted that but for *his* promptings, the employés of the UNION would never have paid their last contribution. In this he wilfully *lies*. The employés of the UNION were in no way instigated to make the donation by their employers, and never contemplated repudiating it. Thursday morning's UNION gave a full list of the men who had donated the money, and the receipt of Mr. Black, Secretary of the Sanitary Fund, attesting that it ($315) had been paid. This should have removed all doubts, if any existed, as to who were the donors. Why does not the editor of the Enterprise accuse Mr. Geo. F. Jones, Mr. DeLong and many other prominent citizens who subscribed repeatedly during the evening, of being influenced to do so by a spirit of rivalry toward his establishment.

We can only view his blackguardism as an attack upon the members of our craft. In asserting that we "Had not intended to pay the bill, but on secondary consideration, and for the sake of saving an entirely imaginary reputation for virtue and honesty, concluded to do so," he has endeavored to misinterpret the generous, patriotic promptings of laboring men who gave their little mite willingly; and in so doing he has proved himself an unmitigated *liar, a poltroon and a puppy.*

PRINTER.

The other "anonymous" *Union* response was an editorial:

THE "HOW IS IT" ISSUE.

When last the Sanitary Commission called for aid, the publishers and employés of the VIRGINIA DAILY UNION unostentatiously united with their generous fellow citizens and contributed the sum of five hundred and fifteen dollars. We have paid that sum in gold to the Treasurer of the Sanitary Fund for Storey county. The Territorial Enterprise newspaper has only pretended to contribute. It has paid nothing of the contributions which it, with great self-show, promised—always in the presence of a crowd. This sort of showing off was not sufficient in itself. The Enterprise must contemptibly boast of its liberality over the UNION, and, in the most unmanly manner, carry its unwarrantable assertions so far as to say that the gentlemen in the employ of the UNION would not pay their subscriptions. We showed the utter and unprecedented meanness of the Enterprise in this instance, and that paper yesterday returned a string of despicable stuff knotted so full of lies that there was not left a space sufficient for the smallest thread of truth. Never before, in a long period of newspaper intercourse—never before in any contact with a cotemporary, however unprincipled he might have been, have we found an opponent in statement or in discussion, who had no gentlemanly sense of professional propriety, who conveyed in every word, and in every purpose of all his words, such a groveling disregard for truth, decency and courtesy, as to seem to court the distinction only of being understood as a vulgar liar. Meeting one who prefers falsehood; whose instincts are all toward falsehood; whose thought is falsification; whose aim is vilification through insincere professions of honesty; one whose only merit is thus described, and who evidently desires to be thus known, the obstacles presented are entirely insurmountable, and whoever would touch them fully, should expect to be abominably defiled.

Clemens himself quotes from this inflammatory essay in 21 May 64 (9:00 P.M.) to Laird. Since both the *Union* editorial and the "PRINTER" letter must have been written on 20 May, the allusions in them to Clemens's *Enterprise* writings of "the last two days" and "yesterday" were meant to refer to "How Is It?" published in the *Enterprise* on 18 May (SLC 1864h, 2), and to Clemens's largely unrecovered 19 May editorial.

³Clemens's good friend Stephen E. Gillis (1838–1918) was raised in Mississippi and Tennessee, where he was trained as a typesetter. He came to San Francisco

with several family members in 1853 and, except for stints as a newspaper editor in Oregon and Arizona, worked on various newspapers there until the end of the decade. When Clemens joined the Virginia City *Enterprise* in 1862, Gillis was the paper's foreman. Equally adept as foreman, compositor, and writer, he spent most of the next thirty years as a news editor, first of the *Enterprise* and then of the Virginia City *Chronicle*. In 1894 he removed to Jackass Hill, California, where he lived with his brothers James and William until his death (William R. Gillis, 7, 19–20, 22, 26–28, 34–35; West, 18). Well known as a scrappy fighter, Gillis acted as Clemens's second during the present dispute with the *Union* and also attempted to become directly involved himself (see 21 May 64 to Laird [9:00 P.M.], n. 2).

To James L. Laird
21 May 1864 • Virginia City, Nev. Terr.
(Virginia City *Territorial Enterprise*, 24 May 64)

ENTERPRISE OFFICE,⎱
SATURDAY EVENING, May 21, 1864 ⎰

JAMES LAIRD, ESQ—*Sir:*—I wrote you a note this afternoon demanding a published retraction of insults that appeared in two articles in the *Union* of this morning—or satisfaction. I have since received what purports to be a reply, written by a person who signs himself "J. W. Wilmington," in which he assumes the authorship and responsibility of one of said infamous articles.[1] Mr. Wilmington is a person entirely unknown to me in the matter, and has nothing to do with it. In the columns of your paper you have declared *your own* responsibility for *all* articles appearing in it, and any farther attempt to make a catspaw of any other individual and thus shirk a responsibility that you had previously assumed will show that *you* are a cowardly sneak. I now *peremptorily* demand of you the satisfaction due to a gentleman—without alternative.

SAM. L. CLEMENS.

[1]Clemens had received the following response, not from Laird (who he presumed had written "The 'How Is It' Issue," the *Union*'s 21 May editorial), but from the author of the "PRINTER" letter, which the paper published the same day:

OFFICE OF THE VIRGINIA DAILY UNION,⎱
VIRGINIA, May 21, 1864. ⎰

SAMUEL CLEMENS, ESQ.—Mr. James Laird has just handed me your note of this date. Permit me to say that I am the *author* of the article appearing in this morning's *Union*. I am responsible for it. I have nothing to retract. Respectfully,

J. W. WILMINGTON.

(Wilmington 1864b, 3:146)

To James L. Laird
21 May 1864 • Virginia City, Nev. Terr.
(Virginia City *Territorial Enterprise*, 24 May 64)

ENTERPRISE OFFICE, VIRGINIA CITY,⎫
May 21, 1864—9 o'clock, P. M. ⎬

JAMES L. LAIRD, ESQ.—*Sir:* Your reply to my last note—in which I *peremptorily demanded satisfaction of you, without alternative*—is just received, and to my utter astonishment you still endeavor to shield your craven carcass behind the person of an individual who in spite of *your* introduction is entirely unknown to me, and upon whose shoulders you *cannot* throw the whole responsibility. You acknowledge and reaffirm in this note that "For all *editorials* appearing in the *Union*, the *proprietors are personally responsible.*"[1] Now, sir, had there appeared no *editorial* on the subject endorsing and reiterating the slanderous and disgraceful insults heaped upon me in the "communication," I would have simply called upon you and demanded the name of its author, and upon your answer would have depended my farther action. But the "editorial" alluded to was equally vile and slanderous as the "communication," and being an "Editorial" would naturally have more weight in the minds of readers. It was the following undignified and abominably insulting slander appearing in your "Editorial" headed "The 'How is it' issue," that occasioned my sending you first an *alternative* and then a *peremptory challenge:*

"Never before in a long period of newspaper intercourse—never before in any contact with a cotemporary, however unprincipled he might have been, have we found an opponent in statement or in discussion, who had no gentlemanly sense of professional propriety, who conveyed in every word, and in every purpose of all his words, such a groveling disregard for truth, decency and courtesy as to seem to court the distinction, only, of being understood as a vulgar liar. Meeting one who prefers falsehood; whose instincts are all toward falsehood; whose thought is falsification; whose aim is villification through insincere professions of honesty; one whose only merit is thus described, and who evidently desires to be thus known, the obstacles presented are entirely insurmountable, and whoever would touch them fully, should expect to be abominably defiled."—*Union, May* 21

You assume in your last note, that I "have challenged Mr. Wilmington," and that he has informed me "over his own signature," that he is quite ready to afford me "satisfaction." Both assumptions are utterly false. I have twice challenged *you*, and you have twice attempted to shirk the responsibility. *Mr. W's* note could not possibly be an answer to my demand for satisfaction from *you*; and besides, his note simply avowed authorship of a certain "communication" that appeared simultaneously with your libelous "editorial," and stated that its author had "nothing to retract." For your gratification, however, I will remark that Mr. Wilmington's case *will be attended to in due time* by a distant acquaintance of his who is not willing to see him suffer in obscurity.[2] In the meantime, if you do not wish yourself posted as a coward, you will *at once accept my peremptory challenge, which I now reiterate.*

SAM. L. CLEMENS.[3]

[1] Laird had sent the following reply to Clemens's second letter:

OFFICE OF THE VIRGINIA DAILY UNION, }
Virginia, Saturday evening, May 21st, 1864. }

SAM'L. CLEMENS, ESQ.:—Your note of this evening is received. To the first portion of it I will briefly reply, that Mr J. W. Wilmington, the avowed author of the article to which you object, is a gentleman now in the employ of the *Union* office. He formerly was one of the proprietors of the Cincinnati *Enquirer*. He was Captain of a Company in the Sixth Ohio Regiment, and fought at Shiloh. His responsibility and character can be vouched for to your abundant satisfaction.

For all editorials appearing in the *Union*, the proprietors are personally responsible; for communications, they hold themselves ready, when properly called upon, either to give the name and address of the author, or failing that, to be themselves responsible.

The editorial in the ENTERPRISE headed "How is it?" out of which this controversy grew, was an attack made upon the printers of the *Union*. It was replied to by a *Union* printer, and a representative of the printers, who in a communication denounced the writer of that article as a liar, a poltroon and a puppy. You announce yourself as the writer of the article which provoked this communication, and demand "satisfaction"—which satisfaction the writer informs you, over his own signature, he is quite ready to afford. I have no right, under the rulings of the code you have invoked, to step in and assume Mr. Wilmington's position, nor would he allow me to do so. You demand of me, in your last letter, the satisfaction due to a gentleman, and couple the demand with offensive remarks. When you have earned the right to the title by complying with the usual custom, I shall be most happy to afford you any satisfaction you desire at any time and in any place. In short, Mr. Wilmington has a prior claim upon your attention. When he is through with you, I shall be at your service. If you decline to meet him after challenging him, you will prove yourself to be what he has charged you with being: "a liar, a poltroon and a puppy," and as such, cannot of course be entitled to the consideration of a gentleman.

Respectfully,
JAMES L. LAIRD.

(Laird 1864a, 3:146)

[2] This "distant acquaintance" was apparently Steve Gillis, who issued a futile challenge to Wilmington:

OFFICE TERRITORIAL ENTERPRISE, ⎱
VIRGINIA, May 21, 1864. ⎰

J. W. WILMINGTON—*Sir:* You are, perhaps, far from those who are wont to advise and care for you, else you would see the policy of minding your own business and letting that of other people alone. Under these circumstances, therefore, I take the liberty of suggesting that you are getting out of your sphere. A *contemptible ass and coward* like yourself should only meddle in the affairs of *gentlemen* when called upon to do so. I approve and endorse the course of my principal in this matter, and if your sensitive disposition is aroused by any proceeding of his, I have only to say that I can be found at the ENTERPRISE office, and always at your service.

S. E. GILLIS.

[To the above, Mr. Wilmington gave a verbal reply to Mr. Millard—the gentleman through whom the note was conveyed to him—stating that he had no quarrel with Mr. Gillis; that he had written his communication only in defense of the craft, and did not desire a quarrel with a member of that craft; he showed Mr. G.'s note to Mr. Millard, who read it, but made no comments upon it.] (Stephen E. Gillis, 3:146)

³ Laird answered this letter as follows:

OFFICE OF THE VIRGINIA DAILY UNION, ⎱
MONDAY MORNING, May 23, 1864. ⎰

SAMUEL CLEMENS, ESQ.:—In reply to your lengthy communication, I have only to say that in your note opening this correspondence, you demanded satisfaction for a communication in the *Union* which branded the writer of an article in the ENTERPRISE as a *liar*, a *poltroon* and a puppy. You declare yourself to be the writer of the ENTERPRISE article, and the avowed author of the *Union* communication stands ready to afford satisfaction. Any attempt to evade a meeting with him and force one upon me will utterly fail, as I have no right under the rulings of the code, to meet or hold any communication with you in this connection. The *threat* of being posted as a coward cannot have the slightest effect upon the position I have assumed in the matter. If you think this correspondence reflects credit upon *you*, I advise you by all means to publish it; in the meantime you must excuse me from receiving any more long epistles from you.

JAMES L. LAIRD.

(Laird 1864b, 3:146)

Clemens published his own letters as well as Laird's, Wilmington's, and Gillis's, numbering them "I" through "VII," under the title "Personal Correspondence" in the *Territorial Enterprise* for 24 May. He appended this final commentary:

I denounce Mr. Laird as an unmitigated liar, because he says I published an editorial in which I attacked the printers employed on the *Union*, whereas there is nothing in that editorial which can be so construed. Moreover, he is a liar on general principles, and from natural instinct. I denounce him as an abject coward, because it has been stated in his paper that its proprietors are responsible for all articles appearing in its columns, yet he backs down from that position; because he acknowledges the "code," but will not live up to it; because he says himself that he is responsible for all "editorials," and then backs down from that also; and because he insults me in his note marked "IV" [Laird's letter of 21 May], and yet refuses to fight me. Finally, he is a fool, because he cannot understand that a publisher is bound to stand responsible for any and all articles printed by him, whether he wants to do it or not.

SAM. L. CLEMENS.

(SLC 1864j, 3:146)

In 1872 Clemens described the *Enterprise* office while he awaited the first response from Laird:

All our boys—the editors—were in our office, "helping" me in the dismal business, and telling about duels, and discussing the code with a lot of aged ruffians who had had experience in such things, and altogether there was a loving interest taken in the matter, which made me unspeakably uncomfortable. . . . I sent him another challenge, and another and another; and the more he did not want to fight, the bloodthirstier I became. But at last the man's tone changed. He appeared to be waking up. It was becoming apparent that he was going to fight me, after all. I ought to have known how it would be—he was a man who never could be depended upon. Our boys were exultant. I was not, though I tried to be.

Clemens alleged that a duel was averted only when, during early morning pistol practice, Steve Gillis shot the head off a sparrow and managed to convince Laird's seconds that Clemens had done it (SLC 1872b, 90–91).

To Ellen G. Cutler
23 May 1864 • Virginia City, Nev. Terr.
(*MTL*, 1:97–98)

Virginia, May 23rd, 1864.

Mrs. W. K. Cutler:[1]

Madam—I address a lady in every sense of the term. Mrs. Clemens has informed me of everything that has occurred in Carson in connection with that unfortunate item of mine about the Sanitary Funds accruing from the ball, and from what I can understand, you are almost the only lady in your city who has understood the circumstances under which my fault was committed, or who has shown any disposition to be lenient with me. Had the note of the ladies been properly worded, I would have published an ample apology instantly—and possibly I might even have done so anyhow, had that note arrived at any other time—but it came at a moment when I was in the midst of what ought to have been a deadly quarrel with the publishers of the Union, and I could not come out and make public apologies to any one at such a time. It is bad policy to do it even now (as challenges have already passed between myself and a proprietor of the Union, and the matter is still in abeyance,) but I suppose I had better say a word or two to show the ladies that I did not wilfully and maliciously do them a wrong.[2]

But my chief object, Mrs. Cutler, in writing you this note (and you will pardon the liberty I have taken,) was to thank you very kindly and sincerely for the consideration you have shown me in this matter, and for your continued friendship for Mollie while others are disposed to withdraw theirs on account of a fault for which I alone am responsible.

Very truly yours,

Sam. L. Clemens.

¹ Ellen G. (Mrs. William K.) Cutler was president of the Carson City Sanitary Ball committee. She had earned some celebrity in Nevada and California for the "entertainments" at which she sang ballads and read from authors as diverse as Edgar Allan Poe, Richard Brinsley Sheridan, Robert Browning, and Orpheus C. Kerr. Widely applauded as a "charming and cultivated woman," Mrs. Cutler was said to have "no superior on the coast" ("Mrs. Cutler's Concert and Readings," San Francisco *Evening Bulletin*, 18 Dec 62, 5; Angel, 220; Nevada City [Calif.] *Transcript*: "Ballad Singing and Readings," 11 June 63, 3; "Sierra Seminary," 27 Dec 63, 2).

² On 24 May Clemens published the following article in the *Enterprise*:

"MISCEGENATION."—We published a rumor, the other day, that the moneys collected at the Carson Fancy Dress Ball were to be diverted from the Sanitary Fund and sent forward to aid a "miscegenation" or some other sort of Society in the East. We also stated that the rumor was a hoax. And it was—we were perfectly right. However, four ladies are offended. We cannot quarrel with ladies—the very thought of such a thing is repulsive; neither can we consent to offend them—even unwittingly—without being sorry for the misfortune, and seeking their forgiveness, which is a kindness we hope they will not refuse. We intended no harm, as they would understand easily enough if they knew the history of this offense of ours, but we must suppress that history, since it would rather be amusing than otherwise, and the amusement would be at our expense. We have no love for that kind of amusement—and the same trait belongs to human nature generally. One lady complained that we should at least have answered the note they sent us. It is true. There is small excuse for our neglect of a common politeness like that, yet we venture to apologize for it, and will still hope for pardon, just the same. We have noticed one thing in this whole business—and also in many an instance which has gone before it—and that is, that we resemble the majority of our species in the respect that we are very apt to get entirely in the wrong, even when there is no seeming necessity for it; but to offset this vice, we claim one of the virtues of our species, which is that we are ready to repair such wrongs when we discover them. (SLC 1864k, 3:146)

Despite the public and private apologies from Clemens, the 18 May letter from the Sanitary Ball committee was published on three consecutive days at the end of May by the Virginia City *Union* (see 20 May 64 to MEC, n. 2).

To Orion and Mary E. (Mollie) Clemens
25 May 1864 • Virginia City, Nev. Terr.
(MS: CU-MARK)

Va, Wednesday A.M.

My Dear Bro.

Don't stump for the Sanitary Fund—Billy Clagett says he certainly will not. If I have been so unlucky as to rob you of some of your popġularity by that unfortunate item, I claim at your hands that you neither increase nor diminish it by so fruitless a proceeding as making speeches for the Fund. I am mighty sick of that fund—it has caused me all my d—d troubles—& I shall leave the Territory when your first speech is announced, & leave it for good.[1]

I see by the Union of this morning, that those ladies have seduced from me what I consider was a sufficient apology, ~~under~~ coming from a man open to a challenge from three persons, & already awaiting the issue of such a message to another[2]—they got out of me what no *man* would ever have got, & then—well, they are ladies, & I shall not speak harshly of them.[3] Now although the Union folks have kept quiet this morning, (much against my expectations,) I still have a quarrel or two on hand—so that this flour sack business may rest, as far as Carson is concerned. I shall take no notice of it ,at, all, except to mash Mr Laird over the head with my revolver for publishing it ~~to~~ if I meet him to-day—otherwise, I do nothing. I consider that I have triumphed over those ladies at last, & I am quits with them. But when I forgive the injury—or forget it— ~~may~~ or fail to set up a score against it, as opportunity offers—may I be able to console myself for it with the consciousness that I have become a marvellously better man. ~~At~~ I have no intention of *hunting* for the puppy, Laird, Mollie, but he had better let me have 24 hours unmolested, to get cool in.

~~We await the result of~~

But for Heaven's sake give me at least the ₫ peace & quiet it will afford me to know that no stumping is to be done for the unlucky Sanitary Fund.

Yro Bro

Sam

[1] Orion Clemens had been appointed president of the Ormsby County sanitary committee on 14 April. In this capacity he was expected to help organize "a thorough Territorial Sanitary Commission through every city and town in the Territory" ("The Union Territorial Convention—Concluded," Virginia City *Union*, 16 Apr 64, 2).

[2] Three of these adversaries were James L. Laird and J. W. Wilmington, of the *Union*, and William K. Cutler, husband of the president of the Sanitary Ball committee (see 28 May 64 to Cutler). As the next letter indicates, Clemens was also anticipating challenges from the husbands of the other committee members. Years later—alluding to this sanitary-fund imbroglio but mistakenly placing it during his March–April 1864 tenure as *Enterprise* chief editor—Clemens claimed, "When I laid down my editorial pen I had four horse-whippings and two duels owing to me" (AD, 19 Jan 1906, CU-MARK, in *MTA*, 1:360).

[3] Clemens was tempted to speak harshly of the Carson City women because their complaint about his "miscegenation society" remarks appeared in the 25 May Virginia City *Union*, despite his apology in the *Enterprise* of the twenty-

fourth. In belatedly airing the women's protest, the *Union* had to adopt the lame pretext that Clemens's "individual" apology was insufficient atonement for the *Enterprise*'s offense in printing his "scurrilous item." The awkwardness of this attempt to prolong the dispute evidently helped Clemens feel, as he goes on to tell Orion here, that he had "triumphed over those ladies at last."

To Orion Clemens
26 May 1864 • Virginia City, Nev. Terr.
(MS: CU-MARK)

Va, May 26, 1864.

My Dear Bro—

Send me two hundred dollars *if you can spare it comfortably*. However, never mind—you can send it to San Francisco if you prefer. Steve & I are going to the States. We leave Sunday morning per Henness Pass.[1] Say nothing about it, of course. We are not afraid of the grand jury, but Washoe has long since grown irksome to us, & we want to leave it anyhow.[2]

We have thoroughly canvassed the Carson business, & concluded we dare not do anything, either to Laird or Carson men without spoiling our chances of getting away. However, if there is any chance of the husbands of those women challenging *me*, I don't want a straw put in the way of it. I'll wait for them a month, if th necessary, & fight them with *any* weapon they choose. I thought of challenging one of them & then crossing the line to await the result, but Steve says it would not be safe, situated as we are.[3]

When I get to the Bay—where we shall remain a month—I will fix the Hale & Norcross in a safe shape.[4]

My best love to Mollie,

Sam

[1] A principal passage through the Sierra Nevada, named for Patrick Henness, one of the men who discovered it in 1850 ("The Henness Pass," North San Juan [Calif.] *Hydraulic Press*, 9 June 60, 2; Gudde, 131–32). Clemens probably chose the Henness Pass route to California because it bypassed Carson City, where he would have been persona non grata at this time (Mack 1947, 323).

[2] In his later explanations of his departure from Nevada Territory, Clemens expanded upon the motives suggested here. In chapter 55 of *Roughing It* he professed to have been bored with his reportorial duties and eager to travel, so that

he was happy to accept Dan De Quille's offer of a chance to go to New York with two others to sell a Nevada silver mine on commission. (Purportedly an unlucky double failure in communication caused Clemens to miss the San Francisco–New York steamer and lose his opportunity to participate in the enterprise.) In 1906, however, Clemens claimed that he and Gillis had to leave Nevada because he had sent a challenge to James L. Laird and Gillis had carried it, making them both subject to "two years apiece in the penitentiary, according to the brand-new law" against dueling (AD, 19 Jan 1906, CU-MARK, in *MTA*, 1:359). There was such a law in effect—section 35 of "An Act concerning Crimes and Punishments"— although it was not "brand-new," having been passed on 26 November 1861. It established a penalty of from two to ten years' imprisonment for both the sending and the delivering of a challenge (*Laws* 1862, 61). Enforcement of this law was sufficiently strict to make some antagonists cross from Nevada into California to do battle. For Clemens's and Gillis's accounts of their dueling experiences see: SLC 1872b, 90–91; *MTB*, 1:250–52; and Fulton, 54. A discussion of Clemens's versions, and their factual basis, can be found in Krauth, 141–53.

³ This stratagem was not "safe" because of another law passed on 26 November 1861—"An Act to Regulate Proceedings in Criminal Cases in the Courts of Justice in the Territory of Nevada." Section 84 of this act stipulated: "When an inhabitant or resident of this territory shall, by any previous appointment or engagement, fight in a duel without the jurisdiction of this territory, and in such duel a wound shall be inflicted upon any person whereof he shall die within this territory, the jurisdiction of the offense shall be in the county where the death shall happen" (*Laws* 1862, 444). Clemens may have witnessed one duel fought in California, the 28 September 1863 encounter in which Joseph T. Goodman wounded Thomas Fitch (see *ET&S1*, 263–64).

⁴ The Hale and Norcross Silver Mining Company was incorporated in March 1861. Its relatively small but well-developed claim of 400 feet was located on the southern portion of the Comstock lode. Clemens had explored the mine in early July 1863 in his capacity as *Enterprise* "local" (see SLC 1863c, 1). The company was known for its relative freedom from mining litigation and its powerful machinery, which soon penetrated the Comstock lode to the greatest depth then attained by any company. It was also known for the frequent assessments it levied on stockholders as a means of raising operating capital. In 1868 Clemens remembered owning six shares of Hale and Norcross stock—a fact that his 1864–65 assessments substantiate (see 28 Sept 64 to OC and MEC, n. 5, and 11 Nov 64 to OC, n. 5)—and claimed to have sold them for $300 a share (SLC 1868, 2). Almost forty years later, however, he recalled that on a tip from mining speculator Herman Camp he had acquired fifty shares at that price, buying them on margin by putting up twenty percent. This purchase, which he indicated came during his May–June 1863 sojourn in San Francisco, "exhausted my funds. I wrote Orion and offered him half, and asked him to send his share of the money." Clemens "waited and waited" for the money, which never reached him, although Orion had sent it. In the meantime the stock rose thousands of dollars and then began to fall steadily "until it fell below the price I had paid for it. Then it began to eat up the margin, and when at last I got out I was very badly crippled" (AD, 5 Apr 1906, CU-MARK, in *MTA*, 2:319–20). Although this account certainly exaggerates the number of shares purchased, it accords with a major boom in Hale and Norcross stock during the two months in 1863 that Clemens lived in San

Francisco. In early May, when he arrived, the stock was quoted at $915 per share, and at the end of June, just before he departed for Virginia City, it was selling for over $2,000 per share. By the time of the present letter, however, the bid price had fallen to $500 (*By-laws*, 1; Hague, 99, 174; "San Francisco Stock and Exchange Board," San Francisco *Alta California*: 1 May 63, 4; 30 June 63, 4; 26 May 64, 6). Apparently Clemens attempted to "fix the Hale & Norcross in a safe shape" by putting part of the stock in Orion's name (see 13 and 14 Aug 64 to OC and MEC).

To William K. Cutler
28 May 1864 • Virginia City, Nev. Terr.
(MS, *draft not sent:* CU-BANC)

Virginia, May 28, 1864.

W. K. Cutler—

Sir—To-day, I have received a letter from you, in which you assume that you have been offended and insulted by certain acts of mine. Having apologized ~~one~~ once for that offensive conduct, I shall not do it again. Your recourse is in a challenge. I am ready to accept, it.

Having made my arrangements—before I ~~reci~~ received your note— to leave for California, & having ~~to~~ no time to fool away on a common bummer like you, I want an immediate reply to this.[1]

[*in Dan De Quille's hand on letter back:*] Mark Twain to Cutler. First draft of document left on my desk when a second was written and sent. Nothing came of the matter. | Dan De Quille.

[1]Clemens later claimed that a duel with Cutler was averted because his opponent was intimidated by Steve Gillis:

Mr. Cutler had come up from Carson City, and had sent a man over with a challenge from the hotel. Steve went over to pacify him. Steve weighed only ninety-five pounds, but it was well known throughout the territory that with his fists he could whip anybody that walked on two legs, let his weight and science be what they might. Steve was a Gillis, and when a Gillis confronted a man and had a proposition to make the proposition always contained business. When Cutler found that Steve was my second he cooled down; he became calm and rational, and was ready to listen. Steve gave him fifteen minutes to get out of the hotel, and half an hour to get out of town or there would be results. So *that* duel went off successfully, because Mr. Cutler immediately left for Carson a convinced and reformed man. (AD, 19 Jan 1906, CU-MARK, in *MTA*, 1:360)

NO LETTERS are known to survive for the next seven weeks. Clemens left Virginia City bound for San Francisco on 29 May 1864. The Gold Hill *Evening News* of the following day observed:

> Among the few immortal names of the departed—that is, those who departed yesterday morning per California stage—we notice that of Mark Twain. We don't wonder. Mark Twain's beard is full of dirt, and his face is black before the people of Washoe. Giving way to the idiosyncratic eccentricities of an erratic mind, Mark has indulged in the game infernal—in short, "played hell." Shifting the *locale* of his tales of fiction from the Forest of Dutch Nick's to Carson City; the *dramatis personae* thereof from the Hopkins family to the fair Ladies of the Ladies' Fair; and the plot thereof from murder to miscegenation—he slopped. The indignation aroused by his enormities has been too crushing to be borne by living man, though sheathed with the brass and triple cheek of Mark Twain. . . . He has *vamosed*, cut stick, absquatulated; and among the pine forests of the Sierras, or amid the purlieus of the city of earthquakes, he will tarry awhile, and the office of the *En[ter]prise* will become purified, and by the united efforts of Goodman and Dan De Quille once more merit the sweet smiles of the ladies of Carson. ("An Exile," 2, in *MTEnt*, 204–5)

The journey was marked by conviviality, however, not by penitence. Clemens had the companionship of Joseph T. Goodman as well as Steve Gillis. Goodman later recalled: "We all sat on the seat behind the driver on a Concord Coach. I intended to go only a little way out on the Geiger Grade [the road between Virginia City and Steamboat Springs, a distance of seven miles]; but the company was too good and I kept clear on to San Francisco" (Goodman to Albert Bigelow Paine, 7 Apr 1911, in Davis 1956d, 4).

In San Francisco, Clemens and Gillis initially settled at the Occidental Hotel, which, Clemens informed his *Territorial Enterprise* readers around the middle of June, was "Heaven on the half shell"—a welcome respite from the sagebrush and desolation of Washoe ("'Mark Twain' in the Metropolis," *ET&S2*, 10). Around 6 June Clemens took a job as local reporter, which paid forty dollars a week, for the San Francisco *Morning Call*. The work soon proved tedious, and by July he was having serious doubts about pursuing his career as a writer. For a while Clemens even considered accepting "an appointment to act as a government pilot on the Mississippi, for a salary of $300 a month" (*ET&S1*, 28). Nevertheless, he remained with the *Call* for four months, during which time, as the next sequence of letters shows, he affirmed his decision to live by his pen (see also *ET&S1*, 26–29, and *CofC*, esp. 1–35).

To William Wright (Dan De Quille)
15 July 1864 • San Francisco, Calif.
(MS, *damage emended:* CU-BANC)

Occidental,[1] S F, 15[th.]

Dear Dan:

Tell Dawson[2] to stir his old stumps & send me that money now if he possibly can. I have almost got that old debt of mine cleared up, & with his assistance & my wages, I can finish the job now. Don't you fail to tell him.

Steve & I have moved our lodgings. ~~The~~ Steve did not tell his folks he had moved, & the other day his father[3] went to our room, & finding it locked, he hunted up the old landlady (Frenchwoman,) & asked her where those young men were. She [*in bottom margin:* (over]) didn't know who he was, & she got her gun off without mincing matters. Said she— "They are gone, thank God—& I hope I may never see them again. I did not know anything about them, or they never should have entered this house. Do you know, Sir, (dropper her voice to a ghastly confidential tone,) they were a couple of desperate characters from Washoe—gamblers & murd[er]ers of the very worst description! I never saw such a countenance as the smallest one[4] had on him. They just took the premises, & lorded it over everything—they didn't care a snap for the rules of the house. One night when they were carrying on in their room with some more roughs, my husband went up to remonstrate with them, & that small man told him to take his head out of the door (pointing a revolver,) because he wanted to shoot in that direction. O, I never saw such creatures. Their room was never vacant long enough to be cleaned up—one of them always went to bed at dark & got up at sunrise, & the other went to bed at sunrise & got up at dark—& if the chamber-man disturbed them they would just set up in bed & level a pistol at him & tell him to get scarce! They used to bring loads of beer bottles up at midnight, & get drunk, & shout & fire off their pistols in the room, & thei throw their empty bottles out of the window at the Chinamen below. You'd hear them count 'One—two—three—fire!' & then you'd hear the bottles crash on the China roofs & see the poor Chinamen scatter like flies. O, it was dreadful! They kept a nasty foreign sword & any number of revolvers & bowie knives in their room, & I know that small one must have murdered los lots of people. They always had women run[n]ing to their room— sometimes in broad daylight—bless you, *they* didn't care. They had no respect for God, man, or the devil. Yes, Sir, they are gone, & the good g God was kind to me when He sent them away!"

There, now—what in the hell is the use of wearing away a lifetime in building up a good name, if it is to be blown away at a breath by an ignorant foreigner who is ignorant of the pleasant little customs that adorn & beautify a state of high ṣcivilization?

The old man told Steve all about it in his dry, unsmiling way, & Steve laughed himself sick over it.

Walter Leman sails for the Sandwich Islands tomorrow—just going for recreation.[5]

Give my great love to Joe & Put[6] & all the boys—& write, you bilk.

But don't I want to go ˏtoˏ Asia, or somewhere—Oh no, I guess not. I have got the "Gypsy" only in a mild form. It will kill me yet, though.

Yr old friend

Sam

[1] It is clear from the contents of this letter that Clemens was no longer at the Occidental Hotel, but since he and Gillis changed lodgings frequently during this period it is likely that he was receiving his mail there.

[2] George F. Dawson, an Englishman, was an editorial writer and assistant editor on the *Territorial Enterprise* and later librarian of the United States Senate (Daggett, 15; William Wright 1893b, 13). According to Dan De Quille, Dawson boxed as a hobby and "particularly prided himself upon being a hard hitter." De Quille described a painful encounter Clemens had with him, probably in late April 1864, at a Virginia City gymnasium:

One day some imp induced Mark Twain to put on a pair of boxing gloves, and with them all the airs of a knight of the prize ring. He had no thought of boxing with any one. Having seen more or less sparring on the stage, a good deal of amateur boxing, and probably one or two prize fights, Mark had got some of the motions. No sooner had he the gloves on than he began capering about the hall. Dawson observed his antics with astonishment not unmixed with awe. He evidently considered that they were made for his special benefit and intimidation. Perhaps he may have thought that he detected Mark regarding him interrogatively from beneath his bushy brows at the end of each series of cabezal rotations. At all events, in view of Mark's movements of a supposed warlike import, Dawson kept a wary eye on him;

never once suspecting that the ex-Mississippi pilot was merely making a bid for his admiration.

Presently Mark squared off directly in front of Dawson and began working his right like the piston of a steam engine, at the same time stretching out his neck and gyrating his curly pate in a very astonishing manner.

Dawson took this to be a direct act of defiance—a challenge to a trial of skill that could not be ignored. Desperately, therefore—and probably not without a secret chill of fear at his heart—Dawson drew off and with full force planted a heavy blow squarely upon Mark's offered nose, the latter not making the least movement toward a guard.

The result was a "plentiful flow of claret" and a nose "like an egg-plant," which supposedly so embarrassed Clemens that he accepted a reportorial assignment outside Virginia City just "to get his nose out of town" (William Wright 1893b, 13–14). See also *ET&S1*, 357–58.

³ Angus Gillis (see 25 Sept 64 to JLC and PAM, n. 3).

⁴ Steve Gillis.

⁵ Walter M. Leman, a popular San Francisco actor, had played for several weeks in April and May 1864 at Maguire's Opera House in Virginia City, where he "made a great many friends" ("Theatrical Record," San Francisco *Morning Call*, 15 May 64, 1). Leman sailed for the Sandwich Islands on 16 July aboard the bark *Onward*, arriving in Honolulu on 1 August. He lectured on "The Drama" and twice gave readings from Shakespeare and other dramatists before departing for San Francisco on 21 September ("Marine Intelligence," San Francisco *Evening Bulletin*, 16 July 64, 5; Honolulu *Pacific Commercial Advertiser*: "Passengers" and "To the Public of Honolulu—A Card!" 6 Aug 64, 2; "The Lecture on the Drama," 13 Aug 64, 2; "Mr. W. M. Leman," 17 Sept 64, 2; "Passengers," 24 Sept 64, 2).

⁶ Joseph T. Goodman and Charles A. V. Putnam.

To Jane Lampton Clemens
12 August 1864 • San Francisco, Calif.
(*Author's copy* and MS: CU-MARK and NPV)

. . . .

My Dear Mother—You have portrayed to me so often & so earnestly the benefit of taking frequent exercise, that I know it will please you to learn that I belong to the San F. Olympic Club, whose gymnasium is one of the largest & best appointed in the United States.¹ I am glad, now, that you put me in the notion of it, Ma, because if you had not, I never would have thought of it myself. I think it nothing but right to give you the whole credit of it. It has been a great blessing to me. I feel like a new man. I sleep better, I have a healthier appetite, my intellect is clearer, & I have become so strong & hearty that I fully believe twenty years have been added to my life. I feel as if I ought to be very well satisfied with this result, when I reflect that I never was in that gymnasium but once in my life, & that was over three months ago.[2]

[*seven-eighths MS page (about 135 words) missing*]

The place where my laugh comes in, though, is where a resident of ~~Milton Place~~ ˌSan José˴ read that article & commented on it. He is one of these fellows who is impervious to humor, & he takes everything he finds in a newspaper in dead earnest. Some fellow handed him that article just to see what he would say. ~~(He lives alongside the house the rocket crashed through.)~~ He read it with oppressive solemnity until he came to where the neighbors were expecting the man that went up with the rocket & moved their families out of his way, & then he threw down the paper & turned angrily to his friend & says he: "Moved their families out to give him a *show!* Was expectin'ˌg of him *down!* Now look-a-here,[3]

· · · ·

---

[1] The Olympic Club was organized in 1860 and had about four hundred members. The club's gymnasium on Sutter Street near Montgomery offered classes in gymnastics, boxing, and fencing. Clemens's "exercising was confined to studying up jokes to play on his fellow members" (Treat, 31; Langley 1864, 566).

[2] It probably was this letter that Jane Clemens acknowledged on 28 September: "We recived Sam's scolding letter dated 12th of August if we cant make him write only by making him mad we will have to try that for we would rather have a scolding letter than none" (JLC to OC, MEC, and SLC, 28 Sept 64, NPV, in *MTBus*, 82). The "scolding," as opposed to the teasing about the benefits of exercise, may have filled at least part of the gap that follows.

[3] The article referred to was Clemens's "What a Sky-Rocket Did," published in the San Francisco *Morning Call* on 12 August. It is a hoax about an expended rocket crashing through the roof of a tenement on "Milton Place, Bush street," San Francisco. The object of its satire is William Crawley Hinckley, a former member of the city's board of supervisors (see *ET&S2*, 34–37). Clemens's account of a humorless response to this article survives on a stray manuscript page numbered "3" (NPV). Since a similar account appears in the following letter to Orion and Mollie, which derives in part from the present letter, this stray page probably belongs here. Clemens must have enclosed clippings of "What a Sky-Rocket Did" in this letter and in the next one.

To Orion and Mary E. (Mollie) Clemens
13 and 14 August 1864 • San Francisco, Calif.
(MS: CU-MARK)

San F, Aug. ~~12~~ 13.[1]

My Dear Bro & Sister:

I have managed to write another valuable letter to Ma, as follows:

"My Dear Mother—You have portrayed to me so often & so earnestly the benefit of taking frequent exercise, that I know it will please you to learn that I belong to the San F. Olympic Club, whose gymnasium is one of the largest & best appointed in the United States. I am glad, now, that you put me in the notion of it, Ma, because if you had not, I never would have thought of it myself. I think it nothing but right to give you the whole credit of it. It has been a great blessing to me. I feel like a new man. I sleep better, I have a healthier appetite, my intellect is clearer, & I have become so strong & hearty that I fully believe twenty years have been added to my life. I feel as if I ought to be very well satisfied with this result, when I reflect that I never was in that gymnasium but once in my life, & that was over three months ago."

How's that? I think I can see the old lady pluming herself as she reads the first page ∄ aloud, & perhaps commenting to the auditory (they generally make my private letters pretty public at home,): "Thar, now, I always told Sam it would be so, & in those very ~~wort~~ words, I expect, but he was so headstrong he never would listen to me before; I guess he's found out that I know some things worth knowing." Oh, no—I guess she won't snort, though, when she turns the page over, it ain't likely.[2] It takes *me* to make *her* life interesting to her. I wonder why she never inquired about the sequel to that mystery wherein the fellow was going to blow the young woman's head off with a double-barreled shotgun through the back window?[3] I guess she was ruther down on that little novelette. She never encouraged me to go on with it.

I have got D[r] Bellows stuck after my local items.[4] He says he never fails to read them,—said he went into "convulsions of laughter" over the account of "What a Sky-Rocket Did." He told me he would consider me a benefactor to him if I would publish a book. I itched to tell him an anecdote about that sky-rocket article, but I didn't dare to. Somebody showed it to an old fellow down at San José, who is perfectly impervious to humor, just to see what he would say. He takes everything he finds in a newspaper in dead earnest. He read the article ˏ(it was published day before yesterday—Friday,ˏ with oppressive solemnity until he came to where the neighbors were expecting the fellow that went up with the rocket, & moved their families out of his way, & then he slammed the paper on the floor & rose up & ᴄᴏ angrily confronted the man—ˏ& says he,ː ꞌꞋWꞋ with ᵇⁱᵗᵗᵉʳ measureless scorn in his tones: "Was expect'n of him do̭wn! They druther he'd fall in the *alley!* Moved ther families out to give him a *show!* Now look-a-here, my friend, you may go on & believe that, if you think you can stand it, but you'll excuse ME. I just think it's a *God dam lie!*"

I enclose the Hale & Norcross stock. It is all in your name, you see, so if I want to leave here at any time, there'll be no bother about it. Put it in the safe, & if I get a chance to sell it well, endorse it & send it to me.[5]

Yr Bro,

Sam

I wouldn't have had Ma & Pamela publish that letter of mine for a thousand dollars—but I shan't say anything now to make them feel bad about it.[6]

[1] The fact that Clemens was about to copy his 12 August letter to his mother into the present letter accounts for his momentary misdating here. His statement, in paragraph four, that "What a Sky-Rocket Did" was published "day before yesterday—Friday" indicates that at least that interlined phrase was written on Sunday, 14 August.

[2] Clemens ended the first manuscript page of this letter with the words "with this result, when," thereby allowing Orion and Mollie to experience the prank he was describing.

[3] See 2? Jan 64 to JLC.

[4] The Reverend Henry Whitney Bellows (1814–82) was the founder and president of the United States Sanitary Commission. From May to September 1864 he conducted a western fund-raising campaign for the commission while also filling the pulpit of San Francisco's First Unitarian Church. As part of this campaign, he lectured in Nevada Territory in July, appearing in Virginia City (twice) and several other towns, but evidently not in Carson City, where Orion and Mollie were living (Virginia City *Union*: "Lectures!" 16 July 64, 2; "Dr. Bellows' Lecture," 21 July 64, 3; "Another Lecture from Dr. Bellows," 23 July 64, 3). Clemens probably admired Bellows's religious philosophy, which placed high value on humor, "the inner side of laughter," asserting that it was indispensable to the health of "mind and heart" and that "the want of it is a calamity, and an injury to the sober and solid interests of society . . . to scholarship, economy, virtue, and reverence. . . . The intellect that plays a part of every day, works more powerfully

and to better results, for the rest of the time; the heart that is gay for an hour, is more serious for the other hours of the day" (Bellows, 6–8). For details of Clemens's friendship with Bellows, see *CofC*, 61–62, 66–68, 256–58.

[5]The bid price for Hale and Norcross stock (see 26 May 64 to OC, n. 4) had continued to plummet and currently was $300 per share ("San Francisco Stock and Exchange Board, August 13, 1864," San Francisco *Alta California*, 14 Aug 64, 6). Clemens expressed his frustration with the unprofitability of this stock and with the company's repeated assessments—$25, and occasionally $50, per share every two months—in the San Francisco *Morning Call* of 19 August:

The Hale & Norcross officers decide to sink a shaft. They levy forty thousand dollars. Next month they have a mighty good notion to go lower, and they levy a twenty thousand dollar assessment. Next month, the novelty of sinking the shaft has about worn off, and they think it would be nice to drift a while—twenty thousand dollars. The following month it occurs to them it would be so funny to pump a little—and they buy a forty thousand dollar pump. Thus it goes on for months and months, but the Hale & Norcross sends us no bullion, though most of the time there is an encouraging rumor afloat that they are "right in the casing!" ("What Goes with the Money?" *ET&S2*, 455)

Despite his present claim to have transferred all of his Hale and Norcross holdings to Orion, Clemens still had two shares in his own name in May 1865 (see 11 Nov 64 to OC, n. 5).

[6]The allusion is probably to Clemens's 17 May 1864 letter to his mother and sister.

To William Wright (Dan De Quille)
17 September 1864 • San Francisco, Calif.
(MS facsimile: Mack 1947, facing 256)

Ɏ   San F., Sept 17.

Dear Dan—

If you will buy my furniture at $55, I'll send you a bill of sale, & then you can sell it to somebody who will suit you*t* better as a bedfellow than Dawson.[1]

If you consent, go to Paxton & Thornburgh, Bankers, & assume a debt I owe them of $55, (provided Harry Blodgett has not already paid it,) & write me word & the bill of sale shall go up by return mail.[2] Ⱦ Mr Daggett cannot prove that I owe him a cent, & of course he cannot hold my furniture.[3]

Put. has gone back to Sac. Say, look in Cohen's notary book, & tell me how much money he has received from the first beginning. His book is open to inspection by anybody. All well. Give our love to old Joe & Dennis.[4] I don't work after 6 in the evening, now on the "Call." ₐI got disgusted with night work.ₐ[5]

Yr old friend

Sam L. Clemens.

[1] Apparently George F. Dawson of the *Territorial Enterprise* was now sharing the lodgings that De Quille had shared with Clemens from late October 1863 through the end of May 1864 (see note 3). De Quille recalled that these quarters consisted of "a large bedroom and a room somewhat smaller for use as a parlor or sitting room" and that Joseph T. Goodman

bossed the job of furnishing these rooms, and piled into them several hundred dollars' worth of stuff. Mark said that as Goodman had been "so keen to do the ordering" of the things we'd "just let him foot the bill." So, whenever the furniture man—good old Moses Goldman—came after us with his bill, we laughed at him, and referred him to Goodman. But one day old Moses sued us and we had to square up with him. Mark said we might have known better than to try such a trick with "a man whose front name was Moses and whose rear name was Goldman."

However, we had a huge double bed, piles of bedding, splendid carpets and fine fittings of all kinds. This, in comparison with the bunks in which we roosted in an old tumble-down shed when I first began work on the *Enterprise*, was quite palatial.

Mark and I agreed well as room-mates. Both wanted to read and smoke about the same length of time after getting into bed, and when one got hungry and got up to go down town for oysters the other also became hungry and turned out. (William Wright 1893b, 13)

[2] Henry L. Blodgett was a Virginia City deputy sheriff and notary public with whom Clemens briefly shared an office in the spring of 1864 (see 18 Mar 64 to PAM, n. 9). Most of Clemens's indebtedness to John A. Paxton and W. B. Thornburgh, Virginia City banking partners (Kelly 1863, 175, 270, 287), may have been an obligation he incurred in assisting his old friend, Neil Moss, "the Prodigal" of chapters 55 and 59 of *Roughing It* (see 18? May 63 to JLC and PAM, n. 2). *That* debt still remained unpaid late in 1864, for, according to chapter 59 of *Roughing It*, Clemens was haunted at the time by a collector "who had in his hands the Virginia banker's bill for the forty-six dollars which I had loaned my schoolmate, the 'Prodigal.' . . . But he never collected that bill, at last nor any part of it. I lived to pay it to the banker myself."

[3] Originally from New York, Rollin M. Daggett (1831–1901) had spent several years as a San Francisco journalist, founding the *Golden Era* (1852) and the daily *Evening Mirror* (1860). In 1862 he moved to Virginia City and, in partnership with Warren F. Myers, established a brokerage house (Myers and Daggett) specializing in mining stock. That same year Daggett became a part-time reporter for the *Territorial Enterprise*. In 1864 he joined the paper's editorial staff and in 1874 he succeeded Joseph T. Goodman as editor-in-chief. Later he was a Republican congressman from Nevada (1879–81) and United States minister resident to Hawaii (1882–85). Myers and Daggett owned the building at 25 North B Street that housed their offices, the Virginia City Library and Reading Rooms, and Clemens and De Quille's apartment. The two *Enterprise* reporters had made an agreement to rent their quarters, at $30 a month, from 28 October 1863 to 28 November 1864. When Clemens left Virginia City on 29 May 1864 they had paid only $135 of the $210 due to that point. Clemens had paid an additional $25 on 31 August

"pr, Sale of Mining Stock" (statement of rental account, 13 Dec 64, NvHi, photofacsimile in Mack 1947, 246), leaving him owing $12.50 of his share of the rent through May. Possibly Myers and Daggett maintained that he was also responsible for half the rent through 28 November, particularly since De Quille seems to have had trouble finding a satisfactory roommate to replace him (Weisenburger, 2, 5, 52–53, 61; Angel, 317, 322; Daggett 1893b, 15; William Wright 1893b, 13; Kelly 1863, 203, 253, 265; *BDAC*, 771).

[4] Joseph T. Goodman and Denis E. McCarthy. Also mentioned in this paragraph are *Enterprise* assistant editor Charles A. V. Putnam, who returned to Virginia City by early October, and the paper's bookkeeper, Henry P. Cohen (Doten 1973, 1:807). Cohen had been appointed "Notary Public for Storey county *vice* Mark Twain, resigned" ("Still Another," Virginia City *Evening Bulletin*, 22 Apr 64, 3).

[5] Clemens made his arrangments for a shorter work day with George E. Barnes (d. 1897), proprietor of the San Francisco *Morning Call*. As the next letter indicates, their agreement also called for a reduction in Clemens's salary (see also *CofC*, 16–19).

To Jane Lampton Clemens and Pamela A. Moffett
25 September 1864 • San Francisco, Calif.
(MS: NPV)

ˌP. S.—Jerome Rice was an old friend of mine at the Lick House a year ago. We always sat together at table. He used always to pledge his "lost wife & babies" in his wine at dinner, & wonder whether they were living or dead & I used to stand security that he should live to see them again, poor fellow. He was one of the best men in the world. His wife went from the ship to the funeral,—& afterwards lay in a swoon 36 hours. While Rice was here rolling in suddenly acquired wealth, his wife was wearing stockings in Texas which she made out of old pieces of blanket. She was in the enemy'sˌies country, & could not escape. She had a hard time.ˌ[1]

San Francisco,
Sept. 25, ~~188~~ 1864.

My Dear Mother & Sister

You can see by my picture that this superb climate agrees with me. And it ought, after living where I was never out of sight of snow-banks 24 hours during 3 years. Here we have neither snow nor cold weather, fires are never lighted, & yet summer clothes are never worn—you ~~were~~ wear spring clothing the year round.

Steve Gillis, who has been my comrade for 2 years, & who came down here with me, is to be married, in a week or two, to a very pretty girl worth $130,000 in her own right²—& then I shall be alone again, until they build a house, which they will do shortly.

We have been here only 4 months, yet we have changed our lodgings 5 times, & our hotel twice. We are *very* comfortably fixed where we are, &h now, & have no fault to find with the rooms or with the people—we are the only lodgers in a well-to-do private family, with one grown daughter in & a piano in the parlor adjoining our room. But I need a change, & must move again. I have taken rooms further down the street. I shall stay in this little quiet street, because it is full of gardens & shrubbery, & there are none but dwelling houses in it.³

I am taking life easy, now, & I mean to keep it up for a while. I don't work at night any more. I told the "Call" folks to pay me $25 a week, & let me work only in daylight. So I get up at 10 in the morning, & quit work at 5 or 6 in the afternoon. You ask if I work for greenbacks? Hardly. Ⱦ What do you suppose I could do with greenbacks here?⁴

I have engaged to write for the new literary paper—the "Californian"—same pay I used to receive on the "Golden Era"—one article a week, fifty dollars a month. I quit the "Era," long ago. It wasn't high-toned enough. I thought that whether I was a literary "jackleg" or not, I wouldn't class myself with that style of people, anyhow. The "Californian" circulates among the highest class of the community, & is a paper the best weekly literary paper in the United States—& I suppose I ought to know.⁵

I work as I always did—by fits & starts. I wrote two articles last night for the Californian, so that lets me out for 2 weeks.⁶ That would be about seventy-five dollars, in greenbacks, wouldn't it?

Been down to San José (generally pronounced Sanno*zay*—emphasis on last syllable)—today—50 miles from here, by Railroad. Town of 6,000 inhabitants, buried in flowers & shrubbery. The climate is finer than ours here, because it is not so close to the ocean, & is protected from the winds by the coast range.

I had an invitation today, to ⱷ go down on an excursion to San Luis Obispo & from thence to the city of Mexico, to be gone 6 or 8 weeks, or possibly longer, but I could not accept, on account of my contract to act as chief mourner or groomsman at Steve's funeral. wedding.

I have triumphed. They refused me & other reporters some information at a branch of the Coroner's office—Massey's undertaker establishment, a few weeks ago. I published the wickedest article on them I ever wrote in my life, & you can rest assured we got all the information we wanted after that. It made Mr. Massey come to his milk, mighty quick. Next week the Coroner died, & when they came to fill the vacancy, I had a candidate pledged to take the lucrative job out of Massey's hands, & I went into the Board of Supervisors & button-,holed, hold every member & worked like a slave against for my man. When I began he hadn't a friend in the Board,. He was elected, just like a knife, & Mr Massey is out in the cold.[7] I learned to pull wires in the Washoe Legislature, & my ⅄ experience is, that when a bill is to be put through a body like that, the only thing necessary to insure success is to get the reporters to log-roll for it.

What has become of that girl of mine that got married? I mean Laura Wright.

I wrote to Aunt Ella 3 months ago. I don't hear often from Orion & Mollie. I hardly ever write. When you write to me, write through Orion.

By the new census, San Francisco has a population of $ 130,000. They don't count the hordes of Chinamen.

Yrs afftly
Sam.

I send a picture for Annie, & one for Aunt Ella—that is, if she will have it.[8]

---

[1] Clemens had stayed at the Lick House in September 1863 while he was in San Francisco attempting to cure a cold. Jerome Rice was a local auctioneer and real-estate dealer who suffered fatal injuries when his carriage went over an embankment on 7 September 1864. He survived four nights at the site of the accident before being rescued, but died shortly thereafter. Clemens published an account of Rice's ordeal in the *Morning Call* of 13 September, where he commented:

> His wife and family, who have been enduring for four years all the privations and misfortunes that war could entail upon them in a section of Texas desolated alternately by both contending parties, and whom he had not seen and scarcely ever heard from during that time, will arrive here from Boston, (to which port they lately escaped,) day after to-morrow. . . . Who, among all the brave men that shall read this sad chapter of disasters, could carry, with firm nerve, the bitter tidings to the unsuspecting widow and her orphans, and uncoffin before them a mutilated corpse in place of the loving husband and father they are yearning to embrace? ("Sad Accident—Death of Jerome Rice," *CofC*, 124)

Clemens probably enclosed a clipping of this article in his letter.

[2] See 28 Sept 64 to OC and MEC, n. 3.

[3] The San Francisco directory effective October 1864 listed Clemens at 32 Minna Street and Steve Gillis—along with his younger brother, William (1840–1929), and their father, Angus (1800–70)—on Brannan Street, between Seventh and Eighth streets. Clemens's next known move kept him on the "little quiet street": the directory effective December 1865 put him and Steve Gillis at the

rooming house that Angus Gillis was then operating at 44 Minna Street (Langley 1864, 106, 174; Langley 1865, 121, 195; William R. Gillis to Harry A. Williams, 31 May 1924, PH in CU-MARK).

⁴In February and July 1862 the United States government, pressed to meet Civil War costs, had passed laws authorizing the issue of treasury notes unbacked by specie. Although these "greenbacks" were legal tender for all debts public and private, gold coin remained the dominant currency in California (Mitchell, 74–79, 81–98, 142–44). The value of greenbacks in the San Francisco market fluctuated; at the time of this letter a $1.00 greenback was worth $.4775 in gold ("San Francisco Stock and Exchange Board, 24 September, 1864," San Francisco *Alta California*, 25 Sept 64, 6). Federal employees had to accept their pay in greenbacks, but Clemens, like other nonfederal workers, received his salary (reduced fifteen dollars a week under his "daylight" arrangements) in gold. Six times from 31 July to 2 October 1864, he protested in the *Morning Call* on behalf of federal employees, who had to purchase goods and services in gold despite being paid in the depreciated paper currency (see *CofC*, 227–31).

⁵The *Californian* first appeared in May 1864, owned and initially edited by Charles Henry Webb (1834–1905) with Bret Harte (1836–1902) as the principal contributor. Harte also acted as its editor between 10 September and 19 November 1864 and presumably accepted the first nine of Clemens's contributions, eight of which have been identified (see *ET&S2*, 66–71, 72, 79–133). Webb and Harte had been associated with the popular *Golden Era* and hoped to capture its audience with an elegant format and more sophisticated material. In order to accomplish this, the *Californian* "attracted the most able writers of the metropolis during its short but expensive life. Its principal failings—that it confined itself too much to polite essays and satires and that it ignored local color almost entirely—were results of the temper of the period" (Walker 1969, 178). The paper changed hands in 1866, but, unable to achieve financial success, survived only another two years.

⁶Mark Twain's first contribution to the *Californian*, published on 1 October 1864, was "A Notable Conundrum," about the Fourth Industrial Fair of the Mechanics' Institute in San Francisco. The second sketch referred to here cannot now be identified (see *ET&S2*, 66–71, 72).

⁷The "wickedest article" was "A Small Piece of Spite," published in the *Morning Call* on 6 September 1864 (see *CofC*, 233–36). Atkins Massey (1819–92) was San Francisco's leading undertaker; Coroner Benjamin A. Sheldon (1825–64) had an office in Massey's funeral parlor at 651 Sacramento Street. The coroner elected after Sheldon's sudden death on 10 September was Dr. Stephen R. Harris (1802–79), who had been San Francisco's third mayor from 1 January to 9 November 1852 (Heintz, 16–19).

⁸The photographs for Ella Hunter Lampton and Annie Moffett were probably duplicates of the one mentioned in the first paragraph (not the postscript). No copy of the photograph has been found.

To Orion and Mary E. (Mollie) Clemens
28 September 1864 • San Francisco, Calif.
(MS: CU-MARK)

"Call Office"[1]

San F. 28th

My Dear Bro & Sister.

I guess my letter was not under way so long—I never date a letter right.[2]

I *would* commence on my book, but (mind, this is a secret, & must not be mentioned,) Steve & I are getting things ready for his wedding, which will take place on the 24th Oct. He will marry Miss Emmelina Russ, who is worth $100,000, & what is much better, is a good, sensible girl & will make an excellent wife. Of course I shall "stand up" with Steve, at the nuptials, as chief mourner. ₐWe shall take a bridal tour of a week's duration.ₐ[3]

~~Your head~~

Your head is eminently sound on the subject of marriage. I am resolved on that or suicide—perhaps.

I only get $12 an article for the Californian, but you see it makes my wages up to what they were on the Call, ₐwhen I worked at night,ₐ & the paper ~~is~~ has an exalted reputation in the east, & is liberally copied from by papers like the Home Journal.[4]

Orion, the H & N assessment is not ~~due~~ ₐdelinquent,ₐ until the 1st Nov, & I may be able to pay all of it myself. In the meantime I will hold on to the check, & if you should need it, let me know.[5]

Well Mollie I *do* go to church. How's that?

As soon as this wedding business is over, I believe I will send to you for the files, & begin on my book.[6]

Yr Bro

Sam

[1] The offices of the San Francisco *Morning Call* were in "a new brick building at 612 Commercial Street" (*CofC*, 12).

[2] Possibly a reference, perhaps in jest, to the letter of 13 and 14 August to Orion and Mollie which Clemens had misdated by one day. This remark may indicate, however, that he sent them another letter, now lost, subsequent to that one.

[3] Emeline Russ was the daughter of Emanuel Charles Christian Russ (1795–1857), a manufacturing jeweler who became "the most extensive owner of real property in San Francisco" (Swasey, 233). His son Adolph (b. 1826) built the Russ

House, a luxurious hotel on Montgomery Street completed in 1862. Emeline Russ did not marry Steve Gillis; on 28 December 1867 she married Frederick Gutzkow, superintendent of the San Francisco Assaying and Refining Works (Swasey, 229; Bancroft 1891–92, 6:533–40; Langley 1867, 226; "Married," San Francisco *Morning Call*, 31 Dec 67, 3). Gillis, according to his brother William, married "Miss Kate Robinson, a niece of Mrs. J. T. Goodman, in December, 1867. After his marriage he took up his residence in San Francisco, working at the case there until 1871" (William R. Gillis, 34). He then returned with his wife to Virginia City.

[4] The New York *Home Journal*, a literary weekly that had begun publication in 1846 (Mott 1938, 2:349–55).

[5] Clemens had recently criticized the Hale and Norcross company's assessment practices (see 13 and 14 Aug 64 to OC and MEC, n. 5). On 21 September 1864, the following notice had appeared in the San Francisco *Alta California* (4):

Hale and Norcross Silver Mining Company, Virginia District, Nevada Territory.—Notice is hereby given, that at a meeting of the Board of Trustees of said Company, held on the 13th day of September, 1864, an assessment of $25 per share was levied upon the capital stock of said Company, payable forthwith, in United States gold coin, to the Secretary, at his office, No. 60 Exchange Building. Any stock upon which said assessment shall remain unpaid on SATURDAY, the 15th day of October, 1864, will be advertised on that day as delinquent, and unless payment shall be made before, will be sold on Tuesday, the 1st day of November, 1864, to pay the delinquent assessment, together with costs of advertising and expenses of the sale. By order of the Board of Trustees.

JOEL F. LIGHTNER, Sec'y.
Office, No. 60 Exchange Building, San Francisco.

Four shares that Clemens had put in Orion's name (stock certificate number 484) were among those advertised as delinquent in the *Alta California* during the second half of October. The total assessment of $100 on these shares was paid, however, apparently by Clemens, on 21 October (receipted bill in CU-MARK).

[6] An early plan for a book along the lines of *Roughing It*. The "files" were the clippings from Nevada newspapers, including *Territorial Enterprise* articles by Clemens, which Orion had been pasting in scrapbooks since his arrival in the territory. Six scrapbooks, covering the period 1861–64, survive in the Mark Twain Papers (CU-MARK).

To Orion Clemens
18 October 1864 • San Francisco, Calif.
(MS: CU-MARK)

San F, Oct. 18, '64.

My Dear Bro

Capt Blaisdell[1] says they talk some of running you for U S Senate. Do you think you stand any show? If so, maybe you had better make friends with your Carson enemies—that is, if you approve of the Scriptural doctrine which makes it a man's duty to love his enemies.[2]

I am getting along satisfactorily.[3] Send the stock—send the stock. If I don't sell it I will send it back, & I shan't sell without advice from Sam Martin, at Va, who is watching the mine.[4]

My Love to Mollie. I wrote to Ma yesterday.

Yr Bro
Sam.

[1] Henry Goode Blasdel (1825–1900), originally from Indiana, had come to Virginia City in 1860, after eight years as a miner, farmer, and merchant in California. His Nevada mining interests extended as far as Aurora and included, in the Virginia district, the construction of the Empire and Hoosier State mills and the superintendency of the Potosi and the Hale and Norcross mines. On 8 November 1864, eight days after Nevada was admitted to the Union, Blasdel was elected its first state governor. He was reelected in 1866, serving through 1870. Clemens's designation of him here as "Capt" has not been explained; the title may have been a relic of Blasdel's former connection with the steamboat business in Aurora, Indiana (*DAB*, 2:358).

[2] Orion Clemens never became a candidate for senatorial office. It was generally assumed that he would be chosen secretary of state in the election of 8 November 1864, particularly since he had won that office in the voided election of 19 January 1864 (see 2? Jan 64 to JLC, n. 4). Unfortunately, as Samuel Clemens later recalled, Orion

was hit with one of his spasms of virtue on the very day that the Republican party was to make its nominations in the Convention. Orion refused to go near the Convention. He was urged, but all persuasions failed. He said his presence there would be an unfair and improper influence, and that if he was to be nominated the compliment must come to him as a free and unspotted gift. This attitude would have settled his case for him without further effort, but he had another spasm of virtue on the same day, and that made it absolutely sure. . . . On nomination day he suddenly changed from a friendly attitude toward whiskey—which was the popular attitude—to uncompromising teetotalism, and went absolutely dry. His friends besought and implored, but all in vain. He could not be persuaded to cross the threshold of a saloon. The paper next morning contained the list of chosen nominees. His name was not in it. He had not received a vote. (AD, 5 Apr 1906, CU-MARK, in *MTA*, 2:318)

The Republican candidate for secretary of state, elected in November 1864, was Chauncey N. Noteware. Orion was elected to the state assembly in November 1865 and served from 1 January to 1 March 1866 (Andrew J. Marsh, 694 n. 296; Angel, 87, 529; *Journal of the Assembly*, passim).

[3] Clemens had lost the security of his weekly salary from the San Francisco *Morning Call*, having left that paper's employ on or about 10 October (see *CofC*, 23). He later explained: "I neglected my duties and became about worthless, as a reporter for a brisk newspaper. And at last one of the proprietors took me aside, with a charity I still remember with considerable respect, and gave me an opportunity to resign my berth and so save myself the disgrace of a dismissal" (*Roughing It*, chapter 58). George E. Barnes, an editor as well as one of the proprietors of the *Call*, remembered that Clemens, "although at the time a good general writer and correspondent, . . . made but an indifferent reporter. He only played at itemizing." He "parted from THE CALL people on the most friendly terms, when it

was found necessary to make the local department more efficient, admitting his reportorial shortcomings and expressing surprise they were not sooner discovered" (Barnes, 1). Clemens's only source of income now was the *Californian*, which, according to the previous two letters, paid him either $12.00 or $12.50 per article.

⁴Samuel G. Martin was the foreman at the printing office of the Virginia City *Territorial Enterprise* and the first president of the Washoe Typographical Union, organized in May 1863 (Kelly 1863, 256; Doten 1973, 3:2251). The mine he was watching for Clemens was the Hale and Norcross.

To Orion Clemens
11 November 1864 • San Francisco, Calif.
(MS: CU-MARK)

S F 11ᵗʰ—

My Dʳ Bro—

I have been trying to borrow that money, but I do not think—in fact I am pretty certain—that I cannot do it. They all say the same thing: that you have no specific contract law, & they will not send money where there is no protection for it.¹ Steve's brother-in-law, money-lender,² & Geo. Davis, & Henriques the prominent real estate & money broker,³ all say the same thing. Therefore, do not expect anything from my efforts.

Sandy Baldwin is already in Carson—cannot you borrow the money from him on your scrip?

Dawson says Daggett ~~will~~ & Fitch will be likely to euchre you out of the nomination.⁴ He will if lying & swindling can do it. I know Daggett & Fitch both, & I swear a solemn oath that I believe that they would blast the characters of their own mothers & sisters to gain any great advantage in life. I know both dogs well. Look out for them. ₍They are two-faced.₎

I am watching the H & N. in the hope that it may go up a little & sell for enough to set you up in your new home free from debt—if it will do that, it is all I want.⁵ Cook says the mine was looking better some days ago, & he would not be surprised if it turned out well, yet.⁶

Yr Bro

Sam

¹By an act passed on 27 April 1863, California had established that "in an action on a contract or obligation in writing, for the direct payment of money, made payable in a specified kind of money or currency, judgment for the plaintiff,

whether the same be by default or after verdict, may follow the contract or obligation, and made payable in the kind of money or currency specified therein" (*Statutes*, 687). This act protected those who loaned money in gold from being repaid in less valuable greenbacks. As Clemens notes, Nevada did not have similar legislation (Mack 1936, 283–85).

[2] Emeline Russ, supposedly Steve Gillis's fiancée, had five brothers, none of whom has been identified as a "money-lender" (Swasey, 233–41).

[3] David Henriques was a member of the San Francisco stock exchange (Langley 1864, lxix). George Davis has not been identified.

[4] Born and educated in New York City, Thomas Fitch (1838–1923) had been a newspaper editor in Milwaukee, and a newspaper editor, lawyer, and state assemblyman in California before moving to Virginia City in June 1863. That year he became an editor of the Virginia City *Union*. The following year he founded a Sunday literary paper, the *Weekly Occidental*, which Clemens recalled as "a feeble, struggling, stupid journal" that folded after four issues (*Roughing It*, chapter 51). In fact, the *Occidental* seems to have issued at least six times, from 6 March through 10 April 1864 (Rogers 1957, 365–70; "Sheriff's Sale," Virginia City *Territorial Enterprise* of unknown date, reprinting the *Weekly Occidental* of 10 Apr 64, PH in CU-MARK, courtesy of Michael H. Marleau). From 1 July to 8 August 1864, Fitch was copublisher of the Virginia City *Evening Washoe Herald*, a daily crusading reform paper. Famed for his powers as an orator, Fitch served as Washoe County district attorney (1865–66) and as a Republican congressman from Nevada (1869–71) (*BDAC*, 891; Angel, 87–88; Lingenfelter and Gash, 257–58).

[5] The daily reports of the San Francisco Stock and Exchange Board, published in the *Alta California*, show that from a low of $200 per share in late August 1864, the bid price of Hale and Norcross stock had boomed to $1,000 per share the day before Clemens wrote the present letter. On 11 November the price dropped to $940 and then suffered a predominantly downward fluctuation, sagging to $310 by 1 December and averaging slightly less than that for the rest of the year. Clemens evidently was short of funds in November, but by early December, when he went to Jackass Hill, California, he had a substantial amount of cash in hand, perhaps from a sale of some or all of the four shares of Hale and Norcross stock he had put in Orion's name. Unfortunately, a conjecture that Clemens sold stock at that time, however reasonable, does not help reconcile his conflicting accounts of his Hale and Norcross transactions (see 26 May 64 to OC, n. 4). His investment in the company apparently terminated ignominiously in mid-1865 when, according to chapter 62 of *Roughing It*, his income in San Francisco was at low ebb. On 8 May of that year his name was listed in a Hale and Norcross assessment delinquency notice as the owner of two shares (stock certificate 664). On 19 May those two shares were offered for sale by a San Francisco auction firm in order to pay off a total assessment of $50 ("Hale and Norcross Silver Mining Company," San Francisco *Alta California*: 8 May 65, 2; 19 May 65, 3). The bid price for the stock was then $460 per share.

[6] Clemens's informant may have been John Cook, a Virginia City miner (Kelly 1863, 184).

NO LETTERS have been discovered for the next eleven months. As 1864 drew to a close Clemens continued to eke out an existence on the $12.00 or $12.50 per article he received from the *Californian*. Since he published only three articles at this time, on 12 November, 19 November, and 3 December (see *ET&S2*, 108–33), his circumstances must have been straitened indeed. According to the chronology Clemens established in *Roughing It*, in early December 1864 he was coming to the end of his "slinking" period:

> For two months my sole occupation was avoiding acquaintances; for during that time I did not earn a penny, or buy an article of any kind, or pay my board. I became a very adept at "slinking." I slunk from back street to back street, I slunk away from approaching faces that looked familiar, I slunk to my meals, ate them humbly and with a mute apology for every mouthful I robbed my generous land-lady of, and at midnight, after wanderings that were but slinkings away from cheerfulness and light, I slunk to my bed. I felt meaner, and lowlier and more despicable than the worms. During all this time I had but one piece of money—a silver ten cent piece—and I held to it and would not spend it on any account, lest the consciousness coming strong upon me that I was *entirely* penniless, might suggest suicide. I had pawned every thing but the clothes I had on; so I clung to my dime desperately, till it was smooth with handling. (*Roughing It*, chapter 59)

On 4 December Clemens escaped to Jackass Hill, in Tuolumne County, about one hundred miles east of San Francisco, a once-rich placer-mining region. "I took $300 with me," he later recalled (2 July 71 to James N. Gillis, CCamarSJ). Clemens used this money, which possibly came from the sale of stock in the Hale and Norcross Silver Mining Company, to pay his board and other expenses during the next twelve weeks, while he was away from San Francisco and not working. Reportedly he had chosen Jackass Hill

> at the suggestion of his friend, Steve Gillis, who had got into trouble with the San Francisco police by intervening in a saloon fight and whipping a bullying bartend-er. Mark had signed a straw bond for $500 and when it looked as though the police meant business both he and Steve decided to go away from there. Steve himself went back to Virginia City and consigned Sam to the hospitality of his brothers.
>
> James and William Gillis were pocket miners on the hill, and [Richard] Stoker was their partner. Stoker was 46 and "gray as a rat," a quiet, philosophic veteran of forty-nine who had chosen this quiet life and who was destined to spend thirty years more there and to die on the hill in 1896. Billy was only 23, and had joined his older brother, Jim, on the hill the year before. (West, 13, 18)

Clemens remained at Jackass Hill, living in the one-room cabin Stoker
had built in 1850, until 22 January 1865. On that date he accompanied
Jim Gillis (1830–1907) to nearby Angels Camp, in Calaveras County,
where Gillis had a mining claim. Winter rains immediately stranded them
in their lodgings and they were still confined eight days later when Stoker
joined them. The rain stopped on 6 February, and presumably they were
then able to do some mining. Mostly, however, through the rain and after,
they and others passed the time exchanging tall tales and anecdotes. By
the time Clemens and his two friends returned to Jackass Hill on 20 February, his notebook was stocked with material that he used in the months
and years to come (see *N&J1*, 63–90). Billy Gillis later recalled that
Clemens immediately attempted to write out one of the tales he had heard
at Angels Camp: "When Sam came back he went to work on the Jumping
Frog story, staying in the cabin while we went out to work at our claims
and writing with a pencil. He used to say: 'If I can write that story the way
Ben Coon told it, that frog will jump around the world'" (West, 18).
Clemens started back to San Francisco, via Copperopolis and Stockton,
on 23 February, arriving at the Occidental Hotel on the twenty-sixth. In
chapter 62 of *Roughing It* he reported: "After a three months' absence, I
found myself in San Francisco again, without a cent. When my credit was
about exhausted, (for I had become too mean and lazy, now, to work on a
morning paper, and there were no vacancies on the evening journals,) I
was created San Francisco correspondent of the *Enterprise*, and at the end
of five months I was out of debt."

In fact the *Enterprise* assignment was not Clemens's first work after his
return. Before undertaking that he resumed his contributions to the *Californian*, using some of his Tuolumne and Calaveras material in two of the
sketches he published in the spring of 1865—"An Unbiased Criticism"
and "Answers to Correspondents" (see *ET&S2*, 134–43, 187–96). Probably by mid-June he had begun contributing to the *Enterprise* as well and
soon afterward he began the daily correspondence for it that earned him
a welcome $100 a month. That summer and fall he also published brief
items in the San Francisco *Dramatic Chronicle* and the San Francisco
Youths' Companion (see *ET&S2*, 233–35, 297–99, 240–45).

By early September 1865 Clemens's *Californian* articles had won praise
across the continent in the New York *Round Table*. The Angels Camp frog
tale—transformed in mid-October into "Jim Smiley and His Jumping
Frog" and published in the New York *Saturday Press* on 18 November—

was to make him a budding literary celebrity before the end of the year (for detailed discussion and texts of Clemens's 1864–65 publications, see *ET&S1* and *ET&S2*). Not coincidentally, the day after Clemens completed the "Jumping Frog" and saw the *Round Table* praises reprinted in the San Francisco *Dramatic Chronicle*, he acknowledged his " 'call' to literature," albeit ambivalently, in the next letter.

To Orion and Mary E. (Mollie) Clemens
19 and 20 October 1865 • San Francisco, Calif.
(MS, *damage emended:* CU-MARK)

ₐP. S. You had better shove this in the stove—for if we strike a bargain I don't want any absurd "literary remains" & "unpublished letters of Mark Twain" published after I am planted.ₐ

San F.—Oct. 19, 1865.

My Dear Bro & Sister:

Orion there was **genius**—true, unmistakeable **genius**—in that sermon of yours. It was not the gilded base metal that passes for intellectual gold too generally in this world of ours. It is one of the few sermons that I have read with pleasure—I do not say profit, because I am beyond the reach of argument now. But seven or eight years ago that single sermon would have saved me. It even made me **think**—yea, & *regret*, for a while, as it was. (Don't preach from ~~this~~ ₐthe above, text, next time.) Viewed as a **literary** production, that sermon was first-class.

And now let me preach *you* a sermon. I never had but two **powerful** ambitions in my life. One was to be a pilot, & the other a preacher of the gospel. I accomplished the one & failed in the other, **because** I could not supply myself with the necessary stock in trade—*i.e.* religion. I have given it up forever. I never had a "call" in that direction, anyhow, & my aspirations were the very ecstasy of presumption. ~~An~~ But I *have* had a "call" to literature, of a low order—*i.e.* humorous. It is nothing to be proud of, but it is my strongest suit, & if I were to listen to that maxim of stern *duty* which says ~~it is m~~ that to do right you **must** multiply the one or the two or the three talents which the Almighty entrusts to your keeping,[1]

I would long ago have ceased to meddle with things for which I was by nature unfitted & turned my attention to seriously scribbling to excite the **laughter** of God's creatures. Poor, pitiful business! Though the Almighty did His part by me—for the talent is a mighty engine when supplied with the steam of **education,**—which I have not got, & so its pistons & cylinders & shafts move feebly & for a holiday show & are useless for any good purpose.

But as I was saying, it is **human nature** to yearn to be what we were never intended for. It is singular, but it is so. I wanted to be a pilot or a preacher, & I was about as well calculated for either as is poor Emperor Norton for Chief Justice of the United States.[2] Now *you* aspire to be a **lawyer,** when the voice of God is thundering in your ears, & you are wilfully deaf & will not hear. *You* were **intended** for a preacher, & lo! you would be a scheming, groveling, mud-cat of a **lawyer.** A man **never is** willing to do what his Creator intended him to do. You are honest, pious, virtuous—what would you have more? **Go forth & preach.** When you preach from a pulpit, I will listen to you & not before. Until that time, I will read your sermons with sincere pleasure, but only as **literary gems.** That is my ultimatum. Ever since I got acquainted with you—which was in the autumn of 1861—I have thought many & many & **many** a time ~~what~~ how you would tower head & shoulders above any of the small-fry preachers of my experience! I know what I am talking about. It is the nature of man to see as by the light of noonday the talents of his neighbor, (& to which that neighbor is blind as night,) & at the same time to be unaware of his own talents while he is gazing afar off at those of ~~his~~ ₓthatₓ neighbor ,ₗ, as aforesaid. *You* see in me a talent for humorous writing, & urge me to cultivate it. But I always regarded it as brotherly partiality, ₓon your part,ₓ & attached no value to it. It is only now, when editors of standard literary papers in the distant east give me high praise, & who do not know me & cannot of course be blinded by ~~partiality~~ the glamour of partiality, that I really begin to believe there must be something in it.[3]

But I'll toss up with you. Your letter has confirmed me. I *know*—I don't suppose—I *know* you would be great & useful as a minister of the gospel, & I am satisfied you will never be any better lawyer than a good many others. Now I don't know how you regard the ministry, but *I* would rather be a shining light in that department than the greatest lawyer that ever trod the earth. What is the pride of saving the widow's property or the homicide's trivial life, to snatching an immortal soul in mercy from the jaws of hell? Bah! the one is the ~~insignificant~~ ˌfeebleˌ glitter of the firefly, & the other the regal glory of the sun.

But as I said, I will toss up with you. I will drop all trifling, & sighing after vain impossibilities, & strive for a fame—unworthy & evanescent though it must of necessity be—if you will record your promise to go hence to the States & preach the gospel when circumstances shall enable you to do so? I am in earnest. Shall it be so?

I am also in debt. But I have gone to work in dead earnest to get out. Joe Goodman pays me $100 a month for a daily letter, and the Dramatic Chronicle pays me $ —or rather *will* begin to pay me, next week—$40 a month for dramatic criticisms. Same wages I got on the *Call*, & more agreeable & less laborious work.[4]

Mollie, my dear, I send you slathers of love. Wrote to Ma to-night.

> Yr Bro
> Sam.

[in pencil, on back of letter as folded:]

Friday—Have just got your letter. The "prospects" are infernal, Mollie. "Confidence" is down low. I saved on the Ophir $25, but *not* losing the $100 assessment I would have had to pay had I held it a few days longer. All stocks have their day, & "Confidence" will, too—I *did* want to wait on *one* stock till its day arrived, but your prospects do not look encouraging.[5] ~~Go on, I~~

I read all your sermons—and I shall continue to read them, but of course as unsympathetically as a man of stone. I have a religion—but you will call it blasphemy. It is that there is a God for the rich man but none for the poor.

You are in trouble, & in debt—so am I. I am utterly miserable—so are you. ~~Koe~~ Perhaps your religion will sustain you, will feed you—I place no dependence in mine. Our religions are alike, though, in one respect—neither can make a man happy when he is out of luck. If I do not get out of debt in 3 months,—pistols or poison for one—exit *me*. [There's a text for a sermon on Self-Murder—Proceed.][6]

---

[1] Matthew 25:14–30, the parable of the talents.

[2] Joshua A. Norton came to San Francisco in 1849 and was soon a successful merchant and real-estate speculator. In 1853 he lost his entire fortune, reportedly in a scheme to corner the local rice market, after which he disappeared for about

four years. He returned in uniform, calling himself "Norton I, Emperor of the United States." For twenty-three years he remained a San Francisco fixture, a kindly lunatic who paraded the streets, attended public functions, circulated his own currency, and issued sometimes visionary proclamations. His death in 1880 was the occasion of an elaborate public funeral (Dickson, 141–48; Cowan, Bancroft, and Ballou, 30–59, 91–103).

[3] On 18 October the San Francisco *Dramatic Chronicle* ("Recognized," 3) reprinted the following remarks by the editor of the New York *Round Table*:

> The enterprising State of California, which follows as closely as she can upon the steps of her older Eastern sisters, has produced some examples of our national humor which compare favorably with those already mentioned. They are but little known in this region, and few, if any, have yet appeared "between covers." The foremost among the merry gentlemen of the California press, as far as we have been able to judge, is one who signs himself "Mark Twain." Of his real name we are ignorant, but his style resembles that of "John Phoenix" more nearly than any other, and some things we have seen from his pen would do honor to the memory of even that chieftain among humorists. He is, we believe, quite a young man, and has not written a great deal. Perhaps, if he will husband his resources and not kill with overwork the mental goose that has given us these golden eggs, he may one day take rank among the brightest of our wits. ("American Humor and Humorists," *Round Table*, 9 Sept 65, 2)

[4] The demands of producing a daily *Enterprise* letter made it difficult for Clemens to meet other commitments. After contributing four pieces to the *Californian* in May 1865 and four more in June, he managed to write only seven original articles for that journal over the next six months (see *ET&S2*, 144–232, 250–61, 359–66, 405–12, and Howell, 188–90). No drama reviews by him have been located in the San Francisco *Dramatic Chronicle*, although between 26 October and 19 December he did contribute several dozen unsigned brief items to that paper, which on 17 October had published his "Earthquake Almanac." He also published three letters in the *Napa County Reporter*, on 11 and 25 November and 2 December (see *ET&S2*, 297–99, 371–75, 380–84, 481–512).

[5] Orion Clemens's circumstances in Carson City were worse than his brother's in San Francisco. No longer collecting a salary and fees as territorial secretary and having failed to secure an office under the state government elected in November 1864, Orion was forced to strike out on his own. Samuel Clemens later remembered that "he put up his sign as attorney at law, but he got no clients" (AD, 5 Apr 1906, CU-MARK, in *MTA*, 2:318–19). Five months after the present letter Orion left Nevada (see 22 May 66 to MEC, n. 1).

[6] On 21 April 1909, in a marginal note in his copy of the *Letters of James Russell Lowell*, Clemens recalled an "experience of 1866" when "I put the pistol to my head but wasn't man enough to pull the trigger. Many times I have been sorry I did not succeed, but I was never ashamed of having tried. Suicide is the only really sane thing the young or the old ever do in this life" (SLC 1909b, 1:375). This attempt must have come no later than the first days of 1866. Surely by 20 January, when he boasted of his literary success to his mother and sister and outlined an array of short- and long-term literary projects, Clemens was no longer disposed to consider "Self-Murder."

To Orion and Mary E. (Mollie) Clemens
13 December 1865 • San Francisco, Calif.
(MS: CU-MARK)

ₐSend the memoranda *at once.*ₐ

San F. Dec. 13. Wednes.

My Dear Bro.

I have just made a proposition to an old friend of mine—a "rustler," an energetic, ~~untr~~ untiring business man & a man of capital & large ⱡNew York business associations & facilities. He ~~lev~~ leaves for the east 5 days hence—on the 19ᵗʰ· I told him we had 30,000 acres land in Tennessee, & there was oil on it⸝—& if he would send me $500 from New York to go east with, $500 more after I got there, & pay all my expenses while I assisted him in selling the land, I would give him one-half of the entire proceeds of the sale of the land.

Herman Camp offered me half, 2 years ago, if I would go with him to New York & help him sell some mining claims, & I, like a fool, refused. He went, & made $270,000 ¢ in two months. He is independent, now, & I had to make *him* a liberal offer. Men from New York tell me that Camp's mines have given better satisfaction than any that were sold in that market; he was shrewd enough to sell them well.[1]

Now I don't want that Tenn land to go for taxes, & I don't want any "slouch" to take charge of the sale of it. I am tired being a beggar—tired being chained to this accursed homeless desert,—I want to go back to a Christian land once more—& so I want you to send me immediately all necessary memoranda to enable Camp to understand the condition, & quantity & resources of the land, & how he must go about finding it. He will visit St Louis & talk with the folks, & then go at once & see the land, & telegraph me whether he closes with my proposition or not. Write me these particulars at once, as he ~~la~~ leaves on the 19ᵗʰ. Send letters of introduction to me for him—to dwellers on the Tenn. land who can assist in showing him over it. He says the land is valuable now that there is peace & no slavery, even if it have no oil in it.[2]

Dear Mollie—It keeps raining, so we can't go shopping, Mrs. B.[3] being unwell. Hold on a day or two.

Yrs Bro

Sam

[1] Herman Camp was an early locator on the Comstock lode and an aggressive speculator in Washoe mining stocks. He had been friendly with Clemens in Virginia City and then in San Francisco while Clemens was staying there in mid-1863. Camp had gone from San Francisco to New York in June 1863, apparently remaining at least until late August 1864. At the end of January 1865 Clemens had made the following notebook record of Camp's mining sales: "Herman Camp has sold some Washoe Stock in New York for $270,000" (*N&J1*, 73; Angel, 58, 59; *ET&S1*, 487; "The Departing Steamer," San Francisco *Alta California*, 3 June 63, 1; Marshall, 1).

[2] Clemens later gave this account of Camp's plans and their outcome:

He agreed to buy our Tennessee land for two hundred thousand dollars, pay a part of the amount in cash and give long notes for the rest. His scheme was to import foreigners from grape-growing and wine-making districts in Europe, settle them on the land, and turn it into a wine-growing country. . . . I sent the contracts and things to Orion for his signature, he being one of the three heirs. But they arrived at a bad time—in a doubly bad time, in fact. The temperance virtue was temporarily upon him in strong force, and he wrote and said that he would not be a party to debauching the country with wine. Also he said how could he know whether Mr. Camp was going to deal fairly and honestly with those poor people from Europe or not?—and so, without waiting to find out, he quashed the whole trade, and there it fell, never to be brought to life again. The land, from being suddenly worth two hundred thousand dollars, became as suddenly worth what it was before—nothing, and taxes to pay. (AD, 5 Apr 1906, CU-MARK, in *MTA*, 2:320–21)

[3] Unidentified.

To Jane Lampton Clemens and Pamela A. Moffett
20 January 1866 • San Francisco, Calif.
(MS: CU-MARK)

San Francisco,

Jan. 20, 1865.[1]

My Dear Mother & Sister:

Ma's last letter was sent me by Mollie to-day.

I don't know what to write—my life is so uneventful. I wish I was back there piloting up & down the river again. Verily, all is vanity and little worth—save piloting. To think that after writing many an article a man might be excused for thinking tolerably good, those New York people should single out a villainous backwoods sketch to compliment me on!—"Jim Smiley & His Jumping Frog"—a squib which would never have been written but to please Artemus Ward, & then it reached New York too late to appear in his book. But no matter—his book was a wretchedly poor one, generally speaking, & it could be no credit to either of us to appear between its covers. This paragraph is from the New York correspondence of the San Francisco *Alta:*[2]

Mark Twain's story in the *Saturday Press* of November 18, called "Jim Smiley and his Jumping Frog," has set all New York in a roar, and he may be said to have made his mark. I have been asked fifty times about it and its author, and the papers are copying it far and near. It is voted the best thing of the day. Cannot the *Californian* afford to keep Mark all to itself? It should not let him scintilate so widely without first being filtered through the California press.

The New York publishing house of Carleton & Co gave the sketch to the "Saturday Press" when they found it was too late for the book.[3]

Bret Harte & I have both quit the "Californian." He will write for a Boston paper hereafter,[4] and I for the "New York Weekly Review"—~~the Saturday~~ and possibly for the "Saturday Press" sometimes. I am too lazy to write oftener than once a month, though. I sent a sketch by yesterday's steamer which will probably appear in the "Review" along about the middle or latter part of February. If it makes Annie mad I can't help it. If it makes Ma mad I can't help it. I don't mean *them* any offence at all—I am only using them as types of a class—I am merely hitting other people over their shoulders. ~~It~~ The Aunt I mention is *not* Aunt Ella or Aunt Betsy Smith—& I think they will see that she bears no resemblance to them.[5]

Though I am generally placed at the head of my breed of scribblers in this part of the country, the place properly belongs to Bret Harte, I think (late editor of the "Californian",[)] though he denies it, along with the rest. He wants me to club a lot of old sketches together with a lot of his, & publish a book together. I wouldn't do it, only he agrees to take all the trouble. But I want to know whether we are going to make anything out of it, first, however. He has written to a New York publisher, & if we are offered a bargain that will pay for a month's labor, we will go to work & prepare the volume for the press. My labor will not occupy more than 24 hours, because I will only have to take the scissors & slash my old sketches out of the Enterprise & the Californian—I burned up a small cart-load of them lately—so *they* are forever ruled out of any book—but they were not worth republishing.[6]

Understand—all this I am telling you is in confidence—we want it to go no further—however, it don't make any difference where you are, I suppose, so far away.

And we have got another secret on hand. We are going to burlesque a book of poems which the publisher, Bancroft, ¢ is to issue in the spring. We know all the tribe of California poets, & understand their different styles, & I think we can just make them get up & howl. If Bancroft prints his book in New York in the spring, ours shall be in press there at the same time, & come out promptly with his volume. Then you'll ⅃ hear these poetical asses here tear around worse than a pack of wildcats. Bancroft's book is to contain a poem by every poet in California. We shall only burlesque a few of the prominent ones, but we will introduce each burlesque poem with a blast of trumpets & some comments that will be eminently worth reading, no doubt. I am willing enough to go into this thing, because there will be *fun* in it.[7]

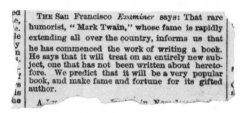

THE San Francisco *Examiner* says: That rare humorist, "Mark Twain," whose fame is rapidly extending all over the country, informs us that he has commenced the work of writing a book. He says that it will treat on an entirely new subject, one that has not been written about heretofore. We predict that it will be a very popular book, and make fame and fortune for its gifted author.

The book referred to in that paragraph is a pet notion of mine—nobody knows what it is going to be about but just myself. Orion don't know. I am slow & lazy, you know, & the bulk of it will not be finished under a year. I expect it to make about three hundred pages, and the last hundred will have to be written in St Louis, because the materials for them can only be got there. If I do not write it to suit me at first I will write it all over again, & so, who knows?—I may be an old man before I finish it. I have not written a line in it for three weeks, & may not for three more. I shall only write when the spirit moves me. I am the Genius of Indolence.[8]

I still write a letter every day for the "Enterprise." Give my love to everybody.

Aff'ly
Sam. Clemens.

P. S. Give the enclosed Enterprise letter to Zeb Leavenworth, or send it to Bill Kribben, Secretary of the Pilot's Association.[9]

That Ajax is the finest Ocean Steamer in America, & one of the fastest. She will make this trip to the Sandwich Islands & back in a month, & it generally take[s] a sailing vessel three months. She had 52 invited guests aboard—the cream of the town—gentleman & ladies both, & a splendid ~~band~~ brass band. I know lots of the guests. I got an invitation, but I could not accept it, because there would be no one to write my correspondence while I was gone. But I am so sorry now. If the Ajax were back I would go—quick!—and throw up the correspondence. Where could a man catch such another crowd together?[10]

Mark

[1]Clemens mistook the year.

[2]The clipping, glued to the manuscript letter, was from "Podgers' Letter from New York," dated 10 December 1865 (San Francisco *Alta California*, 10 Jan 66, 1). "Podgers" was Richard L. Ogden, the *Alta*'s New York correspondent.

[3]Artemus Ward had written Clemens in November 1864 inviting him to contribute to the forthcoming *Artemus Ward; His Travels* (New York: Carleton, 1865). Clemens did not receive Ward's letter until he returned to San Francisco from Jackass Hill and Angels Camp at the end of February 1865. He considered it too late to send a sketch, but when Ward renewed his request Clemens wrote "Jim Smiley and His Jumping Frog" and mailed it to New York on 18 October. It appeared in the New York *Saturday Press* on 18 November 1865. See *ET&S2*, 262–72.

[4]On 30 December 1865 the *Californian* had announced the withdrawal of Bret Harte from the editorship, a position he had probably held for the better part of the year ("With the close . . . ," *Californian* 4 [30 Dec 65]:8; see also *ET&S2*, 144). Harte continued to write for the *Californian* until the late summer of 1866 (his contributions are collected in Howell, 1–102). That year he became the Pacific Coast correspondent of the Boston *Christian Register* and the Springfield (Mass.) *Republican*. Unlike Clemens, however, Harte did not depend on literary work for his livelihood: during this period he enjoyed a secure income, which reached $270 per month, from his undemanding post as secretary to Robert B. Swain, superintendent of the United States Branch Mint in San Francisco (Merwin, 33–34; O'Connor, 93; Walker 1969, 185; Langley 1865, 215, 593).

[5]"An Open Letter to the American People" appeared in the New York *Weekly Review* on 17 February 1866 (*ET&S3*, no. 181). In it Clemens burlesqued the epistolary style of his mother and a fictitious "Aunt Nancy," and he praised the "eminently readable and entertaining" style of thirteen-year-old Annie Moffett. He had already published "The Great Earthquake in San Francisco" in the *Review* (25 Nov 65, *ET&S2*, 300–310) and he later published two additional sketches there—"How, for Instance?" and "Depart, Ye Accursed!" (29 Sept 66 and 15 Dec 66, *ET&S3*, nos. 192 and 199). He published "The Mysterious Bottle of Whiskey" and "A Strange Dream" in the New York *Saturday Press* (3 Mar 66 and 2 June 66, *ET&S3*, nos. 186 and 189). The aunts referred to were Ella Hunter Lampton and Elizabeth W. Smith.

[6]Clemens and Harte never collaboratively produced a volume of sketches. Clemens, however, eventually did "club a lot of old sketches together" into *The Celebrated Jumping Frog of Calaveras County, And other Sketches*, published by Charles H. Webb in 1867 (see *ET&S1*, 503–42).

[7]Hubert H. Bancroft (1832–1918), the San Francisco publisher, book collector, and historian, did not publish an anthology of "all the tribe of California poets." He may initially have been interested in publishing the collection that finally issued as *Poetry of the Pacific* (San Francisco: Pacific Publishing Company, 1867). That volume was edited by May Wentworth (pen name of Mary Richard-

son Newman), a contributor to the San Francisco *Golden Era* and an author of children's books. *Poetry of the Pacific* was to some extent a rebuttal to Harte's controversial collection *Outcroppings: Being Selections of California Verse* (San Francisco: A. Roman and Co., 1866), which had appeared in December 1865. Wentworth's compilation included many poets who were disgruntled over their exclusion from Harte's volume (see Walker 1969, 211–19). The idea for a parody of the forthcoming collection presumably was in part an outgrowth of Harte's burlesque reviews of a supposed seventeen-volume anthology, *Tailings: Being Rejections of California Verse*, in the 23 and 30 December 1865 numbers of the *Californian* (Harte 1865a, 9, and Harte 1865b, 8). The appearance in late January or early February 1866 of *Outcroppings, No. 2*, a burlesque collection ostensibly published by "A Rum-Un and Co." but actually sponsored as an advertising stunt by San Francisco shirt manufacturers S. W. H. Ward and Son, probably forestalled the Clemens-Harte parody (see Smith and Anderson, 65–68).

[8] The *Examiner* report appeared on 12 January. The clipping, glued in place here, is from an unidentified newspaper (possibly the steamer edition of the *Alta California*). The book in progress was evidently about the Mississippi. On 4 March the San Francisco correspondent of the Unionville (Nev.) *Humboldt Register* reported, "Mark Twain told me last night he would leave, in a few days, for the Sandwich Islands, in the employ of The Sacramento Union. Will be gone about two months. Then will go to Montana for same paper, and next Fall down the Missouri river in a Mackinac boat—he's an old Mississippi pilot—to New Orleans; where he intends writing a book" ("Letter from San Francisco," 10 Mar 66, 1). Clemens did not go to Montana after his Sandwich Islands assignment for the *Union*; nor did he go to New Orleans. The Mississippi material had to wait until he began "Old Times on the Mississippi" in 1874 (see SLC 1875).

[9] William J. Kribben, a friend of Clemens's on the Mississippi, was a St. Louis–New Orleans pilot for nearly a quarter of a century before his death from yellow fever in 1878. He was an incorporator of the Western Boatman's Benevolent Association, discussed in chapter 15 of *Life on the Mississippi*, and for many years served as its secretary. Clemens's enclosure may have included "Captain Montgomery," his tribute to the kindliness and generosity of Joseph E. (Ed) Montgomery, who was captain of the *City of Memphis* in March 1860, while Clemens was its pilot. The sketch appeared in one of Clemens's letters to the Virginia City *Territorial Enterprise*, probably in mid-January; it was reprinted in the San Francisco *Golden Era* on the twenty-eighth of the month (*ET&S3*, no. 161).

[10] The *Ajax*, owned by the California Steam Navigation Company, began its maiden voyage on the San Francisco to Honolulu run on 13 January, thereby initiating the first regular steamship service between the Sandwich Islands and the United States. The *Territorial Enterprise* letter Clemens enclosed for his family to read and pass on presumably contained remarks about the *Ajax*. These were omitted when the *Golden Era* reprinted the *Enterprise* text on 28 January. On 22 February, the day of the ship's return, Clemens interviewed its passengers and the following day he wrote an account of their pioneer voyage for the *Enterprise* ("Voyage of the Ajax," *ET&S3*, no. 182). He himself was a passenger on the *Ajax*'s second trip in March 1866.

To William R. Gillis
3? March 1866 • San Francisco, Calif.
(Paraphrase: William R. Gillis, 43)

. . . .

I am leaving San Francisco in a short time for Sandwich Islands in company with a party of U. S. surveyors, as special correspondent of the Alta California.[1] As in the course of human events we may not meet again, I will unburden my conscience of a load it has been carrying ever since the night of the serenade you and your band of troubadors attempted to give me. When you came into the cabin after I had scared the other boys off the hill, I was in a mighty ugly mood and I wanted just the chance you gave me to vent my spleen on somebody or something. I called you some pretty hard names, which I knew at the time were undeserved, and accused you of high crimes and misdemeanors of which I knew you were not guilty. I wanted to ask your pardon the next morning when you called me to breakfast, but courage failed me and I put off doing so to a more "convenient season." That season has now arrived, and I do ask you to forgive me. Tell the boys that I am often with them in my dreams, and that when I return to the city I will come back to them once more on Old Jackass, if I can possibly arrange to do so.[2]

. . . .

[1] Gillis introduced this paraphrase with these words: "Just previous to his departure for Honolulu I received a letter from Sam, which ended as nearly as I can now remember, as follows" (William R. Gillis, 43). In fact, Gillis's recollection of the passage was uneven, and at times mistaken. Clemens, unaccompanied by any surveyors, toured the Sandwich Islands as correspondent for the Sacramento *Union.* He probably wrote the letter represented here around 3 March, by which date he had made public his acceptance of the assignment (see 20 Jan 66 to JLC and PAM, n. 8).

[2] The "serenade" occurred in late 1864 or early 1865, while Clemens was visiting at Jackass Hill, California. Sixty years later William Gillis recalled,

> Getting into Tuttletown at a rather late hour one night on my way home from Sonora, I found a party of half a dozen young men who had been serenading their lady friends in the neighborhood. I suggested that they go with me to Jackass Hill and end the night's program with a serenade to Mark Twain. They readily fell in with my suggestion and we climbed the hill together, and, after our chief musician had tuned up his "old banjo," lined up under Mark's window, and opened up with "Oh, Darkies, hab you seen Ole Massa?"
>
> We had finished this song and "Happy Land O'Canaan" and were well under way with "I'se Gwine to de Shuckin," when that window went up with a bang, and an angry, rasping

voice snarled out, "What do you lot of yapping coyotes mean by disturbing the peace and quiet of the respectable people on the hill with that infernal yowling you're doing out there? Get away from this window, you drunken loafers, and go off to that shuckin you're howling about, and go right now."

This rude reception, it is needless to say, put an abrupt ending to our serenade and my companions left the hill on the double quick. On entering the cabin I found Mark sitting on the side of the bed, cramming his pipe with "Bull Durham" tobacco. "Hello, Sam," said I, "going to have a smoke?"

At my salutation he looked at me with an ugly scowl and greeted me with, "Billy, how did you come to get drunk tonight, and bring that gang of low down rowdies on the hill, to make the night hideous with their horrible racket? Up to this time I have regarded you as a well-behaved, decent young fellow with instincts somewhat approaching those of a gentleman but I have been wakened from that dream tonight to find you nothing but a common, wine guzzling hoodlum." (William R. Gillis, 38–39)

To Jane Lampton Clemens and Pamela A. Moffett
5 March 1866 • San Francisco, Calif.
(MS: NPV)

San Francisco,
March 5, 1866.

My Dr Mother & Sister:

I start to the Sandwich Islands day after to-morrow (I suppose Annie is geographer enough by this time to find them on the map,) in the steamer "Ajax." ~~I~~ We shall arrive there in about 12 days. ~~I have~~ My friends seem determined that I shall not lack acquaintances, for I only decided to-day to go, & they have already sent me letters of introduction to everybody down there worth knowing~~, the King included, I believe~~. I am to remain there a month & ransack the islands, the great cataracts & the volcanoes completely, & write twenty or thirty letters to the Sacramento *Union*— for which they pay me as much money as I would get if I staid at home.[1]

If I come back here I expect to start straight across the continent by way of the Columbia river, the Pen d'Oreille Lakes, through Montana & down the Missouri river—only 200 miles of land travel from San Francisco to New Orleans.[2]

Good bye for the present.

Yrs
Sam.

[1] In 1899 Clemens remembered the Sacramento *Union* as "a rich and influential daily journal which had n't any use" for his letters from the Sandwich Islands "but could afford to spend twenty dollars a week for nothing" (SLC 1899b, 76–

77). He had gone to Sacramento on 24 February, doubtless to formalize this assignment, which may have been conceived as long ago as 20 January when he complained to his mother and sister about missing the first trip of the *Ajax*. Charles Henry Webb, editor of the *Californian*, in 1900 recalled expediting the commission for Clemens: "Didn't I pilot him to Sacramento for an engagement with the *Union* to write letters from the Sandwich Islands? Didn't I get his hat checked to the Islands and back when the *Union* wouldn't advance the money for his fare?" (Webb to Edmund Clarence Stedman, [14? Nov 1900], Stedman and Gould, 2:275). Years later, however, the daughter of *Union* proprietor James Anthony remembered that Clemens was sent to Honolulu "by Papa and Mr Morrill [Paul Morrill, one of Anthony's partners] to write a series of letters for the paper, which he did most effectively—was to receive $50.00 for each letter. He squandered his means to such an extent—that they were obliged to pay his passage home" (Mary Josephine Anthony to Mrs. Bishop, portion of 1925 letter in CU-MARK). Whatever his exact arrangements with the *Union*, Clemens left San Francisco aboard the *Ajax* on 7 March and arrived in Honolulu eleven days later. He remained four months and produced twenty-five letters. These formed the basis for his unpublished 1867 Sandwich Islands book (see p. 361) and, ultimately, for chapters 62–77 of *Roughing It*. (Clemens's *Union* letters are reprinted in *MTH*, 262–420; his Sandwich Islands notebooks are in *N&J1*, 91–237.)

² This trip was to be a prelude to the writing of a book, apparently about the Mississippi (see 20 Jan 66 to JLC and PAM, n. 8).

To Jane Lampton Clemens and Pamela A. Moffett
3 April 1866 • Honolulu, Sandwich Islands
(MS: NPV)

Honolulu, Sandwich
Islands, April 3, 1866.

My Dear Mother & Sister:

I have been here two or three weeks, & like the beautiful tropical climate better & better. I have ₩ ridden on horseback all over this island (Oahu) in the meantime, & have visited all the ancient battle-fields & other places of interest. I have got a lot of human bones which I took from one of these battle-fields—I guess I will bring you some of them.¹ I went with the American Minister to & took dinner this evening with the King's Grand Chamberlain, who is related to the royal family, & although darker than a mulatto, he has an excellent English education & in manners is an accomplished gentleman.² The dinner was as ceremonious as any I ever attended in California—five regular courses, & five kinds of wine and one of brandy. I am to He is to call for me in the morning with his carriage, & we will visit the King at the palace³—both are good Masons—the King is a Royal Arch Mason.[4] After dinner to-night they called in the "singing girls," & we had some beautiful music, sung in the native tongue.

The steamer I came here in sails tomorrow, & ʃ as soon as she is gone I shall s̶e̶ sail for the other islands of the group & visit the great volcano—the grand wonder of the world. Be gone 2 months.[5]

Yrs.

Sam.

[1] Clemens described his "equestrian excursion" around Oahu, with a party of friends, in letters published in the Sacramento *Union* on 21 and 24 April (SLC 1866a, 3, and SLC 1866b, 4). He reported that at one old battleground "the bleached bones of men gleamed white in the moonlight. We picked up a lot of them for mementoes" (SLC 1866b, 4).

[2] The United States minister resident to Hawaii was James McBride (1802–75), commissioned on 9 March 1863. McBride had been replaced on 21 March 1866, just three days after Clemens's arrival, but continued to serve until late July while awaiting his successor (*NCAB*, 13:470; U.S. Department of State, 46; see 22 May 66 to MEC, n. 4). The Hawaiian king was Kamehameha V (1830–72), who reigned from 1863 to 1872. His grand chamberlain, David Kalakaua (1836–91), who later became king (1874–91), was unrelated to the royal family (Day, 201).

[3] Clemens's signature in the guest book at Iolani Palace testifies to his visit there on 4 April.

[4] "This degree is indescribably more august, sublime and important, than all which precede it; and is the summit and perfection of ancient Masonry" (Macoy, 145). As a Master Mason at this time, Clemens was ten degrees short of the king's thirteenth-degree sublimity. Yet even Kamehameha V had not quite reached the summit: depending on which Masonic rite he followed, there may have been as many as fifty-nine degrees beyond his Royal Arch (Macoy, 282–86).

[5] In fact Clemens left in mid-April for Maui, where he visited Haleakala volcano. He returned to Honolulu on 22 May, then left again on 26 May for a three-week visit to Hawaii and Kilauea volcano (see *N&J1*, 100–101).

To W. C. Kimball and W. W. Kimball
26 April 1866 • Island of Maui, Sandwich Islands
(MS: Jacobs)

Wailuku,[1] Apr. 26.

Messrs Kimball[2]—

Gentlemen—Don't you think for a moment of going up on Haleakala without giving me an opportunity of accompanying you! I have waited for & skirmished after some company for some time without avail, & now I hear that you will shortly be at Haiku.[3] So I shall wait for YOU.

Cannot you let me know, just as soon as you arrive, & give me a day or two (or more, even, if possible,) to get there in, with my horse? Because I am told the distance hence to Haiku is 15 miles—to prosecute which will be a matter of time, to my animal, & possibly a matter of eternity. His strong suit is grace & personal ~~comi~~ comeliness, rather than velocity.

                                        Yours Very Truly,
                                        Sam L. Clemens.

(Or "Mark Twain," if you ~~know m~~ have forgotten my genuine name.)

                    ∧ $\left\{ \begin{array}{l} My\ a\,d\,d\,r\,e\,s\,s\ is\ ``Wailuku\ Plan- \\ tation.\text{''} \end{array} \right.$ ════════ ∧

(*Original.*)

I shall send two or three notes ~~for~~ by different parties, for fear one might miss fire—an idea suggested by my own native sagacity.

[1] A town and district on the north coast of the island of Maui.

[2] Aged twenty-seven and thirty respectively, the Kimball brothers had been among Clemens's fellow passengers aboard the *Ajax*. They departed Honolulu for San Francisco on 2 June aboard the bark *D. C. Murray* (*Ajax* passenger list, PH in CU-MARK; "Passengers," Honolulu *Pacific Commercial Advertiser*, 9 June 66, 2).

[3] A village on the coast of Maui on the route to the extinct volcano Haleakala, whose name means "House of the Sun" (*MTH*, 58). Clemens did not describe his visit to Haleakala for the Sacramento *Union*; he did so in chapter 76 of *Roughing It*, but without naming his companions.

To Jane Lampton Clemens and Pamela A. Moffett
4 May 1866 • Island of Maui, Sandwich Islands
(MS: NPV)

                    Wailuku ~~Planta~~ Sugar Plantation $\Big\}$
                    Island of Maui, H. I, May 4, 1866.

My Dear Mother & Sister:

11 o'clock at Night.—This is the infernalest darkest country, when the moon don't shine; I stumbled & fell over my horse's lariat a minute ago & hurt my leg, & so I must stay here to-night; I ~~came~~ went to Ulapalakua Plantation (25 miles,) a few days ago, & returned yesterday afternoon, to Mr. Cornwell's (Waikapu Plantation) & staid all night (it is 2 miles from here) & came here this evening to Mr Peck's, (Honolulu

friends of mine,), & took tea, & we have been playing seven-up & whist (plenty of ladies in his family;) but I only hitched that horse, intending to ride to the further sea-shore, a (this is a narrow peninsula in the middle of the island), & stay all night at the Waihee Plantation, ,5 miles from here,, but as I said, I couldn't even see the horse it was so dark when I came out of Mr Peck's a while ago, & so I fell & hurt my leg.[1] I got the same leg hurt the other last week; I said I hadn't got hold of a spirited horse since I had been on the island, & one of the proprietors loaned me a big, vicious colt; he was altogether too spirited; I went to tighten the cinch before mounting him, when he let out with his left & kicked me across a ten-acre lot. A native rubbed & doctored me so well that I was able to stand on my feet in half an hour. It was then half after 4, & I had an appointment to go 7 miles & get a girl & take her to a pic-nic ,a card party, at 5. If I hadn't had a considerable weakness for her she might have gone to the devil under the circumstances, but as it was, I went after her. I got even with the colt; it was a very rough road, but I got there at 5 minutes past 5, & then had to quit, my leg hurt me so. ,She was ready & her horse was saddled, but we didn't go., But I had a jolly time—played a cribbage nearly all night. If I were worth even $5,000 I would try to marry that plantation—but as it is, I resign myself to a long & useful bachelordom as cheerfully as I may.

I had a pleasant time of it at Ulupalakua Plantation. It is 3,000 feet above the level of the sea (in plain sight from here, 25 miles;) two pretty & accomplished girl's in the family & the plantation yields an income of $60,000 a year—chance for some enterprising scrub.[2] I have been clattering around among the plantations for 3 weeks, now, & next week I am going to visit the extinct crater of Mount Hala Haleakala—the largest in the world; it is ten miles to the foot of the mountain; it rises 10,000 feet above the valley; the crater is 29 miles in circumference & 1,000 feet deep. Seen from the summit, the city of St Louis would look like a picture in the bottom of it.[3]

As soon as I get back from Haleakala (pronounced Hally-ekka-lah,) I will sail for Honolulu again & from thence to the Island of Hawaii (pronounced Hah-*wy*-ye,) to see the greatest *active* volcano in the world—that of Kilauea (pronounced Kee-low-*way*-ah),—& from thence back to San Francisco—& then, doubtless, to the States. I have been on this trip 2 months, & it will probably be 2 more before I get back to California.

Yrs aff'y
Sam.

[1] Sherman Peck (1800–71) was senior partner in Charles Brewer and Company, Honolulu commission merchants and sugar factors. The firm had a controlling interest in the Wailuku Sugar Company, which comprised three of the plantations Clemens mentions here: Wailuku, Waikapu (owned by Henry Cornwell), and Waihee. In addition, Brewer and Company was agent for the plantation at Ulu-palakua, described in the next paragraph (Sullivan, 123–24, 127, 129; Condé and Best, 267; "Waikapu Plantation!" Honolulu *Pacific Commercial Advertiser*, 12 May 66, 1; Adler, 36). Clemens discussed sugar production on these and other plantations in a Sacramento *Union* letter published on 26 September 1866 (SLC 1866g, 1).

[2] James Makee's Rose Ranch, at Ulupalakua on the slopes of Haleakala, was the largest sugar plantation in the Sandwich Islands, with a thousand acres under cultivation. Makee, formerly a Massachusetts whaling captain, had been put ashore in 1843 after suffering a severe injury in a shipboard assault. At the time of Clemens's visit he was famed for his lavish way of life and hospitality at Rose Ranch, which had guest cottages, lush gardens populated by hundreds of peacocks, "a billiard room, a tennis court, and a bowling alley with one small kanaka boy to tend each pin" (Daws, 207). Clemens may have visited Rose Ranch at the recommendation of a San Francisco friend, poet Charles Warren Stoddard (1843–1909). Stoddard had stayed there in 1864 while visiting his sister Sara, who was married to James Makee's son Parker (Lee, 237; Day, 169; Walker 1969, 272).

[3] Modern sources agree on these dimensions for Haleakala: height, 10,023 feet; crater circumference, about twenty miles; crater depth, 2,720 feet. In chapter 76 of *Roughing It* Clemens remarked, "If it had a level bottom it would make a fine site for a city like London."

To William Bowen

7 May 1866 • Island of Maui, Sandwich Islands

(MS facsimile: TxU)

Wailuku P̶l̶ Sugar Plantation 1866
Island of Maui, Sandwich Islands, May 7.

Dear Bill—

I have been mad at you so long that the old anger has about spent itself & I begin to feel friendly again. But you ought to have your d—d neck broken anyhow, my boy.[1]

I expected to be in the States long before this, but things fell out otherwise. I contracted with the Sacramento Union to go wherever they chose & correspond for a few months, & I had a sneaking notion that they would start me east—but behold how fallible is human judgment!—they sent me to the Sandwich Islands. I look for a recall by the next mail, though, because I have written them that I cannot go all over the eight inhabited islands of the group in less than five months & do credit to myself & them, & I don't want to spend so much time. I have been here two months, & yet have only "done" the island of Oahu & part of this island of Maui, & by it is going to take me two weeks more to finish this one & at least a month to "do" the island of Hawaii & the great volcanoes—& by that time, surely, I can hear from them.

But I have had a gorgeous time of it so far. I wish you & Sam[2] were here. We would sail from Island to island for a year & have a merry hell of a time. We would get more invitations from sea captains. Honolulu is a great stopping point for ships, & during the month I was there I was invited to go to every blamed place on the habitable globe, I think. The last was from the captain of a nic fine ship,—he was going round the world—& if either of you bilks had been here I would have thrown up my berth & gone with him.

I have seen a fellow here that you & I knew in Hannibal in childhood—named Martin—he was a carpenter; here he came here busted a year ago & called himself the Wizard of the East & gave a sleight of hand entertainment,—& it was the *d—dest* sli sleight of hand entertainment you ever heard of. He tried to shoot a pocket handkerchief into an a closed oyster-can, & he pretty nearly shot the d—d head off of a Kanaka spectator. None of his apparatus would work. He had a learned pig, ˌwhich he gave out could speak 7 languages,ˌ too—a striped learned pig. He told me he caught that hog in the extinct crater of Haleakala, 10,000 feet above the level of the sea, where the son of a sea horse had been running wild for three generations; he brought him down here into the valley, shaved him close, painted stripes on him with id iodine, ˌ& then greased him,ˌ & advertised that he would give any person in the audience ten dollars ˌwhoˌ would come into the ring & catch the pig & hold him two minutes. A big brawny Kanaka & a gigantic Missourian each got the hog by a hind leg, & the brute held on, notwithstanding the grease, but the hog turned & bit a square meal out of the Kanaka & made him let go, & then started, & took the bold Missourian straight through the audience, squealing, & upsetting people & benches, & raising more hell, & scaring women to death, & broke for high ground on Haleakala, & neither he nor the Missourian were ever heard of afterwards—& Martin wasn't for some time, for in the melee he took his little cash-box & "shoved." He says he likes to live here, "because," says he, "when I'm busted I can go through a Kanaka lord of the soil; & when I can't do that, I can always rig a purchase to swindle one of them d—d Missionaries." I am of the opinion that Mr Martin ⚹ is a brick.[3]

I wouldn't write you so much about Martin, only I haven't anything else to write about—except the islands, & that is cash, you know, & goes in the "Union."

Give my regards to my Christian friends, ˌSam & Bart especiallyˌ & drop me a line to San Francisco, "Care of Occidental Hotel."[4]

Yr old friend
Sam L. Clemens.

[1] Bowen, who had served as a Union pilot during the Civil War, currently was a steamboat captain. He remained a captain until 1868, when he left the Mississippi and soon after went into the insurance business (Bowen data, captains' file, MoSHi, PH in CU-MARK). Clemens's anger may have been the residue of a disagreement he and Bowen had in early 1861, while they were piloting the *Alonzo Child* (see 11 and 12 May 62 to OC, n. 22). Possibly, however, his irritation was part of the "misunderstanding all around" concerning his 1861 loan to Bowen (see 25 Aug 66 to Bowen).

[2] Bowen's younger brother.

[3] Daniel Martin's stage name was "Martin the Wizard." No details of his residence in Hannibal have been recovered: he does not appear in the censuses for 1840–60. In the early and mid-1860s, however, Martin lived and owned a saloon in Como, Nevada (near Carson City), performing there and also on the road. Clemens had visited Como, purpose unknown, from 4 to 7 March 1864, but there is no evidence that he saw Martin then. Following their encounter in the Sandwich Islands, the two men may have met in Virginia City in the second week of November 1866, while Clemens was staying there during his lecture tour of the area and Martin arrived en route to San Francisco (Doten 1973, 1:718–70 passim, esp. 763, 767, 2:849, 871–72, 903–4; "Martin the Wizard," Virginia City *Territorial Enterprise*, 9 Nov 66, 3). Martin performed in Virginia City, but not until 13 November, the day after Clemens left. The *Territorial Enterprise* called his show—which featured "magic cups, rings and queer arrangements, performing pigeons, rabbits, and all that sort of thing"—"meritorious in the highest degree" and "unequaled" for "startling novelty and brilliant effect" ("Martin the Wizard," 14 Nov 66, 3; "The Great Wizard," 16 Nov 66, 3).

[4] Barton S. Bowen (b. 1829 or 1830, d. 1868 or 1869), elder brother of William (1836–93) and Samuel (1838?–78). He had preceded them as a Mississippi steamboat pilot and captain and was widely known for his heroism in preventing loss of life when the *Garden City* burned on 14 January 1855 (Lytle, 244; Way 1983, 177). Sobieski Jolly called him "that Prince of good Fellows . . . splendid Master and a No. 1 *Pilot*" (Jolly, no page). Bowen had assisted Clemens financially at the time of Henry Clemens's fatal injury, and Clemens afterward served on boats piloted and captained by Bowen (see 18 June 58 to MEC, n. 3, and the Steamboat Calendar). Remarking in 1907 that Bowen had "stepped down a grade" from pilot when

he became a captain, Clemens noted, "I never lost any part of my respect & affection for him on account of that retrogression; no, he was a high-minded, large-hearted man, & I hold him in undiminished honor to this day" (25–28 Feb 1907 to John B. Downing, CU-MARK).

To Mary E. (Mollie) Clemens
22 May 1866 • Honolulu, Sandwich Islands
(MS: NPV)

Honolulu, May 22.

My Dear Sister:

I have just got back ~~fo~~ from a sea voyage—from the beautiful island of Maui. I have spent 5 weeks there, riding backwards & forwards among the sugar plantations—looking up the splendid scenery & visiting the lofty crater of Haleakala. It has been a perfect jubilee to me in the way of pleasure. I have not written a single line, & have not once thought of business, or care, or human toil or trouble or sorrow or weariness. Few such months come in a lifetime.

I set sail again, a week hence, for the island of ~~M~~ Hawaii, to see the great active volcano of Kileaua. I shall not get back here for 4 or 5 weeks, & shall not reach San Francisco before the latter part of July. So it is no use to wait for me to go home. Go on yourselves.[1] It is Orion's duty to attend to that land, & after shutting me out of my attempt to sell it (for which I shall never entirely forgive him,) if he lets it be sold for taxes, all his religion will not wipe out the sin.[2] It is no use to quote Scripture to me, Mollie, ~~with~~—I am in poverty & exile now because of Orion's religious scruples. Religion & poverty cannot go together. I am satisfied Orion will eventually save himself, but in doing it he will ~~damm~~ damn the balance of the family. I want no such religion. He has got a duty to perform by us—will he perform it?

I have crept into the old subject again, & opened the old sore afresh that cankers within me. It has got into many letters to you & I have burned them. But it is no use disguising it—I always feel bitter & malignant when I think of ~~that~~ Ma & Pamela grieving at our absence & the land going to the dogs when I could have sold it & been at home now, instead of drifting about the outskirts of the world, battling for bread. If I were in the east, now, I could stop the publication of a piratical book which has stolen some of my sketches.[3]

I saw the American Minister today & he says Edwin McCook, of Colorado Ter. has been appointed to fill his place—so there is an end to *that* project.[4]

It is late—good-bye, Mollie.

                                                         Yr Bro
                                                          Sam.

[1] In 1906 Clemens gave this account of Orion and Mollie's return to Keokuk, Iowa:

I came East in January, 1867. Orion remained in Carson City perhaps a year longer. Then he sold his twelve-thousand-dollar house and its furniture for thirty-five hundred in greenbacks at about 30 per cent discount. He and his wife took first-class passage in the steamer for New York. In New York they stopped at an expensive hotel; explored the city in an expensive way; then fled to Keokuk, and arrived there about as nearly penniless as they were when they had migrated thence in July, '61. (AD, 5 Apr 1906, CU-MARK, in *MTA*, 2:322)

In fact, Orion and Mollie left Carson City on 13 March 1866 and, after a stopover in Virginia City, arrived at Heaton's Station (in Placer County, just inside the California border) on the seventeenth of the month. There they separated, Mollie going on an extended excursion to Sacramento, San Francisco, and other points, while Orion settled in at Meadow Lake, in the Excelsior mining district of Nevada County, California. When Mollie joined him on 16 June, he had still not been able to sell their house in Carson City. Through most of that summer Orion tried to raise money for their journey home. Under the pen names "Noiro" and "Snow Shoe" he wrote articles about local mines for the Meadow Lake *Morning Sun* and corresponded with the San Francisco *Morning Flag* (see OC 1866a–n), while simultaneously attempting to practice law and prospect. He tried to liquidate part of his holdings in the Mount Blanc Gold and Silver Consolidated Mining Company, explaining that he intended to use the capital "to go to the States on the next Steamer, with my wife, to attend to our Tennessee land" (OC to J. A. Byers, 12 July 66, CU-MARK). He and Mollie finally left for San Francisco on 26 July, presumably having disposed of the Mount Blanc stock or the Carson City house, or both. They sailed from San Francisco on 30 August aboard the steamer *Golden City*, which made connections in Panama for New York (OC to JLC and PAM, 19 and 20 Mar 66, ViU; MEC, 15–17; OC to MEC, 7 June 66, 12 June 66, and 13 June 66, CU-MARK; "Sailing of the 'Golden City,'" San Francisco *Evening Bulletin*, 29 Aug 66, 5).

[2] The reference is to Orion's rejection of Herman Camp's proposal for the Tennessee land (see 13 Dec 65 to OC and MEC, n. 2).

[3] *Beadle's Dime Book of Fun No. 3*, copyrighted on 19 April 1866 by Beadle and Company of New York, had reprinted a condensed and edited version of "Jim Smiley and His Jumping Frog," all of "Fitz Smythe's Horse," and part of "'Mark Twain' on the Launch of the Steamer 'Capital'" (see *ET&S2*, 282–88, 343–46, 359–66).

[4] Edward M. McCook (1833–1909) was commissioned on 21 March 1866 to replace James McBride as United States minister resident to Hawaii. McCook, a distinguished Union general, was governor of Colorado Territory from 1869 to 1875 (U.S. Department of State, 46). Clemens's frustrated "project" probably was a scheme to secure the ministerial office for Orion.

To Jane Lampton Clemens and Pamela A. Moffett
21 June 1866 • Honolulu, Sandwich Islands
(MS: NPV)

Honolulu, Sandwich Islands, ⎰
June 21, 1866.   ⎱

My Dear Mother & Sister—

I expect I have made ~~Mollie~~ Orion mad, but I don't care a cent. He wrote me to go home & sell the Tenn. land & I wrote him to go to thunder & take care of it himself. I *tried* to sell it once & he broke up the trade.

I have just got back from a hard trip through the Island of Hawaii, begun on the 26th May & finished on the ~~1~~ 18th of June—only 6 or 7 days at sea—all the balance horseback, & the hardest mountain roads in the world. I staid at the Volcano ~~4 days &~~ ˄about a week &˄ witnessed the greatest eruption that has occurred for years.[1] I lived well there. They charge $4 a day ~~but the~~ for board & a dollar or two extra for guides & horses. I had a pretty good time. They didn't charge me anything. I have got back sick—went to bed as soon as I arrived here—shall not be strong again for several days yet. I rushed too fast. I ought to have taken five or six weeks on that trip.[2]

A week hence I start for the Island of Kaui, to be gone 3 weeks—& *then* I go back to California.[3]

The Crown Princess is dead, & thousands of natives cry & wail & dance the dance for the dead around the King's palace all night & every night. They will keep it up for a month, & then she will be buried.[4]

Hon. Anson Burlingame ~~M~~ U.S. Minister to China, & Gen. Van Valkenburgh, Minister to Japan, with their families & suits, have just arrived here *en route*.[5] They were going to do me the honor to call on me this morning, & that accounts for my being out of bed now. You know what condition my room is always in when you are not around—so I climbed out of bed & dressed & shaved pretty quick & went up to the residence of the American Minister & called on *them*. Mr. Burlingame told me a good deal about Hon. Jere Clemens & that Virginia Clemens who was wounded in a duel. He was in Congress years together with both of them.[6] Mr. B. sent for his son, to introduce him—said he could tell that frog story of mine as well as anybody.[7] I told him I was glad to hear it, for I never tried to tell it myself, without making a botch of it. At his request I have loaned Mr Burlingame pretty much everything I ever wrote. I guess he will be an almighty wise man if ˄by the time˄ he wades through that lot.

If the new United States Minister to the Sandwich Islands (Hon Edwin MᶜCook,) were only here, now, so that I could get his views on this new condition of Sandwich Islands politics, I would sail for California at once. But he will not arrive for two weeks yet, & so I am going to spend that interval on the island of ~~Kauu~~ Kauai.[8]

I stopped 3 days with Hon. Mr. Cony, Deputy Marshal of the Kingdom, at Hilo, Hawaii, last week, & by a funny circumstance, he knew everybody that ever I knew in Hannibal & Palmyra. We used to sit up all night talking, & then sleep all day. He lives like a Prince.[9] Confound that island, I had a streak of fat & a streak of lean all over it—got lost several times & had to sleep in huts with the natives & live like a dog.[10] Of course I couldn't speak fifty words of the language. Take it altogether, though, it was a mighty hard trip.

Yrs aff^{ly}

Sam

[1]Clemens had arrived at the Volcano House, the three-month-old hotel near Kilauea crater, on Sunday, 3 June, and remained until Thursday, 7 June. The eruption he witnessed had begun on 22 May and continued throughout his stay in the Sandwich Islands. Clemens described his visit to Kilauea in letters published in the Sacramento *Union* on 25 October and 16 November (SLC 1866h, 1, and SLC 1866i, 1). Moreover, even before seeing the volcano, he had used it as the setting for "A Strange Dream," written in April, a sketch about an imaginary search for the bones of Kamehameha I (1737?–1819), the conqueror of the Hawaiian Islands (New York *Saturday Press*, 2 June 66, *ET&S3*, no. 189). Later Clemens made a description of Kilauea a set piece in his Sandwich Islands lecture and redescribed his visit to it in chapters 74 and 75 of *Roughing It* (*MTH*, 72–74, 117–22; Honolulu *Pacific Commercial Advertiser*: "Volcano Hotel," 10 Mar 66, 2; "The Volcano in Eruption Again," 9 June 66, 3; "Ho for the Volcano!" 4 Aug 66, 3).

[2]Clemens was suffering a severe case of saddle boils.

Volcano House, Island of Hawaii, 1866.
Lyman House Memorial Museum, Hilo, Hawaii.

[3] The trip to Kauai was canceled; Clemens remained on Oahu until his departure from the Sandwich Islands on 19 July.

[4] Victoria Kaahumanu Kamamalu (b. 1838), heir presumptive to the Hawaiian throne, had died on 29 May (Korn, 302–3). In his notebook Clemens wrote, "Pr. V. died in forcing abortion—kept half a dozen bucks to do her washing, & has suffered 7 abortions" (*N&J1*, 129). He attended her funeral in Honolulu on 30 June and described the month-long mourning period and the funeral procession in his letters published in the Sacramento *Union* on 16 July, 30 July, and 1 August (SLC 1866c, 1; SLC 1866e, 1; and SLC 1866f, 1). He later used some of this material in chapter 68 of *Roughing It*.

[5] Anson Burlingame and Robert B. Van Valkenburgh had arrived in Honolulu on 18 June. Van Valkenburgh (1821–88), former Republican congressman from New York (1861–65) and commander of the 107th Regiment, New York Volunteer Infantry, at the battle of Antietam (1862), was on his way to Japan to take up his duties as American minister resident there. He had been commissioned on 18 January 1866 and served until 11 November 1869. Burlingame (1820–70), former American party and Republican congressman from Massachusetts (1855–61) and minister resident to China since 1861, was returning to his post after a leave of absence in the United States. He held his ministerial office until 21 November 1867. On 1 December of that year the Chinese government appointed him its ambassador to negotiate treaties with foreign powers (Honolulu *Pacific Commercial Advertiser*: "Passengers," 23 June 66, 2; "Our Diplomatic Guests," 30 June 66, 2; *BDAC*, 631, 1750; U.S. Department of State, 42, 47). Clemens was much impressed by Burlingame and after his death on 22 February 1870 published a

long tribute to him in the Buffalo *Express* (SLC 1870a, 2). In 1906 he remembered Burlingame as a "wise and just and humane and charming man and great citizen and diplomat" who had offered this advice, "which I have never forgotten, and which I have lived by for forty years": " 'Avoid inferiors. Seek your comradeships among your superiors in intellect and character; always *climb*' " (AD, 20 Feb 1906, CU-MARK, in *MTA*, 2:123, 125).

[6] Jeremiah Clemens (1814–65), an Alabaman, was a lawyer, army officer, Democratic senator from Alabama (1849–53), newspaper editor, and author of several historical romances. Sherrard Clemens (1820–80), a Virginian, was a lawyer and a Democratic congressman from Virginia (1852–53, 1857–61). He was seriously wounded in the thigh in a duel he fought on 17 September 1858 with O. Jennings Wise, one of the editors of the Richmond *Enquirer*, after Wise accused him in print of political trickery. Anson Burlingame served in Congress with Sherrard Clemens, but not with Jeremiah. Both men were third cousins to Clemens (*BDAC*, 706; "Duel," Richmond *Dispatch*, 18 Sept 58, 1; "The Late Duel," Richmond *Dispatch*, 28 Sept 58, 1; "Sherrard Clemens," New York *Times*, 3 June 80, 5; Bell, 31, 34, 36, 37).

[7] Edward L. Burlingame (1848–1922) accompanied his father to China as his private secretary. He later became the first editor of *Scribner's Magazine* (1887–1914).

[8] In fact McCook did not arrive in Honolulu until 22 July, three days after Clemens left for San Francisco ("Passengers," Honolulu *Pacific Commercial Advertiser*, 28 July 66, 2).

[9] Clemens's host probably was John H. Coney, sheriff of the island of Hawaii (Parke, 95, 103). "A tall handsome man, who carried himself like a soldier," he was "titular executive head of government next to the Governess of Hawaii and her Lieut. Governor" (Austin, 203–4). Coney's Missouri connection has not been documented.

[10] Edward Howard, an Englishman who met Clemens at the Volcano House at Kilauea, complained of one such "streak of lean":

> Before leaving the Volcano . . . I suggested that we have a guide. He [Clemens] wouldn't hear of it, said the trail was so plainly worn on the rocks that we couldn't miss it, but before noon we were lost in the forest, following goat and cattle trails in every direction, riding around great cracks, some of which we nearly fell into. . . . When it came night, even he thought we had better not go on for fear of falling into a lava crack. He pulled his saddle off his horse and made a pillow of it after scraping up some leaves, as if he were used to this sort of thing, and put his raincoat over him. Even then the man wanted to tell me a story, that he was reminded of, hungry as we were. This most improvident man had thrown our lunch away, that had been given us at the Volcano House, early in the day; said we'd be at the Half Way House before noon.
>
> Next morning, fortunately, a native came along with a gun, hunting goats, and we persuaded him to lead us to the Half Way House. It was only a few miles away. Here we got something to eat . . . roast pig and boiled taro and some nasty paste he [the native] called "poi" which Sam seemed to relish. (Austin, 253)

To Jane Lampton Clemens and Pamela A. Moffett
27 June 1866 • Honolulu, Sandwich Islands
(MS: NPV)

ˌP. S.—Now *please* don't read this to anybody—I am always *afraid* to write to you—you always show my letters.ˏ

Honolulu, June 27, 1866.

My Dear Mother & Sister:

I enjoy being in the Sandwich Islands because I don't r

[*three-fourths MS page (about 80 words) missing*]

& Gen. Van Valkenburgh, the United States Ministers to China & Japan say that California is proud of Mark Twain, & that some day America will be too, no doubt.

[*four and three-fourths MS pages (about 530 words) missing*]

tub, with a gill of water a day to each man. I got the whole story from the third mate & ten of the sailors. If my account gets to the Sacramento Union first, it will be *published* first all over the United States, France, England, Russia and Germany—all over the world, I may say. You will see it. Mr. Burlingame went with me all the time, & helped me question the men—throwing away invitations to dinner with the princes & foreign dignitaries, & neglecting all sorts of things to accommodate me[1]—& you know I appreciate that kind of thing—especially from *such* a man, who is acknowledged to have no superior in the diplomatic circles of the world, & obtained from China concessions in favor of America which were refused to Sir Frederick Bruce & the Envoys of France & Russia until procured for them by Burlingame himself—which service was duly acknowledged by those dignitaries.[2] He hunted me up as soon as he came here, & has done me a hundred favors since, & says if I will come to China in the ~~great~~ first trip of the great mail steamer next January & make his house in Pekin ~~hi~~ my home, he will afford me facilities that few men can have ~~then~~ there for seeing & learning.[3] He will give me letters to the chiefs of the great Mail Steamship Company which will be of service to me in this

matter. I expect to do all this, but I expect to go to the States first,—&
from China to the Paris World's Fair.[4]

Don't show this letter.[5]

Yrs aff[ty]

Sam.

P.S. The crown Princess of this Kingdom will be buried tomorrow with
great ceremony—after that I sail in 2 weeks for California.

---

[1] On 3 May 1866 the clipper *Hornet*, en route from New York to San Francisco
with a cargo of candles and kerosene, burned and sank in the Pacific Ocean. The
fifteen survivors of the disaster reached the Sandwich Islands on 15 June after a
harrowing journey of four thousand miles in a longboat (*MTH*, 102–5; Brown,
9). Clemens gave a brief, secondhand account of their ordeal in his letter dated 22
June to the Sacramento *Union* (SLC 1866c, 3). The following day *Hornet* third
mate John S. Thomas and ten other survivors arrived in Honolulu, and Clemens,
still suffering from saddle boils, managed to obtain an interview. Anson Burlingame, he later recalled,

came and put me on a stretcher and had me carried to the hospital where the shipwrecked
men were, and I never needed to ask a question. He attended to all of that himself, and I had
nothing to do but make the notes. . . .

We got through with this work at six in the evening. I took no dinner, for there was no
time to spare if I would beat the other correspondents. I spent four hours arranging the
notes in their proper order, then wrote all night and beyond it; with this result: that I had a
very long and detailed account of the *Hornet* episode ready at nine in the morning, while the
correspondents of the San Francisco journals had nothing but a brief outline report—for
they did n't sit up. The now-and-then schooner was to sail for San Francisco about nine;
when I reached the dock she was free forward and was just casting off the stern-line. My fat
envelop was thrown by a strong hand, and fell on board all right, and my victory was a safe
thing. All in due time the ship reached San Francisco, but it was my complete report which
made the stir and was telegraphed to the New York papers. (SLC 1899b, 77)

Clemens's scoop appeared on the front page of the Sacramento *Union* on 19 July
(SLC 1866d, 1). No New York printing of this report has been located, but a
condensed version of it did appear in the Stamford (Conn.) *Advocate* on 17 August
("The Hornet," 2).

[2] Burlingame had first arrived in Peking as United States minister resident in
July 1862. He enlisted the cooperation of the other foreign ministers in the "Burlingame plan" of noninterference and goodwill toward the Chinese government.
He also redefined the trade concessions due to foreign powers. "Under his moni-
tion the 'Four B's,' as they were called,—Balluzeck [L. de Balluzeck, Russian
minister], Berthemy [Jules François Gustave Berthemy, French minister], Bruce
[Frederick William Adolphus Bruce, English minister], and Burlingame,—con-
stituted a self-appointed committee of safety for China, and insured her passage
into a peaceful period of internal reconstruction which endured for twenty years"
(Frederick Wells Williams, 36, 20–37; Morse, 2:50; Cordier, 1:69 n. 1).

[3] The Pacific Mail Steamship Company inaugurated its Japan-China mail route
on 1 January 1867 with the sailing of the *Colorado* from San Francisco (San Francisco *Morning Call*: "The Grand Banquet," 1 Jan 67, 1; "For Japan and China," 1
Jan 67, 3).

[4] The Paris Universal Exposition opened on 1 April 1867. Clemens visited it briefly in July that year, while on the *Quaker City* excursion, and subsequently gave it passing mention in chapter 13 of *The Innocents Abroad* (see Ganzel, 102–3, 112–13).

[5] Conceivably Jane Clemens and Pamela Moffett excised "sensitive" passages from this letter—the missing five and one-half manuscript pages—before ignoring Clemens's admonition.

To Samuel C. Damon
19 July 1866 • Honolulu, Sandwich Islands
(*The Friend*, 1 Aug 66)

HONOLULU July 19, 1866.

REV. MR. DAMON:[1]—Dear Sir—I return herewith the last book I borrowed, with many thanks for its use and for all your kindness. I take your Jarves' History with me, because I may not be able to get it at home.[2] I "cabbage" it by the strong arm, for fear you might refuse to part with it if I asked you. This is a case of military necessity, and is therefore admissible. The honesty of the transaction may be doubtful, but the policy of it is sound—sound as the foundation upon which the imperial greatness of America rests.

So just hold on a bit. I will send the book back within a month, or soon after I arrive.[3]

. . . . .

[1] Samuel Chenery Damon (1815–85) was pastor of the Oahu Bethel Church and chaplain of the Honolulu American Seamen's Friend Society. Since 1843 he had published and edited *The Friend: A Monthly Journal, Devoted to Temperance, Seamen, Marine and General Intelligence*. Clemens became friendly with Damon and for "part of his sojourn . . . roomed on the corner of Fort Street and Chaplain Lane next to the Damon home" (Damon, 61). This gave him easy access to the chaplain and his large library, important sources of information about the Sandwich Islands (see *N&J1*, 199–203, 215). Damon prefaced Clemens's letter with these words: "This noted correspondent of the Sacramento *Union*, has left for the coast, but we may expect he will continue to write about the islands and people. On his departure, he sent us the following epistle."

[2] Clemens was preparing to depart from Honolulu aboard the clipper *Smyrniote*, which sailed the day he wrote this letter ("Passengers," Honolulu *Pacific Commercial Advertiser*, 21 July 66, 2). The borrowed book was the third edition of *History of the Hawaiian Islands* (Honolulu: Charles Edwin Hitchcock, 1847), by James Jackson Jarves (1818–88), a journalist, historian, art critic, and art collec-

tor. It was this edition that Clemens used in writing his Sandwich Islands letters to the Sacramento *Union*, the final eight of which were not published until after his return to San Francisco on 13 August (see *MTH*, 256, 365–420). In 1884 Clemens used the second edition of Jarves's book—*History of the Hawaiian or Sandwich Islands* (Boston: James Munroe and Company, 1844)—while trying to write a Sandwich Islands novel (see *N&J1*, 103–5). That copy survives in the Mark Twain Papers (CU-MARK).

³"We sincerely wish that all who borrow books were equally conscientious," Damon remarked following the letter. "May this remind others who have books in their possession belonging to our Sanctum, to return them instanter." It was not until 20 May 1867, however, that Clemens could report: "I am growing more worthy every day. I have mailed to Father Damon, in the Sandwich Islands, the Hawaiian History I stole from him" (SLC 1867b, 1). In the meantime, his theft provoked some chaffing in the Hawaiian press (see *MTH*, 156–63).

To Jane Lampton Clemens and Pamela A. Moffett
30 July, 6, 7, 8, 10, and 20 August 1866 • *Smyrniote* en route from Honolulu to San Francisco, and San Francisco, Calif.
(MS: NPV)

On Board Ship Smyrniote, ⎱
At Sea, July 30, 1866. ⎰

Dear Mother & Sister:

I write, now, because I must go hard at work as soon as I get to San Francisco, & then I shall have no time for other things—though truth to say I have nothing *now* to write which will be calculated to interest you much. We left the Sandwich Islands 8 or ten days—or 12 days ago—I don't know which, I have been so hard at work until to-day (at least *part* of each day,) that the time has slipped away almost unnoticed.) At̶f̶ The first few days we came at a whooping gait—being in the latitude of the "North-East trades," but we soon ran out of them. We used them as long as they lasted—hundreds of miles—& came dead straight north until exactly abreast of San Francisco—precisely straight west of the city in a ſ bee-line—but a *long* bee-line, as we are about ~~eighteen hundred miles west~~ ₐtwo thousand milesₐ i̶t̶ at sea—consequently, we are not a hundred yards nearer San Francisco than *you* are. And here we lie becalmed on a glassy sea—we do not move an inch—y̶ we ~~through~~ ₐthrowₐ banana & orange peel overboard & it lies still on the water by the vessel's side.

Sometimes the ocean is as dead level as the ~~th~~ Mississippi river, & ~~gla~~ glitters glassily like it was ~~possib~~ polished—but usually, of course, no matter how calm the weather is, we roll & surge over the grand ground-swell. We amuse ourselves catching vast sea-birds with a hook-&-line, & by tying pieces of tin to the ship's log & sinking them to see how far we can distinguish them under water—86 feet was the deepest we could see a ₐa small ₐ piece of tin, but a white plate would show about as far down as the steeple of Dr Bullard's church would reach, I guess.[1] The sea is very dark & blue here. I played whist & euchre at night until the passengers all tire out & go to bed, & then walk the quarter-deck & smoke with the mates & swap lies with them till 2 oclock (as I call it) but ~~"fore~~ "four bells in the middle watch["] (as they call it.) Get up at 8 in the morning— always the last man, & never quick enough for the first table—& breakfast with servants, children & subordinate officers. This is better than I do ~~at hom~~ in San Francisco, though—always get up at noon, there.

Ever since we got becalmed—~~4~~ 5 days—I have been copying the diary of one of the young Fergusons (the two boys who starved & suffered, with 13 others, in an open boat at sea for 43 days, lately, after their ship, the "Hornet," was burned on the equator.) Both these boys, & Capt Mitchell, are passengers with us. I am copying the diary to publish in Harper's Magazine if I have time to fix it up properly when I get to San F.[2]

I suppose, from present appearances,—light winds & calms—that we shall be two ~~weeks~~ or three weeks at sea, yet,—and I hope so—I am in no hurry to go to work.

Sunday Morning, Aug. ~~5~~ 6.

This is rather slow. We still drift, drift, drift along—at intervals a spanking breeze, & then—drift again—hardly move for half a day. But I enjoy it. We have such snowy moonlight, & such gorgeous sunsets. And the ship is so easy—even in a gale, she rolls very little, compared to other vessels—& in this calm we could dance on deck, if we chose. You can walk a crack, so steady is she. Very different from the Ajax. My trunk used to get loose in the stateroom & rip & tear around the place as if it had life in it, & I always had to take my clothes off in bed because I could not stand up & do it.

There is a ship in sight—the first object we have seen since we left Honolulu. We are still 1300 or 1400 miles from land, & so anything like this that varies the vast solitude of the ocean makes all hands light-hearted & cheerful. We think the ship is the *"Comet,"* which left Honolulu several hours before we did. She is about twelve miles away, & so we cannot see her hull, but the sailors think it~~s~~ is the Comet because of some peculiarity about her fore-top-gallant-sails. We have watched her all the forenoon.

Afternoon—We had preaching on the quarter-deck by Rev. Mr. Rising, of Virginia City, old friend of mine.[3] Spread a flag on the booby-hatch, which made a very good pulpit, & then ranged the chairs on either side against the bulwarks; last Sunday we had the shadow of the mainsail, but today we were on the opposite tack, close-hauled, & had the sun. I am leader of the choir on this ship, & a sorry lead it~~s~~ is. I hope they will have a better opinion ~~in h~~ of the music in h̸ Heaven than I have down here. If they don't a thunderbolt will come down & knock the vessel endways.

The other ship *is* the Comet—she is right abreast, 3 miles away, sailing on our course—both of us in a dead calm. With the glasses we can see what we take to be men & women on her decks. I am ~~ac~~ well acquainted with nearly all her passengers, & being so close seems right sociable.

Monday 7—I had just gone to bed a little after midnight when the 2ᵈ mate came & roused up the captain & said "The Comet has come round & is standing away on the other tack." I went up immediately, & so did all our passengers, without waiting to dress—men, women & children. There was a perceptible breeze. Pretty soon the other ship swept down upon us with all her sails set, & made a fine show in the luminous starlight. She passed within a hundred yards of us, so we could faintly see persons on her decks. We had two minutes chat with each other, through the medium of hoarse shouting, & then ~~the gallant vessels~~ she bore away to windward.

In the morning she was only a little black peg standing out of the glassy sea in the distant horizon—an almost invisible mark in the bright sky. Dead calm. So the ships have stood, all day long—have not moved 100 yards.

Aug. ∅ 8—The calm continues. Magnificent weather. The gentlemen have all turned boys. They play boyish games on the poop and quarter-deck: For instance: They lay a knife on the fife-rail of the mainmast—stand off 3 steps, shut one eye, walk up & strike at it with the forefinger; (seldom hit it); also they lay a knife on the deck & walk 7 or 8 steps with eyes close shut, & try to find it. They kneel—place elbows against knees—extend~~s~~ hands in front along the deck—place knife against end of fingers—then clasp hands behind back & bend forward &

try to pick up the knife with their teeth & rise up from knees without rolling over or losing their balance. They tie a string to the shrouds—stand with back against it—walk 3 steps (eyes shut)—turn around 3 times and go & put finger on the string; only a military man can do it. If you want to know how perfectly ˏridiculous˅ a grown man looks performing such absurdities in the presence of ladies, get one to try it.

Afternoon—The calm is no more. There are 3 vessels in sight. It is so sociable to have them hovering about us on this ~~waste of~~ broad waste of waters. It is sunny & pleasant, but blowing hard. Every rag about the ship is spread to the breeze & she is speeding over the sea like a bird. There is a large brig right astern of us with all her canvas set & chasing us at her best. She came up fast while the winds ~~are~~ were light, but now it is hard to tell whether she gains or not. We can see the people on the forecastle with the glass. The race is exciting.[4] ˏI am sorry to know that we shall soon have to quit the vessel & go ashore if she keeps up this speed.˅

~~Friday~~

Friday, Aug. 10—We have breezes & calms alternately. The brig is 2 miles to 3 astern, & just stays, there. We sail *directly* east—this brings the brig, with all her canvas set, almost in the eye of the sun, when it sets—beautiful. She looks sharply cut & black as coal ~~in the midst of a~~ ˏagainst a˅ background of fire & in the midst of a sea of blood.

San Francisco, Aug. 20.

We never saw the Comet again till the 13th, in the morning, 3 miles away. At 3 oclock that afternoon, 25 days out from Honolulu, both ships entered the Golden Gate of San Francisco *side by side*, & 300 yards apart. There was a gale blowing, & both vessels clapped on every stitch of canvas & swept up through the channel & past the fortresses at a magnificent gait.

Under that day's date I find the following terse & irreverent remark: "Ashore again, & devilish sorry for it."[5]

I have been up to Sacramento & squared accounts with the *Union*. They paid me a great deal more than they promised me. I suppose that means that I gave satisfaction, but they did not say so.[6]

Orion & Mollie are here. They leave for Santa Cruz tomorrow.[7]

I have sent Captain Mitchell's log overland to the N.Y. *Times*, but told them not to put my name to it, because if I get time I am going to write the whole story of the *Hornet* disaster for Harper's Magazine.[8]

I Looking over my note-book, I find the following:

"On board ship Emmeline, off Hawaii, Sandwich Islands: Corn-bread brick-bats for dinner today—I wonder what Margaret would think of *such* corn-bread?"[9]

That reminds me that I went to reading your letters a while ago at dinner, but there was so little cheerful news in them that I lost my appetite & came away with an empty stomach.[10]

Yrs aff

Sam

[1] The First Presbyterian Church of St. Louis, on the corner of Fourteenth Street and Lucas Place, "was, at the time of its erection, the finest church edifice in the Mississippi Valley; it cost, for its erection, alone, over $100,000. It was a stately Gothic edifice, surmounted by a beautifully proportioned tower and spire. It was dedicated to the worship of Almighty God, on October 21, 1855" (Conard, 5:212). Construction of this lavish church—which Pamela Moffett and Jane Clemens occasionally attended—came during the "vigorous and efficient ministry" (1838–55) of the Reverend Artemas Bullard (b. 1802), a "wise master builder," who died in a railroad disaster less than two weeks after the dedication (Conard, 5:212–13, 1:421–22, 3:3; Varble, 226–27).

[2] Clemens identified the Ferguson brothers, of Stamford, Connecticut, in a notebook entry evidently made on 28 July: "Sam' Ferguson is about 28—a graduate of Trinity College, Hartford—Henry is 18—a student of same college" (*N&J1*, 142). Samuel Ferguson, who had sailed on the *Hornet* to restore his health after "a severe attack of lung fever," died at Santa Clara, California, on 1 October 1866, of "Consumption" that developed "after his exposure" in the *Hornet* longboat (Henry Ferguson to SLC, 8 Dec 99, CU-MARK). Henry Ferguson lived until 1917, becoming an Episcopal clergyman, a professor of history and political science at Trinity College, and rector of St. Paul's School in Concord, New Hampshire. Captain Josiah A. Mitchell, aged fifty-three, of Freeport, Maine, continued his maritime career until his death in 1876 (Brown, 230–31; *MTH*, 102–3, 107–8 n. 5). Clemens's literary use of the Mitchell and Ferguson diaries is discussed in note 8.

[3] The Reverend Franklin S. Rising (1833?–68) was the prototype of the "fragile, gentle, spirituel new fledgling" minister in chapter 47 of *Roughing It*. He had arrived in Virginia City in mid-April 1862 and had become rector of St. Paul's Episcopal Church. In February 1866, in ill health and suffering from a badly sprained knee, Rising had sailed for Hawaii. He reached Honolulu on 16 March, just two days before Clemens, who probably in early April made a note of his condition: "Mr. Rising—first sprained & nervous prostration—worn out with study & labor—health not much improved" (*N&J1*, 197). In June Rising had accepted the post of financial secretary and general agent of the American Church Missionary Society. He was now returning to San Francisco to embark for New York, where the society had its offices. He died in December 1868 in the collision of the steamers *America* and *United States* on the Ohio River. (For a study of Rising's friendship with and possible influence on Clemens, see Muir, 317–22.)

[4] This paragraph and part of the paragraph beginning "Friday, Aug. 10" appear, with some differences, in the notebook Clemens was using aboard the *Smyrniote*—evidently copied from this letter (see *N&J1*, 162–63).

[5] In fact Clemens's notebook entry reads: "Aug 13—San Francisco—Home again. No—*not* home again—in prison again—and all the wild sense of freedom gone. The city seems so cramped, & so dreary with toil & care & business anxiety. God help me, I wish I were at sea again!" (*N&J1*, 163).

[6] Although he had agreed to spend a month in the Sandwich Islands gathering material for twenty or thirty letters and in fact had stayed four months, Clemens clearly had given satisfaction. By 20 August the Sacramento *Union* had published eighteen letters, with another seven, at least some of them written by this time, to appear between 24 August and 16 November (see *MTH*, 256). Years later, in "My Début as a Literary Person," Clemens recalled:

> When I returned to California by and by, I went up to Sacramento and presented a bill for general correspondence at twenty dollars a week. It was paid. Then I presented a bill for "special" service on the *Hornet* matter of three columns of solid nonpareil at *a hundred dollars a column*. The cashier did n't faint, but he came rather near it. He sent for the proprietors, and they came and never uttered a protest. They only laughed in their jolly fashion, and said it was robbery, but no matter; it was a grand "scoop" (the bill or my *Hornet* report, I did n't know which); "pay it. It's all right." The best men that ever owned a newspaper. (SLC 1899b, 77)

James Anthony (1823–76), Henry W. Larkin (1819–78), and Paul Morrill—operating as James Anthony and Co.—were the proprietors and publishers of the *Union* (masthead, Sacramento *Union*, 20 Aug 66, 1; "James Anthony," Sacramento *Record-Union*, 5 Jan 76, 4; "Death of H. W. Larkin," Sacramento *Record-Union*, 12 Nov 78, 3; Willis, 152–53).

[7] Orion and Mollie presumably were sightseeing before leaving for the East on 30 August (see 22 May 66 to MEC, n. 1).

[8] The New York *Times* did not print Clemens's submission. He used lengthy extracts from the diaries of Mitchell and the Ferguson brothers to tell the "whole story" of the *Hornet* disaster in "Forty-three Days in an Open Boat." That article appeared anonymously in the December 1866 number of *Harper's Monthly* (SLC 1866j, 104–13) and was credited to "Mark Swain" in the magazine's annual index. Clemens later reworked the material in "My Début as a Literary Person" (SLC 1899b, 79–87). For an account of Henry Ferguson's objections to both articles, see *N&J1*, 149 n. 118. The Ferguson and Mitchell journals are published in Brown, passim.

[9] This entry appears in neither of Clemens's surviving Hawaiian notebooks, but may have been in a notebook now lost which covered the months of April and May 1866 (see *N&J1*, 100–101). The *Emeline* was the schooner on which Clemens traveled from Honolulu to the island of Hawaii in late May (*MTH*, 59). Margaret was "the German maid" in the Moffett home in St. Louis (*MTBus*, 47), not Margaret Sexton, the Clemenses' former boarder, as previously conjectured (*N&J1*, 101).

[10] None of the letters that so disturbed Clemens is known to survive.

To the Publishers of the Sacramento *Union*
(James Anthony, Henry W. Larkin, and Paul Morrill)
13 August 1866 • San Francisco, Calif.
(MS facsimile, *draft telegram:* Gates)

ₐPRIVATE.ₐ

San Francisco, Monday Aug 13.
Arrived in Smyrniote this afternoon,—go up to Sacramento tomorrow.

Mark Twain

HONOLULU ITEMS.—Through a note just received from our correspondent at Honolulu, ₐdated July 19,ₐ we learn that the aged father of the reigning King of the Hawaiian Islands, and Mrs. Rooke, the mother of Queen Emma, were both lying at the point of death. H. H. the Governess of Hawaii was also very ill, perhaps even dangerously so. ~~The~~

The Hawaiian Legislature was still in session.

The *Smyrniote* & the *Comet* both sailed for San Francisco ~~of~~ on the 19ᵗʰ of July.[1]

---

[1] The Sacramento *Union* did not publish this news bulletin. It can be updated, however, as follows: Mataio Kekuanaoa (1791–1868)—father of Kamehameha V—recovered, but not until late September; Grace Kamaikui Young Rooke—foster mother of Kamehameha IV's widow, Emma Naea Rooke (1836–85)—died on 26 July; Princess Ruth Keelikolani (1826–83)—daughter of Mataio Kekuanaoa, half-sister of Kamehameha V, and governess of the island of Hawaii since 1855—although rumored to be seriously ill, had merely sprained her ankle (Korn, 298–99, 302–4; Honolulu *Pacific Commercial Advertiser*: "Reports having been in circulation . . ." and "Her excellency the Governess of Hawaii . . . ," 7 July 66, 2; "Mrs. Rooke . . . ," 28 July 66, 2; "Notes of the Week," 21 July 66, 3, 28 July 66, 3, 29 Sept 66, 3). On the back of the sheet on which he composed this telegram and bulletin, Clemens later in August drafted a portion of "How, for Instance?"—a sketch satirizing accident insurance which appeared in the New York *Weekly Review* on 29 September (*ET&S3*, no. 192).

To William Bowen
25 August 1866 • San Francisco, Calif.

(MS, *damage emended:* TxU)

San Francisco—
Aug. 25, 1866—

Bill, My Boy—

There has been a misunderstanding all around. You know I didn't want to take your note, but you insisted on it. And when I started across the plains to be gone 3 months & have the recreation we all needed (thinking the war would be closed & the river open again by that time,) I turned over a lot of notes for money I had loaned (for I did not know *what* might happen,) ~~& among~~ to Ma, & among them yours—but I charged her earnestly never to call on you for a cent save in direst emergency, because, in all justice you could not be said to owe me a cent. And I told her that if the note remained in my possession I never *would* present it. I was under too many obligations (those of old & tried friendship included,) to you & Bart, to ever have anything like sordid *business* engagements with you.[1]

Well, Maś don't understand the case as we do, Bill, but she will when I go home in October. I know she don't, because she has a larger soul that God usually gives to women.

I generally get up at eleven o'clock, because I am naturally lazy, as you well know, & because the pleasantest of my acquaintances at the hotel breakfast at that hour—but this morning I overslept myself & did not get down until a little after noon—just time enough to miss my breakfast by a scratch.[2] You know how d—d savage a man feels under such circumstances, & so you will appreciate it when I say that when the clerk sent me your letter it answered for breakfast, restored my temper & made me comfortable & at peace with all the world. Thank you right heartily, my lad.

Bill, of course with so much rubbing against antagonistic natures, I have at last come to smothering my feelings & choking them down from showing on the surface—but the news about the Association "fetched" me. I don't know when anything has made me feel so badly as the paragraph that told me the Association had fallen from its high estate—had lost its more than regal power. I say *more* than royal power, Bill, & I speak advisedly—for no king ever ~~wil~~ wielded so absolute a sway over subject & domain as did that old Association. I have compared its machinery with that of other governments—royal, republican & ecclesiastic—& did not find its match. These had their rotten places, their weak spots—but *it* was perfect. It was a beautiful system—beautiful—& I am sorry enough that its greatness hath departed from it.[3]

I am sorry, too, that the instrument of its undoing was found among its own subjects.[4] I am sorry to hear *any* harm of any pilot—for I hold those old river friends above all others, & I know that in genuine *manliness* they assay away above the common multitude. You know, yourself, Bill— or you *ought* to know it—that *all* men—kings & serfs alike—are *slaves* to ~~cir~~ other men & to circumstances—save, alone, the pilot—who comes at no man's beck or call, obeys no man's orders & scorns all men's suggestions. The king *would* do this thing, & he *would* do that: but a cramped treasury overmasters him in the one case & a seditious people in the other. The Senator must hob-nob with **canaille** whom he despises, & banker, priest & statesman trim their actions by the breeze of the world's will & the world's opinion. It is a strange study,—a singular phenomenon, if you please, that the only real, independent & genuine **gentlemen** in the world go quietly up & down the Mississippi river, asking no homage of any one, seeking no popularity, no notoriety, & not caring a damn whether school keeps or not.[5]

Beck Jolly is President—long may the distinguished traveler, the mighty hunter of lions, the brilliant Chinese linguist & the dreaded scourge of the nations of the Orient flourish! Amen. You ask Zeb[6] if he believes there is anybody who can fence with pokers, or talk Chinese, or quell insurrections or eat tiger meat like Beck & me. But who is the Secretary?

"You "write me of the boats, thinking I may yet feel an interest in the old business." You bet your life I do. It is about the only thing I *do* feel any interest in & yet I can hear least about it. If I were two years younger, I would come back & learn the river over again. But it is too late now. I am too lazy for 14-day trips—too fond of running all night & sleeping all day—too fond of sloshing around, talking with people.

Why in the mischief don't O'Neil ~~did~~ die? Is that d—d Fenian going to live forever? But he was a bully boy, if ever there *was* one. You ought to have seen him & me bring the (d—n the boat's name, I can't think of it now—Alonzo, or Child, or something like that,) up the river, through the ice, drawing all the water. He was the whitest Captain I ever sailed with, & in this stiff "earthquake cobbler" I drink present joy & final salvation to him![7]

Do you recollect the old hoss that died in the wilderness? I have made that famous in Washoe, & didn't I make those solemn missionaries' eyes bug out with it? I think so.[8] While I was there, the American Ministers to China & Japan—Mr Burlinggame & Gen. Van Valkenburg came along, & we just made Honolulu howl. I only got tight once, though. I know better than to get tight oftener than once in 3 months. It sets a man back in the esteem of people whose good opinions are worth having.

Didn't have much fun coming up, because we had light winds & calms all the way & were at sea 25 days, on the voyage.

Why the devil didn't you say something about Sam & Bart?[9]

I am very, very sorry you cannot get well[10]—but *don't* despond—it is *poison*, rank *poison* to knuckle down to care & hardships. They must come to us all, albeit in different shapes—& we may not escape them—it is not possible—but we may swindle them out of half their puissance with a stiff upper lip.

Marry be d—d. I am too old to marry. I am nearly 31. I have got gray hairs in my head. Women appear to like me, but d—n them, they don't *love* me.

Well, I have only been back a week, & I have got to stir around some & see the boys. Good bye, Bill. I hope to start to the States about the time you receive this letter—but I don't know—the world is an uncertain institution.

Yrs,
Mark

Old Ed Montgomery did me a genuine kindness once, Bill, if you recollect,[11]

—⁓⁓—

~~Sam~~ Mark

[1] Bowen had borrowed $200 from Clemens, apparently early in 1861. Jane Clemens had preserved Bowen's note—in which he promised to repay her son "one day after" 25 February 1861 "on order"—in Clemens's 1860–61 piloting notebook. On the back of the note she recorded $77.15 in interest, accrued at 10 percent per year by 4 January 1865, as well as the only reimbursement Bowen is known to have made: $100, paid to her on 7 March 1865 (see *N&J1*, 61).

[2] Clemens was probably again staying at the Occidental Hotel.

[3] Chapter 15 of *Life on the Mississippi* summarizes the rise and fall of the Western

Boatman's Benevolent Association, described there as "perhaps the compactest, the completest, and the strongest commercial organization ever formed among men." Concurrent with the growth of railroad and river-tow commerce, the monopolistic power of this organization of St. Louis and New Orleans steamboat pilots, to which Clemens belonged, rapidly eroded after the end of the Civil War, although its demise did not come until July 1875.

⁴William J. Kribben, secretary of the Western Boatman's Benevolent Association, absconded with the association's funds. Clemens's remarks here suggest that the defalcation was recent; clearly he had only recently learned of it from Bowen. He mentioned the treacherous act in 1883 in chapter 15 of *Life on the Mississippi* and in 1897 in "Villagers of 1840–3" (*Inds*, 97).

⁵Chapter 14 of *Life on the Mississippi* opens with a restatement of the assertions in this paragraph. The entire chapter is devoted to the thesis that a pilot "was the only unfettered and entirely independent human being that lived in the earth."

⁶Zebulon Leavenworth.

⁷Clemens had piloted the *Alonzo Child* under James O'Neal in early 1861 while its regular captain, David DeHaven, was ill.

⁸Clemens had entertained with a song about an old horse he called both "Jerusalem" and "Methusalem" at least since his piloting days. Annie Moffett recalled the version he sang then:

> When I think of Uncle Sam during those early years it is always as a singer. He would sit at the piano and play and sing by the hour, the same song over and over:—
>
>> There was an old horse
>> And his name was Jerusalem.
>> He went to Jerusalem,
>> He came from Jerusalem.
>> Ain't I glad I'm out of the wilderness! Oh! Bang!
>
> (*MTBus*, 39)

Other, briefer descriptions of his performances, on the Mississippi and in Nevada, can be found in *MTB*, 1:129, 295–96; *ET&S1*, 197; William Wright 1893b, 14; and Doten 1973, 2:997. While in Hawaii, Clemens presumably had ample opportunity to make "eyes bug out" with this song since "as he went about the Islands" he "called on or stayed over night with many missionaries and their descendants" (*MTH*, 134). "Jerusalem/Methusalem" possibly derived from a song Clemens might have learned in his childhood—for example, the slave song "The Old Gray Mare Came Tearin' out the Wilderness," melodic source of the popular "Old Gray Mare" (Sandburg, 102).

⁹Bowen's pilot brothers.

¹⁰In 1897 Clemens recalled in "Villagers of 1840–3" that Bowen was "Diseased" (*Inds*, 97). His ailment has not been identified.

¹¹For Captain Joseph E. Montgomery's kindness to Clemens, see 27? June 60 to OC, n. 5. In "Captain Montgomery," written for the Virginia City *Territorial Enterprise* in January 1866, Clemens had said that "whenever he commenced helping anybody, Captain Ed. Montgomery never relaxed his good offices as long as help was needed" (*ET&S3*, no. 161). Clemens added the present remark about Montgomery on the back of the first page of the letter, possibly in reference to an enclosed copy of his *Enterprise* contribution.

🐾

No LETTERS are known to survive for the next two months. In chapter 78 of *Roughing It* Clemens gave short shrift to the interval between his return from Honolulu on 13 August 1866 and the delivery of his first formal lecture on 2 October: "I was home again, in San Francisco, without means and without employment. I tortured my brain for a saving scheme of some kind, and at last a public lecture occurred to me!" In fact, Clemens was demonstrably busy during this period and, given his liberal settlement with the proprietors of the Sacramento *Union*, was not without funds (see 30 July . . . 20 Aug 66 to JLC and PAM, n. 6). In the second half of August he presumably finished writing his Sandwich Islands letters to the *Union* and possibly began drafting "Forty-three Days in an Open Boat," published by *Harper's Monthly* in December (SLC 1866j, 104–13). Also in August he resumed his contributions to the New York *Weekly Review* with "How, for Instance?" (published 29 Sept 66, *ET&S3*, no. 192). The Sacramento *Union* employed him again in September to help report the thirteenth annual fair of the California State Agricultural Society, held in Sacramento from the tenth to the fifteenth of the month. Clemens devoted his attention to the stock shows and horse races: James Anthony, one of the *Union* proprietors, called him "the best reporter of a horse-race that ever was made" (Mary Josephine Anthony to Mrs. Bishop, portion of 1925 letter in CU-MARK; for Clemens's probable contributions to the *Union*'s coverage of the fair, see Branch 1969, 179–86.) After the fair, Clemens conceivably did some preliminary work on the book made up of his Sandwich Islands letters which he submitted to the New York publishers Dick and Fitzgerald in 1867, only to withdraw it because of what he termed the "dull publishing times" (see *N&J1*, 176–77 n. 166). He concluded his September efforts with "Origin of Illustrious Men," published in the *Californian* on the next-to-last day of the month (*ET&S3*, no. 193).

On 2 October—with the encouragement of his friend John McComb (1829–96), soon to become a proprietor and the supervising editor of the San Francisco *Alta California*—Clemens took a step that had a profound effect on his life and career. He delivered his first lecture, on the Sandwich Islands, to a packed house at Maguire's Academy of Music in San Francisco. The rousing success of this lecture (comically described in chapter 78 of *Roughing It*) resulted in a quickly arranged tour of California and

Nevada towns under the management of Denis E. McCarthy, formerly co-owner of the Virginia City *Territorial Enterprise*. In the first two weeks of the tour Clemens lectured in Sacramento (11 October), Marysville (15 October), Grass Valley (20 October), Nevada City (23 October), Red Dog (24 October), and You Bet (25 October), all in California, before moving on to Virginia City, where he wrote the next letter (*MTB*, 1:291–94; "The Alta California," Virginia City *Territorial Enterprise*, 4 Nov 66, 2; *MTH*, 421–22; Fatout 1960, 33–54).

To Robert M. Howland
29 October 1866 • Virginia City, Nev.
(MS: NvHi)

Virginia, Oct. 29.

Dear Bob

I have just received your dispatch—& I'm all right—how are *you?*

I expect to lecture here day after to-morrow—(Wednesday) pro-vided I can get the theatre—can't tell yet—& lecture in Gold Hill Thurs-day, Silver City Friday and in Carson Saturday if you think I can get a good audience there. What do you think of it?[1] Ask old Abe Curry if the people will turn out—I hunted for him in Sacramento but I could only *hear* of him at every corner but never catch him.[2]

Good Bye— Take a drink at my expense.

Yr old Friend

Mark

---

[1]Clemens amended these lecture plans somewhat, appearing in: Virginia City on Wednesday, 31 October; Carson City on Saturday, 3 November; Dayton on Thursday, 8 November; Silver City on Friday, 9 November; and Gold Hill on Saturday, 10 November. (For further details of his itinerary at this time, see 2 Nov 66 to JLC and family.) Since he had left Nevada in May 1864 under the imputation of having slandered the ladies of Carson City, he was understandably concerned about how he would now be received (*MTH*, 422; Fatout 1960, 54–55; Doten 1973, 2:901, 903).

[2]Abraham (sometimes Abram) V. Z. Curry (1814?–73), a principal founder (in 1858) and leading citizen of Carson City, had been active in territorial affairs. His generosity in providing the first Territorial Legislature (1861) with a furnished

meeting place and free transportation to it was the basis of Clemens's assertion, in chapter 25 of *Roughing It*, that "but for Curry the government would have died in its tender infancy" (Marsh, Clemens, and Bowman, 478 n. 133; Mack 1936, 178–79, 228–29; *ET&S1*, 463–64).

To Abraham V. Z. Curry and Others
per Telegraph Operator
1 November 1866 • Virginia City, Nev.
(Transcript: CU-MARK)

CALIFORNIA STATE TELEGRAPH COMPANY

Virginia Nov. 1st 186 6
3:15 P M

TO A Curry, J. Neely Johnson
R M Howland & others

Been on sick list off now—I accept for Saturday with many thanks—will be there tomorrow[1]

Mark Twain

17 Pd. 85 J

---

[1] Clemens was responding to the following letter:

CARSON CITY, October 30, 1866.

MARK TWAIN, Esq.: Dear Sir—The undersigned, Citizens of Carson City, respectfully invite you to favor them with a repetition of the Address or Lecture which you have so acceptably presented to the People of San Francisco and other places, on the subject of the Sandwich Islands, and its People, *or any other man*, at such time as may comport with your other engagements in this respect. An early reply to this invitation will the more satisfactorily enable us to make such announcement of the fact of your acceptance (if agreeable to you) as will secure the attendance on such an occasion, of the people of Carson City, who remember you in times gone by as one of its citizens, and who have none other than the most kindly remembrances of you. (Carson City *Daily Appeal*, 31 Oct 66, 3, clipping in Scrapbook 1:71, CU-MARK)

More than one hundred individuals signed this invitation, including Curry, Johnson, Howland, and, at the head of the list, the addressees of the next letter.

To Henry G. Blasdel and Others
1 November 1866 • Virginia City, Nev.
(Virginia City *Territorial Enterprise*, 4 Nov 66)

VIRGINIA, November 1.[1]

His Excellency H. G. Blasdel, Governor, and Messrs. A. Helm,
   O. A. F. Gilbert, H. F. Rice and others:[2]

GENTLEMEN: Your kind and cordial invitation to lecture before my
old friends in Carson has reached me, and I hasten to thank you gratefully
for this generous recognition—this generous toleration, I should say—of
one who has shamefully deserted the high office of Governor of the Third
House of Nevada and gone into the Missionary business, thus leaving you
to the mercy of scheming politicians—an act which, but for your forgiv-
ing disposition, must have stamped my name with infamy.

I take a natural pride in being welcomed home again by so long a list
of old personal friends, and shall do my level best to please them, hoping
at the same time that they will be more indulgent toward my shortcomings than they would feel called upon to be toward those of a stranger.

Kindly thanking you again, gentlemen, I gladly accept your invitation, and shall appear on the stage of the Carson Theatre on Saturday
evening, November 3d, and disgorge a few lines and as much truth as I
can pump out without damaging my constitution.

Yours, sincerely,
MARK TWAIN.

Ex-Gov. Third House, and late Independent Opposition Missionary
   to the Sandwich Islands.

P. S.—I would have answered yesterday, but I was on the sick list,
and I thought I had better wait a day and see whether I was going to get
well or not.

M. T.

---

[1] In publishing this letter the Virginia City *Territorial Enterprise* noted: "The
following characteristic card from Mark Twain is in reply to a general invitation
of the residents of Carson extended to him to visit the State Capital and deliver his
lecture on the Sandwich Islands." Clemens's letter was a formal reply to the invitation that he had already answered with the preceding telegram.

[2] Henry G. Blasdel was governor of Nevada. Alfred Helm, a Carson City businessman and theater owner, was clerk of the second district court of Nevada

Territory in 1862 and 1863, and since 1864 had been clerk of the Nevada state supreme court. Henry F. Rice (1817?–77), for many years the Wells, Fargo and Company agent in Carson City, served several terms as an Ormsby County commissioner between 1861 and 1866. O. A. F. Gilbert was a clerk at a Carson City dry-goods establishment in 1862; his occupation in 1866 has not been determined (Angel, 87, 89, 529, 555; Marsh 1972, 694 n. 294; Kelly 1862, 10, 70, 72; Kelly 1863, 9).

To Jane Lampton Clemens and Family
2 November 1866 • Virginia City, Nev.
(MS: NPV)

Va, Nov. 1.

All the Folks, Affectionate Greeting:

You know the flush times are past, & it has long been impossible to more than half fill the Theatre here, with any sort of attraction—but they filled it for me, night before last,—full—dollar all over the house.

I was mighty dubious about Carson, but the enclosed call & some telegrams set that all right—I lecture there tomorrow night.[1]

They offer me a full house & no expenses, in Dayton—go there next.[2]

Sandy Baldwin says I have made the most sweeping success of any man he knows of.

I have lectured in San Francisco, Sacramento, Marysville, Grass Valley, Nevada, You Bet, Red Dog & Virginia. I am going to talk in Carson, Gold Hill, Silver [*in bottom margin:* (over) City, Dayton, & Washoe,[3] San Francisco again, & again here if I have time to re-hash the lecture.[4]

Then I am bound for New York—lecture on the Steamer, maybe. I'll leave toward 1st December—but I'll telegraph you.

Love to all.

Yrs

Mark

---

[1]Clemens was writing on 2 November: the Carson City lecture of "tomorrow night," scheduled in the preceding two letters, took place on 3 November; the Virginia City lecture of the "night before last" took place on 31 October. In Virginia City, at Maguire's Opera House, Clemens had an audience of about eight

hundred. Alfred Doten, writing in the *Territorial Enterprise* of 1 November, called it "one of the largest and most fashionable audiences that ever graced the Opera House":

> The entire dress circle and the greater portion of the parquette were filled with ladies, while all the available space for extra seats and standing room was occupied. It was a magnificent tribute to the lecturer from his old friends. Of the lecture itself we can only speak in general terms, as its points are too numerous and varied to admit of special mention. Combining the most valuable statistical and general information, with passages of drollest humor—all delivered in the peculiar and inimitable style of the author—and rising occasionally to lofty flights of descriptive eloquence—the lecture constitutes an entertainment of rare excellence and interest. (Doten 1866, 3; see also Doten 1973, 2:901)

[2] On 8 November.

[3] Clemens was "the guest of Thomas Fitch at the latter's home in Washoe City for a week during the Nevada lecture tour":

> Thomas Fitch secured the courthouse of Washoe City. Here Mark Twain gave his lecture on the Sandwich Islands. Fitch introduced his friend, who had arrived at the point where he needed no introduction to the Western side of America, at least. . . .
> On their way back to Fitch's home after the lecture Twain was depressed. He had not liked his lecture.
> "Well, Sam, it was a great success," said Thomas Fitch, who had acted as doorkeeper, cheerily. "I have taken in over $200."
> "Yes, and I have taken in over 200 people," returned Twain gloomily.
> "Now, Sam, don't belittle yourself. You know you rank as one of the foremost humorists of the day," returned his friend.
> "I know. But as a lecturer I am a fraud, ain't I?" insisted Twain.
> "You have a tendency that way," said Fitch, laughingly.
> Mark Twain bubbled over with sudden humor.
> "I know, Tom," he said, "but there are over two hundred towns in the United States and all have over five thousand inhabitants, and maybe I can play all of them at once." (Wells, 13)

Fitch, whom Clemens had once characterized as an unscrupulously ambitious "two-faced" dog, was now district attorney of Washoe County, Nevada (see 11 Nov 64 to OC). The lecture in Washoe City must have occurred between 4 and 7 November, Clemens's only free dates before his departure from Nevada on 12 November.

[4] On 10 November, following his lecture in Gold Hill, Clemens was the victim of a prank concocted by Denis E. McCarthy, Steve Gillis, and several other friends, who waylaid him on the "Divide," a "lonesome, windswept road" between Gold Hill and Virginia City, ostensibly to relieve him of the evening's proceeds. Their real intention, Gillis claimed in 1907, was to provide him with a ready subject for a second Virginia City lecture, since he had refused to give his Sandwich Islands talk again, "saying that he would not repeat himself in the same town, that he was tired of the old lecture, and that he had neither time nor material to prepare a new one" (Gillis to Albert Bigelow Paine, ca. June 1907, in Davis 1956a, 3; see also *MTB*, 1:297–302). According to Alfred Doten, Clemens lost "about $125 in coin, & a very valuable gold watch . . . worth $300" as well as "two jacknives, & three lead pencils" and he put "a card in the paper in morning [11 November], offering to negociate for the watch" (Doten 1973, 2:903). Furious when he learned of the joke and unplacated by the return of his property, Clemens left Virginia City on 12 November. He arrived the following night in San Francisco, where, a month later, he unexpectedly profited from the Gillis-McCarthy

"robbery" (see 14 Dec 66 to JLC and family, n. 1). He delivered his Sandwich Islands lecture in San Francisco on 16 November, in San Jose on 21 November, in Petaluma on 26 November (not 23 or 24 November, as previously thought), in Oakland on 27 November, and again in San Francisco on 10 December ("Robbed," San Francisco *Morning Call*, 15 Nov 66, 1; Petaluma *Journal and Argus*: "Mark Twain," 22 Nov 66, 2; "Reprehensible," 29 Nov 66, 2; *MTH*, 422–23; Fatout 1960, 56–66). For the dates of the earlier lectures mentioned here see p. 362 and 29 Oct 66 to Howland, n. 1.

To Catherine C. (Kate) Lampton and Annie E. and Samuel E. Moffett
2? November 1866 • Virginia City, Nev.
(MS: NPV)

[*first four MS pages (about 400 words) missing*]¹

will all come straight anyway. How is old Moses that was rescued from the bulrushes & keeps a second-hand clothing-store in Market Street?²

Dear Sammy—Keep up your lick & you will become a great minister of the gospel some day, & then I shall be satisfied. I wanted to be a minister myself—it was the only genuine ambition I ever had—but somehow I never had any qualification for it *but* the ambition. I always missed fire on the ministry. *Then* I hoped *some* member of the family would take hold of it & succeed. Orion would make a preacher, & I am ready to swear he will never make anything else in the world. But he won't touch it. I am utterly & completely disgusted with a member of the family who *could* be carry out my old ambition & won't. If I only had his chance, I would make the abandoned sinner get up & howl. But you may succeed, & I am determined Pamela shall make you try it anyhow.

Yrs Affly
Sam.

¹This is almost certainly the letter to "Annie & Sammy & Katie" mentioned in the next letter. Kate Lampton (b. 1856), Clemens's first cousin, was the daughter of James A. H. Lampton and Ella Hunter Lampton (*Inds*, biographical directory). She may have kept some or all of the pages missing here.

²Annie Moffett later recalled this long-standing joke, dating from Clemens's piloting days:

I was very fond of Uncle Sam, but I did not think he was the genius of the family. I remember when I was about eight I thought he needed a little religious instruction and started to tell him the story of Moses. Uncle Sam was strangely obtuse, and finally I went to my father and said, "Papa, Uncle Orion has good sense and Mama has good sense, but I don't think Uncle Sam has good sense. I told him the story of Moses and the bullrushes and he said he knew Moses very well, that he kept a secondhand store on Market Street. I tried very hard to explain that it wasn't the Moses I meant, but he just *couldn't* understand." (*MTBus*, 38–39)

In the model letter attributed to her in "An Open Letter to the American People," Annie assures her uncle: "If you was here I could tell you about Moses in the Bulrushers again, I know it better, now" (New York *Weekly Review*, 17 Feb 66, *ET&S3*, no. 181).

To Jane Lampton Clemens and Family
4 December 1866 • San Francisco, Calif.
(MS, *damage emended:* NPV)

San.f., Dec. 4, 1866.
My Dear folks—

I have written to Annie & Sammy & Katie some time ago—also to the balance of you.[1]

I called on Rev. Dr Wadsworth last night with the City College man, but the old rip wasn't at home. I was sorry, because I wanted to make his acquaintance. I am thick & thieves with the Rev. Stebbings, & I am laying for the Rev. Scudder & the Rev. Dr Stone.[2] I am running on preachers, now, altogether. I find them gay. Stebbings is a regular brick. I am taking letters of introduction to Henry Ward Beecher, Rev. Dr Tyng, & other eminent parsons in the east.[3] Whenever anybody offers me a letter to a preacher now, I snaffle it on the spot. I shall make Rev. Dr Bellows trot out the fast nags of the cloth for me when I get to New York. Bellows is ~~cons~~ an able, upright & eloquent man—a man of imperial intellect & matchless power—he is Christian in the truest sense of the term & is unquestionably a brick.[4]

I lectured in Oakland the other night,[5]—guest of J. Ross Browne & his charming family, & a Mrs. Porter was to have been there to see me, but it rained & she couldn't—he says she ~~is~~ knew me in Hannibal. I wonder who it is—ₐneéₐ Lavinia Honeyman, maybe—I cannot think of any other.[6]

Gen. Drum has arrived in Philadelphia & established his head-quarters ~~á~~ there, as ~~Aj~~ Adjutant Genl. ~~under~~ to Maj. Gen. Meade. Col. Leonard has received a letter from him in which he offers me a complimentary benefit if I will come there. I am much obliged, really, but I am afraid I shan't lecture much in the States.[7]

The China Mail Steamer is getting ready & everybody says I am throwing away a fortune in not going in her. I firmly believe it myself.

I sail for the States in the Opposition steamer of the 15th inst., positively & without reserve. My room is already secured for me, & is the choicest in the ship. I know all the officers.[8]

Yrs Aff^{ly}

Mark

[1] Evidently the preceding two letters.

[2] The prominent San Francisco clergymen mentioned here were: Charles Wadsworth (1814–82), pastor of Calvary Presbyterian Church; Horatio Stebbins (1821–1902), pastor of the First Unitarian Church; Henry Martyn Scudder (1822–95), pastor of Howard Presbyterian Church; and Andrew Leete Stone (1815–92), pastor of the First Congregational Church (*ET&S2*, 536–37; Langley 1865, 600; Langley 1867, 655). In "Important Correspondence," published in the *Californian* on 6 May 1865, Clemens had facetiously claimed: "I have a great deal of influence with the clergy here, and especially with the Rev. Dr. Wadsworth and the Rev. Mr. Stebbins—I write their sermons for them" (*ET&S2*, 150). Wadsworth, Stebbins, and Stone were among the signers of a 5 December "call" soliciting Clemens's final San Francisco lecture (see 6 Dec 66 to Low and others, n. 2).

[3] Beecher (1813–87), the most widely known minister of his time, was pastor of the fashionable Plymouth Congregational Church in Brooklyn. Clemens apparently first heard him preach on 3 February 1867 and described the experience in a letter of 18 February to the San Francisco *Alta California* (SLC 1867a, 1). Stephen Higginson Tyng (1800–85), rector of St. George's Episcopal Church in New York City, was a renowned preacher and the first president of the National Freedman's Relief Association, founded in February 1862 to assist slaves freed by Union forces (*NCAB*, 2:187–88; "National Freedman's Association," New York *Times*, 22 Feb 62, 8).

[4] Clemens's friend Henry W. Bellows in 1866 became editor of the *Christian Examiner*, published in New York. This bimonthly was "one of the most important of American religious reviews not alone because of its exposition of the Unitarian point of view in theology throughout more than half a century, but because of its distinctive work in literary criticism, and its comment on social, philosophical, and educational problems" (Mott 1939, 284–85). Bellows continued as editor through 1869.

[5] On 27 November Clemens had lectured on the Sandwich Islands at the College of California in Oakland. Chartered in 1855, the college had developed from the Contra Costa Academy, a private school for boys founded by Congregational cler-

gyman Henry Durant two years earlier. It grew into the University of California (established 1868), which Durant served as first president ("Mark Twain's Lecture," Oakland *News*, 28 Nov 66, 3; Hart, 120–21).

⁶Travel writer J. Ross Browne (1821–75) lived with his large family on a rambling property in Oakland. He was serving the United States Treasury Department as a "special commissioner to collect mining statistics in the States and Territories west of the Rocky mountains," having been appointed on 28 July 1866 (Browne and Taylor, 3). Lavinia Honeyman (b. 1835 or 1836) had been one of Clemens's childhood friends in Hannibal (Wecter, 184; *Hannibal Census*, 310). In "Villagers of 1840–3" he recalled that she "captured 'celebrated' circus-rider—envied for the unexampled brilliancy of the match—but he got into the penitentiary at Jefferson City and the romance was spoiled" (*Inds*, 102). It is not known if she was Mrs. Porter.

⁷Brevet Brigadier General Richard Coulter Drum (1825–1909) had been assistant adjutant general of the Department of California in the Division of the Pacific of the United States Army. He had been transferred from San Francisco to Philadelphia to assume the same post in the Division of the Atlantic under General George G. Meade (1815–72). Brevet Colonel Hiram Leonard (d. 1883) was deputy paymaster general of the Department of California in the Division of the Pacific (*NCAB*, 12:359; Langley 1865, 159, 274, 622; Heitman, 384, 628). He was among those who signed the 5 December "call" for Clemens's Sandwich Islands lecture.

⁸Clemens sailed on the first leg of the trip to the East Coast on 15 December aboard the *America*, captained by Edgar Wakeman (1818–75). The *America* belonged to the North American Steamship Company, which offered passage to the East via Nicaragua, in "opposition" to the Pacific Mail Steamship Company's older Panama route. The day Clemens left, the San Francisco *Alta California* described the commission it had recently given him:

> "Mark Twain" goes off on his journey over the world as the Travelling Correspondent of the ALTA CALIFORNIA, not stinted as to time, place or direction—writing his weekly letters on such subjects and from such places as will best suit him; but we may say that he will first visit the home of his youth—St. Louis—thence through the principal cities to the Atlantic seaboard again, crossing the ocean to visit the "Universal Exposition" at Paris, through Italy, the Mediterranean, India, China, Japan, and back to San Francisco by the China Mail Steamship line. That his letters will be read with interest needs no assurance from us—his reputation has been made here in California, and his great ability is well known; but he has been known principally as a humorist, while he really has no superior as a descriptive writer—a keen observer of men and their surroundings—and we feel confident his letters to the ALTA, from his new field of observation, will give him a world-wide reputation. ("'Mark Twain's' Farewell," 15 Dec 66, 2, in Benson, 213)

Clemens's account of his harrowing voyage to New York is preserved in his notebook of the trip and in his correspondence for the *Alta* (see *N&J1*, 238–99, and *MTTB*, 11–81). His plan to visit the Far East, in acceptance of Anson Burlingame's invitation, and then return to San Francisco by the China Mail Steamship line was not accomplished. He did, however, visit his family in St. Louis during March and April 1867, and he visited the Paris exposition, Italy, and the Mediterranean later that year as a member of the *Quaker City* excursion.

To Isabella A. Cotton
4 December 1866 • San Francisco, Calif.
(MS: CU-MARK)

San f. Dec. 4.

Dear Miss Bella[1]

I have had your letter several days, & have been intending to call—but I am still unwell & take no pleasure in going out.

I leave for New York in the ~~Opposition~~ Opposition steamer of the ~~13th~~ 15th inst., & I do hope I shall be well by that time.

I enclose the picture. Have you seen Henry M℃Farlane? He is clerk at Wm. B. Cooke & Co's, Stationers, Montgomery Block, Montgomery street above Washington.[2]

Remember me kindly to Mrs Blanchard,[3] & believe, that although I may not see you more, I shall always hold you in happy remembrance & not soon forgøet the pleasant voyage we made in Company ~~for th~~ in the good ship Smyrniote.

Yr friend

Sam L. Clemens[4]

---

[1] Little is known of Isabella A. Cotton, one of Clemens's companions during the *Smyrniote* voyage from Honolulu to San Francisco. She was still in San Francisco more than a year after the ship's arrival, but the listing for her in the 1867–68 city directory merely read "dwl [dwelling] with Lott Blanchard" (Langley 1867, 145), and her name did not appear in subsequent directories. Lott Blanchard was keeper of the lighthouse at Fort Point, in San Francisco, in 1865–66, and for several years afterward was a messenger in the collector's office of the United States Custom House in that city ("Passengers," Honolulu *Pacific Commercial Advertiser*, 21 July 66, 2; Langley 1865–Langley 1873).

[2] The son of Henry MacFarlane, a Honolulu liquor dealer. He had been one of Clemens's companions on his "equestrian excursion" on the island of Oahu in March 1866 (SLC 1866b, 4, and SLC 1866c, 3). His name appeared for the last time in the San Francisco city directory in 1867–68 (Langley 1867, 314). The picture, which Clemens actually enclosed in the next letter, has not been identified.

[3] Mrs. A. Blanchard, perhaps the wife or mother of Lott Blanchard, had arrived in Honolulu from San Francisco aboard the bark *Cambridge* on 24 April 1866. She returned to San Francisco aboard the *Smyrniote* with Clemens and Cotton ("Passengers," Honolulu *Pacific Commercial Advertiser*, 21 July 66, 2).

[4] This letter is annotated on the back, in an unknown hand: "F. H. B. 26." The initials may stand for Frank H. Blanchard, who from the mid-1860s to the early 1870s lived at the same San Francisco and Oakland addresses as Lott Blanchard. It seems likely that the men were brothers, or even father and son. In 1865–66

Frank Blanchard was a messenger in the surveyor's department of the United States Custom House in San Francisco. Afterward he was a ticket clerk for the Pacific Mail Steamship Company and then a real estate agent, notary public, and commissioner of deeds (Langley 1865–Langley 1874).

To Isabella A. Cotton
4 December 1866 • San Francisco, Calif.
(MS: CU-MARK)

Dec. 4.

Dear Miss Bella

By some strange oversight I *forgot* to enclose the picture. I hasten to correct the blunder.

Yr friend

Sam L. Clemens

To Frederick F. Low and Others
6 December 1866 • San Francisco, Calif.
(San Francisco *Alta California*, 8 Dec 66)

SAN FRANCISCO, December 6, 1866.

HIS EXCELLENCY GOV. LOW, GOV. BLASDEL, GEN. WM. H. FRENCH, HON. OGDEN HOFFMAN, ETC.[1]—GENTLEMEN: I cannot too highly appreciate the invitation you have honored me with, coming, as it does, from citizens who rarely permit their names to be used in this manner, and I gratefully accept your call. San Francisco has already given me a reception or two which I may be pardoned for feeling very proud of, and whether I have deserved this further generosity or not, I shall none the less industriously endeavor to persuade strangers that I have, anyhow.

I shall be happy to repeat my first lecture at CONGRESS HALL, Bush street, just above Montgomery, on MONDAY EVENING, December 10th, and will do my best, on that occasion, to merit the high favor you have shown me.[2]

Very respectfully,

Your obliged servant,

MARK TWAIN.

[1] Frederick F. Low (1828–94), a former gold miner and banker, governor of California (1863–67); Henry G. Blasdel, governor of Nevada; Brevet Major General William H. French (1815–81), a former Union commander, now serving with the Second United States Artillery on the Pacific Coast; Ogden Hoffman (1822–91), since 1851 judge of the United States District Court for the northern district of California (*NCAB*, 4:49–50; Heitman, 437; Shuck 1889, 315–18; Shuck 1901, 472–73; Langley 1865, 595).

[2] Clemens was responding to the following invitation, signed by Low, Blasdel, French, and Hoffman, heading a list of twenty:

SAN FRANCISCO, December 5th, 1866.

Mark Twain, Esq.—Sir: Several of the undersigned were present, two months ago, when you delivered your first Lecture on the Sandwich Islands, and would like much to hear it again; the remainder were unable to attend at that time, and desire that you will afford them the pleasure thus forfeited. Therefore, for these reasons, and also as a testimony to the strangers among whom you are going, of the esteem in which your abilities are held among your friends here at home, we invite you to repeat that Lecture before your departure for the Eastern States, and request that in your reply to this note you will name the day which will be most convenient for the purpose. ("Correspondence," San Francisco *Alta California*, 8 Dec 66, 2)

Clemens gave satisfaction with this repeat performance. The *Alta California* remarked on 11 December: "In every respect, whether in regard to the subject matter of the lecture, manner of delivery, and amendment of some blemishes apparent on the first occasion, this lecture was a decided success" ("'Mark Twain's' Lecture," 1). Clemens concluded with a "farewell" in which he gave his "sincerest thanks and acknowledgments" for the "extreme kindness and cordiality" San Francisco had shown him, and predicted a brilliant future for the city ("'Mark Twain's' Farewell," San Francisco *Alta California*, 15 Dec 66, 2, in Benson, 212–13).

To Jane Lampton Clemens and Family
15 December 1866 • San Francisco, Calif.
(MS: NPV)

Dec. 14th—

Sanf—Midnight

Dear folks—

I sail tomorrow per Opposition—telegraphed you to-day—leaving more friends behind me than any newspaper man that ever sailed out of the Golden Gate,[1] Phoenix not excepted.[2] The reason I mention this with so much pride is because our fraternity generally leave ~~not~~ none but enemies here when they go—as, for instance, Webb,.[3] I stepped in at the great church Fair at Platt's Hall,[4] to-night, & all the Cannibals (I mean ladies & gentlemen of Sandwich Island nativity) I ever knew & 30 or 40 I never heard of before, came forward, without the formality of introductions, & bade me good bye & God speed. Somehow these people touch me mighty close to home with their eloquent eyes & their cordial words & the fervent clasp of their hands.

Love to all

Yrs

Sam[5]

[1] Evidence of the affection that San Franciscans felt for Clemens is provided by the following anecdote:

How "Mark Twain" Got ahead of the Highwaymen.—That robbery of the "Philosopher," on the Divide, was generally considered a good joke by every one, except the subject of it. He kept his temper, however, and fate has made him even at last. The story of his robbery travelled East, and a warm-hearted and impulsive friend in New York, before the explanation of the story reached there, immediately dispatched the following:

New York, December 12th.

Mark Twain:—Go to Nudd, Lord & Co., Front street, collect amount of money equal to what highwaymen took from you.

A. D. N.

On receipt of this very comforting telegram, the "Philosopher," who is remarkable for the fidelity with which he obeys orders, collected a hundred dollars from the firm, and will give tickets to his lectures for that amount on the other side. He leaves for New York to-day, and of course will lecture there. The "hundred in coin" will be a capital starter, when mutual explanations will have been made. As the darkey might say, "Mark" would not object to "a nudder" message on the same terms. (San Francisco *Morning Call*, 15 Dec 66, 1)

Asa D. Nudd, Charles S. Lord and Company were "importers and wholesale dealers [in] wines and liquors" (Langley 1867, 372). The "robbery" was the prank Denis E. McCarthy and Steve Gillis had played on Clemens in November (see 2 Nov 66 to JLC and family, n. 4).

[2] George Horatio Derby (1823–61), a graduate of West Point who attained the rank of captain in the United States Army Corps of Topographical Engineers, was best known for his humorous writings under the pseudonym "John Phoenix." His sketches, widely reprinted in newspapers during the 1850s, were collected in two volumes: *Phoenixiana; Or, Sketches and Burlesques* (New York: D. Appleton and Company, 1856) and, posthumously, *The Squibob Papers* (New York: Carleton, 1865). Although Derby acquired his reputation while stationed on the Pacific Coast (1849–56), St. Louis citizens and newspapers took a special interest in his writings because of his connections to the area: he had married a St. Louis woman and his family was living near Carondelet at the time of his death. The St. Louis press prominently reported his burial in Bellefontaine Cemetery early in June 1861—the month before Clemens, who knew Derby's work well, left Missouri for Carson City ("Military Burial To-day, of Capt. George H. Derby," St. Louis *Missouri Democrat*, 3 June 61, 2).

[3] Charles Henry Webb had relinquished the editorship of the faltering *Californian* in April 1866, leaving San Francisco on the eighteenth of the month and settling permanently in the East ("Sailing of the 'Sacramento,'" San Francisco *Evening Bulletin*, 18 Apr 66, 3; Webb, 8–9). His departure was not mourned, for

during his three-year stay he had given offense in the *Californian* with caustic criticism of the local scene (see Walker 1969, 183–84).

[4] A "Festival and Fair," featuring food, music, and "tableaux vivants," was put on from 10 to 15 December by the women of the Reverend Henry Martyn Scudder's Howard Presbyterian Church to "raise funds for upholstering the new church" ("Platt's Music Hall," San Francisco *Alta California*, 11 Dec 66, 4). This building on Mission Street, erected in 1866 and dedicated on 6 January 1867, was described as "an elegant brick structure, in the Anglo-Norman style, the auditorium of which is in the form of an ellipse, with a concave roof, which gives it a peculiar appearance" (Langley 1867, 15, 659).

[5] Mollie Clemens added the following note to Orion before forwarding this letter to him:

I believe Mela is writing. All told me to forward you their love in the last letter but, "O! I forgot" But I send it now all the same. Mother is very anxious to see you. Pa and Will sold their Tennessee lands to Jo. I told them they were to write you what you were to do, as you were authorised to sell and would if you could get $1.^{00} or 50$^{¢}$ per acre. They are responsible to Jo for that, they did not tell me to write any thing about it. Jo asked me to tell you to write to him. Please do so.

A copy of the S F Times came yesterday

At the time she wrote this note, probably in February 1867, Mollie Clemens seems to have been in Keokuk, Iowa, with her family. Orion was in Tennessee, trying to dispose of his family's Fentress County land and corresponding with the San Francisco *Times* under the pen name "Cumberland" (OC 1867a–c). Mentioned in this passage are: Pamela Moffett ("Mela"); William Stotts (1799–1888) and Mary Patterson (Polly) Stotts (1797–1869), Mollie's parents; and William L. Stotts (b. 1829) and Joseph Patterson Stotts (1824–93), two of Mollie's brothers.

Appendixes

Appendix A

Genealogy of the Clemens Family

THE FOLLOWING documents and published sources have been used to establish the names and dates in this genealogy.

Documents: Various of Clemens's notebooks and letters, letters from members of his family (especially at CU-MARK and NPV, but also at other collections); Clemens's will of 17 August 1909 (Probate Court, Redding, Conn., PH in CU-MARK, courtesy of Isabelle Budd); births, deaths, and marriages recorded in Mollie Clemens's journal (MEC, 3, 8, 15, 20–21) and in Bibles that belonged to John Marshall Clemens and Jane Lampton Clemens, to Samuel E. and Mary Mantz Moffett (both in CU-MARK), and to Orion and Mollie Clemens (PH in CU-MARK); Annie Moffett Webster's "Family Chronicle" (Webster 1918, 1–3, 24, 28, 38); the announcements of Clara Clemens's marriages to Ossip Gabrilowitsch and Jacques Alexander Samossoud (CU-MARK); George E. Dutton, Jr., to John E. Landon, 10 July 1967, reporting the death of Doris Webb Webster (PH in CU-MARK); Annie Moffett Webster's death certificate (NPV); an acknowledgment of condolences upon the death of William Luther Webster (NPV); handwritten notes by Ralph Connor accompanying the 10 June 1916 will of his mother-in-law, Alice Jane (Jean) Webster McKinney (NPV).

Published Sources: Standard biographical dictionaries (for example, *DAB*, *NCAB*) and works on Mark Twain (for example, *MTA*, *MTB*, *MTBus*); two genealogical studies (Bell, 26–27; Selby, passim); a study of Mark Twain's connection with Elmira, New York (Jerome and Wisbey, 172, 236–37); and obituaries for: Henry Clemens (in "The Victims," Memphis [Tenn.] *Appeal*, 22 June 58, 2); Ossip Gabrilowitsch (New York *Times*, 15 Sept 1936, 29); Alice Jane (Jean) Webster McKinney (New York *Times*, 12 June 1916, 11); Glenn Ford McKinney (New York *Times*, 16 Feb 1934, 19); Anita Moffett (*Antiquarian Bookman* 9 [19 Apr 1952]: 1491); Francis Clemens Moffett (New York *Times*, 6 Mar 1927, 26); Mary

Mantz Moffett (New York *Times*, 3 Oct 1940, 25); Pamela A. Moffett (New York *Times*, 3 Sept 1904, 7); Samuel Erasmus Moffett (*Collier's* 41 [15 Aug 1908]: 23); Clara Clemens Samossoud (New York *Times*, 21 Nov 1962, 30); Jacques Alexander Samossoud (New York *Times*, 15 June 1966, 47); and Samuel Charles Webster (New York *Times*, 26 Mar 1962, 31).

Otherwise authoritative sources give mistaken information about four of the individuals in this genealogy:

Henry Clemens. Samuel Clemens's 21 June 1858 telegram to William A. Moffett (p. 85) establishes that Henry died that morning. This date is confirmed by the report of his death in the Memphis (Tenn.) *Appeal* of 22 June ("The Victims," 2). Clemens subsequently misrecorded the date as 20 June in his mother's Bible. Orion recorded the same incorrect date in his and Mollie's Bible, Mollie repeated it in her journal (MEC, 8), and Albert Bigelow Paine used it in his account of Henry's death (*MTB*, 1:141–42). In 1876, Clemens mistakenly dated Henry's death as 19 June (10 June 76 to John L. RoBards, MoHM).

Pleasant Hannibal Clemens. The only one of Clemens's brothers and sisters for whom no birth or death dates were entered in the family Bibles. He was born after Pamela and before Margaret Clemens, late in 1828 or early in 1829, and died at three months of age. Some confusion exists about his name. Orion called him "Pleasant" (18 May 85 to SLC, CU-MARK), Clemens simply called him "Han" in "Villagers of 1840–3" (*Inds*, 104), and Annie Moffett Webster called him both "Hannibal Pleasant" and "Pleasants Hannibal" (Webster 1918, 2; *MTBus*, 44). Both of his names were family names—John Marshall Clemens's two brothers were Pleasant (1800–1811) and Hannibal (1803–36)—but since he was named after his paternal great-uncle Pleasant Goggin (1777–1831), it is most likely that his first name was "Pleasant" (Bell, 26–27; Selby, 77, 79, 93).

Ossip Gabrilowitsch. Gabrilowitsch's birth date is given as 7 February 1878 in his New York *Times* obituary (15 Sept 1936, 29) and, with one exception, in standard biographical dictionaries. The date appears as 8 February on his headstone in the Langdon-Clemens family plot in Wood-lawn Cemetery, Elmira, New York. At least two studies adopt the date on the headstone (Selby, 89; Jerome and Wisbey, 236 [but see also 172]), and one biographical dictionary also specifies 8 February (*NCAB*, 27:80).

Pamela A. Moffett. Pamela died on 31 August 1904 (New York *Times*, 3 Sept 1904, 7; Webster 1918, 3). Clemens mistakenly recorded her death date in his notebook as 1 September 1904, and Paine published this inaccurate notebook entry twice (*MTB*, 3:1224; *MTN*, 392; the original document is in CU-MARK).

Orion Clemens
b. 17 July 1825
d. 11 Dec 1897

m. 19 Dec 1854 ─────────────────────

Mary Eleanor (Mollie) Stotts
b. 4 Apr 1834
d. 15 Jan 1904

Pamela Ann Clemens
b. 13 Sept 1827
d. 31 Aug 1904

m. 20 Sept 1851 ────────────────────

William Anderson Moffett
b. 13 July 1816
d. 4 Aug 1865

Pleasant Hannibal Clemens
b. 1828 or 1829
d. aged 3 months

John Marshall Clemens
b. 11 Aug 1798
d. 24 Mar 1847

m. 6 May 1823 ─────────

Jane Lampton
b. 18 June 1803
d. 27 Oct 1890

Margaret L. Clemens
b. 31 May 1830
d. 17 Aug 1839

Benjamin L. Clemens
b. 8 June 1832
d. 12 May 1842

SAMUEL LANGHORNE CLEMENS
b. 30 Nov 1835
d. 21 Apr 1910

m. 2 Feb 1870 ────────────────────

Olivia Louise (Livy) Langdon
b. 27 Nov 1845
d. 5 June 1904

Henry Clemens
b. 13 July 1838
d. 21 June 1858

Jennie Clemens
b. 14 Sept 1855
d. 1 Feb 1864

Alice Jane (Jean) Webster
b. 24 July 1876
d. 11 June 1916

m. 7 Sept 1915 ——————— [1 child]

Glenn Ford McKinney
b. 15 Feb 1869
d. 15 Feb 1934

Annie E. Moffett
b. 1 July 1852
d. 24 Mar 1950

m. 28 Sept 1875

Charles Luther Webster
b. 24 Sept 1851
d. 26 Apr 1891

William Luther Webster
b. 15 Oct 1878
d. ? Mar 1945

Samuel Charles Webster
b. 8 July 1884
d. 24 Mar 1962

m. 1920?

Doris Webb
b. ?
d. 9 July 1967

Samuel Erasmus Moffett
b. 5 Nov 1860
d. 1 Aug 1908

m. 13 Apr 1887

Mary Emily Mantz
b. 19 Aug 1863
d. 2 Oct 1940

Anita Moffett
b. 4 Feb 1891
d. 26 Mar 1952

Francis Clemens Moffett
b. 1 Oct 1895
d. 4 Mar 1927

Langdon Clemens
b. 7 Nov 1870
d. 2 June 1872

Olivia Susan (Susy) Clemens
b. 19 Mar 1872
d. 18 Aug 1896

Clara Langdon Clemens
b. 8 June 1874
d. 19 Nov 1962

m. 6 Oct 1909 ——————— Nina Gabrilowitsch
b. 18 Aug 1910
d. 16 Jan 1966

1) Ossip Gabrilowitsch
b. 7 Feb 1878
d. 14 Sept 1936

m. 11 May 1944

2) Jacques Alexander Samossoud
b. 8 Sept 1894
d. 13 June 1966

Jane Lampton (Jean) Clemens
b. 26 July 1880
d. 24 Dec 1909

Appendix B

Steamboat Calendar:
Clemens's Piloting Assignments, 1857–1861

THE FOLLOWING record of arrivals and departures is based on currently available evidence, both factual and conjectural, about Clemens's employment, first as a cub (or steersman), then as a licensed pilot, on Mississippi River steamboats from April 1857 to May 1861. Comparatively strong evidence places him on fourteen of the listed boats: the *Paul Jones*, *Crescent City*, *R.J. Lackland*, *John J. Roe*, *Pennsylvania*, *John H. Dickey*, *White Cloud*, *Aleck Scott*, *Alfred T. Lacey* (in 1859), *Edward J. Gay*, *A. B. Chambers*, *City of Memphis*, *Arago*, and *Alonzo Child*. Somewhat less compelling evidence points to his employment on the *William M. Morrison*, *D. A. January*, *Alfred T. Lacey* (in 1858), *New Falls City* (both assignments), and *J. C. Swon*. While the inclusive dates of Clemens's service on a few of these eighteen boats are known with certainty, many of the dates on which he either began or ended his employment on the others remain uncertain. Particularly uncertain are the conjectural dates of his employment on the *Morrison* and the *New Falls City* (in October–December 1858), since his known movements on the river appear to allow for several periods when he might have worked on them. A departure or arrival date printed here in *italic type* indicates uncertainty about Clemens's conjectural *presence* on a given boat at that time, not about the arrival or departure date itself.

Clemens was trained to navigate the river between St. Louis and New Orleans (the "Lower Mississippi"). Customarily he steered or piloted boats engaged in trade between those cities, with three exceptions. The *John H. Dickey* and its temporary replacement, the *White Cloud* (normally a Missouri River boat), were St. Louis-Memphis packets; and when Clemens was a pilot on the *Arago*, it was a St. Louis-Vicksburg packet that nevertheless made Cairo and New Orleans its terminals on one of his trips. For the *Dickey* and *White Cloud*, making weekly round trips between St. Louis and Memphis, departure dates only are supplied.

Most of the departure and arrival dates in the calendar were taken from the port lists and river columns of contemporary newspapers, primarily the St. Louis *Missouri Republican, Missouri Democrat,* and *Evening News;* the Memphis *Appeal,* and *Avalanche;* and the New Orleans *Crescent, Picayune, Delta,* and *True Delta.* On rare occasions, these newspapers failed to report the date of a boat's arrival or departure, and at times they reported conflicting dates. Sometimes the information they supplied was simply incorrect, perhaps because it was carried over by mistake from the day before or published in mistaken anticipation of an arrival or a departure. Errors are also traceable to differing press deadlines (morning and evening), to unexpected scheduling changes or delays, and to boats' arriving shortly before or after midnight, when river reporters were off duty and therefore easily mistaken about (or indifferent to) the actual date. Finally, broken or incomplete newspaper runs or illegible microfilm copy occasionally result in the loss of port lists and river columns necessary for a date or span of dates. Every attempt has nevertheless been made to repair these discrepancies and omissions to achieve the greatest possible accuracy and completeness. (A detailed discussion of the evidence used to determine all dates may be found in Branch 1987, forthcoming).

                                                                           E. M. B.

	DEPART	ARRIVE	DEPART	ARRIVE
PAUL JONES	*Cincinnati*	*N. Orleans*	*N. Orleans*	*St. Louis*
15 Apr–9 May 1857	15 Apr	26 Apr	30 Apr	9 May
SLC cub under Horace E. Bixby; capt., Hiram K. Hazlett				
CRESCENT CITY	*St. Louis*	*N. Orleans*	*N. Orleans*	*St. Louis*
22 May–7 July 1857	22 May	27 May	1 June	9 June
SLC cub under Bixby; co-pilot prob. Strother Wiley; capt., R. C. Young	*17 June*	*23 June*	*28 June*	*7 July*
RUFUS J. LACKLAND				
11 July–3 Aug 1857	11 July	19 July	23 July	3 Aug
SLC cub under unknown pilot, poss. Bixby; capt., William B. Miller				
JOHN J. ROE				
5 Aug–24 Sept 1857	5 Aug	14 Aug	18 Aug	29 Aug
SLC cub under Zebulon Leavenworth and/or Sobieski Jolly; capt., Mark Leavenworth	2? Sept[1]	10 Sept	15 Sept	24 Sept
WILLIAM M. MORRISON				
9–26 Oct 1857	*9 Oct*	*16 Oct*	*19 Oct*	*26 Oct*
SLC cub, poss. under Bixby; co-pilot poss. Isaiah Sellers; capt., John N. Bofinger				
PENNSYLVANIA				
2–26 Nov 1857	*2 Nov*	*8 Nov*	*10 Nov*	*16 Nov*
SLC cub under William Brown; co-pilot, George G. Ealer; capt., John S. Klinefelter	18 Nov	24 Nov	26 Nov	
D. A. JANUARY				
13–22 Dec 1857			*13 Dec*	*22 Dec*
SLC cub under Joseph Edward Montgomery; capt., Patrick Yore				
NEW FALLS CITY				
14–20 Jan 1858	*14 Jan*	*20 Jan*		
SLC cub under co-pilots Isaac Chauncy Cable and Zebulon Leavenworth; capt., Montgomery				
PENNSYLVANIA				
6 Feb–5 June 1858			6 Feb	14 Feb
SLC cub under Brown; co-pilot Ealer; capt., Klinefelter	17 Feb	25 Feb	27 Feb	9 Mar
	11 Mar	17 Mar	20 Mar	27 Mar

[1] The *Roe*'s departure is not noted in the newspapers. Its presence at Hickman, Kentucky, on 5 September suggests the date of 2 September.

	DEPART *St. Louis*	ARRIVE *N. Orleans*	DEPART *N. Orleans*	ARRIVE *St. Louis*
	31 Mar	6 Apr	10 Apr	16 Apr
	20 Apr	26 Apr	30 Apr	5 May
	10 May	16 May	20 May	27 May
	30 May	5 June		

ALFRED T. LACEY

11–28 July 1858

SLC cub, poss. under Barton S.
Bowen; co-pilot poss. Ealer; capt.,
John P. Rodney

	11 July	*16 July*	*21 July*	*28 July*

JOHN H. DICKEY

4 Aug–19 Oct 1858

SLC cub under Samuel A. Bowen;
co-pilot poss. Strother Wiley;
capt., Daniel Able

	St. Louis	*Memphis*
	4 Aug	*7 Aug*
	11 Aug	*14 Aug*
	18 Aug	*21 Aug*
	25 Aug	28 Aug
	1 Sept	4 Sept
	8 Sept	11 Sept
	15 Sept	18 Sept
	22 Sept	25 Sept
	29 Sept	2 Oct
	6 Oct	9 Oct
	13 Oct	16 Oct

WHITE CLOUD

20–26 Oct 1858

SLC cub, prob. under Samuel A.
Bowen; capt., Able

	20 Oct	23 Oct

NEW FALLS CITY

30 Oct–8 Dec 1858

SLC cub, prob. under Bixby;
capt., James B. Woods

	St. Louis	*N. Orleans*	*N. Orleans*	*St. Louis*
	30 Oct	*8 Nov*	*10 Nov*[2]	*17 Nov*
	19 Nov	*26 Nov*	*29 Nov*	*8 Dec*

ALECK SCOTT

13 Dec 1858–8 Apr 1859

SLC cub under Bixby; capt.,
Robert A. Reilly

	13 Dec	*21 Dec*	*24 Dec*	*1 Jan*
	4 Jan	*11 Jan*	*15 Jan*	*27 Jan*
	1 Feb	*11 Feb*	*16 Feb*	*27 Feb*
	1 Mar	8 Mar	11 Mar	19 Mar
	21 Mar	27 Mar	31 Mar	*8 Apr*[3]

[2] The *New Falls City*'s memoranda reports this date, whereas the New Orleans daily newspapers give 9 November.

[3] Clemens acquired his pilot's license on 9 April 1859.

	DEPART *St. Louis*	ARRIVE *N. Orleans*	DEPART *N. Orleans*	ARRIVE *St. Louis*
ALFRED T. LACEY 4–21 May 1859 SLC pilot; co-pilot, Barton S. Bowen; capt., Rodney	4 May	10 May	14 May	21 May
J. C. SWON 25 June–28 July 1859 SLC pilot; capt., Isaac H. Jones	*25 June* *13 July*	*1 July* *19 July*	*3 July* *21 July*	*9 July* *28 July*
EDWARD J. GAY 2 Aug–1 Oct 1859 SLC pilot; capt., Barton S. Bowen	2 Aug 24 Aug 13 Sept	10 Aug 1 Sept 21 Sept	12 Aug 3 Sept 23 Sept	19 Aug 9 Sept 1 Oct
A. B. CHAMBERS 26 Oct 1859–24 Feb 1860 SLC pilot; co-pilots for one trip each, James C. DeLancey and Wil- liam Bowen; capt., George W. Bowman	26 Oct 23 Nov 20 Dec[4] *1 Feb*	7 Nov 4 Dec 7 Jan *11 Feb*	9 Nov 8 Dec 10 Jan *14 Feb*	20 Nov 17 Dec 20 Jan *24 Feb*
CITY OF MEMPHIS 25 Mar–1 or 2 July 1860 SLC pilot; co-pilot, Wesley Jacobs; capt., Montgomery	*25 Mar* *14 Apr* *4 May* 24 May 13 June	*2 Apr* *21 Apr* *14 May* 31 May 22 June	*4 Apr* *24 Apr* *15 May* 3 June 24 June	*11 Apr* *1 May* *22 May* 10 June 1–2 July
ARAGO 28 July–31 Aug 1860 SLC pilot; co-pilot, J. W. Hood; capt., George P. Sloan	*St. Louis* 28 July *Cairo* 12 Aug	*Vicksburg* 3 Aug *N. Orleans* 20 Aug	*Vicksburg* 4 Aug *N. Orleans* 22 Aug	*Cairo* 11 Aug *St. Louis* 31 Aug
ALONZO CHILD 19 Sept 1860–8 May 1861 SLC pilot; co-pilots, Bixby, Wil- liam Bowen, Sam Brown; capts., David DeHaven and James O'Neal	*St. Louis* 19 Sept 9 Oct 31 Oct *23 Nov* 14 Jan 8 Feb[6]	*N. Orleans* 28 Sept 20 Oct 9 Nov *1 Dec* 24 Jan 16 Feb	*N. Orleans* 29 Sept 21 Oct 10 Nov *4 Dec*[5] 29 Jan 18 Feb	*St. Louis* 6 Oct 28 Oct 18 Nov *11 Jan* 5 Feb 25 Feb

[4] Having run aground at Power's Island and Goose Island below St. Louis, the *Chambers* resumed its trip south on 31 December from Cairo.

[5] The *Child* laid up at Cairo from 11 December to 8 January.

[6] The 5 February arrival and 8 February departure of the *Child* were at Cairo, not St. Louis, because of poor river conditions.

DEPART	ARRIVE	DEPART	ARRIVE
St. Louis	*N. Orleans*	*N. Orleans*	*St. Louis*
27 Feb	6 Mar	8 Mar	15 Mar
20 Mar	26 Mar	28 Mar	5 Apr
9 Apr	16 Apr	18 Apr	25 Apr
2 May	8 May		

Appendix C

Maps of Nevada Territory, 1864

THE FOLLOWING maps depict the most developed and populated areas of Nevada Territory as of May 1864, when Clemens ended his residence of almost three years and moved to San Francisco. But they also represent the territory essentially as it was throughout his stay—excepting the boundary with California, not established until 1863; the town of Austin, also established in 1863; Roop County, called Lake County through 1862; and Lander and Nye counties, created in 1862 and 1864. Map 1, *Principal Mining Regions of Nevada Territory, 1864*, provides an overview of the areas in which Clemens lived and worked between 1861 and 1864, first as Orion Clemens's legislative clerk, then as a miner, and finally as a journalist. Map 2, *Carson City, Virginia City, and Environs*; Map 3, *Humboldt Mining Region*; and Map 4, *Esmeralda Mining Region*, correspond to the boxes on Map 1 and provide greater detail.

All four maps are based on *DeGroot's Map of Nevada Territory, Exhibiting a Portion of Southern Oregon & Eastern California* (San Francisco: Warren Holt, 1863), the most detailed and accurate contemporary map of the territory. Its creator, Henry DeGroot, was Nevada's pioneer cartographer, commissioned by the Territorial Legislature in 1861 to do the first map of the region (*Journal of the Council*, 54, 76). The base map has been corroborated by, and in a few instances corrected or supplemented from, other contemporary maps (three of them by DeGroot himself) as well as modern maps prepared by the United States Geological Survey. For example: DeGroot's misplacement of Unionville in Star District and his mislabeling of Rough Creek have been corrected on Maps 3 and 4, respectively; his omission of Devil's Gate, King's Cañon, Gold Cañon, and Clear Creek District has been remedied on Map 2. DeGroot's representation of lakes, sinks, sloughs, and tributaries sometimes differs from other maps, both contemporary and modern, but the mutable, even seasonal, nature of these features obviates any correction. On the other

hand, his perfunctory and idiosyncratic notation for mountain ranges is
here replaced with a notation that better indicates size and extent. In
reducing the dimensions of DeGroot's map (ca. 32″ × 38″) we have necessarily omitted some details—such as "American Flat," "Chalk Knoll,"
and "Blue Supper D[istrict]" in the congested area around Virginia City
on Map 2—but all details relevant to Clemens's Nevada letters have been
retained. Place names and county and territorial boundaries have been
corroborated by the standard historical sources (Angel, Carlson, Swackhamer). And some elements on Map 3 have been supplied from Clemens's
own accounts of his journey to the Humboldt mining region (see pp. 147–
50 here and chapter 27 of *Roughing It*) as well as from an anonymous
account of the same trip, published in "Letter from Nevada Territory"
(San Francisco *Alta California*, 18 June 63, 1). To help coordinate these
maps with the letters and with each other, we have added legends like
"SLC's route to Ragtown" and "To Aurora and Mono Lake," which are
not in DeGroot. The draft maps prepared at the Mark Twain Papers were
redrawn by John R. Parsons and Mark Williams of Eureka Cartography,
Berkeley, California.

M.B.F.

Source Maps

Bancroft, H. H.

1862. *Bancroft's Map of the Washoe Silver Region of Nevada Territory*.
San Francisco: H. H. Bancroft and Co.

1868. *Bancroft's Map of California, Nevada, Utah and Arizona*. San
Francisco: H. H. Bancroft and Co.

Colton, J. H.

1864. *Colton's Map of the States and Territories West of the Mississippi
River to the Pacific Ocean*. New York: J. H. Colton.

DeGroot, Henry.

1861. *Map of Nevada Territory*. PH of hand-drawn map in CU-BANC.

1863. *DeGroot's Map of Nevada Territory, Exhibiting a Portion of Southern Oregon & Eastern California*. San Francisco: Warren Holt.

1863. *A Tracing of a Map of Nevada & Eastern California*. Hand-drawn
map in CU-BANC.

1864. *Map of the State of Nevada*. Hand-drawn map in CU-BANC.

Lloyd, H. H.

1865. *New Map of the U.S. Territories and Pacific States.* New York: H. H. Lloyd and Co.

Milleson, M.

1863. *Milleson and Washburn's Map of the Celebrated Humboldt Silver Mines. Compiled from Recent Surveys of Messrs Fine and Epler, County Surveyors of Humboldt County, N.T.* Drawn by M. Milleson. Drawn on stone by Edward Fairman. San Francisco: B. F. Butler.

Ransom, Leander, and A. J. Doolittle.

1863. *New Map of the State of California, Exhibiting the Rivers, Lakes, Bays and Islands, with the Principal Towns, Roads, Railroads and Transit Routes to the Silver Mining Districts of Nevada Territory.* San Francisco: W. Holt.

U.S. Department of the Interior. General Land Office.

1866. *Map of the State of Nevada to Accompany the Annual Report of the Comm^r. Genl. Land Office.* New York: Major and Knapp.

U.S. Department of the Interior. U.S. Geological Survey.

1970. *Western United States 1:250,000; Walker Lake.* Washington, D.C.

1974. *Western United States 1:250,000; Reno.* Edition 3. Reston, Va.

1978. *State of Nevada 1:500,000.* Reston, Va.

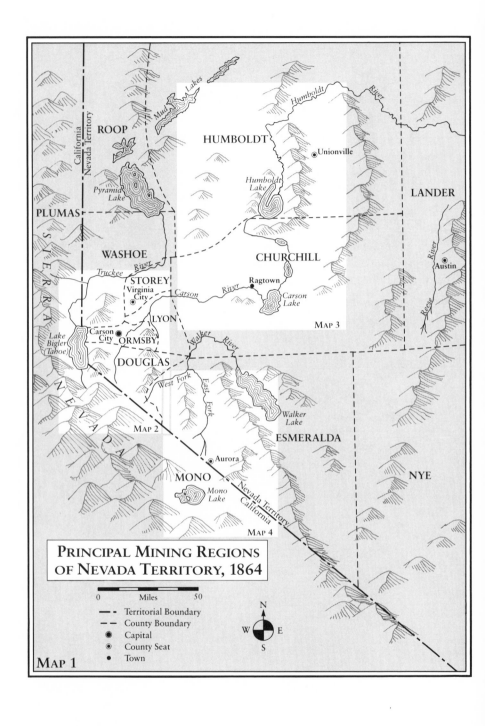

ROOP

HUMBOLDT

Mud Lakes

Humboldt River

Unionville

Humboldt Lake

LANDER

PLUMAS

Pyramid Lake

WASHOE

Truckee River

STOREY

Virginia City

Carson River

Ragtown

CHURCHILL

Carson Lake

MAP 3

Austin

Reese River

LYON

SIERRA

Carson City

ORMSBY

Lake Bigler (Tahoe)

DOUGLAS

Walker River

Walker River

NEVADA

West Fork

East Fork

Walker Lake

MAP 2

ESMERALDA

Aurora

NYE

MONO

Mono Lake

Nevada Territory California

MAP 4

Principal Mining Regions of Nevada Territory, 1864

0   Miles   50

— · — Territorial Boundary
— — County Boundary
◉ Capital
◉ County Seat
• Town

N
W   E
S

Map 1

California Nevada Territory

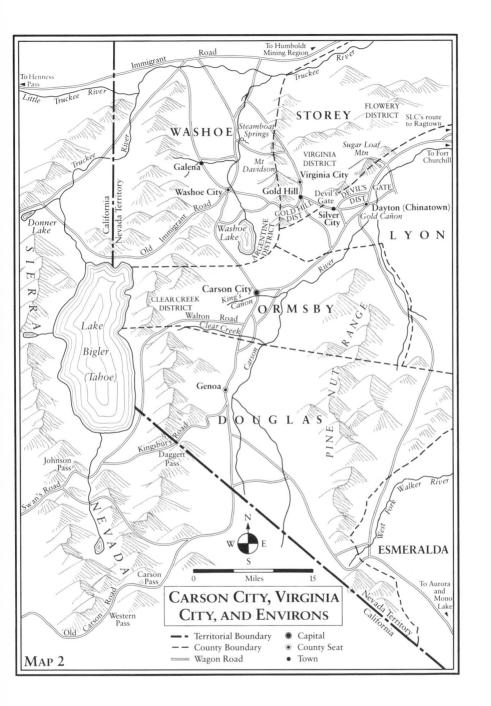

To Henness
◄ Pass

Little Truckee River

Immigrant   Road

To Humboldt
Mining Region

Truckee   River

California
Nevada Territory

Truckee   River

WASHOE

Steamboat
Springs

STOREY

FLOWERY
DISTRICT

SLC's route
to Ragtown

Galena

Mt
Davidson

VIRGINIA
DISTRICT

Sugar Loaf
Mtn

To Fort
Churchill

Washoe City

Virginia City

Road

Old   Immigrant

Gold Hill

Devil's
Gate

DEVIL'S
DIST.

GATE

Dayton (Chinatown)

Donner
Lake

Washoe
Lake

GOLD HILL
DIST.

Silver
City

Gold Cañon

LYON

ARGENTINE
DISTRICT

River

S I E R R A

Lake

CLEAR CREEK
DISTRICT

Carson City

King's
Cañon

O R M S B Y

Bigler

Walton   Road

Clear Creek

Carson

(Tahoe)

Genoa

D O U G L A S

P I N E   N U T   R A N G E

Johnson
Pass

Kingsbury Road

Daggett
Pass

Swan's Road

Walker   River

West   Fork

N E V A D A

Carson
Pass

N
W E
S

ESMERALDA

Carson   Road

Western
Pass

Old   Carson   Road

0   Miles   15

Nevada Territory
California

To Aurora
and
Mono
Lake ◄

CARSON CITY, VIRGINIA
CITY, AND ENVIRONS

- - ● Territorial Boundary   ● Capital
- - - County Boundary   ◉ County Seat
=== Wagon Road   ● Town

MAP 2

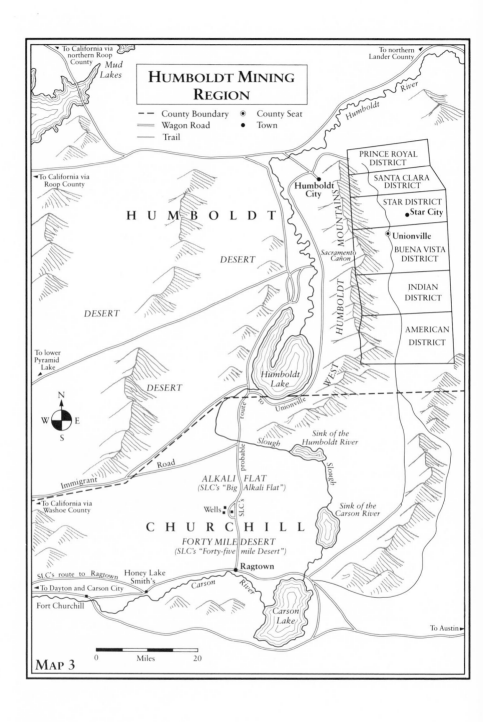

HUMBOLDT MINING REGION

- – – County Boundary
- ≡≡ Wagon Road
- — Trail
- ◉ County Seat
- • Town

To California via northern Roop County

Mud Lakes

To northern Lander County

Humboldt River

To California via Roop County

HUMBOLDT

Humboldt City

PRINCE ROYAL DISTRICT

SANTA CLARA DISTRICT

STAR DISTRICT

• Star City

◉ Unionville

BUENA VISTA DISTRICT

INDIAN DISTRICT

AMERICAN DISTRICT

HUMBOLDT MOUNTAINS

DESERT

Sacramento Cañon

DESERT

DESERT

To lower Pyramid Lake

Humboldt Lake

WEST

DESERT

route to Unionville

N
W E
S

Sink of the Humboldt River

Slough

probable

Immigrant Road

Slough

ALKALI FLAT
(SLC's "Big Alkali Flat")

Sink of the Carson River

To California via Washoe County

Wells

SLC's

CHURCHILL

FORTY MILE DESERT
(SLC's "Forty-five mile Desert")

• Ragtown

SLC's route to Ragtown

Honey Lake Smith's

To Dayton and Carson City

Fort Churchill

Carson River

Carson Lake

To Austin

0   Miles   20

MAP 3

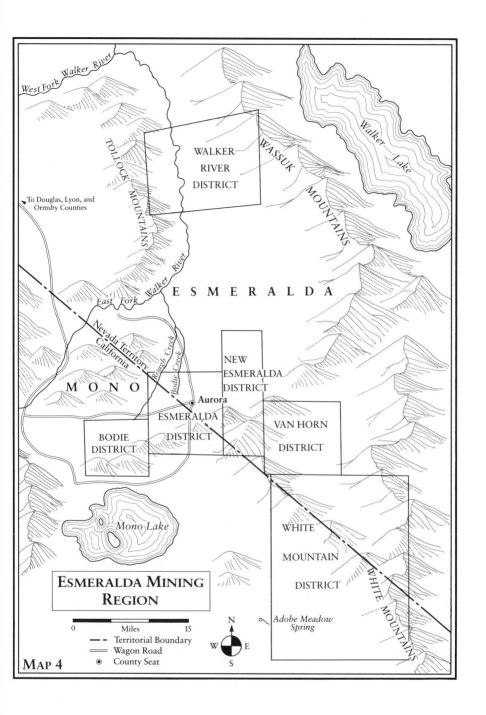

West Fork Walker River

TOLLOCK MOUNTAINS

WALKER
RIVER
DISTRICT

WASSUK MOUNTAINS

Walker Lake

To Douglas, Lyon, and
Ormsby Counties

E S M E R A L D A

East Fork Walker River

Nevada Territory
California

Rough Creek

Bodie Creek

M O N O

NEW
ESMERALDA
DISTRICT

Aurora

ESMERALDA
DISTRICT

VAN HORN
DISTRICT

BODIE
DISTRICT

Mono Lake

WHITE

MOUNTAIN

DISTRICT

WHITE MOUNTAINS

Adobe Meadow
Spring

ESMERALDA MINING REGION

0   Miles   15

- - - Territorial Boundary
═══ Wagon Road
◉ County Seat

N
W · E
S

MAP 4

Appendix D

Photographs and Manuscript Facsimiles

REPRODUCED HERE are two dozen contemporary images—photographs, engravings from photographs, an oil painting, and one printed document—chiefly of Clemens's immediate family, friends, or close associates during the period of these letters. Several of the photographs have not been published before.

Immediately following these documents are photographic facsimiles of nine complete letters in Clemens's holograph, a representative selection. We reproduce these documents partly for their inherent interest, and partly to afford the reader a chance to see for himself what details of the original the transcription includes, and how, as well as what it omits. Because of the imperfect nature of facsimiles, close comparison with the transcription will almost certainly turn up apparent discrepancies between the two. The textual commentaries for all nine letters therefore undertake to resolve such differences and to give a full physical description of the original document.

Samuel L. Clemens, 1851 or 1852. Copy in the Mark Twain Papers,
The Bancroft Library (CU-MARK).

1858. Courtesy of Vassar College Library (NPV).

1863.   1865 or 1866.
Mark Twain Papers, The Bancroft Library (CU-MARK).

Samuel L. Clemens's Pilot's Certificate, awarded 9 April 1859. Courtesy of Mariners' Museum, Newport News, Virginia (ViNeM).

Jane Lampton Clemens, 1858 or 1859, portrait by St. Louis artist
Edwin Brady. Courtesy of Vassar College Library (NPV).

Henry Clemens, 1858. Courtesy of Vassar College Library (NPV).

Pamela A. Moffett, probably early 1860s. Courtesy of Mrs. Kate Gilmore and Mark Twain Museum, Hannibal, Missouri (MoHM).

William A. Moffett, probably 1864 or 1865.
Courtesy of Vassar College Library (NPV).

Samuel E. Moffett and Annie E. Moffett, probably 1863.
Courtesy of Vassar College Library (NPV).

Orion Clemens, early 1860s.
Courtesy of Nevada State Historical Society (NvHi).

Mary E. (Mollie) Clemens, 1866.
Courtesy of Nevada State Historical Society (NvHi).

Jennie Clemens, probably 1863.
Courtesy of Nevada State Historical Society (NvHi).

Laura Wright, May 1861. Mark Twain Papers, The Bancroft Library
(CU-MARK), gift of Mrs. Helen Jackson.

Samuel A. Bowen, ?1860. Courtesy of Mark Twain Museum,
Hannibal, Missouri (MoHM).

Robert M. Howland, 1861. Mark Twain Papers, The Bancroft Library
(CU-MARK), courtesy of Mr. and Mrs. Robert M. Gunn.

James W. Nye, probably 1862. Signature evidently not Nye's. The Bancroft Library (CU-BANC).

William Wright (Dan De Quille), 1864. Signed and dated by Wright. The Bancroft Library (CU-BANC).

Joseph T. Goodman, ?1863 (Mack 1947, facing 193).

Charles Farrar Browne (Artemus Ward), mid-1860s, engraving from a photograph (Charles Farrar Browne, frontispiece).

Bret Harte, probably 1870. The
Bancroft Library (CU-BANC).

Daniel Martin (Martin the Wizard),
1864. Courtesy of Doten Collection,
University Library, University of
Nevada Reno (NvU).

Kamehameha V, king of the Hawaiian
Islands, 1865. Courtesy of Hawaii
State Archives, Honolulu.

Anson Burlingame, 1868, engraving
from a photograph (*Eclectic Magazine*
71 [September 1868]: facing 1037).
Courtesy of New York Public Library,
Astor, Lenox and Tilden Foundations
(NN).

Clemens to Pamela A. Moffett, 8 October 1853, New York, New York. Mark Twain Papers, The Bancroft Library (CU-MARK). The oldest surviving document in Clemens's handwriting, the letter consists of four unnumbered pages on two leaves of a folded sheet, silked and patched to prevent further damage. Transcribed on pp. 16–17; reproduced at 61 percent of actual size.

6 A(838)

thias—the former character being his greatest.
He appears in Philadelphia on Monday night.

I have not received a letter from
home lately, but got a "Journal" the other
day in which I see the office has been sold.
I suppose Ma, Orion and Henry are in St.
Louis now. If Orion has no other project
in that his head, he ought to take the contract
for getting out some weekly paper, if he
can't get a foremanship. Now, for
such a paper as the "Presbyterian" (containing about 60,000) he could get $20 or $25
a week, and he and Henry could easily
do the work—nothing to do but set the type
and make up the forms. I mean they
could easily do the work if $5.00 for 25,000
(per week) could beat a little work into (no
offence to him) Henry's lazy bones! Orion
must get him. Wolfe a sit. in St. Louis.—
He can get 20 cents per 1,000. The foreman
of Gray's office has taken a great fancy to go
to St. Louis and has got everything out of me
that I knew about the place, and I shouldn't
be surprised if he should go there.

If my letters do not come often,
you need not bother yourself about me; for
if you have a brother nearly eighteen years,

Manuscript page 2, to Pamela A. Moffett, 8 October 1853. Verso of the first leaf.

of age, who is not able to take care of him
a few miles from home, such a brother
not worth one's thoughts: and if I don't manage to take care of № 1, be assured you will
never know it. I am not afraid, however: I
shall ask favors from no one, and endeavor
to be, (and shall be,) as "independent as a wood
sawyer's clerk."

　　　　　I never saw such a place for military companies, as New York. Go on the street
when you will, you are sure to meet a company
in full uniform, with all the usual appendages of drums, fifes, &c. I saw a large company of soldiers of the war of 1812, the other
day, with a '76 veteran p scate here and
there in the ranks.　　　　　　　assed through
one of the parks lately, I came upon a company of boys on parade. Their uniforms
were neat, and their muskets about half
the common size. Some of them were
not more than seven or eight   as of
age; but had evidently been well dri

　　　　　Passage to Albany & 60 mile
finest steamers that ply the Hudson, is from
25 cents — cheap enough, but is generally
cheaper than that in the summer.
　　　　　I want you to write as soon as I

Manuscript page 3, to Pamela A. Moffett, 8 October 1853. Recto of the second leaf.

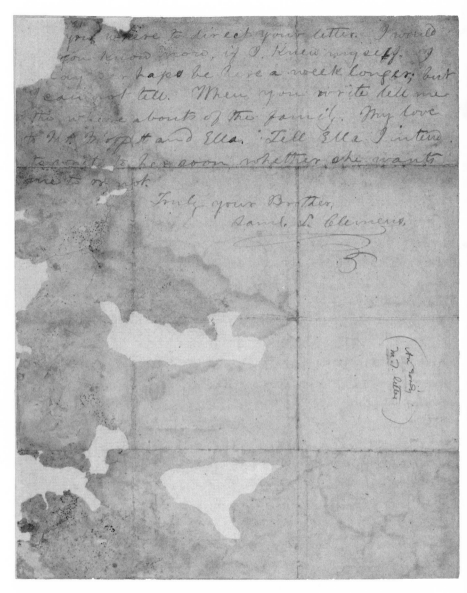

you where to direct your letter. I would
you knew more, if I knew myself. I
may perhaps be here a week longer; but
I cannot tell. When you write tell me
the whereabouts of the family. My love
to Mr. Moffett and Ella. Tell Ella I intend
to write to her soon whether she wants
me to or not.

      Truly your Brother,
         Saml. L. Clemens.

Manuscript page 4, to Pamela A. Moffett, 8 October 1853. Verso of the second leaf.

Memphis, Tenn., Friday, June 18th, 1858.

Dear Sister Mollie:

Long before this reaches you, my poor Henry, —my darling, my pride, my glory, my _all_, will have finished his blameless career, and the light of my life will have gone out in utter darkness. O, God! this is hard to bear. Hardened, hopeless,—aye, lost—lost—lost and ruined sinner as I am—I, even _I_, have humbled myself to the ground and prayed as never man prayed before, that the great God might let this cup pass from me—That he would strike me to the earth, but spare my brother—That he would pour out the fulness of his just wrath upon my wicked head, but have mercy, mercy, mercy upon that unoffending boy. The horrors of three days have swept over me—They have blasted my youth and left me an old man before my time. Mollie, there are grey hairs in my head to-night. For forty-eight hours I labored at the bedside of my poor burned and bruised, but uncomplaining brother, and then the star of my hope went out and left me in the gloom of despair. Then poor wretched me, that was once so proud, was humbled to the very dust— lower than the dust—for the vilest beggar in the streets of Saint Louis could never conceive of a humiliation like mine. Men take me by the hand and congratulate me, and call me "lucky" because I was not on the Pennsylvania when she blew up! My God forgive them, for they know not what they say.

Mollie you do not understand why I was not on that boat—I will tell you. I left Saint Louis on her, but on the way down, Mr. Brown, the pilot that was killed by the explosion (poor fellow,) quarreled with Henry without cause, while I was steering — Henry started out of the pilot-house — Brown jumped up and collared him — turned him half-way around and struck him in the face! — and him nearly six feet high — struck my little brother. I was wild from that moment. I left the boat to steer herself, and avenged the insult — and the Captain said I was right — that he would discharge Brown in N. Orleans if he could get another pilot, and would do it in St. Louis anyhow. Of course both of us could not return to St. Louis on the same boat — no pilot could be found, and the Captain sent me to the A. T. Lacey, with orders to her Captain to bring me to Saint Louis. Had another pilot been found, poor Brown would have been the "lucky" man.

I was on the Pennsylvania five minutes before she left N. Orleans, and I must tell you the truth, Mollie — Three hundred human beings perished by that fearful disaster. Henry was asleep — was blown up — then fell back on the hot boilers, and I suppose that rubbish fell on him, for he is injured internally. He got into the water and swam to shore, and got into the flatboat with the other survivors. He had nothing on but his wet shirt, and he lay there burning up with a southern sun and freezing in the wind till the Kate Frisbee came along. His wounds were not dressed till he got to Memphis, 15 hours after the explosion. He was senseless and motionless for 12 hours after that. But may God bless Memphis, the noblest city on the

Manuscript page 2, to Mary E. Clemens, 18 June 1858. Verso of the first leaf.

face of the earth. She has done her duty by these poor afflicted creatures — especially Henry, for he has had five — aye, ten, fifteen, twenty times the care and attention that any one else has had. Dr. Peyton, the best physician in Memphis (he is exactly like the portraits of Webster,) sat by him for 36 hours. There are 32 scalded men in that room, and you would know Dr. Peyton better than I can describe him, if you could follow him around and hear each man murmur as he passes — "May the God of Heaven bless you, Doctor!" The ladies have done well, too. Our second Mate, a handsome, noble-hearted young fellow, will die. Yesterday a beautiful girl of 15 stooped timidly down by his side and handed him a pretty bouquet. The poor suffering boy's eyes kindled, his lips quivered out a gentle "God bless you, Miss," and he burst into tears. He made them write her name on a card for him, that he might not forget it.

Pray for me, Mollie, and pray for my poor sinless brother.

Your unfortunate Brother,
Saml. L. Clemens.

P.S. I got here two days after Henry.

Manuscript page 3, to Mary E. Clemens, 18 June 1858. Recto of the second leaf; verso blank.

1863

Lick House June 20.

My Dear Bro.

The Echo progresses! The terms of compromise were agreed on yesterday — I don't know what they are, yet — only that they are rather severe on us. But every inch saved is bully, you bet. You can make money at trading Emma for Echo at 5 feet for one. But I don't want to trade at that rate — nor any other, for that matter. Gould & Curry, it is conjectured, will advance to the neighborhood of a thousand dollars an inch within the next twelve months — and take my word for it, the Echo will make 'em hunt their holes within the next twenty-four. It is on the main Gold Hill lead, and the nastiest old ledge in Nevada Territory. I have stores of information on hand, but it is not for publication just yet. I have played my cards with a stiff upper lip since my arrival here — sometimes flush, sometimes dead broke & in debt — have spent eight hundred dollars, & sent Ma two hundred — was strapped day before yesterday, but I'm on the upper side of the wheel again to-day, with twelve hun-

Clemens to Orion and Mary E. (Mollie) Clemens, 20 June 1863, San Francisco, California. Mark Twain Papers, The Bancroft Library (CU-MARK). The letter is written on the unnumbered recto and verso of a leaf torn from a folded sheet. Transcribed on p. 258; reproduced at 56 percent of actual size.

dred dollars in the bank & out of debt —
nine-tenths of it will be invested to-morow,
& then I'll hold up & start home in a
day or two. But through it all, I have
kept strict watch over the Echo, & when
money was to be spent in order to get into
anybody's good graces or gain a point in
the way of information, I have spent it like
a Lord, & trusted to luck to get even again.
Oh, I tell you I'm on it. And mind, if you
can't sell your Echo at $3,000 a foot fifteen
months from now, do you pack up your
traps & go home — because then it will be
proved that all promises fail in this
country. As I told you before, let people
imagine that you own about a thousand
feet in it if they will. I've got Echo on my
brain — That's what's the matter with me.

Mollie, my dear, I enclose some
more pictures for those girls, if they
want them. All hearty — how are you?

Yr Bro
Sam

Clemens to Jane Lampton Clemens and Pamela A. Moffett, 18 July 1863, Virginia City, Nevada Territory. Mark Twain Papers, The Bancroft Library (CU-MARK). The letter is written on two leaves of a folded sheet using only the first and fourth pages, both unnumbered. Transcribed on pp. 259–60; reproduced at 57 percent of actual size.

would have brought me $10,000 — but I have carelessly let it go down to nothing again. I don't think I am any account, any how. Now, I raised the price of "North Ophir" from $13 foot to $45 a foot, to-day, & they gave me five feet. That will go the way of all the rest. I shall probably mislay it or throw it in my trunk & never get a dollar out of it. But I am telling you too many secrets, & I'll stop. One more. A gentleman in San Francisco told me to call at his office, & he would give me five feet of "Overman." Well, do you know I never went after it? The stock is worth $400 a foot, now — $2,000 thrown away! I don't care a straw, for myself, but I ought to have had more thought for you. Never mind, though, Ma — I will be more careful in future. I will take care that your expenses are paid — sure.

You and Pamela only pay $8 a week apiece for board (& lodging too?) Well, you are not in a very expensive part of the world, certainly. My room-mate & I pay, together, $70 a month for our bedchamber, & $50 a month, each, for board, besides. Put in my washing, & it costs me $100 a month to live.
Affectionately, Mark

Manuscript page 2, to Jane Lampton Clemens and Pamela A. Moffett, 18 July 1863. The signature is the oldest known private use of Clemens's pen name. Verso of the second leaf.

No. 11 — $20 enclosed   Va. Aug 5.

My Dear Mother & Sister

I got burned out about ten days ago — saved nothing but the clothes I had on — lost a couple of handsome suits that I had made in San Francisco. The fire resulted in no benefit to me except that Judge Ferris' wife offered me the use of one of the spare chambers in her house until the Superintendent of the Ophir, who occupies it, returns from San Francisco. Therefore, I shall live in some style for a while, at any rate, free of charge, in rooms worth $200 or $250 a month, I guess. I board at the Collins House. They only charge me $10 a week there — so much for being a reporter. Mrs. Ferris (and every body else,) has gone to Lake Bigler, & I shall go myself if I can get any one to report for me. However, I didn't lose so very much by the fire. A man whom I never saw before, gave me some "feet" as I went down town, & I sold the batch for $200 & fitted myself out again half as good as new. The unknown scoundrel couldn't have done me a favor of the kind when I needed it more.

Clemens to Jane Lampton Clemens and Pamela A. Moffett, 5 August 1863, Virginia City, Nevada Territory. Mark Twain Papers, The Bancroft Library (CU-MARK). The letter is written on two leaves of a folded sheet using only the first and fourth pages, both unnumbered. Transcribed on pp. 261–62; reproduced at 56 percent of actual size.

Orion is in town. I saw him at the Theatre to-night. He says he has a letter from home at Carson.

He sent me your last the other day, with a fearful lecture to me on the subject of dissipation, from himself. As I don't dissipate, & never expect to, & am man enough to have a good character & keep it, I didn't take the trouble to answer it. He will learn after a while, perhaps, that I am not an infant, that I know the value of a good name as well as he does, & stop writing such childish nonsense to me.

Now, I don't ~~really~~ really work more than two hours a day, but then I am busy all the time, gadding about, you know, & consequently I don't expect to write you very often. You can hear from me by the paper, though. When I was in San Francisco I believe they thought I wasn't coming back any more, & stopped your paper — but I started it again pretty suddenly when I returned. — I am glad to hear you are all improving in health. I wish you would stay with the Grass.

aff'ete Sam

Manuscript page 2, to Jane Lampton Clemens and Pamela A. Moffett, 5 August 1863. Verso of the second leaf.

Va, Wednesday A.M.

My Dear Bro.

Don't stump for the
Sanitary Fund — Billy Clagett
says he certainly will not.
If I have been so unlucky
as to rob you of some of
your popularity by that unfortunate item, I claim at
your hands that you neither
increase nor diminish it
by so fruitless a proceeding
as making speeches for the
Fund. I am mighty sick of that
fund — it has caused me all
my d—d troubles — & I shall
leave the Territory when your
first speech is announced,
& leave it for good.

I see by the Union of
this morning, that those ladies
have seduced from me what
I consider was a sufficient
apology, ~~coming~~ coming from a

Clemens to Orion and Mary E. (Mollie) Clemens, 25 May 1864, Virginia City,
Nevada Territory. Mark Twain Papers, The Bancroft Library (CU-MARK). The
letter consists of three unnumbered pages on two leaves of a folded sheet. Transcribed on pp. 297–98; reproduced at 60 percent of actual size.

man open to a challenge from three persons, & already awaiting the issue of such a message to another — They got out of me what no man would ever have got, & then — well, they are ladies & I shall not speak harshly of them. Now although the Union folks have kept quiet this morning, (much against my expectations,) I still have a quarrel or two on hand — so that this flour sack business may rest, as far as Carson is concerned. I shall take no notice of it at all, except to mash Mr Laird over the head with my revolver for publishing it if I meet him to-day — otherwise, I do nothing. I consider that I have triumphed over those ladies at last, & I am quits with them. But when I forgive

the injury — or forget it — ~~xxxx~~
or fail to set up a score a—
gainst it as opportunity offers
— may I be able to console myself
for it with the consciousness
that I have become a mar-
vellously better man. ~~xx~~
I have no intention of hunting
for the puppy, Laird, Mollie,
but he had better let me
have 24 hours unmolested,
to get cool in.

~~xxxxxxxxxxxxxx~~
But for Heaven's
sake give me at least the
peace & quiet it will afford
me to know that no stumping
is to be done for the un-
lucky Sanitary Fund.
Yr Bro
Sam

Manuscript page 3, to Orion and Mary E. Clemens, 25 May 1864. Recto of the second leaf; verso blank except for an address probably in Orion's hand (see the textual commentary).

Occidental, 7, 15 th

Dear Dan:

Tell Dawson to stir
his old stumps & send me
that money now if he pos-
sibly can. I have almost
got that old debt of mine
cleared up, & with his assistance & my wages I can
finish the job now. Don't
you fail to tell him.

Steve & I have moved
our lodgings. The Steve did
not tell his folks he had
moved, & the other day his
father went to our room,
& finding it locked, he hunted
up the old landlady (Frenchwoman) & asked her where
those young men were. She
over

Clemens to William Wright (Dan De Quille), 15 July 1864, San Francisco, California. William Wright Papers, The Bancroft Library (CU-BANC). The letter
consists of six pages written on both sides of three leaves torn from folded sheets,
repaired along the crease where the paper had torn. Transcribed on pp. 303–4;
reproduced at 63 percent of actual size.

didn't know who he was, & she got her gun off without mincing matters. Said she— "They are gone, thank God— & I hope I may never see them again. I did not know anything about them, or they never should have entered this house. Do you know, Sir, (dropped her voice to ghastly confidential tone,) they were a couple of desperate characters from ____ —gamblers & murderers of the very worst description! I never saw such a countenance as the smallest one had on him. They just took the premises, & lorded it over everything— they didn't care a snap for the rules of the house! One night when they

Manuscript page 2, to William Wright, 15 July 1864. Verso of the first leaf.

were carrying on in their
room with some more
roughs, my husband went
up to remonstrate with
them, & that small man told
him to take his head out
of the door (pointing a
revolver) because he wanted
to shoot in that direction.
O, I never saw such
creatures. Their room
was never vacant long
enough to be cleaned up
— one of them always
went to bed at dark &
got up at sunrise, & the
other went to bed at sun-
rise & got up at dark —
& if the chamber-man dis-
turbed them they would just
set up in bed & level a pistol

Manuscript page 3, to William Wright, 15 July 1864. Recto of the second leaf.

at him & tell him to get scarce!
They used to bring loads of
beer bottles up at midnight,
& get drunk, & shout &
fire off their pistols in the
room, & throw their empty
bottles out of the window
at the Chinamen below.
You'd hear them count 'One
— two — three — five!' & then
you'd hear the bottle crack
on the China roofs & see
the poor Chinamen scatter
like flies. O, it was dreadful! They kept a nasty
foreign sword & any number
of revolvers & bowie knives
in their room, & I know that
small one must have mur-
dered lots of people. They always had women coming to their
room — sometimes in broad

Manuscript page 4, to William Wright, 15 July 1864. Verso of the second leaf.

daylight — bless you, they
didn't care. They had no
respect for God, man
or the devil. Yes, Sir,
they are gone, & the good God
was kind to me when He
sent them away!"

"There, now — what
in the hell is the use of
wearing away a lifetime
in building up a good name,
if it is to be blown away at
a breath by an ignorant
foreigner who is ignorant
of the pleasant little customs that adorn & beautify
a state of high civilization?"

The old man told Steve
all about it in his dry unsmiling
way & Steve laughed himself
sick over it.

Manuscript page 5, to William Wright, 15 July 1864. Recto of the third leaf.

6

Walter Leman sails for the Sandwich Islands to morrow — just going for recreation.

Give very great love to Geo & Put & all the boys — & write, you bilk.

But don't I want to go to Asia, or somewhere — Ah no, I guess not. I have got the "Gypsy" only in a mild form. It will kill me yet, though.

yr old friend

Sam

Manuscript page 6, to William Wright, 15 July 1864. Verso of the third leaf.

P.S. You had better shove this in the stove — for if we strike a bargain I don't want any absurd "literary remains" & unpublished letters of Mark Twain published after I am planted.

Oct. 19, 1865.

My Dear Bro & Sister:

Orion there was genius — true, unmistakeable genius — in that sermon of yours. It was not the gilded base metal that passes for intellectual gold too generally in this world of ours. It is one of the few sermons that I have read with pleasure — I do not say profit, because I am beyond the reach of argument now. But seven or eight years ago that single sermon would have saved me. It even made me think — yea, & regret for a while, as it was. (Don't preach from the above text, next time.) Viewed as a literary production, that sermon was first-class.

And now let me preach you a sermon. I never had but two powerful ambitions in my life. One was to be a pilot, & the other a preacher of the gospel. I accomplished the one & failed in the other, because I could not supply myself with the necessary stock in trade — i.e. religion. I have given it up forever. I never had a "call" in that direction, anyhow, & my aspirations were the very ecstasy of presumption. But I have had a "call" to literature, of a low order — i.e. humorous. It is nothing to be

---

Clemens to Orion and Mary E. (Mollie) Clemens, 19 and 20 October 1865, San Francisco, California. Mark Twain Papers, The Bancroft Library (CU-MARK). The letter consists of five pages written on four leaves torn from folded sheets. The first three leaves, with writing on rectos only, are repaired with stiff paper backing. The fourth leaf, badly damaged, is unrepaired: although Clemens originally inscribed only the recto, he added to the verso after folding the letter for mailing. Transcribed on pp. 322–24; the first four pages reproduced at 51 percent, the fifth page at 72 percent of actual size.

proud of, but it is my strongest
suit, & if I were to listen to that maxim of stern duty which says ~~also~~
that to do right you _must_ multiply
the one or the two or the three talents
which the Almighty entrusts to your
keeping, I would long ago have
ceased to meddle with things for
which I was by nature unfitted
& turned my attention to seriously
scribbling to excite the laughter of
God's creatures. Poor, pitiful
business! Though the Almighty
did it & is part ly me — for the talent
is a mighty engine when supplied
with the steam of _education_ — which
I have not got, & so its pistons & cylinders & shafts move feebly, & for a
holiday show & are useless for any
good purpose.

But as I was saying, it is
human _nature_ to yearn to be what
we were _never_ intended for. It is singular, but it is so. I wanted to be a
pilot or a preacher, & I was about
as well calculated for either as is
poor Emperor Norton for Chief Justice of the United States. Now _you_
aspire to be a _lawyer,_ when the voice
of God is thundering in your ears
& you are wilfully deaf & will not
hear. _You_ were _intended_ for a
preacher, & lo! you would be a scheming,
groveling, mud-cat of a _lawyer._ A man

Manuscript page 2, to Orion and Mary E. Clemens, 19 and 20 October 1865.
Recto of the second leaf.

never is willing to do what his Creator ³
intended him to do. You are honest,
pious, virtuous — what would you
have more? *Go forth* & *preach.* When
you preach from a pulpit, I will listen
to you & not before! Until that time, I
will read your sermons with sincere
pleasure, but only as *literary* gems.
That is my ultimatum. Ever since I
got acquainted with you — which was
in the autumn of 1861 — I have thought
many & many & many a time
how you would tower head & shoulders above any of the small-fry
preachers of my experience! I
know what I am talking about.
It is the nature of man to see as by the
light of noonday the talents of his
neighbor, (& to which that neighbor is
blind as night) & at the same time to
be unaware of his own talents, while
he is gazing afar off at those that of his
neighbor, as aforesaid. You see in me
a talent for humorous writing, & urge
me to cultivate it. But I always regarded it as brotherly partiality, in your part &
attached no value to it. It is only
now, when editors of standard literary
papers in the distant east give me
high praise, & who do not know me
& cannot of course be blinded by
the glamour of partiality, that I
really begin to believe there must be
something in it.

Manuscript page 3, to Orion and Mary E. Clemens, 19 and 20 October 1865.
Recto of the third leaf.

But I'll toss up with you. 4

Your letter has confirmed me. I *know* — I don't suppose — I *know* you would be great & useful as a minister of the gospel, & I am satisfied you will never be any better lawyer than a good many others. Now I don't know how you regard the ministry, but *I* would rather be a shining light in that department than the greatest lawyer that ever trod the earth. What is the pride of saving the widow's property or the homicide's trivial life, to snatching an immortal soul in mercy from the jaws of hell? Bah! The one is the pitiful people glitter of the fire-fly, & the other the regal glory of the sun.

But as I said, I will toss up with you. I will drop all trifling, & sighing after vain impossibilities, & strive for a fame — unworthy, & evanescent though it must of necessity be — if you will record your promise to go hence to the States & preach the gospel when circumstances shall enable you to do so? I am in earnest. Shall it be so?

I am also in debt. But I have gone to work in dead earnest to get out. Joe Goodman pays me $100 a month for a daily letter, and the Dramatic Chronicle pays me + or rather will begin to pay me, next week — $40 a month for dramatic criticisms. Same wages I got on the Call, & more agreeable & less laborious work. Mollie, my Dear, I send you slathers of love. Wrote to ma to-night. Yr Bro Sam.

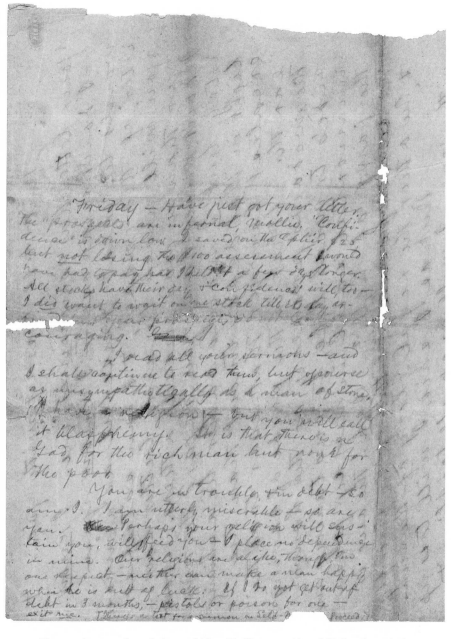

Friday — Have just got your letter,
the "prospects" are infernal, Mollie, "Confidence" is down low. I saved on the Split $25
but not losing the $100 assessment I would
have had to pay had I held it a few days longer.
All stocks have their day & "confidence" will too —
I did want to wait on one stock till its day arrived, but your prospects are not very encouraging.

I read all your sermons — and
I shall continue to read them, but of course
as unsympathetically as a man of stone.
I have a nephew — but you will call
it blasphemy. It is that there is a
God for the rich man but none for
the poor.

You are in trouble, & in debt — so
am I. I am utterly miserable — so are
you. Perhaps your religion will sustain you, will feed you — I place no dependence
in mine. Our religions are alike, though, for
one is perfect — neither can make a man happy
when he is out of luck. If I do not get out of
debt in 3 months, — pistols or poison for one —
exit me.

Manuscript page 5, to Orion and Mary E. Clemens, 19 and 20 October 1865.
Verso of the fourth leaf; only the inscribed portion reproduced.

San F. Dec. 4 (1866)

Dear Miss Bella,

I have had your letter several days, & have been intending to call — but I am still unwell & take no pleasure in going out.

I leave for New York in the ~~Opposition~~ steamer of the 15th inst., & I do hope I shall be well by that time.

I enclose the picture. Have you seen Henry McFarlane? He is clerk at Wm. B. Cooke & Co's, Stationers, Montgomery Block, Montgomery Street above Washington.

Remember me kindly to Mrs Blanchard, & believe that although I may not see you more, I shall always hold you in happy remembrance, & not soon forget the pleasant voyage we made in Company ~~in the~~ good ship Emyrniote.

Yr Friend
Sam L. Clemens

Clemens to Isabella A. Cotton, 4 December 1866, San Francisco, California. Mark Twain Papers, The Bancroft Library (CU-MARK). The letter is written on the recto of one leaf, mounted on a stiff paper backing and partially trimmed. Transcribed on p. 371; reproduced at 59 percent of actual size.

Editorial Apparatus

Guide to the Textual Commentaries

THE TEXTUAL COMMENTARIES treat three closely related matters: how and on what evidence the texts of the letters have been established for this edition; when and where they have been previously published, if at all; and where, and by whose hand, the original documents have been preserved, or not, as the case may be. Under the following heading, Rules and Procedures, we describe the content and purpose of the five standard sections in each commentary, and define the special symbols and terms used in them. Under the next two headings, Description of Texts and Description of Provenance, we summarize information about prior publication and provenance that would otherwise have to be frequently repeated in the commentaries for letters in this volume. The editorial rationale for the texts is given in the Guide to Editorial Practice, pages xxv–xlvi.

1. Rules and Procedures

■ *Heading.* Each commentary begins with the same editorial information that heads the letter itself, except that here the date of composition comes first and the *Union Catalog of Clemens Letters (UCCL)* record number has been added at the end. These headings identify each commentary with its proper text, but collectively they also provide a calendar of letters for this volume, superseding the relevant part of the *UCCL* date-list. For while the record number of each letter remains unchanged, some of the *UCCL* assigned dates, addressees, places, and sources have inevitably been corrected or supplemented.

■ *Copy-text.* This section identifies the document or documents that serve as copy-text for the letter. There are really only two possible kinds of copy-text for any letter: the original document sent, or some kind of copy (or draft) of it, ranging all the way from Clemens's own holograph draft to facsimiles or photocopies of the original document to transcriptions that only paraphrase or describe it.

No *more* authoritative text can exist for a letter than the document actually transmitted. When it survives and is accessible, it is therefore always copy-text, meaning the text from which the editors depart *as little as possible*, chiefly in response to the limitations of transcription itself, listing these changes item by item as emendations of the copy-text (barring only such changes as are described on pages xl–xlv). The text of such a document includes all of its words and word fragments, numerals, punctuation, and nonsemantic signs (such as indention), whether or not any of these was deleted, or adopted rather than inscribed (as in the case of printed letterhead), or added during the time of the original transmission (postmarks, dockets, and so forth). The text *excludes* any subsequent additions or changes made by Clemens or anyone else, which would be reported only under certain conditions specified below. Roughly eighty percent of all letters in this edition survive and are accessible in their original documents.

But if the original document sent is lost or unavailable, either wholly or in part, copy-text for the missing letter or part thereof becomes one or another kind of *copy* of it. Thus if only the author's draft survives, it is perforce copy-text, even though it may be only a partial copy of the letter before it was sent—always signaled in the source line of the editorial heading by the word "*draft*." In such a case, emendation of the copy-text is confined to changes required by the nature of transcription, and is not designed to recover the text of the document actually sent, but to reproduce the draft faithfully *as* a draft.

But in the much commoner and more various case, the most authoritative available copy of the letter sent serves as copy-text and is emended, again to make any changes required by the nature of transcription, but also to recover and restore the text as it was in the lost original, insofar as the evidence permits, with all departures from the copy-text recorded as above. Copy-texts in this category exhibit such a wide range of authority that few generalizations about them hold without exception, but most *facsimiles* of a lost original are more likely to preserve its details unaltered than are most *transcriptions* of it, and facsimiles or photocopies of an original are therefore preferred as copy-text whenever they exist, even for small or discontinuous parts of a letter. When the choice is instead between two or more transcriptions of an original document, the one judged closest to the lost original in a single line of descent from it is always preferred as copy-text, unless it can be established that two or more of these transcriptions derive *independently* from the lost original, a fundamentally different situation.

For if two transcriptions descend independently from a common source (not necessarily the lost MS itself, but from a single document nearer to the MS than any other document in the line of descent from it), each might preserve readings from the original which are not preserved in the other, and these cannot be properly excluded from any text that attempts the fullest possible fidelity to the original. In such cases, no copy-text is designated; all texts judged to have derived independently from the MS are identified in chronological order and are assigned an abbreviation (to be used in the full record of their variants); and the text is established by selecting the most persuasively authorial readings from among all variants, substantive and accidental. Before this alternative method is followed, however, we require that the independence of the variant texts be demonstrated by at least one persuasively authorial variant occurring uniquely in each, thereby excluding the possibility that either text actually derives from the other. There are indubitably variant texts that *do* probably descend independently from a common source and ultimately from the original, but that still do not meet this rather stiff test. So where independent descent is suspected, even likely but not demonstrable in this way, the facts may be mentioned, but whichever text has the preponderance of persuasively authorial readings is designated copy-text, and the others are treated *as if* they simply derived from it, and their variants are not published.

A special case occurs when the original document survives but only in a more or less damaged state, with parts of the original text now invisible, lost, or otherwise obscured by physical means. In such a case, the original document is copy-text throughout, and where undamaged it is emended only as an original document would be, but the damaged parts, being in effect imperfect copies of the original, are emended as necessary and possible to restore the original text, either by drawing on transcriptions made before the damage occurred, or on various forms of documentary evidence still in the damaged document, or both.

Unless the copy-text is here explicitly defined as a "PH" or "facsimile," all documents cited as copy-text have been directly examined and the edited text verified against them. When two or more documents of differing authority (a transcription and a partial MS facsimile, for instance) must be frequently intercalated, either document may be designated copy-text, as convenient, and emended to reflect the superior authority of MS (see, for example, 1 June 57 to Ann E. Taylor). If both the original and a draft survive, copy-text is normally the document sent, with variants of the draft separately reported in the commentary. If a letter survives only in a paraphrase, summary, or description, it is included only if the nonoriginal document is judged to preserve at least some *words* of the original. Like the author's draft, it is not necessarily emended to bring its text closer to the text that was sent, since its nonauthorial words usually provide a necessary context for the authorial words it has, in part, preserved.

When two or more documents serve in turn as copy-text for a single letter, they are identified in the order each is first used in the transcription. When the copy-text is a unique, or virtually unique document, its location is always given. If it is perforce a printed text known to survive in multiple examples, the specific copy used and its location are given, either here or, for books or journals providing several texts in the same volume of *Letters*, in Description of Texts, where it may be referred to as necessary in each relevant commentary. Physical descriptions of copy-text documents are *not* routinely provided unless the documents are also reproduced in facsimile within the volume, or unless some such description bears on how the text has been established. In either of these cases, a physical description is provided: complete for the facsimile letters, partial and as needed for the other. Unless one or both of these conditions apply, therefore, inscriptions and alterations imposed by another hand on a manuscript subsequent to its first transmission and receipt are not necessarily described, transcribed, or otherwise recorded. Physical damage to a copy-text is always described and, if possible, the damaged portions of the document are reproduced in facsimile, so that anyone may test the editors' conjectural restoration of what is otherwise lost. Since such conjectures are emendations of the copy-text and are therefore listed in detail under ■ *Emendations and textual notes*, the facsimile may be given in that section.

■ *Previous publication.* As appropriate, this section cites in chronological order and briefly characterizes three kinds of prior publication: the earliest known, no matter how fragmentary; the most complete known; and any that are well known and reasonably accessible in works such as

MTL and *MTEnt*. When the copy-text is wholly or in part published, it is normally mentioned here only if it is the sole instance of previous publication. The word "known" in this context necessarily signifies "known to the editors," because this section is emphatically *not* a complete record of previous publication, but rather a deliberately selective report to suggest roughly how and when the letter was first made public and therefore accessible to scholarship.

■ *Provenance*. This section likewise gives what is reported or known about the history of ownership and location of the copy-text, especially any original MS, but in addition for nonoriginal copy-texts, what if anything is known of the ownership, existence, and present whereabouts of the MS from which the copy-text derives. When a single description of provenance can suffice, at least in part, for two or more letters in a volume, it is given once under Description of Provenance and referred to as necessary in each relevant commentary.

■ *Emendations and textual notes*. This section records, in a list keyed by page and line number to the edited text, all deliberate departures from the copy-text (barring only those described on pages xl–xlv). Words and characters that have been *interpolated* within editorial brackets are manifestly editorial and are not recorded as emendations. In addition, this section includes (a) editorial *refusals* to emend the copy-text, identified by "*sic*," only when readings are especially at risk of being mistaken for typographical errors in the edited text, and (b) *textual notes*, which are [*always italicized and within square brackets*] and which aim to clarify or explain the reasoning behind any particular emendation of, or refusal to emend, the copy-text. When evidence affects the emendation of two or more letters in the same volume, it is given once for that volume under Description of Texts and referred to in each relevant commentary. When evidence affects a single letter at more than one point, it is ordinarily treated in this section, just before the list of emendations for that letter. When two or more documents alternate as copy-text, they are re-identified at each relevant interval within this list. When no copy-text has been designated because two or more documents descend independently from the lost original, *all variants* are recorded and identified by the abbreviations assigned under ■ *Copy-text*, and this section is renamed ■ *Emendations, adopted readings, and textual notes* to signify that no preferred text or copy-text exists for that letter.

All entries in this list begin with a page and line cue (for example,

120.3, meaning page 120, line 3), followed by the word or passage to be documented (called the "lemma") exactly as it stands in the edited text, except where it is necessary to signify indention [¶], line ending (|), or to shorten the lemma by elision ("Write . . . is"). As far as possible, the lemma is confined to the words and punctuation being documented (whether emended, or otherwise explained). But when more than one instance of a word appears in the same line of the edited text, the lemma includes one or more preceding or succeeding words sufficient to identify which instance in that line is meant. Line numbers include every line of letter text on a page, even when the page contains text from more than one letter, and they also include lines consisting wholly of editorial description, such as "[*about one page (150 words) missing*]," "[*in pencil*]," or the editorial ellipsis (. . . .) indicating an unknown amount of missing text. Line numbers *exclude* all other editorial matter, both in the letter heading and in the notes.

The lemma is separated by a centered bullet (•) from the matter to its right, which is either a textual note or, more often, the corresponding reading of the copy-text, *transcribed* without change or emendation so far as our notation permits, and for matters not susceptible of transcription, *described* within brackets [*in italic type*]. For example, a typical entry documenting emendation (a) to simplify the form used in the transcription and (b) to record deletion by superimposition, appears thus:

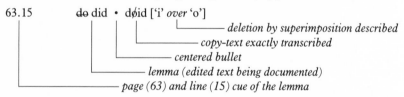

Any reading that appears in the edited text, including any of the special typographical characters used in the transcription, may appear in the lemma to the left of the bullet. (Authorial and editorial signs used in the text are defined or explained on pages xxxviii–xl of the Guide to Editorial Practice.)

Editorial Signs

Some editorial signs used only rarely in the transcription appear more frequently, and with a slightly changed significance, to the right of the bullet; a few editorial signs appear exclusively there.

[¶]   A paragraph sign within brackets is editorial shorthand for "paragraph indention" and may appear to the left or the right of the bullet, with or without negation, as in [*no* ¶].

~   The wavy (or swung) dash is used to the right of the bullet, signifying a word or number identical to the word on the left (for this purpose, hyphenated compounds are defined as one word). It is used *only* when the variant concerns exclusively punctuation or lineation.

∧   The sans serif inferior caret, not to be confused with (ˏ) meaning insertion, is used *only* in conjunction with the swung dash to indicate where punctuation present in the lemma is absent in the copy-text, hence supplied by emendation.

[d◊◊m◊nd]   In letter text the diamond appears only rarely, signifying any alphabetical character, numeral, or punctuation mark which the editors cannot read or reliably conjecture. In the apparatus, however, the diamond appears more frequently to the right of the bullet, always within square brackets, and there it means *just* "unreadable," since the lemma shows what has been conjectured for it. "Unreadable" characters are defined as those which the editors cannot see, or see clearly enough to *identify at least conjecturally*, whether because they are deleted, badly inked, faded, stained, blotted, torn away, or the like. Diamonds are usually enclosed by brackets with ordinary alphabetical characters, which signify conjecturally identifiable characters. Diamonds *never* stand for space between words, which is represented by the standard word-space. When the word-space is also within the brackets, it is to be understood as conjectural, not literally visible.

17.23	eight years • eigh[t y◊]ars [*torn*]	
170.2	"nurse" • ["]nurse" [*dry pen*]	
359.24	I don't know • I [d◊◊'◊] | know [*torn*]	

A partly obscured character still visible enough to ensure its identity beyond a reasonable doubt is transcribed without any record of emendation.

| The vertical rule signifies the end of a line in either the edited text or the copy-text, to the left or right of the bullet, respectively. Line endings in the copy-text often clarify, and are sometimes essential to understanding, both authorial errors and editorial emendations. For instance:

16.3	any of the • any [◊f] | the [*torn*]
35.19	Churchyard • Church-|yard
42.34	appropriate • appro-|propriate
186.5	*witness* • *wit*-|ness
90.22	*ond*ersthand • *on*-|dersthand
17.5	Louis. He • ~.—|~

The vertical rule appears in the lemma only when line endings in the edited text have created an ambiguous form. The record of emendations may resolve the ambiguity by giving the unambiguous reading of the copy-text or, when the copy-text is also ambiguous, by an editorial decision (signaled by "*i.e.*,") based on evidence of Clemens's contemporary practice or, lacking evidence for that, on the contemporary practice of others as documented in dictionaries and the like.

21.33-34	water-|wheels • water-wheels
369.1-2	head-|quarters • head-|quarters [*i.e.*, 'headquarters']

‖   The double vertical rule signifies the end of a line at the end of a page, and supplants the vertical rule whenever a line ending to be reported also occurs at a page ending.

87.2	beginning • [*previous page missing*] ‖ ginning

DESCRIPTIVE TERMS

The following terms appear frequently to the right of the bullet in the (*italicized*) descriptive portion of an entry, always in the purposefully narrow sense defined here:

above   Interlined or written in the space above something else in the manuscript, either with or without a caret. Compare '*over*' and '*across*'.

across   Written over and at an angle to previously inscribed text: so-called 'cross writing,' which is always identified within the transcription itself.

doubtful   Uncertain by an order of magnitude *more* than that signified by '*possible*' and '*possibly*'; applied either to the reading transcribed in the text or to a reading omitted from it as too conjectural to be reliable.

false start   A start made too soon, requiring a new beginning, as in a race. Usually corrected by Clemens, false starts are *never* transcribed in the text because they cannot be rendered fully intelligible there (present methods would not, for instance, enable a reader to distinguish them from revisions).

implied	Not signaled explicitly in the manuscript, but implicitly, by means that are themselves untranscribable, such as word spacing: 'They have Herndon's Report, now.' (66.30). Here Clemens did not strike out the period after 'Report', but implied its deletion by the way he spaced the next word. The last word of any sentence and the first word of the next would normally be spaced more than any two words within a sentence.
inserted	Placed between two previously inscribed words or characters, or between them and a previously fixed point in the manuscript, such as the top of the page. Insertions may be interlined (with or without a caret), squeezed in, or superimposed on deleted characters—methods not distinguished in the edited text and not recorded except when pertinent.
inserted over	Inserted by superimposing on characters which are thereby deleted. Unlike most alterations achieved by superimposition, the timing of such a change is manifestly not immediate, but on review, as the carets in the transcription show.
miswritten	Malformed, misshapen—*not* mistaken in any other sense. The author may have traced over to correct such characters, or deleted and rewritten them, but they are *never* transcribed in the text because they cannot be rendered intelligible there (not distinguishable from a revision, for instance). Authorial corrections of miswritten characters are mentioned in the emendations list only when (a) corrected miswriting has not been transcribed in the text but is possibly a revision; and (b) *vice versa*:

247.31   If • ⟠ If ['If' *over one or two characters, probably* 'If' *miswritten, possibly* 'O']

258.14   Ma𝑠 • [*possibly* 'Ma'; *the canceled* 's' *may be merely a superfluous stroke*]

over   Superimposed on, written on top of, some other char-
                 acters, thereby deleting them. Distinct from written
                 '*above*' or written '*across.*'

not in   By itself to the right of the bullet, this signifies that the
                 reading of the lemma is absent from the copy-text. It may
                 also describe text specified to the right of the bullet, as
                 with '[*not in* MTL]'

partly formed   Characters begun but not completed, hence necessarily
                 conjectural. Partly formed characters are transcribed in
                 the text as if they had been completed, without emen-
                 dation, unless no conjecture is deemed reliable, in which
                 case they are omitted from the text and given along with
                 some of the competing alternatives in the record of
                 emendations.

possible,   Uncertain by an order of magnitude *less* than that signi-
    possibly   fied by '*doubtful*'; applied either to something tran-
                 scribed in the text, or to alternatives deemed more or less
                 on a par and necessarily omitted from the transcription
                 as too uncertain to be reliable.

sic   Confirmation that the copy-text has been deliberately
                 transcribed without emendation, either because it is the
                 author's error that cannot be corrected by interpolation
                 within brackets, or because, appearances notwithstand-
                 ing, it is intentional. Only readings deemed at unusual
                 risk of being mistaken for typographical errors in the ed-
                 ited text are confirmed in this way: routine authorial er-
                 rors, such as omitted apostrophes and the like, are not.

2. Description of Texts

Individual commentaries may designate as copy-text one or both of the
following publications. When the information given here is pertinent for
any reason, the reader is specifically referred to it.

MTB   *Mark Twain: A Biography. The Personal and Literary Life
                 of Samuel Langhorne Clemens by Albert Bigelow Paine,
    with Letters, Comments and Incidental Writings Hitherto Unpublished; Also*

New Episodes, Anecdotes, etc. 3 vols. New York and London: Harper and Brothers, 1912. *BAL*, p. 251. *Copy used:* copy #1, CU-MARK. Where *MTB* has served as copy-text, copy #1 (publisher's code H-M on the copyright page of volume 1, signifying the first impression, ordered in August 1912) has been collated against copy #2 (code K-K, signifying an impression ordered in October 1935, which is the latest impression located). In 1935 Paine made a few corrections in the plates, but no variants in the texts of these letters have been found.

MTB was first issued in three volumes, then in four and later in two, all with the same pagination.[1] Paine said that he had "obtained his data from direct and positive sources: letters, diaries, account-books, or other immediate memoranda" (1:xv). His industry in this respect was such that several letters he published have not since been found in their original form and are therefore known, for all practical purposes, only from his transcriptions (or occasional facsimiles) in *MTB* and *MTL*. Although the printer's copy for *MTB* has not been found, it is known that Paine's general method of acquiring letter texts was to borrow the original whenever possible, presumably transcribing it himself, probably on a typewriter, before returning the manuscript to its owner.[2] He presumably had full access both to the documents (now in the *Mark Twain Papers*) that Clemens himself defined and set aside for his official biographer, and to those now in the *McKinney Family Papers*. He also had access to at least some of the letters in the *Moffett Collection*, but it is not known whether these were ever fully in his hands or transcribed for him. Although he

---

[1] Pagination is continuous and is the same in all sets, regardless of volume number, except for (a) the preliminary pages and (b) pages 832–38, where difficulty in dividing three volumes into four caused the following differences:

3 vols:	832		833	834	[*no #*]	835	836	837	838	[*no #*]	839
4 vols:	[*no #*]	832	833	834		835	836	837	838	[*no #*]	839
2 vols:	[*no #*]	832	833	[*not in*]	834	835	836	837	838		839

The two-volume set was presented as "four volumes in two" with spines printed "I–II" and "III–IV," respectively, but there is no indication within the text where volumes II and IV begin.

[2] For example, Paine must have been relying on transcriptions when he edited Clemens's 25 Oct 61 letter to PAM and JLC, for he printed the two parts of the letter as if they were discrete letters, even though the end of the first part to PAM and the beginning of the concluding part to JLC are on the two sides of a single leaf of MS. It seems unlikely, therefore, that he had direct access to the MS of the letter, at least not when he edited it as separate letters for *MTB* in 1912 and for *MTL* in 1917.

published many of the letters now in the *McKinney Family Papers*, he published relatively few of those in the *Moffett Collection*.

MTB is necessarily copy-text for a few letters not republished in *MTL*. But letter texts in *MTB* are generally excerpts and, judging from collation with letters that are still extant in manuscript, they were more freely edited than the corresponding passages published in *MTL*. Excerpts from *MTB* appeared in *Harper's Monthly Magazine* in thirteen installments, running from November 1911 through November 1912, hence largely before *MTB* appeared in September 1912. Collation shows that when the book and the magazine both include text for a letter, they sometimes contain evidence of having each derived independently from a common source (very likely a typescript and its carbon copy), even though each has also been separately copy-edited. Whenever persuasively authorial variants are found uniquely in both texts, the transcription is based on both. When such variants cannot be found, *MTB* is designated copy-text and the magazine, which was generally edited more heavily than the book, is treated as if it simply derived from *MTB* instead of their common source.

MTL   *Mark Twain's Letters, Arranged with Comment by Albert Bigelow Paine*. 2 vols. New York and London: Harper and Brothers Publishers, 1917. *BAL* 3525. *Copy used:* copy #1, CU-MARK. As indicated under *MTB* above, the letters published in *MTL* are generally more complete as well as more reliable than those extracted or published in full in *MTB*. Because printer's copy for *MTL* has likewise not been found, it is not always clear what relation it bore to the printer's copy for *MTB*. Transcriptions are based on both *MTL* and *MTB* only when persuasively authorial variants occur uniquely in both, thus establishing their independent derivation from the lost MS. Otherwise, if a letter text appears both in *MTL* and *MTB*, *MTL* is chosen as copy-text and *MTB* treated as if it simply derived from *MTL* instead of their common source.

Most of the letters published in *MTL* survive in their original manuscripts. Collation of these documents with their transcriptions in *MTL* shows, in addition to the expected errors and omissions, that a uniform style for the date line, greeting, complimentary closing, and signature lines was *always* imposed on the *MTL* transcription. The uniformity of this house styling is established by a very large body of letter manuscript, and Clemens's consistency in using certain forms is likewise established by an even larger body of evidence. When the copy-text is necessarily *MTL*, this evidence is considered sufficient to permit the conjectural restoration of the likely forms in the original letter, at least in these uniformly styled lines. All emendations to remove this nonauthorial styling in *MTL* are, of course, recorded.

3. Description of Provenance

When more than one letter in a volume is of like provenance, the relevant commentaries give it, at least in part, by referring to one or more of the principal collections described here.

McKinney   The Jean Webster McKinney Family Papers, housed in
Family Papers   the Francis Fitz Randolph Rare Book Room, Helen D.
Lockwood Library, Vassar College, Poughkeepsie, New York (NPV). This collection was given to Vassar in 1977 by Jean and Ralph Connor, of Tymor Farm, LaGrangeville, New York. Jean Connor inherited the papers from her mother, Jean Webster McKinney, who had in turn inherited them from her mother, Annie Moffett Webster, Clemens's niece and the wife of Charles L. Webster, his business partner from 1884 to 1888. The letters and other Clemens materials in the collection represent one of the three principal caches of family letters, having passed from Clemens to his mother, Jane Lampton Clemens (d. 1890), his brother Orion (d. 1897) and sister-in-law Mollie Clemens (d. January 1904), and ultimately to his sister Pamela A. Moffett (d. August 1904). Some of these documents went eventually to her son, Samuel E. Moffett (see the *Moffett Collection*, below) and some to her daughter, Annie E. Moffett, later Webster. Not surprisingly, therefore, several manuscript letters are now found partly in the *McKinney Family Papers* and partly in the *Moffett Collection*.

Mollie Clemens wrote her nephew Samuel Moffett on 31 July 1899 that "We never destroyed Sams letters—*excepting* at by his request, or a few no one should see" (CU-MARK). At least one partly destroyed (censored) letter survives in this collection (see pages 347–49), but by far the larger toll was probably taken by accidental physical damage or loss, and by the deliberate destruction, following Mollie Clemens's death in 1904, of most of Clemens's letters to his mother. As early as 1881, Orion Clemens had assembled a number of his brother's letters written between about 1853 and 1865 as part of a sprawling manuscript for his own autobiography (never published), finding even then that not all the letters had been preserved intact. On 6 October 1899, Pamela Moffett sent an unknown number of original letters to her son, Samuel Moffett, then a journalist in California, saying in part that she "was sorry to see that parts of some of the letters were missing" (CU-MARK). Moffett tried to publish at least a few of these letters in biographical sketches of Clemens, but was eventually told to preserve them for publication after Clemens's death. Some, if not all, of these letters must eventually have become part of the *Moffett Collection*, described below.

But in 1904, according to a 1935 Associated Press story in an unidentified newspaper, Mollie Clemens's executor, John R. Carpenter, burned "almost four trunks" of Clemens's letters to his mother, "as requested by the famous humorist." Carpenter confided his story, according to this report, to Dr. G. Walter Barr of Keokuk, who gave this account:

> When Mrs. Clemens died [in 1890], . . . her carefully preserved personal and family treasures went into the possession of her son, Orion. When Orion died, his wife had the succession and kept it inviolate until her own death in 1904.
>
> John R. Carpenter was administrator of Orion's wife's estate and the treasured archives of Mother Clemens were delivered to him. One item was a collection of letters from Mark Twain to his mother, running through many decades, from youth to worldwide fame.
>
> But with those three or four trunks of letters was an admonition. Mark Twain had enjoined his mother that she always burn his letters to her. She had not done so, but had passed on the mandamus to Orion and to the wife of the latter, and Carpenter was familiar with it.
>
> He had a treasure of incalculable value and an imperative order to destroy it.
>
> Carpenter realized fully the value of the material he was about to burn in his library grate. When I exclaimed that to destroy all those letters was a monstrous crime against biography, history and the record of a man who belonged to the whole world, he answered that he agreed with me—but what could be done under the circumstances?
>
> Mark Twain had written those letters to his mother in perfect candor—and about the whole sum of his candid writing was in them—intending and believing that nobody else would ever see them, and had ordered them burned.
>
> And so Carpenter burned every one. It took him several long evenings to complete the job thoroughly.[3]

---

[3] "Mark Twain Letters to Mother Burned at Direction of Author," unidentified clipping, datelined December 14, PH in CU-MARK. The New York *Times* also published an abbreviated version of this story on 15 December 1935 (2:8).

That this story was not a fiction is suggested, at any rate, by the postscript of Clemens's letter to Carpenter on 14 February 1904, the original draft of which survives in the Mark Twain Papers: "If there are any letters of mine, I beg that you will destroy them."

The *McKinney Family Papers* consist of Clemens documents typically left by him, at various times, with his sister. They include his earliest surviving notebook (probably written in 1855; see *N&J1*, 11–39); half a dozen literary manuscripts, incomplete and unpublished, written principally between 1859 and 1868 (see *ET&S1–3*); more than six hundred letters and telegrams from Clemens to various members of his family, and to business associates like Webster, as well as family photographs and mementoes, and letters and documents by other family members and close associates (Simpson, 6–14).

Mark Twain   The Mark Twain Papers, The Bancroft Library, Univer-
Papers   sity of California, Berkeley, California (CU-MARK).

The core of this collection is the body of documents that Clemens made available to Albert Bigelow Paine for the official biography Paine was to produce, and from which Paine eventually published, selectively, an edition of letters, one of notebooks, and one of the autobiography. Since Clemens's death in 1910, these papers have been successively in the care of Paine (1910–37); Bernard DeVoto at Harvard (1938–46); Dixon Wecter at the Huntington Library, San Marino, and later at the University of California, Berkeley (1946–50); Henry Nash Smith (1953–63); and Frederick Anderson (1963–79), both of the latter at the University of California in Berkeley, and both successors to Paine, DeVoto, and Wecter as the official literary executor for the Clemens estate. Upon the death of Clara Clemens Samossoud in 1962, the papers were bequeathed to the University of California, and in 1971 they became part of The Bancroft Library, where they now reside.

The original collection segregated by Clemens for Paine included forty-five of the approximately fifty extant notebooks kept by Clemens between 1855 and 1910; approximately seventeen thousand letters received by Clemens or his family; an estimated six hundred literary manuscripts, most of them unpublished, including the autobiographical dictations; as well as photographs, clippings, contracts, and a variety of other documents originally owned by Clemens. Since Paine's tenure, primary and secondary documents have been added to this assemblage in various ways, ranging from gifts both of photocopy and original manuscripts and documents, to large purchases and bequests comprising many hundreds of letters, to the systematic compilation of a secondary archive of photocopies collected from the owners of original manuscripts and other documents around the world. Four major acquisitions of original letter manuscripts are especially pertinent here.

Samossoud Collection (c. 1952), The Mark Twain Papers. Among the documents apparently *not* made wholly available to Paine were the letters written by Clemens to his fiancée and wife, Olivia Langdon, and later to their daughters Susie, Clara, and Jean. The letters to Olivia were sold to the University of California in about 1952 by Clara's husband, Jacques Samossoud. Other parts of this large cache of family letters still held by Clara and her husband were sold or given by them to other persons and institutions, not all yet identified. No letters from the Samossoud Collection appear in the first volume of *Mark Twain's Letters*, but every subsequent volume will contain at least one.

Moffett Collection (1954), The Mark Twain Papers. This collection represents that portion of Pamela Moffett's papers that was given to her son Samuel instead of her daughter Annie (see *McKinney Family Papers*, above). The collection became the property of Samuel Moffett's daughter Anita Moffett (d. 1952), either upon his death in 1908, or upon the death of her younger brother, Francis Clemens Moffett, in 1927. The papers were discovered in 1954, in a warehouse sale that included some of her effects: sixteen hundred letters by Clemens, his family, and associates, including Pamela Moffett's letters to her son and daughter; ten scrapbooks of newspaper clippings for the period 1858–1898, evidently compiled by Orion Clemens and containing original printings of Clemens's and his brother's western journalism; deeds to the brothers' 1860s Nevada mining claims; family photographs and a family Bible. This acquisition was made possible for the University of California in 1954 by a group of anonymous donors. The inventory of Clemens letters made at the time was not always specific enough to enable the editors now to be certain whether some letters were part of the Moffett Collection or were already in the Mark Twain Papers.

Tufts Collection (1971), The Mark Twain Papers. This collection was assembled chiefly by James Tufts, at one time managing editor of the San Francisco *Examiner* and an acquaintance of Clemens's. It was purchased in 1971 from Tufts' son, Dr. John M. Tufts, Kentfield, California. The collection includes twenty-three original letters by Clemens, literary manuscripts, first printings of his sketches, first editions of his books, and photographs.

Appert Collection (1973 and 1977), The Mark Twain Papers. The gift of Mr. and Mrs. Kurt E. Appert, Pebble Beach, California, the collection includes more than fifty letters by Clemens, literary manuscripts, photographs, letters to Clemens, first editions of his works, and books from his library.

Textual Commentaries

■ 24 August 1853 · To Jane Lampton Clemens · New York, N.Y. ·
UCCL 02711

■ *Copy-text:* "Letter from New York," Hannibal *Journal*, 5 Sept 53, 2, at the State
Historical Society of Missouri, Columbia (MoHi). "Letter from New York,"
Hannibal *Journal* (weekly), 8 Sept 53, 2 (MoHi) is a reimpression from the same
type and is textually identical. ■ *Previous publication:* Ridings, 183–84; Brashear
1934, 153–55. A partial facsimile of the first *Journal* printing appears in Brashear
facing 154 (misdated 8, instead of 5, September 1853). ■ *Provenance:* This letter
was unknown to Paine as late as 1917: "It is not believed that a single number of
Orion Clemens's paper, the Hannibal *Journal*, exists to-day" (*MTL*, 1:20). In
1926, however, a file of the *Journal* kept by William T. League (to whom Orion
had sold the paper in September 1853) came to light and was given by the League
family to the State Historical Society of Missouri (Armstrong, 485). This letter
and the next one were republished shortly thereafter. ■ *Emendations and textual
notes:*

3.7	Orion . . . Sam • O. and H. C— | but take S. [*Collation of the parts of Clemens's 26–?28 Oct 53 letter to OC and HC that survive both in MS and in a Muscatine* Journal *printing (see below in the apparatus to that letter) shows the degree of freedom Orion assumed in revising his brother's private letters for publication. In this letter, there can be little doubt that the names elided in the Hannibal* Journal *were given in full in Clemens's MS, nor that* 'Orion', 'Henry', *and* 'Clemens' *were the MS forms of those names; neither of the brothers seems to have had a nickname. The form* 'Sam' *is almost as certain. Clemens was always referred to as* 'Sam' *in his family's early letters, and he evidently thought of himself by that name, for he almost invariably signed himself* 'Sam' *in personal letters, using* 'Sam'' *or* 'Saml.' *only for more formal communications.*]
3.9	didn't • did'nt
3.19	awful • awlul
4.11–12	Harvel Jordan's • F.———J———'s [*As at 3.7, the* Journal *disguised a name, but this time the compositor apparently misread the name when eliding it. Clemens's* 'H' *and* 'F' *were sometimes similar in*

form, as the following examples, isolated from the MS of his 8 Oct 53
letter to his sister and reproduced here at actual size, illustrate:]

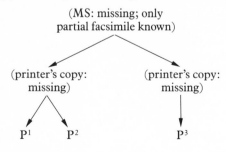

4.13   seems • [sic]

5.4   [closing and signature missing] • [Even though Clemens probably
            signed this letter 'Sam', the exact form of his closing and signature in
            what may well be his first letter to his mother cannot be reliably conjec-
            tured, especially since only one other original letter to her (p. 63) has
            survived for the eight years following this one.]

■ 31 August 1853 · To Jane Lampton Clemens · New York, N.Y. ·
UCCL 02712

■ *Copy-text:* Hannibal *Journal*, 10 Sept 53, 2, at the State Historical Society of
Missouri, Columbia (MoHi). A reimpression from the same type in the Hannibal
Journal (weekly), 15 Sept 53, 2 (MoHi) is textually identical. ■ *Previous publica-
tion:* Minnie M. Brashear, "An Early Mark Twain Letter," *Modern Language
Notes* 44 (April 1929): 257–58; Armstrong, 498–99; Brashear 1934, 155–57.
■ *Provenance:* see the previous letter. ■ *Emendations and textual notes:*

9.8   but • bnt

■ 3? September 1853 · To Pamela A. Moffett · New York, N.Y. ·
UCCL 02713

■ *Copy-text:* Except for a partial facsimile of the MS in *MTL*, 1:31, containing
'Where . . . by it.' (14.7–13), the text is based on three printed transcriptions,
none of them complete, that appear to derive independently from the lost MS:

                    P¹   Paine, 48–49
                    P²   *MTB*, 1:94–95
                    P³   *MTL*, 1:21–22

For a general description of these printed texts, see pp. 456–59. Collation shows
that they are in approximately the following relation to the MS:

                        (MS: missing; only
                        partial facsimile known)

            (printer's copy: (printer's copy:
            missing)   missing)

            P¹   P²   P³

Variants recorded at 13.20, 13.22–23, 13.31–14.5, 14.6, and 14.8 attest to this or a similar path of derivation. Although all three texts were edited by Paine, each was copy-edited independently. P^1 was a condensation of P^2 appearing in advance of book publication. Consequently readings in P^1 and P^2 frequently agree against the reading of P^3, but since P^1 and P^2 derive independently of one another only from the same transcription of the MS, their agreement gives them no greater authority than resides in a reading in P^3, which likewise derives from the MS through an intervening transcription. In fact, since P^1 and P^2 appear to have been edited more freely than P^3, for example in variants recorded at 13.3, 13.6, 13.30, 14.9, and 14.10, the readings of P^3 are adopted more often. When P^1 and P^2 disagree, on the other hand, agreement of P^3 with either of them is persuasive evidence of the MS reading. ■*Previous publication:* see *Copy-text.* ■*Provenance:* Paine must have had the MS, or a photograph of at least part of it, in his possession when he published the partial facsimile in *MTL* in 1917. The first part of the MS was lost before 1912, when Paine introduced the surviving text with the comment, "A portion of a letter to his sister Pamela has been preserved," referred to it as a "fragment," and identified it as "the earliest existing specimen of his composition" (*MTB*, 1:94). ■*Emendations, adopted readings, and textual notes:*

13.1   [¶] . . . From (P^3) • [¶] From ($P^{1,2}$)
13.3   &c., (P^3) • etc., ($P^{1,2}$)
13.3   tis (P^3) • 'tis ($P^{1,2}$)
13.5   Machinery (P^3) • machinery ($P^{1,2}$)
13.6   1 (P^2) • one (P^1); 8 (P^3) [*Clemens's subsequent comment that* 'It has just struck 2 A.M.' *(14.5) rules out the reading of* P^3. *The entries at 13.12 and 14.6 suggest that* P^1 *styled many of Clemens's numerals as words.*]
13.6   o'clock.) (P^3) • $\sim$). ($P^{1,2}$)
13.7   as (P^3) • [*not in*] ($P^{1,2}$)
13.8   to-night, • $\sim$. ($P^{1,2}$); tonight, (P^3)
13.9   and ($P^{1,3}$) • $\sim$, (P^2)
13.10   Palace ($P^{2,3}$) • palace (P^1)
13.12   50 ($P^{2,3}$) • fifty (P^1)
13.13   Palace ($P^{2,3}$) • palace (P^1)
13.14   round (P^3) • around ($P^{1,2}$)
13.17   county (P^3) • County ($P^{1,2}$)
13.18   course, (P^3) • $\sim_\wedge$ ($P^{1,2}$)
13.19   county (P^3) • County ($P^{1,2}$)
13.19   reservoir, (P^3) • $\sim_\wedge$ ($P^{1,2}$)
13.19   *thirty-eight* (P^3) • thirty-eight ($P^{1,2}$)
13.20   miles ! (P^3) • $\sim$, (P^1); $\sim_\wedge$ (P^2)
13.20   and (P^3) • $\sim$, ($P^{1,2}$)
13.20   easily ($P^{1,2}$) • [*not in*] (P^3)

13.21   *one . . . day!* (P³) • one hundred barrels of water per day. (P¹);
               one hundred barrels of water per day! (P²)

13.22–23   Write . . . is. • [*follows* 'by it.' *(14.13)*] (P¹,²); [*not in*] (P³) [*The
               position of this sentence in the MS remains problematic. Although* P¹
               and P² *print it as the second sentence of the postscript, the MS facsim-
               ile—which appears to reproduce the postscript—does not include it.
               While the sentence may have been accidentally or deliberately excluded
               from the facsimile, the more likely explanation is that it was actually
               written elsewhere, probably in the margin of the passage within which
               it has been here transcribed, and that in 1912, Paine printed it in the
               postscript only as an editorial convenience.*]

13.24   exercise; (P³) • ~, (P¹,²)

13.25   do, (P²,³) • ~∧ (P¹)

13.26   one (P³) • a (P¹,²)

13.26   day, (P³) • ~∧ (P¹,²)

13.27   miles, *is* exercise— (P³) • miles is exercise. (P¹,²)

13.27   it now (P¹,²) • ~, ~ (P³)

13.28   kept; (P¹,²) • ~, (P³)

13.30   Jim (P³) • Jim (Wolfe) (P¹,²)

13.30   write, (P²,³) • ~∧ (P¹)

13.31–14.5   news. I . . . offices. (It (P³) • news. [*three ellipsis points*] [¶] (It
               (P¹,²)

14.5   A.M. (P³) • A.M., (P¹,²)

14.6   6, (P²,³) • six (P¹)

14.6   7 (P²,³) • seven (P¹)

14.6   ask (P¹,²) • ask me (P³)

               [*MS facsimile is copy-text for* 'Where . . . by it.' *(14.7–13)*]

14.7   printers' (MS facsimile, P³) • printer's (P¹,²)

14.8   me, (MS facsimile, P²,³) • ~∧ (P¹)

14.9   I . . . Ella soon. (MS facsimile, P³) • [*not in*] (P¹,²)

14.10   Brother (MS facsimile, P³) • Brother, (P¹); brother, (P²)

14.11   Sam (MS facsimile) • SAM. (P¹⁻³)

14.12   P.S (MS facsimile) • P. S. (P¹,³); P.S.— (P²)

■ 8 October 1853 · To Pamela A. Moffett · New York, N.Y. · *UCCL*
00001

■*Copy-text:* MS, Mark Twain Papers, The Bancroft Library, University of California, Berkeley (CU-MARK). The MS, which is damaged and has been silked,
is reproduced in facsimile on pp. 417–20. It consists of a single folder of cream-
colored wove paper, 7⅝ by 9¾ inches (19.3 by 24.8 cm), inscribed on all four
pages. The folder is blind embossed in the upper left corner with a five-pointed

star enclosed in a circle of words, of which 'OAKLAND' is the only one legible. The paper is probably the same as that used in 26–?28 Oct 53 to OC and HC. The letter was written in black ink, now faded to brown. ■ *Previous publication: MTB*, 1:97, excerpts; and *MTL*, 1:23–25, with minor omissions indicated by ellipses. Collation shows that both printings derive from a common source with the same errors, presumably Paine's transcription of the original. This transcription may have been made when the MS was in a less damaged state, for the paper had not cracked when Paine penciled an *x* following 'revenge,)' (16.16), but nothing in Paine's texts establishes that he was able literally to copy anything that must now be wholly conjectured. Consequently, for the now missing portions of the MS, Paine's texts must be regarded as without authority. The few cases in which their readings differ from the present text and are not clearly refuted by the surviving manuscript evidence are reported in the record of emendation. ■ *Provenance:* In about 1880, Orion Clemens incorporated this letter MS in the draft of his autobiography then in progress: his page numbers appear in purple ink atop each page. The penciled notations are by Paine, probably added when he had the letter transcribed for publication. The circled '2' canceled at the top of the first page probably refers to the position of this letter in *MTB* or *MTL*, in both of which it is the second letter printed. On the first page the note '3½″ wide' and the *x*s inserted before 'Edwin' (16.11) and after 'revenge,)' (16.16) suggest that Paine may have been planning to publish a facsimile of part of the letter; both *MTB* and *MTL* are printed with a type line 3½ inches wide. No such facsimile is known to exist, however. On the last page Paine wrote '(An early M. T. letter)'. The MS may have been in the Mark Twain Papers since Paine's service as literary executor of the Mark Twain Estate (1910–37). It is more probable, however, that it is part of the Moffett Collection; see p. 462. ■ *Emendations and textual notes:*

16.1–2   1853. [¶] My • 18[◊◊◊] | [¶] My [*torn*]
16.3   any of the • any [◊f] | the [*torn*]
16.7   time I • tim[◊] | I [*torn*]
16.7   or so, from • o[◊ ◊◊◊] | from [*torn; possibly* 'or two from']
16.8   is just as • is [◊◊◊◊] | as [*MTL reads* 'is as'. *Although the paper is now torn away following* 'is', *there was space at the end of the line for about three or four characters. (The character now partly visible after* 'is' *is not part of the inscription at this point; see the next entry.) Clemens must have written something in this space, for he was obliged to put the next word,* 'as', *at the beginning of the next line.*]
16.9   York as it • York [a◊] | it [*During the process of silking, the letter* 'a' *on a small, detached fragment of paper was mistakenly placed following* 'is' (16.8) *on the line above its proper place, which is probably here as part of the missing word* 'as'.]
16.15   brother's • br[◊t◊]er's [*torn*]
16.18   and Pythias • and | [◊y]thias [*torn*]
16.25   he cannot • he | [ca◊]not [*torn*]
16.25   for such • for | [◊◊c]h [*torn*]

17.1	~~he cou~~ (containing • ~~he cou~~ (con-|[◊◊◊]ning [*torn;* 'con-' *over* 'he cou']
17.1	$25 per • $25 | [p◊]r [*torn*]
17.4	~~in to~~ into • ['in to' *marked by Clemens to close up*]
17.5	Louis. He • ~.—|~
17.7	Louis, • Lo[◊◊◊], [*torn*]
17.7	that I • tha[t] I [*torn*]
17.8	go, there. • ~. ~. [*deletion implied*]
17.9	yourself about • yourse*f*lf abo*f*ut ['l' *over* 'f'; 'u' *over* 't']
17.11	himself a • him[s◊◊◊] | a [*torn*]
17.11	brother is not • brother [◊◊] | not [*torn*]
17.13	*b* ask • ['a' *over* 'b']
17.14	independent as • independen[t] as [*torn*]
17.14–15	wood-|sawyer's • wood-|sawyer's [*i.e.,* 'wood-sawyer's']
17.18	appendages • appe[n-]|dages [*torn*]
17.18	company • co[m◊]|pany [*torn*]
17.19	~~the~~ soldiers • ['so' *over* 'the']
17.19–20	veteran scattered here • vetera[◊] scatt[◊◊◊d] here [*torn*]
17.20	And when I passed through one • [An◊ ◊◊◊◊ ◊ ◊]assed throug[h] one [*torn; MTL reads* 'And as I passed through one']
17.23	eight years • eigh[t y◊]ars [*torn*]
17.24–25	well drilled. [¶] Passage • well[◊rill◊d◊] [¶] Passage [*torn; MTL reads* 'well-drilled. [¶] Passage']
17.25	Albany • A[l]bany [*torn*]
17.25	miles) in the finest • mile[◊◊ ◊◊ ◊◊◊] | finest [*torn; MTL reads* 'miles on the finest']
17.28	I tell you • I ‖ [◊◊◊◊] you [*torn*]
17.29	would let you • would | [◊◊◊] you [*torn*]
17.29	myself • myse*f*lf ['l' *over* 'f']
17.29	I may • I | [◊]ay [*torn*]
17.30	*f* write • ['w' *over* 'r']

■ 26–?28 October 1853 · To Orion and Henry Clemens · Philadelphia, Pa. · *UCCL* 00002

■ *Copy-text:* MS, Jean Webster McKinney Family Papers, Vassar College Library (NPV), is copy-text for the first part of the letter, 'Philadelphia . . . Sam' (19.1–23.4), and for the note 'Please . . . Sam' (24.9–11). A contemporary transcript presumably set from the MS, "From Philadelphia," Muscatine *Journal* (weekly) (11 Nov 53), 1, is copy-text for the remainder of the letter, 'Philadelphia . . . S. C.' (23.6–24.8). Newsprint was examined in the collections of the P. M. Musser

Public Library, Muscatine, Iowa (IaMu), and the Historical Library, The State Historical Society of Iowa, Des Moines. The *Journal* text appeared under the heading:

From Philadelphia.
Tomb of Franklin—Planted Cannon—The Exchange —Ride to Fairmount—Philadelphia Marble—Fairmount Water Works—Revolutionary Associations, &c.
Extract from a private letter to the senior editor, dated

PHILADELPHIA, Oct. 26, 1853.

The *Journal* text itself consists of: '* * * * * The grave . . . Exchange.' (20.16–22.19) followed with no break or sign of omission by the section for which the *Journal* is copy-text. Orion Clemens, being "the senior editor," was probably the one primarily responsible for the editing of this letter as it was printed in the *Journal*. He may even have set the type for the letter himself. Collation of the MS and the *Journal* printing, presented below, shows the nature and extent of the changes Orion felt free to make when publishing his brother's letter, and suggests the kinds of changes he probably imposed on the parts of this letter, as well as on other letters, for which MS does not survive. Besides correcting lapses, he altered sentence breaks, paragraphing, hyphenation of compound words, and other punctuation. He sometimes misread the MS, changed the language to suit his own taste, omitted words he may have found offensive, such as 'infernal' (21.8), and deleted personal remarks addressed to himself and discussion of the personal affairs of his brother or other members of the family. ■ *Previous publication:* in addition to the copy-text, *MTB*, 1:99–100, excerpts from MS; *MTL*, 1:25–28, text of MS, with omissions; Lorch 1929a, 410–13, text of Muscatine *Journal*. ■ *Provenance:* see McKinney Family Papers, pp. 459–61. About 1880, Orion Clemens numbered each page of the MS in ink for inclusion in his autobiography. He also used a pencil to make eleven changes in the MS and to write 'Transfer to end' in the upper left corner of the first MS page, with a line running to Clemens's note 'Please . . . Sam' (24.9–11). Orion was evidently directing a transcriber or compositor where to place Clemens's note, which is written across the first paragraph of the letter. For several reasons, it is probable that Orion marked the MS in pencil at the same time he added the ink page numbers, in 1880, not in 1853. Orion's marks in the MS do not correspond to the *Journal* text: most of the changes in the *Journal* text were not marked in the MS, and most of the changes marked in the MS were made in passages not printed in the *Journal*. The *Journal* did not print the end of the letter or the cross-written note Orion wanted placed there, nor did it include the passages in which Orion made seven of his eleven MS changes. True, the *Journal* text does incorporate the four changes Orion made in the part of the MS printed there, but all are changes of the sort an editor would have to make to produce a corrected and grammatically conventional text: three (21.10, 21.23, and 22.10) are necessary corrections of lapses in the MS, and one, the addition of a comma following 'That is' (20.31) where the MS all but calls out for a

comma, is virtually a correction as well. Finally, the entire texture of the two sets of changes—the ones made in the *Journal* text and those marked in the MS—is different. Orion edited the letter for the *Journal* with a free hand, shaping it to suit himself, but he marked the MS scarcely at all. Besides the added comma at 20.31, he made only one other change in the MS that is not a necessary correction: he replaced Clemens's somewhat idiosyncratic 'of' by more conventional 'from' at 19.20. In 1880 Clemens felt that Orion had followed his advice to write the autobiography "in a plain, simple, truthful way, suppressing none of the disagreeables" (9 June 80 to W. D. Howells, MH-H, in *MTHL*, 1:312); Orion's light editing of the MS of this letter for inclusion in the autobiography is evidently part of that simplicity. Interestingly enough, where Clemens omitted a necessary verb at 22.10, Orion supplied 'looks' in the *Journal* text, but he penciled 'is', a less suitable choice, in the MS. This difference suggests that Orion did not have a copy of the *Journal* text at hand when marking the MS for inclusion in his autobiography. Orion sold his interest in the Muscatine *Journal* in June 1855; the publisher's file of the *Journal* is probably the one now in the Musser Public Library.
■ *Emendations and textual notes:*

[*MS is copy-text for* 'Philadelphia . . . Sam' *(19.1–23.4)*)]

19.10	~~the~~ three • thᴇ́ree ['r' *over* 'e']
19.11	ƀ devil • ['d' *over partly formed* 'b' *or* 't']
19.13	~~del~~ deal • deʎal ['a' *over* 'l']
19.13	ɱMonday • ['M' *over* 'm']
19.15	hankerchief • [*sic*]
19.19	State. On • ~.—|~
19.23	~~will~~ (when • ~~wₕenₕ~~ ₍(when₎ ['hen' *over* 'ill'. *Although* 'wₕenᵢₗₗ' *was only marginally legible, Clemens let it stand and continued the sentence, perhaps until, the closing parenthesis following* 'Ky;' *(19.24) having made an opening parenthesis necessary, he rewrote* 'when' *as* '(when'.]
19.24	and • and | and
20.7	*encouraging* • *encₕouraging* ['o' *over* 'u']
20.7	ń "it's • [*quotation mark above possible partly formed* 'n']
20.14	than • [*sic*]
20.19	~~th~~ it • ['it' *over* 'th']
20.24–25	side walk • [*possibly* 'sidewalk']
20.25	~~on~~ in • ǿin ['i' *over* 'o']
20.30	~~we~~ where • wᴇ́here ['h' *over* 'e']
20.32	parts, of • ~. ~ [*deletion implied*]
20.35	out-skirts • out-|skirts
20.36	is. We • ~.—|~
20.36	ħ large • ['l' *over* 'h']

20.37   p̸ building • ['b' *over* 'p']

21.4   ~~this~~ these • thisese ['e' *over* 'is']

21.7   massy • [*Clemens wiped something out before writing this word in the same space, but no trace of any prior inscription is legible; as many as three characters could have been written in the space, or Clemens may have wiped away something as meaningless as a blot of ink.*]

21.9   building • biluilding ['u' *over* 'il']

21.16   ~~lie~~ like • li¢ke ['k' *over* 'e']

21.17   ~~pe~~ prepared • p¢repared ['r' *over* 'e']

21.21   you, know • [*sic*]

21.24   n̸ quite • ['q' *over* 'n']

21.27   ~~every~~ upward • ['upwa' *over* 'every']

21.28   ∅ a well • ['a' *over unrecovered wiped out character*]

21.33–34   water-|wheels • water-wheels

21.34   b̸Book • ['B' *over* 'b']

22.1   W̶a̶ Wissahickon • W̸aissahickon ['i' *over* 'a']

22.9   ~~the~~ her • ſher [*originally* 'the' *but* 't' *never crossed;* 't' *canceled;* 'r' *added*]

22.11   situationed • ['ion' *over* 'ed']

22.14   distributin • [*sic*]

22.26   ~~star~~ stagger • staſgger ['g' *over* 'r']

22.27   and • [*sic*]

22.29   hands • [*sic*]

22.29   is • [*sic*]

22.31   ~~re~~ your • ['yo' *over* 're']

22.33   bell,! • [*exclamation point over comma*]

     [*Muscatine* Journal *is copy-text for* 'Philadelphia . . . S. C.' (*23.6–24.8*)]

23.11   liberty • libert[y]

24.4   looked • looĸed

24.4   Clemens's • C——'s [*As in 24 Aug 53 to JLC, Orion's newspaper disguised the personal name.*]

24.5   track • tracĸ

     [*MS is copy-text for* 'Please . . . Sam' (*24.9–11*)]

■ *Collation:* This collation reports variants of four kinds: Samuel Clemens's inscription in the MS (labeled MS); Orion Clemens's changes in the MS (MS—OC); the readings of the Muscatine *Journal* (J); and the readings of this edition when they differ from all three texts.

19.1   Philadelphia, Pa. (MS) • PHILADELPHIA, (J)

19.2–20.16   My . . . home. [¶] The (MS) • [¶] * * * * * The (J)

19.3   I[t] • I (MS); It (MS—OC)

19.20	of the (MS) • ~~of~~ ˌfromˌ the (MS—OC)
19.24	and • and	and (MS); ~~and~~	and (MS—OC)
20.3	the[y] • the (MS); they (MS—OC)
20.14	than (MS) • thatⱨ (MS—OC) ['t' *over* 'n']
20.16	Church-yard (MS) • Church yard (J)
20.16	cor. (MS) • corner (J)
20.24	cannons (6 pounders) (MS) • ~ , (~ ~,) (J)
20.24–25	side walk (MS) • sidewalk, (J)
20.25	st. (MS) • street, (J)
20.25	ground, (MS) • ~∧ (J)
20.27	water; they (MS) • water. They (J)
20.28	manner, (MS) • ~∧ (J)
20.29	churches, (MS) • ~∧ (J)
20.29	N.Y. (MS) • New York. (J)
20.31	That is (MS) • ~ ~ˌ (MS—OC); ~ ~, (J)
20.32	parts, of • ~. ~ (MS); ~∧ ~ (J)
20.32	[*no* ¶] Well (MS) • [¶] Well (J)
20.34	heathen (MS) • heathens (J)
20.35	get towards (MS) • near (J)
20.35	out-skirts • out-|skirts (MS); outskirts (J)
20.36	*always* (MS) • always (J)
20.36	is. We (J) • ~.—|~ (MS)
21.2	beautiful (MS) • ~, (J)
21.3	base, (MS) • ~∧ (J)
21.3–4	about . . . windows. (MS) • 25 or 30 feet high. (J)
21.5	and then the (MS) • with (J)
21.6	the other was (MS) • others are (J)
21.7	massy; (MS) • ~, (J)
21.7	imagination, (MS) • ~∧ (J)
21.8	the infernal (MS) • [*not in*] (J)
21.9	[*no* ¶] Marble (MS) • [¶] Marble (J)
21.9	Phila. (MS) • Philadelphia. (J)
21.10	I[t] • I (MS); Iₜ (MS—OC); It (J)
21.15	dwellings) (MS) • ~,) (J)
21.15	stoop (MS) • stoops (J)
21.16	sun, (MS) • ~∧ (J)
21.17	Fairmount,—got • ~,|—~ (MS); ~,∧~ (J)
21.17	stage, (MS) • ~∧ (J)
21.18	hill, (MS) • ~∧ (J)

21.18   great (MS) • [*not in*] (J)

21.19   road, (MS) • ~∧ (J)

21.20–22   (or . . . am) (MS) • [*not in*] (J)

21.23   dam, (MS) • ~∧ (J)

21.23   hold[s] • hold (MS); holds̜ (MS—OC); holds (J)

21.25   entered—and (MS) • ~∧~ (J)

21.27   stands (MS) • ~, (J)

21.27–28   (is that proper?) (MS) • [*not in*] (J)

21.28   well executed (MS) • well-executed (J)

21.32   pump-house (MS) • ~, (J)

21.32   it) (MS) • ~,) (J)

21.33–34   water-|wheels • water-wheels (MS); water wheels (J)

21.34   back-number (MS) • back number (J)

21.35   Works, (MS) • ~∧ (J)

21.35   give you. [*no* ¶] I (MS) • give. [¶] I (J)

21.36   steamboats (MS) • steam | boats (J)

21.37   Manayunk (MS) • Wamoyunk (J)

21.37   Geo. (MS) • George (J)

22.1   Wissahickon (MS) • Wassahickon (J)

22.1   in (MS) • to (J)

22.2   trip,—as (MS) • ~,∧~ (J)

22.4   up—of (MS) • ~, ~ (J)

22.5   rock, (MS) • ~; (J)

22.6   say (MS) • ~, (J)

22.6   nice (MS) • [*not in*] (J)

22.9   [*no* ¶] Well (MS) • [¶] Well (J)

22.10   respectable-sized (MS) • respectably-sized (J)

22.10   [looks] • [*not in*] (MS); ∧is∧ (MS—OC); looks (J)

22.11   *nothing* (MS) • nothing (J)

22.11   either:—for (MS) • ~∧—~ (J)

22.13   5 or six (MS) • five or six (J)

22.14   (distributin) (MS) • (distributing) (J)

22.15   [*no* ¶] Passing (MS) • [¶] Passing (J)

22.16   "House of Refuge," (MS) • ∧~ ~ ~,∧ (J)

22.16   of which . . . at (MS) • which . . . about at (J)

22.17   School),—then (MS) • ~;)∧∧~ (J)

22.18   'bus, (MS) • ~∧ (J)

22.20–23.4 There . . . Sam (MS) • [*not in*] (J)

22.27   and (MS) • and̸ (MS—OC)

22.29   hands (MS) • hands̸ (MS—OC)

23.6–24.8   Philadelphia . . . S. C. (J) • [*not in*] (MS)
24.9–11   Please . . . Sam (MS) • [*not in*] (J)

■ **28 November 1853 · To Orion Clemens · Philadelphia, Pa. · *UCCL* 00003**

■ *Copy-text:* MS, Jean Webster McKinney Family Papers, Vassar College Library (NPV). The MS, a single leaf inscribed on both sides, has been damaged by moisture along the bottom edge, where a piece has also been torn out, affecting four words, which are emended at 29.2 and 29.3. The MS leaf was probably already torn in 1912: the passage damaged in the MS is among those omitted from both *MTB* and *MTL*. In *MTBus*, S. C. Webster coped with the MS damage by quoting only part of a sentence, beginning with the word that immediately follows the gap caused by the tear: '. . . take Ma . . . too.' (29.3–4). The faded ink is somewhat more legible in the original than in the illustration of the bottom of the first page, reproduced here at 51 percent of actual size.

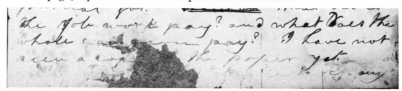

■ *Previous publication: MTB*, 1:101, excerpts; *MTL*, 1:29, with omissions; *MTBus*, 18, 28, brief excerpts. ■ *Provenance:* see McKinney Family Papers, pp. 459–61. ■ *Emendations and textual notes:*

28.3   to-day • to-|day
28.12   were • [*sic*]
28.12   foreighner • [*sic*]
28.12–13   every o̶t̶ φ̶ American • ~ ~ ~| ~ [*Possible miswritten* 'ot' *followed by a partly formed character, possibly* 'o' *or* 'a'. *Clemens implicitly deleted* 'ot' *by beginning the partly formed character; he explicitly deleted both together, apparently when he ran out of space at the end of the line.*]
29.1   t̶h̶ does • ['d' *over* 'th']
29.2   copy of • cop[y ◊f] [*torn*]
29.3   I intend to take • I [in◊◊◊◊ to] take [*torn*]
29.3   anyhow • any[◊]|how [*water-stained*]
29.6   this • th/is ['i' *over* 's']
29.11   uprightness/; • [*semicolon over period*]
29.12   b̶e̶l̶o̶w̶ before • belowfore ['fore' *over* 'low']
29.16   "free-soil? I • "~?—|~
29.17   negro." • [*sic*]

■ 4 December 1853 · To the Muscatine *Journal* · Philadelphia, Pa. ·
UCCL 00004

■ *Copy-text:* "*Original*. Correspondence," Muscatine *Journal*, 16 Dec 53, 1, in the
P. M. Musser Public Library, Muscatine, Iowa (IaMu), and the Historical Library, The State Historical Society of Iowa, Des Moines. ■ *Previous publication:*
Branch 1942, 12–14. ■ *Provenance:* The Musser Public Library file of the Muscatine *Journal* may be the one kept by the publisher. ■ *Emendations and textual notes:*

30.14	design • d[e]sign
30.16	Delaware • Delware
30.19	street. • ~,
30.26	stranger • stanger
31.11	evening, • ~[,]

■ 5 December 1853 · To Pamela A. Moffett · Philadelphia, Pa. · *UCCL*
00005

■ *Copy-text:* MS, Jean Webster McKinney Family Papers, Vassar College Library
(NPV). A piece torn out of the top edge of the leaf affects words on both sides,
which are emended at 33.1, 33.2, and 33.14. The illustrations show the damaged

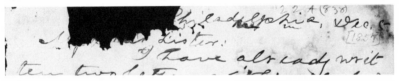

text in the first lines on the recto and verso of the leaf, reproduced at 53 percent
of actual size. ■ *Previous publication: MTB*, 1:101, excerpts; *MTL*, 1:30. ■ *Provenance:* see McKinney Family Papers, pp. 459–61. In about 1880, Orion Clemens incorporated this letter MS in the draft of his autobiography then in progress;
his page numbers appear in purple ink atop each page. ■ *Emendations and textual notes:*

33.1	Philadelphia • [P]hiladelphia [*torn*]
33.2	My Dear • M[y De]ar [*torn*]
33.7	is • is is
33.9	and know • [*sic*]
33.11	interesting [letter] to • interesting | to

33.13   places in • places [i]n [*torn*]
33.14   wanted to spend • wante[◊ ◊◊ ◊◊◊n]d [*torn*]
33.14   warm climate; • warm [cl◊mat◊]; [*torn*]
33.15   ~~wh~~ weather • w|heather ['e' *over partly formed* 'h']

■ 24 December 1853 · To the Muscatine *Journal* · Philadelphia, Pa. ·
UCCL 00006

■ *Copy-text:* "Correspondence," Muscatine *Journal*, 6 Jan 54, 1, in the P. M.
Musser Public Library, Muscatine, Iowa (IaMu), and the Historical Library,
The State Historical Society of Iowa, Des Moines. ■ *Previous publication:* Branch
1942, 15–17. ■ *Provenance:* The Musser Public Library file of the Muscatine *Journal* may be the one kept by the publisher. ■ *Emendations and textual notes:*

34.1–2   1853. [¶] The • 1853. | *The Weather—Fire and Loss of Life—*
          Christmas Preparations—"Chew's House"—Lydia Darrah's House
          —The Old "Slate Roof House"—"Carpenter's Hall," &c. [¶] The
          [*Although these subheadings were printed between the dateline and the*
          text, they were almost certainly Orion Clemens's (or his partner's) ad-
          dition. Similar headings were added to 26–?28 Oct 53 to OC and
          HC.]
34.6   building • huilding
34.19   selling • selli[n]g
35.11   John Penn • John P[e]nn
35.19   Churchyard • Church-|yard
35.25   should • s[h]ould
35.33   their • [*sic*]
35.35   upon • npon
35.35   time-honored • time-honord

■ 3 February 1854 · To the Muscatine *Journal* · Philadelphia, Pa. ·
UCCL 09400

■ *Copy-text:* "From Philadelphia. Correspondence of the Journal," Muscatine
Journal (weekly), 17 Feb 54, 1, in the Historical Library, The State Historical Society of Iowa, Des Moines. ■ *Previous publication:* Branch 1984, 2. ■ *Provenance:*
unknown. ■ *Emendations and textual notes:*

37.25   thirty-three • thi[r]ty-three
37.25–26 England • [E]ngland
37.30   "death" • "~["]
38.1   dry • d[r]y
38.2   brother • b[◊]other

38.2	before · b[e]fore
38.5	What · W[◇]at
38.5	you · yo[u]
38.7	it, · ~[,]
38.9	curiosity. · ~[.]

■ 17 and 18 February 1854 · To the Muscatine *Journal* · Washington, D.C. · *UCCL* 00007

■ *Copy-text:* "For the Journal. Washington Correspondence," Muscatine *Journal* (weekly), 24 Mar 54, 1, in the P. M. Musser Public Library, Muscatine, Iowa (IaMu), and the Historical Library, The State Historical Society of Iowa, Des Moines. ■ *Previous publication:* Branch 1942, 18–22. ■ *Provenance:* The Musser Public Library file of the Muscatine *Journal* may be the one kept by the publisher. ■ *Emendations and textual notes:*

40.8	thought · tho[u]ght
40.18	indeed · inde[e]d
40.25	somewhere · s[◇]mewhere
40.28	nineteen · ninet[e]en
40.31	dish-rag · dish-|rag
41.6–7	described · deecribed
41.13	Pocahontus · [*sic*]
41.21	Senators · S[e]nators
41.22	have · have
41.23–24	Douglass · D[o]uglass
41.24	Seward · Sewa[r]d
41.36	Church of · Church-| of
42.1	also · a[l]so
42.6	States. The · ~.—|~
42.7	building · buildings
42.11	hair was · hair wes
42.13	impossible · imposs[i]ble
42.16	ago · a[g]o
42.16	notice. The · ~.—|~
42.34	feet · foet
42.34	appropriate · appro-|priate
42.35–36	it in · it | n
43.1	of · [*not in*]

■ 16 February 1855 · To the Editors of the Muscatine *Tri-Weekly Journal*
(Orion Clemens and Charles E. H. Wilson) · St. Louis, Mo. · *UCCL*
00008

■ *Copy-text:* PH, "Correspondence of the 'Journal'," Muscatine *Tri-Weekly Journal*, 28 Feb 55, 2, in the P. M. Musser Public Library, Muscatine, Iowa (IaMu). Although the microfilm was made from the file of the *Journal* in the Musser Public Library, the original of this issue could not be located to provide the copy-text for this edition. ■ *Previous publication:* Branch 1942, 23–25. ■ *Provenance:* The Musser Public Library file of the Muscatine *Journal* may be the one kept by the publisher. ■ *Emendations and textual notes:*

47.4	yesterday, from · ~[◊] | ~
47.19	started · strated
47.24–25	perished, among · perished,among
47.25–26	horse, valued · horse [,]valued
47.29	horses · horscs
47.34	wanted. Late · ~.—|~
48.1	shoulders. The · ~.—|~
48.3	kind · ki[n]d
48.17	wasn't · was'nt
48.21	soon · so[o]n

■ 24–26 February 1855 · To the Muscatine *Tri-Weekly Journal* · St.
Louis, Mo. · *UCCL* 09994

■ *Copy-text:* "Correspondence of the 'Journal'," Muscatine *Tri-Weekly Journal*, 9 Mar 55, 1, in the Historical Library, The State Historical Society of Iowa, Des Moines. ■ *Previous publication:* Branch 1984, 4–5. ■ *Provenance:* unknown. The file of the Muscatine *Journal* in the P. M. Musser Public Library, Muscatine, Iowa (IaMu), presumably the one kept by the publisher, does not include this issue. ■ *Emendations and textual notes:*

50.3	overhauled · over-|hauled
50.4	case · casc
50.11	Berthoud · Bea-|thoud
50.12	gentlemen · gentlem[e]n
50.13	will · wil
50.13	Louis · L[o]uis
50.19	side walk · side wall
50.19	Main · Main Main
50.21	feet, · ~⌄
50.26	posse · pesse

51.3–4	enchantingly • enchnntingly
51.5	carried • carriɛd
51.5	finished, in • ~. ~
51.6–7	foot-|steps • footsteps
51.7	Banvard • Bauvard
51.10	Court • Cour[t]
51.18	Highly • Htghly
51.22	children • chidren
51.24	Apaches • Apachas
51.36–37	quarters • quartsrs
52.10–11	do, $5 50 • ~∧ $~, ~
51.11	at • a[t]
52.14	pound • pouud

■ 1 March 1855 · To the Muscatine *Tri-Weekly Journal* · St. Louis, Mo. · *UCCL* 09995

■*Copy-text:* "Correspondence of the 'Journal'. Special Correspondence. *Murder—Deputy Marshal of St. Louis Killed by Bob O'Blennis!*" Muscatine *Tri-Weekly Journal*, 12 Mar 55, 2, in the Historical Library, The State Historical Society of Iowa, Des Moines. ■*Previous publication:* Branch 1984, 6. ■*Provenance:* unknown. The file of the *Journal* in the P. M. Musser Public Library, Muscatine, Iowa (IaMu), presumably the one kept by the publisher, does not include this issue. ■*Emendations and textual notes:*

54.9–10	it." Brand • ~."—|~
54.14	bone. Brand • ~.—|~
54.15	frantic. Mr. • ~.—|~
54.21	outlaw • out-|law
54.26	s. l. c. • s. c. l.

■ 5 March 1855 · To the Muscatine *Tri-Weekly Journal* · St. Louis, Mo. · *UCCL* 00009

■*Copy-text:* "Correspondence of the 'Journal'," Muscatine *Tri-Weekly Journal*, 14 Mar 55, 2, in the P. M. Musser Public Library, Muscatine, Iowa (IaMu), and the Historical Library, The State Historical Society of Iowa, Des Moines. ■*Previous publication:* Branch 1942, 26–27. ■*Provenance:* The Musser Public Library file of the Muscatine *Journal* may be the one kept by the publisher. ■*Emendations and textual notes:*

55.3	out. Yesterday • ~.—|~
55.4	season. March • ~.—|~

55.5	lion." The • ~."—|~
55.19–56.1	terminate • terminato
56.4	hanging, people • hanging,people
56.6	cemetery • cemetry
56.11	Jamieson • Jameison
56.11	tragedian • trag[e]dian
56.19	to-day. Hyde • ~.—|~
56.23	$5 50. Flour • $~ ~.—|~
56.26	lbs. Potatoes • ~.—|~

■ 21 and 25 May 1856 · To Ann E. Taylor · Keokuk, Iowa · *UCCL* 00010

■*Copy-text:* "Letters Young Mark Twain Wrote in 1857," Kansas City (Mo.) *Kansas City Star Magazine,* 21 Mar 1926, 4, in Jean Webster McKinney Family Papers, Vassar College Library (NPV). The article printed this letter and the letter of 1 June 57. ■*Previous publication:* "Personal Glimpses: Sam Clemens in 'Sideburns' to 'Dear Friend Annie,' " *Literary Digest* 89 (8 May 1926): 38 and 42; Lorch 1929a, 422–25; and Brashear, 167–69. ■*Provenance:* see McKinney Family Papers, pp. 459–61. According to the *Star Magazine* article, this letter was one of five Clemens wrote to Ann E. Taylor which were found by Mrs. Catherine Blackwell among the papers of her brother, Judge C. A. Cunningham of Carrollton, Mo., after his death in 1920. Cunningham was married to Ann E. Taylor, who died in 1916. In fact there were probably no more than four letters: what Mrs. Blackwell took to be a fifth letter must have been the now missing portion of this one. That part and two additional letters—perhaps the letters Clemens wrote from Cincinnati which he mentions in 1 June 57 to Taylor (pp. 71–72)— disappeared after Mrs. Blackwell sent them to cousins living in the state of Washington (*Star Magazine,* 3). None of the four (or five) MSS has been found. ■*Emendations and textual notes:* Comparison of the *Star Magazine* printing of the 1 June 57 letter with the MS facsimiles of parts of it shows that the newspaper styled dateline and signature. Emendations at 59.4 and 62.5 reverse the same typographic styling apparently imposed by the *Star Magazine* on this letter.

| 59.2–4 | of . . . "Royal George" . . . requiem. • "of . . . 'Royal George' . . . requiem." [*Printed in the body of the* Kansas City Star Magazine *article with the introduction:* "The last three lines of one of the letters sent to Washington ran over to the first page of one of the remaining letters. Apparently 'Sam' was adding a few pages to one long letter every day or two. These three lines read:". *Although the article only implies that this passage belongs to this letter, the facsimile of the first MS page of 1 June 57 to Taylor (the only other possibility) shows clearly that the passage is not part of that one. These words must* |

have been written at the head of the lost MS page above the 25 May dateline of the present letter.]

59.5   Sunday, May 25. • ~, | ~ ~. [*A runaround at this point in the* Star Magazine *made the type column too narrow to accommodate the dateline all on one line, but the narrow column was probably not the only reason it was printed in two lines. The* Star Magazine *also printed the dateline of 1 June 57 to Taylor in two lines, even though at that point in the article the type column was amply wide enough to print the dateline on one line as Clemens wrote it. Since Clemens can be seen to have written short datelines all on one line in all letters of this period for which MS or facsimile survives, he probably did so in this instance as well, and we have emended to restore the likely reading of the original.*]

61.16–17   Detch-|man • *Detch*-man

61.26   Mane • Marie [*The* Star Magazine's *misspelling, not surprising in view of the oddity of the nickname 'Mane' and its resemblance in Clemens's hand to 'Marie', has been corrected on the basis of two instances of Clemens's spelling (at 72.11 and 73.30) that appear in the MS facsimiles of 1 June 57 to Taylor, and with the confirmation of the nickname and its spelling from family tradition provided by Gladys Hill.*]

61.35   Mane • Marie [*See previous entry.*]

62.5   Sam. • SAM. [*Although Clemens used double underscores to signify small capitals when marking MS for a printer, he seldom drew them under the signatures of personal letters. The MS facsimile of the end of 1 June 57 to Taylor shows that he did not do so in that case, but the* Star Magazine *styled that signature in capitals and small capitals when printing it. It is highly probable that Clemens also wrote this signature in the normal way and that the small capitals are the result of styling by the* Star Magazine, *which is here emended.*]

■ 10 June 1856 · To Jane Lampton Clemens and Pamela A. Moffett · Keokuk, Iowa · *UCCL* 00011

■ *Copy-text:* MS, Jean Webster McKinney Family Papers, Vassar College Library (NPV). ■*Previous publication: MTB,* 1:108–9, excerpt; *MTL,* 1:32–33, with omissions. ■*Provenance:* see McKinney Family Papers, pp. 459–61. ■*Emendations and textual notes:*

63.1   THE • 52. | THE

63.13   and manage • and̶m̶a̶ manage [*false start 'ama' corrected:* 'm' *mended to* 'n' *by* 'd' *written over third arch of* 'm' *and partly formed* 'a']

63.15   d̶o̶ did • dø̶id ['i' *over* 'o']

63.15   would the • [*Clemens inadvertently left out a word following* 'would', *possibly* 'make', 'see', *or* 'have'. *In MTL Paine emended to* 'would have the'. *The sentence is not part of the excerpt in MTB.*]

63.15   book hands • bo̶k̶ok hands ['o' *over* 'k']

63.16   drop. • [*A word may be missing. For example, Clemens could have
            meant to write* 'drop them.' *In* MTL *Paine emended to* 'drop it.'
            which seems less likely. The sentence is not part of the excerpt in
            MTB.]
63.19   t̶w̶ five • ['fi' *over* 'tw']
63.25   just • [*possibly* 'j̸' just'; 'j' *over* 'y']
63.29   ran • [*sic*]

■ 5 August 1856 · To Henry Clemens · Keokuk, Iowa · *UCCL* 00012

■*Copy-text:* MS, Jean Webster McKinney Family Papers, Vassar College Library
(NPV). ■*Previous publication: MTB*, 1:110, brief excerpts and paraphrase;
MTL, 1:34–35, with omissions; *MTBus*, 28–29, including only text not pub-
lished in *MTL*. ■*Provenance:* see McKinney Family Papers, pp. 459–61.
■*Emendations and textual notes:*

66.4   else,— • [*dash over period*]
66.7   n̶e̶v̶ knew • ['kn' *over* 'nev']
66.10   Orion. She • ~.—|~
66.13   a̶ ̶h̶ fifty • ['fif' *over* 'a h']
66.16   time. Though • ~.—|~
66.17   wishȩṣịng • ['es' *over* 'ing']
66.21   l̶u̶ "love • [' "l' *over* 'lu']
66.27   o̶v̶e̶r̶ with • ['with' *over* 'over']
66.30   Report, now. • ~. ~. [*deletion implied*]
66.31   to-night, at • ~. ~ [*deletion implied*]
66.36   b̶o̶ big • ['bi' *over* 'bo']
66.37   f̶o̶r̶ to • ʃto̸ ['t' *over* 'f']
66.37   s̶i̶n̶k̶ single • sinʲgle ['g' *over* 'k']
67.1   b̶e̶ I • ['I' *over* 'be']
67.1   w̸ allow • ['a' *over* 'w']

■ 1 June 1857 · To Ann E. Taylor · New Orleans, La. · *UCCL* 00013

■*Copy-text:* Transcript and two partial MS facsimiles in "Letters Young Mark
Twain Wrote in 1857," Kansas City (Mo.) *Kansas City Star Magazine*, 21 Mar
1926, 3 and 4–5, in Jean Webster McKinney Family Papers, Vassar College Library (NPV). The transcript is copy-text for 'P. S. . . . it.' (71.2–3) and for '—
and . . . spent' (72.13–73.25); the facsimile of the first MS page, reproduced below, is copy-text for 'New . . . reply' (71.4–72.13); and the facsimile of the lower
right corner of the last MS page is copy-text for 'half . . . Clemens.' (73.25–33).
This second facsimile, which shows only the ends of the last eleven lines of the

P. S.—I have just returned from another cemetery—brought away an orange leaf as a memorial—I inclose it.

1 June 1857 to Ann E. Taylor. Facsimile of the first MS page, the same size as it appeared in the *Kansas City Star Magazine*. Clemens's penciled postscript is just visible at the top of the page. The text of the postscript is printed above the facsimile for comparison.

MS, is reproduced here together with a version of the entire passage printed line for line as in the MS and marked to show the portions that are in the facsimile and those that are not. The MS probably consisted of a single folder inscribed on all four pages. Not counting the postscript, the text on the first MS page fills 35 lines of type in the *Star Magazine* printing, while the rest of the letter fills 119 lines, or about three times as much, making four MS pages in all. The facsimile of the corner of the last page shows that Clemens's inscription completely filled that page. In the facsimile of the first MS page, two leaves can be discerned, the edge of the second peeping out from behind the first. These must have been the two leaves of a folder, for had they been separate, the photographer would not have pinned the second leaf to the backing board behind the first when photographing the first page. In the same facsimile the laid paper can be seen to have separated along the fold as though it were relatively stiff, and both facsimiles suggest an opaque paper with little show-through. Therefore, although Clemens sometimes wrote only on the first and fourth pages of a folder when his paper was very thin, in this case he probably wrote on all four pages of one folder. The body of the letter was written in ink; the postscript was written at the top of the first page in pencil. In the facsimile its presence can be detected, but it is too faint to read (see entry below for 71.2–3). ■*Previous publication:* in addition to the copy-text, "Personal Glimpses: Sam Clemens in 'Sideburns' to 'Dear Friend Annie,'" *Literary Digest* 89 (8 May 1926): 38, 44; Lorch 1929a, 429–31; Brashear, 176–79. ■*Provenance:* see McKinney Family Papers, pp. 459–61, and note on provenance, 21 and 25 May 56 to Ann E. Taylor. ■*Emendations and textual notes:*

> [*Transcript is copy-text for* 'P. S. . . . it.' *(71.2–3)*]

71.2–3   P. S. . . . it. • [*Written in pencil at the top of the first MS page. In the facsimile, traces of the inscription can be made out. If one already knows from the printed text just what must be there, the shadowy words* '◊◊metery—brought away a◊ orange' *can just be discerned at the end of the line above the dateline and, more faintly, what is probably the ghost of* 'I inclose' *to the left of the dateline, although* 'inclose' *is not clear enough to enable one to verify its spelling. If, however, the transcript were not available as a gloss of the inscription, no part of the postscript could with confidence be read in the facsimile; consequently the transcript is copy-text for this passage.*]

> [*MS facsimile is copy-text for* 'New . . . reply' *(71.4–72.13)*]

71.6   being • [◊]eing [*blotted; the transcript reads* 'being']
72.4   beside • [*sic*]

> [*Transcript is copy-text for* '—and . . . spent' *(72.13–73.25)*]

72.14   Mane • Marie [*The* Star Magazine's *misspelling, not surprising in view of the oddity of the nickname* 'Mane' *and its resemblance in Clemens's hand to* 'Marie', *has been corrected on the basis of two instances of Clemens's spelling (at 72.11 and 73.30) that appear in the MS facsimiles (see illustrations), and the confirmation of the name and its spelling from family tradition provided by Gladys Hill.*]

dead *seven years*. I spent half an hour watching
the chameleons—strange animals, to change
their clothes so often! I found a dingy looking
one, drove him on a black rag, and he turned
black as ink—drove him under a fresh leaf,
and he turned the brightest green color you ever saw.
   I wish you would write to me at St.
Louis (I'll be there next week) for I don't believe
you have forgotten how, yet. Tell Mane and Ete
"howdy" for me.   Your old friend
                              Sam. L. Clemens.

1 June 1857 to Ann E. Taylor. Facsimile of the lower right corner of the last MS page, the
same size as it was printed in the *Kansas City Star Magazine*. The entire passage is printed
line for line below the facsimile. The box superimposed on the right side of the printed version encloses the text included in the facsimile. The beginnings of the MS lines, which do
not appear in the facsimile, are outside the box on the left. The choice of 'dead' to begin the
first line of the passage is conjectural. The line down the center of the printed version representing the straight left edge of the facsimile is distorted because the regularity of type
does not reflect the variability of handwriting.

73.9   graveyard • grave-|yard
                [*MS facsimile is copy-text for* 'half . . . Clemens.' (73.25–33)]
73.25   watching . . . strange (Transcript) • watching | [*not in*] ange
73.26   change . . . I (Transcript) • change | [*not in*] I
73.26–27   looking . . . black (Transcript) • looking | [*not in*] lack
73.27   turned . . . him (Transcript) • turned | [*not in*] [i]m
73.28   leaf, . . . brightest (Transcript) • leaf, | [*not in*] [t◇]st
73.28–29   saw. [¶] I . . . would • saw. | [*not in*] [u]ld [*The transcript reads*
                'saw. [*no* ¶] I . . . would'. *As transcribed, the MS line* 'I wish you
                would write to me at St.' (73.29) *contains markedly less text than the
                other lines partially visible in the MS facsimile, although it ends as
                close to the right edge of the leaf as they do. Differences in word spacing
                in the several lines are not great enough to account for the differences in
                line length. The beginning of the line (which is outside the area of the
                MS facsimile) must have contained something that does not appear in
                the transcript—possibly a word inadvertently omitted during transcrip-
                tion, a MS cancellation, or a word illegible to the transcriber. It is at
                least equally probable, however, and a simpler conjecture, that the line
                was indented as a paragraph, although the* Star Magazine *does not so
                indent it. We have emended to reflect the probable MS paragraph in-
                dentation.*]
73.29   St. . . . next week) (Transcript) • St. | [*not in*] week) [*The tran-
                script includes a comma after* 'week'.]
73.30   believe . . . how, yet (Transcript) • believe | [*not in*] [w], yet
73.30–32   ͺTell . . . Ete "howdy" for me.ͺ Your old (Transcript) • ͺTell . . .
                Eteͺ | [*not in*] old (MS facsimile) [*The partial MS facsimile shows
                that* 'Tell . . . Ete' *was inserted in the available space above the sig-
                nature; the remainder of the sentence, outside the area of the facsimile,
                must have been inserted as well and has been so marked.*]

■ 9 March 1858 · To Orion and Mary E. (Mollie) Clemens · St. Louis,
Mo. · *UCCL* 00014

■ *Copy-text:* MS, Jean Webster McKinney Family Papers, Vassar College Library
(NPV). ■*Previous publication: MTB*, 1:133–34, excerpts; *MTL*, 1:36–38.
■*Provenance:* see McKinney Family Papers, pp. 459–61. About 1880 Orion
Clemens marked the MS for inclusion in the autobiography he was then writing.
■*Emendations and textual notes:* Clemens wrote the letter in pencil; unfortunately
Orion also wrote on the MS in pencil. Orion's hand here can usually be readily
distinguished, but positive identification sometimes becomes difficult in very
short additions like those discussed below at 76.13, 77.17, and 77.34.

76.13   5̶0̶ 20 • ['20' *over* '50'. *The handwriting of the correction could be
                that of either brother, but only Samuel Clemens would have had reason
                and the knowledge to change the sense of the passage in this way.*]

76.18	ƀ Brown	• [‘B’ *over* ‘b’]
76.23	ₐ island	• [‘i’ *over* ‘a’]
77.6	sleeting	• sleḟeting [*second* ‘e’ *over* ‘t’]
77.14	yawl	• yaⱡwl [‘w’ *over* ‘l’]

77.17 ¶ • [*Possibly inserted by Orion, but probably by Samuel Clemens, who usually wrote the paragraph sign so that it resembled a large, bold* P, *as this one does.*]

77.17 ∅ • [*possibly miswritten* ‘2’ *or* ‘3’]

77.20 woodpiles • [*possibly* ‘wood piles’]

77.30–31 hope will • [*sic*]

77.34 had had • had | had [*Clemens may have intended either* ‘have had’ *or simply* ‘had’*;* ‘ve’ *was inserted over* ‘d’ *of first* ‘had’, *almost certainly by Orion Clemens.*]

■ 15 June 1858 · To William A. Moffett *per* Telegraph Operator · Memphis, Tenn. · *UCCL* 00015

■ *Copy-text:* MS telegram blank filled out in the hand of a telegraph operator and presumably received by William Moffett, Moffett Collection, Mark Twain Papers, The Bancroft Library, University of California, Berkeley (CU-MARK). ■ *Previous publication:* none known. ■ *Provenance:* see Moffett Collection, p. 462. ■ *Emendations and textual notes:*

80.10 5 ẇ a .50 & 110 Col • [‘a’ *over* ‘w’]

■ 18 June 1858 · To Mary E. (Mollie) Clemens · Memphis, Tenn. · *UCCL* 00016

■ *Copy-text:* MS, Moffett Collection, Mark Twain Papers, The Bancroft Library, University of California, Berkeley (CU-MARK). A photographic facsimile of the MS is on pp. 421–23. The MS consists of a folder of blue-lined off-white laid paper, 7¾ by 9¾ inches (19.6 by 24.9 cm), inscribed on the first three pages in a black ink, now faded to brown. ■ *Previous publication: MTB*, 1:141–42, with omissions; *MTL*, 1:39–41. ■ *Provenance:* see Moffett Collection, p. 462. ■ *Emendations and textual notes:*

81.1	me,—	• [*dash over period*]
81.10	dust,—	• [*dash over period*]
81.13	beg because	• beǥcause [‘c’ *over possible* ‘g’]
81.14	My	• [*sic; MTL reads* ‘May’]
81.16	they	• [*sic;* ‘y’ *canceled in pencil, probably not by Clemens*]
81.16	was way	• wayṣ [‘y’ *over* ‘s’]

81.20   B̶r̶o̶ and • ['and' *over* 'Bro']
81.37   M̶ he • ['he' *over partly formed* 'M']
82.4   s̶t̶ sat • s̶l̶at ['a' *over* 't']
82.6   ϕ man • ['m' *over* 'o']

■ 21 June 1858 · To William A. Moffett *per* Telegraph Operator · Memphis, Tenn. · *UCCL* 00017

■ *Copy-text:* MS telegram blank filled out in the hand of a telegraph operator and presumably received by William Moffett; Moffett Collection, Mark Twain Papers, The Bancroft Library, University of California, Berkeley (CU-MARK). ■ *Previous publication:* none known. ■ *Provenance:* see Moffett Collection, p. 462. ■ *Emendations and textual notes:*

85.2   LINES. • [*Below the company name on the telegram blank is printed:* 'TERMS AND CONDITIONS ON WHICH MESSAGES ARE RECEIVED BY THIS COMPANY FOR TRANSMISSION. The public are notified, that, in order to guard against mistakes in the transmission of messages, every message of importance ought to be repeated, by being sent back from the station at which it is to be received to the station from which it is originally sent. Half the usual price for transmission will be charged for repeating the message. This company will not be responsible for mistakes or delays in the transmission or delivery of unrepeated messages, from whatever cause they may arise; nor will it be responsible for damages arising from mistakes or delays in the transmission or delivery of a repeated message, beyond an amount exceeding two hundred times the amount paid for sending the message; nor will it be responsible for delays arising from interruptions in the working of its Telegraphs, nor for any mistake or omission of any other Company over whose lines a message is to be sent to reach the place of destination. All messages will hereafter be received by this Company for transmission, subject to the above conditions.']

85.5   Moffitt • [*sic*]

■ 9 and 11 March 1859 · To Pamela A. Moffett · New Orleans, La. · *UCCL* 00019

■ *Copy-text:* MS, Moffett Collection, Mark Twain Papers, The Bancroft Library, University of California, Berkeley (CU-MARK). ■ *Previous publication:* Fender, 738–39 (excerpt). ■ *Provenance:* see Moffett Collection, p. 462. ■ *Emendations and textual notes:*

87.2	beginning • [*previous pages missing*] ‖ginning
88.11	~~rep~~ removed • rep̸moved ['m' *over partly formed* 'p']
88.12	~~loth~~ loath • lot~~h~~ath ['at' *over* 'th']
88.14	before,⸺ • [*dash inserted over comma*]
88.21	clowns,— • [*comma possibly inserted*]
88.24	stalwart̸d • ['t' *over* 'd']
88.25	ɼ splendidly • ['s' *over* 'r']
88.29–30	~~were~~ was • wer~~e~~as ['as' *over* 'ere']
88.30	Ɨ At • ['A' *over* 'I']
89.7	tip-toeing • tip-|toeing
89.9	~~come~~ get • ['get' *over* 'come']
89.9	now,⸺ • [*dash inserted over comma*]
89.9	far • ɼar ['f' *canceled inadvertently*]
89.10–11	~~seeming some a little sun~~ spreading • s[eem]ing s[◇◇◇] [◇] little ‖ sun spreading ['spr' *over possible* 'sun'; *other text canceled heavily*]
89.20	stripes • ['r' *and* 'i' *written as one character*]
89.22	queern̸ • ['r' *over* 'n']
89.32	followed • folɨ-|lowed [*hyphen over* 'l']
89.36	m̸May-tree • ['M' *over* 'm']
89.36–37	m̸May-|pole • m̸May-pole ['M' *over* 'm']
89.37	Ҡ a • ['a' *over* 'K']
90.2	&̸ again • ['a' *over* '&']
90.3	~~whole~~ long • ['long' *over* 'whole']
90.9	street, ˌyesterday.ˌ • ∼.ˌ∼.ˌ [*deletion implied*]
90.16	sorry • sa̸lorry ['or' *over* 'al']
90.22	*on*dersthand • *on*-|dersthand
90.26	acknowlege • [*sic*]

■ 6 July 1859 · To John T. Moore · Memphis, Tenn. · *UCCL* 02714

■*Copy-text:* PH, "A Mark Twain Letter," *Arkansaw Traveler* 3 (14 July 83): 4.
■*Previous publication:* Paine, 224, excerpt; *MTB*, 1:156, same excerpt. ■*Provenance:* Collation of the *Arkansaw Traveler* text with the excerpt published by Paine provides no evidence that the copy of this letter sent by Stephen E. Gillis to Paine in 1907 was anything other than a copy of the *Arkansaw Traveler* or a text derived from it (see pp. 92–93, n. 2); there is no indication that Paine or Gillis ever saw the MS. ■*Emendations and textual notes:*

91.9	flatboat • flat-|boat
92.12	luxurient • [*sic*]

■ 13? October 1859 · To Elizabeth W. Smith · St. Louis, Mo. · *UCCL* 00021

■ *Copy-text:* MS facsimile; MS in the collection of Robert Daley. ■ *Previous publication: MTL*, 1:44–45, misdated (see p. 94, n. 1), with omissions. ■ *Provenance:* Robert Daley provided CU-MARK with a photographic facsimile of the MS in August 1976. ■ *Emendations and textual notes:*

94.7   —very well are in the · —very [◇◇◇ll] are in the ['are in the' *over* '—very' *and possible* 'well']

94.10   myself—*I* · myself|[—]*I* [*dash obscured on photocopy by crease in MS; MTL reads* 'myself—*I*']

94.12   *I*— · [*dash over* 'I']

■ 27? June 1860 · To Orion Clemens · *City of Memphis* en route from Memphis, Tenn., to St. Louis, Mo. · *UCCL* 00018

■ *Copy-text: MTB*, 1:146, is copy-text for the first part of the letter, 'What . . . devil.' (96.2–97.5); MS, Jean Webster McKinney Family Papers, Vassar College Library (NPV) is copy-text for the remainder of the letter, 'self . . . in it.' (97.7–98.11). The relation of the two fragments is discussed in n. 1, p. 98. ■ *Previous publication: MTL*, 1:42–44, prints all the text of the MS except the sentence fragment with which the MS begins, but it does not include the passage for which *MTB* is copy-text. ■ *Provenance:* for the surviving MS, see McKinney Family Papers, pp. 459–61. The whereabouts of the MS for the rest of the letter is unknown; when marking the MS in 1880 for insertion in his autobiography, Orion Clemens noted that "the balance is lost." ■ *Emendations and textual notes:* Orion Clemens replaced 'I' with 'me' to tidy up the grammar at 97.11. Although his dark pencil can usually be distinguished from the lighter pencil in which the letter was written, some doubt remains about the capitalization of 'prosperity' (97.38) reported below.

            [MTB *is copy-text for* 'What . . . devil.' *(96.2–97.5)*]
96.2   energy? · energy? [he says]. [*The square brackets are in* MTB.]
            [MS *is copy-text for* 'self . . . in it.' *(97.7–98.11)*]
97.7   yourself · [*previous pages missing*] ‖self
97.9   meddlers*₁*, · [*comma over period*]
97.11   and any · any*d* ['y' *over* 'd']
97.12   came*₁*, · [*comma over period*]
97.15   con awakened · con-| awakened
97.16   that know · ['know' *over* 'that']
97.22   me her · ['her' *over* 'me']
97.24   *e* take · ['t' *over* 'e']
97.25   to that · t*h*hat ['h' *over* 'o']

97.26	somewhere. I • ~.—|~
97.38	ẇ vast • ['v' *over* 'w']
97.38	₱Prosperity • ['P' *over* 'p', *probably by Samuel, but possibly by Orion Clemens*]

■ 11 August 1860 · To Susan I. (Belle) Stotts · Cairo, Ill. · *UCCL* 00024

■ *Copy-text:* MS, Jean Webster McKinney Family Papers, Vassar College Library (NPV). ■ *Previous publication: MTBus*, 34–35, misdated 1857; someone, probably Paine, wrote '[1857]' in the top margin of the first MS page. ■ *Provenance:* see McKinney Family Papers, pp. 459–61. ■ *Emendations and textual notes:*

100.7–8	water-|melon • watermelon
100.17	It • ['t' *inserted in pencil. Clemens wrote the letter in pencil and probably corrected it himself, but the contrast between the block-letter form of the 't' and the cursive text around it raises the possibility that someone else, possibly Paine, made the change.*]
100.18	I̶f̶ *I'll* • *I͵'ll͵* f ['͵'ll͵' *over* 'f' *before underscore was written;* 'I f' *possibly* 'If']
100.25	h̶a̶ be • ['be' *over* 'ha']
100.30	bluff. ᐱSomebody • ~.—|ᐱ~
100.30	̲"̲A "Snag • "͵Snag͵Ⱥ ['S' *over possible* 'A']
100.32	me • [me] [*torn*]
100.34–35	Vicksburgh • [*sic*]

■ 29 September 1860 · To Orion Clemens · New Orleans, La. · *UCCL* 00025

■ *Copy-text:* MS, Jean Webster McKinney Family Papers, Vassar College Library (NPV). ■ *Previous publication: MTB*, 1:155, brief quotation; *MTL*, 1:48, with omission. ■ *Provenance:* see McKinney Family Papers, pp. 459–61. ■ *Emendations and textual notes:*

102.4	₃̸2 • ['2' *over* '3']
102.8	d̶i̶s̶a̶ dissipating • dis͛sipating [*second* 's' *over* 'a']

■ 21 November 1860 · To Orion Clemens and Family · St. Louis, Mo. · *UCCL* 00026

■ *Copy-text:* MS, Appert Collection, Mark Twain Papers, The Bancroft Library, University of California, Berkeley (CU-MARK). ■ *Previous publication:* Sotheby and Co., London, *Catalogue of Nineteenth Century and Modern First Editions, Presentation Copies, Autograph Letters and Literary Manuscripts*, sale of 5 and 6 July 1971, lot 682, brief excerpts. ■*Provenance:* see Appert Collection, p. 463. The letter was probably still in Orion's possession in about 1880, for he crossed out his wife's contemporary marginalia (see p. 106, n. 10) and pasted to the MS a note that suggests he intended to include the letter in the autobiography he was then writing: "My wife has penciled in the margin of this letter: 'Orion seems low-spirited again.'" The MS, however, does not bear any of the other markings, such as page numbers and directions for the printer, that letters intended for insertion in the autobiography usually contain, and Orion's additions may have been made at some other time. ■*Emendations and textual notes:*

103.6	nearly • n[◊]arly [*torn*]
103.10–11	to-|day • to-day
103.18	*Ł* Trip • ['T' *over* 'L']
103.20	40ᶜ • [*sic*]
104.12	~~ther~~ their • the*ŕ*ir ['i' *over* 'r']
104.19	~~the~~ simply • ['sim' *over* 'the']
104.34	No,—*M* no • [*dash over comma;* 'M' *partly formed*]
105.7	bivuac • [*sic*]

■ 26 December 1860 · To the Worshipful Master, Wardens, and Brethren of Polar Star Lodge No. 79 of the Ancient, Free, and Accepted Order of Masons, *per* John M. Leavenworth · St. Louis, Mo. · *UCCL* 10665

■*Copy-text:* MS facsimile in "Mark Twain the Mason," *Masonic Light* (Kansas City, Mo.: Masonic Light Publishing Co., February 1926), 9, in Iowa Masonic Library, Grand Lodge of Iowa, Cedar Rapids (IaCrM). ■*Previous publication:* Almost two years before publication of the MS facsimile in 1926, a transcript was published in Denslow, 56. ■*Provenance:* The location of the MS is unknown. ■*Emendations and textual notes:*

106.2	Bretheren • [*sic*]
106.6	voluntary • [*sic*]
107.9	Wannall • [*possibly* 'Waunall']

■ 6 February 1861 · To Orion and Mary E. (Mollie) Clemens · Cairo, Ill. · *UCCL* 00027

■*Copy-text:* MS, Jean Webster McKinney Family Papers, Vassar College Library (NPV). ■*Previous publication: MTB*, 1:157–59, with omissions; *MTL*,

1:48–51, with omissions; *MTBus*, 52–57. ▪*Provenance:* see McKinney Family Papers, pp. 459–61. About 1880 Orion marked the MS for inclusion in his autobiography. ▪*Emendations and textual notes:* Orion superimposed in pencil what he judged were necessary corrections or clarifications of his brother's handwriting, which was also in pencil. This circumstance makes it impossible always to discriminate certainly between what Orion superimposed and what Clemens originally wrote and may have corrected himself before sending the letter. Four especially difficult cases (reported below at 110.29, 110.33, 111.7, and 112.10–11) each concern either a correction that might have been made by Clemens but that is here assigned to Orion and therefore does not appear in the text, or a word or correction that is indubitably by Clemens but that has been obscured by Orion's overwriting and therefore appears in the text, or not, according to its degree of uncertainty.

107.10	A̸ Steamer •	['S' *over* 'A']
108.3	ø̸ to •	['t' *over* 'o']
108.5	~~in town~~ on business •	['on business' *over* 'in town']
108.7–8	~~remembered~~ happened •	['happened' *over* 'remembered']
108.11	enchantress∮'s •	[*apostrophe over* 'e']
108.12	whereabouts •	where-|abouts
108.12	~~ot~~ simpler •	['s' *over* 'ot']
108.12	language •	langauˌuage ['ua' *over* 'au']
108.29	y̸ have •	['h' *over* 'y']
108.31–32	constitution,ˌ; •	[*semicolon over comma*]
108.33	youˌr ~~are~~ strength •	['r' *in* 'your' *and* 'str' *in* 'strength' *over* 'are']
108.39–109.1	long-|lived •	long-lived
109.2	~~with~~ who •	['who' *over* 'with']
109.16	thousandˌgh •	['s' *over* 'gh']
109.19	yourself •	yourse∮lf ['l' *over* 'f']
109.20	~~wis~~ never •	['ne' *over* 'wis']
109.22	cheerful∮ness •	['n' *over second* 'l']
109.24	Y̸ Up •	['Y' *mended to* 'U']
109.29	~~had this ca~~ it was well •	['it was we' *over* 'had this ca']
109.33	y̸ in •	['i' *over* 'y']
109.38	~~im~~ will •	['wi' *over* 'im']
110.2	~~on~~ or •	orˌ∮ ['r' *over* 'n']
110.3	~~you will be~~ *a child will* •	['a child w' *over* 'you will be']
110.29	you[r] •	[*possibly* 'yourˌ'. *The needed* 'r' *squeezed in, probably by Orion.*]
110.33	*fond* •	[*Probable but not certain: two folds in the MS intersect, obscuring the text at this point, and Orion mistakenly wrote* 'proud' *heavily over the original word, further obscuring it.*]

111.7   instability • [*possibly* 'u̶n̶ instability', 'un̜in̜stability', *or*
             'un̜in̜stability'; 'in' *or* 'ins' *over possible* 'un' *or miswritten* 'in'. *Orion
             traced over* 'ins', *presumably because some such underlying change by
             Clemens made the letters unclear, but the overwriting has made the
             original inscription and its correction or repair too uncertain to include
             in the text.*]

112.10–11   (which . . . (like . . . characters,) . . . Another's? [)] • [*possibly*
             '(̸[~ . . . (~ . . . ~,) . . . ~?]'; *an opening square bracket written
             over the first opening parenthesis and a closing bracket added following
             the question mark. The form of the brackets and the dark, blunt pencil
             with which they were inscribed suggest that Orion, rather than his
             brother, probably supplied them.*]

112.15   p̸ have • ['h' *over* 'p']

112.19–20   ⌄several⌄ years • ⌄sever[al]⌄ years [*torn*]

112.29   Y̶ Votre • ['V' *over* 'Y']

112.34   V̶ Ton • ['T' *over* 'V']

112.34   b̸ F̸ • [*canceled* 'F' *or* 'T' *over doubtful* 'b' *or* 'le']

■ 18 March 1861 · To Orion Clemens · St. Louis, Mo. · *UCCL* 00022

■ *Copy-text: MTL*, 1:45–47, is copy-text for 'St. Louis . . . willing' (116.1–
118.2) and for 'at . . . cars.' (118.5–15); MS, Jean Webster McKinney Family Papers, Vassar College Library (NPV), is copy-text for 'for . . . aimed' (118.2–4)
and for 'Your . . . one !' (118.16–19). The surviving MS is a fragment cut from
the bottom of the last leaf, which, as the illustration shows, was inscribed on both
sides. Calculations based on a comparison of the partial MS text with the text
published in *MTL* indicate that the MS was probably originally four pages, presumably two leaves inscribed on both sides, and that the surviving fragment is
about one-fourth of the second leaf. The remainder of the MS is missing. ■ *Previous publication:* in addition to the copy-text, *MTB*, 1:155 and 156, and Paine,
224, excerpts. ■ *Provenance:* see McKinney Family Papers, pp. 459–61. Orion
traced over Clemens's faint complimentary close and signature in the purple ink
he used in 1880 when numbering the pages of many of his brother's letters for
inclusion in his own autobiography. Traces of the same ink below the cut edge of
the MS fragment where Orion made changes (discussed in the entry for 118.1–2)
indicate that the MS was physically intact at that time. The MS must also have
been intact when the transcript was made from which the *MTL* text derives,
since *MTL* includes text both from the portion of the MS now lost and from the
surviving fragment. It cannot now be determined, however, when the MS was cut
apart, or whether Paine made the transcript himself directly from the MS or relied on a transcript made by someone else. Even if he never saw the whole MS,
Paine probably had access to the surviving fragment, as he did to all the other
MSS that are now in the McKinney Family Papers, although he might not have
recognized it as part of this letter. ■ *Emendations and textual notes:* The rationale
for emendations to remove *MTL* styling is given on pp. 458–59. Since, so far as

is known, the MS has always remained in the family's possession, probably a family member was the one who cut it apart, but exactly who that person was, and why and when the MS was cut, remain unknown. Someone could have cut off the complimentary close and signature that were boldly inscribed in purple ink, to save them as a souvenir, but since a family member would probably have recognized that these were not written by Clemens, this seems unlikely. A stronger possibility is that someone cut away part of the text altogether, perhaps to suppress it. Support for this conjecture comes from calculations, based on the length of the lines in the MS fragment, of the amount of *MTL* text that must have been on each of the four MS pages, from which it appears that the fourth MS page contained as much as three fewer lines than each of the first three MS pages, and that therefore the text in *MTL* may silently omit not only the postscripts but up to three other lines, or about twenty words, as well. If this is what happened, the most likely point where such a cut might have been made seems to be following the now somewhat abrupt ending of the last paragraph (118.5). But if what looks like a shortfall in the calculated length of the fourth MS page was due to some other cause—the space could have been filled by the now missing top of Clemens's elaborate signature flourish, for example, or the calculations, based as they are on a small sample, may be in error for undetectable reasons—then the text as we have it may be complete, and the motivation of the person who cut the MS apart must be sought elsewhere. The recto and verso of the MS fragment are reproduced at 90 percent of actual size.

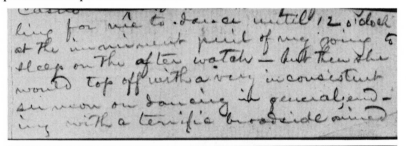

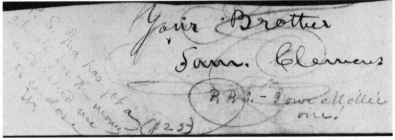

[MTL *is copy-text for* 'St. Louis . . . willing' *(116.1–118.2)*]

116.1   St. Louis, Mch 18. • Sᴛ. Lᴏᴜɪs, *Mch 18. 1860.* [*Since Clemens indubitably wrote the letter in 1861 (see p. 118, n. 1), he is unlikely to have dated it 1860; nor would his normally clear handwriting lend it-*

self to a misreading of 'ɪ' for 'o'. It is more likely that Clemens omitted the year, which Paine then supplied, erroneously, on the copy for MTL. The year has therefore been emended.]

116.2-3   My Dear Bro., [¶] Your • My dear Bro.,—[*no* ¶] Your

118.1-2   Castle and me. She was perfectly willing • Castle and myself. She was perfectly willing (MTL); Cas[tle ◇◇◇ ◇◇◇ S◇◇ was p◇◇f◇◇◇◇y ◇◇◇◇]||ling (MS) [*MS cut off; the bottom parts of a few letters are visible, as indicated here, but most are entirely lost (see illustration). The traces of Clemens's inscription surviving on the cut edge support or at least do not contradict the MTL readings 'Castle and' and 'She was perfectly willing'. Between 'and' and 'She', however, the evidence of the MS contradicts the MTL reading 'myself' and supports the conjectural reading 'me'. The only survivals from Clemens's inscription in this space are two small marks that are spaced wrong to have been part of 'myself' or 'self' and in any case are really too small to help much in determining what was written there. Two other marks, in the purple ink used by Orion Clemens, do appear at the edge of the leaf: a sublinear caret about halfway between 'Castle' and 'She', and the loop of a descender about halfway between the caret and 'She'. Paine presumably had some warrant in the MS for 'myself'; he may have been following Orion's revision. The descender loop shows that Orion wrote something over at least the end of the word originally written by his brother, while the caret shows that he inserted something approximately where the space would have fallen between 'and' and the next word. Orion could have written 'self' over the word Clemens had written and inserted 'my' before it, or he could have inserted 'myself' partly above the line and partly over Clemens's inscription. The most likely conjecture is that Clemens wrote 'me' and his brother, marking the MS for inclusion in his autobiography, amended the reading to the more hightoned 'myself'. The conjecture 'me' has been adopted in place of MTL's manifestly non-authorial 'myself'.*]

[*MS is copy-text for* 'for me . . . aimed' *(118.2–4)*]

[*MTL is copy-text for* 'at . . . cars.' *(118.5–15)*]

[*MS is copy-text for* 'Your . . . one!' *(118.16–19)*]

118.16-17 Your Brother | Sam. Clemens • Your [B]rother | Sam. Clemens ['*Sam.*' *possibly* '*Sam*'; '*Clemens*' *possibly* '*Clemens.*'. Orion traced over Clemens's inscription, which is extremely faint and is embellished by several flourishes so ornate they impair legibility.*]

■ 26 April 1861 · To Orion Clemens · *Hannibal City* en route from St. Louis to Hannibal, Mo. · *UCCL 00028*

■*Copy-text:* MS, Jean Webster McKinney Family Papers, Vassar College Library (NPV). ■*Previous publication: MTBus*, 61. ■*Provenance:* see McKinney Family Papers, pp. 459–61. The MS was in the possession of Orion Clemens at least as late as 1880, when he added a note to it (see p. 121, n. 3). ■*Emendations and textual notes:* none.

■ 12? September 1861 · To Mary E. (Mollie) Clemens · Carson City, Nev. Terr. · *UCCL* 02715

■ *Copy-text:* MS, Jean Webster McKinney Family Papers, Vassar College Library (NPV). Only the last leaf of the MS survives. As the illustration shows, a piece has been torn out of the leaf at the upper right corner, affecting seven lines; the missing text has been conjecturally supplied by emendation. Accompanying the MS facsimile is a type facsimile of the same lines with the emended readings in place. ■ *Previous publication:* none known. ■ *Provenance:* see McKinney Family Papers, pp. 459–61. ■ *Emendations and textual notes:*

> well, although I believe I never had the pleasure of
> her acquaintance,) and left for California the same
> day, and I told him plainly that I did not be-
> lieve it, and wouldn't, if he swore it—for I didn't,
> Mollie, and did think Billy could be as stupid
> as that. On the contrary, I thought he was the
> most talented boy that Keokuk had ever pro-
> duced. But when I got back, Orion confirmed

12? September 1861 to Mary E. (Mollie) Clemens. Facsimile of the top of the MS leaf reproduced at 76 percent of actual size. Jean Webster McKinney Family Papers, Vassar College Library (NPV). The type facsimile of the same lines, including the missing text supplied by emendation, is marked to show where the leaf was torn. Because the regularity of type only approximates the handwriting, the curve of the torn MS edge appears somewhat distorted in the type facsimile. To avoid unnecessary misalignment of the text, the type facsimile does not report the 'w' overwritten by 'swore' in the fourth line and shows the MS reading 'did' in the fifth line rather than the interpolated correction 'did[n't]' that appears in the text.

123.2   pleasure of her • ple[◇◇◇◇◇ ◇◇] | her [*torn*]

123.3   California the same day; • California [◇◇◇ ◇◇◇◇] | day; [*Although the available space would also permit* 'the next', *external evidence rules out* 'next' *and supports at least the sense of* 'the same'; *see p. 123, n. 1.*]

123.3–4   did not believe • did [n◇◇ ◇◇◇]|lieve [*torn*]

123.4   ẉ swore • ['s' *over* 'w']

123.4   for I didn't, Mollie • fo[◇ ◇ ◇◇◇◇◇◇◇] | Mollie [*torn*]

123.5   as stupid as • as [◇◇◇◇◇◇] | as [*torn*]

123.6	was the most • w[a◊ ◊◊◊]	most [*torn*]	
123.6	ever produced • ever [p◊◊◊]|duced [*torn*]	
123.8	~~ever~~ ˄were to˄ • ['were' *inserted over* 'ever' *and* 'to' *interlined*]	
123.8–9	~~should~~ would • ['would' *over* 'should']	

■ 18–21 September 1861 · To Jane Lampton Clemens · Carson City, Nev. Terr. · *UCCL* 00029

■ *Copy-text: MTL*, 1:56–59. ■ *Previous publication:* Paine, 228, and *MTB*, 1:178 and 180, brief excerpts. ■ *Provenance:* As early as 1917, Paine reported that the beginning of the letter was missing (*MTL*, 1:56). ■ *Emendations and textual notes:* The rationale for emendations to remove *MTL* styling is given on pp. 458–59. 'Bella' and 'Renson', emended at 125.37 and 126.11, respectively, are probably typographical errors in *MTL*. Clemens would not have made such mistakes, and Paine is scarcely more likely to have done so. Both names are correctly spelled elsewhere: 'Belle' in the last paragraph of this letter (126.13; *MTL*, 1:59), and 'Benson' in 25 Oct 61 to PAM and JLC (132.8; *MTL*, 1:62). The excerpts quoted in *MTB* and Paine do not include the passages in which the names were misspelled in *MTL*.

124.1–2	standard-|bearers • standard-bearers	
124.11	to-night • tonight	
124.12	he was • [*sic*]	
124.25	swears. But • ∼.—∼	
125.11	to. *I* • ∼.—∼	
125.11	the ——— thieving • the———thieving	
125.23	sundown • sun-|down	
125.34	happen. I • ∼.—∼	
125.35	tea-pot • tea-|pot	
125.37	Belle • Bella	
126.11	Benson • Renson	
126.19	Sam • SAM	

■ 18–30 September 1861 · From George Turner (*per* William M. Gillespie) and Samuel L. Clemens to Orion Clemens · Carson City, Nev. Terr. · *UCCL* 00033

■ *Copy-text:* MS, Moffett Collection, Mark Twain Papers, The Bancroft Library, University of California, Berkeley (CU-MARK). ■ *Previous publication:* none known. ■ *Provenance:* see Moffett Collection, p. 462. Clemens wrote this note on a handwritten form pasted in a scrapbook kept by Orion Clemens (see p. 129, n. 3). The paste caused the edge of the form to wrinkle. Slight variations in the weight of Clemens's pencil line inscribing '—I send' and 'the devil' (128.17 and 128.18) correspond to the wrinkles in the paper, indicating that the form was already pasted into the scrapbook when Clemens wrote his note. The leaf has never been folded and therefore can never have been mailed, in an ordinary envelope at any rate. No evidence survives to indicate when or why it was torn out of the scrapbook. ■ *Emendations and textual notes:* The shaded text is in the hand of William M. Gillespie, presumably at dictation from George Turner (see p. 128, n. 1).

128.8	~~sends~~ transmits	• ['trans-|' *over* 'sends']
128.8	~~for the concurr~~ herewith for the	• ['herewith for the' *over* 'for the concurr']
128.13	Respl'y	• [*sic*]

■ 25 October 1861 · To Pamela A. Moffett and Jane Lampton Clemens · Carson City, Nev. Terr. · *UCCL* 00030

■ *Copy-text:* MS, Jean Webster McKinney Family Papers, Vassar College Library (NPV). ■ *Previous publication: MTB*, 1:175–76 and 180–81, excerpts; *MTL*, 1:53–55 and 59–62, with omissions. ■ *Provenance:* see McKinney Family Papers, pp. 459–61. The MS was already incomplete by 1917, when Paine reported the "Remainder missing" (*MTL*, 1:55). Both *MTB* and *MTL* print the sections of the letter addressed respectively to Pamela Moffett and Jane Clemens (or excerpts from them) as though they were separate letters. *MTL* even begins the section to Jane Clemens with a substitute dateline: "(Date not given, but *Sept.* or *Oct., 1861*.)" Paine must have been working from transcripts which did not show that the last page of the section addressed to Pamela and the first page of the section addressed to Jane Clemens were written on the two sides of a single sheet of paper. Paine also did not know about the complete, revised version of the section to Jane Clemens, dated 26 October 1861, published in the Keokuk *Gate City* (pp. 136–39). ■ *Emendations and textual notes:*

129.11–12	~~two o~~ three	• ['three' *over* 'two o']
130.1	region. I	• ~.—|~
130.4	~~v~~ever	• ['e' *over* 'v']
130.13	~~m~~ feet	• ['f' *over doubtful* 'm']
130.16	them,	• [*comma over period*]
130.33	~~I~~ we	• ['w' *over* 'I']
130.35	~~money~~ month	• mont~~he~~y ['th' *over* 'ey']
131.11	~~loose~~ lose	• ['lose' *over* 'loose']
131.23	Perry	• [*doubtful; possibly* 'Percy']
131.25	first,—	• [*dash over period*]
131.30	where there's	• where there's ['e' *over* 's']

131.34   ₵ Certainly • ['C' *over* 'c']
132.9   l̶o̶ life • l∅ife ['i' *over* 'o']
132.23   m̶e̶a̶n̶ intend • ['intend' *over* 'mean']
132.24   ⫏ Lake • ['L' *over* 'l']
132.31   Chinamen • China-|men
132.31–32   {̶y̶ ki-|yo-ties • {̶y̶ ki-yo-ties [*parenthesis canceled and* 'k' *over* 'y']
132.32   c̶h̶i̶n̶ poets • ['poets' *over* 'chin']
132.33–34   s̶o̶ sun."—and • s∅un."—|—and ['u' *over* 'o'; *dittography emended*]
133.14   o̶f̶ in • ['in' *over* 'of']
133.20   a̶n̶ in • ['i' *over* 'an']
133.21   o̶f̶ again • ['ag' *over* 'of']
133.24–25   you ˌandˌ begin • you ˌ[a◇◇]ˌ begin [*torn*]
133.25–26   e̶x̶t̶e̶n̶ expanding • exˌpandingt̶e̶n̶ ['pan' *over* 'ten']
133.28–29   c̶a̶ Carson • ['C' *over* 'ca']
133.32   t̶h̶a̶n̶ that • thaṭ n̶ ['t' *over* 'n']
133.32   ƕ *run* • ['r' *over* 'h']
133.33   ∅ greatest • ['g' *over* 'p']
133.35   w̶i̶l̶ rural • ['r' *over possible* 'wil']
133.36   p̶r̶o̶m̶e̶ pass • ['pass' *over* 'prome']
133.36   s̶t̶r̶e̶e̶t̶s̶ dusty • ['dusty' *over* 'streets']
134.4   v̶e̶g̶i̶ vegetable • vegʲetable [*possibly* 'vegʲetable'; 'e' *over* 'i', *possibly inserted*]
134.8   s̶o̶w̶ sewed • sˌeweḓo̶w̶ ['ew' *over* 'ow']
134.9   Occasionallyly̶ • ['al' *over* 'ly']
134.11   ⫏ short • ['s' *over* 'j']

■ 26 October 1861 · To Jane Lampton Clemens · Carson City, Nev. Terr. · *UCCL* 00031

■ *Copy-text:* PH, "Nevada Correspondence," Keokuk *Gate City*, 20 Nov 61, 2. Newsprint of the *Gate City* is in the Iowa State Historical Department, Division of the State Historical Society, Iowa City (IaHi), and the Historical Library, The State Historical Society of Iowa, Des Moines. We have not been able to use the original newspaper as copy-text. ■ *Previous publication:* Lorch 1929a, 453–56; Rogers 1961, 22–26. ■ *Provenance:* unknown. ■ *Emendations and textual notes:* Clemens based this letter on the part of the previous one that was addressed to his mother (25 Oct 61 to PAM and JLC, pp. 132–34). Most of the substantive variants between the MS of that letter and the newspaper text of this one show that he deliberately revised the text, presumably in a separate MS, now lost, that served the *Gate City* as printer's copy. Typographical errors in the *Gate City*, identified by collation with the MS of the 25 Oct 61 letter wherever the two texts overlap, have been corrected; the unrevised MS of the 25 Oct 61 letter is cited as (MS 25 Oct) whenever the correction adopted is corroborated by it.

136.4	everything (MS 25 Oct) • every thing
136.5	alone. Very • ~.—|~
137.1	quartz (MS 25 Oct) • quarts
137.1	vicinity, • ~.
137.2	10 • Io
137.2	Territory • Territiory
137.3	marble, (MS 25 Oct) • ~∧
137.4	gypsum (MS 25 Oct) • gympsum
137.5	Christians (MS 25 Oct) • christians
137.16	through (MS 25 Oct) • thorugh
137.18	desert. When (MS 25 Oct) • ~.—|~
137.20–21	grease-|wood • grease-wood
137.23	and • aad
137.25	barring (MS 25 Oct) • bar-|ing
137.26	ain't (MS 25 Oct) • aint
138.7	very (MS 25 Oct) • verry
138.17	unplastered (MS 25 Oct) • un-|plastered
138.28	Christian • christian [*The* Gate City *printed* 'christians' *for MS* 'Christians' *at 137.5 and probably made the same change here, whether because of deliberate styling or simple misreading.*]
138.33	but (MS 25 Oct) • [b]ut
139.3	days. And • ~.—|~

■ 29 October 1861 · To Horatio G. Phillips · Carson City, Nev. Terr. · *UCCL* 00032

■ *Copy-text:* MS, Harry G. Ransom Humanities Research Center, University of Texas, Austin (TxU). ■ *Previous publication:* Sotheby and Co., London, *Catalogue of a Selected Portion of the Well-Known Library of the Late John Francis Neylan of San Francisco*, sale of 28 May 1962, lot 112, brief excerpts. ■ *Provenance:* see *Previous publication.* ■ *Emendations and textual notes:*

140.9	~~when~~ by the • ['by the' *over* 'when']
141.1	~~sell~~ sacrifice • ['sac' *over* 'sell']
141.1	a̸ feet • ['f' *over* 'a']
141.3	y̸ and • ['a' *over* 'y']
141.20	s̸Slander • ['S' *over* 's']

141.20   in whose presence against whom • ['against whom' *over* 'in whose presence']

141.21   Mali∱ce • ['c' *over* 'f']

■ 29, 30, and 31 January 1862 · From Orion and Samuel L. Clemens to Mary E. (Mollie) Clemens · Carson City, Nev. Terr. · *UCCL* 00035

■ *Copy-text:* MS, Mark Twain Papers, The Bancroft Library, University of California, Berkeley (CU-MARK). ■ *Previous publication:* none known. ■ *Provenance:* date of acquisition unknown. Probably in Moffett Collection; see p. 462. The MS was evidently in the possession of Orion Clemens as late as 1880, when he was preparing his autobiography. ■ *Emendations and textual notes:* On a sheet once pinned to the first page of the MS Orion wrote, "The following is from myself to my wife, with an addendum by Sam:". He canceled the clipping glued to the MS, which is therefore reproduced in type facsimile, and most of his own part of the letter, 'The Silver . . . 31—' (143.12–144.7) and 'It . . . woman.' (144.13–18).

144.7   ∤ that • ['t' *over* 'a']

144.14   better • ∤ better [*first* 'b' *written faintly with drying pen; deletion implied*]

144.25   ∉ he • ['h' *over* 'e']

144.25   insignificant • insi∉gnificant ['g' *over* 'c']

144.29   his he • he͜is ['e' *over* 'i']

144.33   Mine • [*Clemens gave this word and 'Mine' at 144.34 some unrecovered special significance by inscribing the 'M' of each in a peculiar block form, shown below at actual size. In each case, he may have written '_ine' before supplying the 'M'. His remark '(as I perceive by your language)' (144.31–32) suggests that the oddly formed letters were his response to something Mollie had written him, perhaps a pun.*]

144.33   was there • ['the' *over* 'was']

144.34   Mine • [*See the note at 144.33.*]

144.36   it was the cinch • ['the cin' *over* 'it was']

144.37   up one • ['one' *over* 'up']

144.38   ∤ great • ['g' *over* 'a']

145.5   ∱ board • ['b' *over* 'f']

145.8   Han He • He͜an ['e' *over* 'an']

145.13   Nye, says • ~ , | ~ [*sic*]

145.15   ∰ how • ['h' *over* 'w' *or possibly* 'm' *or* 'n']

145.20   ∤Being • ['B' *over* 'b']

145.26   Millenium • [*sic*]

145.29   such subject • su͜bject͜ch ['bj' *over* 'ch']

■ 30 January 1862 · To Jane Lampton Clemens · Carson City, Nev.
Terr. · *UCCL* 00034

■*Copy-text:* PH, "Model Letter from Nevada," Keokuk *Gate City*, 6 Mar 62, 4.
Newsprint of the *Gate City* is in the Iowa State Historical Department, Division
of the State Historical Society, Iowa City (IaHi), and the Historical Library, The
State Historical Society of Iowa, Des Moines. We have not been able to use the
original newspaper as copy-text. ■*Previous publication:* Paine, 419–20, and
MTB, 1:183–84, paraphrase and excerpts; Lorch 1938, 345–49; Rogers 1961,
29–34. ■*Provenance:* Paine cites the Keokuk *Gate City* as his source for the excerpts published in *MTB*; he evidently did not see the MS, which is not known
to survive. ■*Emendations and textual notes:* The name printed as 'Fillon' in the
Gate City has been emended in five places to the correct form 'Tillou'. Although
in this letter Clemens referred to Clagett and Oliver by first names only, he did
not conceal their identities, and it seems unlikely that he meant to conceal Tillou's identity either. More probably the *Gate City* compositor simply misread
Clemens's handwriting, in which 'T' and 'F' are easily mistaken for one another.

147.13	Tillou · Fillon	
147.17	*carminia* · [*sic*]	
148.12	Tillou's · Fillon's	
148.20	Tillou's · Fillon's	
148.24	wrenched · wer enched	
149.11	Ma.) And · ~.)—|~	
149.21	Tillou · Fillon	
149.26	Tillou · Fillon	
149.30	mien · mein	
150.10	fortunes · fortuncs	

■ 30 January–1 February 1862 · To William A. Moffett · Carson City,
Nev. Terr. · *UCCL* 00038

■*Copy-text:* MS, Jean Webster McKinney Family Papers, Vassar College Library (NPV). ■*Previous publication:* none known. ■*Provenance:* see McKinney
Family Papers, pp. 459–61. ■*Emendations and textual notes:*

153.5	i̶n̶ a · ['a' *over* 'in']
153.6	their · [*sic*]
153.12	Virginia, City · Virginia, City [*sic;* 'i' *over* 'a']
153.15	and is · an̶d̶i̶s̶ is ['d' *over possible* 'is'; *false start*]
153.15	railway · a̶n̶d̶ ̶i̶s̶ railway ['railw' *over* 'and is'; *probably a false start inadvertently echoing* 'and is' *(153.15) directly above in the previous MS line*]

153.16	~~its~~ throughout • ~~its~~ throughou~~t~~ʃ ['th' *over* 'its'; *terminal* 't' *over* 'g']
153.16	whole • who*s*le ['l' *over* 's']
153.16	~~who~~ which • wh*ø*ich ['i' *over* 'o']
153.22	*k* have • ['h' *over* 'k']
153.25	~~Sunday~~ Saturday • S̩atur~~unda~~y ['atur' *over* 'unda', *inadvertently covering too much*]
153.26	our • our̩*ɳ* ['r' *over doubtful* 'n']
153.28	~~told~~ took • took̩l̩d ['ok' *over* 'ld']
154.1	⁼("First • "⁅First ['F' *over possible opening parenthesis*]
154.7	~~at~~ per • ['per' *over* 'at']
154.12	rhumatic • [*sic*]
154.12	~~The~~ Some • ['So' *over* 'The']
154.14	⁁National • ⁁Nat*ø*ional ['N' *over opening quotation marks;* 'i' *over* 'o']

■ 8 and 9 February 1862 · To Jane Lampton Clemens and Pamela A. Moffett · Carson City, Nev. Terr. · *UCCL* 00036

■*Copy-text:* MS, Jean Webster McKinney Family Papers, Vassar College Library (NPV). ■*Previous publication: MTB*, 1:190–92, excerpts; *MTL*, 1:63–68, with omissions; *MTBus*, 64, 66, brief excerpts of text not published by Paine. ■*Provenance:* see McKinney Family Papers, pp. 459–61. ■*Emendations and textual notes:*

156.25	~~al~~ amount • a*m*mount ['m' *over* 'l']
156.38	~~ne~~ have • ['ha' *over* 'ne']
157.1	its • [*sic*]
157.3	*w* have • ['h' *over doubtful partly formed* 'w']
157.7	40-horse • 40-hor*ø*se ['s' *over* 'e']
157.9	*y* then • ['t' *over* 'y']
157.28	take, • take, | ~~take,~~
157.31	Jerusalem • Jeru*s*salem ['s' *over* 'l']
157.32	~~watch~~ send • ['send' *over* 'watch']
157.33	~~th~~ over • ['ov' *over* 'th']
157.38	~~man~~ ̩male̩ • male̩*ɳ* ['le' *over* 'n']
157.38	~~woman,~~ ̩female,̩ • ~~woman,~~ ̩female̩ ['female' *inserted over* 'woman'; *the comma retained*]
157.38–158.1	~~fe~~ ̩man or woman,̩ you • ~~fe-~~ ̩man or woman,̩ || you ['fe-' *canceled at end of page*]
158.4	*f* Folsom • ['F' *over* 'f']
158.8	want to • want~~to~~ t̩o ['t' *over* 'to'; *false start*]

158.8–9 water-|mill • water-mill
158.10 $~~25,000,~~ • ['25' *doubtful*]
158.11 location. What • ~.—|~
158.14 so much • ~~som~~ so much ['so m' *over* 'som'; *false start*]
158.17 $~~2~~ $4 • $4̸ ['4' *over* '2']
158.17 ta/king • ['l' *canceled*]
158.25 wood-chopper • wood-|chopper
158.34 ~~there~~ their • the͜irr͜e ['ir' *over* 're']
159.1 rich. $ Twenty • rich.—|$ Twenty ['T' *over* 'S']
159.3 ~~wort~~ for • ['for' *over* 'wort']
159.17 ɟ homesick • ɟ home-|sick ['h' *over* 's']
159.19 matter,⸺ • [*dash inserted over comma*]
159.20 ~~does~~ never • ['never' *over* 'does']
159.28 wouldn't,). • [*sic*]
159.28 its • [*sic*]
159.30 haven't̶ been • ['n't' *wiped away;* 'b' *over* 't']
159.32 ɟ̷ is • ['is' *over* 'w']
159.35 ~~coat,~~ boots, • ['boots,' *over* 'coat,']
159.36 was • was̸ ['s' *over* 't']
160.17 ~~Go~~ any • ['an' *over* 'Go']
160.24 ~~na~~ sex • ['se' *over* 'na']
160.25 spell • spe̸ll ['l' *over* 'e']
160.31 cockroaches • cock-|roaches
160.32 ~~the~~ it • ['it' *over* 'the']
160.35 ~~I have~~ we have • ['we ha' *over* 'I have']
160.38 ~~you know.~~ Madam. • ['Madam.' *over* 'you know.']
161.1 ~~and~~ so that • ['so t' *over* 'and']

■ 28 February 1862 · To William H. Clagett · Carson City, Nev. Terr. ·
UCCL 00037

■ *Copy-text:* MS, Clifton Waller Barrett Library, University of Virginia (ViU). Damage emended at 164.1, 164.13, and 164.21–22 where the MS is heavily worn along the folds. ■ *Previous publication:* none known. ■ *Provenance:* deposited at ViU on 23 Apr 1960. ■ *Emendations and textual notes:* Although the MS itself is not especially difficult to read, discoloration in the damaged areas makes the best attainable photographs virtually illegible and thus not worth publishing here.

163.8 ~~my~~ getting • ['ge' *over* 'my']
163.11 necess͜it͜ary • [*originally* 'necessary'; 'it' *over* 'ar']
164.1 think . . . is much . . . best • t[h]ink . . . i[s m]uch . . . b[est] [*torn*]

164.3–4	sell,— • [*dash over period*]
164.5	to-morrow • to-|morrow
164.11	again,, • [*comma over period*]
164.13	country • coun[◇r]y [*torn*]
164.17	v̵i̵ ravish • ['ra' *over* 'vi']
164.21	s̵o̵ long-legged • ['lo' *over* 'so']
164.21–22	Tom ! . . . good, kind • To[m] ! . . . goo[d, k]ind [*torn*]
164.31	mind, you, • [*sic*]
164.33–34	*Pro*digious • *Pro-*|digious
164.36	w̵e̵ Orion • ['Or' *over* 'we']
165.6	a̸ is • ['i' *over* 'a']
165.11	A̸ Amen. • ['A' *over* 'a']
165.12	"̵A̵ "So • "So̸A̸ ['S' *over possible* 'A']
166.2	i̵f̵ though • ['t' *over* 'if']
166.5	7̸ 8 • ['8' *over* '7']
166.6	purpose • pu̸rpose ['r' *over possible* 'p']
166.6	r̸ Sunrise • ['S' *over* 'r']
166.7	bed, ,again., • ∼. ,∼. , [*deletion implied*]
166.8	some, time • [*sic*]
166.11	T̸ However • ['H' *over possible* 'T']
166.12	o̵f̵ after • ø̸after ['a' *over* 'o' *and* 'ter' *added*]
166.30	b̵y̵ at • ['at' *over* 'by']
166.36	a̵i̵r̵ heir • ['heir' *over* 'air']
167.3	"made over" jintly;" • [*possibly* ' "made over "jintly;" ']

■ 8 and 9 March 1862 · To William H. Clagett · Carson City, Nev. Terr.
· *UCCL* 00039

■*Copy-text:* MS, Clifton Waller Barrett Library, University of Virginia (ViU).
■*Previous publication:* none known. ■*Provenance:* deposited at ViU on 23 Apr
1960. ■ *Emendations and textual notes:*

169.7–8	to-|morrow • to-morrow
170.2	"nurse" • ["]nurse" [*dry pen*]
170.9	f̵o̵ from • f̸rom ['r' *over* 'o']
170.11	naturaly • [*sic*]
170.23	you [make of] that • you | that
171.1	this *do* • [*Clemens may have meant* 'things *do*'.]
171.11	a̵ ̵d̵u̵c̵k̵s̵ water slides • ['water s' *over* 'a ducks']
171.15	o̵f̵ over • o̸ver ['v' *over* 'f']
171.15	Tillou̸w̸ • ['u' *over* 'w']

■ 20 March 1862 · To Jane Lampton Clemens · Carson City, Nev. Terr.
· *UCCL* 00040

■ *Copy-text:* PH, Keokuk *Gate City*, 25 June 62, 1. Newsprint of the *Gate City* is in the Iowa State Historical Department, Division of the State Historical Society, Iowa City (IaHi), and the Historical Library, The State Historical Society of Iowa, Des Moines. We have not been able to use the original newspaper as copy-text. ■ *Previous publication:* Lorch 1930, 270–76; Rogers 1961, 35–40. ■ *Provenance:* unknown. ■ *Emendations and textual notes:*

175.5	dead-wood • dead-|wood
175.19	Madam. For • ~.—|~
175.32–33	bob-|tails • bob-tails
175.33	dear. And • ~.—|~
175.37	turkey-buzzards. And • ~.—|~
176.10	portly • patly
176.21	savvy • savery
177.1	in • is
177.22	names.) They • names,) they
177.23	rabbit • rabit
177.26–27	necklace • neck-lace
177.27	shapelessness • shapeless
177.27	them • them | them
177.31	juvenile muff, • ~, ~_∧_
177.37	Princesses • Princcsses
178.5	occasionally. After • ~.—|~
178.6	principal article • principal | article article
178.11	unfractured • unfractur-|aed
178.16	cards. They • ~.—|~
178.26–27	commenced, • ~;
178.30	of • o[f]

■ 2 April 1862 · To Jane Lampton Clemens · Carson City, Nev. Terr. ·
UCCL 00041

■ *Copy-text:* MS, Jean Webster McKinney Family Papers, Vassar College Library (NPV). ■ *Previous publication: MTL,* 1:69–70, with major omissions; *MTBus,* 65, excerpt not published in *MTL.* ■ *Provenance:* see McKinney Family Papers, pp. 459–61. The MS was in the possession of Orion Clemens as late as about 1880, when he marked it for inclusion in his autobiography. ■ *Emendations and textual notes:*

180.3	been received • been ~~re~~| received
180.7	~~make~~ explain • ['expla' *over* 'make']

180.14   s̶h̶ said   •   ['sa' *over* 'sh']
180.24   n̶o̶t̶ ̶a̶ but not   •   ['but n' *over* 'not a']
180.24   p̶Providence   •   ['P' *over* 'p']
181.3   "̶B̶ "Roll   •   "B̶Roll ['R' *over* 'B']
181.3–4   Moo-|oon   •   Moo-oon
181.4–5   t̶u̶n̶e̶ melody   •   ['melo' *over* 'tune']
181.7–8   a̶s̶ ̶a̶ ̶s̶o̶ as something   •   ['as som' *over* 'as a so']
181.17   d̶ business   •   ['b' *over* 'd']
181.23   Conradṅ   •   ['d' *over* 'n']
181.28   black,̶—   •   [*dash over period*]
181.30–31   fire-|proof   •   fire-proof
181.35   ȯ when   •   ['w' *over* 'o']
182.6   headache,̶—̶   •   [*dash inserted over comma; possibly* 'headache,—']
182.9   with, ˌhim.ˏ   •   ～. ˌ～.ˏ [*deletion implied*]
182.11–12   guests. ˌȦnd we didn't drill.ˏ   •   ['and . . . drill' *interlined with a caret following* 'guests'; 'A' *over* 'a' *and period added after* 'drill'; *caret left standing between* 'guests' *and original period*]
182.17   w̶e̶ our   •   ['our' *over* 'we']
182.34   i̶f̶ I   •   ['I' *over* 'if']
182.35   a̶l̶ too   •   ['too' *over* 'al']
183.7   t̶h̶a̶n̶ that   •   thatṅ ['t' *over* 'n']

■ 10? April 1862   ·   To Orion Clemens   ·   Aurora, Calif./Nev. Terr.   ·
UCCL 11364

■*Copy-text: MTB*, 1:198. ■*Previous publication:* none known except the copy-text. ■*Provenance:* unknown. ■*Emendations and textual notes:* none.

■ 13 April 1862   ·   To Orion Clemens   ·   Aurora, Calif./Nev. Terr.   ·
UCCL 00042

■*Copy-text:* MS, Jean Webster McKinney Family Papers, Vassar College Library (NPV). ■*Previous publication: MTB*, 1:196, excerpts; *MTL*, 1:70–72, with omissions. ■*Provenance:* see McKinney Family Papers, pp. 459–61. ■*Emendations and textual notes:*

185.8   &̶ A   •   ['A' *over possible* '&']
185.15   enemy̶i̶e̶s̶   •   enemyi̇es ['y' *over* 'es'; *deletion of* 'i' *implied*]
185.16   O̶n̶e̶ Noble's   •   ['No' *over* 'One']
185.18   t̶h̶a̶ this   •   thi̇is ['i' *over* 'a']

186.3	~~he's~~ he'll • he'$ll [*first* 'l' *over* 's']
186.5	*witness* • *wit-*|ness
186.9	~~$20~~ $40 • $$40 ['4' *over* '2']
186.14	much work • ˄ much ~~wo~~ work [*canceled* 'wo' *doubtful, apparently miswritten*]
186.24	Young's • [*sic*]
186.30	~~And~~ • [*doubtful*]
186.38	foget • [*sic*]

■ 17 and 19 April 1862 · To Orion Clemens · Aurora, Calif./Nev. Terr.
· *UCCL* 00043

■ *Copy-text:* MS, Moffett Collection, Mark Twain Papers, The Bancroft Library, University of California, Berkeley (CU-MARK). ■ *Previous publication: MTB*, 1:198–99, brief excerpt. ■ *Provenance:* see Moffett Collection, p. 462. ■ *Emendations and textual notes:*

190.3	tunnell • [*sic*]
190.10	~~tun~~ seventeen-thousand-dollar • ['sev' *over* 'tun']
190.18	~~wil~~ we'll • [' we'' *over* 'wil']
190.22	~~ma~~ figure • ['fig' *over* 'ma']
190.28	~~and~~ if any • ['if a' *over* 'and']
190.37	~~¢~~ Karson • ['K' *over* 'C']

■ 18 April 1862 · To William H. Clagett · Aurora, Calif./Nev. Terr. ·
UCCL 00044

■ *Copy-text:* MS, Clifton Waller Barrett Library, University of Virginia (ViU); damage emended. ■ *Previous publication:* none known. ■ *Provenance:* deposited at ViU on 23 Apr 1960. ■ *Emendations and textual notes:*

192.7	two, • two[,] [*torn*]
192.9	~~will~~ can • ['can' *over* 'will']
192.9	~~or $15.~~ • ['15' *doubtful*]
192.10	₦ But • ['B' *over partly formed* 'N']
192.15	Billy • Bi*f*lly ['l' *over* 'f']
192.23	~~though~~ think • th˄ink~~ough~~ ['ink' *over* 'ugh'; *deletion of* 'o' *implied*]
193.5	˄myself˄—that • ˄myself—˄—that
193.22	possible. • possible[.] [*torn*]
193.23	~~it~~ machinery • ['m' *over* 'it']
193.32	Co. • C[o◊] [*torn*]

■ 24 and 25 April 1862 · To Orion Clemens · Aurora, Calif./Nev. Terr.
 · *UCCL* 00045

■ *Copy-text:* MS, Jean Webster McKinney Family Papers, Vassar College Library
(NPV). ■ *Previous publication: MTB*, 1:199, brief excerpts; *MTL*, 1:79–81, with
omissions; *MTBus*, 70–71, with extensive omissions. ■ *Provenance:* see Mc-
Kinney Family Papers, pp. 459–61. ■ *Emendations and textual notes:*

194.10   ~~I,~~ I do · ['I d' *over* 'I,']
194.18   ~~know that y~~ knew, at that · ['knew, at tha' *over* 'know that y']
195.4   ~~that~~ this · th{is}at ['is' *over* 'at']
195.6   ~~be~~ as · ['as' *over* 'be']
195.7–8   ~~such~~ prospecting · ['pros' *over* 'such']
195.8   ~~in~~ &c. · ['&c' *over* 'in']
195.10–11   ~~asking~~ getting · ask{gett}ing ['gett' *over* 'ask']
195.11   tried · tri{ed}ied ['ed' *over* 'ied']
195.14   ṃMountain · ['M' *over* 'm']
195.16   ~~that~~ there · th{er}eat ['er' *over* 'at']
195.28   revisit · re-|visit
196.3   thin{k}king · ['k' *over* 'g']
196.14   it.? · [*sic*]
196.15   ~~did~~ suppose · ['sup' *over* 'did']
196.17   office{;}; · [*period mended to semicolon*]
196.19   ~~it~~ if · if{f} ['f' *over* 't']
196.33   hang to until · [*sic*]
196.36   ~~tell~~ ask · ['ask' *over* 'tell']
197.17   ¶ · [*paragraph sign mistakenly inscribed as a* 'P']
197.19   ~~charge~~ custody · ['custody' *over* 'charge']
197.25   {C Carson · ['C' *over* partly formed 't']
197.31   ṇ Naval · ['N' *over* 'n']

■ 28 April 1862 · To Orion Clemens · Aurora, Calif./Nev. Terr. ·
 UCCL 00046

■ *Copy-text:* MS, Jean Webster McKinney Family Papers, Vassar College Library
(NPV). ■ *Previous publication: MTB*, 1:196–97, excerpt; *MTBus*, 69, brief excerpt. ■ *Provenance:* see McKinney Family Papers, pp. 459–61. ■ *Emendations
and textual notes:*

200.1   to-morrow · to-|morrow
200.2   ~~is~~ it · i{t}t ['t' *over* 's']
200.10   be · [*sic*]

■ 4 and 5 May 1862 · To Orion Clemens · Aurora, Calif./Nev. Terr. · *UCCL* 00047

■ *Copy-text:* MS, Jean Webster McKinney Family Papers, Vassar College Library (NPV). ■ *Previous publication: MTL*, 1:76–78, with omissions; *MTBus*, 66, brief excerpt not in *MTL*. ■ *Provenance:* see McKinney Family Papers, pp. 459–61. ■ *Emendations and textual notes:*

201.5	~~D—d—~~ Well— • [‘Well—’ *over* ‘D—d—’]
201.9	expenses, • expense~~es~~s, [‘s,’ *over doubtful* ‘es’]
201.11	be • b[◇] [*gold sample covers* ‘e’]
202.7	~~bo~~ broke • bo̸roke [‘r’ *over* ‘o’]
202.19	it.̸— • [*dash over period*]
202.21	~~know~~ knew • k‸new‸~~now~~ [‘new’ *over* ‘now’*; doubtful* ‘o’]
202.22	~~that~~ they • th‸ey‸~~at~~ [‘ey’ *over* ‘at’]
202.33	e̸ angle • [‘a’ *over doubtful* ‘e’]
203.1	notion • noth̸ion [‘i’ *over* ‘h’]
203.4	It’s • [*sic*]
203.8	$20 • [‘2’ *over very doubtful* ‘1’]
203.9	~~first~~ once • [‘once’ *over* ‘first’]
203.12	Do~~nt~~ you • [‘y’ *over* ‘nt’]
203.15	h̸ those • [‘t’ *over doubtful* ‘h’]
203.17	~~wi~~ must • [‘mu’ *over doubtful* ‘wi’]
203.18–19	~~until you~~ at all • [‘at all’ *over* ‘until you’]
204.6	~~da~~ d—n • da̸—n [*dash over* ‘a’]

■ 11 and 12 May 1862 · To Orion Clemens · Aurora, Calif./Nev. Terr. · *UCCL* 00048

■ *Copy-text:* MS of letter, Jean Webster McKinney Family Papers, Vassar College Library (NPV); MS of envelope, Mark Twain Papers, The Bancroft Library, University of California, Berkeley (CU-MARK). ■ *Previous publication: MTB*, 1:197–98, excerpts; *MTL*, 1:73–76, with omissions. ■ *Provenance:* see McKinney Family Papers, pp. 459–61. The envelope is probably part of the Moffett Collection; see p. 462. ■ *Emendations and textual notes:*

205.6	privi̸ations • [‘a’ *over* ‘i’]
205.12	8̸ 6 • [‘6’ *over* ‘8’]
206.12	~~the~~ work • [‘wor’ *over* ‘the’]
206.12	~~led~~ leads • le‸ads‸d̸ [‘a’ *over* ‘d’]
206.18	~~$16~~ $18 • $1‸86̸ [‘8’ *over* ‘6’]
206.19	~~lately~~ • [*doubtful*]
206.24	doe̸ • [‘e’ *doubtful*]

206.27–28   Sam. [¶] I • ~.—[¶]~
206.28 $150? • [*sic*]
206.38   N̶ S. • ['S' *over* 'N']
207.5   w̶a̶l̶l̶ was • wasll̶ ['s' *over* 'll']
207.13   fortune?" • [*sic*]
207.16   ¢ anybody • ['a' *over* 'e']
207.29   ¢ Clear • ['C' *over* 'c']
207.32   A̶ R. • ['R' *over* 'a']
207.36–37   c̶o̶ can't • cø̶an't ['a' *over* 'o']
208.8   you ‚but . . . rock‚. • you. ‚but . . . rock‚ [*possibly* 'you‚, ‚but
             . . . rock‚,'; 'but . . . rock' *inserted with a caret misplaced following
             the period; possibly a comma over the period*]
208.8   1̶1̶ 12 • 12/̶ ['2' *over doubtful* '1']
208.11   rock is • rock̶i̶s̶ is ['is' *over* 'is'; *false start*]
208.16   s̶ it • ['i' *over* 's']
208.33–34   bed-|room • bedroom
208.36   c̶l̶ contrabands • ['co' *over* 'cl']
209.17   i̶n̶ when • ['w' *over* 'in']
209.19   a̶l̶t̶h̶ as we • ['as w' *over* 'alth']
209.27–28   f̶o̶r̶ from • fromo̶r̶ ['ro' *over* 'or']
209.28   a̶ w̶h̶ which • ['whi' *over* 'a wh']
209.34   invincible • [*a stroke above the first* 'i' *appears to be a crossbar mis-
             takenly added to create a* 't']
210.1   m̶o̶r̶e̶ t̶h̶a̶n̶ p̶a̶y̶ at least pay • ['at least pay' *over* 'more than pay']
210.4   M‚— • [*dash over period*]
210.12–16   but . . . stand it. • [*canceled lightly; intended to be read. The orig-
             inal MS is reproduced at 50 percent of actual size.*]

210.14   t̶h̶i̶s̶ that • thatis̶ ['at' *over* 'is']
210.14   properly • propf̶erly ['e' *over* 'r']
210.17   pay‚ it. • ~. ~. [*deletion implied*]
210.17   thoughts; • [*semicolon possibly a comma*]

210.20	~~to~~ I • ['I' *over* 'to']
210.20	~~take~~ have • ['ha' *over* 'take']
210.23	debt • ȡ debt ['d' *over doubtful* 'd']
210.24	~~pr~~ peremptorily • p/eremptorily ['e' *over* 'r']
210.26	ẇ is • ['i' *over* 'w']
210.37	~~th~~ on • ['on' *over* 'th']
211.1	Swon*ı*,"— • [*dash over period*]
211.1–2	bomb-|shell • bomb-shell

■ 17 May 1862 · To Orion Clemens · Aurora, Calif./Nev. Terr. · *UCCL* 00049

■*Copy-text:* MS, Jean Webster McKinney Family Papers, Vassar College Library (NPV). ■*Previous publication: MTL*, 1:78–79, excerpts; *MTBus*, 67–69, omitting *MTL* text. ■*Provenance:* see McKinney Family Papers, pp. 459–61. ■*Emendations and textual notes:*

213.4	good*ı*— • [*dash over period*]
213.8	J̵ Gov. • ['G' *over* 'J']
213.10	ȼ sent • ['s' *over* 'c']
214.25	~~rea~~ found • ['fou' *over* 'rea' *or possibly* 'rec']
214.27	~~and~~ or • ['or' *over* 'and']
215.2	~~cul~~ consult • consultᵾl ['on' *over doubtful* 'ul']
215.7	~~too~~ to • tọọo ['o' *over* 'oo']
215.7	ʃ it • ['i' *over* 't']

■ 2 June 1862 · To Orion Clemens · Aurora, Calif./Nev. Terr. · *UCCL* 00050

■*Copy-text:* MS, Jean Webster McKinney Family Papers, Vassar College Library (NPV). ■*Previous publication: MTB*, 1:201, excerpt; *MTL*, 1:79, same excerpt. ■*Provenance:* see McKinney Family Papers, pp. 459–61. ■*Emendations and textual notes:*

216.8	J̵ Mr. • ['M' *over* 'I']
216.9	ȿ 6 • ['6' *over* 's']
216.10	~~the~~ when • ['whe' *over* 'the']
216.11	~~It~~ me • ['me' *over* 'I t']
217.10	~~ab~~ perhaps • ['pe' *over* 'ab']
217.12	sublet • sub-|let
217.13	sharping • [*sic*]

■ 9 June 1862 · To Orion Clemens · Aurora, Calif./Nev. Terr. · *UCCL* 02778

■ *Copy-text:* MS, Jean Webster McKinney Family Papers, Vassar College Library (NPV). ■ *Previous publication:* none known. ■ *Provenance:* see McKinney Family Papers, pp. 459–61. ■ *Emendations and textual notes:*

218.6	prrice •	[*sic*]
218.7	feet, •	[*comma doubtful*]
219.9	~~wort~~ word • wor{d ['d' *over* 't']
219.11	Calfornia •	[*sic*]
219.13	seend •	[*sic*]

■ 22 June 1862 · To Orion Clemens · Aurora, Calif./Nev. Terr. · *UCCL* 00052

■ *Copy-text:* MS, Clifton Waller Barrett Library, University of Virginia (ViU). ■ *Previous publication:* none known. ■ *Provenance:* deposited at ViU on 17 Dec 1963. ■ *Emendations and textual notes:*

220.11	~~These~~ These • Thes̬es̬e	['se' *canceled, possibly to produce* 'The'; *then* 'se' *added over cancellation*]
221.15	~~on~~ old • old̬d̬	['l' *over* 'n']
221.23	ø̸ business •	['b' *over* 'p']
221.34	~~th~~ a •	['a' *over doubtful partly formed* 'th']
221.37	₿ Your •	['Y' *over* 'B']

■ 25 June 1862 · To Orion Clemens · Aurora, Calif./Nev. Terr. · *UCCL* 00053

■ *Copy-text:* MS of letter, Jean Webster McKinney Family Papers, Vassar College Library (NPV); MS of envelope, Mark Twain Papers, The Bancroft Library, University of California, Berkeley (CU-MARK). ■ *Previous publication: MTBus*, 69–70. ■ *Provenance:* letter, see McKinney Family Papers, pp. 459–61; envelope, probably Moffett Collection but possibly in Mark Twain Papers since Paine's service as executor of the Mark Twain Estate (1910–37); see p. 462. ■ *Emendations and textual notes:*

223.7	$4 • $4ø̸	[*originally* '$ o'; '4' *over letter* 'o'; *false start*]
223.7	ẅ could •	['c' *over* 'w']
223.11–12	Fly-|away • Flyaway	

■ 9 July 1862 · To Orion Clemens · Aurora, Calif./Nev. Terr. · *UCCL* 00054

■ *Copy-text:* MS, Moffett Collection, Mark Twain Papers, The Bancroft Library, University of California, Berkeley (CU-MARK). ■ *Previous publication: MTB*, 1:199–200, brief paraphrase and excerpt. ■ *Provenance:* see Moffett Collection, p. 462. ■ *Emendations and textual notes:*

224.1	1862 •	[*possibly* '1862.']
224.9	₳ him •	['h' *over* 'a']
225.3–4	steam-|boat •	steamboat
225.7	a̶t̶ that •	['th' *over deleted* 'at']
225.16	(100)̸ miles •	['m' *over closing parenthesis*]
225.30	they done •	[*sic*]
226.1	d̶o̶ during •	dǿuring ['u' *over* 'o']
226.5	Lewis is •	Lewis̸ is [*false start*]

■ 23 July 1862 · To Orion Clemens · Aurora, Calif./Nev. Terr. · *UCCL* 00055

■ *Copy-text:* MS, Jean Webster McKinney Family Papers, Vassar College Library (NPV). ■ *Previous publication: MTB*, 1:202, brief excerpts; *MTL*, 1:81–82, with omissions. ■ *Provenance:* see McKinney Family Papers, pp. 459–61. ■ *Emendations and textual notes:*

228.12	ᵈᵒ ᵈᵒ •	[*below* 'Johnson' (*228.12*) *in line above in MS*]
228.21	I̶ ̶w̶ If •	If ψ̸ [*originally* 'I w'; 'f' *over* 'w']
228.29	matter,̸, •	[*comma over period*]
228.32	$̶2̶0̶ $25 •	$25¢ ['5' *over* '0']
229.15	cheaper. •	[*sic*]

■ 30 July 1862 · To Orion Clemens · Aurora, Calif./Nev. Terr. · *UCCL* 00056

■ *Copy-text:* MS, Jean Webster McKinney Family Papers, Vassar College Library (NPV). ■ *Previous publication: MTB*, 1:203, brief excerpt; *MTL*, 1:83, same excerpt. ■ *Provenance:* see McKinney Family Papers, pp. 459–61. ■ *Emendations and textual notes:*

231.4–5	l̶o̶c̶a̶l̶ post •	['post' *over* 'local']
232.10	I̶f̶ ̶h̶e̶ ̶s̶a̶y̶ ̶t̶h̶e̶ ̶w̶◊◊◊◊ ̶h̶e̶ I told my agent •	[*sequence of revision*

       doubtful; 'he say' *doubtful;* 'the' *over* 'say'; 'I told my agent' *over* 'If
. . . he']

232.17	t̶o̶ for • ['f' *over* 'to']
232.18	ill-natured • ill-|natured
232.22	t̸ as • ['a' *over* 't']
232.24	wide. • [*sic*]

■ 7 August 1862 · To Orion Clemens · Aurora, Calif./Nev. Terr. ·
UCCL 00057

■ *Copy-text:* MS, Jean Webster McKinney Family Papers, Vassar College Library
(NPV). ■ *Previous publication: MTB*, 1:204, brief excerpt; *MTL*, 1:83–84, with
omissions. ■ *Provenance:* see McKinney Family Papers, pp. 459–61. ■ *Emendations and textual notes:*

233.4	t̶o̶ ̶l̶e̶t̶ that • ['that' *over* 'to let']
233.4	l̶o̶ how • ['h' *over* 'lo']
233.6	to-night • to-|night
233.8	facilities • facili̸ties ['t' *over* 'e']
233.12	yonnder • [*possibly* 'younder']
234.2	w̸ although • ['a' *over* 'w']
234.9	Hang to • [*sic*]
234.18	B̶u̶n̶k̶e̶r̶ Bully for • Bu̬lly̬nker̶ for ['lly f' *over* 'nker']
234.19–20	to-|night • to-night
234.31	t̸ a • ['a' *over possible* 't']
234.35	f̸ should • ['s' *over* 'f']

■ 15 August 1862 · To Pamela A. Moffett · Aurora, Calif./Nev. Terr. ·
UCCL 00058

■ *Copy-text: MTL*, 1:85–86. ■ *Previous publication:* Paine, 425, and *MTB*, 1:203,
same brief quotation and paraphrase; Fender, 740, 742, excerpts. ■ *Provenance:*
unknown. ■ *Emendations and textual notes:* The rationale for emendations to remove *MTL* styling is given on pp. 458–59.

235.1	Esmeralda, Cal., Aug. 15, 1862. • ESMERALDA, CAL., *Aug. 15, 1862.*
235.2–3	My Dear Sister: [¶] I • MY DEAR SISTER,—I
236.17	10 × 12 • 10×12
237.6	Beck • Beack

237.6   Jolly? • Jolly?[1] [*and footnote:* '[1]A pilot.']
237.8   Sam • SAM

■ 9 September 1862 · To William H. Clagett · Aurora, Calif./Nev. Terr.
  · *UCCL* 00059
■ *Copy-text:* MS, Clifton Waller Barrett Library, University of Virginia (ViU).
■ *Previous publication:* "Two Civil War Letters," *American Heritage* 8 (Oct 1957):
62, with omissions; Fatout 1964, 67, excerpt paraphrased. ■ *Provenance:* depos-
ited at ViU on 23 Apr 1960. ■ *Emendations and textual notes:*

238.4   represented • ['ed' *doubtful*]
238.17   ¢ Confederacy • ['C' *over* 'c']
238.20   battle-field • battle-|field
238.22   they were • they they were
238.24   frantic • fra¢ntic ['n' *over* 'c']
238.26   ѱWashington • ['W' *over* 'w']
238.31   ҏPennsylvania • ['P' *over* 'p']
239.1   than that • thatﾌ ['t' *over* 'n']
239.3   subject. Let • ~.—|~
239.3–4   ev endeavor • eᵧndeavor ['n' *over* 'v']
239.14   mill mild • mil／d ['d' *over* 'l']
239.19   les let's • leｵt's ['t's' *over* 's']
239.20   weeks • weekshi ['ee' *over* 'hi']
240.6   Humbol／dt • ['d' *over* 't']

■ 21 October 1862 · To Orion and Mary E. (Mollie) Clemens · Virginia
  City, Nev. Terr. · *UCCL* 00060
■ *Copy-text:* MS, Jean Webster McKinney Family Papers, Vassar College Library
(NPV). Only the first two pages of the manuscript have survived. ■ *Previous publication: MTBus*, 75–76, with omission. ■ *Provenance:* see McKinney Family Papers, pp. 459–61. The missing part of the MS was lost before 1946; the text
printed in *MTBus* ends where the present text does with the note, "Remainder
missing" (76). ■ *Emendations and textual notes:*

241.6–7   say,— • [*dash over period*]
241.13–14   thin wrong • ['wro' *over* 'thin']
241.14   night, was. • ~. ~. [*deletion implied*]
241.14   appealed— I • ['I' *over dash*]
242.2   Davidson! • Davidson[!] [*torn*]

■ 16 February 1863 · To Jane Lampton Clemens and Pamela A. Moffett
· Virginia City, Nev. Terr. · *UCCL* 00061

■ *Copy-text:* MS, Jean Webster McKinney Family Papers, Vassar College Library
(NPV). ■ *Previous publication: MTBus*, 77–78. ■ *Provenance:* see McKinney
Family Papers, pp. 459–61. ■ *Emendations and textual notes:*

244.11	~~dol~~ doing · do/ing ['i' *over* 'l']
245.3	m̸Madamₗ, · ['M' *over* 'm'; *comma over period*]
245.9	W̸ one · ['o' *over possible* 'w']
245.22	Louis · Louʃis ['i' *over* 's']
245.25	not? · [*sic*]
245.33	myself, · [*possibly* 'myselfₗ,'; *comma over period*]
245.34	affctnly · [*scrawled;* 'ctnl' *not certain*]

■ 11 and 12 April 1863 · To Jane Lampton Clemens and Pamela A. Moffett · Virginia City, Nev. Terr. · *UCCL* 00063

■ *Copy-text:* MS, Jean Webster McKinney Family Papers, Vassar College Library
(NPV) and Mark Twain Papers, The Bancroft Library, University of California,
Berkeley (CU-MARK). The surviving MS is demonstrably incomplete. It consists of two folders of onionskin paper, both inscribed on the first and fourth sides
only. Since the second of these folders begins with a page numbered '5', a third
(middle) folder containing pages 3 and 4 is presumed missing. The first extant
folder, through the first two syllables of 'California' (247.32), is at Vassar; the second, 'of great' (247.34) to the end, is in the Mark Twain Papers. ■ *Previous publication: MTB*, 1:227–28, 229, 232, brief excerpts; *MTL*, 1:88–89, excerpt mistakenly combined with a paragraph from 18 Mar 64 to PAM; *MTBus*, 66, brief
excerpt. All these excerpts are taken from the first folder; no publication is
known of the missing middle folder or of the last one. ■ *Provenance:* see Mc-
Kinney Family Papers, pp. 459–61. The MS in CU-MARK was probably acquired in the Moffett Collection; see p. 462. ■ *Emendations and textual notes:*
Since the folder of pages 3 and 4 that would demonstrate the link between the surviving fragments is lost, it must remain an uncertain although plausible conjecture that the two fragments are in fact parts of one letter. The surviving MS fragments were written in the same ink and on identical paper, but unfortunately this
evidence does little to confirm the conjecture, for Clemens used the same kinds
of ink and paper often in this period. Two other factors support the conjecture
more strongly: no other MS fragment that could complement either of these two
has been found; and the two surviving fragments each contain references (documented on pp. 249–50, notes 5 and 7) that appear to belong to a single letter.

246.3–4	~~Mi~~ Jackson · ['Jac' *over doubtful* 'Mi']
246.4	m̸Missourian · ['M' *over* 'm']

247.8	you. That's • ~.—|~
247.21	~~if I~~ whether • ['wh' *over* 'if I']
247.24	ton. I • ~.—|~
247.28	~~is~~ it • it$ ['t' *over* 's']
247.28–29	$ minted • ['m' *over partly formed* 'y']
247.29	much • mu$ch ['c' *over partly formed* 'h']
247.29	but • ~~but~~ | but [*first* 'but' *wiped out, possibly miswritten*]
247.31	If • $$ If ['If' *over one or two characters, probably* 'If' *miswritten, possibly* 'O']
247.32	California • Cali-| [*next page missing*]
247.36	~~should~~ she could • ['she c' *over* 'should']
247.37	little • litt$le ['le' *over* 'e']
247.37	daylight • day-|light
248.10	whopper-j$awed • whopper-jo$wed ['aw' *over* 'o' *and a partly formed character*]
248.11	*blast* • [*underscore heavily traced over*]
248.12	~~if s~~ when • ['wh' *over* 'if s']
248.15	~~wh~~ you • ['y' *over* 'w' *and partly formed* 'h']
248.17	~~Emma Ro Rowe,~~ • ['Row' *over* 'Ro']
248.18	~~Espec~~ I mean • ['I mea' *over* 'Espec']
248.19	~~as~~ me • ['m' *over* 'as']
248.24	easy-going • easy-|going
248.26	~~kid~~ kindly • ki$ndly ['n' *over* 'd']

■ 16 April 1863 · To Jane Lampton Clemens · Virginia City, Nev. Terr.
· *UCCL* 00064

■ *Copy-text:* MS, Jean Webster McKinney Family Papers, Vassar College Library (NPV). The MS is a single, unnumbered leaf inscribed on both sides. ■ *Previous publication: MTBus*, 79. ■ *Provenance:* see McKinney Family Papers, pp. 459–61. The MS was incomplete in 1946 when Webster printed the fragment given here with the comment that "the head and tail of the next letter are missing" (*MTBus*, 78). ■ *Emendations and textual notes:*

251.2	~~othe~~ at • ['at' *over* 'othe']
251.2	~~whe~~ who • who$ ['o' *over* 'e']
251.18	$ kind • ['k' *over* 'y']
251.22	$ Mr. • ['M' *over* 'm']
251.22	$ advance • ['a' *over possible* 'l']

■ 18? May 1863 · To Jane Lampton Clemens and Pamela A. Moffett ·
San Francisco, Calif. · *UCCL* 00065

■*Copy-text:* MS, Moffett Collection, Mark Twain Papers, The Bancroft Library,
University of California, Berkeley (CU-MARK). ■*Previous publication:* none
known. ■*Provenance:* see Moffett Collection, p. 462. ■*Emendations and textual
notes:* The surviving MS consists of a single leaf inscribed on both sides, the first
of which is numbered '3'. Jane Clemens may have passed on the first two pages
for someone else to read, retaining the second leaf so as not to expose her son's
predatory practices.

252.8	be̶ did	• ['di' *over* 'be']
252.11	t̶h̶e̶ ̶s̶t̶r̶ Montgomery	• ['Mont' *over* 'the str']
253.2	Virginia,ˌ	• [*comma over period*]
253.3–4	[*about . . . away*]	• [*A narrow strip was carefully torn away across the bottom of the MS leaf. The illustration reproduces the original MS at 51 percent of actual size.*

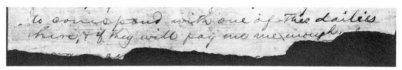

Parts of letters too fragmentary to read survive on the torn edge, indicating that the lost strip bore writing. The paper appears to be the same
as that used for Clemens's letters of 11 and 12 April, 1 June, and 4 June
63, all of which are 27 cm long. This leaf varies in length from 24.7 to
26.2 cm because of the unevenness of the torn edge, but clearly just
enough paper was torn away to accommodate one line of writing plus
perhaps one word at the end of the preceding line. Clemens himself
probably tore the strip away before mailing the letter, presumably as the
quickest and most complete method of cancellation. Since the sentence
from which the words were torn is complete as it stands, running up to
the torn edge at the foot of MS page 3 and concluding at the top of page
4, he may have torn away the strip before finishing that sentence. At any
rate, he probably tore it before finishing the letter, for the letter ends just
at the torn edge on the other side of the leaf, with no sign of any inscription below the signature.*]

253.3	me	• me me
253.7	M̶r̶.̶	• [*period doubtful*]
253.9	t̶h̶e̶ ̶M̶r̶.̶	• ['Mr.' *over* 'the']
253.12	m̶o̶n̶t̶h̶s̶—	• [*possibly* 'm̶o̶n̶t̶h̶s̶,—']
253.16	m̸ʰ have	• ['h' *over* 'm']
253.21	affctiny	• ['ny' *scrawled; doubtful*]
253.22	Sam	• [*written just above the torn edge, with no sign that any text was removed when the sheet was torn*]

■ 1 June 1863 · To Jane Lampton Clemens and Pamela A. Moffett · San Francisco, Calif. · *UCCL* 00066

■*Copy-text:* MS, Jean Webster McKinney Family Papers, Vassar College Library (NPV). ■*Previous publication: MTB*, 1:232–33, excerpts; *MTL*, 1:90–91, with omission. ■*Provenance:* see McKinney Family Papers, pp. 459–61. ■*Emendations and textual notes:*

255.1	N⁰· 2—[$20°° Enclosed] • [*possibly inserted;* 'E' *possibly* 'e']
255.9	ȼ fag • ['f' *over partly formed* 'g']
255.19–20	excursion • excursi⁄on ['o' *over doubtful* 'n']
255.21–22	"Oh . . . "gentleman . . . wagon!" • [*sic*]
255.23	dinner, • [*followed by stray marks, canceled by Clemens, that were apparently caused by offset of wet ink from some other document laid on the MS*]
255.24	champaign • [*sic*]
255.29	ships • [*possibly* 'ships.'; *followed by a canceled stray mark (see note at 255.23)*]
255.29	~~here~~ about • ['about' *over* 'here']
255.30	wet • we⁄st ['t' *over* 's']

■ 4 June 1863 · To Jane Lampton Clemens and Pamela A. Moffett · San Francisco, Calif. · *UCCL* 00067

■*Copy-text:* MS, Moffett Collection, Mark Twain Papers, The Bancroft Library, University of California, Berkeley (CU-MARK). ■*Previous publication: MTB*, 1:233, brief excerpt; Fender, 746, excerpt not in *MTB*. ■*Provenance:* see Moffett Collection, p. 462. ■*Emendations and textual notes:*

256.13	havent • [*sic*]
257.3	Nash • N⁄ash ['a' *over probably malformed* 'a']
257.17–18	~~bel~~ beheld • be⁄held ['h' *over* 'l']

■ 20 June 1863 · To Orion and Mary E. (Mollie) Clemens · San Francisco, Calif. · *UCCL* 00068

■*Copy-text:* MS, Mark Twain Papers, The Bancroft Library, University of California, Berkeley (CU-MARK). A photographic facsimile of the MS is on pp. 424–25. The MS consists of a half sheet of thin blue-lined off-white laid paper, 8¼ by 10⅝ inches (20.9 by 27 cm), inscribed on both sides in black ink, now faded to brown. At the top of the first page Paine wrote '1863' in pencil. ■*Previous publication:* none known. ■*Provenance:* probably Moffett Collection; see p. 462. ■*Emendations and textual notes:*

258.11   h̷ stores • ['s' *over* 'h']
258.12   i̶s̶ it • it$̷ ['t' *over* 's']
258.13   I̷ my • ['m' *over* 'I']
258.14   Ma$̷ • [*possibly* 'Ma'; *the canceled* 's' *may be merely a superfluous stroke*]
258.17   +̶ & • ['&' *over dash*]

■ 18 July 1863 · To Jane Lampton Clemens and Pamela A. Moffett ·
Virginia City, Nev. Terr. · *UCCL* 00069

■ *Copy-text:* MS, Mark Twain Papers, The Bancroft Library, University of California, Berkeley (CU-MARK). A photographic facsimile of the MS is on pp. 426–27. The MS consists of a folder of off-white onionskin faintly lined in blue, 8 3/16 by 10 1/2 inches (20.8 by 26.8 cm), inscribed on first and fourth pages only in black ink. ■ *Previous publication: MTB*, 1:233, 234, excerpts. ■ *Provenance:* probably Moffett Collection; see p. 462. ■ *Emendations and textual notes:*

259.4   you • y̷ you ['y' *over partly formed, possibly miswritten* 'y']
259.5   money!̷? • [*question mark over exclamation point*]
260.6   m̶y̶ mighty • m̷ighty ['i' *over* 'y']
260.7   *reputation* • [*broken underscore*]
260.12   w̶o̶u̶ in • ['in' *over* 'wou']
260.12   last ◇ months • [*an ink blot covers possible* '2' *or* '3']
260.14–15 $13 a foot • $13 | [◇ f]oot [*torn*]
260.15   they gave • they | [◇◇v]e [*torn*]
260.15–16   way of • wa[y] of [*torn*]
260.18   I̷ A • ['A' *over* 'I']
260.23   paid,̶— • [*dash over period*]
260.25   I̷ My • ['M' *over* 'I']

■ 5 August 1863 · To Jane Lampton Clemens and Pamela A. Moffett ·
Virginia City, Nev. Terr. · *UCCL* 00070

■ *Copy-text:* MS, Mark Twain Papers, The Bancroft Library, University of California, Berkeley (CU-MARK); damage emended. A photographic facsimile of the MS is on pp. 428–29. The MS consists of a folder of white onionskin, 8 5/16 by 10 9/16 inches (21.2 by 26.9 cm), watermarked overall in a small grid pattern. In the upper right corner the folder is blind embossed with a crown above a shield within which a viking ship sails beneath a pattern of stars. The folder is inscribed on the first and fourth sides only in black ink, now somewhat faded to brown. ■ *Previous publication:* none known. ■ *Provenance:* probably Moffett Collection; see p. 462. ■ *Emendations and textual notes:*

261.6	M̶r̶ • {◌}r̶ [*blotted and torn; doubtful*]
261.7	t̶h̶e̶ ̶s̶p̶a̶r̶e̶ one of • ['one of' *over* 'the spare']
262.3	rooms • ro[o]ms [*torn*]
262.9	m̶e̶ myself • mÿyself ['y' *over* 'e']
262.10	ⱴ when • ['w' *over partly formed character, possibly* 'n' *or* 'm']
262.15	dissipation⸝, • [*comma over period*]
262.20	w̶o̶ really • w̶o̶ ̶r̶e̶a̶l̶l̶y̶ really ['re' *over* 'wo'; 'really' *blotted, canceled, then rewritten for clarity*]
262.24	ⱴ any • ['a' *over* '&']
262.25	returned. I • ∼.—|∼
262.26	ⱴ with • ['w' *over* 'a']

■ 19 August 1863 · To Jane Lampton Clemens and Pamela A. Moffett · Steamboat Springs, Nev. Terr. · *UCCL* 00071

■*Copy-text:* MS, Jean Webster McKinney Family Papers, Vassar College Library (NPV). A facsimile of the first MS page (through 'life' at 264.4) is in Branch 1950, facing 230. ■*Previous publication: MTB*, 1:238–39, excerpts; *MTL*, 1:91–93, with omissions. ■*Provenance:* see McKinney Family Papers, pp. 459–61.
■*Emendations and textual notes:*

263.6	any • ⱴ| any [*ran out of space*]
263.8	¢ may • ['m' *over* 'c']
263.9	day." There's • ∼."—|∼
264.24	steamboat's • steam-|boat's

■ 2? January 1864 · To Jane Lampton Clemens · Carson City, Nev. Terr. · *UCCL* 00072

■*Copy-text:* MS, pages 3–4, 'ment . . . know.' (267.1–28), Jean Webster McKinney Family Papers, Vassar College Library (NPV); MS, pages 5–6, Mark Twain Papers, The Bancroft Library, University of California, Berkeley (CU-MARK). Pages 1–2 of the MS are missing. ■*Previous publication: MTB*, 1:243–44, excerpt; *MTBus*, 79–80, excerpt not in *MTB*. ■*Provenance:* see McKinney Family Papers, pp. 459–61. The last two MS pages were probably acquired in the Moffett Collection; see p. 462. ■*Emendations and textual notes:*

267.8	p̶ & • ['&' *over* 'p']
267.11	t̶h̶ nobody • ['n' *over* 'th']
267.11	tell⸝— • [*dash over period*]
267.11	¢Enrolling • ['E' *over* 'e']
267.14	under • un¢der ['d' *over* 'e']

267.23	semi-occasionally · semi-|occasionally
267.26	provided something · provided ꞩ something ['s' *written prematurely and canceled before* 'd' *was inserted; false start*]
268.13	ꞁ her · ['h' *over partly formed* 'w']
268.14	w̶o̶r̶k̶ worm · wormk̶ ['m' *over* 'k']
268.17	ꞁ care · ['c' *over* 'w']
268.17	care worn · [*possibly* 'careworn']
268.22	a̶t̶ ̶s̶u̶n̶ at twilight · ['at twi' *over* 'at sun']
268.23–24	[*illegible deletion, torn*]—I · [*Dash over heavy cancellation; the presence of actual characters under the cancellation is not certain; see p. 270, n. 9. The illustration reproduces the original MS at 50 percent of actual size.*]

■ 9 and 10 January 1864 · To Jane Lampton Clemens and Pamela A. Moffett · Carson City, Nev. Terr. · *UCCL* 00073

■ *Copy-text:* MS, Mark Twain Papers, The Bancroft Library, University of California, Berkeley (CU-MARK). ■ *Previous publication: MTB*, 1:243, brief excerpt. ■ *Provenance:* see Mark Twain Papers, pp. 461–62. ■ *Emendations and textual notes:*

271.4	d̶ Dear · ['D' *over* 'd']
271.17	use,— · [*dash over period*]
271.20	s̶h̶ you · ['y' *over* 's' *and another character, possibly partly formed* 'h' *or* 'l']
271.23	L̶e̶g̶e̶ Legislature · Legꞔislature ['i' *over* 'e']

■ 23 January 1864 · To Seymour Pixley and G. A. Sears · Carson City, Nev. Terr. · *UCCL* 00074

■ *Copy-text:* "Local Matters," Carson City *Independent*, 24 Jan 64, undated clipping headed "Daily Independent" in Scrapbook 4:3, Moffett Collection, Mark Twain Papers, The Bancroft Library, University of California, Berkeley (CU-MARK). ■ *Previous publication:* China [pseud.], "Carson Correspondence," Gold Hill (Nev. Terr.) *News*, 25 Jan 64, 2; *MTB*, 1:245; *MTL*, 1:96. ■ *Provenance:* see Moffett Collection, p. 462. The Gold Hill *News* establishes the source and date of the undated clipping that serves as copy-text. Datelined "Carson City, Jan. 25.," the column begins: "Editor Gold Hill News.—The following correspondence published in the *Independent* of this place, yesterday morning, speaks for itself. . . ." No complete copy of the *Independent* is known to survive for the period 23–25 Jan 64 (Lingenfelter and Gash, 33–34). ■*Emendations and textual notes:* Collation shows that the Gold Hill *News*, *MTB*, and *MTL* all derive from the *Independent* and may therefore be ignored.

272.4   I am • ɪ am
272.5   I take • ɪ take

■ 29 February 1864 · To J. T. Goodman and Company · Virginia City, Nev. Terr. · *UCCL* 00075

■*Copy-text:* MS, Mark Twain Papers, The Bancroft Library, University of California, Berkeley (CU-MARK). ■*Previous publication:* none known. ■*Provenance:* acquisition date unknown; possibly Moffett Collection; see p. 462. Orion Clemens wrote on the verso of the leaf, 'Sam's order for $150'. Since there is no mark on this document indicating that it was negotiated, it is possible that Orion did not deliver it for payment, and that therefore it remained in the family's possession. There is, however, no reason to suppose that Orion did not collect the money. ■*Emendations and textual notes:*

273.2   28̶ 29 • 29̸8̸ ['9' *over* '8']
273.3   Goodman ̂ • Good&̶m̶man ['ma' *over* '&m']

■ 18 March 1864 · To Pamela A. Moffett · Virginia City, Nev. Terr. · *UCCL* 00076

■*Copy-text:* MS, pages 1–2, 5–8, Moffett Collection, Mark Twain Papers, The Bancroft Library, University of California, Berkeley (CU-MARK); MS, pages 3–4, 'of much . . . If' (274.18–37), Jean Webster McKinney Family Papers, Vassar College Library (NPV). ■*Previous publication:* *MTB*, 1:248, brief excerpts; *MTL*, 1:89, a single paragraph, 'Pamela . . . sisters.' (274.20–30), mistakenly printed as part of 11 and 12 Apr 63 to Jane Clemens and Pamela Moffett. The excerpts printed in *MTB* and *MTL* do not overlap. They were in separate collections when Paine saw them, and he evidently did not realize they were parts of the same letter. ■*Provenance:* see Moffett Collection, p. 462, and McKinney Family Papers, pp. 459–61. ■*Emendations and textual notes:*

273.8   M̶o̶t̶ Sister • ['Sis' *over* 'Mot']
273.9   b̶e̶c̶ this • ['th' *over* 'bec']
274.1   Orpheus • Op̸rpheus ['r' *over* 'p']
274.4   n̶o̶t̶e̶ brief • ['brief' *over* 'note']
274.7   cap/, • [*comma over period*]
274.11   handwriting • hand-|writing

274.12–13   door-|plate • door-plate
274.20   d̶o̶ you • ['yo' *over* 'do']
274.22   t̶h̶e̶n̶ not • ['not' *over* 'then']
275.2   would‚n't‚ • ['n't' *squeezed in at end of line, probably inserted*]
275.2   such • such such
275.3   G̶o̶ his • ['his' *over* 'Go']
275.8   i̶t̶ to • ['to' *over* 'it']
275.13   had • hai̶dd [*possibly* 'haadd'*;* 'd' *over* 'id' *or possibly* 'ad']
275.17   t̶h̶i̶e̶v̶i̶n̶g̶,̶ ̶l̶o̶u̶s̶y̶ slow‚‚,̶going‚‚ r̶a̶t̶t̶y̶ ̶p̶o̶p̶u̶l̶ careless • t̶h̶i̶e̶v̶i̶n̶g̶,̶
             slow‚‚|‚going‚‚ l̶o̶u̶s̶y̶ ̶r̶a̶t̶t̶y̶ ̶p̶o̶p̶u̶l̶ careless [*originally* 'thieving, |
             lousy'*;* 'slow,' *over* 'thieving,' *and* 'ratty' *over* 'lousy'*;* 'popul'
             added, making 'slow, | ratty popul'*; hyphen over comma after* 'slow'
             and 'going, careless' *over* 'ratty popul' *to make* 'slow-going, care-
             less']
275.19   h̶e̶r̶ hearing • hefaring ['a' *over* 'r']
275.25   P̶ & • ['&' *over possible* 'P']
275.26   to-day • to-|day
275.26   f̶l̶a̶s̶ flakes • flaskes ['k' *over* 's']
276.1   there • [*sic*]
276.4   f feel • ['f' *over* 'r']
276.6   ̶(̶b̶e̶l̶ (beware • (befware ['w' *over* 'l']
276.8   thankful • thfankful ['a' *over* 'n']

■ **14 April 1864 · To Orion Clemens · Virginia City, Nev. Terr. · *UCCL*
11066**

■ *Copy-text:* Transcript (including signature) in an unknown hand, in *Proclama-
tions, Appointments, Messages, 1861–1864*, 251, in Executive Records of Governor
James Warren Nye (1861–1864), Nevada State Library and Archives, Division of
Archives and Records, Carson City (Nv-Ar). ■ *Previous publication:* Rocha and
Smith, 88. ■ *Provenance:* Clemens's MS is not known to survive. ■ *Emendations
and textual notes:* none.

■ **17 May 1864 · To Jane Lampton Clemens and Pamela A. Moffett ·
Virginia City, Nev. Terr. · *UCCL* 00077**

■ *Copy-text:* "History of the Gold and Silver Bars—How They Do Things in
Washoe," clipping from an unidentified newspaper in Scrapbook 1:59, Moffett
Collection, Mark Twain Papers, The Bancroft Library, University of California,
Berkeley (CU-MARK). ■ *Previous publication: MTEnt*, 186–89. ■ *Provenance:*
see Moffett Collection, p. 462. References in the clipping to "a lady of this city"
and "our Sanitary Fair" (p. 284, n. 1) establish that the story was written for and

presumably published in a St. Louis newspaper. The copy-text clipping, however, could be of a reprint in a Nevada or other newspaper. A search of microfilms of the *Missouri Democrat* and the *Missouri Republican* failed to locate the article, but the typography of the clipping resembles that of the *Democrat* and not that of the *Republican*. No other St. Louis newspaper microfilm for the period could be located, and no other English-language newspaper for the period is listed in the files of the State Historical Society of Missouri, Columbia. ■ *Emendations and textual notes:*

282.3	Storey • Story [*As a newspaper reporter in Storey County, Clemens certainly knew the correct spelling.*]
282.9	know. Then • ~.—|~
282.15	RUEL • [*also 'Ruel' at 282.24, 282.26, 282.27, 282.29, 282.36, and 283.2. The name is correctly spelled 'Reuel' in chapter 45 of* Roughing It *(SLC 1872a, 316); misspelled 'Ruel' in Clemens's 1897 notebook (Notebook 41, TS p. 36, CU-MARK); and correctly spelled in a 1906 typescript (AD, 16 Mar 1906). No evidence has been found, however, to show whether Clemens knew the correct spelling in 1864 or was responsible for the correct spelling in 1872 or 1906. The only located instance of the name in his handwriting is the notebook entry, when he misspelled it as here. Consequently the misspelling in the newspaper has not been emended.*]
282.17	as • [*not in*]
282.17	himself, • him
282.18	sympathies." He • ~."—|~
283.7	couldn't • could'nt
283.8	$500 dollars • [*sic*]
283.17	blocked up • blockedup
283.25	hers • her's
283.37	in the • on the
284.5	Enterprise • enterprise [*Clemens sometimes wrote initial 'e' in a form similar to his 'E'; someone not familiar with his hand might therefore have difficulty telling whether a word in his MS began with 'e' or 'E'. Presumably the St. Louis compositor, not realizing that 'the Enterprise' was a newspaper, misread Clemens's 'E' as 'e' and missed the underline. We have emended to style 'Enterprise' like the other newspaper titles mentioned, as Clemens probably did.*]

■ 20 May 1864 · To Mary E. (Mollie) Clemens · Virginia City, Nev. Terr. · *UCCL* 00078

■ *Copy-text:* MS, Mark Twain Papers, The Bancroft Library, University of California, Berkeley (CU-MARK). ■ *Previous publication: MTEnt,* 190–91. ■ *Provenance:* probably Moffett Collection; see p. 462. ■ *Emendations and textual notes:*

287.4   thousand • thou-|ßsand ['s' *over* 's']
287.7   ladies • [*sic*]
288.1   *I* item • ['i' *over* 'I']
288.10   handwriting • hand-|writing
288.21   dealt • dealltt ['t' *over* 'lt']
288.22   wound • woulnd ['n' *over* 'l']
288.31   day,, • [*comma over period*]
288.34   pu the • ['the' *over* 'pu']

■ 21 May 1864 · To James L. Laird · Virginia City, Nev. Terr. · *UCCL* 00079

■ *Copy-text:* "Personal Correspondence," letter I, Virginia City *Territorial Enterprise*, 24 May 64, clipping in Scrapbook 3:146, Moffett Collection, Mark Twain Papers, The Bancroft Library, University of California, Berkeley (CU-MARK). ■ *Previous publication: MTEnt,* 191–92. ■ *Provenance:* see Moffett Collection, p. 462. ■ *Emendations and textual notes:* none.

■ 21 May 1864 · To James L. Laird · Virginia City, Nev. Terr. · *UCCL* 02773

■ *Copy-text:* "Personal Correspondence," letter III, Virginia City *Territorial Enterprise*, 24 May 64, clipping in Scrapbook 3:146, Moffett Collection, Mark Twain Papers, The Bancroft Library, University of California, Berkeley (CU-MARK). ■ *Previous publication:* Benson, 183, reprinted from the Sacramento *Union,* 26 May 64, 2; *MTEnt,* 192. ■ *Provenance:* see Moffett Collection, p. 462. ■ *Emendations and textual notes:*

292.15   L. CLEMENS • L[◊] CLEMENS

■ 21 May 1864 · To James L. Laird · Virginia City, Nev. Terr. · *UCCL* 02774

■ *Copy-text:* "Personal Correspondence," letter V, Virginia City *Territorial Enterprise*, 24 May 64, clipping in Scrapbook 3:146, Moffett Collection, Mark Twain Papers, The Bancroft Library, University of California, Berkeley (CU-MARK). ■ *Previous publication:* Benson, 184–85, reprinted from the Sacramento *Union,* 26 May 64; *MTEnt,* 193–95. ■ *Provenance:* see Moffett Collection, p. 462. ■ *Emendations and textual notes:*

293.18   issue • is[◊]|sue
293.27   liar. Meeting • liar[◊] Meeting
294.9   retract." • retract[◊]"

■ 23 May 1864 · To Ellen G. Cutler · Virginia City, Nev. Terr. · *UCCL* 00080

■ *Copy-text: MTL*, 1:97–98. ■ *Previous publication:* none known except the copy-text. Paine observed in 1917 that the letter had "never before been published" (*MTL*, 1:97). ■ *Provenance:* unknown. ■ *Emendations and textual notes:* The rationale for emendations to remove *MTL* styling is given on pp. 458–59.

296.1	Virginia, May 23rd, 1864. •	VIRGINIA, *May 23rd, 1864.*
296.2	Mrs. W. K. Cutler: •	MRS. W. K. CUTLER:
296.3	Madam— •	MADAM,—
296.25	Sam. L. Clemens. •	SAM. L. CLEMENS.

■ 25 May 1864 · To Orion and Mary E. (Mollie) Clemens · Virginia City, Nev. Terr. · *UCCL* 00081

■ *Copy-text:* MS, Mark Twain Papers, The Bancroft Library, University of California, Berkeley (CU-MARK). A photographic facsimile of the MS is on pp. 430–32. The MS consists of a folder of blue-lined off-white laid paper, $7\frac{3}{4}$ by $9\frac{3}{4}$ inches (19.7 by 24.8 cm), blind embossed in the upper left corner with the word 'BANCROFT' in a decorative lozenge. The folder is inscribed on the first three pages in black ink, now faded to brown. ■ *Previous publication: MTEnt*, 201–2. ■ *Provenance:* probably Moffett Collection; see p. 462. On the last page of the MS folder someone, probably Orion, wrote in pencil: 'For Mr & Mrs Sam'l L. Clemens, Care of Mrs Crane Elmira n y'. This address could have been written in almost any year during the period from 1871 to 1897, when the Clemenses spent many summers at Susan Crane's Elmira home. Orion Clemens died on 11 December 1897. Next to the address Paine wrote in pencil '1864'. Also on the last page, a penciled note that may have been in Paine's hand has been erased: 'These letters are not to be published or used in any way. They are to be destroyed.' At the top of the first MS page Paine wrote in pencil 'May '64' and '[May 25? 1864]'. ■ *Emendations and textual notes:*

297.5	popⱷularity •	['u' *inserted over* 'o']
298.12	t̶o̶ if •	['if' *over* 'to']
298.20	q̶ peace •	['p' *over* 'q']
298.23	Yro •	[*sic*]

■ 26 May 1864 · To Orion Clemens · Virginia City, Nev. Terr. · *UCCL* 00082

■ *Copy-text:* MS, Mark Twain Papers, The Bancroft Library, University of California, Berkeley (CU-MARK). ■ *Previous publication: MTEnt*, 203. ■ *Provenance:* see Mark Twain Papers, pp. 461–62. A penciled underscore below 'Henness Pass' (299.5) may have been added by Orion Clemens, either when he received the letter or perhaps when he was preparing his autobiography in 1880; Clemens wrote the letter in ink. Although Paine did not publish this letter, two notes on the MS, '[Thursday]' above the date and '*Imp.*' below it, appear to be in his hand. Since Clemens announces in the letter his secret plan to leave Virginia City on Sunday, it is indeed important—if that is what '*Imp.*' means—to know that the letter was written on Thursday. ■*Emendations and textual notes:*

299.3–4   *comfortably.* However • ~.—|~
299.6   it/, • [*comma over period*]
299.7   us/, • [*comma over period*]
299.11   ẇ̸ away • ['a' *over partly formed* 'w']

■ 28 May 1864 · To William K. Cutler · Virginia City, Nev. Terr. · *UCCL* 00083

■*Copy-text:* MS, *draft not sent,* William Wright Papers, The Bancroft Library, University of California, Berkeley (CU-BANC). ■*Previous publication: MTEnt,* 204. ■*Provenance:* The William Wright Papers were acquired by The Bancroft Library in November 1953. The collection includes correspondence, manuscripts, notebooks, and clippings of articles by Wright (Dan De Quille) as well as letters and other documents by members of his family (*The William Wright Papers: Report and Key to Arrangement,* typescript, The Bancroft Library). The second draft of this letter, which was actually sent, is not known to survive. ■*Emendations and textual notes:*

301.5   o̶n̶e̶ once • onȼe ['c' *over* 'e']
301.6   accept/ it. • ~. ~. [*deletion implied*]
301.7   r̶e̶c̶i̶ received • recḭeived ['e' *over* 'i']
301.8   t̶o̶ no • ['no' *over* 'to']

■ 15 July 1864 · To William Wright (Dan De Quille) · San Francisco, Calif. · *UCCL* 00084

■*Copy-text:* MS, William Wright Papers, The Bancroft Library, University of California, Berkeley (CU-BANC). Repeated foldings have worn holes in the MS where the creases intersect, affecting some characters, which have been emended. A photographic facsimile of the MS is on pp. 433–38. The MS consists of three half sheets of poor-quality off-white wove paper, 7⅜ by 9 7/16 inches (18.8 by 24 cm), each inscribed on both sides in black ink, now faded to brown. The paper, soiled and much folded, was formerly stitched together roughly where it had separated along the folds; some of the holes through which the thread passed are visible in the facsimile. ■*Previous publication:* Fender, 752, excerpts. ■*Provenance:* see the previous commentary. ■*Emendations and textual notes:*

303.9	Frenchwoman • French-|woman
303.14	dropper • [*sic*]
303.15	desperate • despe*r*-|rate [*hyphen over* 'r']
303.25	sunrise • sun-|rise
304.2	~thei~ throw • the*i*row ['ro' *over* 'ei']
304.4	hear • [he]ar [*torn*]
304.4	bottles • bo[t]tles [*torn*]
304.7	knives • kni*v*es ['v' *over* 'e']
304.8	~los~ lots • lo*t*s ['t' *over* 's']
304.10–11	*G* God • ['G' *over* 'g']
304.12	lifetime • l[◇]fetime [*torn*]
304.15	*c*ivilization • ['c' *over* 's']

■ 12 August 1864 · To Jane Lampton Clemens · San Francisco, Calif. ·
UCCL 10993

■ *Copy-text:* Author's copy, in MS of 13 and 14 Aug 64 to OC and MEC (307.4–
15), Mark Twain Papers, The Bancroft Library, University of California, Berkeley (CU-MARK), is copy-text for 'My . . . ago.' (305.1–306.4); a leaf of MS inscribed on one side only, Jean Webster McKinney Family Papers, Vassar College
Library (NPV), is copy-text for 'The . . . look-a-here,' (306.6–15). It is conjectural but probable that the leaf at Vassar is from the MS of this letter (see p. 306,
n. 3); the remainder of the MS is missing. Since Clemens revised the text of this
MS leaf when copying it into his 13 and 14 Aug 64 letter to Orion and Mollie, it
is likely that he also changed the first paragraph of this letter, when copying it into
that one, in ways not now detectable. ■ *Previous publication:* none known. ■ *Provenance:* MS of the salutation and first paragraph probably acquired in the Moffett
Collection; see p. 462. See McKinney Family Papers, pp. 459–61. ■ *Emendations
and textual notes:* In 13 and 14 Aug 64 to OC and MEC, Clemens enjoys imagining
how his mother will discover she is being teased only when she turns to the second
page of this letter (see p. 307.16–22). Therefore, the second page of the missing
MS must have begun about at 'I reflect' (306.3), as Clemens contrived for the second page of his letter to Orion and Mollie to do (see p. 308, n. 2). Since the surviving MS leaf of this letter bears the page number '3', the gap between the two
surviving parts of the letter represents all but a line or two of the missing second
page of the MS. An unknown amount of text is missing at the end of the letter.

305.2	My • "~
306.4	ago. • ~."
306.9	newspaper • news-|paper
306.15	expectin'*g* • [*possibly* 'expecti'n*g*'; *apostrophe inserted above* 'n'. *This ambiguous placement may foreshadow the reading* 'expect'n' *in the revision of the passage included in 13 and 14 Aug 64 to OC and MEC (308.8)*]

■ 13 and 14 August 1864 · To Orion and Mary E. (Mollie) Clemens · San Francisco, Calif. · *UCCL* 00085

■ *Copy-text:* MS, Mark Twain Papers, The Bancroft Library, University of California, Berkeley (CU-MARK). ■ *Previous publication:* none known. ■ *Provenance:* probably Moffett Collection; see p. 462. ■ *Emendations and textual notes:*

307.1	~~12~~ 13 • 13̸ ['2' *mended to* '3']
307.17	a̸ • ~~alodẃ a~~ ['d' *over* 'w' *or possibly* 'u'; 'a' *may have been canceled because it was too close to the canceled miswriting for legibility*]
307.19	~~wort~~ words • wor/ds ['d' *over partly formed* 't']
307.25	shotgun • [*possibly* 'shot gun']
307.26	ruther • [*sic*]
307.29	them,— • [*dash over period*]
307.29	went into • went/ into [*false start*]
307.32	sky-rocket • sh̸ky-rocket ['k' *over possible* 'h']
308.3	(it • [*no closing parenthesis*]
308.7	~~co~~ angrily • ['an' *over possible* 'co']
308.8	he,~~;~~ "W̶ with • ['w' *over colon; open quotation marks and a partly formed character, probably* 'W', *canceled. Clemens probably meant to cancel all three marks at once by writing over them but had to cancel the quotation marks and the partly formed character separately when* 'with' *fit below them without touching them.*]
308.18	wouldn't • would/n't ['n' *over partly formed* 't']

■ 17 September 1864 · To William Wright (Dan De Quille) · San Francisco, Calif. · *UCCL* 00086

■ *Copy-text:* photographic facsimile of MS, Mack 1947, facing 256. ■ *Previous publication:* none known except the copy-text. ■ *Provenance:* unknown. ■ *Emendations and textual notes:*

309.4	bedfellow • bed-|fellow
309.8	T̸ Mr • ['M' *over partly formed* 'T']

■ 25 September 1864 · To Jane Lampton Clemens and Pamela A. Moffett · San Francisco, Calif. · *UCCL* 00087

■ *Copy-text:* MS, Jean Webster McKinney Family Papers, Vassar College Library (NPV). ■ *Previous publication: MTB*, 1:256, excerpts; *MTL*, 1:99–100, with omissions. ■ *Provenance:* see McKinney Family Papers, pp. 459–61. ■ *Emendations and textual notes:*

311.6	funeral,— • [*dash over period*]
311.9	enemy'sies • ['y's' *over* 'ies']
311.11	188 1864 • 1864,8 ['6' *over* '8']
311.14	snow-banks • snow-|banks
311.16	were wear • werear ['ar' *over* 'er']
312.7	& h now • ['now' *over* '& h']
312.16–17	I What • ['W' *over* 'I']
312.18–19	"Californian"— • [*possibly* ' "Californian"—; *close quotation marks above dash*]
312.20–21	high-|toned • high-toned
312.30	Railroad • Railroaidd ['d' *over* 'id']
312.32	because it • becausit it [*false start*]
312.34	to d • ['d' *partly formed*]
313.7	button-holedhold • button-hold|holed
313.9	Board,. • [*period over comma*]
313.10–11	x experience • ['e' *over* 'x']

■ 28 September 1864 · To Orion and Mary E. (Mollie) Clemens · San Francisco, Calif. · *UCCL* 00088

■*Copy-text:* MS, Mark Twain Papers, The Bancroft Library, University of California, Berkeley (CU-MARK). ■*Previous publication:* none known. ■*Provenance:* probably Moffett Collection; see p. 462. ■*Emendations and textual notes:*

315.11–12	We shall take a bridal . . . duration., [¶] Your head • ['ke a bridal' *over* 'Your head']

■ 18 October 1864 · To Orion Clemens · San Francisco, Calif. · *UCCL* 00090

■*Copy-text:* MS, Mark Twain Papers, The Bancroft Library, University of California, Berkeley (CU-MARK). ■*Previous publication:* none known. ■*Provenance:* probably Moffett Collection; see p. 462. ■*Emendations and textual notes:* none.

■ 11 November 1864 · To Orion Clemens · San Francisco, Calif. · *UCCL* 00091

■*Copy-text:* MS, Mark Twain Papers, The Bancroft Library, University of California, Berkeley (CU-MARK). ■*Previous publication:* none known. ■*Provenance:* probably Moffett Collection; see p. 462. ■*Emendations and textual notes:* none.

■ 19 and 20 October 1865 · To Orion and Mary E. (Mollie) Clemens ·
San Francisco, Calif. · *UCCL* 00092

■*Copy-text:* MS, Mark Twain Papers, The Bancroft Library, University of California, Berkeley (CU-MARK); damage emended. A photographic facsimile of
the MS is on pp. 439–43. The MS consists of four sheets of thin, poor-quality
white wove paper, 9 1/16 by 11 inches (22.9 by 28 cm), having the word 'PARIS' in a
decorative lozenge blind embossed in the upper left corner of each leaf. The first
three leaves are inscribed on one side only in a black ink, now faded to brown; the
fourth leaf is inscribed on the recto in the same ink and on the verso in black pencil. The first three leaves have been mounted on supporting sheets; the fourth
leaf, bearing Clemens's inscription on the back, has not been mounted. All four
leaves are creased and chipped, especially along the right edge where one crucial
fragment is missing (324.34). ■*Previous publication:* SLC 1961, 6–9. ■*Provenance:* probably Moffett Collection; see p. 462. ■*Emendations and textual notes:*

322.12   preach · ['e' *and* 'a' *written as one character*]
322.19   A̶n̶ But · ['Bu' *over* 'An']
322.20   litera/ture · ['t' *over* 'r']
322.22   m̶ that · ['th' *over* 'm']
322.22   multiply · mul/tiply ['t' *inserted over* 'l']
323.5   **education**͵— · [*dash over period*]
323.20   autumn · [*possibly* '/ autumn'*; the* 'a' *is blotted and smeared and
            probably was not written over another character, but it might possibly
            be over* 's']
323.26   neighbor͵, · [*comma over period*]
323.30   p̶a̶r̶t̶i̶a̶l̶i̶t̶y̶ the glamour · ['the glam' *over* 'partiality']
323.32   toss · t[o]ss [*torn*]
323.37   property · [*possibly* 'property,']
324.2   i̶n̶s̶i̶g̶n̶i̶f̶i̶c̶a̶n̶t̶ · ins[ig]n[i]fic[ant] [*torn*]
324.2–3   fire-|fly · fire-fly
324.8   do so? · [*sic*]
324.12 $̶— · [*dash over dollar sign*]
324.20   but · [*sic*]
324.23   arrived, but · ar[ri◇◇d], [b]ut [*torn*]
324.24   G̶o̶ ̶o̶n̶,̶ ̶I̶ · ['on' *doubtful*]
324.34   Self-Murder—Proceed.] · Self-[M◇◇d◇◇—]Proceed.[]] [*Clem-
            ens's closing bracket is extremely faint. A fragment of paper where
            'Murder' was written is missing; a mark on the surviving edge might
            be the top of the* 'd'. *A crease runs the full length of the page about* 1/8
            *inch from the edge in all four leaves of the MS, and fragments have bro-
            ken away from all four leaves along the crease, but only at this point has
            any text been lost for that reason. This fragment could have broken
            away accidentally, because the paper is brittle, but the possibility that
            someone tore it deliberately cannot be ruled out.*]

■ 13 December 1865 · To Orion and Mary E. (Mollie) Clemens · San Francisco, Calif. · *UCCL* 00093

■*Copy-text:* MS, Mark Twain Papers, The Bancroft Library, University of California, Berkeley (CU-MARK). ■*Previous publication:* none known. ■*Provenance:* probably Moffett Collection; see p. 462. ■*Emendations and textual notes:*

326.5	untr untiring • unt⁄iring ['i' *over* 'r']	
326.6	⁄New • ['N' *over* 'n']	
326.6	lev leaves • le⁄aves ['a' *over* 'v']	
326.8	it⁄— • [*dash over period*]	
326.13	mining • mi⁄-|ning [*hyphen over* 'i']	
326.14	∅ in • ['i' *over* 'o']	
326.26	la leaves • l⁄eaves ['e' *over* 'a']	

■ 20 January 1866 · To Jane Lampton Clemens and Pamela A. Moffett · San Francisco, Calif. · *UCCL* 00094

■*Copy-text:* MS, Mark Twain Papers, The Bancroft Library, University of California, Berkeley (CU-MARK). ■*Previous publication: MTB*, 1:278–79, 280, 281, excerpts; *MTL*, 1:101–2, with omissions. ■*Provenance:* probably Moffett Collection; see p. 462. ■*Emendations and textual notes:*

327.2	1865 • [*sic*]	
327.9	backwoods • back-|woods	
328.13	Weekly • Wee⁄kly ['k' *over* 'l']	
328.13–14	the Saturday • the | Saturday [*Both words were canceled with identical looping scrawls, presumably together, not separately.*]	
329.2	you'll ⁄ hear • you'll ⁄ hea hear ['h' *of* 'hea' *over* 'y'; 'hea' *rewritten for clarity*]	
329.3	wildcats • wild-|cats	
329.28	write • writt write	

■ 3? March 1866 · To William R. Gillis · San Francisco, Calif. · *UCCL* 00095

■*Copy-text:* Paraphrase in William R. Gillis, 43. ■*Previous publication:* William R. Gillis, *Gold Rush Days with Mark Twain* (New York: Boni, 1930), 75–76, a later edition of the same paraphrase with minor variants that are without authority. ■*Provenance:* unknown. ■*Emendations and textual notes:*

332.2	I • "∼	
332.2	for Sandwich • [*sic*]	

332.14   "convenient season." • '~ ~.'
332.17   so. • ~."

■ 5 March 1866 · To Jane Lampton Clemens and Pamela A. Moffett ·
San Francisco, Calif. · *UCCL* 00096

■*Copy-text:* MS, Jean Webster McKinney Family Papers, Vassar College Library (NPV). ■*Previous publication: MTB*, 1:282, brief excerpt; *MTL*, 1:103.
■*Provenance:* see McKinney Family Papers, pp. 459–61. ■*Emendations and textual notes:*

333.4   to-morrow • to-|morrow
333.6   J̵ We • ['I' *doubtful*]
333.6   I̶ ̶h̶a̶v̶e̶ My friends • ['My frie' *over* 'I have']

■ 3 April 1866 · To Jane Lampton Clemens and Pamela A. Moffett ·
Honolulu, Sandwich Islands · *UCCL* 00097

■*Copy-text:* MS, Jean Webster McKinney Family Papers, Vassar College Library (NPV). ■*Previous publication: MTB*, 1:283, 284, excerpts; *MTL*, 1:104.
■*Provenance:* see McKinney Family Papers, pp. 459–61. ■*Emendations and textual notes:*

334.5   ẅ ridden • ['r' *over* 'w']
334.14   I̶ ̶a̶m̶ ̶t̶o̶ He is to • ['He is to' *over* 'I am to']
335.1   to-night • to-|night
335.3   ₰ as • ['a' *over* 's']
335.4   s̶e̶ sail • sₐ́ail ['a' *over* 'e']

■ 26 April 1866 · To W. C. Kimball and W. W. Kimball · Island of
Maui, Sandwich Islands · *UCCL* 00098

■*Copy-text:* MS, collection of Victor and Irene Murr Jacobs, Dayton, Ohio.
■*Previous publication: Autographs and Modern Signed Editions. Catalogue 70*
(Bridgewater, Mass.: Paul C. Richards Autographs, [1972]), item 174, with
omissions. ■*Provenance:* Victor Jacobs acquired the MS from Paul C. Richards
Autographs, which had acquired it from Rodney C. Eaton, a great-nephew of the
Kimballs'. In 1971 Mr. Eaton sent a photographic facsimile of the MS to the
Mark Twain Papers. ■*Emendations and textual notes:*

336.5   c̶o̶m̶i̶ comeliness • comₑ́eliness ['e' *over* 'i']
336.8   k̶n̶o̶w̶ ̶m̶ have forgotten • ['have for' *over* 'know m']

■ 4 May 1866 · To Jane Lampton Clemens and Pamela A. Moffett · Island of Maui, Sandwich Islands · *UCCL* 00099

■*Copy-text:* MS, Jean Webster McKinney Family Papers, Vassar College Library (NPV). ■*Previous publication: MTL*, 1:104–5, with omissions; *MTBus*, 85–86, with omissions; *MTH*, 40–41, brief excerpt. ■*Provenance:* see McKinney Family Papers, pp. 459–61. ■*Emendations and textual notes:*

336.14	P̶l̶a̶n̶t̶a̶ Sugar •	['Sugar' *over* 'Planta']
336.14	Plantation • Plandtation	['t' *over* 'd']
336.19	c̶a̶m̶e̶ went •	['went' *over* 'came']
336.19–20	Ulapalakua •	[*sic*]
337.1	mine,), •	[*close parenthesis over comma*]
337.3	₫ (this •	[*open parenthesis over* 'a']
337.7	t̶h̶e̶ ̶o̶t̶h̶e̶r̶ last week •	['last week' *over* 'the other']
337.18	₫ cribbage •	['c' *over* 'a']
337.23	girl's •	[*sic*]
337.26	H̶a̶l̶a̶ Haleakala • Haldeakala	['e' *over* 'a']
337.34	Kee-low-*way*-ah),— •	[*dash over period*]

■ 7 May 1866 · To William Bowen · Island of Maui, Sandwich Islands · *UCCL* 00100

■*Copy-text:* Photographic facsimile of MS, Harry Ransom Humanities Research Center, University of Texas, Austin (TxU). ■*Previous publication: MTLBowen*, 11–12. ■*Provenance:* The University of Texas acquired the facsimile from Royden Burwell Bowen, son of William Bowen, about 1940 (*MTLBowen*, 10). ■*Emendations and textual notes:*

338.1	P̶l̶ Sugar •	['Su' *over* 'Pl']
339.13	n̶i̶c̶ fine •	['fine' *over doubtful* 'nic']
339.19	s̶l̶i̶ sleight • sldeight	['e' *over* 'i']
339.27	i̶d̶ iodine • idlodine	['o' *over* 'd']
340.3	₫ is •	['i' *over* 'a']
340.6	"Union." •	[*possibly italicized, but what might be an underscore appears more likely to be a crossbar mistakenly written by Clemens across* 'h' *in* 'Christian' *(340.7) in the line below, presumably under the momentary impression that it was a* 't']

■ 22 May 1866 · To Mary E. (Mollie) Clemens · Honolulu, Sandwich Islands · *UCCL* 00101

■*Copy-text:* MS, Jean Webster McKinney Family Papers, Vassar College Library (NPV). ■*Previous publication: MTL*, 1:105–6, with omissions; *MTBus*,

87–88, with omissions; *MTH*, 42, excerpt. ∎*Provenance:* see McKinney Family Papers, pp. 459–61. ∎*Emendations and textual notes:*

341.3	~~fo~~ from • f∮rom ['r' *over* 'o']
341.10	Ж Hawaii • ['H' *over* 'M']
341.11	Kileaua • [*sic*]
341.19	~~damm~~ damn • damn̖m̸ [*final* 'm' *mended to* 'n']
341.25	~~that~~ Ma • ['Ma' *over* 'that']

∎ 21 June 1866 · To Jane Lampton Clemens and Pamela A. Moffett · Honolulu, Sandwich Islands · *UCCL* 00102

∎*Copy-text:* MS, Jean Webster McKinney Family Papers, Vassar College Library (NPV). ∎*Previous publication: MTL*, 1:106–8, with omissions. ∎*Provenance:* see McKinney Family Papers, pp. 459–61. ∎*Emendations and textual notes:*

343.8	ʒ 18ᵗʰ • ['1' *over partly formed* '2']
343.9	horseback • horse-|back
343.17	Kaui • [*sic*]
343.22	Ж U.S. • ['U' *over partly formed* 'M']
344.15	~~Kauu~~ Kauai • Kau∦ai ['u' *mended to* 'a']
344.16	Cony • [*sic*]

∎ 27 June 1866 · To Jane Lampton Clemens and Pamela A. Moffett · Honolulu, Sandwich Islands · *UCCL* 00103

∎*Copy-text:* MS, pages 1–2 (in part), 7–9, Jean Webster McKinney Family Papers, Vassar College Library (NPV). The bottom three-fourths of the first leaf has been cut away, truncating the text of MS pages 1 and 2, which were written on the two sides of the leaf. MS pages 3 through 6 are missing. ∎*Previous publication: MTB*, 1:285 and 287, brief excerpts and paraphrase; *MTL*, 1:108–9, with omissions; *MTBus*, 86, brief excerpt. ∎*Provenance:* see McKinney Family Papers, pp. 459–61. The cut-away parts were probably already missing when Paine saw the MS, for he printed almost all the surviving text but none of what is missing. In 1912 he quoted 'California . . . doubt.' (347.8–9) among the excerpts in *MTB*, and in 1917, observing that "only a fragment" of the letter then survived, he printed the bulk of the text from 'with a gill' (347.11) to the end in *MTL*. S. C. Webster introduced the fragment 'Gen. . . . doubt.' (347.8–10) with the comment, "Another letter to his mother has been largely cut away, probably because a warning postscript says that it must not be shown to anybody. My family, unfortunately, were very conscientious about following Uncle Sam's instructions" (*MTBus*, 86). ∎*Emendations and textual notes:*

347.5	don't r • [*The remainder of the leaf is cut away.*]
347.9	doubt. • [*The remainder of the leaf is cut away. The top of some character survives on the cut edge where the next line would have begun, indicating that* 'doubt.'*, which falls at the end of a line, was not the end of a paragraph.*]
347.15	it. Mr. • ~.—|~.
347.22–23	acknowledged • ack-‖kno̶nowledged ['now' *over* 'know']
347.26–27	t̶h̶e̶n̶ there • there̸ ['re' *over* 'n']
348.1	first̸,— • [*dash over period*]

■ 19 July 1866 · To Samuel C. Damon · Honolulu, Sandwich Islands · *UCCL* 00104

■*Copy-text:* " 'Mark Twain,' at the Confessional!" *The Friend* 17 n.s. (1 Aug 66): 65. ■*Previous publication: MTH*, 156. ■*Provenance:* unknown. ■*Emendations and textual notes:*

349.2	Mr. • ~,
349.6–7	admissable • [*sic*]

■ 30 July, 6, 7, 8, 10, and 20 August 1866 · To Jane Lampton Clemens and Pamela A. Moffett · *Smyrniote* en route from Honolulu to San Francisco, and San Francisco, Calif. · *UCCL* 00105

■*Copy-text:* MS, Jean Webster McKinney Family Papers, Vassar College Library (NPV). ■*Previous publication: MTB*, 1:289, brief excerpt; *MTL*, 1:115–19, with omissions. ■*Provenance:* see McKinney Family Papers, pp. 459–61. ■*Emendations and textual notes:* Someone, probably not Clemens, drew a single thin line through two passages: 'I am . . . San F.' (351.20–21) and 'Orion . . . Magazine.' (353.34–37). The lines were drawn so lightly that they leave the passages quite unobscured; their similar appearance indicates they were probably drawn by the same person. They are in a black ink, faded to brown, now indistinguishable from the ink in which Clemens wrote the letter, but they are unlike the marks Clemens normally used for cancellation. When he canceled a passage so as actually to delete it, it was his habit to write heavily with loops and swirls or repeated overscores, making the text hard to read. The purpose of *these* lines, however, is not clear, and context is of little help in understanding them. The only other mark in the MS not obviously by Clemens is a penciled *X* before 'I played whist' (351.9) marking the first of three places where Paine omitted text in *MTL*. Paine probably wrote the *X*, and he may also have drawn the anomalous lines when editing the letter. He published only a brief excerpt not related to either of these passages in *MTB*, but in *MTL* he published the whole letter except for three silent omissions: 'I played . . . there.' (351.9–15); 'Under . . . it.' "

(353.28–29); and 'I suppose . . . stomach.' (353.31–354.7). The last of these includes the second passage lined through in the MS. Observing that the passages are at least partly redundant, Paine might have marked them while deciding whether to omit one. If Paine was the one who lined through the MS passages, however, the fact cannot be proved and his reasons remain conjectural.

350.8–9	(at . . . day,) . . . unnoticed.) • [*sic*]
350.9	At f The • ['T' *over* 'f']
350.13–14	I bee-line • ['b' *over* 'l']
350.15	it at • *l*at ['a' *over undotted* 'i' *of* 'it']
350.17	y we • ['w' *over* 'y']
351.1	m Mississippi • ['M' *over* 'm']
351.1–2	gla glitters • gl*i*tters ['i' *over* 'a']
351.2	possib polished • polishedssib ['lished' *over* 'ssib']
351.3–4	ground-|swell • ground-swell
351.9	played whist • ['w' *over* 'd']
351.11	oclock • [*sic*]
351.11	"fore "four • "four*r*e ['ur' *over* 're']
351.15	at hom in San • ['in San' *over* 'at hom']
351.16	4 5 • ['5' *over* '4']
351.20–21	I am . . . San F. • [*lightly lined through but not canceled, probably not by Clemens; see textual commentary*]
351.25	5 6 • ['6' *over* '5']
352.5–6	booby-|hatch • booby-hatch
352.10	in h of • ['of' *over* 'in h']
352.10	h Heaven • [*Clemens started to write* 'h' *but completed the character as* 'H']
352.14	ac well • ['we' *over* 'ac']
352.22–23	star-|light • starlight
352.24	minutes • [*sic*]
352.25	the gallant vessels she • ['she' *over* 'the']
352.31	9 8 • ['8' *over* '9']
352.33–34	main-|mast • mainmast
352.36	close • [*sic*]
353.4	finger • finge*r* ['r' *over* 's']
353.8	waste of broad • ['broad' *over* 'waste of']
353.14–16	‚I am sorry . . . speed.‚ [¶] Friday • ['sorry' *over* 'Friday']
353.24	oclock • [*sic*]
353.34–37	Orion . . . Magazine. • [*lightly lined through but not canceled, probably not by Clemens; see textual commentary*]
354.1	I Looking • ['L' *over* 'I']

354.2   Emmeline • [*sic*]

354.2–3   Corn-|bread • Corn-bread

■ 13 August 1866 · To the Publishers of the Sacramento *Union* (James Anthony, Henry W. Larkin, and Paul Morrill) · San Francisco, Calif. · *UCCL* 10676

■ *Copy-text:* MS facsimile, *draft telegram;* MS in the collection of Robert A. Gates. ■ *Previous publication:* none known. ■ *Provenance:* Mr. Gates provided a photograph of the MS to the Mark Twain Papers in 1984. The recipients' copy of the telegram is not known to survive. ■ *Emendations and textual notes:* The MS is a folder of which one page contains the draft telegram and the other three pages contain a draft of part of Clemens's sketch "How, For Instance?" first published in the New York *Weekly Review* (29 Sept 66, 1).

356.1   PRIVATE • ['Private' *with three underscores*]

356.3   afternoon,— • [*dash over period*]

■ 25 August 1866 · To William Bowen · San Francisco, Calif. · *UCCL* 00106

■ *Copy-text:* MS, Harry Ransom Humanities Research Center, University of Texas, Austin (TxU). The corner of the last leaf is torn off, affecting three lines that are emended at 359.24, 24–25, and 27. ■ *Previous publication: MTLBowen,* 12–15. ■ *Provenance:* The University of Texas acquired the MS in the summer of 1940 from William Bowen's daughter Mrs. Louis Knox, the former Eva Laura Bowen (*MTLBowen,* 7 n. 12, 10). ■ *Emendations and textual notes:*

357.16   that • [*sic*]

357.21   miss • m~~ſ~~iss miss ['i' *over* 's'; *rewritten for clarity*]

357.22–23   circumstances • ci~~c~~rcumstances ['rc' *over* 'cu']

358.1   ~~wil~~ wielded • wi/elded ['e' *over* 'l']

358.12   ~~cir~~ other • ['oth' *over* 'cir']

358.18   phenomenonṃ • ['m' *mended to* 'n']

358.23   traveler • trave/ler ['l' *over* 'r']

358.32   g̸ again • ['a' *over* 'g']

358.35   Ṃ Why • ['W' *over partly formed character, possibly* 'M', 'N', *or* 'A']

358.35   O'Neil • [*sic*]

358.35   ~~did~~ die • di~~e~~d ['e' *over* 'd']

359.7   Burling g̸ame • ['a' *over* 'g']

359.7   Valkenburg • [*sic*]

359.24   I don't know • I [d◇◇'◇] | know [torn; see illustration, which repro-
              duces the damaged part of the MS at 83 percent of actual size]
359.24–25   uncertain institution • unce[◇◇◇◇◇] | institution [torn; see illustra-
              tion]
359.27   Mark • M[a◇◇] [torn; see illustration]
359.31   S̶a̶m̶ Mark • ['Mark' over 'Sam']

■ 29 October 1866 · To Robert M. Howland · Virginia City, Nev. ·
UCCL 00107

■ Copy-text: MS, Nevada Historical Society, Reno (NvHi). A facsimile of the MS
is in Branch 1950 following 130. ■ Previous publication: Hutcheson, 1–2. ■ Provenance: Louise Howland, Robert M. Howland's daughter, gave the MS to the
Nevada State Museum in about 1948. It was deposited at the Nevada Historical
Society in the 1970s and subsequently became the property of the Historical Society (Hutcheson, 1–2; Eric Moody, Curator of Manuscripts, Nevada Historical
Society, telephone conversation with K. M. Sanderson, 2 Jan 1987). ■ Emendations and textual notes:

362.4   to-morrow • to-|morrow

■ 1 November 1866 · To Abraham V. Z. Curry and Others per Telegraph
Operator · Virginia City, Nev. · UCCL 00108

■ Copy-text: Transcript, Mark Twain Papers, The Bancroft Library, University
of California, Berkeley (CU-MARK). The transcript is a TS prepared by Dixon
Wecter from the original telegram blank, which was presumably filled out in the
hand of a telegraph operator and received by Curry and the others. ■ Previous
publication: none known. ■ Provenance: In September 1948 Mrs. Charles Gunn
and Louise Howland, daughters of Robert M. Howland, loaned the original of
this document and nine MS Clemens letters to Dixon Wecter, then editor of the
Mark Twain Papers, to enable him to transcribe them. Sometime after Wecter returned the letters, the original of this telegram was lost. ■ Emendations and textual
notes: Wecter was a meticulous and accurate transcriber. His typescript reflects
the style of known telegraph forms in matters like spacing, alignment, typography, and the record of the telegram's word count. Text presumed to have been
printed on the original telegram blank appears in small capitals, and dotted

underscores have been supplied below the portions of the dateline and address line that would normally have been written in blanks provided for them. The emendations report these typographic refinements on Wecter's typescript. A border has also been added to distinguish this text as a telegram, on the model of Clemens's telegrams of 15 and 21 June 58 to William A. Moffett (pp. 80 and 85).

363.1	CALIFORNIA . . . COMPANY •	CALIFORNIA STATE TELE-GRAPH COMPANY
363.2	Virginia Nov. 1st 186 6 •	Virginia [City] Nov. 1st 1866 [*The telegraph operator would have been unlikely to write* '[City]'. *Presumably Wecter added it to avoid ambiguity in the typescript that would not have been a problem in the original.*]
363.4	TO A Curry, J. Neely Johnson •	To A Curry, J. Neely Johnson

■ 1 November 1866 · To Henry G. Blasdel and Others · Virginia City, Nev. · *UCCL* 00109

■*Copy-text:* "Card from Mark Twain," Virginia City *Territorial Enterprise*, 4 Nov 66, 2, University of Nevada Reno (NvU). ■*Previous publication:* "Card from Mark Twain," Sacramento *Union*, 6 Nov 66, 2; Benson, 200. ■*Provenance:* unknown. ■*Emendations and textual notes:*

364.3	*Rice* •	*Ric*[e]
364.6	generous toleration •	gen[◊]rous toleration
364.13–14	shortcomings •	shortcomiugs
364.21	Independent Opposition •	Indep[e]n[◊]en[◊] Op[◊]|position
364.22	Islands •	[I]slands

■ 2 November 1866 · To Jane Lampton Clemens and Family · Virginia City, Nev. · *UCCL* 00110

■*Copy-text:* MS, Jean Webster McKinney Family Papers, Vassar College Library (NPV). ■*Previous publication: MTL*, 1:121, with omissions. ■*Provenance:* see McKinney Family Papers, pp. 459–61. ■*Emendations and textual notes:*

365.5	last,— •	[*dash over period*]

■ 2? November 1866 · To Catherine C. (Kate) Lampton and Annie E. and Samuel E. Moffett · Virginia City, Nev. · *UCCL* 00111

■*Copy-text:* MS, pp. 5–6, Jean Webster McKinney Family Papers, Vassar College Library (NPV). MS pages 1–4 are lost. The extant MS is a single leaf inscribed on both sides and numbered '5' on the recto. ■*Previous publication:* none known. ∎*Provenance:* see McKinney Family Papers, pp. 459–61. ∎*Emendations and textual notes:*

367.3	second-hand • second-|hand
367.9–10	& I . . . touch • [*crossed out with a large penciled* X, *probably by Orion Clemens; the letter was written in ink*]
367.11	b̶e̶ carry • ['ca' *over* 'be']

∎ 4 December 1866 · To Jane Lampton Clemens and Family · San Francisco, Calif. · *UCCL* 00112

∎*Copy-text:* MS, Jean Webster McKinney Family Papers, Vassar College Library (NPV); damage emended. ∎*Previous publication: MTL*, 1:122, with omissions. ∎*Provenance:* see McKinney Family Papers, pp. 459–61. ∎*Emendations and textual notes:* Tears in the MS were once mended with transparent tape which damaged the MS further, staining it and obscuring some text. Conservation treatment improved the legibility of the MS significantly and recovered several readings not formerly visible, but three words that had been clearly legible, 'imperial', 'he', and '&' (368.14, 368.15, and 368.15), were partially or totally lost when the tape was removed, as the accompanying illustration of the first page shows. Fortunately, the MS was examined and a microfilm was made before the MS was treated. The MS was also examined again after the treatment. Text legible during at least one examination of the MS has been transcribed without emendation. Readings obscured or invisible during both examinations have been emended.

368.3	Katie some • Kati[e] some [*torn*]
368.6	the old rip • [*Revised in pencil, probably by Paine:* 't̶h̶e̶ ̶o̶l̶d̶ ̶r̶i̶p̶ ₓhe,' *or possibly* 't̶h̶e̶ ̶o̶l̶d̶ ̶r̶i̶p̶ ₓhe,'. *MTL reads* 'he'.]
368.7	thick & thieves • [*sic*]
368.10	Henry Ward • Henry [W]ard [*torn*]
368.10	Dʳ Tyng • D[◊] | Tyng [*torn*]
368.10	other • oth/er ['e' *over* 'r']
368.12	preacher now • preache[r] | now [*torn*]
368.13	cloth for • cl[◊◊◊] | for [*torn*]
368.14	c̶o̶n̶s̶ an able • ['an able' *over* 'cons']
368.15	Christian • Ch[r]istian [*torn*]
368.17	Oakland • O[a]kland [*torn*]
368.19	i̶s̶ knew • ['k' *over* 'is']
368.20	neé • [*sic*]
369.1–2	head-|quarters • head-|quarters [*i.e.,* 'headquarters']
369.2	∤ there • ['t' *over* 'a']
369.2	A̶j̶ Adjutant • A/djutant ['d' *over* 'j']
369.2	u̶n̶d̶e̶r̶ to Maj. • ['to Maj.' *over* 'under']

San.f. Dec. 4, 1866.

My Dear folks —

I ... are written to An-
nie & Sammy & Katie some time
ago — also to the balance of you.
... I called on Rev. Dr Wadsworth last night with the City College man, but ~~the old rip~~ wasn't
at home. I was sorry, because
I wanted to make his acquaintance.
I am thick & thieves with the Rev.
Stebbings, & I am laying for the
Rev. Scudder & the Rev. Dr Stone.
I am running on preachers, now
altogether. I find them gay. Stebbings is a regular brick. I am
taking letters of introduction to
Henry Ward Beecher Rev. D.
Tyng, & other eminent parsons
in the east. Whenever anybody
offers me a letter to a preacher
now, I snaffle it on the spot.
I shall make Rev. Dr Bellows
trot out the fast nags of the
for me when I get to New York.
Bellows is ~~an~~ able, upright &
eloquent man — a man of im-
p ... intellect & matchless power
... is Christian in the truest sense
of the terms is unquestionably a brick.

4 December 1866 to Jane Lampton Clemens and Family. Facsimile of the first MS page reproduced at 51 percent of actual size.

■ 4 December 1866 · To Isabella A. Cotton · San Francisco, Calif. ·
UCCL 00113

■*Copy-text:* MS, James and John M. Tufts Collection, Mark Twain Papers, The
Bancroft Library, University of California, Berkeley (CU-MARK). A photographic facsimile of the MS is on p. 444. The MS consists of one sheet of very thin
blue-lined white wove paper, 7$\frac{15}{16}$ by 10$\frac{3}{8}$ inches (20.1 by 26.4 cm), inscribed on
one side only in black ink, now faded to brown. The leaf has been mounted on a
stiff backing sheet for support. ■*Previous publication:* none known. ■*Provenance:*
see Tufts Collection, pp. 462–63. ■*Emendations and textual notes:*

371.5	~~Opposition~~ Opposition • ['Opposition' *over wiped out, possibly miswritten* 'Opposition']
371.6	~~13ᵗʰ~~ 15ᵗʰ • 1,5ᵗʰ3ᵗʰ ['3' *mended to* '5', *canceling first* 'ᵗʰ'; 'ᵗʰ' *added*]
371.9	above • aboveᵥ ['e' *over last part of* 'w' *mending it to* 'v']
371.12	forgǿet • ['e' *over* 'o']
371.12	~~for th~~ in the • ['in the' *over doubtful* 'for th']

■ 4 December 1866 · To Isabella A. Cotton · San Francisco, Calif. ·
UCCL 00114

■*Copy-text:* MS, James and John M. Tufts Collection, Mark Twain Papers, The
Bancroft Library, University of California, Berkeley (CU-MARK). ■*Previous
publication:* none known. ■*Provenance:* see Tufts Collection, pp. 462–63.
■*Emendations and textual notes:* none.

■ 6 December 1866 · To Frederick F. Low and Others · San Francisco,
Calif. · UCCL 00115

■*Copy-text:* "Correspondence," San Francisco *Alta California*, 8 Dec 66, 2. ■*Previous publication: MTH*, 449–50. ■*Provenance:* The MS is not known to survive.
■*Emendations and textual notes:*

372.18	occasion • occrsion

■ 15 December 1866 · To Jane Lampton Clemens and Family · San
Francisco, Calif. · UCCL 00116

■*Copy-text:* MS, Jean Webster McKinney Family Papers, Vassar College Library
(NPV). ■*Previous publication: MTB*, 1:304, brief excerpt; *MTBus*, 89. ■*Provenance:* see McKinney Family Papers, pp. 459–61. ■*Emendations and textual notes:*

373.7	~~not~~ none • no/ne ['n' *over* 't']
373.8	Webb,. • [*period over comma*]
373.9	to-night • to-|night

References

This LIST defines the abbreviations used in this book and provides full bibliographic information for works cited by the author's name, by the author's name and publication date, or by a short title.

AD   Autobiographical Dictation.

Adler, Jacob.
    1966. *Claus Spreckels: The Sugar King in Hawaii*. Honolulu: University of Hawaii Press.

AMT
    1959. *The Autobiography of Mark Twain*. Edited by Charles Neider. New York: Harper and Brothers.

Anderson, Frederick, and Edgar Marquess Branch, eds.
    1972. *The Great Landslide Case*. Berkeley: The Friends of The Bancroft Library.

Angel, Myron, ed.
    1881. *History of Nevada*. Oakland, Calif.: Thompson and West. See Poulton's *Index to History of Nevada*.

Appleton.
    1885. *Appletons' Annual Cyclopaedia and Register of Important Events of the Year 1884*. New York: D. Appleton and Co.

Armstrong, C. J.
    1930. "Mark Twain's Early Writings Discovered." *Missouri Historical Review* 24 (July): 485–501.

Arrington, Joseph Earl.
    1953. "Leon D. Pomarede's Original Panorama of the Mississippi River." *Bulletin of the Missouri Historical Society* 9 (April): 261–73.

Austin, Franklin H.
    1926. "Mark Twain Incognito—A Reminiscence." *Friend* 96 (September, October, November): 201–4, 224–29, 248–54. Partly reprinted in *MTH*, 75–79.

Baetzhold, Howard G.

1972. "Found: Mark Twain's 'Lost Sweetheart.' " *American Literature* 44 (November): 414–29.

Baker, William.

1979. "Mark Twain in Cincinnati: A Mystery Most Compelling." *American Literary Realism* 12 (Autumn): 299–315.

BAL

1957. *Bibliography of American Literature.* Compiled by Jacob Blanck. Vol. 2. New Haven: Yale University Press.

Bancroft, Hubert Howe.

1882–90. *History of the Pacific States of North America.* 34 vols. San Francisco: A. L. Bancroft and Co./ History Company.

1891–92. *Chronicles of the Builders of the Commonwealth.* 7 vols. San Francisco: History Company.

1892. *Index to Chronicles of the Builders of the Commonwealth.* San Francisco: History Company.

Barnes, George E.

1887. "Mark Twain. As He Was Known during His Stay on the Pacific Slope." San Francisco *Morning Call*, 17 April, 1.

Bassford, Homer.

1899. "Mark Twain as a Cub Pilot: A Talk with His Old Chief, Captain Horace Bixby." *Saturday Evening Post* 172 (16 December): 515.

Bates, Allan C.

1967. "Sam Clemens, Pilot-Humorist of a Tramp Steamboat." *American Literature* 39 (March): 102–9.

1968. *Mark Twain and the Mississippi River.* Ph.D. diss., University of Chicago.

BBC

1966. *British Broadcasting Corporation Song Catalogue.* 4 vols. London: British Broadcasting Corporation.

BDAC

1961. *Biographical Directory of the American Congress, 1774–1961.* Washington, D.C.: Government Printing Office.

Belcher, Wyatt Winton.

1947. *The Economic Rivalry between St. Louis and Chicago 1850–1880.* Studies in History, Economics and Public Law, edited by the Faculty of Political Science of Columbia University, publication no. 529. New York: Columbia University Press.

Bell, Raymond Martin.

1984. *The Ancestry of Samuel Clemens, Grandfather of Mark Twain.* TS in CU-MARK.

Bellows, Henry Whitney.

1857. *The Relation of Public Amusements to Public Morality, Especially of the Theatre to the Highest Interests of Humanity.* New York: C. S. Francis and Co.

Benson, Ivan.
1938. *Mark Twain's Western Years*. Stanford University: Stanford University Press.

Biographical Review
1905. *Biographical Review of Lee County, Iowa, Containing Biographical and Genealogical Sketches of Many of the Prominent Citizens of To-day and Also of the Past*. Chicago: Hobart Publishing Company.

[Bixby, Horace E.]
1882. "How the Boy Became a Pilot and the Pilot a Humorist." New Orleans *Times-Democrat*, 7 May, 3.

1910. "Learned River for $500." St. Louis *Missouri Republican*, 22 April, 3.

Bowers, Fredson.
1976. "Transcription of Manuscripts: The Record of Variants." *Studies in Bibliography* 29:212–64.

Branch, Edgar Marquess.
1942. *Mark Twain's Letters in the Muscatine "Journal."* Chicago: Mark Twain Association of America.

1950. *The Literary Apprenticeship of Mark Twain*. Urbana: University of Illinois Press.

1969. "Mark Twain Reports the Races in Sacramento." *Huntington Library Quarterly* 32 (February): 179–86.

1982a. "Sam Clemens, Steersman on the *John H. Dickey*." *American Literary Realism* 15 (Autumn): 195–208.

1982b. "A New Clemens Footprint: Soleather Steps Forward." *American Literature* 54 (December): 497–510.

1983–84. "Did Sam Clemens Write 'Learning Grammar'?" *Studies in American Humor* 2 (Winter): 201–5.

1984. "Three New Letters by Samuel L. Clemens in the Muscatine *Journal*." *Mark Twain Journal* 22 (Spring): 2–7.

1985a. *Men Call Me Lucky: Mark Twain and the "Pennsylvania."* Oxford, Ohio: Friends of the Library Society, Miami University.

1985b. "Fact and Fiction in the Blind Lead Episode of *Roughing It*." *Nevada Historical Society Quarterly* 28 (Winter): 234–48.

1987, forthcoming. "A Proposed Calendar of Samuel Clemens's Steamboats, 15 April 1857 to 8 May 1861, with Commentary." *Mark Twain Journal* 24 (Fall 1986).

Brashear, Minnie M.
1934. *Mark Twain, Son of Missouri*. Chapel Hill: University of North Carolina Press.

Brigham, Clarence S.
1962. *History and Bibliography of American Newspapers, 1690–1820*. 2 vols. Reissue, with additions and corrections, of 1947 American Antiquarian Society edition. Hamden, Conn.: Archon Books.

Briton [pseud.].
1863. "Letter from Esmeralda District." Letter dated 27 March. San Francisco *Alta California*, 28 March, 1.

Brooks, Ida L.
1906. "Did Mark Twain's Laziness Cost Him a Fortune?" San Francisco *Chronicle*, 25 March, 1–2.

Brown, Alexander Crosby.
1974. *Longboat to Hawaii: An Account of the Voyage of the Clipper Ship "Hornet" of New York Bound for San Francisco in 1866.* Cambridge, Md.: Cornell Maritime Press.

Browne, Charles Farrar [Artemus Ward, pseud.].
1898. *The Complete Works of Artemus Ward, (Charles Farrar Browne.) With a Biographical Sketch.* Rev. ed. New York: G. W. Dillingham Company.

Browne, J[ohn] Ross.
1860–61. "A Peep at Washoe." Articles 1–3. *Harper's New Monthly Magazine* 22 (December–February): 1–17, 145–62, 289–305.

Browne, J[ohn] Ross, and James W. Taylor.
1867. *Reports upon the Mineral Resources of the United States.* Washington, D.C.: Government Printing Office.

Bunker, William M.
[1879]. *From Report upon the Aurora Mining District, Esmeralda Co., Nevada.* San Francisco: Barry, Baird, and Co.

Burns, Shannon.
1980. "A Fraudulent Mark Twain Letter." *American Literary Realism* 13 (Spring): 90–92.

By-laws
1868. *By-laws of the Hale and Norcross Silver Mining Company.* San Francisco: Commercial Herald.

Campbell and Richardson.
1863. *Campbell & Richardson's St. Louis Business Directory for 1863.* St. Louis: Campbell and Richardson.

Carlson, Helen S.
1974. *Nevada Place Names: A Geographical Dictionary.* Reno: University of Nevada Press.

CCamarSJ   Estelle Doheny Collection, The Edward Laurence Doheny Memorial Library, Saint John's Seminary, Camarillo, California.

Chalfant, Willie Arthur.
1928. *Outposts of Civilization.* Boston: Christopher Publishing House.

Clagett   Collection of Fred Clagett.

Clark, Dennis.
1973. *The Irish in Philadelphia: Ten Generations of Urban Experience.* Philadelphia: Temple University Press.

Clemens, Mary E. (Mollie). See MEC.

Clemens, Orion. See OC.

Clemens, Samuel L. See SLC.

CofC
1969. *Clemens of the "Call": Mark Twain in San Francisco.* Edited by Edgar M. Branch. Berkeley and Los Angeles: University of California Press.

Colcord, R. K.
1928. "Reminiscences of Life in Territorial Nevada." *Nevada Historical Society Quarterly* 7 (June): 112–19.

Collins, Lewis.
1874. *History of Kentucky.* 2 vols. Rev. and enl. ed. Covington, Ky.: Collins and Co. Citations are to the 1966 reprint edition, Frankfort, Ky.: Kentucky Historical Society.

Conard, Howard L., ed.
1901. *Encyclopedia of the History of Missouri.* 6 vols. New York: Southern History Company.

Condé, Jesse C., and Gerald M. Best.
1973. *Sugar Trains: Narrow Gauge Rails of Hawaii.* Felton, Calif.: Glenwood Publishers.

Congressional Globe
1835–73. *Congressional Globe.* 46 vols. Washington, D.C.: Globe Office.

Copp, Samuel.
1864. Letter to Almarin B. Paul, 6 June, in "The Gold and Silver Bars from Nevada." St. Louis *Missouri Republican*, 8 June, 3.

Cordier, Henri.
1901–2. *Histoire des relations de la Chine avec les puissances occidentales, 1860–1900.* 3 vols. Paris: Felix Alcan, Éditeur.

Covici, Pascal, Jr.
1960. "Dear Master Wattie: The Mark Twain–David Watt Bowser Letters." *Southwest Review* 45 (Spring): 106–9.

Cowan, Robert Ernest, Anne Bancroft, and Addie L. Ballou.
1964. *The Forgotten Characters of Old San Francisco.* Los Angeles: Ward Ritchie Press.

Cox, Samuel S.
1862. *Speech of Hon. S. S. Cox, of Ohio, in Vindication of Gen. McClellan from the Attacks of Congressional War Critics.* Washington, D.C.: Towers and Co.

Crone, John S.
1937. *A Concise Dictionary of Irish Biography.* Rev. and enl. ed. Dublin: Talbot Press. Citations are to the 1970 reprint edition, Nendeln / Liechtenstein: Kraus Reprint.

CTcHi   North Lake Tahoe Historical Society, Tahoe City, California.

CtY   Yale University Library, New Haven, Connecticut.

CU-BANC   The Bancroft Library, University of California, Berkeley.

CU-MARK   Mark Twain Papers, CU-BANC.

Curtis, William E.
1888. "The Gate City of Iowa: Keokuk and Her Famous Sons." Chicago *News* ("Morning Issue"), 2 August, 1, clipping in Scrapbook 20:80–83, CU-MARK.

DAB
1928–36. *Dictionary of American Biography*. Edited by Allen Johnson and Dumas Malone. 20 vols. New York: Charles Scribner's Sons.

Daggett, Rollin M.
1893. "Daggett's Recollections," in "The Passing of a Pioneer." San Francisco *Examiner*, 22 January, 15. Reprinted as "*Enterprise* Men and Events" in Lewis, 11–16.

DAH
1940. *Dictionary of American History*. Edited by James Truslow Adams and R. V. Coleman. 5 vols. New York: Charles Scribner's Sons.

Dale, Lily [pseud.].
1863. "Letter from Esmeralda." Letter dated 30 November. San Francisco *Alta California*, 11 December, 3.

Daley   Collection of Robert Daley.

Damon, Ethel M.
1966. *Samuel Chenery Damon*. Honolulu: Hawaiian Mission Children's Society.

Davis, Chester L.
1956a. "Mark Twain's Highway Robbery as Told by Steve Gillis." *Twainian* 15 (January–February): 3–4.

1956b. "Letters from Steve Gillis." *Twainian* 15 (March–April): 1–3.

1956c. "Mining Days Sweetheart of Mark Twain." *Twainian* 15 (May–June): 1–2.

1956d. "Goodman's Assistance on the Biography." *Twainian* 15 (May–June): 2–4.

1981. "Mark's Mother in Keokuk." *Twainian* 40 (January–February): 1–4.

Davis, Walter B., and Daniel S. Durrie.
1876. *An Illustrated History of Missouri*. St. Louis: A. J. Hall and Co.

Daws, Gavan.
1968. *Shoal of Time: A History of the Hawaiian Islands*. New York: Macmillan Company.

Day, A. Grove.
1968. *Hawaii and Its People*. Rev. ed. New York: Meredith Press.

DeLaney, Wesley L.
1948. "The Truth about That Humboldt Trip as Told by Gus Oliver to A. B. Paine." *Twainian* 7 (May–June): 1–3.

De Vinne, Theodore Low.
1910. *Correct Composition: A Treatise on Spelling Abbreviations, the Compound-*

ing and Division of Words, the Proper Use of Figures and Numerals, Italic and Capital Letters, Notes, Etc. 3d ed. New York: Century Company.

Dickson, Samuel.
1947. *San Francisco Is Your Home.* Stanford, Calif.: Stanford University Press.

Dillon, William.
1888. *Life of John Mitchel.* 2 vols. London: Kegan Paul, Trench, and Co.

Dixon, W. W.
1903. "Sketch of the Life and Character of William H. Clagett." *Contributions to the Historical Society of Montana* 4:249–57.

Doten, Alfred.
1866. "Mark Twain's Lecture—An Immense Success." Virginia City *Territorial Enterprise,* 1 November, 3.
1973. *The Journals of Alfred Doten, 1849–1903.* Edited by Walter Van Tilburg Clark. 3 vols. Reno: University of Nevada Press.

Eberlein, Harold Donaldson, and Cortlandt Van Dyke Hubbard.
1939. *Portrait of a Colonial City: Philadelphia, 1670–1838.* Philadelphia: J. B. Lippincott Company.

Edwards, Richard.
1864. *Edwards' Annual Director to the Inhabitants, Institutions, Incorporated Companies, Manufacturing Establishments, Business, Business Firms, &c., in the City of St. Louis, for 1864.* St. Louis: Richard Edwards.
1865. *Edwards' Annual Director to the Inhabitants, Institutions, Incorporated Companies, Manufacturing Establishments, Business, Business Firms, etc., etc., in the City of St. Louis, for 1865.* St. Louis: Richard Edwards.

Elliott, Russell R.
1973. *History of Nevada.* Lincoln: University of Nebraska Press.

Emrich, Duncan, ed.
1950. *Comstock Bonanza.* New York: Vanguard Press.

Estavan, Lawrence, ed.
1938–42. *San Francisco Theatre Research.* 18 vols. San Francisco: Work Projects Administration.

ET&S1
1979. *Early Tales & Sketches, Volume 1 (1851–1864).* Edited by Edgar Marquess Branch and Robert H. Hirst, with the assistance of Harriet Elinor Smith. The Works of Mark Twain. Berkeley, Los Angeles, London: University of California Press.

ET&S2
1981. *Early Tales & Sketches, Volume 2 (1864–1865).* Edited by Edgar Marquess Branch and Robert H. Hirst, with the assistance of Harriet Elinor Smith. The Works of Mark Twain. Berkeley, Los Angeles, London: University of California Press.

ET&S3
1988, forthcoming. *Early Tales & Sketches, Volume 3 (1866–1868).* Edited by Edgar Marquess Branch and Robert H. Hirst, with the assistance of Harriet

Elinor Smith. The Works of Mark Twain. Berkeley, Los Angeles, London: University of California Press.

Exhibition Catalogue
1853. *Official Catalogue of the New York Exhibition of the Industry of All Nations*. 1st rev. ed. New York: G. P. Putnam and Co.

Fatout, Paul.
1960. *Mark Twain on the Lecture Circuit*. Bloomington: Indiana University Press.
1964. *Mark Twain in Virginia City*. Bloomington: Indiana University Press.

Fender, Stephen.
1976. "'The Prodigal in a Far Country Chawing of Husks': Mark Twain's Search for a Style in the West." *Modern Language Review* 71 (October): 737–56.

Ferris, Ruth.
1965. "Captain Jolly in the Civil War." *Missouri Historical Society Bulletin* 22 (October): 14–31.

Foster, John G.
1872. Testimony of 20 February, in *Report of the Commissioners and Evidence Taken by the Committee on Mines and Mining of the House of Representatives of the United States, in Regard to the Sutro Tunnel*. Washington, D.C.: Government Printing Office.

Fulton, Robert.
1914. "Glimpses of the Mother Lode." *Bookman* 39 (March): 49–57.

Gallaher, Ruth A.
1922. "Hummer's Bell." *Palimpsest* 3 (May): 155–64.

Ganzel, Dewey.
1968. *Mark Twain Abroad: The Cruise of the "Quaker City."* Chicago: University of Chicago Press.

Garrett, Thomas E.
1879. *A Memorial of James Andrew Hayes Lampton, Past Master of George Washington Lodge, No. 9, A.F. & A.M.* St. Louis: Woodward, Tiernan and Hale.

Garrison, Raymond E.
1959. *Tales of Early Keokuk Homes*. Hamilton, Ill.: Hamilton Press.

Gates   Collection of Robert A. Gates.

Gianella, Vincent P.
1960. "The Site of Williams Station, Nevada." *Nevada Historical Society Quarterly* 3 (October–December): 5–10.

Gillis, Stephen E.
1864. "Personal Correspondence," Item VI. Virginia City *Territorial Enterprise*, 24 May, clipping in Scrapbook 3:146, CU-MARK.

Gillis, William R.
1924. *Memories of Mark Twain and Steve Gillis*. Sonora, Calif.: Banner.

Goode, George Brown, ed.
1897. *The Smithsonian Institution, 1846–1896: The History of Its First Half Century.* Washington, D.C.: [Smithsonian Institution].

Goodman, Joseph T.
1892. "Artemus Ward: His Visit to the Comstock Lode." San Francisco *Chronicle*, 10 January, 1.

Greeley, Horace.
1853. *Art and Industry as Represented in the Exhibition at the Crystal Palace New York—1853–4.* New York: J. S. Redfield.

Green.
1850. *Green's St. Louis Directory for 1851.* St. Louis: Charles and Hammond.

Greene, C. P., ed.
1905. *A Mirror of Hannibal.* Hannibal: C. P. Greene.

Gregory, Ralph.
1963. "Mark Twain's Last Visit to Florida." Paris (Mo.) *Monroe County Appeal*, 3 January, 9.
1971. "Sam Clemens and the Florida Girls." Paris (Mo.) *Monroe County Appeal*, 5 July, 3.

Gregory, Winifred, ed.
1937. *American Newspapers, 1821–1936: A Union List of Files Available in the United States and Canada.* New York: H. W. Wilson Company. Citations are to the 1967 reprint edition, New York: Kraus Reprint Corporation.

Gribben, Alan.
1980. *Mark Twain's Library: A Reconstruction.* 2 vols. Boston: G. K. Hall and Co.

Griffin, Lloyd Wilfred.
1941. "Matthew Franklin Whittier, 'Ethan Spike.'" *New England Quarterly* 14 (December): 646–63.

Grimes, Absalom.
1926. *Absalom Grimes: Confederate Mail Runner.* Edited by M. M. Quaife. New Haven, Conn.: Yale University Press.

Grissom, Daniel M.
1924. "Personal Recollections of Distinguished Missourians." *Missouri Historical Review* 19 (October): 94–98.

Gudde, Erwin G.
1960. *California Place Names.* Berkeley and Los Angeles: University of California Press.

Gunn   Collection of Mr. and Mrs. Robert M. Gunn.

Hague, James D.
1870. *Mining Industry.* Washington, D.C.: Government Printing Office.

Hall, Frank.
1889–95. *History of the State of Colorado.* 4 vols. Chicago: Blakely Printing Company.

Hannibal Census
[1850] 1963. "Free Inhabitants in the City of Hannibal." *Population Schedules of the Seventh Census of the United States, 1850. Roll 406. Missouri: Marion, Mercer, Miller, and Mississippi Counties.* National Archives Microfilm Publications, Microcopy no. 432. Washington, D.C.: General Services Administration.

Hanson, Joseph Mills.
1946. *The Conquest of the Missouri.* 2d ed. New York: Murray Hill Books, Rinehart and Co.

Harris, Faye Erma.
1965. *A Frontier Community: The Economic, Social, and Political Development of Keokuk, Iowa, from 1820 to 1866.* Ph.D. diss., University of Iowa.

Harrison, George C.
1858. "The Disaster to the Steamer Pennsylvania: Statement of an Eyewitness." Memphis *Morning Bulletin*, 22 June, 2. Facsimile in Branch 1985a, 27–30.

Hart, James D.
1978. *A Companion to California.* New York: Oxford University Press.

Harte, Bret.
1865a. "A New California Book." *Californian* 4 (23 December): 9. Reprinted in Howell, 86–89.

1865b. "Tailings. Second Notice." *Californian* 4 (30 December): 8. Reprinted in Howell, 89–91.

Harvey, Frederick L.
1902. *History of the Washington National Monument and of the Washington National Monument Society.* Washington, D.C.: Norman T. Elliott Printing Company.

HC   Henry Clemens.

Heintz, William F.
1975. *San Francisco Mayors, 1850–1880.* Woodside, Calif.: Gilbert Richards Publications.

Heitman, Francis B.
1903. *Historical Register and Dictionary of the United States Army, from Its Organization, September 29, 1789, to March 2, 1903.* 2 vols. Washington, D.C.: Government Printing Office.

Herndon, William Lewis, and Lardner Gibbon.
1853–54. *Exploration of the Valley of the Amazon, Made under Direction of the Navy Department.* 2 vols.: vol. 1 by Herndon, vol. 2 by Gibbon. Washington, D.C.: Robert Armstrong/A.O. P. Nicholson.

HF
1988, forthcoming. *Adventures of Huckleberry Finn.* Edited by Walter Blair and Victor Fischer. The Works of Mark Twain. Berkeley, Los Angeles, London: University of California Press.

History of Lee County
1879. *The History of Lee County, Iowa.* Chicago: Western Historical Company.

Hoe, Robert.
1902. *A Short History of the Printing Press.* New York: Robert Hoe.

Holcombe, Return I.
1884. *History of Marion County, Missouri.* St. Louis: E. F. Perkins. Citations are to the 1979 reprint edition, Hannibal and Marceline: Marion County Historical Society and Walsworth Publishing Company.

Howell, John, ed.
1927. *Sketches of the Sixties by Bret Harte and Mark Twain.* San Francisco: John Howell.

Howland, Louise.
[1906]. Untitled recollections of Mark Twain and Robert M. Howland, MS of five pages, Gunn.

Hudson, Frederic.
1873. *Journalism in the United States, from 1690 to 1872.* New York: Harper and Brothers. Citations are to the 1968 reprint edition, New York: Haskell House Publishers.

Huntington, David C.
1966. *The Landscapes of Frederic Edwin Church: Vision of an American Era.* New York: George Braziller.

Hutcheson, Austin E.
1948. "Twain Letter to Bob Howland Asks about Good Audience for Carson City Lecture." *Twainian* 4 (September–October): 1–2.

Hyde, William, and Howard L. Conard, eds.
1899. *Encyclopedia of the History of St. Louis.* 4 vols. New York: Southern History Company.

IaCrM   Iowa Masonic Library, Grand Lodge of Iowa, Cedar Rapids.

IaHi   State Historical Society of Iowa, Iowa City.

IaMu   P. M. Musser Public Library, Muscatine.

ICMM
1964. *The International Cyclopedia of Music and Musicians.* Edited by Robert Sabin. 9th ed. New York: Dodd, Mead, and Co.

Inds
1988, forthcoming. *Huck Finn and Tom Sawyer among the Indians, and Other Unfinished Stories.* Edited by Dahlia Armon and Walter Blair. The Mark Twain Library. Berkeley, Los Angeles, London: University of California Press.

Irvine, Leigh H., ed.
1905. *A History of the New California: Its Resources and People.* 2 vols. New York: Lewis Publishing Company.

Ivins, Virginia Wilcox.
[191_]. *Yesterdays: Reminiscences of Long Ago.* [Keokuk?]: n.p.

Jackson, Joseph.
1931–33. *Encyclopedia of Philadelphia.* 4 vols. Harrisburg: National Historical Association.

Jacobi, Charles Thomas.
   1888. *The Printers' Vocabulary: A Collection of Some 2500 Technical Terms, Phrases, Abbreviations and Other Expressions Mostly Relating to Letterpress Printing*. London: Chiswick Press.

Jacobs   Collection of Victor and Irene Murr Jacobs.

James, George Wharton.
   1910. *Heroes of California*. Boston: Little, Brown, and Co.

Jerome, Robert D., and Herbert A. Wisbey, Jr., eds.
   1977. *Mark Twain in Elmira*. Elmira, N.Y.: Mark Twain Society.

Jewett, Charles C.
   1851. *Notices of Public Libraries in the United States of America*. Smithsonian Reports. Washington, D.C.: Printed for the House of Representatives.

JLC   Jane Lampton Clemens.

Jolly, Sobieski.
   n.d. "Reminiscence of My Life as Master and Pilot on the Ohio and Mississippi Rivers." TS of MS, MoSHi.

Jones, Alexander E.
   1954. "Mark Twain and Freemasonry." *American Literature* 26 (November): 363–73.

Journal of the Assembly
   1866. *Journal of the Assembly during the Second Session of the Legislature of the State of Nevada*. Carson City: John Church.

Journal of the Council
   1862. *Journal of the Council of the First Legislative Assembly of the Territory of Nevada*. San Francisco: Valentine and Co.

Journal of the House
   1862. *Journal of the House of Representatives of the First Legislative Assembly of the Territory of Nevada*. San Francisco: Valentine and Co.

Kane, Elisha Kent.
   1853. *The U.S. Grinnell Expedition in Search of Sir John Franklin: A Personal Narrative*. New York: Harper and Brothers.

   1856. *Arctic Explorations: The Second Grinnell Expedition in Search of Sir John Franklin, 1853, '54, '55*. Philadelphia: Childs and Peterson.

Kelly, J. Wells, comp.
   1862. *First Directory of Nevada Territory*. San Francisco: Valentine and Co.

   1863. *Second Directory of Nevada Territory*. San Francisco: Valentine and Co.

Kennedy, Anthony.
   1908. "'Mark Twain' a Poor Typo." *Inland Printer* 40 (January): 560.

Kennedy, Robert V., comp.
   1857. *Kennedy's Saint Louis City Directory for the Year 1857*. St. Louis: R.V. Kennedy.

   1859. *St. Louis Directory, 1859*. St. Louis: R.V. Kennedy.

   1860. *St. Louis Directory, 1860*. St. Louis: R. V. Kennedy and Co.

Keokuk Census

[1850] 1963. "Free Inhabitants in the City of Keokuk." *Population Schedules of the Seventh Census of the United States, 1850. Roll 186. Iowa: Lee and Linn Counties*. National Archives Microfilm Publications, Microcopy no. 432. Washington, D.C.: General Services Administration.

[1860] 1967. "Free Inhabitants in . . . Keokuk City." *Population Schedules of the Eighth Census of the United States, 1860. Roll 330. Iowa: Kossuth and Lee Counties*. National Archives Microfilm Publications, Microcopy no. 653. Washington, D.C.: General Services Administration.

Kerr, Howard.

1972. *Mediums, and Spirit-Rappers, and Roaring Radicals: Spiritualism in American Literature, 1850–1900*. Urbana: University of Illinois Press.

Keseph [pseud.].

1863. "Our Letter from Esmeralda." Letter dated 18 January. San Francisco *Alta California*, 25 January, 1.

Knox, T. H., comp.

1854. *The St. Louis Directory, for the Years 1854–5*. St. Louis: Chambers and Knapp.

Korn, Alfons L.

1958. *The Victorian Visitors: An Account of the Hawaiian Kingdom, 1861–1866*. Honolulu: University of Hawaii Press.

Kouwenhoven, John A.

1953. *The Columbia Historical Portrait of New York*. Garden City, N.Y.: Doubleday and Co.

Krauth, Leland.

1980. "Mark Twain Fights Sam Clemens' Duel." *Mississippi Quarterly* 33 (Spring): 141–53.

Laird, James L.

1864a. "Personal Correspondence," Item IV. Virginia City *Territorial Enterprise*, 24 May, clipping in Scrapbook 3:146, CU-MARK.

1864b. "Personal Correspondence," Item VII. Virginia City *Territorial Enterprise*, 24 May, clipping in Scrapbook 3:146, CU-MARK.

Langley, Henry G., comp.

1859. *The San Francisco Directory for the Year Commencing June, 1859*. San Francisco: Valentine and Co.

1860. *The San Francisco Directory for the Year Commencing July, 1860*. San Francisco: Valentine and Co.

1861. *The San Francisco Directory for the Year Commencing September, 1861*. San Francisco: Valentine and Co.

1862. *The San Francisco Directory for the Year Commencing September, 1862*. San Francisco: Valentine and Co.

1863. *The San Francisco Directory for the Year Commencing October, 1863*. San Francisco: Towne and Bacon.

1864. *The San Francisco Directory for the Year Commencing October, 1864*. San Francisco: Towne and Bacon.

1865. *The San Francisco Directory for the Year Commencing December, 1865*. San Francisco: Towne and Bacon.

1867. *The San Francisco Directory for the Year Commencing September, 1867*. San Francisco: Henry G. Langley.

1868. *The San Francisco Directory for the Year Commencing October, 1868*. San Francisco: Henry G. Langley.

1869. *The San Francisco Directory for the Year Commencing December, 1869*. San Francisco: Henry G. Langley.

1874. *A Directory of the City of Oakland and the Town of Alameda, for the Year Ending December 31st, 1874*. Oakland, Calif.: Henry G. Langley.

Laws
1862. *Laws of the Territory of Nevada, Passed at the First Regular Session of the Legislative Assembly*. San Francisco: Valentine and Co.

1863. *Laws of the Territory of Nevada, Passed at the Second Regular Session of the Legislative Assembly*. Virginia City: J. T. Goodman and Co.

1864. *Laws of the Territory of Nevada, Passed at the Third Regular Session of the Legislative Assembly*. Virginia City: John Church and Co.

Lax, Roger, and Frederick Smith.
1984. *The Great Song Thesaurus*. New York: Oxford University Press.

Lee, W. Storrs.
1966. *The Islands*. New York: Holt, Rinehart and Winston.

Lewis, Oscar.
1971. *The Life and Times of the Virginia City "Territorial Enterprise": Being Reminiscences of Five Distinguished Comstock Journalists*. Ashland, Ore.: Lewis Osborne.

Lex
1963. *A Mark Twain Lexicon*. By Robert L. Ramsay and Frances G. Emberson. New York: Russell and Russell.

Liberal [pseud.].
1861. "Letter from Salt Lake." Letter dated 7 September. Sacramento *Union*, 12 September, 3.

Lincoln, Abraham.
1953–55. *The Collected Works of Abraham Lincoln*. Edited by Roy P. Basler. 9 vols. New Brunswick, N.J.: Rutgers University Press.

Lingenfelter, Richard E., and Karen Rix Gash.
1984. *The Newspapers of Nevada: A History and Bibliography, 1854–1979*. Reno: University of Nevada Press.

Litwack, Leon F.
1979. *Been in the Storm So Long*. New York: Alfred A. Knopf.

Lockwood, Charles.
1978. *Suddenly San Francisco: The Early Years of an Instant City*. San Francisco: San Francisco Examiner Division of the Hearst Corporation.

Lorch, Fred W.
1929a. "Mark Twain in Iowa." *Iowa Journal of History and Politics* 27 (July): 408–56.

1929b. "Orion Clemens." *Palimpsest* 10 (October): 353–88.

1946. "Mark Twain's Philadelphia Letters in the Muscatine *Journal*." *American Literature* 17 (January): 348–52.

Lord, Eliot.
1883. *Comstock Mining and Miners*. Washington, D.C.: Government Printing Office. Citations are to the 1959 reprint edition, introduction by David F. Myrick, Berkeley: Howell-North.

Ludlow, Fitz Hugh.
1863. "A Good-bye Article." *Golden Era* 11 (22 November): 4.

Ludlow, Noah M.
1880. *Dramatic Life as I Found It*. St. Louis: n.p. Citations are to the 1966 reprint edition, edited by Francis Hodge and Richard Moody, New York: Benjamin Blom.

Lyman, George D.
1934. *The Saga of the Comstock Lode: Boom Days in Virginia City*. New York: Charles Scribner's Sons.

Lytle, William M., comp.
1952. *Merchant Steam Vessels of the United States, 1807–1868*. Edited by Forrest R. Holdcamper. Publication no. 6. Mystic, Conn.: Steamship Historical Society of America.

McDermott, John Francis.
1949. "Leon Pomarede, 'Our Parisian Knight of the Easel.' " *Bulletin of the City Art Museum of St. Louis* 34 (Winter): 8–18.

McDougall, Marion Gleason.
1891. *Fugitive Slaves (1619–1865)*. Publications of the Society for the Collegiate Instruction of Women, Fay House Monographs, no. 3. Boston: Ginn and Co.

Mace, William R.
1960. "Mark Twain: One of Our Great Freemasons." *California Freemason* 7 (Autumn): 160–64.

McElroy.
1854. *McElroy's Philadelphia Directory for 1854*. Philadelphia: Edward C. and John Biddle.

McGrath, Roger D.
1984. *Gunfighters, Highwaymen, and Vigilantes: Violence on the Frontier*. Berkeley, Los Angeles, London: University of California Press.

Mack, Effie Mona.
1936. *Nevada: A History of the State from the Earliest Times through the Civil War*. Glendale, Calif.: Arthur H. Clark Company.

1947. *Mark Twain in Nevada*. New York: Charles Scribner's Sons.

1961a. "James Warren Nye, 1814–1876: A Biography." *Nevada Historical Society Quarterly* 4 (July–December): 7–59.

1961b. "Orion Clemens, 1825–1897: A Biography." *Nevada Historical Society Quarterly* 4 (July–December): 61–108.

1964. "William Morris Stewart, 1827–1909." *Nevada Historical Society Quarterly* 7 (January–June): 11–110.

Macoy, Robert.
1870. *True Masonic Guide*. New York: Clark and Maynard.

Maitland, James.
1891. *The American Slang Dictionary*. Chicago: R. J. Kittredge and Co.

Mantle, Burns, and Garrison P. Sherwood, eds.
1944. *The Best Plays of 1899–1909 and the Year Book of the Drama in America*. Philadelphia: Blakiston Company.

Marsh, Andrew J.
1972. *Letters from Nevada Territory, 1861–1862*. Edited by William C. Miller, Russell W. McDonald, and Ann Rollins. [Reno]: Legislative Counsel Bureau, State of Nevada.

Marsh, Andrew J., Samuel L. Clemens, and Amos Bowman.
1972. *Reports of the 1863 Constitutional Convention of the Territory of Nevada*. Edited by William C. Miller, Eleanore Bushnell, Russell W. McDonald, and Ann Rollins. [Reno]: Legislative Counsel Bureau, State of Nevada.

Marsh, Grant.
1878. "Sam Clemens' Pard." St. Louis *Missouri Republican*, 8 December, 7.

1881. "Mark Twain's Steamboating Days." Unidentified clipping enclosed in John B. Downing to SLC, 15 August, CU-MARK.

Marshall, George M.
1864. "Letter from New York." Virginia City *Daily Union*, 14 October, 1.

Mattson, J. Stanley.
1968. "Twain's Last Months on the Mississippi." *Missouri Historical Review* 62 (July): 398–409.

MEC (Mary E. [Mollie] Clemens).
1862–66. "Mrs. Orion Clemens. 'Journal.' For 1862." Location unknown, PH of MS in CU-MARK. Partly printed in Lorch 1929b, 357–59.

Merwin, Henry Childs.
1911. *The Life of Bret Harte*. Boston and New York: Houghton Mifflin Company.

MH-H   Houghton Library, Harvard University, Cambridge, Massachusetts.

Miller, Hunter, ed.
1931–48. *Treaties and Other International Acts of the United States of America*. 8 vols. Washington, D.C.: Government Printing Office.

Miller, William C.
1973. "Samuel L. and Orion Clemens vs. Mark Twain and His Biographers (1861–1862)." *Mark Twain Journal* 16 (Summer): 1–9.

Milleson, M.
1863. *Milleson and Washburn's Map of the Celebrated Humboldt Silver Mines. Compiled from Recent Surveys of Messrs Fine and Epler, County Surveyors of Humboldt County, N.T.* Drawn by M. Milleson. Drawn on stone by Edward Fairman. San Francisco: B. F. Butler.

Mining Laws
1863. *Mining Laws of Esmeralda District.* San Francisco: Towne and Bacon.

Mitchell, Wesley Clair.
1903. *A History of the Greenbacks.* Chicago: University of Chicago Press. Citations are to the 1960 reprint edition, University of Chicago Press.

MoCgS   Southeast Missouri State University, Cape Girardeau.

MoHi   Missouri State Historical Society, Columbia.

MoHM   Mark Twain Museum, Hannibal.

Montague, William L.
1853. *The Saint Louis Business Directory for 1853–4.* St. Louis: E. A. Lewis.

Morgan, Charlotte E.
1930. *The Origin and History of the New York Employing Printers' Association: The Evolution of a Trade Association.* Studies in History, Economics and Public Law, edited by the Faculty of Political Science of Columbia University, publication no. 319. New York: Columbia University Press.

Morrison.
1852. *Morrison's St. Louis Directory, for 1852.* St. Louis: Missouri Republican.

Morse, Hosea Ballou.
1918. *The International Relations of the Chinese Empire.* 3 vols. London: Longmans, Green, and Co.

MoSHi   Missouri Historical Society, St. Louis.

Motheral, J. G.
1971. *Fort Point: "Gibraltar of the Pacific."* [San Francisco]: Fort Point Museum Association.

Mott, Frank Luther.
1938. *A History of American Magazines, 1850–1865.* Cambridge: Harvard University Press.

1939. *A History of American Magazines, 1741–1850.* Cambridge: Harvard University Press.

1962. *American Journalism, a History: 1690–1960.* 3d ed. New York: Macmillan Company.

MS   Manuscript.

MSM
1969. *Mark Twain's Mysterious Stranger Manuscripts.* Edited by William M. Gibson. The Mark Twain Papers. Berkeley and Los Angeles: University of California Press.

MTA

1924. *Mark Twain's Autobiography*. Edited by Albert Bigelow Paine. 2 vols. New York: Harper and Brothers.

MTB

1912. *Mark Twain: A Biography*. By Albert Bigelow Paine. 3 vols. New York: Harper and Brothers. [*Volume numbers in citations are to this edition; page numbers are the same in all editions.*]

MTBus

1946. *Mark Twain, Business Man*. Edited by Samuel Charles Webster. Boston: Little, Brown, and Co.

MTE

1940. *Mark Twain in Eruption*. Edited by Bernard DeVoto. New York: Harper and Brothers.

MTEnt

1957. *Mark Twain of the "Enterprise."* Edited by Henry Nash Smith, with the assistance of Frederick Anderson. Berkeley and Los Angeles: University of California Press.

MTH

1947. *Mark Twain and Hawaii*. By Walter Francis Frear. Chicago: Lakeside Press.

MTL

1917. *Mark Twain's Letters*. Edited by Albert Bigelow Paine. 2 vols. New York: Harper and Brothers.

MTLBowen

1941. *Mark Twain's Letters to Will Bowen*. Edited by Theodore Hornberger. Austin: University of Texas.

MTN

1935. *Mark Twain's Notebook*. Edited by Albert Bigelow Paine. New York: Harper and Brothers.

MTSpk

1976. *Mark Twain Speaking*. Edited by Paul Fatout. Iowa City: University of Iowa Press.

MTTB

1940. *Mark Twain's Travels with Mr. Brown*. Edited by Franklin Walker and G. Ezra Dane. New York: Alfred A. Knopf.

Muir, Andrew Forest.

1955. "Note on Twain and Rising." *California Historical Society Quarterly* 34 (December): 317–22.

N&J1

1975. *Mark Twain's Notebooks & Journals, Volume I (1855–1873)*. Edited by Frederick Anderson, Michael B. Frank, and Kenneth M. Sanderson. The Mark Twain Papers. Berkeley, Los Angeles, London: University of California Press.

N&J2
   1975. *Mark Twain's Notebooks & Journals, Volume II (1877–1883)*. Edited by Frederick Anderson, Lin Salamo, and Bernard L. Stein. The Mark Twain Papers. Berkeley, Los Angeles, London: University of California Press.

NAW
   1971. *Notable American Women 1607–1950: A Biographical Dictionary*. Edited by Edward T. James, Janet Wilson James, and Paul S. Boyer. 3 vols. Cambridge: Belknap Press of Harvard University Press.

NCAB
   1898–1984. *The National Cyclopedia of American Biography*. Volumes 1–62 and A–M plus index. New York: James T. White and Co.

Nevada [pseud.].
   1864. "Letter from Carson City." Letter dated 16 February. San Francisco *Evening Bulletin*, 22 February, 5.

Neville, Amelia Ransome.
   1932. *The Fantastic City: Memoirs of the Social and Romantic Life of Old San Francisco*. Boston: Houghton Mifflin Company.

NGD
   1980. *The New Grove Dictionary of Music and Musicians*. Edited by Stanley Sadie. 20 vols. London: Macmillan Publishers.

NIM
   1978. *Newspapers in Microform: United States, 1973–1977*. Washington, D.C.: Library of Congress.

NN   The New York Public Library, Astor, Lenox and Tilden Foundations, New York City.

NN-B   Henry W. and Albert A. Berg Collection, NN.

NNPM   Pierpont Morgan Library, New York City.

Nomad [pseud.].
   1863. "Letter from Nevada Territory." Letter dated 17 February. Sacramento *Union*, 24 February, 1.

NPV   Jean Webster McKinney Family Papers, Francis Fitz Randolph Rare Book Room, Vassar College Library, Poughkeepsie, New York.

Nv-Ar   Nevada State Library and Archives, Division of Archives and Records, Carson City.

NvHi   Nevada State Historical Society, Reno.

NvU   University of Nevada Reno.

NvU-NSP   Nevada State Papers, NvU.

Nye, James W.
   1862. *Second Annual Message of Governor James W. Nye, to the Legislature of Nevada Territory, November 13, 1862*. Carson City: J. T. Goodman and Co.

Nye-Starr, Kate.
   1888. *A Self-Sustaining Woman; or, The Experience of Seventy-two Years*. Chicago: Illinois Printing and Binding Company.

OC (Orion Clemens).

1853a. "Notice." Announcement dated 7 September. Hannibal *Journal*, 10 September, 2.

1853b. "Notice to the Public." Hannibal *Tri-Weekly Messenger*, 29 September, 3, reprinting the Hannibal *Journal* of 22 September.

1855. "Good Bye." Muscatine *Tri-Weekly Journal*, 8 June, 2.

1856. *Keokuk City Directory, for 1856–7*. Keokuk: O. Clemens.

1857. *Keokuk Directory and Business Mirror for the Year 1857*. Keokuk: O. Clemens.

1862. "Matters in Nevada Territory." Letter dated 10 May. Keokuk *Gate City*, 19 June, 2. Reprinted in Rogers 1961, 41–45.

1866a. "Meadow Lake." Letter dated 28 May. San Francisco *American Flag*, 7 June, clipping in Scrapbook 6:96–97, CU-MARK.

1866b. "Letter from Meadow Lake." Letter dated 3 June, signed "Snow Shoe." San Francisco *American Flag*, 12 June, clipping in Scrapbook 6:98–99, CU-MARK.

1866c. "Our Ledges.—No. 1." Undated letter signed "Noiro." Meadow Lake (Calif.) *Morning Sun*, 9 June, clipping in Scrapbook 6:97, CU-MARK.

1866d. "Our Ledges.—No. 2." Undated letter signed "Noiro." Meadow Lake (Calif.) *Morning Sun*, 12 June, clipping in Scrapbook 6:98, CU-MARK.

1866e. "Our Ledges.—No. 3." Undated letter signed "Noiro." Meadow Lake (Calif.) *Morning Sun*, 15 June, clipping in Scrapbook 6:100, CU-MARK.

1866f. "Our Ledges.—No. 4." Undated letter signed "Noiro." Meadow Lake (Calif.) *Morning Sun*, 18 June, clipping in Scrapbook 6:100–101, CU-MARK.

1866g. "Our Ledges.—No. 5." Undated letter signed "Noiro." Meadow Lake (Calif.) *Morning Sun*, 23 June, clipping in Scrapbook 6:101, CU-MARK.

1866h. "Our Ledges.—No. 6." Undated letter signed "Noiro." Meadow Lake (Calif.) *Morning Sun*, 26 June, clipping in Scrapbook 6:101–2, CU-MARK.

1866i. "Our Ledges.—No. 7." Undated letter signed "Noiro." Meadow Lake (Calif.) *Morning Sun*, 29 June, clipping in Scrapbook 6:102, CU-MARK.

1866j. "Our Ledges.—No. 8." Undated letter signed "Noiro." Meadow Lake (Calif.) *Morning Sun*, 2 July, clipping in Scrapbook 6:104, CU-MARK.

1866k. "Our Ledges.—No. 9." Undated letter signed "Noiro." Meadow Lake (Calif.) *Morning Sun*, 4 July, clipping in Scrapbook 6:104, CU-MARK.

1866l. "Our Ledges.—No. 10." Undated letter signed "Noiro." Meadow Lake (Calif.) *Morning Sun*, 10 July, clipping in Scrapbook 6:106, CU-MARK.

1866m. "Our Ledges.—No. 11." Undated letter signed "Noiro." Meadow Lake (Calif.) *Morning Sun*, 16 July, clipping in Scrapbook 6:107, CU-MARK.

1866n. "Letter from Meadow Lake." Letter dated 26 July, signed "Noiro." San Francisco *American Flag*, 8 August, clipping in Scrapbook 6:123–24, CU-MARK.

1867a. "Letter from Tennessee." Letter dated 28 December 1866, signed "Cumberland." San Francisco *Times*, 26 January, 2, clipping in Scrapbook 4:38, CU-MARK.

1867b. "Letter from Tennessee." Letter dated 4 January, signed "Cumberland." San Francisco *Times*, 2 February, 4, clipping in Scrapbook 4:38–39, CU-MARK.

1867c. "Letter from St. Louis." Unsigned letter dated 11 March. San Francisco *Times*, 13 April, 2.

OC (Orion Clemens) and Charles E. H. Wilson.
1855. "Introduction." Muscatine *Tri-Weekly Journal*, 4 June, 2.

O'Connor, Richard.
1966. *Bret Harte: A Biography*. Boston: Little, Brown, and Co.

Odell, George C. D.
1927–49. *Annals of the New York Stage*. 15 vols. New York: Columbia University Press.

Oehser, Paul H.
1983. *The Smithsonian Institution*. 2d ed. Boulder, Colo.: Westview Press.

Orton, Richard H.
1890. *Records of California Men in the War of the Rebellion, 1861 to 1867*. Sacramento: State Office.

Paine, Albert Bigelow.
1911. "Mark Twain: Some Chapters from an Extraordinary Life." *Harper's Monthly Magazine* 124 (December): 42–53.

PAM   Pamela Ann Moffett.

Parke, William Cooper.
1891. *Personal Reminiscences of William Cooper Parke, Marshal of the Hawaiian Islands, from 1850 to 1884*. Cambridge, Mass.: University Press.

Paul, Almarin B. [Cosmos, pseud.].
1861. "Washoe: Its Mines, Mills and Machinery." San Francisco *Evening Bulletin*, 1 November, 1.

1864a. "A Great Sanitary Fair in St. Louis—The Union People of Nevada Are Called!" Virginia City *Union*, 24 March, 2.

1864b. "Affairs in Washoe." San Francisco *Evening Bulletin*, 25 May, 1.

1864c. Telegram to Samuel Copp, 6 June, in "The Gold and Silver Bars from Nevada." St. Louis *Missouri Republican*, 8 June, 3.

1927. "My First Two Years in California." *Quarterly of the Society of California Pioneers* 4 (March): 24–54.

PH   Photocopy.

Phillips, Michael J.
1920. "Mark Twain's Partner." *Saturday Evening Post* 193 (11 September): 22–23, 69–70, 73–74.

Pioneer [pseud.].
1863a. "The Esmeralda Mining Region." Letter dated 7 January. San Francisco *Evening Bulletin*, 15 January, 2.

[1863b]. "Unionville, Then and Now." Unidentified clipping, [16 May], in Bancroft Scraps: Nevada Mining (set W, vol. 94:1), 84, CU-BANC.

Portrait
1899. *Portrait and Biographical Record of the State of Colorado.* Chicago: Chapman Publishing Company.

Poulton, Helen J.
1966. *Index to History of Nevada.* Reno: University of Nevada Press.

Primm, James Neal.
1981. *Lion of the Valley: St. Louis, Missouri.* Boulder, Colo.: Pruett Publishing Company.

Proclamations
1861–64. *Proclamations, Appointments, Messages, 1861–1864,* in Executive Records of Governor James Warren Nye (1861–64), Nv-Ar.

Quartz [pseud.].
1863a. "Letter from Nevada Territory." Letter dated 1 February. San Francisco *Alta California*, 8 February, 1.
1863b. "Notes on the Mines of Nevada Territory—No. 2." Letter dated 6 February. San Francisco *Alta California*, 11 February, 1.

Ratay, Myra Sauer.
1973. *Pioneers of the Ponderosa: How Washoe Valley Rescued the Comstock.* Sparks, Nev.: Western Printing and Publishing Company.

Raymond, Rossiter W.
1881. *A Glossary of Mining and Metallurgical Terms.* Easton, Pa.: American Institute of Mining Engineers.

[Read, Opie P.]
1883a. "A Mark Twain Letter." *Arkansaw Traveler* 3 (14 July): 4.
1883b. "That Mark Twain Letter." *Arkansaw Traveler* 3 (4 August): 4.

Reed, Mort.
1969. *Cowles Complete Encyclopedia of U.S. Coins.* Foreword by Gilroy Roberts. New York: Cowles Book Company.

Rees, Thomas.
1908. *Sixty Days in Europe and What We Saw There.* Springfield, Ill.: State Register Company.

Reid, J. M.
1876. *Sketches and Anecdotes of the Old Settlers, and New Comers, the Mormon Bandits and Danite Band.* Keokuk: R. B. Ogden.

RI
1972. *Roughing It.* Edited by Franklin R. Rogers and Paul Baender. The Works of Mark Twain. Berkeley, Los Angeles, London: University of California Press.

Rice, Clement T. [Carl, pseud.].
1863a. "Mineral Wealth of Washoe." Sacramento *Union*, 10 April, 4, reprinting the Virginia City *Union* of 2 April.
1863b. "The Late Fire at Virginia City (N.T.)." Sacramento *Union*, 30 July, 2, reprinting the Virginia City *Union* of unknown date.
1864. "Letter from Carson." Virginia City *Union*, 30 January, 1.

Ridings, J. Willard.
1930. "Missouri History Not Found in Textbooks." *Missouri Historical Review* 25 (October): 180–99.

Ringwalt, J. Luther, ed.
1871. *American Encyclopaedia of Printing.* Philadelphia: Menamin and Ringwalt, J. B. Lippincott and Co.

Rocha, Guy Louis, and Roger Smith.
1983. "Mark Twain and the Nevada Notary Stampede." *Nevada Historical Society Quarterly* 26 (Summer): 83–90.

Rode, Charles R., comp.
1852. *The New York City Directory, for 1852–1853.* New York: Charles R. Rode.

1853a. *The New-York City Directory, for 1853–1854.* New York: Charles R. Rode.

1853b. *Rode's New York Business Directory, 1853–1854.* At end of Rode 1853a.

Rogers, Franklin R.
1957. "Washoe's First Literary Journal." *California Historical Society Quarterly* 36 (December): 365–70.

1961. *The Pattern for Mark Twain's "Roughing It": Letters from Nevada by Samuel and Orion Clemens, 1861–1862.* Berkeley and Los Angeles: University of California Press.

Rosecrans, William S.
1864. Certificate dated 27 April, in "Sanitary Appointment." Virginia City *Union*, 19 May, 3.

Sahab [pseud.].
1863. "The Esmeralda Region." Letter dated 24 January. San Francisco *Evening Bulletin*, 3 February, 1.

Samuels, Peggy, and Harold Samuels.
1976. *The Illustrated Biographical Encyclopedia of Artists of the American West.* Garden City, N.Y.: Doubleday and Co.

Sandburg, Carl.
1927. *The American Songbag.* New York: Harcourt, Brace, and Co.

Saunders, Frederick.
1853. *New-York in a Nutshell; or, Visitors' Hand-Book to the City.* New York: T. W. Strong.

Scharf, J. Thomas.
1883. *History of Saint Louis City and County, from the Earliest Periods to the Present Day.* 2 vols. Philadelphia: Louis H. Everts and Co.

Scharf, J. Thomas, and Thompson Westcott.
1884. *History of Philadelphia: 1609–1884.* 3 vols. Philadelphia: L. H. Everts and Co.

Scott, Charles M., and William Gallaher.
1857. "To the Public." St. Louis *Missouri Republican*, 6 October, 2.

Scott, Edward B.
1957. *The Saga of Lake Tahoe*. Crystal Bay, Nev.: Sierra-Tahoe Publishing Company.

Sears, Minnie Earl, ed.
1926. *Song Index*. New York: H. W. Wilson Company.

Seitz, Don C.
1919. *Artemus Ward (Charles Farrar Browne): A Biography and Bibliography*. New York: Harper and Brothers.

Selby, P. O., comp.
1973. *Mark Twain's Kinfolks*. Kirksville, Mo.: Missouriana Library, Northeast Missouri State University.

Shuck, Oscar T.
1889. *Bench and Bar in California*. San Francisco: Occident Printing House.

1901. *History of the Bench and Bar of California*. Los Angeles: Commercial Printing House.

Silliman, B., Jr., and C. R. Goodrich, eds.
1854. *The World of Science, Art, and Industry Illustrated from Examples in the New-York Exhibition, 1853–54*. New York: G. P. Putnam and Co.

Silversmith, J.
1861a. "Joshua A. Clayton." *Mining and Scientific Press* 3 (30 March): 4.
1861b. "The Veatch Process." *Mining and Scientific Press* 3 (20 April): 4.

Simmons, A. J.
1861a. "Letter from the Humboldt Mines." Letter dated 5 August. Sacramento *Union*, 27 August, 3.

1861b. "The Humboldt Mines." Letter dated 22 September. Sacramento *Union*, 3 October, 1.

Simpson, Alan.
1977. *Mark Twain Goes Back to Vassar: An Introduction to the Jean Webster McKinney Family Papers*. Poughkeepsie, N.Y.: Vassar College.

SLC (Samuel Langhorne Clemens).
1853. "Our Assistant's Column." Hannibal *Journal*, 26 May, 3.

1856a. "Correspondence." Letter dated 18 October. Keokuk *Saturday Post*, 1 November, 4. Reprinted in *TJS*, 3–16.

1856b. "Snodgrass' Ride on the Railroad." Letter dated 14 November. Keokuk *Post*, 29 November, 2; reprinted in Keokuk *Saturday Post*, 6 December, 4. Reprinted in *TJS*, 19–33.

1857. "Snodgrass, in a Adventure." Letter dated 14 March. Keokuk *Post*, 10 April, 2; reprinted in Keokuk *Saturday Post*, 18 April, 4. Reprinted in *TJS*, 37–48.

[1858]. "My brother, Henry Clemens . . . ," in an incomplete, unidentified newspaper clipping, [July?], Scrapbook 1:15, CU-MARK. Facsimile in Branch 1985a, 36.

1859. "Soleather Cultivates His Taste for Music." New Orleans *Crescent*, 21 July, 4. Reprinted in Branch 1982b, 498–502.

1862. Letter dated 13 July, in "Late from Washoe." Sacramento *Union*, 22 July, 2, reprinting the Virginia City *Territorial Enterprise* of 20 July, not extant.

1863a. "From the Humboldt River Region." San Francisco *Evening Bulletin*, 3 March, 2, reprinting the Virginia City *Territorial Enterprise* of 26 February, not extant.

1863b. "Latest from Washoe." San Francisco *Alta California*, 20 April, 1, reprinting the Virginia City *Territorial Enterprise* of 17 April, not extant.

1863c. "The Comstock Mines." Marysville (Calif.) *Appeal*, 12 July, 1, reprinting the Virginia City *Territorial Enterprise* of unknown date, not extant. Reprinted in Fatout 1964, 75–76.

1863d. "'Mark Twain's' Letter." Letter dated 12 July. San Francisco *Morning Call*, 15 July, 1. Reprinted in *Twainian* 11 (January–February 1952): 2–3.

1863e. "'Mark Twain's' Letter." Letter dated 16 July. San Francisco *Morning Call*, 18 July, 1. Reprinted in *Twainian* 11 (January–February 1952): 3.

1863f. "'Mark Twain's' Letter." Letter dated 19 July. San Francisco *Morning Call*, 23 July, 1. Reprinted in *Twainian* 11 (January–February 1952): 3–4.

1863g. "'Mark Twain's' Letter." Letter dated 8 August. San Francisco *Morning Call*, 13 August, 1. Reprinted in *Twainian* 11 (March–April 1952): 3.

1863h. "Letter from Mark Twain." Letter dated 13 September. Virginia City *Territorial Enterprise*, [17] September, clipping in Scrapbook 2:78, CU-MARK. Reprinted in *MTEnt*, 75–80.

1863i. "First Annual Fair of the Washoe Agricultural, Mining and Mechanical Society." Letter dated 19 October. Virginia City *Territorial Enterprise*, 20 October, clipping in Scrapbook 2:99, CU-MARK. Reprinted in *MTEnt*, 80–86.

1863j. "Letter from Mark Twain." Letter dated 7 November. Virginia City *Territorial Enterprise*, 10 November, clipping in Scrapbook 2:110–11, CU-MARK. Reprinted in *MTEnt*, 86–89.

1863k. "Letter from Mark Twain." Letter dated 15 November. Virginia City *Territorial Enterprise*, [17] November, clipping in Scrapbook 1:71, CU-MARK. Reprinted in *MTEnt*, 90–92.

1863l. "Letter from Mark Twain." Letter dated 5 December. Virginia City *Territorial Enterprise*, 8 December, clipping in Scrapbook 3:28, CU-MARK. Reprinted in *MTEnt*, 92–95.

1863m. "Letter from Mark Twain." Letter dated 12 December. Virginia City *Territorial Enterprise*, 15 December, clipping in Scrapbook 3:42–43, CU-MARK. Reprinted in *MTEnt*, 95–100.

1863n. "Nevada State Constitutional Convention. Third House." Report dated 13 December. Virginia City *Territorial Enterprise*, 19 December, clipping in Scrapbook 3:55, CU-MARK. Reprinted in *MTEnt*, 100–110.

1863o. "The Bolters in Convention." Virginia City *Territorial Enterprise*, 30 December, clipping in Scrapbook 3:60–61, CU-MARK. Reprinted in *MTEnt*, 112–17.

1864a. "Letter from Mark Twain." Letter dated 10 January. Virginia City *Territorial Enterprise*, [11] January, clipping in Scrapbook 4:4, CU-MARK. Reprinted in *MTEnt*, 126–30.

1864b. "Legislative Proceedings." Virginia City *Territorial Enterprise*, 14 January, clipping in Scrapbook 4:3, CU-MARK. Reprinted in *MTEnt*, 131–34.

1864c. "House—Seventeenth Day." Report dated 28 January. Virginia City *Territorial Enterprise*, 29 January, clipping in Scrapbook 3:140, CU-MARK. Reprinted in *MTEnt*, 144–47.

1864d. "Doings in Nevada." Letter dated 4 January. New York *Sunday Mercury*, 7 February, 3. Reprinted in *MTEnt*, 121–26.

1864e. "Letter from Mark Twain." Letter dated "Saturday night" [6 February]. Virginia City *Territorial Enterprise*, 9 February, clipping in Scrapbook 3:103, CU-MARK. Reprinted as "Concerning Notaries" in Walker 1938, 67–70.

1864f. "Letter from Mark Twain." Letter dated "Monday" [25 April]. Virginia City *Territorial Enterprise*, 28 April, clipping in Scrapbook 3:144, CU-MARK. Reprinted in *MTEnt*, 178–82.

1864g. "Grand Austin Sanitary Flour-Sack Progress through Storey and Lyon Counties." San Francisco *Evening Bulletin*, 19 May, 5, reprinting the Virginia City *Territorial Enterprise* of 17 May, not extant.

1864h. "How Is It?" in " 'How Is It?'—How It Is." Virginia City *Union*, 19 May, 2, reprinting the Virginia City *Territorial Enterprise* of 18 May, not extant.

1864i. "Travels and Fortunes of the Great Austin Sack of Flour." San Francisco *Evening Bulletin*, 20 May, 1, reprinting the Virginia City *Territorial Enterprise* of 18 May, not extant.

1864j. "Personal Correspondence." Virginia City *Territorial Enterprise*, 24 May, clipping in Scrapbook 3:146, CU-MARK.

1864k. "Miscegenation." Virginia City *Territorial Enterprise*, 24 May, clipping in Scrapbook 3:146, CU-MARK. Reprinted in *MTEnt*, 196–98.

1864l. "Suit against a Mining Superintendent." San Francisco *Morning Call*, 20 August, clipping in Scrapbook 5:41, CU-MARK.

1864m. "Answer to a Mining Company's Suit." San Francisco *Morning Call*, 28 September, 1.

1866a. "Scenes in Honolulu—No. 6." Letter dated March. Sacramento *Union*, 21 April, 3. Reprinted in *MTH*, 284–90.

1866b. "Scenes in Honolulu—No. 7." Letter dated March. Sacramento *Union*, 24 April, 4. Reprinted in *MTH*, 291–95.

1866c. "Scenes in Honolulu—No. 13." Letter dated 22 June. Sacramento *Union*, 16 July, 3. Reprinted in *MTH*, 328–34.

1866d. "Letter from Honolulu." Letter dated 25 June. Sacramento *Union*, 19 July, 1. Reprinted in *MTH*, 335–47.

1866e. "Scenes in Honolulu—No. 14." Letter dated 30 June. Sacramento *Union*, 30 July, 1. Reprinted in *MTH*, 348–55.

1866f. "Scenes in Honolulu—No. 15." Letter dated 1 July. Sacramento *Union*, 1 August, 1. Reprinted in *MTH*, 356–64.

1866g. "From the Sandwich Islands." Letter dated 10 September. Sacramento *Union*, 26 September, 1. Reprinted in *MTH*, 398–407.

1866h. "From the Sandwich Islands." Letter dated June. Sacramento *Union*, 25 October, 1. Reprinted in *MTH*, 408–15.

1866i. "Letter from Honolulu." Letter dated 3 June. Sacramento *Union*, 16 November, 1. Reprinted in *MTH*, 416–20.

1866j. "Forty-three Days in an Open Boat." *Harper's New Monthly Magazine* 34 (December): 104–13.

1866k. "Mark Twain's Interior Notes—No. 2." San Francisco *Evening Bulletin*, 6 December, 1.

1867a. "'Mark Twain' in New York." Letter dated 18 February. San Francisco *Alta California*, 30 March, 1. Reprinted in part in *MTTB*, 90–100.

1867b. "Letter from 'Mark Twain.'" Letter dated 20 May. San Francisco *Alta California*, 7 July, 1. Reprinted in *MTTB*, 202–13.

1867c. "Letter from 'Mark Twain.'" Letter dated 28 May. San Francisco *Alta California*, 28 July, 1. Reprinted in *MTTB*, 238–48.

1867d. "Mark Twain's Letters from Washington. Number I." Letter dated 4 December. Virginia City *Territorial Enterprise*, 22 December, clipping in Willard S. Morse Collection, Beinecke Rare Book and Manuscript Library, CtY.

1868. "Letter from Mark Twain." Letter dated 2 May. Chicago *Republican*, 31 May, 2.

1869a. *The Innocents Abroad; or, The New Pilgrims' Progress.* Hartford: American Publishing Company.

1869b. "A Fair Career Closed," in "Browsing Around." Letter dated November. Buffalo *Express*, 27 November, 2.

1870a. "Anson Burlingame." Buffalo *Express*, 25 February, 2. Reprinted in SLC 1923, 17–23.

1870b. "A Couple of Sad Experiences." *Galaxy* 9 (June): 858–61.

1870c. "Post-Mortem Poetry." *Galaxy* 9 (June): 864–65.

1872a. *Roughing It.* Hartford: American Publishing Company.

1872b. "How I Escaped Being Killed in a Duel." In *Tom Hood's Comic Annual for 1873*, 90–91. London: Fun Office.

1873. "Samuel Langhorne Clemens." Autobiographical sketch, January, MS of eleven pages, NNPM.

1874. *The Gilded Age: A Tale of Today.* Charles Dudley Warner, coauthor. Hartford: American Publishing Company.

1875. "Old Times on the Mississippi." Articles 1–7. *Atlantic Monthly* 35 (January–June): 69–73, 217–24, 283–89, 446–52, 567–74, 721–30; *Atlantic Monthly* 36 (August): 190–96.

1880. *A Tramp Abroad.* Hartford: American Publishing Company.

1883. *Life on the Mississippi.* Boston: James R. Osgood and Co.

1885a. "Remarks" at Actors' Fund Fair, Academy of Music, Philadelphia, 9 April, in *MTSpk*, 194.

1885b. "The Private History of a Campaign That Failed." *Century Magazine* 31 (December): 193–204.

1894. *The Tragedy of Pudd'nhead Wilson and the Comedy Those Extraordinary Twins*. Hartford: American Publishing Company.

[1898?]. Autobiographical notes, MS of seven pages (beginning "Talk about going . . ."), CU-MARK.

1899a. "Samuel Langhorne Clemens." Autobiographical sketch, March, MS of fourteen pages, NN-B. Printed in *BAL* 3521.

1899b. "My Début as a Literary Person." *Century Magazine* 59 (November): 76–88.

1909a. *Is Shakespeare Dead?* New York: Harper and Brothers.

1909b. Marginalia, 21 April, in *Letters of James Russell Lowell*. Edited by Charles Eliot Norton. 2 vols. New York: Harper and Brothers. Photofacsimile in Sotheby Parke Bernet, lot 16, PH in CU-MARK. See Gribben, 1:425–26.

1912. "My Platonic Sweetheart." *Harper's Monthly Magazine* 126 (December): 14–20.

1923. *Europe and Elsewhere*. New York: Harper and Brothers.

1961. "My Dear Bro: A Letter from Samuel Clemens to His Brother Orion." Edited by Frederick Anderson. Berkeley: Berkeley Albion.

Smith, Elizabeth H.
1965. "Reuel Colt Gridley." *Tales of the Paradise Ridge* 6 (June): 11–18.

Smith, Henry Nash, and Frederick Anderson, eds.
1957. *Mark Twain: San Francisco Correspondent*. San Francisco: Book Club of California.

Smith, R. A.
1852. *Philadelphia as It Is, in 1852*. Philadelphia: Lindsay and Blakiston.

Smith, Solomon F.
1868. *Theatrical Management in the West and South for Thirty Years*. New York: Harper and Brothers. Citations are to the 1968 reprint edition, edited by Arthur Thomas Tees, New York: Benjamin Blom.

Sotheby Parke Bernet.
1976. *Printed Books and Autograph Letters*. Sale number 3482, 25 February. New York: Sotheby Parke Bernet.

Stanford, Leland.
1863. Message to the California legislature, 30 March, unidentified clipping in Scrapbook 3:35, CU-MARK.

Statutes
1863. *The Statutes of California Passed at the Fourteenth Session of the Legislature, 1863*. Sacramento: Benj. P. Avery.

Stedman, Laura, and George M. Gould.
1910. *Life and Letters of Edmund Clarence Stedman*. 2 vols. New York: Moffat, Yard, and Co.

Stevens, George A.
1912. *New York Typographical Union No. 6: Study of a Modern Trade Union and Its Predecessors*. New York State Department of Labor, Annual Reports of De-

partment Bureaus for the Twelve Months Ended September 30, 1911, vol. 2, pt. 1. Albany: State Department of Labor.

Stevens, Walter B.
1911. *St. Louis: The Fourth City, 1764–1911.* 2 vols. St. Louis: S. J. Clarke Publishing Company.

Stiles, Edward H.
1916. *Recollections and Sketches of Notable Lawyers and Public Men of Early Iowa.* Des Moines: Homestead Publishing Company.

Stillé, Charles J.
1866. *History of the United States Sanitary Commission.* Philadelphia: J. B. Lippincott and Co.

Stokes, I. N. Phelps.
1939. *New York Past and Present: Its History and Landmarks, 1524–1939.* New York: New York Historical Society.

A Subscriber [pseud.].
1863. "The Ophir Monopoly." Letter dated 20 August. San Francisco *Alta California,* 4 September, 1, reprinting the Virginia City *Union* of 1 September.

Sullivan, Josephine.
1926. *A History of C. Brewer & Company Limited: One Hundred Years in the Hawaiian Islands.* Edited by K. C. Leebrick. Boston: Walton Advertising and Printing Company.

Swackhamer, William D.
1973. *Political History of Nevada.* 6th ed. Carson City: State Printing Office.

Swasey, William F.
1891. *The Early Days and Men of California.* Oakland, Calif.: Pacific Press Publishing Company.

Titus, Edna Brown, ed.
1965. *Union List of Serials in Libraries of the United States and Canada.* 3d ed. 5 vols. New York: H. W. Wilson Company.

TJS
1928. *The Adventures of Thomas Jefferson Snodgrass.* Edited by Charles Honce. Chicago: Pascal Covici.

Townsend, John Wilson.
1913. *Kentucky in American Letters, 1784–1912.* 2 vols. Cedar Rapids, Iowa: Torch Press.

Treat, Archibald J.
1893. "Historical Sketch," in *The History of the Olympic Club,* 13–51. San Francisco: Art Publishing Company.

TS Typescript.

Tucker, John W.
1863. "A 'Pioneer' Mining Shark!" San Francisco *Alta California,* 16 January, 2.

TxU   Harry Ransom Humanities Research Center, University of Texas, Austin.

UCCL
1986. *Union Catalog of Clemens Letters.* Edited by Paul Machlis. Berkeley, Los Angeles, London: University of California Press.

U.S. Congress, Senate.
1859. "Report of the Supervising Inspectors of Steamboats for the Year 1859," in *The Executive Documents, Printed by Order of the Senate of the United States, Second Session, Thirty-fifth Congress, 1858–'59.* 18 vols. Washington, D.C.: William A. Harris.

U.S. Department of State.
1870. *Register of the Department of State.* Washington, D.C.: Government Printing Office.

Van Der Zee, Jacob.
1915. "History of Presbyterianism in Iowa City." *Iowa Journal of History and Politics* 13 (October): 529–80.

Van Ravenswaay, Charles.
1967. "Years of Turmoil, Years of Growth: St. Louis in the 1850's." *Bulletin of the Missouri Historical Society* 23 (July): 303–24.

Varble, Rachel M.
1964. *Jane Clemens: The Story of Mark Twain's Mother.* Garden City, N.Y.: Doubleday and Co.

Veni, Vidi [pseud.].
1862a. "Esmeralda Correspondence." Letter dated 23 June. Sacramento *Bee*, 2 July, 1.

1862b. "Mono County Correspondence." Letter dated 3 July. Sacramento *Bee*, 12 July, 3.

1862c. "Esmeralda Correspondence." Letter dated 13 July. Sacramento *Bee*, 21 July, 1.

1862d. "Esmeralda Correspondence." Letter dated 13 August. Sacramento *Bee*, 20 August, 1.

ViNeM   Mariners' Museum, Newport News, Virginia.

ViU   Clifton Waller Barrett Library, Alderman Library, University of Virginia, Charlottesville.

Vox Populi [pseud.].
1862a. "Letter from Esmeralda Mining District." Letter dated 7 April. Sacramento *Union*, 14 April, 8.

1862b. "Letter from Esmeralda." Letter dated 13 April. Sacramento *Union*, 22 April, 4.

1862c. "Letter from Esmeralda." Letter dated 21 April. Sacramento *Union*, 28 April, 5.

Walker, Franklin.
1938. *The Washoe Giant in San Francisco.* San Francisco: George Fields.

1969. *San Francisco's Literary Frontier*. Rev. ed. Seattle: University of Washington Press.

Wasson, Joseph.
1878. *Bodie and Esmeralda*. San Francisco: Spaulding, Barto, and Co.

Way, Frederick, Jr.
1975. "Mississippi Scene." *S & D Reflector* 12 (September): 40–46.
1983. *Way's Packet Directory, 1848–1983*. Athens: Ohio University.

WBD
1967. *Webster's Biographical Dictionary*. Springfield, Mass.: G. and C. Merriam Company.

Webb, Charles H. [Inigo, pseud.].
1866. "Inigoings." *Californian* 4 (5 May): 8–9.

Webster, Annie Moffett.
1918. "Family Chronicle Written for Jean Webster McKinney by Her Grandmother." TS dated 26 October, NPV.
1949. "Recollections of the Clemens Family in St. Louis When Sam Was a River Pilot." *Twainian* 8 (March–April): 1–2.

Wecter, Dixon.
1952. *Sam Clemens of Hannibal*. Boston: Houghton Mifflin Company, Riverside Press.

Weisenburger, Francis Phelps.
1965. *Idol of the West: The Fabulous Career of Rollin Mallory Daggett*. Syracuse: Syracuse University Press.

Wells, Evelyn.
1921. "The Silver Sixties." San Francisco *Call and Post*, 6 April, 13.

West, George P.
1924. "Bret Harte's 'Roaring Camp' Still Producing: Mother Lode Country Rich in Reminiscences of Mark Twain's Youth." San Francisco *Call and Post*, 24 May, section 2:13, 18.

Westcott, Thompson.
1877. *The Historic Mansions and Buildings of Philadelphia, with Some Notice of Their Owners and Occupants*. Philadelphia: Porter and Coates.

Wheat, Margaret M.
1967. *Survival Arts of the Primitive Paiutes*. Reno: University of Nevada Press.

Williams, C. S.
1861. *Williams' Cincinnati Directory, City Guide and Business Mirror . . . for 1861*. Cincinnati: C. S. Williams.
1863. *Williams' Cincinnati Directory, City Guide and Business Mirror, for Year Commencing June, 1863*. Cincinnati: Williams and Co.

Williams, Frederick Wells.
1912. *Anson Burlingame and the First Chinese Mission to Foreign Powers*. New York: Charles Scribner's Sons.

Willis, William L.
1913. *History of Sacramento County, California*. Los Angeles: Historic Record Company.

Wilmington, J. W. [Printer, pseud.].
1864a. "How It Is." Virginia City *Union*, 21 May, 2.
1864b. "Personal Correspondence," Item II. Virginia City *Territorial Enterprise*, 24 May, clipping in Scrapbook 3:146, CU-MARK.

Wilson, H., comp.
1853. *Trow's New York City Directory . . . for 1853–1854*. New York: John F. Trow.

Wilson, James Grant, and John Fiske, eds.
1887–89. *Appletons' Cyclopaedia of American Biography*. 6 vols. New York: D. Appleton and Co.

Wilson, Joseph M.
1875. *The Masterpieces of the Centennial International Exhibition*. Vol. 3, *History, Mechanics, Science*. Philadelphia: Gebbie and Barrie.

WIM
1973. *What Is Man? and Other Philosophical Writings*. Edited by Paul Baender. The Works of Mark Twain. Berkeley, Los Angeles, London: University of California Press.

Wright, James W. A.
1960. *The Cement Hunters: Lost Gold Mine of the High Sierra*. Edited by Richard E. Lingenfelter. Los Angeles: Glen Dawson.

Wright, William [Dan De Quille, pseud.].
1863. "Letter from Dan De Quille!" Letter dated 24 February. Virginia City *Territorial Enterprise*, undated clipping in Scrapbook 2:33, CU-MARK.
1876. *The Big Bonanza*. Hartford: American Publishing Company. Citations are to the 1947 reprint edition, introduction by Oscar Lewis, New York: Alfred A. Knopf.
1893a. "Reminiscences of the Comstock," in "The Passing of a Pioneer." San Francisco *Examiner*, 22 January, 15. Reprinted as "The Story of the *Enterprise*" in Lewis, 5–10.
1893b. "Salad Days of Mark Twain." San Francisco *Examiner*, 19 March, 13–14. Reprinted in Lewis, 37–52.

Writers' Program.
1942. *Lee County History*. Compiled and written by the Iowa Writers' Program. Lee County: Work Projects Administration.

Wyoming [pseud.].
1862a. "Letter from the Humboldt Mines." Letter dated 23 March. Sacramento *Union*, 1 April, 4.
1862b. "Letter from the Humboldt Mines." Letter dated 20 April. Sacramento *Union*, 29 April, 1.

Zimmer, Ethel, ed.
1959. "Colonel Samuel Youngs' Journal." *Nevada Historical Society Quarterly* 2 (April–June): 27–67.

Index

THE FOLLOWING have not been indexed: citations and cross-references; fictional characters; the Guide to Editorial Practice; the Guide to the Textual Commentaries and the commentaries themselves; proper names on the Maps of Nevada Territory, 1864; and the facsimiles of letter manuscripts. Place names are included when they are important biographically, particularly as Clemens's residences or the subject of his commentary, but they are excluded when mentioned only in passing.

Alphabetizing is *word-by-word*, except for the following. (1) When persons, places, or things share the same name, they are indexed in that order, regardless of alphabetical consequences: thus "Kinkead, John H." precedes "Kinkead, Harrington and Company"; "St. Louis" the city precedes "*St. Louis*" the ship. (2) Formal titles (Mr., Mrs., Dr., Sergeant, Captain, Sir, and so forth) may be included with a name, but are ignored when alphabetizing, except for wives identified by their husband's name: thus "Blanchard, Mrs. A." precedes "Blanchard, Frank H."; but "Bohon, Thomas B." precedes "Bohon, Mrs. Thomas B." (3) When subheadings appear for "letters to" (or "by," "from," or "*per*"), they *precede* all other subheadings; when the subheading for "mentioned" appears, it *follows* all other subheadings.

Recipients of Clemens's letters are listed in **boldface type;** boldface numbers (**191n1**) indicate principal identifications; numbers linked by ampersand (347 & 348n2) indicate that the allusion in the letter text can best be located by reading the note first. Works written by Mark Twain are indexed separately by title *and* under "Clemens, Samuel Langhorne: works," as well as, when appropriate, under the publishing journal. Works written by others are indexed both under the title and the author's name. Daily newspapers are indexed by their location (city or town); all other periodicals by title.

The text of this book is set in Mergenthaler Linotype Plantin. Headings are in Plantin Light. Plantin was originally designed for the Monotype Company by F. H. Pierpont in 1913. The paper is Perkins & Squier High Opaque Offset, acid free, manufactured by the P. H. Glatfelter Company. The book was composed by Wilsted & Taylor Publishing Services of Oakland, California, using Data General Nova 4c and Nova 4x computers, Penta software, and a Linotron 202 typesetter. It was printed and bound by Maple-Vail Book Manufacturing Group in Binghamton, New York.